LEADERSHIP
Enhancing the Lessons of Experience

LEADERSHIP
Enhancing the Lessons of Experience

Richard L. Hughes
Robert C. Ginnett
Gordon J. Curphy

Boston • Burr Ridge, IL • Dubuque, IA • Madison, WI
New York • San Francisco • St. Louis • Bangkok • Bogotá
Caracas • Lisbon • London • Madrid • Mexico City
Milan • New Delhi • Seoul • Singapore • Sydney
Taipei • Toronto

Irwin/McGraw-Hill

*A Division of The **McGraw-Hill** Companies*

LEADERSHIP: ENHANCING THE LESSONS OF EXPERIENCE

This book is printed on acid-free paper.

2 3 4 5 6 7 8 9 0 QPF/QPF 9 3 2 1 0 9

ISBN 0-256-26143-1

Vice president and editor in chief: *Michael W. Junior*
Publisher: *Craig S. Beytien*
Senior sponsoring editor: *John E. Biernat*
Editorial assistant: *Erin Riley*
Marketing manager: *Ellen Cleary*
Marketing coordinator: *Christine Witt*
Project manager: *Paula M. Buschman*
Production supervisor: *Scott M. Hamilton*
Freelance design coordinator: *Laurie J. Entringer*
Cover designer: *James Shaw*
Supplement coordinator: *Jennifer L. Frazier*
Compositor: *GAC Shepard Poorman*
Typeface: *10/12 Palatino*
Printer: *Quebecor Printing Book Group/Fairfield*

Library of Congress Cataloging-in-Publication Data

Hughes, Richard L.
    Leadership: enhancing the lessons of experience / Richard L. Hughes, Robert C. Ginnett, Gordon J. Curphy.—3rd ed.
        p.   cm.
    Includes bibliographical references and index.
    ISBN 0-256-26143-1
    1. Leadership.   I. Ginnett, Robert C.   II. Curphy, Gordon J.
III. Title.
HM141.H78 1999
303.3'4—dc21   98-36084

http://www.mhhe.com

We dedicate this book to our families:
Georgeann, Anne, Amy, and Sarah
Sherry, Laura, and Brad
Dianne, Chelsea, Ian, and McLaren

Rich Hughes is Director of Research and a Senior Research and Program Associate at the Colorado Springs Branch of the Center for Creative Leadership (CCL). CCL is an international, nonprofit educational institution devoted to behavioral science research and leadership education. Rich manages CCL's Developing the Strategic Leader program, and trains in a variety of programs for senior executives. He joined the Center in 1995 after having served for the previous decade as the Associate Dean for Quality and Head of the Department of Behavioral Sciences and Leadership at the U.S. Air Force Academy. He is a licensed clinical psychologist, and a graduate of the Air Force Academy. He has an M.A. from the University of Texas and a Ph.D. from the University of Wyoming.

Robert Ginnett is a Senior Fellow in Applied Research at the Center for Creative Leadership. In addition to his work with senior executives, he has been engaged in ongoing research on high-performing teams. His research has found wide applicability—from surgical teams to top management teams. Previously, Robert was a tenured professor at the U.S. Air Force Academy. He has an undergraduate degree in psychology, and an MBA and a Ph.D. in organizational behavior from Yale University.

Gordy Curphy is Vice President and General Manager for Personnel Decisions , Inc. (PDI). PDI is a psychologically based management consulting firm providing consultation and programs in selection, assessment, and coaching for managers and executives, training and development, organizational reengineering, assessment centers, and outplacement services. Gordy's responsibilities include managing PDI's Denver office, serving the Rocky Mountain region. He has his undergraduate degree from the U.S. Air Force Academy and his Ph.D. from the University of Minnesota.

Often the only difference between chaos and a smoothly functioning operation is leadership; this book is about that difference.

The authors are psychologists; therefore the book has a distinctly psychological tone. You, as a reader, are going to be asked to think about leadership the way psychologists do. There is much here about psychological tests and surveys, about studies done in psychological laboratories, and about psychological analyses of good (and poor) leadership. You will often run across common psychological concepts in these pages, such as personality, values, attitudes, perceptions, and self-esteem, plus some not-so-common "jargon-y" phrases like double-loop learning, expectancy theory, and perceived inequity. This is not the same kind of book that would be written by coaches, sales managers, economists, political scientists, or generals.

Be not dismayed. Because these authors are also teachers with a good eye and ear for what students find interesting, they write clearly and cleanly, and they have also included a host of entertaining, stimulating snapshots on leadership: cartoons, quotes, anecdotal highlights, and personal glimpses from a wide range of intriguing people, each offered as an illustration of some scholarly point.

Also, because the authors are, or have been at one time or another, together or singly, not only psychologists and teachers but also children, students, Boy Scouts, parents, professors (at the U.S. Air Force Academy), Air Force officers, pilots, church members, athletes, administrators, insatiable readers, and convivial raconteurs, their stories and examples are drawn from a wide range of personal sources, and their anecdotes ring true.

As psychologists and scholars, they have reviewed here a wide range of psychological studies, other scientific inquiries, personal reflections of leaders, and philosophic writings on the topic of leadership. In distilling this material, they have drawn many practical conclusions useful for current and potential leaders. There are suggestions here for goal setting, for running meetings, for negotiating, for managing conflict within groups, and for handling your own personal stress, to mention just a few.

All leaders, no matter what their age and station, can find some useful tips here, ranging over subjects such as body language, keeping a journal, and how to relax under tension.

In several ways the authors have tried to help you, the reader, feel what it would be like "to be in charge." For example, they have posed quandaries such as the following: You are in a leadership position with a budget provided by an outside funding source. You believe strongly in, say, Topic A, and have taken a strong, visible public stance on that topic. The head of your funding source takes you aside and says, "We disagree with your stance on Topic A. Please tone down your public statements, or we will have to take another look at your budget for next year."

What would you do? Quit? Speak up and lose your budget? Tone down your public statements and feel dishonest? There's no easy answer, and it's not an unusual situation for a leader to be in. Sooner or later, all leaders have to confront just how much outside interference they will tolerate in order to be able to carry out programs they believe in.

The authors emphasize the value of experience in leadership development, a conclusion I thoroughly agree with. Virtually every leader who makes it to the top of whatever pyramid he or she happens to be climbing does so by building on earlier experiences. The successful leaders are those who learn from these earlier experiences, by reflecting on and analyzing them to help solve larger future challenges.

In this vein, let me make a suggestion. Actually, let me assign you some homework. (I know, I know, this is a peculiar approach in a book foreword but stay with me, I have a point.)

YOUR ASSIGNMENT: To gain some useful leadership experience, persuade eight people to do some notable activity together for at least two hours that they would not otherwise do without your intervention. Your only restriction is that you cannot tell them why you are doing this.

It can be any eight people: friends, family, teammates, club members, neighbors, students, working colleagues. It can be any activity, except that it should be something more substantial than watching television, eating, going to a movie, or just sitting around talk-

ing. It could be a roller-skating party, an organized debate, a songfest, a long hike, a visit to a museum, or volunteer work such as picking up litter or visiting a nursing home.

If you will take it upon yourself to make something happen in the world that would not have otherwise happened without you, you will be engaging in an act of leadership with all of its attendant barriers, burdens, and pleasures, and you will quickly learn the relevance of many of the topics that the authors discuss in this book. In fact, if you try the eight-person-two-hour experience first and read this book later, you will have a much better understanding of how complicated an act of leadership can be. You will learn about the difficulties of developing a vision ("Now that we are together, what are we going to do?"), of motivating others, of setting agendas and timetables, of securing resources, of the need for follow-through. You may even learn about "loneliness at the top." However, if you are successful, you will also experience the thrill that comes from successful leadership. One person *can* make a difference by enriching the lives of others, if only for a few hours. And for all of the frustrations and complexities of leadership, the tingling satisfaction that comes from success can become almost addictive. The capacity for making things happen can become its own motivation. With an early success, even if it is only with eight people for two hours, you may well be on your way to a leadership future.

The authors believe that leadership development involves reflecting on one's own experiences. Reading this book in the context of your own leadership experience can aid in that process. Their book is comprehensive, scholarly, stimulating, entertaining, and relevant for anyone who wishes to better understand the dynamics of leadership, and to improve her or his own personal performance.

David P. Campbell

Our third edition is different in a number of ways from the second edition. We have reorganized the sequencing of chapters within the overall structure of the book to enhance its continuity. We have woven issues of women's leadership and cultural diversity throughout the text rather than concentrating them in just one chapter at the end. We have consolidated what were three separate chapters on leadership skills into one large section at the end of the book. A final major change involves the addition of a continuing focus on three world-class leaders across several different chapters to further enhance the book's currency and integration. Amid all the changes, however, one thing has remained constant: our commitment that the book be comprehensive and balanced in its treatment of the leadership literature *and* that it also be engaging in its presentation to the reader. Now let us examine features of the third edition in somewhat greater detail.

Several significant improvements have been made to Part I ("Leadership Is a Process, Not a Position"). As noted above, one change involves continuing attention to three leaders—Madeleine Albright, Colin Powell, and Konosuke Matsushita—across several chapters. This addition allows a greater depth of analysis of several world-class leaders, from several different perspectives (i.e., in terms of the different topics of various chapters). Furthermore, this mechanism also enhances continuity and integration across chapters. Another major change to Part I is the inclusion of the chapter on contingency theories of leadership as the third chapter. Feedback from our first two editions recommended that these theories be introduced at a relatively early point in the book rather than near the end.

Most of the improvements in Part II ("Focus on the Leader") involve changes within the respective chapters. For example, each chapter includes updated research findings, new textual examples and Highlights where appropriate, as well as general improvements to chapter readability and relevance. Chapter 7, "Ethics, Values, and Attitudes," is significantly expanded, and now addresses how gender and cross-cultural differences affect leadership. Furthermore, this chapter now immediately follows the chapter entitled "Power and Influence" (Chapter 6), a logical and natural sequence. The latter chapter, too, includes greater attention to gender and leadership, as do several others, including "Leadership Behavior" (Chapter 10) and "Charisma and Transformational Leadership" (Chapter 11).

In Part III ("Focus on the Followers"), Chapter 12, "Followers and Followership," has been expanded to include a section on social exchange and leader–member relations. It also includes additional material on partnering, stewardship, and courageous followership. Chapter 13, "Groups, Teams and Their Leadership," includes an improved graphic representation of the Team Effectiveness Leadership Model, a major focus of that chapter. In addition, there is a new section on geographically dispersed teams.

Part IV ("Focus on the Situation") includes major revisions to Chapter 15, "Characteristics of the Situation." The chapter was extensively rewritten to increase its relevance to leadership issues and decrease its "feel" as merely a summary of organizational behavior topics. This was accomplished partly through the addition of the Congruence Model as a major topic in the chapter and also by decreasing (but not eliminating) attention to customary organizational behavior topics. The last chapter in this section is totally new for the third edition. Called "A Final Word: Leadership in the Future," it uses a hypothetical scenario to achieve the dual ends of integrating preceding textual material and looking at what sorts of challenges leaders in the not-so-distant future might face.

The final section of the book, Part V, presents all of the leadership skills in one place. The primary reason for this change is to improve continuity across the more topical chapters of the text. In both previous editions, a chapter on leadership skills concluded each section dealing with the leader, the followers, or the situation, respectively. This inevitably disrupted the transition between major parts of the book. Furthermore, grouping leadership skills at the end of the book allows professors greater latitude in introducing skills lessons at *their* discretion. Two other changes

to this part of the book include a very general (and admittedly somewhat arbitrary) categorization of skills into "basic" and "advanced" groupings, and the addition of sections on several leadership skills not presented in earlier editions. These newest skills include motivating others, rewards, team building, empowerment, coaching, credibility, and developmental planning.

Acknowledgments

Many people have shared their thoughts, criticisms, words of encouragement, and energy in helping us on this project and, more generally, influencing our thinking about leadership. From the Air Force Academy faculty (at one time or another), we would like to thank Bill Clover, Dave Porter, Tom McCloy, Bill Rosenbach, Jeff Austin, Fred Harburg, Bob Gregory, John Anderson, and Chip Wood. We are also especially indebted to Laura Neal for her technical assistance, undying patience, and consistently good humor in helping in the preparation of this edition.

From the Center for Creative Leadership we would like to thank Henry Browning, David Campbell, Dianne Nilsen, Glenn Hallam, Robert Kraus, Peter Neary, Karen McNeill-Miller, Jodi Taylor, and John Alexander.

We also deeply appreciate the enthusiastic encouragement, guidance, and support of numerous individuals from Irwin/McGraw-Hill, including John Biernat, Craig Beytein, Erin Riley, Paula Buschman, Ellen Cleary, and Christine Witt. We feel fortunate and proud to be associated with such a thoroughly professional editorial and publishing staff.

We are indebted to a number of individuals whose evaluations and constructive suggestions about earlier editions provided the foundations of our revisions. We are grateful for the scholarly and insightful comments of Lawrence B. Carroll, Thomas J. Cosgrove, Ken Eastman, Joseph A. Petrick, and Anson Sears for their comments about the first edition. We are similarly grateful for the equally scholarly and insightful re-views by Ken Eastman, Linda Neider, Doug McConnell, Anne Cowden, Nell Tabor-Hartley, and David Van Fleet for their comments about the second edition. These individuals share a significant amount of credit for improvements in this third edition.

We would like to make a few more personal acknowledgments. RCG would like to thank Richard Hackman, of Harvard University, for his work on team effectiveness. GJC would like to thank all of the people who have shaped his thinking about leadership, and most particularly Robert and Joyce Hogan, Fred Fiedler, Gary Yukl, Bernie Bass, Bruce Avolio, John Campbell, Marv Dunnette, Fred Gibson, Tom Daniel, Dale Thompson, Jeanette and Jack Curphy, and the staff at PDI-Denver.

Richard Hughes
Robert Ginnett
Gordon Curphy

CONTENTS IN BRIEF

C O N T E N T S

3   Contingency Theories of Leadership   50

4   Leadership Is Developed through Education and Experience   78

5   Assessing Leadership and Measuring Its Effects   103

FOCUS ON THE LEADER

6   Power and Influence   137

PART III

Focus on the Followers

I   LEADERSHIP IS A PROCESS, NOT A POSITION

If any single idea is central to this book, it is that leadership is a process, not a position. The entire first part of the book, in fact, explores that idea. One is not a leader – except perhaps in name only – merely because one holds a title or position. Leadership involves something happening as a result of the interaction between a leader and followers.

In Chapter 1 we define leadership and explore its relationship to concepts such as management and followership. We also suggest that better leadership is something everyone shares responsibility for. In Chapter 2 we discuss how leadership involves complex interactions between the leader, the followers, and the situation they are in. We also present an interactional framework for conceptualizing leadership which becomes an integrating theme throughout the rest of the book. Chapter 3 examines how several different formal theories of leadership extend this concept of interaction very systematically to make various predictions about leadership effectiveness. Chapter 4 looks at how we can become

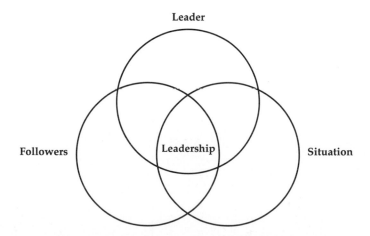

better leaders by profiting more fully from our experiences, which is not to say that either the study or the practice of leadership is simple. Part I concludes with a chapter examining basic concepts and methods used in the scientific study of leaders and leadership.

1   LEADERSHIP IS EVERYONE'S BUSINESS

Chapter Outline

Introduction

In the spring of 1972, an airplane flew across the Andes mountains carrying its crew and 40 passengers. Most of the passengers were members of an amateur Uruguayan rugby team en route to a game in Chile. The plane never arrived. It crashed in snow-covered mountains, breaking into several pieces on impact. The main part of the fuselage slid like a toboggan down a steep valley, finally coming

3

to rest in waist-deep snow. Although a number of people died immediately or within a day of the impact, the picture for the 28 survivors was not much better. The fuselage initially offered little protection from the extreme cold, food supplies were scant, and a number of passengers had serious injuries from the crash. Over the next few days, several of the passengers became psychotic and several others died from their injuries. Those passengers who were relatively uninjured set out to do what they could to improve their chances of survival.

Several worked on "weatherproofing" the wreckage, others found ways to get water, and those with medical training took care of the injured. Although shaken from the crash, the survivors initially were confident they would be found. These feelings gradually gave way to despair, as search and rescue teams failed to find the wreckage. With the passing of several weeks and no sign of rescue in sight, the remaining passengers decided to mount several expeditions to determine the best way to escape. The most physically fit were chosen to go on the expeditions, as the thin mountain air and the deep snow made the trips extremely taxing. The results of the trips were both frustrating and demoralizing; the expeditionaries determined they were in the middle of the Andes mountains, and walking out to find help was believed to be impossible. Just when the survivors thought nothing worse could possibly happen, an avalanche hit the wreckage and killed several more of them.

The remaining survivors concluded they would not be rescued and their only hope was for someone to leave the wreckage and find help. Three of the fittest passengers were chosen for the final expedition, and everyone else's work was directed toward improving the expedition's chances of success. The three expeditionaries were given more food and were exempted from routine survival activities; the rest spent most of their energies securing supplies for the trip. Two months after the plane crash, the expeditionaries set out on their final attempt to find help. After hiking for 10 days through some of the most rugged terrain in the world, the expeditionaries stumbled across a group of Chilean peasants tending cattle. One of the expeditionaries stated, "I come from a plane that fell in the mountains. I am Uruguayan. . . ." Eventually, 14 other survivors were rescued.

When the full account of their survival became known, it was not without controversy. It had required extreme and unsettling measures; the survivors had lived only by eating the flesh of their deceased comrades. Nonetheless, their story is one of the most moving survival dramas of all time, magnificently told by Piers Paul Read in *Alive* (1974). It is a story of tragedy and courage, and it is a story of leadership.

Perhaps a story of survival in the Andes is so far removed from everyday experience that it does not seem to hold any relevant lessons about leadership for you personally. But consider for a moment some of the basic issues the Andes survivors faced: tension between individual and group goals, dealing with the different needs and personalities of group members, and keeping hope alive in the face of adversity. These issues are not so very different from those facing many groups we're a part of. We can also look at the Andes experience for examples of the emergence of informal leaders in groups. Before the flight, a boy named Parrado was awkward and shy, a "second-stringer" both athletically and socially. Nonetheless, this unlikely hero became the best loved and most respected among the survivors for his courage, optimism, fairness, and emotional support. Persuasiveness in group decision making also was an important part of leadership among the Andes survivors. During the difficult discussions preceding the agonizing decision to survive on the flesh of their deceased comrades, one of the rugby players made his reasoning clear: "I know that if my dead body could help you stay alive, then I would want you to use it. In fact, if I do die and you don't eat me, then I'll come back from wherever I am and give you a good kick in the ass" (Read, 1974, p. 77).

The Purpose of This Book

Few of us will ever be confronted with a leadership challenge as dramatic as that faced by the Andes survivors. We may frequently face, however, opportunities for leadership that involve group dynamics which are just as complex. This purpose of this book is to help you be more effective in leadership situations by helping you better understand the complex challenges of leadership.

More specifically, we hope this book will serve as a sort of guide for interpreting leadership theory and research. The book describes and critically evaluates a number of leadership theories and research articles, and also offers practical advice on how to be a better leader. This book is designed to fill the gap between books that provide excellent summaries of leadership research but little practical advice on how to be a better leader, and those that are not based on theory or research but primarily offer just one person's views on how to be a better leader (in "how to" books, memoirs, etc.).

Three Leaders

One way we will bridge that gap between leadership research and more personalized accounts of leadership will be through personal glimpses of individual leaders (also see Highlight 1–1). Dozens of different leaders are mentioned illustratively throughout the text, but three particular individuals will be a continuing focus across many chapters. They are Colin Powell, Madeleine Albright, and Konosuke Matsushita. Let us introduce you to them now.

Colin Powell

Colin Powell is a former chairman of the Joint Chiefs of Staff, the highest ranking officer in the U.S. armed forces, and the first African American ever to hold that position. He has commanded soldiers, advised presidents, and considered running for president of the United States himself in 1996. He still may, and millions hope he will. Much of his work today involves leading an army of volunteers to improve the future for disadvantaged youth.

We might wonder, however, will he act differently leading civilian volunteers from the way he acted when he wore stars on his shoulders? We might also wonder, what is it about him that inspired so many to hope he would run for elective office himself? And we might wonder, was he always a great leader, or did even Colin Powell need to learn a few things along the way? These are some of the questions we will consider ahead.

Madeleine Albright

Madeleine Albright is the U.S. secretary of state, the highest ranking woman official in the nation's history. A naturalized citizen, she was born in Czechoslovakia in the days immediately preceding World War II. Fleeing the tyranny of both nazi Germany and Soviet communism, her family escaped to England and later emigrated to the United States. Remaining in Europe, her grandparents died in concentration camps.

Influencing others' views of foreign policy always has been an interest of Albright's, perhaps because she grew up in four different countries and speaks five languages. In the eighth grade she won a contest for correctly naming all the members of the United Nations, and as a ninth grader she started an international-relations club at her school, naming herself its president. As secretary of state she is known for her candor and charm as well as her grasp of complex issues. Before becoming secretary of state, Albright served in several other governmental roles. She also served on the faculty at Georgetown University, where she won numerous awards for outstanding teaching.

Konosuke Matsushita

Although you never may have heard of Konosuke Matsushita by name, John Kotter has called him the most remarkable entrepreneur of the 20th century. Despite only four years of formal education, he founded Matsushita Electric in 1917 and saw his company build revenue of nearly $50 billion. On a purely financial basis this exceeded the success of such other well known entrepreneurs as Soichiro Honda, Sam Walton, J. C. Penney, Henry Ford, and Bill Gates. Matsushita's legacy, however, is far more than business success.

He was more than just wildly successful. He was an innovative leader who instituted radically unconventional management practices that even today are considered modern. He was a philanthropist, creating a Nobel Prize–like organization and an institute to develop leadership in government and politics for the 21st century. By comparison, graduates of the Matsushita Institute of Government and Management are 100 times more likely to serve in the Japanese Diet than graduates of the Kennedy School of Government at Harvard University are to serve in the U.S. Congress.

What accounts for the success of this remarkable man? Did he possess extraordinary qualities? Did certain unique circumstances or events favor him? We will examine these and other questions about Konosuke Matsushita.

Leadership Quotes, Chapter 1

The halls of fame are open wide and they are always full. Some go in by the door called "pushed" and some by the door called "pull."

Stanley Baldwin

Stow this talk. Care killed a cat. Fetch ahead for the doubloons.

Long John Silver, in Robert Louis Stevenson's *Treasure Island*

Progress always involves risks. You can't steal second base and keep your foot on first.

Frederick B. Wilcox

If you miss seven balls out of ten, you're batting three hundred and that's good enough for the Hall of Fame. You can't score if you keep the bat on your shoulder.

Walter B. Wriston

If you want some ham, you gotta go into the smokehouse.

Huey Long

He who would eat the fruit must climb the tree.

Scottish Proverb

*Lives of great men all remind us
We can make our lives sublime,
And, departing, leave behind us
Footprints on the sands of time.*

Henry Wadsworth Longfellow

Remember the difference between a boss and a leader: a boss says "Go!"—a leader says, "Let's go!"

E. M. Kelly

Never reveal all of yourself to other people; hold back something in reserve so that people are never quite sure if they really know you.

Michael Korda

A democracy cannot follow a leader unless he is dramatized. A man to be a hero must not content himself with heroic virtues and anonymous action. He must talk and explain as he acts—drama.

William Allen White

Nurture your mind with great thoughts. To believe in the heroic makes heroes.

Benjamin Disraeli

Any fool can keep a rule. God gave him a brain to know when to break the rule.

General Willard W. Scott

Never try to teach a pig to sing; it wastes your time and it annoys the pig.

Paul Dickson

What Is Leadership?

The Andes story and the lives of the three leaders we just introduced provide numerous examples of leadership. But just what *is* leadership? People who do research on leadership actually disagree more than you might think about what leadership really is. Most of this disagreement stems from the fact that leadership is a complex phenomenon involving the leader, the followers, and the situation. Some leadership researchers have focused on the personality, physical traits, or behaviors of the leader; others have studied the relationships between leaders and followers; still others have studied how aspects of the situation affect the ways leaders act. Some have extended the latter viewpoint so far as to suggest there is no such thing as leadership; they argue that organizational successes and failures often get falsely attributed to the leader, but the situation may have a much greater impact on how the organization functions than does any individual, including the leader (Meindl & Ehrlich, 1987).

Perhaps the best way for you to begin to understand the complexities of leadership is to see some of the ways leadership has been defined. Leadership researchers have defined leadership in the following different ways:

- The creative and directive force of morale (Munson, 1921).
- The process by which an agent induces a subordinate to behave in a desired manner (Bennis, 1959).
- The presence of a particular influence relationship between two or more persons (Hollander & Julian, 1969).
- Directing and coordinating the work of group members (Fiedler, 1967).
- An interpersonal relation in which others comply because they want to, not because they have to (Merton, 1969; Hogan, Curphy, & Hogan, 1994).
- Transforming followers, creating visions of the goals that may be attained, and articulating for the followers the ways to attain those goals (Bass, 1985; Tichy & Devanna, 1986).
- The process of influencing an organized group toward accomplishing its goals (Roach & Behling, 1984).
- Actions that focus resources to create desirable opportunities (Campbell, 1991).
- The leader's job is to create conditions for the team to be effective (Ginnett, 1996).

As you can see, these definitions differ in many ways, and these differences have resulted in various researchers exploring very different aspects of leadership. For example, if we were to apply these definitions to the Andes survival scenario described earlier, researchers adopting Munson's definition would focus on the behaviors Parrado used to keep up the morale of the survivors. Researchers using Roach and Behling's definition would examine how Parrado managed to convince the group to stage and support the final expedition. One's definition of leadership might also influence just *who* is considered an appropriate leader for study. For example, researchers who adopted Merton's definition might not be interested in studying Colin Powell's leadership as an army general. They might reason that the enormous hierarchical power and authority of an army general makes every order or decision a "have to" response from subordinates. Thus, each group of researchers might focus on a different aspect of leadership, and each would tell a different story regarding the leader, the followers, and the situation.

Although such a large number of leadership definitions may seem confusing, it is important to understand that there is no single correct definition. The various definitions can help us appreciate the multitude of factors that affect leadership, as well as different perspectives from which to view it. For example, in Bennis's definition, the word *subordinate* seems to confine leadership to downward influence in hierarchical relationships; it seems to exclude informal leadership. Fiedler's definition emphasizes the directing and controlling aspects of leadership, and thereby may deemphasize emotional aspects of leadership. The emphasis Merton placed on subordinates' "wanting to" comply with a leader's wishes seems to exclude coercion of any kind as a leadership tool. Further, it becomes problematic to identify ways in which a leader's actions are really leadership if subordinates voluntarily comply when a leader with considerable potential coercive power merely asks others to do something without explicitly threatening them. Similarly, Campbell used the phrase *desirable opportunities* precisely to distinguish between leadership and tyranny.

All considered, we believe the definition provided by Roach and Behling (1984) to be a fairly comprehensive and helpful one. Therefore, this book also defines leadership as "the process of influencing an organized group toward accomplishing its goals." There are several implications of this definition which are worth further examination.

Leadership Is Both a Science and an Art

Saying leadership is both a science and an art emphasizes the subject of leadership as a field of scholarly inquiry, as well as certain aspects of the practice of leadership. The scope of the science of leadership is reflected in the number of studies—approximately 8,000—cited in a recent edition of an authoritative reference work, *Bass & Stogdill's Handbook of Leadership: Theory, Research, & Managerial Applications* (Bass, 1990). However, being an expert on leadership research is neither a necessary nor a sufficient condition for being a good leader. Some managers may be effective leaders without ever having taken a course or training program in leadership, and some scholars in the field of leadership may be relatively poor leaders themselves.

This is not to say that knowing something about leadership research is irrelevant to leadership effectiveness. Scholarship may not be a prerequisite for leadership effectiveness, but understanding some of the major research findings can help individuals better analyze situations using a variety of perspectives. That, in turn, can give leaders insight about how to be more effective. Even so, because the skill in analyzing and responding to situations varies greatly across leaders, leadership will always remain partly an art as well as a science.

Leadership Is Both Rational and Emotional

Leadership involves both the rational and emotional sides of human experience. Leadership includes actions and influences based on reason and logic as well those based on inspiration and passion. We do not want to cultivate leaders like Commander Data of *Star Trek: The Next Generation*, who always responds with logical predictability. Because people differ in their thoughts and feelings, hopes and dreams, need and fears, goals and ambitions, and strengths and weaknesses, leadership situations can be very complex. Because people are both rational and emotional, leaders can use rational techniques and/or emotional appeals in order to influence followers, but they must also weigh the rational and emotional consequences of their actions.

A full appreciation of leadership involves looking at both these sides of human nature. Good leadership is more than just calculation and planning, or following a "checklist," even though rational analysis can enhance good leadership. Good leadership also involves touching others' feelings; emotions play an important role in leadership too. Just one example of this is the civil rights movement of the 1960s. It was a movement based on emotions as well as on principles. Dr. Martin Luther King, Jr., *inspired* many people to action; he touched people's hearts as well as their heads.

Aroused feelings, however, can be used either positively or negatively, constructively or destructively. Some leaders have been able to inspire others to deeds of great purpose and courage. On the other hand, as images of Adolph Hitler's mass rallies or present-day angry mobs attest, group frenzy can readily become group mindlessness. As another example, emotional appeals by the Reverend Jim Jones resulted in approximately 800 of his followers volitionally committing suicide.

The mere presence of a group (even without heightened emotional levels) can also cause people to act differently than when they are alone. For example, in airline cockpit crews, there are clear lines of authority from the captain down to the first officer (second in command) and so on. So strong are the norms surrounding the authority of the captain that some first officers will not take control of the airplane from the captain even in the event of impending disaster. Foushee (1984) reported a study wherein airline captains in simulator training intentionally feigned incapacitation so that the response of the rest of the crew could be observed. The feigned incapacitations occurred at a predetermined point during the plane's final approach in landing, and the simulation involved conditions of poor weather and visibility. Approximately 25 percent of the first officers in these simulated flights allowed the plane to crash. For some reason, the first officers did not take control even when it was clear the captain was allowing the aircraft to deviate from the parameters of a safe approach. This example demonstrates how group dynamics can influence the behavior of group members even when emotional levels are *not* high. (Believe it or not, airline crews are so well-trained, this is *not* an emotional situation.) In sum, it should be apparent that leadership involves followers' feelings and nonrational behavior as well as rational behavior. Leaders need to consider *both* the rational and the emotional consequences of their actions.

Leadership and Management

In trying to answer, "What is leadership?" it is natural to look at the relationship between leadership and management. To many, the word *management* suggests words like *efficiency, planning, paperwork, procedures, regulations, control,* and *consistency.* Leadership is often more associated with words like *risk taking, dynamic, creativity, change,* and *vision.* Some say leadership is fundamentally a value-choosing, and thus a value-laden, activity, whereas management is not. Leaders are thought to *do the right things,* whereas managers are thought to *do things right* (Bennis, 1985; Zaleznik, 1983). Here are some other distinctions between managers and leaders (Bennis, 1989):

- Managers administer; leaders innovate.
- Managers maintain; leaders develop.
- Managers control; leaders inspire.
- Managers have a short-term view; leaders, a long-term view.
- Managers ask how and when; leaders ask what and why.
- Managers imitate; leaders originate.
- Managers accept the status quo; leaders challenge it.

Zaleznik (1974, 1983) goes so far as to say these differences reflect fundamentally different personality types, that leaders and managers are basically different kinds of people. He says some people are managers *by nature;* other people are leaders *by nature.* This is not at all to say one is better than the other, only that they are different. Their differences, in fact, can be quite useful, since organizations typically need both functions performed well in order to be successful. For example, consider again the civil rights movement in the 1960s. Dr. Martin Luther King, Jr., gave life and direction to the civil rights movement in America. He gave dignity and hope of freer participation in our national life to people who before had little reason to expect it. He inspired the world with his vision and eloquence, and changed the way we live together. America is a different nation today because of him. Was Dr. Martin Luther King, Jr., a leader? Of course. Was he a manager? Somehow that does not seem to fit, and the civil rights movement may have failed if it had not been for the managerial talents of his supporting staff. Leadership and management complement each other, and both are vital to organizational success.

With regard to the issue of leadership versus management, we take a middle-of-the-road position. We think of leadership and management as closely related but distinguishable functions. Our view of the relationship is

FIGURE 1–1

*Leadership and
Management
Overlap*

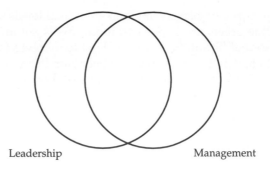

Leadership   Management

depicted in Figure 1–1. It shows leadership and management as two over-lapping functions. Although some of the functions performed by leaders and managers may be unique, there is also an area of overlap.

Leadership and Followership

One aspect of our text's definition of leadership is particularly worth noting: Leadership is a social influence process shared among *all* members of a group. Leadership is not restricted to the influence exerted by someone in a particular position or role; followers are part of the leadership process, too. In recent years, both practitioners and scholars have emphasized the relatedness of leadership and followership. As Burns (1978) observed, the idea of "one-man leadership" is a contradiction in terms.

Thus, the question *What is leadership?* cannot be separated from the question *What is followership?* There is no simple line dividing them; they merge. The relationship between leadership and followership can be represented by borrowing a concept from topographical mathematics: the Möbius strip. You are probably familiar with the curious properties of the Möbius strip: When a strip of paper is twisted and connected in the manner depicted in Figure 1–2, it proves to have only one side. You can prove this to yourself by putting a pencil to any point on the strip and tracing continuously. Your pencil will cover the entire strip (i.e., both "sides"), eventually returning to the point at which you started. In order to demonstrate the relevance of this curiosity to leadership, cut a strip of paper. On one side write *leadership*, and on the other side write *followership*. Then twist the strip and connect the two ends in the manner of the figure. You will have created a leadership/followership Möbius strip wherein the two concepts merge one into the other, just as leadership and followership can become indistinguishable in organizations (adapted from Macrorie, 1984).

This does not mean leadership and followership are the same thing. When top-level executives were asked to list qualities they most look for and admire in leaders and followers, the lists were similar but not identical (Kouzes & Posner, 1987). Ideal leaders were characterized as honest, competent, forward looking, and inspiring; ideal followers were described as honest, competent,

FIGURE 1–2

*The Leadership/
Followership
Möbius Strip*

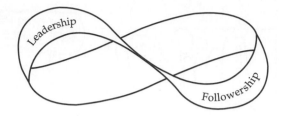

dependent, and cooperative. The differences could become critical in certain situations, as when a forward-looking and inspiring subordinate perceives a significant conflict between his own goals or ethics and those of his superiors. Such a situation could become a crisis for the individual and the organization, demanding choice between leading and following.

Leadership on Stages Large and Small

Great leaders sometimes seem larger than life. Charles de Gaulle, a leader of France during and after World War II, was such a figure (see Highlight 1–2). Not all good leaders are famous or powerful, however, and we believe leadership can be best understood if we study a broad range of leaders, some famous, and some not-so-famous (see Highlight 1–3). Most leaders, after all, are not known outside their own particular sphere or activity, nor should they be. Here are a few examples of leadership on the small stage, where individuals influenced and helped their respective groups attain their goals.

- An elderly woman led an entire community's effort to organize an advocacy and support group for parents of mentally ill adult children and provide sheltered living arrangements for these people. She helped these families while also serving an invaluable role in educating state legislators and social agencies about the needs of this neglected constituency. There had been numerous parents with mentally ill children in this community before, but none had had the idea or took the initiative to organize among themselves. As a result of this woman's leadership, many adults live and work in more humane conditions than they did before.

- A seasoned air force sergeant took two young, "green" enlistees under her wing after they both coincidentally reported for duty on the same day. She taught them the ropes at work and took pride as they matured. One of them performed so well that he went on to be commissioned as an officer. Unfortunately, the sergeant discovered the other pilfering cash from the unit gift fund. Though it pained her to do so, the sergeant took action for the enlistee to be discharged from the service. Leadership involves significant intrinsic rewards such as seeing others blossom under your tutelage, but with its rewards also goes the responsibility to enforce standards of conduct.

Highlight 1–2

The Stateliness of Charles de Gaulle

Certain men have, one might almost say from birth, the quality of exuding authority, as though it were a liquid, though it is impossible to say precisely of what it consists. In his fascinating book *Leaders,* former president Richard Nixon described the French president Charles de Gaulle as one of the great leaders he had met. Following are several aspects of de Gaulle's leadership based on Nixon's observations.

- *He conveyed stately dignity.* De Gaulle had a resolute bearing that conveyed distance and superiority to others. He was at ease with other heads of state but never informal with anyone, even close friends. His tall stature and imperious manner conveyed the message he was not a common man.

- *He was a masterful public speaker.* He had a deep, serene voice and a calm, self-assured manner. He used the French language grandly and eloquently. According to Nixon, "He spoke so articulately and with such precision that his message seemed to resonate apart from his words" (p. 59).

- *He played the part.* De Gaulle understood the role of theater in politics, and his meetings with the press (a thousand at a time!) were like audiences with royalty. He staged them in great and ornate halls, and he deftly crafted public statements that would be understood differently by different groups. In one sense, perhaps, this could be seen as a sort of falseness, but that may be too narrow a view. Nixon reflected on this aspect of de Gaulle's leadership: "General de Gaulle was a facade, but not a false one. Behind it was a man of incandescent intellect and a phenomenal discipline. The facade was like the ornamentation on a great cathedral, rather than the flimsy pretense of a Hollywood prop with nothing behind it" (p. 60).

Source: R. Nixon, *Leaders* (New York: Warner Books, 1982).

- The office manager for a large advertising agency directed its entire administrative staff, most of whom worked in the reception area. His engaging personality and concern for others made everyone feel important. Morale in the office was high, and many important customers credit their positive "first impression" of the whole agency on the congeniality and positive climate among the office staff. Leaders set the tone for the organization, and followers often model the behaviors displayed by the leader. This leader helped create an office mood of optimism and supportiveness that reached outward to everyone who visited.

These examples are representative of the opportunities every one of us has to be a leader. To paraphrase John Fitzgerald Kennedy, we all can make a difference

---
Highlight 1–3

> # Lights, Camera, Action!
>
> The director's role is probably the most critical one in the production of any motion picture. Being a director means wearing many hats: visionary, encourager, taskmaster, coach, and numerous others. What kind of person becomes a movie director? Take the case of Matty Rich, whose major credit is *Straight out of Brooklyn*. Rich is just 20 years old, but he is one of the talented young directors following Spike Lee's lead in making passionate and pointed films about life in the inner city. Rich grew up in Brooklyn watching drugs and crime infect the lives of people close to him. Not liking what he saw, he declared war with his weapon of choice—a camera. "I was angry that everybody around me got destroyed, and I wanted to show that everyday struggle."
>
> Despite his youth, Rich has years of experience in his trade. He began reading books about filmmaking a decade ago. Then, when he was 17, he gambled that those years of study had prepared him well. He got $16,000 in cash advances from relatives' credit cards to finance supplies and a small film crew. Then, out of money, he made an appeal for help over a local black radio station. It worked; Rich collected $77,000 from contributors. He completed his movie, then fortunate breaks led to its screening at a major film festival. Now several studios are pursuing him. "It's kind of weird when you're 19 and you're being wooed . . . If I hadn't done this movie, I'd be just another black kid on the street with a gold tooth and a funny haircut."
>
> Source: R. Corliss , "Boyz of New Black City," *Time*, June 17, 1991, pp. 64–68.

and each of us should try. However, this book is more than an exhortation for each of us to play a more active leadership role on the various stages of our lives. It is a review of what is known about leadership from available research, a review we hope is presented in a way that will foster leadership development. We are all more likely to make the kind of difference we want if we understand what leadership is and what it is not, how you get it, and what improves it (see Highlight 1–4 for a contrasting view of how much of a difference leaders really make). Toward that end, we will look at leaders on both the large and the small stages of life throughout the book. We will look at leaders on the world stage like Albright, Powell, and Matsushita; and we will look at leaders on those smaller stages closer to home like principals, coaches, and managers at the local store. You also might want to see Highlight 1–5 for a listing of women leaders throughout history from many different stages.

Myths That Hinder Leadership Development

Few things pose a greater obstacle to leadership development than certain unsubstantiated and self-limiting beliefs about leadership. Therefore, before we begin examining what leadership and leadership development are in more

Highlight 1–4

The Romance of Leadership

This text is predicated on the idea that leaders can make a difference. Interestingly, though, while people in the business world generally agree, not all scholars do.

People in the business world attribute much of a company's success or failure to its leadership. One study counted the number of articles appearing in *The Wall Street Journal* that dealt with leadership and found nearly 10 percent of the articles about representative target companies addressed that company's leadership. Furthermore, there was a significant positive relationship between company performance and the number of articles about its leadership; the more a company's leadership was emphasized in *The Wall Street Journal*, the better the company was doing. This might mean the more a company takes leadership seriously (as reflected by the emphasis in *The Wall Street Journal*), the better it does.

However, the authors were skeptical about the real utility of leadership as a concept. They suggested leadership is merely a romanticized notion, an obsession people want and need to believe in. Belief in the potency of leadership may be a sort of cultural myth, which has utility primarily insofar as it affects how people create meaning about causal events in complex social systems. The behavior of leaders, the authors contend, does not account for very much of the variance in an organization's performance. Nonetheless, people seem strongly committed to a sort of basic faith that individual leaders shape organizational destiny for good or ill.

Source: J. R. Meindl, S. B. Ehrlich, and J. M. Dukerich, "The Romance of Leadership." *Administrative Science Quarterly* 30 (1985), pp. 78–102.

detail, we will consider what they are not. We will examine several beliefs (we call them myths) that stand in the way of fully understanding and developing leadership.

Myth: Good Leadership Is All Common Sense

At face value, this myth says one needs only common sense to be a good leader. It also implies, however, that most if not all of the studies of leadership reported in scholarly journals and books only confirm what anyone with common sense already knows.

The problem, of course, is with the ambiguous term *common sense*. It implies a common body of practical knowledge about life that virtually any reasonable person with moderate experience has acquired. A simple experiment, however, may convince you that common sense may be less common than you think. Ask a few friends or acquaintances whether the old folk wisdom "Absence makes the heart grow fonder" is true or false. Most will say it is true. After that ask a different group whether the old folk wisdom "Out of sight, out of mind" is true

Highlight 1–5

Women and Leadership
A Few Women Leaders throughout History

69 B.C.   Cleopatra, Queen of Egypt, is born and ascends the throne at age 17.

1429   Joan of Arc is finally granted an audience with Charles the Dauphin of France and subsequently captains the army at the siege of Orleans.

1492   Queen Isabella of Spain finances Columbus's voyage to the new world.

1558–1603   England's Queen Elizabeth I establishes England as a dominant sea power and defeats the Spanish Armada.

1638   Religious dissident Anne Hutchinson leads schismatic group from Massachusetts Bay Colony into wilderness and establishes Rhode Island.

1775–1781   Catherine the Great of Russia adopts an "Armed Neutrality" policy, which undermines the British blockade of the colonies during the American Revolution.

1803–1806   Sacajawea leads the Lewis and Clark expedition.

1837   Educator Mary Lyons founds Mount Holyoke Female Seminary (later Mount Holyoke College), the first American college exclusively for women.

1843   Dorothea Dix reports to Massachusetts legislature on treatment of criminally insane resulting in a significant reform of American mental institutions.

1849   Harriet Tubman escapes from slavery and becomes one of the most successful "conductors" on the Underground Railroad. She helps more than 300 slaves to freedom.

1854   Florence Nightingale, the founder of modern nursing, organizes a unit of women nurses to serve in the Crimean War.

1869   Susan B. Anthony is elected president of the National American Woman Suffrage Association.

1900   Carry Nation gains fame destroying saloons as head of the American Temperance Movement.

1919   Mary Pickford becomes the first top-level female executive of a major film studio.

1940   Margaret Chase Smith is the first woman elected to Congress.

1966   National Organization of Women (NOW) is founded by Betty Friedan.

1969   Golda Meir is elected prime minister of Israel.

1979   Mother Teresa receives Nobel Prize for her three decades of work leading the Congregation of Missions of Charity in Calcutta, India.

1979   Margaret Thatcher becomes the United Kingdom's first female prime minister.

1981   Jeane Kirkpatrick is appointed U.S. ambassador to the United Nations.

1981   Sandra Day O'Connor is appointed to the U.S. Supreme Court.

1988   Benazir Bhutto is elected first female prime minister of Pakistan.

1992   Hillary Clinton assumes active policy role in federal government as First Lady.

1994   Christine Todd Whitman becomes governor of New Jersey.

1996   Madeleine Albright is appointed U.S. secretary of state.

Source: Originally adapted from the *Colorado Education Association Journal*, February–March 1991. Based on original work by the Arts and Entertainment Network.

or false. Most of that group will answer true as well, even though the two proverbs are contradictory.

A similar thing sometimes happens when people hear about the results of studies concerning human behavior. On hearing the results, people may say, "Who needed a study to learn that? I knew it all the time." However, several experiments by Slovic and Fischoff (1977) and Wood (1979) showed that events were much more surprising when subjects had to guess the outcome of an experiment than when subjects were told the outcome. What seems obvious after you know the results and what you (or anyone else) would have predicted beforehand are not the same thing. Hindsight is always 20/20.

The point might become clearer with a specific example you may now try. Read the following paragraph:

> After World War II, the U.S. Army spent enormous sums of money on studies only to reach conclusions that, many believed, should have been apparent at the outset. One, for example, was that southern soldiers were better able to stand the climate in the hot South Sea islands than northern soldiers were.

This sounds reasonable, but there is just one problem; the statement above is exactly contrary to the actual findings. Southerners were no better than Northerners in adapting to tropical climates (Lazarsfeld, 1949). Common sense can often play tricks on us.

Put a little differently, one of the challenges of understanding leadership may well be to know when common sense applies and when it does not. Do leaders need to act confidently? Of course. But they also need to be humble enough to recognize that others' views are useful, too. Do leaders need to persevere when times get tough? Yes. But they also need to recognize when times change and a new direction is called for. If leadership were nothing more than common sense, then there should be few, if any, problems in the workplace. However, we venture to guess you have noticed more than a few problems between leaders and followers. Effective leadership must be something more than just common sense.

Myth: Leaders Are Born, Not Made

Some people believe being a leader is either in one's genes or not; others believe that life experiences mold the individual, that no one is born a leader. Which view is right? In a sense, both and neither. Both views are right in the sense that innate factors as well as formative experiences influence many sorts of behavior, including leadership. Yet both views are wrong to the extent they imply leadership is *either* innate *or* acquired; what matters more is how these factors *interact*. It does not seem useful, we believe, to think of the world as composed of two mutually exclusive types of people, leaders and nonleaders. It is more useful to address the ways in which each person can make the most of leadership opportunities he or she faces.

It may be easier to see the pointlessness of asking whether leaders are born or made by looking at an alternative question of far less popular interest: Are *college professors* born or made? Conceptually, the issues are the same, and here, too, the answer is that every college professor is both born *and* made. It seems clear enough that college professors are partly "born" since (among other factors) there is a genetic component to intelligence, and intelligence surely plays some part in becoming a college professor (well, at least a *minor* part!). But every college professor is also partly "made." One obvious way is that college professors must have advanced education in specialized fields; even with the right genes one could not become a college professor without certain requisite experiences. Becoming a college professor depends partly on what one is "born with" and partly on how that inheritance is shaped through experience. The same is true of leadership.

More specifically, research indicates that many cognitive abilities and personality traits are at least partly innate (McGue & Bouchard, 1990; Tellegen, Lykken, Bouchard, Wilcox, Segal, & Rich, 1988; McCrae & Foster, 1995). Thus, natural talents or characteristics may offer certain advantages or disadvantages to a leader. Take physical characteristics: A man's above-average height may increase others' tendency to think of him as a leader; it may also boost his own self-confidence. But it doesn't "make" him a leader. The same holds true for psychological characteristics which seem related to leadership. The very stability of certain characteristics over long periods of time (e.g., at school reunions people seem to have kept the same personalities we remember them as having years earlier) may reinforce the impression that our basic natures are fixed, but different environments nonetheless may nurture or suppress different leadership qualities.

Myth: The Only School You Learn Leadership from Is the School of Hard Knocks

Some people skeptically question whether leadership can develop through formal study, believing instead it can only be acquired through actual experience. It is a mistake, however, to think of formal study and learning from experience as mutually exclusive or antagonistic. In fact, they complement each other. Rather than ask whether leadership develops from formal study or from real-life experience, it is better to ask what kind of study will help students learn to discern critical lessons about leadership from their own experience. Approaching the issue in such a way recognizes the critical role of experience in leadership development, but it also admits that certain kinds of study and training can improve a person's ability to discern critical lessons about leadership from experience. It can, in other words, help accelerate the process of learning from experience.

We would argue that one of the advantages of formally studying leadership is that formal study provides students with a variety of ways of examining a particular leadership situation. By studying the different ways researchers have defined and examined leadership, students can use these definitions and theories to better understand what is going on in any leadership situation. For example, earlier in this chapter we used three different leadership definitions as a framework for describing or analyzing the situation facing Parrado and the remaining survivors of the plane crash, and each definition focused on a different aspect of leadership. These frameworks can similarly be applied to better understand the experiences one has as both a leader and a follower. We think it is very difficult for leaders, particularly novice leaders, to examine leadership situations from multiple perspectives, but we also believe developing this skill can help you become a better leader. Being able to analyze your experiences from multiple perspectives may be the greatest single contribution a formal course in leadership can give you.

An Overview of This Book

In order to fill the gaps between leadership research and practice, this book will critically review the major theories of leadership as well as provide practical advice about improving leadership. As our first steps in that journey, the next four chapters of the book describe how: (*a*) leadership is an interaction between the leader, the followers, and the situation; (*b*) various formal theories attempt to explain leadership effectiveness in terms of those interactions; (*c*) leadership develops through experience, and (*d*) leadership can be assessed and studied. The remainder of the book uses the leader–follower-situation interaction model described in Chapter 2 as a framework for organizing and discussing various theories and research findings related to leadership. The chapters in Part II focus on the leader, beginning with an examination of the issues of power and influence, then of ethics, values, and attitudes. Other chapters look at theories and research concerning the leader: how good and bad leaders differ in personality, intelligence, creativity, and behavior. Part II concludes by looking at charismatic leadership. Part III primarily focuses on the followers; it summarizes the research and provides practical advice on such topics as motivating subordinates and using delegation. Part IV examines how the situation affects the leadership process. Part V looks at several dozen specific leadership skills, including practical advice about handling specific leadership challenges. While Part V represents in one sense the "end" of the book, you may want to start reading about and practicing some of the skills right now.

Summary

Although many definitions of leadership exist, we define leadership as the process of influencing others toward achieving group goals. The chapter also looks at the idea that leadership is both a science and an art. Because leadership is an immature science, researchers are still struggling to find out what the important questions in leadership are; we are far from finding conclusive answers to them. Even those individuals with extensive knowledge of the leadership research may be poor leaders. Knowing what to do is not the same as knowing when, where, and how to do it. The art of leadership concerns the skill of understanding leadership situations and influencing others to accomplish group goals. Formal leadership education may give individuals the skills to better understand leadership situations, and mentorships and experience may give individuals the skills to better influence others. Leaders must also weigh both rational and emotional considerations when attempting to influence others. Leadership sometimes can be accomplished through relatively rational, explicit, rule-based methods of assessing situations and determining actions. Nevertheless, there is also an emotional side of human nature that must be acknowledged. Leaders are often most effective when they affect people at both the emotional level and the rational level. The idea of leadership as a whole-person process can also be applied to the distinction often made between leaders and managers. Although leadership and management can be distinguished as separate functions, a more comprehensive picture of supervisory positions could be made by examining the overlapping functions of leaders and managers. Leadership does not occur without followers, and followership is an easily neglected component of the leadership process. Leadership is everyone's business and everyone's responsibility. Finally, learning certain conceptual frameworks for thinking about leadership can be helpful in making your own on-the-job experiences a particularly valuable part of your leadership development. Thinking about leadership can help you become a better leader than you are right now.

Key Terms

leadership   management
followership

Discussion Questions

1. We say leadership involves influencing organized groups toward goals. Do you see any disadvantages to restricting the definition to organized groups?

2. How would you define leadership?

3. Are some people the "leader type" and others not the "leader type"? If so, what in your judgment distinguishes them?

4. Identify several "common-sense" notions about leadership that, to you, are patently self-evident.

5. Does every successful leader have a valid theory of leadership?

6. Would you consider it a greater compliment for someone to call you a good manager or a good leader? Why? Do you believe you can be both?

7. Think of further examples of both rational and emotional aspects of leadership.

8. Do you believe leadership can be studied scientifically? Why or why not?

9. To the extent leadership is an art, what methods come to mind for improving one's "art of leadership"?

2 LEADERSHIP INVOLVES AN INTERACTION BETWEEN THE LEADER, THE FOLLOWERS, AND THE SITUATION

Chapter Outline

Introduction

In Chapter 1, we defined leadership as the process of influencing an organized group toward accomplishing its goals. In this chapter, we will expand on this definition by introducing and describing a three-factor framework of the leadership process. We find this framework to be a useful heuristic both for analyzing various leadership situations and for organizing various leadership theories and supporting research. Therefore, the remainder of this chapter is devoted to providing an overview of the framework, and many of the remaining chapters of this book are devoted to describing the components of the framework in more detail.

Looking at Leadership through Several Lenses

In attempting to understand leadership, scholars understandably have spent much of their energy studying successful and unsuccessful leaders in government, business, athletics, and the military. Sometimes scholars have done this systematically by studying good leaders as a group (see Bennis & Nanus, 1985; Astin & Leland, 1991), and sometimes they have done this more subjectively, drawing lessons about leadership from the behavior or character of an individual leader such as Martin Luther King, Jr., Lee Iacocca, or Golda Meir. The latter approach is similar to drawing conclusions about leadership from observing individuals in one's own life, whether it be a high school coach, a mother or father, or one's boss. It may seem that studying the characteristics of effective leaders is the best way to learn about leadership, but such an approach tells only part of the story.

Consider an example. Suppose a senior minister was told by one of his church's wealthiest and consistently most generous members that he should not preach any more prochoice sermons on abortion. The wealthy man's contributions were a big reason a special mission project for the city's disadvantaged youth had been funded, and we might wonder whether the minister would be influenced by this outside pressure. Would he be a bad leader if he succumbed to this pressure and did not advocate what his conscience dictated? Would the minister be a bad leader if his continued public stand on abortion caused the wealthy man to leave the church and withdraw support for the youth program?

Although we can learn much about leadership by looking at leaders themselves, the preceding example suggests the picture provided by studying only leaders provides just a partial view of the leadership process. Would we really know all we wanted to about the preceding example if we knew everything possible about the minister himself? His personality, his intelligence, his interpersonal skills, his theological training, his motivation? Is it not also relevant to understand a bit more, for example, about the community, his parishioners, the businessman, and so on? This points out how leadership depends on several factors, including the situation and the followers, not just the leader's qualities or characteristics. Leadership is more than just the kind of person the leader is or the things the leader does. Leadership is the process of influencing others toward the achievement of group goals; it is not just a person or a position (also see Highlight 2–1).

If we use only leaders as the lens for understanding leadership, then we get a very limited view of the leadership process. We can expand our view of the leadership process by adding two other complementary lenses: the followers and the situation. However, using only the followers or the situation as a lens also would give us an equally limited view of the leadership process. In other words, the clearest picture of the leadership process occurs only when we use all three lenses to understand it.

The Interactional Framework for Analyzing Leadership

Perhaps the first researcher formally to recognize the importance of the leader, follower, and situation in the leadership process was Fred Fiedler (1967). Fiedler used these three components to develop his contingency model of leadership, a theory of leadership that will be discussed in more detail in Chapter 3. Although we recognize Fiedler's contributions, we owe perhaps even more to Hollander's

FIGURE 2–1

*An Interactional
Framework for
Analyzing
Leadership*

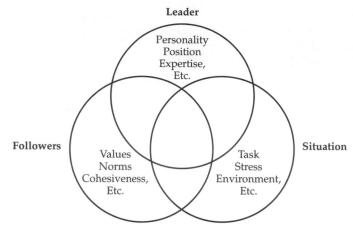

Source: Adapted from E. P. Hollander, *Leadership Dynamics* (New York: Free Press, 1978).

(1978) transactional approach to leadership. We call our approach the **interactional framework.**

There are several aspects of this derivative of Hollander's (1978) approach that are worthy of additional comment. First, as seen in Figure 2–1, the framework depicts leadership as a function of three elements—the leader, the followers, and the situation. Second, a particular leadership scenario can be examined using each level of analysis separately. Although this is a useful way to understand the leadership process, we can have an even better understanding of the process if we also examine the interactions among the three elements, or lenses, represented by the overlapping areas in the figure. For example, we can better understand the leadership process if we not only look at the leaders and the followers but also examine how leaders and followers affect each other in the leadership process. Similarly, we can examine the leader and the situation separately, but we can gain even further understanding of the leadership process by looking at how the situation can constrain or facilitate a leader's actions and how the leader can change different aspects of the situation in order to be more effective. Thus, a final important aspect of the framework is that leadership is the result of a complex set of interactions among the leader, the followers, and the situation. These complex interactions may be why broad generalizations about leadership are problematic; there are many factors that influence the leadership process.

We will now examine each of the three main elements of the interactional framework in turn.

The Leader

This element primarily examines what the leader brings *as an individual* to the leadership equation. This can include unique personal history, interests, character traits, and motivation.

Madeleine Albright

For example, Madeleine Albright displayed an interest and ability in foreign affairs very early in her life. She was also always a hard-working and serious student, from her early school days, through her doctoral training, and as a junior member of the White House staff. In college, for example, she organized her meticulous notes into 15 different colored notebooks. Her self-discipline is further evident in the schedule she followed during her graduate school days. Already the mother of three daughters, she arose each day at 4:30 A.M. to work on her dissertation.

While the specific circumstances of her life were unique to Albright (as they are for each of us), perhaps the general portrait of her qualities may be fairly similar to that of many leaders. Leaders are *not* all alike, but they do tend to share many common characteristics. Research has shown that leaders differ from their followers, and effective leaders differ from ineffective leaders, on various personality traits, cognitive abilities, skills, and values (Stogdill, 1948, 1974; Hogan, Curphy, & Hogan, 1994; Lord, DeVader, & Allinger, 1986; Kanter, 1983; Baltzell, 1980). Another way personality can affect leadership is through temperament, by which we mean whether the leader is generally calm or is instead prone to emotional outbursts. Leaders who have calm dispositions and do not attack or belittle others for bringing bad news are more likely to get complete and timely information from subordinates than are bosses who have explosive tempers and a reputation for killing the messenger.

Another important aspect of the leader is how he or she achieved leader status. Leaders who are appointed by superiors may have less credibility with subordinates and get less loyalty from them than leaders who are elected or emerge by consensus from the ranks of followers. Often, emergent or elected officials are better able to influence a group toward goal achievement because of the power conferred on them by their followers. However, both elected and emergent leaders need to be sensitive to their constituencies if they wish to remain in power.

Did Albright have instant credibility as secretary of state? Not with everyone, even though she'd already been serving as our ambassador to the United Nations. Appointment, even by the president of the United States, does not free one from criticism. Many inside and outside the State Department believed a big reason she got the appointment was that Clinton wanted to appoint a woman to a very senior position. Albright may well have been the very best person for the position, but the varied interests of groups around her inevitably colored their opinions about her selection; for some positively, for others negatively.

More generally, a leader's experience or history in a particular organization is usually important to her or his effectiveness. For example, leaders promoted from within an organization, by virtue of being familiar with its culture and policies, may be ready to "hit the job running." In addition, leaders selected from within an organization are typically better known by others in the organization than are leaders selected from the outside. That is likely to affect, for better or worse, the

Source: The "Bizarro" cartoon by Dan Piraro is reprinted courtesy Chronicle Features, San Francisco, California. All rights reserved.

latitude others in the organization are willing to give the leader; if the leader is widely respected for a history of accomplishment, then she may be given more latitude than a newcomer whose track record is less well known. On the other hand, many people tend to give new leaders a fair chance to succeed, and newcomers to an organization often take time to learn the organization's informal rules, norms, and "ropes" before they make any radical or potentially controversial decisions.

A leader's legitimacy also may be affected by the extent to which followers participated in the leader's selection. When followers have had a say in the selection or election of a leader they tend to have a heightened sense of psychological identification with her, but they also may have higher expectations and make more demands on her (Hollander & Offermann, 1990). We also might wonder what kind of support a leader has from his own boss. If followers sense their boss has a lot of influence with the higher-ups, then subordinates may be reluctant to take their complaints to higher levels. On the other hand, if the boss has little influence with higher-ups, subordinates may be more likely to make complaints to these levels.

I'll be blunt, coach. I'm having a problem with this 'take a lap' thing of yours . . . "

The foregoing examples highlight the sorts of insights one can gain about leadership by focusing on the individual leader as a level of analysis. Even if we were to examine the individual leader completely, however, our understanding of the leadership process would be incomplete. Consider another example, that of Konosuke Matsushita.

Konosuke Matsushita

Konosuke Matsushita began his company in 1917, its first product being a battery-powered electric bicycle lamp. By the 1930s Matsushita Electric had become a thriving corporation despite generally poor economic conditions in Japan. The company's success was due in large part to the fact that Matsushita himself was never one to become complacent with success. He always looked for ways to improve a product's quality or produce it at lower cost, and he always looked for ways to enhance the contribution of the people who worked at his company. Much of his success was due to his creative ways of involving employees in the leadership process. A half-century before concepts like employee empowerment and statements of corporate values became fashionable, he realized that a person's reason for working profoundly affects the quality of the person's work.

His own insight into this truth occurred during a visit in 1932 to a religious community in Japan. What caught his attention was the enthusiastic, reverent, and diligent work of people in the community despite the fact they received no salary. He imagined what the impact on a corporation would be if work within it were made meaningful like a religion. He believed the employees would become both more satisfied and more productive (Kotter, 1997). This prompted deep personal reflection on the fundamental purposes of corporations, and just months later he made a historic speech to everyone in the company. In it he boldly proposed that "the mission of a manufacturer should be to overcome poverty, to relieve society as a whole from misery, and bring it wealth." He recognized such a mission might require even centuries to achieve, but he nonetheless challenged every person in the organization to accept what he considered a sacred calling. Just months later he went on to spell out a set of ideals which he urged all employees to commit themselves to. These were the ideals (Kotter, 1997):

Service to the public.
Fairness and honesty.
Teamwork for the common cause.
Untiring effort for improvement.
Courtesy and humility.

Matsushita's speech was neither eloquent nor inspiring, but its message was consistent with how the organization had been run. More importantly, Matsushita's behavior following it was consistent with his vision and with the ideals he advocated. On an organizational level, he introduced systems like employee ownership of the company, and he encouraged what we now call empowerment among his workers. For example, in 1934 he told employees, "It's not enough to work conscientiously. No matter what kind of job [you have], you should think of yourself as being completely in charge of and responsible for your work, like being president of your own company" (Kotter, 1997, p. 124). Matsushita constantly stressed what he called "collective wisdom," the idea that decisions should be based on input from many employees,

---

Highlight 2–2

Changing Work Roles

John Naisbitt has called the 1990s the decade of women in leadership, and there is no question that women will play an increasingly significant part in both leadership and followership roles in the future. In the first place, in terms of sheer numbers women already are a large and indispensable element of contemporary work life. It is simply erroneous to think of women as a minority in the work force. In fact, as many women in their 20s and 30s work as men; and while just 75 percent of men work, nearly 80 percent of women with no children under 18 do.

Furthermore, women not only compose a major portion of the work force but also are assuming an increasingly significant place as leaders in it, and this will affect the nature of leadership and followership for everyone. Women are reaching a critical mass in all of the white-collar professions. For example, the percentage of women physicians has doubled in the past two decades. Women account for one-third of the M.B.A. degrees and 40 percent of the law degrees awarded. They are advancing fastest in cutting-edge industries like computers and software, where in some cases women compose nearly one-third of a company's management force. And women are starting their own small businesses at a faster rate than men. Some have argued that, thus far this century, corporations have been based on a bureaucratic and authoritarian organizational model compatible with male psychology and that different structures and leadership styles necessarily will evolve as women assume an increasingly large role in corporate leadership. Whether and how men and women differ in their leadership and followership styles are open issues, but it is certain that women's roles in both arenas will only grow.

Sources: J. Naisbitt and P. Aburdene, *Re-inventing the Corporation* (New York: Warner Books, 1985); and *Megatrends 2000* (New York: William Morrow, 1990).

---

as an antidote to self-interested, arbitrary, or misguided actions by individual executives. And on a personal level, too, his interactions with others—his followers included—affirmed their importance and his concern for them.

The foregoing example highlights the sorts of insights one can gain about leadership by focusing on the followers as well as on the individual leader. Still another aspect of this level of analysis is reflected in Highlight 2-2. Even if we were to examine the individual leader completely, however, our understanding of the leadership process would be incomplete. Understanding leadership involves knowing about followers as well as about leaders.

The Followers

Matsushita knew that followers are a critical part of the leadership equation, but their role has not always been appreciated. For example, one can look at history and be struck by the contributions of extraordinary individual leaders. Even the major reviews of the leadership literature show that researchers have paid relatively little attention to the roles followers play in the leadership process (see Bass, 1981, 1990; Stogdill, 1974). However, we know that the followers' expectations, personality traits, maturity levels, levels of competence, and motivation affect the leadership process too (also see Highlight 2–3) (Sutton & Woodman, 1989; Burke, 1965; Moore, 1976; Scandura, Graen, & Novak, 1986; Sales, Levanoni, & Saleh, 1984).

The nature of followers' motivation to do their work is also important. Workers who share a leader's goals and values, and who feel intrinsically rewarded for performing a job well, might be more likely to work extra hours on a time-critical project than those whose motivation is solely monetary.

Even the number of followers reporting to a leader can have significant implications. For example, a store manager having three clerks working for him can spend more time with each of them (or on other things) than can a manager responsible for eight clerks and a separate delivery service; chairing a task force with 5 members is a different leadership activity than chairing a task force with 18 members. Still other relevant variables include followers' trust in the leader and their confidence (or not) that he or she is interested in their well-being.

Changing Roles for Followers

The preceding examples illustrate just a few ways in which followers compose an important and complementary level of analysis for understanding leadership. Such examples should point out how leadership must be understood in the context of a particular group of followers as well as in terms of an individual leader. Now, more than ever before, understanding followers is central to understanding leadership. That is because the leader–follower relationship is in a period of dynamic change (Lippitt, 1982; Block, 1992; Hollander, 1994). One reason for this changing relationship is an increasing pressure on all kinds of organizations to function with reduced resources. Reduced resources and company downsizing have reduced the number of managers and increased their span of control, which in turn leaves followers to pick up many of the functions traditionally performed by leaders. Another reason is a trend toward greater power sharing and decentralized authority in organizations, which in turn creates greater interdependence among organizational subunits and increased need for collaboration among them. Furthermore, the nature of problems faced by many organizations is becoming so complex and the changes are becoming so rapid that more and more people are required to solve them.

These trends suggest several different ways in which followers can take on new leadership roles and responsibilities in the future. For one thing, followers can become much more proactive in their stance toward organizational problems. When facing the discrepancy between the way things are in an organization and the way they could or should be, followers can play an active and constructive role collaborating with leaders in solving problems. In general,

Adjusting to New Roles

Women are rapidly moving into leadership roles that previously had been occupied only by men. Such change, exciting and positive if also overdue, is accompanied by inevitable adjustments. The following is one contemporary woman's account of how it feels to be a trailblazer, a woman leader in a traditionally male-dominated field: the ministry.

"What do you do, Nancy?" the innocent, yet bold, six-year-old asked.

"I am a minister, Jason."

"You're not a ministerette?"

"No, just a minister, Jason. It doesn't matter if you are a girl or a boy . . . it is the same word."

"Oh," Jason replied. "I've never heard of that."

Jason is not alone. And his company is not only those in his age range. To most adults, youths, and children alike, a minister is a man. For anyone who is a pastor, a priest, a rabbi, or who is titled as "clergy," it is virtually assumed that person is male.

I am a woman and I am a minister. I could put those in reverse order, but I was indeed a woman first, and almost everyone I know uses the gender-then-title order: "Our lady minister," "Woman pastor," "Female clergy." Despite our seminaries and theological schools having an average female population of one-third, and despite the fact some Protestant denominations began ordaining women over 30 years ago, it seems strange that I am still a novelty to the average American. Yet, I am reminded of that constantly:

"Here is your change, Father, . . . Sister, . . . Mother, . . ." the awkward-feeling store clerk responds to the woman in a clerical collar.

Part of the problem lies in the limitations of language, but even more, the problem lies in the limitations we place on ourselves and on those around us. Like it or not, clergy is not a traditional role for women. For most folks, there is really no good reason to restrict the ministry to males, only those seven words we hear all too often: "We have always done it that way." In being a minister, and in being female, I am breaking tradition. Not only am I breaking into a traditionally man's world; I am breaking out of a traditionally female world. And like so many women in nontraditional roles, I at times try to fill too many shoes. One of my greatest frustrations is the assumption that because I am female, I must be more sensitive, more caring, more concerned about cooking and our home, and so forth, than my husband. Those assumptions are almost as bad as those which assume I cannot be a good preacher because I am an alto and not a bass. Why cannot people accept me as a minister, as a human being—with all the talents, personality quirks, faults, gifts, and eccentricities thereof?

From one of my first days wearing a clerical collar, and leaving our inner-city apartment to drive to my suburban church, I experienced first the stare, then the double take. I have to deal with the fact that some people will never accept me as they would accept a male minister. I have to deal with the fact that I am asked for identification at local hospitals (when I am not wearing the clerical collar) because I "do not look like a minister."

I am breaking the norm, personifying progress in women's rights; I am doing not only what I want, but what I feel called to do. And I am not letting my gender, not to mention societal norms, get in the way.

making organizations better is a task that needs to be "owned" by followers as well as by leaders.

In addition to helping solve organizational problems, followers can better contribute to the leadership process by becoming better skilled at "influencing upward." Because followers are often at the level where many organizational problems occur, they can provide leaders with relevant information so that good solutions are implemented. Although it is true that some leaders need to become better listeners, it is also true that many followers need training in expressing ideas to superiors more clearly and positively. Still another way followers can assume a greater share of the leadership challenge in the future is by staying flexible and open to opportunities. The future portends more change, not less, and followers who face change with positive anticipation and an openness to self-development will be particularly valued and rewarded (Senge, 1990).

Thus, to an ever increasing degree, leadership must be understood in terms of both leader variables and follower variables, as well as the interactions among them. But even that is not enough. In addition to understanding the leader and the followers, we must also understand the particular situations in which leaders and followers find themselves.

The Situation

The situation is the third critical part of the leadership equation. Even if we knew all we could know about a given leader and a given set of followers, leadership makes sense only in the context of how the leader and followers interact in a given situation (see Highlight 2–4).

The situation may be the most ambiguous aspect of the leadership framework since it can refer to anything from the specific task a group is engaged in all the way to broad situational contexts such as the remote predicament of the Andes survivors. It can include the business challenges facing Matsushita Electric in the 1930s, the complex considerations a president weighs in selecting his cabinet, as in Madeleine Albright's case, or the challenge of establishing a working relationship with your new commander in chief, as in Colin Powell's case.

Madeleine Albright

Let's examine the situation surrounding Albright's selection as secretary of state a bit more closely. We've already noted that President Clinton was probably motivated, at least in part, by the desire to do something dramatic and symbolic—appoint a woman to be secretary of state for the first time ever. Thus, the larger political situation *around* Albright probably created a ripe opportunity for a woman of her talents and credentials to be appointed. On the other hand, there were also pressures from within the State Department working in the opposite direction. Albright had to overcome what may be the hardest "glass ceiling" for women anywhere, that in the State Department. Some saw the Albright appointment initially as mostly cosmetics, maybe good politics but not a choice of substance.

Berkeley in the 1960s

The 1960s were a period of dissent and conflict, and perhaps even today no place epitomizes the decade more than Berkeley, California. But Berkeley did not always have a radical reputation.

The Berkeley campus of the huge University of California system had not always been a center of student protest and large-scale demonstrations. For a long time, it had been relatively sedate and conservative, even if also quite large; more than 20,000 students attended Berkeley in 1960. Campus leaders were clean-cut students who belonged to fraternities and sororities. Berkeley changed, however, in the fall of 1964 when a relatively small number of students launched what became known as the Free Speech Movement. Subsequent protests at other campuses across the country, and later globally, are traceable to the Free Speech Movement at Berkeley. One of its leaders was Mario Savio.

The sources of conflict and radicalism at Berkeley were many, including civil rights and the Vietnam War. But protest in Berkeley first erupted over the issue of whether students could solicit donations and distribute political materials near campus. Whether students could solicit donations or distribute materials on campus had been settled earlier; they could not. In response to having been ordered off campus, however, some student groups set up card tables just off campus, between the university's impressive Sproul Plaza and Berkeley's Telegraph Avenue, with its exciting and bohemian milieu of bookstores and coffeehouses.

Perhaps because their appearance so near the campus offended university officials—the student workers were rarely dressed or groomed in the clean-cut image favored by conservative administrators—even this activity eventually was prohibited. Outraged, a few students defiantly set up tables back in Sproul Plaza, right in the heart of the campus. Disturbed at this open rebuke to its authority, the university directed police to arrest one of the disobedient students. It was October 1, 1964, the birth of the Free Speech Movement.

Presumably, university officials believed this show of force on their part would dishearten the band of student protesters and break them up. As the arrested student got into the awaiting police car, however, someone shouted, "Sit down!" and hundreds of other students immediately did just that. They sat down on the plaza right where they were, effectively blocking the car's movement. The police and administration had never before confronted such massive defiance, and for 32 hours the car stayed put (with the "prisoner," Jack Weinberg, inside) while demonstrators used its roof as a podium from which to speak to the crowd. One who climbed up to speak several times, and who clearly had a gift for energizing the crowd, was Mario Savio. In many ways, the Free Speech Movement, which pitted a rigid university bureaucracy against increasing numbers of alienated students, became a confrontation between just two people: Mario Savio and the university's brilliant but aloof president, Clark Kerr. It was not, however, a fair fight.

As W. J. Rorabaugh has observed, Kerr didn't stand a chance. The student activists were prepared for war, and Kerr wasn't. He was out of touch with the sentiments of increasing numbers of students, sentiments that in part were a direct

(continued)

result of the university's continuing neglect of undergraduate education at the expense of graduate study and government-sponsored research.

The students, on the other hand, had a clear objective—the freedom to be politically active on campus (i.e., free speech). Furthermore, many were politically experienced, seasoned by their participation in civil rights marches in the South. They understood the politics of protest, crowd psychology, the importance of the media, and how to maintain spirit and discipline in their own ranks. Thus, many ingredients for a successful social movement were present. All that was needed was a spark to ignite them and a leader to channel them.

Mario Savio was not a typical undergraduate. His commitment to social reform already was deep, and his experiences were broad. Raised in a devout Catholic family, he had worked in rural Mexico for a church relief organization and had taught in a school for black children in Mississippi. He was proud, cocky, and defiant. It was his ability to articulate his rage, however, that set Savio apart. He could give words and reason to the frustration and anger others were only feeling. Interestingly, Savio was a very different person in private than in public. In private, he seemed cold, hesitant, and self-doubting, but in front of a crowd he could be inspiring.

He may have been at his best at a protest rally in December 1964. Here is what it was like to be in Berkeley in the 60s, listening to a new kind of student leader, one giving voice to the sense of powerlessness and frustration with modern life, which would be a common theme in student revolts throughout the rest of the decade:

> There is a time when the operation of the machine becomes so odious, makes you so sick at heart, that you can't take part; you can't even passively take part, and you've got to put your bodies upon the gears and upon the wheels, upon the levers, upon all the apparatus and you've got to make it stop. And you've got to indicate to the people who run it, to the people that own it, that unless you're free, the machines will be prevented from working at all (Rorabaugh, p. 31).

Earlier that year, Savio had written, "I'm tired of reading history. Now I want to make it." He did. Try to analyze the emergence of Mario Savio in terms of the interactional framework.

Source: W. J. Rorabaugh, *Berkeley at War* (New York: Oxford University Press, 1989).

Not that we should consider gender a negative for Madeleine Albright. She certainly does not, except in that fact that she may have had to work harder than her male counterparts to rise to the level she has. She does not hide her gender, and sometimes uses it effectively to lighten situations, as when she said to the outgoing secretary of state, Warren Christopher, "I only hope that my heels can fill your shoes." This is not to say Albright is a "gentle" secretary, either in her diplomatic role internationally or in her managerial role within the State Department. Very early on in her tenure, in fact, she stunned State Department old-timers with her toughness (which may say as much about them as her!).

One other aspect of the situation surrounding Madeleine Albright's selection is interesting to consider: how she had expanded (perhaps even engineered) her network of professional associations over time, *increasing her visibility to others*. You probably don't realize that for many years before she became ambassador to the United Nations, Albright hosted high-powered dinner discussions at her home near Washington, D.C. Her home was a gathering place for power brokers in the Democratic party and diplomatic establishments. Significantly, among those she hosted was then-governor of Arkansas Bill Clinton.

Colin Powell

We can also understand the interactional framework better by looking more closely at Colin Powell's situation (Powell, 1995). In November of 1997, Bill Clinton had been elected president, but not yet assumed office. He had asked to see Colin Powell, then chairman of the Joint Chiefs of Staff. Powell's political affiliation and preferences at that time were unknown, but he had served faithfully under Presidents Reagan and Bush, and successfully orchestrated a wartime victory for President Bush in Operation Desert Storm.

The president-elect began by complimenting Powell about a speech he had made, and inquired about a few matters of national defense. Clinton particularly asked for Powell's thoughts about a possible nominee to secretary of defense; in other words, about the general's potential next boss. Clinton was inclined to name Congressman Les Aspin, pointedly complimenting Aspin's intelligence. Despite Clinton's evident intent to name Aspin, however, Powell said he had reservations about the nomination. He, too, complimented Aspin's intelligence, but expressed concern that Aspin's disorganized management style would be inappropriate for a person having responsibility for such a large bureaucracy. The two went on to discuss other issues for over an hour, but when Powell rose to leave there was one more thing he needed to say. He felt he needed to address a political promise Clinton had made during the presidential campaign: a promise to end the ban on gays in the military. He said the senior military leadership didn't want it lifted, military people in general didn't want it lifted, and most in Congress didn't want it lifted. The concern, Powell stressed, was privacy. He wondered how the ban could be made to work in the close circumstances of living in army barracks or on naval ships. He asked the president-elect not to make this issue the first priority of the new administration.

Despite Powell's counsel, however, it did become so, and a highly controversial one at that. Through both private negotiation and public media questioning, both Powell and Clinton remained committed to their respective positions. Eventually, a compromise policy was instituted that is still considered hopelessly flawed by many on both sides, popularly known as "don't ask, don't tell." But now let us look at this situation from the perspective of the interactional framework.

First of all, note how much more complex the situation of their meeting was than a mere first meeting between two successful men. One of them was the top military leader in the world at that time, the other would soon be his commander in chief by virtue of free election in a constitutional government which subordinates the military to civilian authority (just to be clear, this is *not* the case for most countries throughout history). In their first face-to-face meeting, which would set a tone for their future working relationship, Powell disagreed with several proposals favored by Clinton (frank and open disagreement, of course, is often the sign of a *constructive* relationship, and that is most likely the way the counsel was both given and received). Perhaps more significantly, both felt obligated to different courses of action and to different groups of stakeholders. Clinton, as a politician and new world leader, must also have been concerned about how the controversy would affect national and international perceptions of his leadership and credibility.

So just what was the situation here? It was the constitutionally mandated nature of their authority relationship. It was the interpersonal context of one person giving unpopular feedback or advice to someone else. It was the very real pressure being exerted on each man independently by different constituencies having different agendas. It was all these things, and more. Leadership, here as everywhere, involves the leader, the followers, and the complex situation they're a part of.

Leadership and Management Revisited

In Chapter 1 we looked at the relationship between leadership and management, and between leaders and managers. While these terms are not mutually exclusive, they do refer to a person's distinctive *style* and *approach*. Even in a particular role, two people may approach it differently; one more like a leader, the other more like a manager. The governor of one state, for example, may function more as a leader, whereas the governor of another state may function more as a manager (and not because there's anything different about the two states). It will be helpful to revisit those concepts in the context of the interactional framework.

Let's begin by reviewing some of the distinctions Bennis makes between leaders and managers.

Leaders	**Managers**
Innovate.	Administer.
Develop.	Maintain.
Inspire.	Control.
Long-term view.	Short-term view.
Ask what and why.	Ask how and when.
Originate.	Initiate.
Challenge the status quo.	Accept the status quo.
Do the right things.	Do things right.

Bennis is hardly alone in contrasting leaders and managers. Numerous other scholars echo the idea of a basic distinction between leadership and management. Kotter (1990), for example, described management in terms of coping with complexity, and leadership in terms of coping with change. Kotter noted how managerial practices and procedures can be traced to the 20th century phenomenon of large organizations, and the need to bring order and consistency to their functioning. Renewed interest in leadership, on the other hand, springs from the challenge of maintaining organizational success in an increasingly dynamic world. He said most U.S. corporations today, for example, are overmanaged and underled; but that "strong leadership with weak management is no better" (p.103). Fairholm (1991) emphasized still other differences between leadership and management when he wrote that

> leadership and management are different in purpose, knowledge base, required skills, and goals. We distinguish leaders as more personal in their orientation to group members than managers. They are more global in their thinking. Leaders, we suggest, focus on values, expectations, and context. Managers, on the other hand, focus on control and results. Leaders impact followers and constituent groups in a way that allows volitional activity of followers, not through formal authority mechanisms. . . . Managers give clear direction, make solitary assignments, and work hard for cooperation. The leader communicates indirectly, gives overlapping and ambiguous assignments, and sometimes sets employees up for internecine strife—to test loyalty and the leader's personal strength. Leaders value cooperation, not just coordination. They foster ideas of unity, equality, justice, and fairness in addition to efficiency and effectiveness, the bastions of management value. (p. 40)

Such differences are just what our framework is all about—*interactions*. In other words, the differences between leaders and managers, or between leadership and management, involve more than just differences between types of individuals. The differences extend to how such individuals *interact with* their followers and the situations they confront. Let's explore how these distinctions affect the other two elements of the framework.

Leader-Follower-Situation Interactions

Leaders create environments within which followers' innovations and creative contributions are welcome. Followers feel a stake in *shaping* something new, not just maintaining a status quo. Leaders also encourage growth and development in their followers in ways broader than what we might call mere job training (e.g., encouraging a follower to take on something really new, something that would stretch the follower but may involve failure on the task; or taking on a developmental experience not directly tied to the follower's present job requirements). Leaders generally are more interested in the big picture of followers' work, and tend to assess their followers' performance less formally and less in terms of specific criteria than managers, and more in terms of holistic, personal, idiosyncratic, or intuitive criteria. Leaders motivate followers more personally and through more personal and intangible factors (e.g., through inspiration, or the reward of just being able to work with the leader, or on a particular project). Leaders redefine the parameters of tasks and responsibilities, both for individual followers and for the entire group. In that sense, leaders actively *change* the situations they're in rather than just optimize their group's adaptation to it. They are forever "moving outside the constraints of structure"

(Fairholm, p. 39). Such redefinitions also may occur through taking a long-term rather than a shorter-term perspective, through accentuating critical values or ends, or by marshalling energy to cope with some new threat.

Manager-Follower-Situation Interactions

Managers are more likely to emphasize routinization and control of followers' behavior. This might be expressed in terms of greater emphasis on making sure followers conform to policies or procedures ("doing it the way we've always done it") or in a tendency to assign narrower rather than broader tasks for followers to perform. It might be expressed in lesser degrees of decision-making discretion or autonomy given to followers, as in a manager's tendency to review *details* of work for them. Managers tend to assess their followers' performance in terms of explicit, fairly specific job descriptions. Managers motivate followers more with extrinsic, even contractual consequences, both positive and negative. Managers tend to accept the definitions of situations presented to them. They might be unlikely, for example, to reorient a group's task or mission in a whole new direction; or to change the whole culture of an organization. When managers do change things, they would be more likely to affect change officially, through control tactics such as developing new policies or procedures.

In reading the preceding paragraphs, it may seem to you that it's better to be a leader than a manager (or, perhaps, vice versa). But such a conclusion would ignore important characteristics of the followers. In some situations leaders are successful and managers are not, but in other situations the opposite is true. Consider, for example, one of Bennis's prototypical leaders: an inspiring individual having a vision of major institutional change that can be achieved only through the energy and creativity of committed followers. Such an inspiring individual may be thwarted, nonetheless, unless her followers share her value-based vision. If they are motivated primarily by economic incentives and are satisfied with their present lot, then the leader may fail to achieve her vision. The whole idea of *interaction* is that the effectiveness of any particular leader approach can be understood only in the context of certain follower and situational conditions. To return to Bennis's distinctions, managers emphasize *stability* whereas leaders emphasize *change*. Managers emphasize consistency and predictability in follower behavior (doing what's expected, doing things right), whereas leaders emphasize *changing* followers. That may mean transforming them or getting them to do more than they thought they could or thought they would. We'll see a similar distinction in Chapter 10 when we contrast transactional and transformational leadership (Bass, 1985).

Leadership, Management, and the Disney Brothers

Walt Disney is surely one of the most familiar names in the world (see Highlight 2–5). Roy Disney is not. Roy was Walt's brother, and he played a vital but different role in the success of the Disney enterprises. In many ways you can think

The Creative Genius of Walt Disney

Walt Disney's creative genius has imprinted our cultural landscape with characters and stories more familiar to many people than their neighbors. Read through this brief description of his life and career, and as you do so think about what different factors contributed to his effectiveness as a creative leader.

Disney built a major studio that produced motion picture masterpieces like *Snow White* and *Fantasia*. Throughout his career, he pioneered technical innovations that set new standards for the industry. These innovations included introducing sound and color to cartoons, inventing special cameras to create new effects in films, and developing sophisticated robotics. He changed the nature of amusement parks in America with Disneyland and Walt Disney World. In fact, these parks are so visionary they've been required study at many schools of architecture. Far more than "fun places," they are serious experiments in urban design, testing radical ideas for solving the problems facing our cities.

For example, the Magic Kingdom at Walt Disney World is really a small city built on top of a huge service-and-utility tunneled infrastructure. The entire park was designed from the start with a quiet and efficient monorail system for mass transit. The area is unique, probably in the world, for setting nearly one-third of its acreage aside for conservation of natural habitat. It is, in sum, a city built with people in mind and a plan for the future. Disney originally intended that EPCOT be a test bed of concepts of planning and living that would always be 25 years ahead of its time and always evolving (EPCOT stands for Experimental Prototype Community of Tomorrow). Walt Disney, who once experimented with drawings that move, became a designer of communities for the 21st century (P. Blake, 1972, 1973).

What kind of a person was Walt Disney? What enabled him to accomplish all this? Certainly his creativity and resourcefulness were apparent early in his life. He was a cartoonist for his school paper, and while serving overseas as an ambulance driver during World War I (he was too young for actual military duty), he built a small business selling souvenir German helmets that appeared to have weathered rough combat. (He actually used new helmets painted to look old and used. A partner pounded dents in the helmets and shot holes in them; they even got human hair from a barber to put in the holes!) (Miller, 1956).

Disney always was committed to making his product the best, from souvenir war helmets to his films. He continuously experimented with new ways of doing things, innovating new technologies to produce the effects he wanted. In the 1930s, he had his special effects staffs make slow-motion pictures of bubbles popping, smoke blowing, and balls bouncing to improve their animation of such actions. He developed rigorous training programs for his animation staffs to help them draw more lifelike cartoons, like learning to blur fast-moving figures. And he had an uncanny sense of timing. For example, Disney profited from the emergence of sound and color in live-action film by seeing their potential application to animated subjects sooner and more clearly than others. He acquired exclusive rights to the Technicolor process because he showed commitment to the new technique when other cartoon producers were skeptical (Thomas, 1976).   *(continued)*

Disney had a genius for spotting talent, and he surrounded himself with other creative people, even eccentric ones. After he found them, though, he was a taskmaster. At work, he was all business, not what you might call a people person. He did not like dealing with others' personal problems, and he had a well-known temper. One of Disney's biographers wrote the following:

> He was incapable of small talk. His employees learned not to engage him in the banter that animators used as relief from the tedium of drawing. His mind was too involved with the problems of the moment—a storyline that defied solution; a cartoon that failed to evoke laughs at the preview; an overdue check from Columbia Pictures that threatened next week's payroll. His workers learned not to be offended if he passed them in the hallway without a word; they knew that he was preoccupied with a studio problem. (Thomas, 1976, p. 111)

Disney also had a sixth sense about what would appeal broadly to the American culture, young and old. He trusted his intuition and judgment to an extraordinary degree, and took great risks with his studio to back them up. Furthermore, he made sure that every project had his personal stamp on it, including such details as what voices to use for the various characters. He was unique in Hollywood for the close personal supervision he gave his work. Walt Disney's name on a film meant it had received his individual touch (Thomas, 1976).

of the differences between them in terms of the distinctions we've been making between leadership and management. In many ways Walt was the creative leader, Roy the manager or "financial guy." The success of the Disney enterprises was due to their *complementary* contributions, and their story provides an interesting illustration of how leaders interact with their followers and situations differently than managers do (Snyder, Dowd, & Houghton, 1994).

One of Walt's distinctive qualities was his drive to experiment and find new ways to improve motion picture quality. He was an innovator himself, but even more importantly he encouraged his staff to be innovative. His studio was always "on the move." He wanted it to be on the technological cutting edge of animation art and never fall prey to a cut-and-dried way of doing things. From the early days, Walt handled the creative side of Disney productions whereas Roy handled the job of securing financing for their cartoons. Walt was never interested in making money as an end in itself, but rather as a means to producing ever-better films. He would not compromise his sense of film quality to increase profit. In fact, he was a gambler willing to risk all for an idea he believed in. Walt's enthusiasm for the creative process was infectious and spread to his staff, who themselves were more dedicated to their art than to the bottom line. Walt's staff believed they were pioneers who were changing the very nature of mass media. He created an energetic and informal environment; he resisted rigid procedures and bureaucracy, yet his staff believed he ran the best studio in the world. One way Walt inspired such commitment among his followers was through his own commitment to *their* development and creative involvement in the studio's work. He brought out the best in them, a quality of work beyond what they believed themselves capable of. He wanted all the people working for him to feel they were making indispensable contributions to the overall project. He encouraged his staff to use their *own* skills to devise original solutions to challenges rather than merely find out what he wanted them to do.

An interesting case in point of the difference between a leader's and manager's orientation may be in the disagreement Walt and Roy Disney had over Walt's idea of a new amusement park. What we now know as Disneyland, and may incorrectly assume looked like a sure fire success as soon as Walt proposed it, was initially opposed by Roy. Roy thought it was just another one of Walt's crazy ideas, and was only willing to risk $10,000 of studio money on what he thought was a harebrained project. Trusting his own vision more than his brother's risk-averse conservatism, Walt scraped together the money needed to finance Disneyland—in part by borrowing on his own life insurance. Even after Walt's death the differences between him and his brother illustrate what's different between leadership and management. Without Walt's creative leadership, the studio fell under the management of "Roy men" who produced moderately successful but uninspired formula pieces for two decades. Only under Michael Eisner, a "Walt man" who understands popular culture, has the studio regained a leading place in American business (see Highlight 2–6).

A Final Word

Fairholm (1991) argued that organizations may need *two different kinds of people at the helm*: good leaders *and* good managers. He wrote, "We need competent, dedicated managers to provide continuity of process, to insure program productivity, and to control and schedule the materials needed for production or service delivery. We also need people who can infuse the organization with common values that define the organization, determine its character, link it to the larger society, and insure its long-term survival" (p. 41). This view is certainly consistent with the success the two Disney brothers had bringing distinctive but complementary sets of competencies and values to their studio. But do examples like this prove that leaders and managers represent inherently different sorts of talents and interests? We think Kotter (1990) is on solid ground when he advises organizations preparing people for executive jobs to "ignore the recent literature that says people cannot manage and lead" (p. 104). He said they should try to develop leader-managers. In other words, it may be useful to distinguish between the functions of leadership and management but still *develop* those complementary functions in the same individuals.

This point may be particularly important with regard to developing the talents of *younger* leader-managers. It would seem inappropriately narrow and limiting for a young person to define himself or herself as "the manager type" or "the leader type." Premature self-definitions of being a leader *or* manager present such *reductio ad absurdum* eventualities as foreclosing real developmental opportunities (e.g., "I guess I shouldn't seek that student body position since it's a leadership role, and I'm really more the management type") or as inappropriate reactions to the sorts of job responsibilities typical for a person early

Highlight 2–6

Passing the Reins at Disney

The mantle of leadership at the Walt Disney Company is now in the hands of Michael Eisner. What was his path to that position, and what has been his imprint on the Disney tradition?

In upbringing, Eisner's personal history was quite different from Walt Disney's. Whereas Disney's family struggled financially, Eisner was born into affluence. Still, Eisner's family stressed discipline and thrift. Family connections did, however, help Eisner secure his first job in show business, as an *usher* for NBC in 1963. After graduating from college, he did such things for the network as keeping track of how frequently different commercials aired, and giving weekend traffic reports.

Eisner's big opportunity came in 1966, when he was picked by 24-year-old Barry Diller, a vice president at ABC (a relatively young network at the time), to refashion the network's children's programming on Saturday mornings. As it turned out, Eisner had a natural aptitude for selecting popular TV programs. He didn't study kids' viewing tastes, he simply trusted his own. It was a successful strategy; in five years he had taken charge of determining ABC's prime time schedule. Eisner succeeded there, too, but eventually both he and Diller left ABC to join Paramount Pictures. Among many successful films he launched at Paramount were those in the Indiana Jones series, beginning with *Raiders of the Lost Ark*.

With his demonstrated grasp of mass appeal, the board of Walt Disney Productions believed Eisner might be the creative genius to return the company to glory. It also brought on another new face, Frank Wells, known for his business savvy. The Eisner-Wells team represented a chemistry of talent echoing the earlier partnership of Walt and Roy Disney.

That is not to say their first days at Disney felt comfortable to the old timers. In fact, Eisner and Wells shook things up, believing the organization had grown too soft and comfortable, even lazy. They brought a new style of management and work to the company. For example, Eisner instituted marathon meetings for generating creative ideas. Eisner's philosophy was to get members of a group to become uninhibited in expressing ideas to each other, a purpose furthered by requiring everyone to work for grueling hours together with little food and water. Difficult and different as the meetings were at first, the approach worked. The management culture at Disney was changing. There were other changes, too. Eisner recruited filmmaker George Lucas, the genius behind the *Star Wars* series, to develop a new ride for the parks that would appeal to teenagers. On other fronts he has vastly expanded the company's hotel operations, and broadened the company's film productions. The result? The company is again regarded as one of the most successful and visionary in the world.

Source: R. Grover, *The Disney Touch* (Chicago: Irwin, 1997).

in her career (e.g., "Boss, you've been giving me too many management-type tasks, and I see myself more as a leader around here"). It seems prudent to note the commonalities—as shown in Figure 1–1—between leadership and management and not focus exclusively on the differences between them, *especially in the early stages of a person's professional development*.

There Is No Simple Recipe for Effective Leadership

As noted above, it is important to understand how the three domains of leadership interact—how the leader, the followers, and the situation are all part of the leadership process. Understanding their interaction is necessary before you can draw valid conclusions from the leadership you observe around you. When you see a leader's behavior (even when it may appear obviously effective or ineffective to you), you should not automatically conclude something good or bad about the leader, or what is the right way or wrong way leaders should act. You need to think about the effectiveness of that behavior in *that* context with *those* followers (see, for example, Highlights 2–7 and 2–8).

As obvious as the above sounds, we often ignore it. Too frequently, we just look at the leader's behavior and conclude that he or she is a good leader or a bad leader apart from the context. For example, suppose you observe a leader soliciting advice from subordinates. Obviously, it seems unreasonable to conclude that good leaders always ask for advice or that leaders who do not frequently ask for advice are not such good leaders. The appropriateness of seeking input from subordinates depends on many factors, such as the nature of the problem or the subordinates' familiarity with the problem. It may be that the subordinates have a lot more experience with this particular problem, and soliciting their input is the correct action to take in this situation.

Consider another example. Suppose you hear that a leader disapproved a subordinate's request to take time off to attend to family matters. Was this bad leadership because the leader did not appear to be "taking care of her people"? Was it good leadership because she did not let personal matters interfere with the mission? Again, you cannot make an intelligent decision about the leader's actions by just looking at the behavior itself. You must always assess leadership in the context of the leader, the followers, and the situation.

The following statements about leaders, followers, and the situation make the above points a bit more systematically.

- A leader may need to respond to various followers differently in the same situation.
- A leader may need to respond to the same follower differently in different situations.
- Followers may respond to various leaders quite differently.
- Followers may respond to each other differently with different leaders.
- Two leaders may have different perceptions of the same followers or situations.

Highlight 2–7

Vince Lombardi Was My Father

Vince Lombardi was one of the greatest football coaches in history. His son, also named Vince Lombardi, is a speaker and consultant on leadership who lives in Bellevue, Washington. Here are a few of the son's reflections on his father's leadership. In reading them, think about coach Lombardi's leadership in terms of our interactional framework.

Contrary to the opinion of many people, leaders are not born. Leaders are made, and they are made by effort and hard work.

Vincent T. Lombardi

Vision

The essence of leadership is vision. Good leaders have a clear, precise vision of what they want for the people they lead. That is my opinion from the vantage point of observing an outstanding leader, my father, Vince Lombardi.

It is generally conceded that my father was one of the great coaches of the modern football era. Yet Vince Lombardi waited until he was 47 years old to become a head coach. Because of the long wait, when he finally became head coach of the Green Bay Packers, he knew precisely what he wanted and he knew exactly how he was going to obtain it.

My father went to Green Bay in 1959, and in 1960 the Packers played for the World Championship. They lost that game, but they never lost another championship game. In the next seven years they won five world championships, three in a row, including the first two Super Bowls.

Mental Toughness

If vision is the essence of leadership, then mental toughness is the one quality that every leader must possess. Vision without mental toughness is nothing more than a good idea. For a leader, mental toughness is holding on to that picture of excellence they have for their people when everyone around them is saying: "Who are you to think you can do that, no one like you has ever done that before?"

Motivation

Vince Lombardi was a consummate motivator. Many times with his players it was "My way or the highway" or "If you can't get the job done I'll find someone who can." They tell the story of the sportswriter interviewing some Packer players and asking, "What is it about Coach Lombardi that makes you so successful?" One of the players thought for a moment and replied, "He treats us all alike, he treats us all the same—like dogs." Coach Lombardi, however, knew that approach would not produce lasting motivation. So after he gained the players' attention with "do it or else," he would focus on the profitability of the task at hand. All good leaders paint great pictures for themselves and the people around them of the rewards for successfully completing the job before them.

An example of this involved Jerry Kramer, an All-Pro guard for many years. Jerry was sitting in front of his locker after an especially poor practice wondering if it was time to move on to a different occupation. My father walked by, sized up the situation, tousled Jerry's hair, and told him, "Son, some day you're going to be one of the greatest guards in football." Jerry Kramer never had to be pushed again. He was recently named to the all-time Super Bowl team.

A Winning Attitude

Vince Lombardi's teams were not a loose collection of individuals. The whole was bigger than the sum of the parts on the Green Bay Packers. Lombardi's teams had trust for one another, they respected one another and they were committed to one another. These elements—trust, respect, and commitment—give a team a winning attitude! When the Green Bay Packers stepped on the field, they didn't hope to win, they expected to win! In their minds they never lost a game. Once in a while they just ran out of time.

There is a corollary to a winning attitude. Leaders can transform a winning attitude into a winning tradition. When new people join the organization, the veterans, the old hands, pass the winning attitude on to the rookies. Either by word or by example they show the new arrivals: "This is how we do things. Around here we expect to win." With a winning tradition, the organization does not succeed just this year; it does not win once in awhile. With a winning tradition you win time after time, year after year after year.

Leaders embodying the quality of mental toughness, projecting a precise picture of the goals to be achieved, and motivating constructively build within their people trust, respect, and commitment. The result is a winning tradition, where the organization does not simply attain their goals, they *maintain* their goals—the mark of true leadership.

Source: Personal communication from Vince Lombardi.

Conclusion: Drawing Lessons from Experience

All of the above leads to one conclusion: The right behavior in one situation is not necessarily the right behavior in another situation. It does *not* follow, however, that any behavior is appropriate in any situation. Although we may not be able to agree on the one best behavior in a given situation, we often can agree on some clearly inappropriate behaviors. Saying that the right behavior for a leader depends on the situation is not the same thing as saying it does not matter what the leader does. It merely recognizes the complexity among leaders, followers, and situations. This recognition is a helpful first step in drawing meaningful lessons about leadership from experience.

Summary

Leadership is a process in which leaders and followers interact dynamically in a particular situation or environment. Leadership is a broader concept than that of leaders, and the study of leadership must involve more than just the study of

---
Highlight 2–8

Has Coaching Changed?

Two of the most respected and successful coaches in today's National Football League are Mike Holmgren of the Green Bay Packers and Bill Cowher of the Pittsburgh Steelers. It is interesting to compare and contrast them with the epitome of excellent coaching from an earlier era, Vince Lombardi (see Highlight 2–7).

In many ways they are all of the same mold. Holmgren and Cowher, just like Lombardi, are coaches with a vision of what they want their team to be; they possess supreme mental toughness; they, too, are consummate motivators; and they have instilled a winning attitude in their respective teams. Nonetheless, there are interesting differences between these modern coaches and the Lombardi image of coaching.

Before he became head coach, Holmgren's personal interest in his players endeared him to them. He said, "When I was coaching in high school, I really thought I could make a difference in kids' lives. Now I just have big little kids. I really have fun coaching. I really like dealing with people—players, in this case." Players on today's Green Bay Packers—Lombardi's old team—say Holmgren's tenure as coach has been marked by discipline, humanity, fairness, and compassion.

Another interesting perspective on how coaching—or coaches—might have changed is in an incident that happened after a 1998 playoff game. The Pittsburgh Steelers barely won the hard-fought game. Coach Bill Cowher made a controversial decision in the last few minutes of the game to go for a touchdown on fourth down when the ball was on the opponent's one-yard line. At the time, the Steelers were ahead by just one point, and a field goal would have been valuable insurance. The Steelers failed in that try and turned the ball over the other team, placing the Steelers defense in a "save the game" mode. The Steelers did hold on to win, but after the game Cowher apologized to his team for what he considered his own poor decision making as a coach. *Apologized to his team.* He said, "I'm a young coach, and I messed up . . . I got caught up in the emotions of the game and I made a mistake. The players bailed me out." It is difficult to imagine such an apology coming from Vince Lombardi.

Do you think coaching has changed? Do you think coaches have changed? What might explain it?

leaders as individuals. The study of leadership must also include two other areas: the followers and the situation. In addition, the interactive nature of these three domains has become increasingly important in recent years and can help us to better understand the changing nature of leader–follower relationships and the increasingly greater complexity of situations leaders and followers face. Because of this complexity, now, more than ever before, effective leadership cannot be boiled down to a simple and constant recipe. It is still true, however, that good leadership makes a difference, and it can be enhanced through greater awareness of the important factors influencing the leadership process.

Key Terms

leader
follower
situation

interaction
interactional framework

Discussion Questions

1. According to the interactional framework, effective leader behavior depends on many variables. It follows there is no simple prescription for effective leader behavior. Does this mean effective leadership is merely a matter of opinion or subjective preference?

2. Generally, leaders get most of the credit for a group's or an organization's success. Do you believe this is warranted or fair?

3. What are some of the other characteristics of leaders, followers, and situations you could add to those listed in Figure 2–1?

3 CONTINGENCY THEORIES OF LEADERSHIP

Chapter Outline

Introduction

In Chapter 2 we saw how leadership involves an interaction between the leader, the followers, and the situation. In Chapter 3 we will see how this basic idea has been elaborated systematically via research in several different theories of leadership.

This will give you a big-picture perspective of research-based leadership theory. Most of the rest of the book, then, will involve more detailed examination of the building blocks of the theories: leaders, followers, and situations.

This chapter reviews four of the more well known contingency theories of leadership. All four address certain aspects of the leader, the followers, and the situation. These four theories also share several other similarities. First, because they are theories rather than someone's personal opinions, these four models have been the focus of a considerable amount of empirical research over the years. Second, these theories implicitly assume that leaders are able to accurately diagnose or assess key aspects of the followers and the leadership situation. Third, with the exception of the contingency model (Fiedler, 1967), leaders are assumed to be able to act in a flexible manner. In other words, leaders can and should change their behaviors as situational and follower characteristics change. Fourth, a correct match between situational and follower characteristics and leaders' behaviors is assumed to have a positive effect on group or organizational outcomes. Thus, these theories maintain that leadership effectiveness is maximized when leaders correctly make their behaviors *contingent* on certain situational and follower characteristics. Because of these similarities, Chemers (1984) argued that these four theories were more similar than they were different. He said they differed primarily in terms of the types of situational and follower characteristics that various leader behaviors should be contingent on (also see Highlight 3–1 for some different perspectives on theories and leadership).

The Normative Decision Model

Obviously, in some situations leaders can delegate decisions to subordinates or should ask subordinates for relevant information before making a decision. In other situations, such as emergencies or crises, leaders may need to make a decision with little, if any, input from subordinates. The level of input subordinates have in the decision-making process can and does vary substantially depending on the issue at hand, followers' level of technical expertise, or the presence or absence of a crisis. Although the level of participation varies due to various leader, follower, and situational factors, Vroom and Yetton (1973) maintained that leaders could often improve group performance by using an optimal amount of participation in the decision-making process. Thus, the normative decision model is directed solely at determining how much input subordinates should have in the decision-making process. Precisely because the normative decision model is limited only to decision making and is not a grand, all-encompassing theory, it is a good model with which to begin the chapter.

Levels of Participation

Like the other theories in this chapter, the **normative decision model** (Vroom & Yetton, 1973) was designed to improve some aspects of leadership effectiveness. In this case, Vroom and Yetton explored how various leader, follower, and

---
Highlight 3–1

Leadership Quotes, Chapter 3

The real world is a messy place—yet, even a messy place can (should?) be attacked systematically.

Alex Cornell

Although people object when a scientific analysis traces their behavior to external conditions and thus deprives them of credit and the chance to be admired, they seldom object when the same analysis absolves them of blame.

B. F. Skinner

There is to me something profoundly affecting in large masses of men following the lead of those who do not believe in men.

Walt Whitman

Disraeli cynically expressed the dilemma when he said: "I must follow the people. Am I not their leader?" He might have added: "I must lead the people. Am I not their servant?"

Edward L. Bernays

Men are marked out from the moment of birth to rule or be ruled.

Aristotle

To act is easy; to think is hard.

Goethe

It is a capital mistake to theorize before one has data.

Sir Arthur Conan Doyle

Irrationally held truths may be more harmful than reasoned errors.

Thomas Huxley

situational factors affect the degree of subordinates' participation in the decision-making process and, in turn, group performance. To determine which situational and follower factors affect the level of participation and group performance, Vroom and Yetton first investigated the decision-making processes leaders use in group settings. They discovered a continuum of decision-making processes ranging from completely autocratic (labeled "AI") to completely democratic, where all member of the group have equal participation (labeled "GII"). These processes are listed in Highlight 3–2.

Decision Quality and Acceptance

After establishing a continuum of decision processes, Vroom and Yetton (1973) established criteria to evaluate the adequacy of the decisions made—criteria they believed would be credible to leaders and equally applicable

---

Highlight 3–2

<hr>

Levels of Participation in the Normative Decision Model

Autocratic Processes

AI: The leader solves the problem or makes the decision by him- or herself using the information available at the time.

AII: The leader obtains any necessary information from followers, then decides on a solution to the problem herself. She may or may not tell followers the purpose of her questions or give information about the problem or decision she is working on. The input provided by them is clearly in response to her request for specific information. They do not play a role in the definition of the problem or in generating or evaluating alternative solutions.

Consultative Processes

CI: The leader shares the problem with the relevant followers individually, getting their ideas and suggestions without bringing them together as a group. Then he makes a decision. This decision may or may not reflect the followers' influence.

CII: The leader shares the problem with her followers in a group meeting. In this meeting, she obtains their ideas and suggestions. Then she makes the decision, which may or may not reflect the followers' influence.

Group Process

GII: The leader shares the problem with his followers as a group. Together they generate and evaluate alternatives and attempt to reach agreement (consensus) on a solution. The leader's role is much like that of a chairman, coordinating the discussion, keeping it focused on the problem, and making sure that the critical issues are discussed. He can provide the group with information or ideas that he has, but he does not try to "press" them to adopt "his" solution. Moreover, leaders adopting this level of participation are willing to accept and implement any solution that has the support of the entire group.

Source: Adapted from V. H. Vroom and P. W. Yetton, *Leadership and Decision Making* (Pittsburgh: University of Pittsburgh Press, 1973).

across the five levels of participation. Although a wide variety of criteria could be used, Vroom and Yetton believed decision quality and decision acceptance were the two most important criteria for judging the adequacy of a decision.

Decision quality means simply that if the decision has a rational or objectively determinable "better or worse" alternative, the leader should select the better alternative. Vroom and Yetton (1973) intended quality in their model to apply when the decision could result in an objectively or measurably better outcome for the group or organization. In the for-profit sector, this criterion can be assessed in several ways, but perhaps the easiest to understand is, Would the decision show up on the balance sheet? In this case, a high-quality (or, conversely, low-quality) decision would have a direct and measurable impact on the organization's bottom line. In the public sector, one might determine if there was a quality component to a decision by asking, "Will one alternative have a greater cost saving than the other?" or "Does this decision improve services to the client?" Although it may seem that leaders should always choose the alternative with the highest decision quality, this is not always the case. Often, leaders are confronted with equally good (or bad) alternatives. At other times, the issue in question is fairly trivial, rendering the quality of the decision relatively unimportant.

Decision acceptance implies that followers accept the decision as if it were their own and do not merely comply with the decision. Acceptance of the decision outcome by the followers may be critical, particularly if it is the followers who will bear principal responsibility for implementing the decision. With such acceptance, there will be no need for superiors to monitor compliance, which can be a continuing and time-consuming activity (and virtually impossible in some circumstances, such as with a geographically dispersed sales staff).

As with quality, acceptance of a decision is not always critical for implementation. For example, most organizations have an accounting form that employees use to obtain reimbursement for travel expenses. Suppose a company's chief financial officer has decided to change the format of the form for reimbursing travel expenses and has had the new forms printed and distributed throughout the company. Further, she has sent out a notice that effective June 1, the old forms will no longer be accepted for reimbursement—only claims made using the new forms will be processed and paid. Assuming the new form has no gross errors, problems, or omissions, our CFO really has no concern with acceptance as defined here. If people want to be reimbursed for their travel expenses, then they will use the new form. This decision, in essence, implements itself.

On the other hand, leaders sometimes assume that they do not need to worry about acceptance because they have so much power over their followers that overt rejection of a decision is not likely to occur. A corporate CEO is not apt to see a junior accountant stand up and openly challenge the CEO's decision to implement a new policy, even though the young accountant may not "buy into" the new policy at all. Because followers generally do not openly object to the decisions made by leaders with this much power, these leaders often mistakenly assume that their decisions have been accepted and will be fully implemented. This is a rather naive view of what really goes on in organizations. Just because the junior subordinate does not publicly voice his opposition does not mean he will rush right out and wholeheartedly implement the

FIGURE 3–1

*Vroom and
Yetton's
Leadership
Decision Tree*

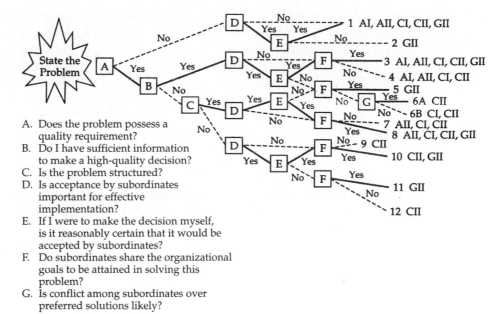

A. Does the problem possess a
   quality requirement?
B. Do I have sufficient information
   to make a high-quality decision?
C. Is the problem structured?
D. Is acceptance by subordinates
   important for effective
   implementation?
E. If I were to make the decision myself,
   is it reasonably certain that it would be
   accepted by subordinates?
F. Do subordinates share the organizational
   goals to be attained in solving this
   problem?
G. Is conflict among subordinates over
   preferred solutions likely?

Source: Reprinted from *Leadership and Decision Making*, by Victor H. Vroom and Philip W. Yetton, by permission
of the University of Pittsburgh Press, © 1973 by the University of Pittsburgh Press.

decision. In fact, the junior accountant has a lot more time to destructively
undermine the policy than the CEO does to check to ensure it is being carried
out to the letter of the law.

The Decision Tree

Having settled on quality and acceptance as the two principal criteria for effective decisions, Vroom and Yetton then developed a normative decision model.
(A normative model is one based on what ought to happen rather than describing what does happen.) They also developed a set of questions to protect quality and acceptance by eliminating decision processes that would be wrong or
inappropriate. Generally, these questions concern the problem itself, the amount
of pertinent information possessed by the leader and followers, and various situational factors.

In order to make it easier for leaders to determine how much participation
subordinates should have to optimize decision quality and acceptance, Vroom
and Yetton (1973) incorporated these questions into a decision tree (see Figure
3–1). To use the decision tree, one starts at the left by stating the problem and
then proceeds through the model from left to right. Every time a box is encountered, the question associated with that box must be answered with either a yes
or a no response. Eventually, all paths lead to a set of decision processes that, if
used, will lead to a decision that protects both quality and acceptance.

Having reached a set of feasible alternatives that meet the desirable criteria for quality and acceptance among followers, the leader may then wish to consider additional criteria. One very practical consideration is the amount of time available. If time is critical, then the leader should select the alternative in the feasible set that is farthest to the *left*, again noting that the feasible set is arranged from AI through GII. It generally takes less time to make and implement autocratic decisions than it does to make consultative or group decisions. Nevertheless, it is important to note that the first step is to protect quality and acceptance (by using the model). Only *after* arriving at an appropriate set of outcomes should leaders consider time in the decision-making process. This tenet is sometimes neglected in the workplace by leaders who overemphasize time as a criterion. Obviously, there are some situations where time is absolutely critical, as in life-or-death emergencies. But too often, leaders ask for a decision to be made as if the situation were an emergency when, in reality, they (the leaders, not the situation) are creating the time pressure. Despite such behavior, it is difficult to imagine a leader who would knowingly prefer a fast decision that lacks both quality and acceptance among the implementers rather than one that is of high quality and acceptable to followers but that takes more time.

Another important consideration is follower development. Again, after quality and acceptance have been considered using the decision tree, and if the leader has determined that time is not a critical element, she may wish to follow a decision process more apt to allow followers to develop their own decision-making skills. This can be achieved by using the decision tree and then selecting the alternative within the feasible set that is farthest to the *right*. As was the case above, the arrangement of processes from AI to GII provides an increasing amount of follower development by moving from autocratic to group decisions.

Finally, if neither time nor follower development is a concern and multiple options are available in the feasible set of alternatives, the leader may select a style that best meets his or her needs. This may be the process with which he is most comfortable ("I'm a CII kind of guy"), or it may be a process in which he would like to develop more skill.

Concluding Thoughts about the Normative Decision Model

Having looked at this model in some detail, we will now look at it from the perspective of the leader-follower-situation (L-F-S) framework. To do this, we have used the different decision processes and the questions from the decision tree to illustrate different components in the L-F-S framework (see Figure 3–2). Several issues become apparent in this depiction. First, for ease of presentation we have placed each question or factor solely within one circle or another. Nevertheless, one could argue that some of the questions could or should be placed in another part of the model. For example, the question "Do I have sufficient information to make a high-quality decision?" is placed in the leader block. It might be argued, however, that no leader could answer this question without some knowledge of the situation. Strictly speaking, therefore, perhaps this question

FIGURE 3–2

Factors from the Normative Decision Model and the Interactional Framework

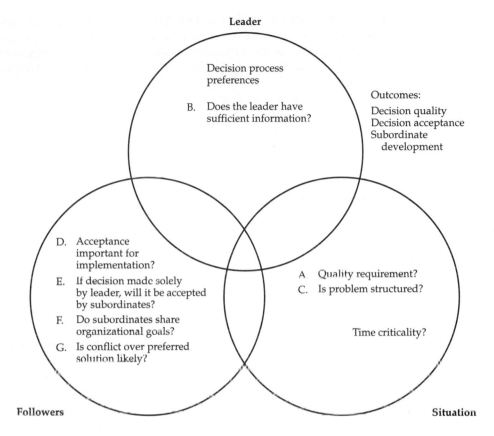

should be placed in the intersection between the leader and the situation. Nonetheless, in keeping with our theme that leadership involves interactions among all three elements, it seems sufficient at this point to illustrate them in their simplest state.

A second issue also becomes apparent when the normative decision model is viewed through the L-F-S framework. Notice how the Vroom and Yetton (1973) model shifts focus away from the leader toward both the situation and, to an even greater degree, the followers. There are no questions about the leader's personality, motivations, values, or attitudes. In fact, the leader's preference is considered only after higher-priority factors have been considered. The only underlying assumption is that the leader is interested in implementing a high-quality decision (when quality is an issue) that is acceptable to followers (when acceptance is critical to implementation). Given that assumption and a willingness to consider aspects of the situation and aspects of the followers, the leader's behavior can be channeled into more effective decision-making processes.

A third issue is that the L-F-S framework organizes concepts in a familiar conceptual structure. This is an advantage even for a theory with as limited a focus as the normative decision model (i.e., decision making); it will be even more helpful later as we consider more complex theories.

Finally, because the normative decision model is a *leadership theory* rather than Vroom and Yetton's personal opinions, a number of empirical studies have investigated the model's efficacy. Research conducted by Field (1982) and Vroom and Jago (1974, 1988) provided strong support for the model, as these studies showed that leaders were much more likely to make effective or successful decisions when they followed its tenets than when they ignored them. Nevertheless, although leaders may be more apt to make more effective decisions when using the model, there is no evidence to show that these leaders are more effective overall than leaders not using the model (Miner, 1975). The latter findings again point out that both the leadership process and leadership effectiveness are complex phenomema; being a good decision maker is not enough to be a good leader (although it certainly helps). Other problems with the model are that it views decision making as taking place at a single point in time (Yukl, 1989), assumes that leaders are equally skilled at using all five decision procedures (Yukl & Van Fleet, 1992), and assumes that some of the prescriptions of the model may not be the best for a given situation. For example, the normative decision model prescribes that leaders use a GII decision process if conflict may occur over a decision, but leaders may be more effective if they instead make an AI decision and avoid intragroup conflict (Couch & Yetton, 1987). Despite these problems, the normative model is one of the best supported of the four major contingency theories of leadership, and leaders would be wise to consider using the model when making decisions.

The Situational Leadership Theory

It seems fairly obvious that leaders do not interact with all followers in the same manner. For example, a leader may give general guidelines or goals to her highly competent and motivated followers but spend considerable time coaching, directing, and training her unskilled and unmotivated followers. Or leaders may provide relatively little praise and few assurances to followers with high self-confidence but high amounts of support to followers with low self-confidence. Although leaders often have different interactional styles when dealing with individual followers, is there an optimum way for leaders to adjust their behavior with different followers and thereby increase their likelihood of success? And if there is, then what factors should the leader base his behavior on—the follower's intelligence? Personality traits? Values? Preferences? Technical competence? Hersey and Blanchard (1969, 1977, 1982) developed the **situational leadership theory** (SLT) to answer these two important leadership questions.

Leader Behaviors

Situational leadership theory has evolved over time. Its roots are in the Ohio State studies, in which the two broad categories of leader behaviors, initiating structure and consideration, were initially identified (see Chapter 10). As SLT

FIGURE 3–3

The SLT Prescriptions for the Most Appropriate Leader Behaviors Based on Follower Maturity

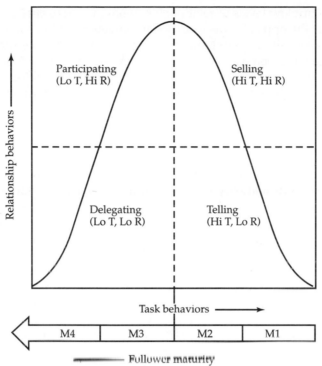

Source: Paul Hersey and Kenneth Blanchard, *Management of Organizational Behavior: Utilizing Human Resources,* 4th ed. (Englewood Cliffs, NJ: Prentice Hall, 1982), p. 152. Adapted by permission.

evolved, so did the labels (but not the content) for the two leadership behavior categories. Initiating structure changed to **task behaviors,** which were defined as the extent to which the leader spells out the responsibilities of an individual or group. Task behaviors include telling people what to do, how to do it, when to do it, and who is to do it. Similarly, consideration changed to **relationship behaviors**, or how much the leader engages in two-way communication. Relationship behaviors include listening, encouraging, facilitating, clarifying, and giving socioemotional support.

When the behavior of actual leaders was studied, there was little evidence to show these two categories of leader behavior were consistently related to leadership success; the relative effectiveness of these two behavior dimensions often depended on the situation. Hersey and Blanchard (1969, 1977, 1982) proposed a model to explain why leadership effectiveness varied across these two behavior dimensions and situations. First, they arrayed the two orthogonal dimensions as in the Ohio State studies, and then they divided each of them into high and low segments (see Figure 3–3). According to Hersey and Blanchard, depicting the two leadership dimensions this way indicated that certain combinations of task and relationship behaviors may be more effective in some situations than in others. For example, in some situations high levels of task behaviors but low levels of relationship behaviors were effective; in other situations, just the opposite was true. So far, however, we have not considered the key follower or situational characteristics with which these combinations of task and relationship behaviors were most effective. Hersey and Blanchard stated that these four combinations of task and relationship behaviors would increase leadership effectiveness if they were made contingent on the maturity level of the individual follower.

Maturity of the Follower

Follower maturity consists of two components: **job maturity** and psychological maturity. **Job maturity** is the amount of *task-relevant* knowledge, experience, skill, and ability that the follower possesses. In a sense, job maturity is much the same as technical expertise. **Psychological maturity** is the follower's self-confidence, commitment, motivation, and self-respect *relative to the task* at hand. Notice that both of these elements of maturity are meaningful only with regard to a particular task. Someone with a medical degree and years of experience as a surgeon might be rated as extremely mature at performing open-heart surgery. That same person might have virtually no job or psychological maturity for the tasks of designing and building a house, piloting a hot-air balloon, or counseling a suicidal patient. It is impossible to assess either job or psychological maturity if the task is unknown. Similarly, because most of us perform multiple tasks, there is no universal level of maturity. Both job and psychological maturity vary according to the task at hand.

Prescriptions of the Theory

Now that the key contingency factor, follower maturity, has been identified, let us move on to another aspect of the figure—combining follower maturity levels with the four combinations of leader behaviors described earlier. The horizontal bar or arrow in Figure 3–3 depicts follower maturity as increasing from right to left (not in the direction we are used to seeing). There are four segments along this continuum, ranging from M1 (the least mature) to M4 (the most mature). Along this continuum, however, the assessment of follower maturity can be fairly subjective. A follower who possesses high levels of both job and psychological maturity relative to the task would clearly fall in the M4 category, just as a follower with neither job nor psychological maturity would fall in M1. The discriminating factors for categories M2 and M3 are less clear, however.

To complete the model, Hersey and Blanchard (1982) added a curved line that represents the leadership behavior that will most likely be effective given a particular level of follower maturity. In order to use SLT, leaders should first assess the maturity level (M1–M4) of the follower relative to the task to be accomplished. Next, a vertical line should be drawn from the center of the maturity level up to the point where it intersects with the curved line in Figure 3–3. The quadrant in which this intersection occurs represents the level of task and relationship behavior that has the best chance of producing successful outcomes. For example, imagine you are a fire chief and have under your command a search-and-rescue team. One of the team members is needed to rescue a backpacker who has fallen in the mountains, and you have selected a particular follower to accomplish the task. What leadership behavior should you exhibit? Assuming this is a responsible and psychologically mature follower who has both substantial training and experience in this type of rescue, you would assess his maturity level as M4. A vertical line from M4 would intersect the curved line in the quadrant where both low-task and low-relationship behaviors by the leader are most apt to be successful. As the leader, you should exhibit a low level of task and relationship behaviors and delegate this task to the follower. On the other hand, you may have a brand-new member of the fire department who still has to learn the ins and outs of firefighting. Because this particular follower has low job and psychological maturity (M1), SLT maintains that the leader should use a high level of task behaviors and a low level of relationship behaviors when initially dealing with this follower.

Hersey and Blanchard suggest one further step leaders may wish to consider. The model described above helps the leader select the most appropriate behavior given the current level of follower maturity. However, there may be cases when the leader would like to see the followers increase their level of maturity. Because more-mature followers are generally more effective than less-mature followers, leaders may wish to implement a series of **developmental interventions** to help boost follower maturity levels. The process would begin by first assessing the follower's current level of maturity and then determining the leader behavior that best suits that follower in that task. Instead of using the behavior prescribed by SLT, however, the leader would select the next higher leadership behavior. Another way of thinking about this would be for the leader to select the behavior pattern that would fit the follower if that follower were one level higher in maturity. This intervention is designed to help followers in their maturity development, hence its name (see Highlight 3–3, on developmental interventions).

Concluding Thoughts about the Situational Leadership Theory

In Figure 3–4, we can see how the factors in SLT fit within the L-F-S framework. In comparison to the Vroom and Yetton model, there are fewer factors to be considered in each of the three elements. The only situational consideration is knowledge of the task, and the only two follower factors are job and psychological maturity. On the other hand, the theory goes well beyond decision making, which was the sole domain of the normative decision model. In fact, Hersey and Blanchard have suggested that their model can even be extended to other applications, such as parenting.

Situational leadership theory is usually appealing to students and practitioners because of its commonsense approach as well as its ease of understanding. Unfortunately, there is little research to support the predictions of SLT in the

---

Highlight 3–3

A Developmental Intervention Using SLT

Dianne is a resident assistant in charge of a number of students in a university dorm. One particular sophomore, Michael, has volunteered to work on projects in the past but never seems to take the initiative to get started on his own. Michael seems to wait until Dianne gives him explicit direction, approval, and encouragement before he will get started. Michael can do a good job, but he seems to be unwilling to start without some convincing that it is all right, and unless Dianne makes explicit what steps are to be taken. Dianne has assessed Michael's maturity level as M2, but she would like to see him develop, both in task maturity and in psychological maturity. The behavior most likely to fit Michael's current maturity level is selling, or high task, high relationship. But Dianne has decided to implement a developmental intervention to help Michael raise his maturity level. Dianne can be most helpful in this intervention by moving up one level to participating, or low task, high relationship. By reducing the amount of task instructions and direction while encouraging Michael to lay out a plan on his own and supporting his steps in the right direction, Dianne is most apt to help Michael become an M3 follower. This does not mean the work will get done most efficiently, however. Just as we saw in the Vroom and Yetton model earlier, if part of the leader's job is development of followers, then time may be a reasonable and necessary trade-off for short-term efficiency.

---

workplace (Vecchio, 1987; Yukl & Van Fleet, 1992). Moreover, follower maturity is poorly defined (Graeff, 1983), and the model provides inadequate rationale or sufficiently specific guidance about *why* or *how* particular levels of task and relationship behaviors correspond to each of the follower maturity levels (Yukl, 1989). Furthermore, Hersey and Blanchard have simply defined leadership effectiveness as those leader behaviors that match the prescriptions of SLT. They have not presented any evidence that leaders who behave according to the model's prescriptions actually have higher unit performance indexes, better-performing or more-satisfied subordinates, or a more-favorable organizational climate (Vecchio, 1987). Nevertheless, even with these shortcomings, SLT is a useful way to get leaders to think about how leadership effectiveness may depend somewhat on being flexible with different subordinates, not on acting the same way toward them all.

The Contingency Model

Although leaders may be able to change their behaviors toward individual subordinates, leaders also have dominant behavioral tendencies. Some leaders may be generally more supportive and relationship-oriented, whereas others may be

FIGURE 3–4

Factors from the Situational Leadership Theory and the Interactional Framework

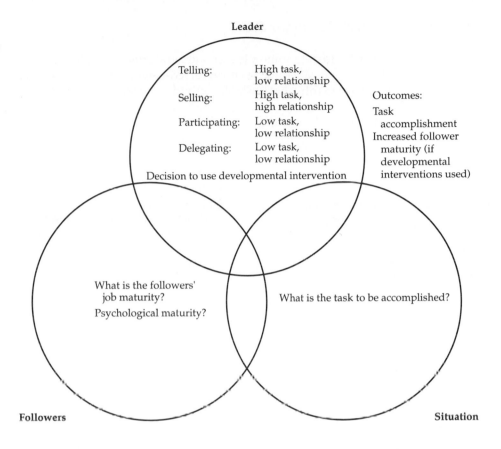

more concerned with task or goal accomplishment. The contingency model (Fiedler, 1967) recognizes that leaders have these general behavioral tendencies and specifies situations where certain leaders (or behavioral dispositions) may be more effective than others.

Fiedler's (1967) **contingency model** of leadership is probably the earliest and most well-known contingency theory, and is often perceived by students to be almost the opposite of SLT. Compared to the contingency model, SLT emphasizes flexibility in leader behaviors, whereas the contingency model maintains that leaders are much more consistent (and consequently less flexible) in their behavior. Situational leadership theory maintains that leaders who *correctly base their behaviors* on follower maturity will be more effective, whereas the contingency model suggests that leader effectiveness is primarily determined by *selecting the right kind of leader for a certain situation or changing the situation* to fit the particular leader's style. Another way to say this is that leadership effectiveness depends on both the leader's style and the favorableness of the leadership situation. Some leaders are better than others in some situations but less effective in other situations. To understand contingency theory, therefore, we need to look first at the critical characteristics of the leader and then at the critical aspects of the situation.

The Least-Preferred-Coworker Scale

In order to determine a leader's general style or tendency, Fiedler developed an instrument called the **least-preferred-coworker (LPC) scale.** The scale instructs a leader to think of the single individual with whom he has had the greatest difficulty working (i.e., the least-preferred coworker) and then to describe that individual in terms of a series of bipolar adjectives (e.g., friendly-unfriendly, boring-interesting, sincere-insincere). Those ratings are then converted into a numerical score.

In thinking about such a procedure, many people assume that the score is determined primarily by the characteristics of whatever particular individual the leader happened to identify as his least-preferred co-worker. In the context of contingency theory, however, it is important to understand that the score is thought to *represent something about the leader, not the specific individual the leader evaluated.*

The current interpretation of these scores is that they identify a leader's motivation hierarchy (Fiedler, 1978). Based on their LPC scores, leaders are categorized into two groups: **low-LPC leaders** and **high-LPC leaders.** In terms of their motivation hierarchy, low-LPC leaders are primarily motivated by the task, which means that these leaders primarily gain satisfaction from task accomplishment. Thus, their dominant behavioral tendencies are similar to the initiating structure behavior described in the Ohio State research or the task behavior of SLT. However, if tasks are being accomplished in an acceptable manner, then low-LPC leaders will move to their secondary level of motivation, which is forming and maintaining relationships with followers. Thus, low-LPC leaders will focus on improving their relationships with followers *after* they are assured that assigned tasks are being satisfactorily accomplished. As soon as tasks are no longer being accomplished in an acceptable manner, however, low-LPC leaders will refocus their efforts on task accomplishment and persist with these efforts until task accomplishment is back on track.

In terms of motivation hierarchy, high-LPC leaders are primarily motivated by relationships, which means that these leaders are primarily satisfied by establishing and maintaining close interpersonal relationships. Thus, their dominant behavioral tendencies are similar to the consideration behaviors described in the Ohio State research or the relationship behaviors in SLT. If high-LPC leaders have established good relationships with their followers, then they will move to their secondary level of motivation, which is task accomplishment. As soon as leader-follower relations are jeopardized, however, high-LPC leaders will cease working on tasks and refocus their efforts on improving relationships with followers.

You can think of the LPC scale as identifying two different sorts of leaders with their respective motivational hierarchies depicted in Figure 3–5. Lower-level needs must be satisfied first. Low-LPC leaders will move "up" to satisfying relationship needs when they are assured the task is being satisfactorily accomplished. High-LPC leaders will move "up" to emphasizing task accomplishment when they have established good relationships with their followers.

FIGURE 3–5

*Motivational
Hierarchies for
Low- and High-
LPC Leaders*

Low-LPC leader motivational hierarchy

High-LPC leader motivational hierarchy

Because all tests have some level of imprecision, Fiedler (1978) suggested that the LPC scale cannot accurately identify the motivation hierarchy for those individuals with certain intermediate scores. Research by Kennedy (1982) suggests an alternative view. Kennedy has shown that individuals within the intermediate range of LPC scale scores may more easily or readily switch between being task- or relationship-oriented leaders than those individuals with more extreme scale scores. They may be equally satisfied by working on the task or establishing relationships with followers.

Situational Favorability

The other critical variable in the contingency model is **situational favorability**, which is the amount of control the leader has over the followers. Presumably, the more control a leader has over followers, the more favorable the situation is, at least from the leader's perspective. Fiedler included three subelements in situation favorability. These were leader-member relations, task structure, and position power.

Leader-member relations is the most powerful of the three subelements in determining overall situation favorability. It involves the extent to which relationships between the leader and followers are generally cooperative and friendly or antagonistic and difficult. Leaders who rate leader-member relations as high would feel they had the support of their followers and could rely on their loyalty.

Task structure is second in potency in determining overall situation favorability. Here the leader would objectively determine task structure by assessing whether there were detailed descriptions of work products, standard operating procedures, or objective indicators of how well the task is being accomplished. The more one could answer these questions affirmatively, the higher the structure of the task.

FIGURE 3–6

Contingency Model Octant Structure for Determining Situational Favorability

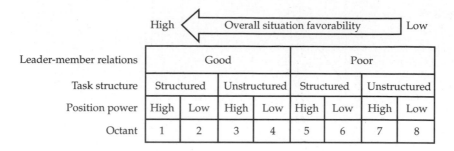

Position power is the weakest of the three elements of situational favorability. Leaders who have titles of authority or rank, the authority to administer rewards and punishments, and the legitimacy to conduct follower performance appraisals have greater position power than leaders who lack them.

The relative weights of these three components, taken together, can be used to create a continuum of situational favorability. When using the contingency model, leaders are first asked to rate items that measure the strength of leader-member relations, the degree of task structure, and their level of position power. These ratings are then weighted and combined to determine an overall level of situational favorability facing the leader (Fiedler & Chemers, 1982). Any particular situation's favorability can then be plotted on a continuum Fiedler divided into octants representing distinctly different levels of situational favorability. The relative weighting scheme for the subelements and how they make up each of the eight octants can be seen in Figure 3–6.

You can see that the octants of situational favorability range from 1 (highly favorable) to 8 (very unfavorable). The highest levels of situational favorability occur when leader-member relations are good, the task is structured, and position power is high. The lowest levels of situational favorability occur when there are high levels of leader-member conflict, the task is unstructured or unclear, and the leader does not have the power to reward or punish subordinates. Moreover, the relative weighting of the three subelements can easily be seen by their order of precedence in Figure 3–6, with leader-member relations appearing first, followed by task structure and then position power. For example, because leader-member relations carries so much weight, it is impossible for leaders with good leader-member relations to have anything worse than moderate situational favorability, regardless of their task structure or position power. In other words, leaders with good leader-member relations will be in a situation that has situational favorability no worse than octant 4; leaders with poor leader-member relations will be facing a leadership situation with situational favorability being no better than octant 5.

Prescriptions of the Model

Fiedler and his associates have conducted numerous studies to determine how different leaders (as described by their LPC scores) have performed in different situations (as described in terms of situational favorability). Figure 3–7 describes

FIGURE 3–7

Leader Effectiveness Based on the Contingency between Leader LPC Score and Situation Favorability

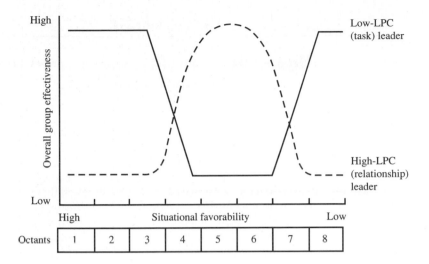

which type of leader (high or low LPC) Fiedler found to be most effective, given a different levels of situation favorability. The solid dark line represents the relative effectiveness of a low-LPC leader, and the dashed line represents the relative effectiveness of a high-LPC leader. It is obvious from the way the two lines cross and recross that there is some interaction between the leader's style and the overall situation favorability. If the situational favorability is moderate (octants 4, 5, 6, or 7), then those groups led by leaders concerned with establishing and maintaining relationships (high-LPC leaders) seem to do best. However, if the situation is either very unfavorable (octant 8) or highly favorable (octants 1, 2, or 3), then those groups led by the task-motivated (low-LPC) leaders seem to do best.

Fiedler suggested that leaders will try to satisfy their primary motivation when faced with unfavorable or moderately favorable situations. This means that low-LPC leaders will concentrate on the task and high-LPC leaders will concentrate on relationships when faced with these two levels of situational favorability. Nevertheless, leaders facing highly favorable situations know that their primary motivations will be satisfied and thus will move to their secondary motivational state. This means that *leaders will behave according to their secondary motivational state only when faced with highly favorable situations* (see Highlight 3–4, "High- and Low-LPC Leaders and the Contingency Model").

There are several interesting implications of Fiedler's (1967) model worthy of additional comment. Because leaders develop their distinctive motivation hierarchies and dominant behavior tendencies through a lifetime of experiences, Fiedler believed these hierarchies and tendencies would be difficult to change through training. Fiedler maintained it was naive to believe that sending someone to a relatively brief leadership training program could substantially alter any leader's personality or typical way of acting in leadership situations; after all, such tendencies had been developed over many years of experience. Instead

---

Highlight 3–4

High- and Low-LPC Leaders and the Contingency Model

Suppose we had two leaders, Tom Low (a low-LPC or task-motivated leader) and Brenda High (a high-LPC or relationship-motivated leader). In unfavorable situations, Tom will be motivated by his primary level and will thus exhibit task behaviors. In similar situations, Brenda will also be motivated by her primary level and as a result will exhibit relationship behaviors. Fiedler found that in unfavorable situations, task behavior will help the group to be more effective, so Tom's behavior would better match the requirements of the situation. Group effectiveness would not be aided by Brenda's relationship behavior in this situation.

In situations with moderate favorability, both Tom and Brenda are still motivated by their primary motivations, so their behaviors will be precisely the same as described: Tom will exhibit task behaviors and Brenda will exhibit relationship behaviors. Because the situation has changed, however, group effectiveness no longer requires task behavior. Instead, the combination of situational variables leads to a condition where a leader's relationship behaviors will make the greatest contribution to group effectiveness. Hence, Brenda will be the most-effective leader in situations of moderate favorability. In highly favorable situations, the explanation provided by Fiedler gets more complex. When leaders find themselves in highly favorable situations, they no longer have to be concerned about satisfying their primary motivations (they already are). In highly favorable situations, leaders switch to satisfying their secondary motivations. Because Tom's secondary motivation is to establish and maintain relationships, in highly favorable situations he will exhibit relationship behaviors.

Similarly, Brenda will also be motivated by her secondary motivation, so she would manifest task behaviors in highly favorable situations. Fiedler believed that leaders who manifested relationship behaviors in highly favorable situations helped groups to be more effective. In this case, Tom is giving the group what they need to be more effective.

---

of trying to change the leader, Fiedler concluded, training would be more effective if it showed leaders how to recognize and change key situational characteristics to better fit their personal motivational hierachies and behavioral tendencies. Thus, according to Fiedler, the content of leadership training should emphazise situational engineering rather than behavioral flexibility in leaders. Relatedly, organizations could become more effective if they matched the characteristics of the leader (in this case LPC scores) with the demands of the situation (i.e., situational favorability) than if they tried to change the leader to fit the situation. These suggestions imply that high- or low-LPC leaders in mismatched situations should either change the situation or move to jobs that better match their motivational hierarchies and behavorial patterns.

FIGURE 3–8

*Factors from
Fiedler's
Contingency
Theory and the
Interactional
Framework*

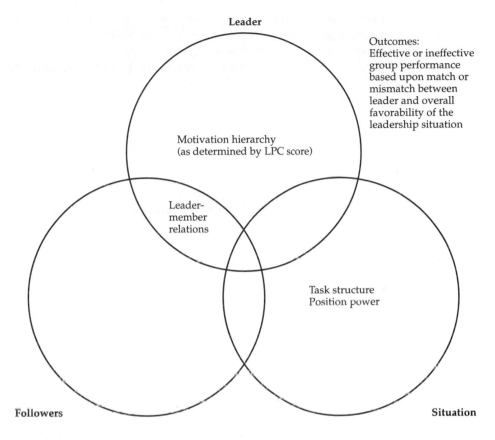

Concluding Thoughts about the Contingency Model

Before reviewing the empirical evidence, perhaps we can attain a clearer understanding of the contingency model by examining it through the L-F-S framework. As seen in Figure 3–8, task structure is a function of the situation and LPC
scores are a function of the leader. Because position power is not a characteristic of the leader but of the situation the leader finds him- or herself in, it is
included in the situational circle. Leader-member relations is a joint function of
the leader and the followers; thus, it best belongs in the overlapping intersection
of the leader and follower circles.

As opposed to the dearth of evidence for Hersey and Blanchard's (1969,
1982) situational theory, Fiedler and his fellow researchers have provided considerable evidence that the predictions of the model are empirically valid, particularly in laboratory settings (Fiedler, 1978, 1995; Fiedler & Chemers, 1982;
Peters, Hartke, & Pohlmann, 1985; Strube & Garcia, 1981). However, a review of
the studies conducted in field settings yielded only mixed support for the model
(Peters, Hartke, & Pohlmann, 1985). Moreover, researchers have criticized the
model for the uncertainties surrounding the meaning of LPC scores (Kennedy,
1982; Rice, 1978; Schriesheim & Kerr, 1977), the interpretation of situational

favorability (Jago & Ragan, 1986a, 1986b), and the relationships between LPC scores and situational favorability (Jago & Ragan, 1986a, 1986b, Vecchio, 1983). Despite such questions, however, the contingency model has stimulated considerable research and is the most validated of all leadership theories.

The Path-Goal Theory

Perhaps the most sophisticated (and comprehensive) of the four contingency models is path-goal theory. The underlying mechanism of **path-goal theory** deals with expectancy, a cognitive approach to understanding motivation where people calculate effort-to-performance probabilities (If I study for 12 hours what is the probability I will get an A on the final exam?), performance-to-outcome probabilities (If I get an A on the final what is the probability of getting an A in the course?), and assigned valences or values to outcome (How much do I value a higher GPA?). Theoretically at least, people were assumed to make these calculations on a rational basis, and the theory could be used to predict what tasks people will put their energies into, given some finite number of options.

Path-goal theory uses the same basic assumptions of expectancy theory. At the most fundamental level, the effective leader will provide or ensure the availability of valued rewards for followers (the "goal") and then help them find the best way of getting there (the "path"). Along the way, the effective leader will help the followers identify and remove roadblocks, and avoid dead ends; the leader will also provide emotional support as needed. These "task" and "relationship" leadership actions essentially involve increasing followers' probability estimates for effort-to-performance and performance-to-reward expectancies. In other words, the leader's actions should strengthen followers' beliefs that if they exert a certain level of effort, then they will be more likely to accomplish a task, and if they accomplish the task, then they will be more likely to achieve some valued outcome.

Although not very complicated in its basic concept, the model added more variables and interactions over time. Evans (1970) is credited with the first version of path-goal theory, but we will focus on a later version developed by House and Dessler (1974). Their conceptual scheme is ideally suited to the L-F-S framework because they described three classes of variables, which include leader behaviors, followers, and the situation. We will examine each of these in turn.

Leader Behaviors

The four types of leader behavior in path-goal theory can be seen in Table 3–1. Like SLT, path-goal theory assumes that leaders not only may use varying styles with different subordinates but might very well use differing styles with the same subordinates in different situations. Path-goal theory suggests that depending on the followers and the situation, these different leader behaviors

TABLE 3–1   The Four Leader Behaviors of Path-Goal Theory

Directive leadership. These leader behaviors are very similar to the task behaviors from SLT. They include telling the followers what they are expected to do, how to do it, when it is to be done, and how their work fits in with the work of others. This behavior would also include setting schedules, establishing norms, and providing expectations that followers will adhere to established procedure and regulations.

Supportive leadership. Supportive leadership behaviors include having courteous and friendly interactions, expressing genuine concern for the followers' well-being and individual needs, and remaining open and approachable to followers. These behaviors, which are very similar to the relationship behaviors in SLT, also are marked by attention to the competing demands of treating followers equally while recognizing status differentials between the leader and the followers.

Participative leadership. Participative leaders engage in the behaviors that mark the consultative and group behaviors described by Vroom and Yetton (1973). As such, they tend to share work problems with followers; solicit their suggestions, concerns, and recommendations; and weigh these inputs in the decision-making process.

Achievement-oriented leadership. Leaders exhibiting these would be seen as both demanding and supporting in interactions with their followers. In the first place, they would set very challenging goals for group and follower behavior, continually seek ways to improve performance en route, and expect the followers to always perform at their highest levels. But they would support these behaviors by exhibiting a high degree of ongoing confidence that subordinates can put forth the necessary effort; will achieve the desired results; and, even further, will assume even more responsibility in the future.

---

can increase followers' acceptance of the leader, enhance their level of satisfaction, and raise their expectations that effort will result in effective performance, which in turn will lead to valued rewards.

The Followers

Path-goal theory contains two groups of follower variables. The first relates to the *satisfaction of followers,* and the second relates to the *followers' perception of their own abilities* relative to the task to be accomplished. In terms of followers' satisfaction, path-goal theory suggests that leader behaviors will be acceptable to the followers to the degree followers see the leader's behavior either as an immediate source of satisfaction or as directly instrumental in achieving future satisfaction. In other words, followers will actively support a leader as long as they view the leader's actions as a means for increasing their own levels of satisfaction. However, there is only so much a leader can do to increase followers' satisfaction levels, as satisfaction also depends on characteristics of the followers themselves.

A frequently cited example of how followers' characteristics influence the impact of leader behaviors on followers' levels of satisfaction involves the trait of locus of control. People who believe they are "masters of their own ship" are said to have an internal locus of control; people who believe they are (relatively speaking) "pawns of fate" are said to have an external locus of control. Mitchell, Smyser, and Weed (1975) found that follower satisfaction was not directly related

Figure 3–9

Interaction between Followers' Locus of Control Scores and Leader Behavior in Decision Making

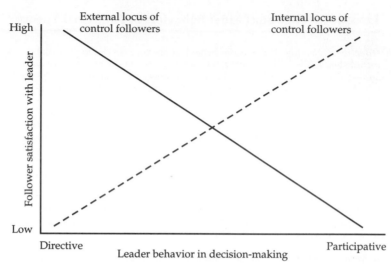

Source: Adapted from T. R. Mitchell, C. M. Smyser, and S. E. Weed, "Locus of Control: Supervision and Work Satisfaction," *Academy of Management Journal* 18 (1975), pp. 623-30.

to the degree of participative behaviors manifested by the leader (i.e., followers with highly participative leaders were not any more satisfied than followers with more autocratic leaders). However, when followers' locus-of-control scores were taken into account, a contingency relationship was discovered. As can be seen in Figure 3–9, internal-locus-of-control followers, who believed outcomes were a result of their own decisions, were much more satisfied with leaders who exhibited participative behaviors than they were with leaders who were directive. Conversely, external-locus-of-control followers were more satisfied with directive leader behaviors than they were with participative leader behaviors.

Followers' perceptions of their own skills and abilities to perform particular tasks can also affect the impact of certain leader behaviors. Followers who believe they are perfectly capable of performing a task are not as apt to be motivated by, or as willing to accept, a directive leader as they would a leader who exhibits participative behaviors. Using the same rationale as for locus of control, one can predict the opposite relationship for followers who do not perceive they have sufficient abilities to perform the task. Once again, the acceptability of the leader and the motivation to perform are in part determined by followers' characteristics. Thus, path-goal theory suggests that both leader behaviors and follower characteristics are important in determining outcomes.

The Situation

Path-goal theory considers three situational factors that impact or moderate the effects of leader behavior on follower attitudes and behaviors. These include the *task, the formal authority system, and the primary work group.* Each of these three factors can influence the leadership situation in one of three ways. These three factors can serve as an independent motivational factor, as a constraint on the behavior of followers (which may be either positive or negative in outcome), or as a reward.

However, it should also be increasingly apparent that these variables can often affect the impact of various leader behaviors. For example, if the task is very structured and routine, the formal authority system has constrained followers' behaviors, and the work group has established clear norms for performance, then leaders would be serving a redundant purpose by manifesting directive or achievement-oriented behaviors. These prescriptions are similar to some of those noted in substitutes for leadership theory (Kerr & Jermier, 1978), as everything the follower needs in order to understand the effort-to-performance and performance-to-reward links is provided by the situation. Thus, redundant leader behaviors might be interpreted by followers as either a complete lack of understanding or empathy by the leader, or an attempt by the leader to exert excessive control. Neither of these interpretations is likely to enhance the leader's acceptance by followers or increase their motivation.

Although we have already described how follower characteristics and situational characteristics can impact leader behaviors, path-goal theory also maintains that follower and situational variables can impact each other. In other words, situational variables, such as the task performed, can also impact the influence of followers' skills, abilities, or personality traits on followers' satisfaction. Although this seems to make perfect sense, hopefully you are beginning to see how complicated path-goal theory can be when one starts considering how situational variables, follower characteristics, and leader behaviors interact in the leadership process. Because these interactions can become extremely complicated and are beyond the scope of this text, readers who wish to learn more about the intricacies of path-goal theory are encouraged to read House and Dessler (1974).

Prescriptions of the Theory

In general, path-goal theory maintains that leaders should first assess the situation and select a leadership behavior appropriate to situational demands. By manifesting the appropriate behaviors, leaders can increase followers' effort-to-performance expectancies, performance-to-reward expectancies, or valences of the outcomes. These increased expectancies and valences will improve subordinates' effort levels and the rewards attained, which in turn will increase subordinates' satisfaction and performance levels and the acceptance of their leaders. Perhaps the easiest way to explain this fairly complicated process is through the use of an example. Suppose we have a set of followers who are in a newly created work unit and do not have a clear understanding of the requirements of their positions. In other words, the followers have a reasonably high level of role ambiguity. According to path-goal theory, leaders should exhibit a high degree of directive behaviors in order to reduce the role ambiguity of their followers. The effort-to-performance link will become clearer when leaders tell followers what to do and how to do it in ambiguous situations, which in turn will cause followers to exert

FIGURE 3–10

Examples of Applying Path-Goal Theory

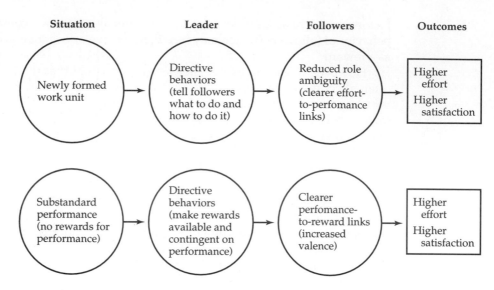

higher effort levels. Because role ambiguity is assumed to be unpleasant, these directive leader behaviors and higher effort levels should eventually result in higher satisfaction levels among followers. Figure 3–10 illustrates this process. Similarly, leaders may look at the leadership situation and note that followers' performance levels are not acceptable. The leader may also conclude that the current situation offers few, if any, incentives for increased performance. In this case, the leader may use directive behaviors to increase the value of the rewards (or valence), which in turn will increase followers' effort levels and performance.

Concluding Thoughts about the Path-Goal Theory

Before getting into the research surrounding path-goal theory, you may wish to examine the theory using the L-F-S framework. As seen in Figure 3–11, the components of path-goal theory fit quite nicely into the L-F-S model. The four leader behaviors fit nicely in the leader circle, the characteristics of the followers fit into the follower circle, and the task and formal authority system fit into the situation circle. Of all the components of path-goal theory, the only "mismatch" with the L-F-S model deals with the primary work group. The norms, cohesiveness, size, and stage of development of groups is considered to be part of the follower function in the L-F-S model but is part of the situation function in path-goal theory. In that regard, we hasten to note we use the L-F-S framework primarily for heuristic purposes. Ultimately, the concepts described in these four theories are sufficiently complex and ambiguous that there probably is no right answer to any single depiction.

In terms of research, the path-goal theory has received only mixed support to date (Schriesheim & DeNisi, 1981; Schriesheim & Kerr, 1977; Yukl, 1989). Although many of these mixed findings may be due to the fact that the path-goal

FIGURE 3–11

*Factors from
Path-Goal
Theory and the
Interactional
Framework*

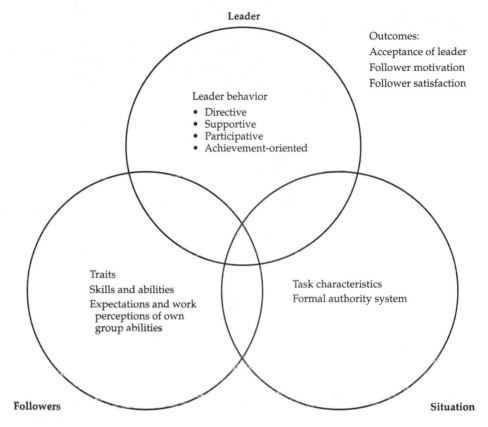

Leader

Leader behavior
- Directive
- Supportive
- Participative
- Achievement-oriented

Outcomes:
Acceptance of leader
Follower motivation
Follower satisfaction

Traits
Skills and abilities
Expectations and work
  perceptions of own
  group abilities

Task characteristics
Formal authority system

Followers   Situation

theory excludes many of the variables found to impact the leadership process, that may also be due to problems with the theory. Yukl (1989) maintained that most of these criticisms deal with the methodology used to study path-goal theory and the limitations of expectancy theory. Moreover, the path-goal theory assumes that the only way to increase performance is to increase followers' motivation levels. The theory ignores the roles leaders play in selecting talented followers, building their skill levels through training, and redesigning their work (Yukl & Van Fleet, 1992).

Nonetheless, path-goal theory is useful for illustrating two points. First, as noted by Yukl (1989), "path-goal theory has already made a contribution to the study of leadership by providing a conceptual framework to guide researchers in identifying potentially relevant situational moderator variables" (p. 104). Path-goal theory also illustrates that as models become more complicated, they may be more useful to researchers and less appealing to practitioners. Our experience is that pragmatically oriented students and in-place leaders want to take something from a model that is understandable and can be applied in their work situation right away. This does not mean they prefer simplicity to validity—they generally appreciate the complexity of the leadership process. But neither do they want a model that is so complex as to be indecipherable.

Summary

This chapter is designed to provide an overview of four of the more well-known contingency theories of leadership, which include the normative decision model (Vroom & Yetton, 1973), the situational leadership model (Hersey & Blanchard, 1984), the contingency model (Fiedler, 1967), and the path-goal theory (House & Dessler, 1974). All four models are fairly similar in that they specify that leaders should make their behaviors contingent on certain aspects of the followers or the situation in order to improve leadership effectiveness. In addition, all four theories implicitly assume that leaders can accurately assess key follower and situational factors. However, as the material regarding perception in Chapter 2 shows, it is entirely possible that two leaders in the same situation may reach very different conclusions about followers' level of knowledge, maturity, the strength of leader-follower relationships, the degree of task structure, or the level of role ambiguity being experienced by followers. These differences in perception could lead these two leaders to reach different conclusions about the situation, which may in turn cause them to take very different actions in response to the situation. Furthermore, these actions may be in accordance or in conflict with the prescriptions of any of these four theories. Also, the fact that leaders' perceptions may have caused them to act in a manner not prescribed by a particular model may be an underlying reason why these four theories have reported conflicting findings, particularly in field settings.

Another reason these theories have generally found mixed support in field settings concerns the fact that they are all fairly limited in scope. Many of the factors that affect leader and follower behaviors in work group, team, or volunteer committee settings are not present in laboratory studies but often play a substantial role in field studies. For example, none of the models take into account how levels of stress, organizational culture and climate, working conditions, technology, economic conditions, or type of organizational design affect the leadership process. Nevertheless, the four contingency theories have been the subject of considerable research, and even if only mixed support for the models has been found, this research has succeeded in adding to our body of knowledge about leadership and has given us a more sophisticated understanding of the leadership process.

Key Terms

normative decision model
decision quality
decision acceptance
situational leadership theory (SLT)
task behaviors
relationship behaviors
job maturity
psychological maturity

developmental interventions
contingency model
least-preferred-coworker (LPC) scale
low-LPC leaders
high-LPC leaders
situational favorability
path-goal theory

Discussion Questions

1. Given the description of the leadership situation facing the airplane crash survivors described in Chapter 1, how would the Vroom-Yetton model, situational leadership theory, the contingency model, and path-goal theory prescribe that a leader should act?

2. Can leaders be flexible in how they interact with others? Do you believe leaders can change their behavior? Their personalities? (These questions will be addressed in upcoming chapters.)

3. Think of a leadership situation you are fairly familiar with. Apply each of the theories in this chapter to the situations; which theory best fits the interaction of the leader, followers, and situation in your example? Does any theory allow you to predict a likely or preferred outcome for a current challenge?

4   LEADERSHIP IS DEVELOPED THROUGH EDUCATION AND EXPERIENCE

Chapter Outline

Introduction

In Chapter 1, we discussed the importance of using multiple perspectives to analyze various leadership situations. Moreover, we argued that it is relatively difficult for leaders to develop this method of analysis on their own and that formal education is one of the best ways to develop multiple perspectives on leadership.

Given the importance of formal education and experience in leadership development, this chapter reviews some of the ways you can better learn about leadership (see also Highlight 4–1). As an overview, we begin this chapter by presenting a general model that describes how we learn from experience. Next, we describe how perceptions can affect a leader's interpretation of, and actions in response to, a particular leadership situation and why reflection is important to leadership development. In addition, this chapter reveals how the people you work with and the task itself can help you become a better leader, and reviews some of the typical content and pedagogy found in many formal leadership education programs. Finally, we discuss how to evaluate and choose between the many different kinds of leadership programs available.

The Action-Observation-Reflection Model

Consider for a moment what a young person might learn from spending a year working in two very different environments: as a staff assistant in the U.S. Congress or as a carpenter on a house construction crew. Each activity has a rich store of leadership lessons there for the taking. Working in Congress, for example, would provide opportunities to observe political leaders both onstage in the public eye and backstage in more private moments. It would provide opportunities to see members of Congress interacting with different constituencies, to see them in political defeat and political victory, and to see a range of leadership styles. A young person could also learn a lot by working on a building crew as it turned plans and materials into the reality of a finished house: watching the coordination with subcontractors, watching skilled craftsmen train younger ones, watching the leader's reactions to problems and delays, watching the leader set standards and assure quality work. At the same time, a person could work in either environment and *not* grow much if he or she is not disposed to. Making the most of experience is key to developing one's leadership ability. In other words, leadership development depends not just on the kinds of experiences one has but also on how one uses them to foster growth. A study of successful executives found that one key quality that characterized them was an "extraordinary tenacity in extracting something worthwhile from their experience and in seeking experiences rich in opportunities for growth" (McCall, Lombardo, & Morrison, 1988, p. 122).

But how does one do that? Is someone really more likely to get the lessons of experience by looking for them? Why is it not enough just to be there? Experiential learning theorists, such as Kolb (1983), believe people learn more from their experiences when they spend time thinking about them. These ideas are extended to leadership in the **action-observation-reflection** (A-O-R) **model**, depicted in Figure 4–1, which shows that leadership development is enhanced when the experience involves three different processes: action, observation, and reflection. If a person acts but does not observe the consequences of her actions or reflect on their significance and meaning, then it makes little sense to say she has learned from an experience. Because some people neither observe the consequences of their actions

Highlight 4–1

Leadership Quotes, Chapter 4

It's not what we don't know that hurts, it's what we know that ain't so.

Will Rogers

If you don't know what you're doing, you keep making the wrong mistakes.

Yogi Berra

An educated man can experience more in a day than an uneducated man in a lifetime.

Seneca

I took a great deal o' pains with his education, sir; let him run the streets when he was very young, and shift for his-self. It's the only way to make a boy sharp, sir.

Charles Dickens, *Pickwick Papers*

Common sense is the collection of prejudices acquired by age 18.

Einstein

*What would a man be wise, let him drink of the river
That bears on its bosom the record of time;
A message to him every wave can deliver.
To teach him to creep till he knows how to climb.*

John Boyle O'Reilly

Teach a highly educated person that it is not a disgrace to fail and that he must analyze every failure to find its cause. He must learn how to fail intelligently, for failing is one of the greatest arts in the world.

Charles F. Kettering

Tell me and I'll forget; show me and I may remember; involve me and I'll understand.

Chinese proverb

Anyone who stops learning is old, whether at 20 or 80. Anyone who keeps learning stays young. The greatest thing in life is to keep your mind young.

Henry Ford

Leadership and learning are indispensable to each other.

John F. Kennedy

*We shall not cease from exploration
And the end of all our exploring
Will be to arrive where we started
And know the place for the first time.*

T. S. Eliot

Good flutists learn from experience; unfortunately, so do bad flutists.

Anonymous

All rising to a great place is by a winding stair.

Francis Bacon

FIGURE 4–1

The Spiral of Experience

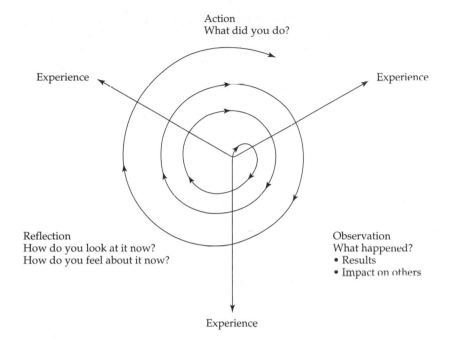

Action
What did you do?

Experience   Experience

Reflection
How do you look at it now?
How do you feel about it now?

Observation
What happened?
• Results
• Impact on others

Experience

nor reflect on how they could change their actions to become better leaders, leadership development through experience may be better understood as the growth resulting from repeated movements through all three phases rather than merely in terms of some objective dimension like time (e.g., how long one has been on the job). We believe the most productive way to develop as a leader is to travel along the **spiral of experience** depicted in Figure 4–1.

Perhaps an example from Colin Powell's life will clarify how the spiral of experience pertains to leadership development. In 1963, Powell was a 26-year-old officer who had just returned to the United States from a combat tour in Viet Nam. His next assignment would be to attend a month-long advanced airborne Ranger course. Near the end of the course, he was to parachute with other troops from a helicopter. As the senior officer on the helicopter, Powell had responsibility for assuring it went well. Early in the flight he hollered for everyone to make sure their static lines were secure, the cables which automatically pulled the chutes open when you jump. Nearing the jump site, he yelled for the men to check their hook-ups one more time. Here are his words describing what happened next:

> Then, like a fussy old woman, I started checking each line myself, pushing my way through the crowded bodies, running my hand along the cable and up to each man's chute. To my alarm, one hook belonging to a sergeant was loose. I shoved the dangling line in his face, and he gasped. . . . This man would have stepped out of the door of the helo and dropped like a rock. (Powell, 1995, p. 109)

So what did Powell learn from this experience? Again, in his own words:

Moments of stress, confusion, and fatigue are exactly when mistakes happen. And when everyone else's mind is dulled or distracted the leader must be doubly vigilant. "Always check small things" was becoming another one of my rules. (p. 109)

Let us now examine this incident in light of the A-O-R model. *Action* refers to Powell's multiple calls for the parachutists to check their lines. We might speculate from his self-description ("like a fussy old woman") that Powell might have felt slightly uncomfortable with such repeated emphasis on checking the lines, even though he persisted in the behavior. Perhaps you, too, sometimes have acted in a certain manner (or were forced to by your parents!) despite feeling a little embarrassed about it; and then, if it was successful, felt more comfortable the next time acting the same way. That seems to be just what happened with Powell here. The *observation* phase refers to Powell's shocked realization of the potentially fatal accident that would have occurred had he *not* double-checked the static lines. And the *reflection* phase refers to the lesson Powell drew from the experience: "always check the small things." Even though it was obviously not a totally new insight, its importance was strongly reinforced by this experience. In a very real sense, Powell was "spiraling" through a lesson he'd learned from other experiences too, but embracing it even more this time, making it part of his style.

We also should note how Powell himself described his learning in a manner consistent with our interactional framework. He emphasized the situational importance of the leader's attention to detail, especially during moments of stress, confusion, and fatigue, when mistakes may be most likely to happen. Finally, it's worth noting that throughout Powell's autobiography he discusses many lessons he learned from experience. One of the keys to his success was his ability to keep learning throughout his career.

The Key Role of Perception in the Spiral of Experience

Experience is not just a matter of what events happen to you; it also depends on how you perceive those events. Perception affects all three phases of the action-observation-reflection model and thus plays a very important role in what anyone will extract from a leadership course or from any leadership situation. Human beings are not passive recorders of experiences that happen to them; rather, people actively shape and construct their experiences. In order to better understand how perception affects experience, we will examine its role in each part of the action-observation-reflection model. We will begin with the stage that seems to correspond most directly with perception—the observation phase.

Perception and Observation

Observation and perception both deal with attending to events around us. Both seem to take place spontaneously and effortlessly, so it is easy to regard them as passive processes. Our common mental images of the perceptual process reflect this implicit view. For example, it is a common misconception that the eye operates essentially like the film in a continuously running camera. The fallacy of this passive view of perception is that it assumes we attend to all aspects of a situation equally. However, we do not see everything that happens in a particular leadership situation, nor do we hear everything. Instead, we are selective in what we attend to and what we, in turn, perceive. One phenomenon that demonstrates this selectivity is called **perceptual set**. Perceptual sets can influence any of our senses, and they are the tendency or bias to perceive one thing and not another. Many factors can trigger a perceptual set, such as feelings, needs, prior experience, and expectations. Its role in distorting what one hears proved a costly lesson when a sympathetic airline pilot told his depressed copilot, "Cheer up!" The copilot thought the pilot had said, "Gear up," and raised the wheels while the plane was still on the ground (Reason & Mycielska, 1982). Try your own ability to overcome perceptual set with the following exercise. Read through the narrative passage below several times:

> FINISHED FILES ARE THE RESULT
> OF YEARS OF SCIENTIFIC STUDY
> COMBINED WITH THE
> EXPERIENCE OF MANY YEARS.

Make sure you have read it to yourself several times *before going any further*. Now, go back to the text and count the number of times the letter F appears.

How many did you count? Three? Four? Five? Six? Most people do not get the correct answer (six) the first time. The most frequent count is three; perhaps that was how many you saw. If you did not find six, go back and try it again. The most common error in this seemingly trivial task is overlooking the three times the word *of* appears. People easily overlook it because the word *of* has a *v* sound, not an *f* sound. Most people unconsciously make the task an auditory search task and listen for the sound of *F* rather than look for the shape of *F*; hence, they find three *F*s rather than six. Listening for the sound constitutes a counterproductive perceptual set for this task, and having read the passage through several times before counting the *F*s only exaggerates this tendency. Another reason people overlook the word *of* in this passage is that the first task was to *read* the passage several times. Because most of us are fairly accomplished readers, we tend to ignore little words like *of*. It disappears from our perceptual set. Then, when we are asked to count the number of *F*s, we have already defined the passage as a reading task, so the word *of* is really not there for us to count.

There are strong parallels between the example of perceptual set above and the perceptual sets that come into play when we are enrolled in a leadership course or observe a leadership situation. For example, your instructor for this class may dress unstylishly, and you may be prejudiced in thinking that poor dressers generally do not make good leaders. Because of your biases, you may discount or not attend to some things your instructor has to say about leadership. This is unfortunate, as your instructor's taste in clothes has little to do with his or her ability to teach (which is, after all, a kind of leadership).

A similar phenomenon takes place when one expects to find mostly negative things about another person (e.g., a problem employee). Such an expectation becomes a perceptual set to look for the negative and look past the positive
things in the process. For example, if you do not believe women and/or minorities are as successful as white males in influencing others, then you may be
biased to identify or remember only those instances where a woman or minority leader failed, and discount or forget those instances where women or minority members succeeded as leaders. Unfortunately, we all have similar biases,
although we are usually unaware of them. Often, we only become aware of our
perceptual sets when we spend time reflecting about the content of a leadership
training program or a particular leadership situation.

Perception and Reflection

Perceptual sets influence what we attend to or do not attend to, what we observe
or do not observe. In addition, perception also influences the next stage of the
spiral of experience—reflection—since reflection deals with how we interpret
our observations. Perception is inherently an interpretive, or a meaning-making,
activity. One important aspect of this deals with a process called **attribution**.

Attributions are the explanations we develop for the behaviors or actions we
attend to. For example, if you see Julie fail in an attempt to get others to form a

"Just don't make any personal appearances until after the election. "
Source: Reprinted from *The Saturday Evening Post* © 1964.

study group, you are likely to attribute the cause of the failure to dispositional factors within Julie. In other words, you are likely to attribute the failure to form a study group to Julie's intelligence, personality, physical appearance, or some other factor even though factors beyond her control could have had played a major part. This tendency to overestimate the dispositional causes of behavior and underestimate the environmental causes when others fail is called the **fundamental attribution error** (Nisbett & Ross, 1980). People prefer to explain others' behavior on the basis of personal attributions, even when obvious situational factors may fully account for the behavior.

On the other hand, if *you* attempted to get others to form a study group and failed, you would be more likely to blame factors in the situation for the failure (e.g., there was not enough time, or the others were not interested, or they would not be good to study with). This reflects a **self-serving bias** (Miller & Ross, 1975), the tendency to make external attributions (i.e., blame the situation) for one's own failures, yet make internal attributions (i.e., take credit) for one's successes. A third factor which affects the attribution process is called the **actor/observer difference** (Jones & Nisbett, 1972). It refers to the fact that people who are observing an action are much more likely than the actor to make the fundamental attribution error. Consider, for example, a student who gets a bad score on an exam. The person sitting *next* to her (i.e., an observer) would tend to attribute the bad score to *internal* characteristics (e.g., not very bright, weak in this subject) whereas the student herself would be more likely to attribute the bad score to *external* factors (e.g., the professor graded unfairly). Putting all these factors together, each of us tends to see our own success as due to our intelligence, personality, or physical abilities, but others' success as more attributable to situational factors or to luck.

We hasten to note in concluding this section that reflection also involves higher functions like evaluation and judgment, not just perception and attribution. We will address these broader aspects of reflection, which are crucial to learning from experience, just ahead.

Perception and Action

We have seen ways perception influences both the observation and reflection stages in the spiral of experience. It also affects the actions we take. For example, Mitchell and his associates (Green & Mitchell, 1979; Mitchell, Green, & Wood, 1981; Mitchell & Wood, 1980) have examined how perceptions and biases affect supervisors' actions in response to poorly performing subordinates. In general, these researchers found that supervisors were biased toward making dispositional attributions about a subordinate's substandard performance and, as a result of these attributions, often recommended that punishment be used to remedy the performance deficit.

Another perceptual variable that can affect our actions is the **self-fulfilling prophecy**. The self-fulfilling prophecy occurs when our expectations or predictions play a causal role in bringing about the events we predict. It is not difficult

FIGURE 4–2

*The Role of
Expectations in
Social
Interaction*

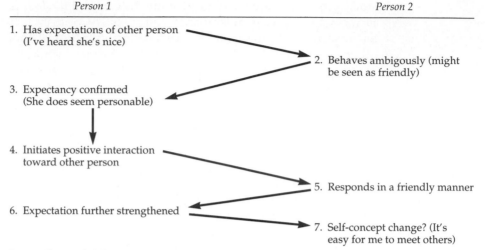

Source: Abstracted with permission from E. E. Jones, "Interpreting Interpersonal Behavior: The Effects of Expectancies," *Science* 234, no. 3 (October 1986), p. 43. Copyright 1986, American Association for the Advancement of Science.

to see how certain large-scale social phenomena may be affected this way. For example, economists' predictions of an economic downturn may, via the consequent decreased investor confidence, precipitate an economic crisis. But the self-fulfilling prophecy occurs at the interpersonal level, too. A person's expectations about another may influence how he acts toward her, and in reaction to his behavior she may act in a way that confirms his expectations (Jones, 1986). One typical interaction sequence is shown in Figure 4–2.

Some of the best evidence to support the effects of the self-fulfilling prophecy on leadership training was collected by Eden and Shani (1982). Eden and Shani conducted a field experiment where they told leadership instructors their students had either unknown, regular, or high command potential. However, the students' actual command potential was never assessed, and unbeknownst to the instructors, the students were actually randomly assigned to the unknown, regular, or high command potential conditions. Nevertheless, students in the high-potential condition had significantly better objective test scores and attitudes than the students in the unknown- or regular-potential conditions, even though instructors simultaneously taught all three types of students. Somehow the students picked up on their instructor's expectations and responded accordingly. Thus, just having expectations (positive or negative) about others can subtly influence our actions, and these actions can, in turn, affect the way others behave.

Reflection and Leadership Development

Perhaps the most important yet most neglected component of the action-observation-reflection model is reflection. Reflection is important because it can provide leaders with a variety of insights into how to frame problems differently, look at situations from multiple perspectives, or better understand subordinates. However, most managers spend relatively little time on this activity, even though the time spent reflecting about leadership can be quite fruitful.

One reason the reflection component is often neglected may be time pressure at work. Leaders are usually very busy people working in pressure-filled situations and often do not have time to ponder all the possible consequences of their actions or reflect on how they could have accomplished a particular action better. In addition, some leaders may not be aware of the value of reflection in leadership development. Hopefully, this section will clarify the value of reflection, and in so doing can complement the emphasis, throughout the remainder of the book, on looking at leadership from different perspectives.

Single- and Double-Loop Learning

It is difficult for leaders to fundamentally change their leadership style without engaging in some kind of reflection. Along these lines, Argyris (1976) described an intensive effort with a group of highly successful chief executive officers who became even better leaders through increased self-awareness. Argyris's model for conceptualizing this growth is applicable to any level of leader and is worth considering in more detail.

Argyris (1976) said that most people interact with others and the environment based on a belief system geared to manipulate or control others, and to minimize one's own emotionality and the negative feelings elicited from others. This belief system also tends to create defensive interpersonal relationships and limits risk taking. People "programmed" with this view of life (as most of us are, according to Argyris) produce group and organizational dynamics characterized by avoidance of conflict, mistrust, conformity, intergroup rivalry, misperceptions and miscommunications with others, ineffective problem solving, and poor decision making. Most important for our purposes here, it generates a certain kind of learning that Argyris called **single-loop learning**.

Single-loop learning describes a kind of learning between the individual and the environment in which learners seek relatively little feedback that may significantly confront their fundamental ideas or actions. There is relatively little public testing of ideas against valid information. Consequently, an actor's belief system becomes self-sealing and self-fulfilling, and little time is spent reflecting about the beliefs. Argyris used the term *single-loop learning* because it operates somewhat like a thermostat; individuals learn only about subjects within the "comfort zone" of their belief systems. They might, for example, learn how well they are achieving a designated goal. They are far less likely, however, to question the validity of the goal or the values implicit in the situation, just as a thermostat does not question its temperature setting. That kind of self-confrontation would involve **double-loop learning**.

Double-loop learning involves a willingness to confront one's own views and an invitation to others to do so, too. It springs from an appreciation that openness to information and power sharing with others can lead to better recognition and definition of problems, improved communication, and increased decision-making effectiveness. Mastering double-loop learning can be thought of as learning how to learn. With considerable collective work, including the difficult task of working through personal blind spots, Argyris's group of leaders did move to this stage. In other words, through reflection they learned how to change their leadership styles by questioning their assumptions about others, their roles in the organization, and their underlying assumptions about the importance of their own goals and those of the organization.

Konosuke Matsushita seems to have perfected the art of double-loop learning despite never thinking of it in such a formal way. Early in his career Matsushita learned, as he said, to "subject my own methods of management to careful scrutiny, finding that there were many ways in which they could be improved" (quoted in Kotter, 1997, p. 83). He always stressed the importance of an open mind, expecting that he could learn something valuable from everyone he met. He was also quite successful in infusing his whole company with a similar value, which made it an extremely adaptive organization. He pushed not only himself but others as well out of comfortable routines. He believed that his company's success depended upon a humble commitment to continuous improvement rather than a corporate culture that was arrogant and rigid.

Thinking Frames and Multiple Perspectives

Another way to conceptualize reflection in leadership development involves **thinking frames**, which refer to the tactics and strategies people use to organize their thinking and to construe the meaning of events (Perkins, 1986). Thinking frames are our mental tools, and they may or may not be useful, just as a hammer or saw may or may not be useful depending on the task at hand. In addition, just as a child with a hammer perceives that the whole world needs hammering, our thinking frames can also represent limits on the ways we can (conceptually) operate on our environment. Leadership development can be thought of as the process of developing more complex and differentiated frames for organizing one's thinking (and hence action) about leadership. Moreover, because some thinking frames are relatively subtle, their development may be better assisted through structured educational experiences. For example, most people would not have thought of the action-observation-reflection model on their own. The development of multiple frames, or perspectives, may be one of the greatest contributions a formal course in leadership can make to a leader's development. The overarching idea in discussing the different definitions and theories of leadership in this text is to help you to develop different frames or perspectives for interpreting leadership situations, which in turn may help you to better influence others to achieve organizational goals. Perhaps one key to leadership success is having a variety of tools to choose from and knowing when and where to use them. Hopefully, the theories and concepts described in this text will give you the tools, and by reflecting about your experiences as a leader, you should begin to gain some insight on when and where to use them.

Leadership Development through Experience

Although using the action-observation-reflection model will help you make the most of your leadership experiences and mature into a better leader, it is also important to realize that some situations are developmentally richer than others. In this section, we will review two developmental factors that make any given experience potent in fostering managerial growth: the people you work with and the characteristics of the task itself (Kouzes & Posner, 1987; Lombardo & Eichinger, 1989). These factors are important because they provide opportunities for a leader or a leader-to-be to apply the action-observation-reflection model and reflect on how to be a better leader.

The People You Work With

The people you associate with can stimulate development in many ways. Kouzes and Posner (1987) noted the diverse ways others nurture our growth:

> Other people have always been essential sources of guidance. We all remember the parent we looked to for advice and support; the special teacher who filled us with curiosity for our favorite subject; the neighbor who always let us watch, even take part in, the tinkering in the garage; the coach who believed that we had promise and inspired us to give our best; the counselor who gave us valuable feedback about our behavior and its impact, the master artisan who instructed us in the fundamentals of a craft; or the first boss who taught us the ropes to skip and the hoops to jump. (p. 286)

Others play an especially important role in personal and professional development at work, so we will focus attention there.

A boss, especially a very good or very bad one, can be a powerful catalyst for growth. Exceptional bosses are vivid examples of how to (or how not to) put values into action. However, bosses are not the only people who contribute to growth and development at work. Working with others who have different backgrounds, perspectives, or agendas can often be a growth experience. Working with problem subordinates can stimulate managerial growth, but so can the need to influence others over whom you have no direct authority or control. You may work on a project and report to a superior other than your own boss, or you may head a team of peers; such situations are particularly helpful in developing negotiation and other informal influence skills. Finally, different management skills are called on when you must make major changes to a group or project such as downsizing it, restructuring it, or starting it from scratch (Lombardo & Eichinger, 1989).

You can learn about effective and ineffective leadership by paying attention to the positive and negative models around you beyond your immediate boss. Watching others in leadership roles may suggest what to do as well as what not to do. Peers, especially, can be a great resource for developing one's effectiveness as a leader. In one program of peer coaching, school principals observed each other interacting in feedback conferences with their respective teachers and then met together afterward to share ideas about how well the conferences went (Gibble & Lawrence, 1987). Such principal-to-principal interaction is especially valuable in that it is rare for any supervisor to get feedback on his or her skill in providing feedback to subordinates. The principals praised their peer coaching as an extremely effective mechanism for enhancing their effectiveness as supervisors.

In an organization, you also can gain valuable perspectives and insights through close association with an experienced person willing to take you under his wing. Such an individual is often called a **mentor**, after the character in Greek mythology whom Odysseus trusted to run his household and see to his son's education when Odysseus went off to fight the Trojans. Now, 3,000 years later, Mentor's name is used to describe the process by which an older and more experienced person helps to socialize and encourage younger organizational colleagues (Wilson & Elman, 1990).

Generally, mentors are highly placed, powerful individuals who develop relatively long-lasting relationships with younger colleagues whose professional careers are influenced and furthered as a result (Hunt & Michael, 1983; Uecker & Dilla, 1985). Typically, the mentoring relationship is informal, though its value has encouraged some to recommend its use formally and systematically in organizations (Clutterbuck, 1982). In terms of value, both mentors and mentorees benefit from having this relationship. Mentors benefit by the greater influence they accrue by having former mentorees in various positions across the organization. Mentors also benefit by having a younger replacement ready to fill their position if they are promoted (Bass, 1990). The mentoree benefits from this relationship by gaining an influential ally and through the mentor's tutoring about the subtler aspects of organizational ethics, influence, and leadership. Having a mentor can also result in more career opportunities for the mentoree (Whitely, Dougherty, & Dreher, 1988; Zey, 1984), and the lack of mentors for women has been cited as one reason there are relatively few women in executive positions (Astin & Leland, 1991). Although some may advocate systematizing mentorship programs to improve the career opportunities for all employees, it remains to be seen whether a formalized program would preserve the essence and qualities of more informal, self-selected mentoring relationships (Rosenbach, 1989).

According to strict definitions of mentoring, perhaps none of our three leaders had a true mentor throughout their careers. Yet Madeleine Albright, for example, was sharpened and toughened by several of her bosses. Two in particular stand out: Zbigniev Brzezinski, a former national security advisor in the Carter White House, and Ed Muskie, former senator from Maine. Both were brilliant, but also had tough-as-nails reputations. Although Ms. Albright was already a person meticulously prepared in advance for anything, her skills and self-confidence were further honed by working for these two very demanding leaders.

An idea somewhat related to mentoring is that of **executive coaching**. Increasingly, executive coaching is seen as a general responsibility of all executives toward managers who report to them The failure to coach managers in their professional development makes as little sense as a football team composed of the best recruited players, going through an entire season without a practice session or coach (Witherspoon & White, 1996). More simply, good coaching is nothing more than good management. It is investment that can help change counterproductive behavior, often interpersonal, that threatens to derail an otherwise valued manager (Waldroop and Butler, 1996).

The Task Itself

In addition to the various sorts of relationships with other people, certain kinds of work-related tasks can also be particularly developmental. Developmental tasks are often more complex and ambiguous than those one has faced before. In addition, leadership development can be enhanced if the environment one works in is changing, dynamic, uncontrollable, and unpredictable. The nature of the task may require new and creative solutions; old answers may not work anymore. Projects involving strategic planning and projections into an uncertain future can be quite challenging intellectually and can contribute to a leader's development (Lombardo & Eichinger, 1989).

Although we have emphasized the importance of applying the action-observation-reflection model to enhance one's learning from experience, the developmental value of the challenging tasks themselves cannot be denied. The best developmental opportunities are those that stretch individuals and allow them to test themselves against new and difficult tasks (Kouzes & Posner, 1987). Of course, the difficulty level of tasks and how much one will be stretched by doing them is meaningful mostly in the context of a given individual's maturity and experience. The following are the words of one college student who was in charge of the flag section of her school's marching band:

> I have 30 people under me broken into four sections. I am responsible for conducting our rehearsals, teaching flag routines, taking care of any problems, recruiting new members, and motivating my people. I do some of this through my four section leaders, so I have to make sure they are doing their jobs properly. The biggest challenge of all this is keeping motivation high and making sure that everyone learns what they are supposed to and performs it well. It is really giving me a lot of experience in interacting with people.

Another student described his own best leadership experience in terms of his unique background as an instructor on his collegiate parachute team:

> During this period I learned a lot about what it takes to teach a person to jump out of an airplane successfully and injury free. The foremost concern and responsibility is the welfare of the student, so I had to be certain that they learned the procedures correctly, and be thoroughly convinced that they would be safe once out the door no matter what situation may arise. I was responsible for someone else's life. I had to be very patient and understanding many times when they would not grasp an idea or a procedure properly, spending a lot of time in certain areas until they were proficient. Other times I had to be stern and strict to emphasize certain emergency procedures

and safety hazards in order to be sure they were aware of the seriousness of the situation. During this period I experienced everything that goes into leadership. I had to work with many people. Many of them were my peers, which makes things more difficult in some cases.

Feeling responsible for someone else's life certainly increases one's personal pressure, and it was partly this pressure that made this student-instructor's role such a valuable leadership experience. Whether or not a particular task is perceived as developmentally challenging and generates a high level of personal pressure depends on several factors. The most commonly cited developmental challenge mentioned by managers was a task where both success and failure were possible and would be obvious to others. The risk of possible failure is a strong incentive for managers to learn. Managers also mentioned deadlines, travel requirements, and longer hours as factors that, while adding to personal pressure, also contributed to professional growth (Lombardo & Eichinger, 1989).

One last aspect of leadership-developing tasks should be mentioned. Just as mentoring relationships fail to develop for all members, organizations may not provide the same developmental opportunities for all their members. In particular, there is a striking difference between large and small organizations in the opportunities they offer. This is apparent, for example, in the chances of having a significant responsibility in the school play in schools with either large or small student bodies. In small schools, virtually anyone who wants to have a significant part in putting on the play will be able to do so. In large schools, though, the number of students far exceeds the number of important functions; many motivated students will miss out on the chance to participate and grow from the experience. As John Gardner (1990) has pointed out, the sheer size and impersonalness of some of our organizations does not provide the soil in which a young person's leadership can grow.

Making the Most of Your Leadership Experiences:
Learning to Learn from Experience

This section builds on the ideas previously introduced in this chapter by providing leadership practitioners with a few suggestions to enhance learning from experience (see Highlight 4–2 for a description of some executives who apparently did not learn enough from experience). For well over a decade, researchers at the Center for Creative Leadership have been studying the role of learning from experience as an important developmental behavior for people in executive positions. While this research has contributed a great deal to *what* people need to learn to be successful (see Highlight 4–3 for a comparison of lessons men and women managers learn from experience), less is known about the process of learning or *how* we learn to be successful. Bunker and Webb (1992) asked successful executives to list adjectives describing how they felt while working through powerful learning events and potent developmental

Executive Derailment:
Knocking Yourself off the Track to Success

Some executives on an apparently clear track to the top never make it. They become derailed. For more than a decade, researchers at the Center for Creative Leadership have studied executives who had fallen short of the levels of success predicted of them earlier in their careers. Typically, their derailments were the result of several factors, though insensitivity to others was the most frequent problem. Sometimes styles that served them well earlier became liabilities in new circumstances, and sometimes long-standing liabilities, previously outweighed by other aspects, eventually took their career toll. A 1996 study expanded the work and included samples of European as well as North American executives. In general, the derailment themes in Europe and North America were consistent:

Characteristics of Successful Leaders	Characteristics of Derailed Leaders
Ability to develop or adapt.	Inability to develop or adapt.
Ability to establish collaborative relations.	Poor working relations.
Ability to build and lead a team.	Inability to build and lead a team.
Nonauthoritarian.	Authoritarian
Consistent exceptional performance.	Poor performance.
Ambitious.	Too ambitious.

How would you interpret these executives' derailments in terms of the action-observation-reflection model? Do you think the problem was in their actions? Their observation or awareness of the consequences of their actions? Or something else?

Source: Adapted from J. B. Leslie and E. Van Velsor, *A Look at Derailment Today: North America and Europe* (Greensboro, NC: The Center for Creative Leadership, 1996).

experiences. Their typical responses were a combination of both positive and negative feelings.

Negatives	Positives
Pained	Challenged
Fearful	Successful
Frustrated	Proud
Stressed	Capable
Anxious	Growing
Overwhelmed	Exhilarated
Uncertain	Talented
Angry	Resourceful
Hurt	Learning

Highlight 4–3

What Do Men and Women Managers Learn From Experience?

For a quarter century or so, significant numbers of women have been represented in the management ranks of companies. During that period companies have promoted large pools of high-potential women, but relatively few of them have achieved truly top-level positions. Several factors probably account for this, but one possibility is that men and women learn differently from their work experiences. Researchers at the Center for Creative Leadership have studied how male and female executives describe the important lessons they've learned from their career experiences, and there are some interesting differences between the genders as well as significant overlap.

Twelve Most Frequent Lessons for Men and Women
Directing and motivating employees.

Self-confidence.

Basic management values.

How to work with executives.

Understanding other people's perspective.

Dealing with people over whom you have no authority.

Handling political situations.

For Men Only	**For Women Only**
Technical/professional skills.	Personal limits and blind spots.
All about the business.	Taking charge of career.
Coping with ambiguous situations.	Recognizing and seizing opportunities
Shouldering full responsibility.	Coping with situations beyond your control.
Persevering through adversity.	Knowing what excites you.

Why would there be any learning differences between the genders? One hypothesis is that men and women managers tend to have somewhat different career patterns. For example, there is some evidence that women receive fewer truly challenging developmental opportunities. You will also be able to read more about how gender differences affect promotion within organizations in Chapter 7.

Source: Adapted from E. Van Velsor, and M. W. Hughes, *Gender Differences in the Development of Managers: How Women Managers Learn from Experience* (Technical Report No. 145), Greensboro, NC: The Center for Creative Leadership, 1990.

This pattern strongly supports the long-hypothesized notion of a meaningful link between stress and learning (Janis, 1971). The learning events and developmental experiences that punctuate one's life are usually, perhaps always, stressful (Grey & Gordon, 1978; Hambrick, 1981; Jennings, 1971; Schein, 1978).

FIGURE 4–3

Anatomy of a Learning Experience

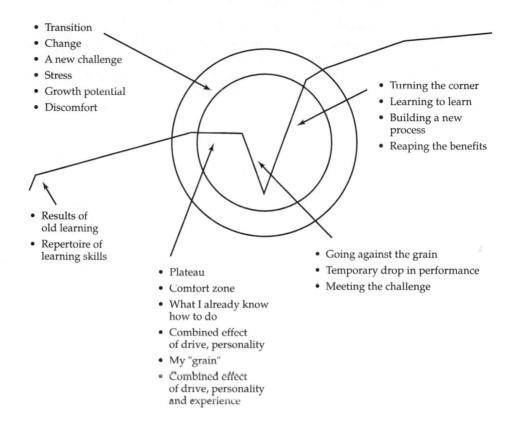

- Transition
- Change
- A new challenge
- Stress
- Growth potential
- Discomfort

- Turning the corner
- Learning to learn
- Building a new process
- Reaping the benefits

- Results of old learning
- Repertoire of learning skills

- Plateau
- Comfort zone
- What I already know how to do
- Combined effect of drive, personality
- My "grain"
- Combined effect of drive, personality and experience

- Going against the grain
- Temporary drop in performance
- Meeting the challenge

Bunker and Webb (1992) note that executives try to be successful without experiencing stress. They are most comfortable when they can draw upon a proven repertoire of operating skills to tackle a challenge they have conquered in the past. Combined with the organizational pressure to have "proven performers" in important positions, there is a tremendous initial pressure to "continue to do what we've always done." In stressful situations, this tendency may become even more powerful. What results is one of the great Catch-22s of adult development: The times when people most need to break out of the mold created by past learning patterns are the times when they are most unwilling to do so. Being able to *go against the grain* of one's personal historic success requires an unwavering commitment to learning and a relentless willingness to let go of the fear of failure and the unknown.

Figure 4–3 depicts the Center for Creative Leadership's work on the process of "learning to learn from experience." Bunker and Webb (1992) describe the figure as a segment of life containing a series of learning opportunities. The circled segment represents a stressful episode of life—a potentially dramatic learning-to-learn event. The left side of the curve represents the growth and development that was stimulated by prior learning experiences. Also represented is a flattening out of learned skill value that often occurs; over time, new skills often become mere routinized habits. People operating in this stabilizing period, called the comfort zone, must overcome the caution generated by ongoing success and the fear of challenging what they already know how to do. The smaller concentric circle represents the tension created by the appearance of a new learning challenge—often arising out of a transition or a stressful experience that requires a response. The sharp dip in success depicts the performance regression that generally accompanies attempts at learning a new set of responses and strategies. One gets through this period (and thus performs at a higher level with broader skills) by coping with the stress or letting go of short-term expectations in favor of more long-term learning. Of course, if one is not willing to go against the grain and tolerate a small dip in performance, then the learning curve becomes flat—no learning.

To be successful, learning must continue throughout life, beyond the completion of one's formal education.

> The end of extrinsically applied education should be the start of an education that is motivated intrinsically. At that point the goal of studying is no longer to make the grade, earn a diploma, and find a good job. Rather, it is to understand what is happening around one, to develop a personally meaningful sense of what one's experience is all about. (Csikszentmihalyi, 1990, p. 142)

There may be no better way to conclude this section than by turning again to the life of Konosuke Matsushita. John Kotter (1997) characterized Matsushita's whole life as one of continual learning, and suggested it may well be the future model for all of us:

> Forget . . . naive notions about success being a simple linear journey upward. KM's economic fortunes crashed twice, in 1899 and 1946. His health, psychological well-being, and personal happiness also fluctuated many times. In a volatile 21st century, this pattern could become more common.
>
> Most of all, forget the mid-20th-century model of learning, careers, and growth. If current trends continue, the success stories of the next few decades will not be about people who are educated from age five to twenty-five and who then apply that schooling until they retire forty years later. Winners will be those who are both willing and able to grow throughout their lifetimes.
>
> If there is any single lesson from his life that Matsushita himself seems to have thought would be particularly applicable and important in the future, it was this: don't assume that we cannot continue to develop, and develop greatly, as we age. (pp. 245–46)

Leadership Development through Education and Training

Although we believe experience plays a large role in leadership development, we believe formal education can play an important role, too. For example, Bray, Campbell, and Grant (1974); Howard (1986); and Wakabayashi and Graen (1984) all found that education level or academic performance in college was positively related to future managerial success. Furthermore, in a major review of the effectiveness of managerial training programs, Burke and Day (1986) found that educational programs generally had a positive effect on leadership development. Thus, formal education and training programs can help one become a better leader. However, it is important to note that these programs vary substantially in both content and pedagogy, and not all programs are appropriate for all leaders. The content of different leadership programs varies considerably, depending on the target audience; university-level courses generally provide a survey of the major leadership findings, programs for first-level supervisors often focus on how to train subordinates and give them feedback about their progress, and programs for senior executives often focus on strategic planning and public relations. In this regard, Brungardt (1996) helpfully distinguished between leadership development and leadership education, the latter being a component of the former. Programs also vary in the extent to which they are based on well-established and professionally accepted practices and standards. Some leadership training programs represent little more than fads or popularized pseudoscience. In the following pages, we will review some of the more common educational and training techniques used to teach and develop leadership.

University Courses in Leadership

Spitzberg (1987) estimated that over 500 colleges or universities offer some type of leadership training program. Often these programs consist of extracurricular leadership activities run out of the student development office or are courses much like the one for which you are using this book. The extracurricular activities can vary greatly, but the leadership courses often have a high degree of overlap in both content and pedagogy. In terms of content, the topics covered in most leadership courses are similar to the subjects addressed in this book and include how personality traits, cognitive abilities, values, behaviors, motivation, group dynamics, communication, situational factors, and different theories of leadership can all be used to describe the leadership process. In addition, many universities offer specialized courses that focus primarily on historical, business, minority, or female leaders.

The techniques, or pedagogy, used to impart these different leadership concepts to students can vary greatly. Many courses use the standard lecture method, and Burke and Day (1986) found this method to be an effective way of imparting knowledge about leadership. Some courses also provide **individualized feedback** to students in the form of personality, intelligence, values, or interests test scores or leadership behavior ratings. A relatively new twist to individualized feedback is to have subjects compare the results of their personality or behavior self-ratings with those given to them by their peers (Curphy, 1991). **Case studies** consist of descriptions of various leadership situations and are used as a vehicle for leadership discussions. **Role playing** is also a popular methodology. In role playing, participants are assigned parts to play (e.g., a supervisor and an unmotivated subordinate) in a job-related scenario. Role playing has the advantage of letting trainees actually practice relevant skills and thus has greater transferability to the workplace than do didactic lectures or abstract discussions about leadership. **Simulations** and **games** are other methods of training. These are relatively structured activities designed to mirror some of the challenges or decisions commonly faced in the work environment. One of the better known leadership simulations is the Center for Creative Leadership's "Looking Glass" (McCall & Lombardo, 1982), in which participants play different leadership roles in a glass manufacturing plant. A newer approach to leadership development puts participants in relatively unfamiliar territory (e.g., outdoors rather than offices) and presents them physical, emotionally arousing, and often team-oriented challenges.

Leadership Training Programs

There are numerous leadership training programs aimed particularly toward leaders and supervisors in industry or public service. In many ways, these have strong parallels to both the content and techniques used in university-level courses on leadership. However, these programs are usually much shorter (typically less than a week), and the content tends to be more focused than that of a university course. The content of these programs also depends on the organizational level of the recipients; programs for first-level supervisors focus on developing supervisory skills such as training, monitoring, giving feedback, and conducting performance reviews with subordinates. Generally, these programs use lectures, case studies, and role-playing exercises to improve leadership skills.

The programs for midlevel managers often focus on improving interpersonal, oral-communication, and written-communication skills, as well as giving tips on time management, planning, and goal setting. These programs rely more heavily on individualized feedback, case studies, presentations, role playing, simulations, **in-basket exercises**, and **leaderless group discussions** as techniques to help leaders develop. In in-basket exercises, participants are given a limited amount of time to prioritize and respond to a number of notes, letters, and phone messages from a fictitious manager's in-basket. This technique is particularly useful in assessing and improving a manager's planning and time management skills. In leaderless group discussions, facilitators and observers rate participants on the degree of persuasiveness, leadership, followership, or conflict each member manifests in a group that has no appointed leader. These ratings are used to provide managers with feedback about their interpersonal and oral-communication skills.

Leadership programs for senior executives and CEOs tend to focus on strategic planning, public relations, and interpersonal skills. Many times, the entire senior leadership of a company will go through a leadership program at the same time. One goal of such a group might be to learn how to develop a strategic plan for their organization. In order to improve public relations skills, some programs have CEOs undergo simulated, unannounced interviews with television reporters and receive feedback on how they could have done better.

Evaluating Leadership Development Programs

Although a number of leadership training programs are based on sound theory and research, some other programs have no basis in science and should be considered speculative at best. Still others are based on unwarranted and simplistic extensions of scientific findings. Perhaps the best way to guarantee that a leadership program will be useful to you or your organization is to adopt a systematic approach to leadership training. There is value in being an informed consumer, and this is just as true for investing one's time, energy, and money in leadership programs as it is for other products and services. To this end, Campbell (1988) has described a systematic model of training that can easily be adapted to leadership development programs. Some of the major steps in Campbell's model are (*a*) determining what needs to be learned, (*b*) determining the training objectives, (*c*) specifying the learning methods and media, and (*d*) evaluating the training outcomes. The following discussion is an adaptation of these steps in leadership development.

Although specifying what needs to be learned in a training program sounds straightforward enough, it is surprising how infrequently this step is actually taken with respect to leadership training. Instead, many organizations send employees to leadership training programs because (*a*) other companies are sending their employees (and maybe gaining some advantage), (*b*) the senior staff went to the training and liked it, or (*c*) the employees deserve a reward for their good work. Unfortunately, none of these is a particularly good reason for choosing a leadership training program. Better questions to ask involve the goals of the organization, the current level of leadership skills in the organization, and the gaps that need to be filled through training in order to accomplish the organization's goals. Systematically determining what leadership gaps need to be filled can be done by accomplishing a needs analysis. Although the details of a needs analysis are beyond the scope of this book, such an analysis will provide answers to the question, *What needs to be learned?*

After determining what gaps need to be filled, the next step in Campbell's (1988) model is to determine the training objectives. In other words, what specific objectives does the training program hope to accomplish, and how do these objectives match up with the leadership gaps to be filled? If the training objectives are not tied to the gaps identified in the needs analysis, then the training will probably have little, if any, positive impact. In addition, if the training program does not offer any specific training objectives, then it will be difficult to evaluate whether or not the training was successful. Tying the training objectives to the gaps identified in the needs analysis is one way to ensure the training program is good for the organization and will be salient to the participants.

Another way to increase the salience of education and training programs is to integrate the material better with a person's ongoing work experience. That is the basis for an approach to management education called **action learning** (Margerison, 1988). Coca-Cola and TRW are two companies, among others, that have adopted such an action-oriented approach to management development

(Berry, 1990; Clover, 1991). Coca-Cola did so, for example, because traditional management development programs often failed to add value to the company. The traditional management development programs did not help because they were not linked to the organization's actual challenges or problems, had objectives that stressed increases in awareness and understanding but did not build competence, and focused on individuals rather than teams or operating units. As an alternative, Coca Cola's approach to management development involves attendance by whole management teams and analysis of current business issues. In general, relative to traditional management development programs, action learning is more work-based than classroom-based, more group-oriented than individual-oriented, more active than passive, and more action-based than knowledge-based (Margerison, 1988).

An overlooked component of Campbell's (1988) model of training is specifying the learning methods and media. Too often, companies buy a leadership development program for their employees because the program makes heavy use of interactive videodiscs, simulations, videotapes, and other types of high-tech training methods. Whether or not this high-tech-based training actually results in improved leadership training remains to be seen. The bottom line is that the needs of the organization and the training objectives determine the techniques to be used in training, rather than permitting the available techniques and equipment to determine the training content.

A final point to consider regarding leadership training involves evaluating the success or effectiveness of any training program. At a minimum, one should ask whether the training successfully accomplished all of the objectives. This again points out the importance of having clear objectives for any training program. According to Kirkpatrick (1967), reaction, learning, behavioral, and results criteria can all be used to evaluate a training program. Asking participants to subjectively rate a program's effectiveness exemplifies reaction criteria, and test scores (e.g., scores on a final exam) exemplify learning criteria. Either or both can be used to evaluate whether a leadership program accomplished its objectives. Determining whether leaders behaved or acted differently in the workplace after training exemplifies a behavioral criteria for evaluation, and the effect on a company's revenues exemplifies results criteria.

Although multiple criteria can and should be used to evaluate a training program, several additional points need to be considered. First, it is possible to get favorable reaction data but unfavorable learning, behavioral, and results data for a training program. Second, just because the impact of a leadership development program is not apparent using results criteria does not mean the program was unsuccessful. There are a number of factors that affect an organization's success, and some (such as market forces) may be relatively insensitive to a change in a leader's style. Finally, none of Kirkpatrick's (1967) four criteria really measure whether or not a leader has developed more thinking frames or perspectives as a result of the leadership training program. This may be the greatest contribution to leadership development a formal leadership course or program can make, yet none of the four criteria really tap this contribution.

Recent developments in training evaluation and assessment are beginning to use more of a thinking-frames or multiple-perspectives approach to evaluate training (Kraiger, Ford, & Salas, 1992), and hopefully these advances will be applied to evaluating leadership development programs.

Building Your Leadership Self-Image

This chapter has explored how leadership develops through experience and formal education. Before concluding, however, we should acknowledge that not everyone wants to be a leader or believes he can be. John Gardner (1965) has argued that many of our best and brightest young people actually have been immunized against, and dissuaded from, seeking leadership opportunities and responsibilities. Other young people, even if they want to be leaders, may not believe they have what it takes. Both groups, we believe, are selling themselves short.

For those who merely want to avoid the responsibilities of leadership, we encourage an openness of mind about leadership's importance and pervasiveness. We hope this book offers ways of thinking about leadership that make it at once more immediate, more relevant, and more interesting than it may have seemed before. For others, we encourage flexibility in self-image. Do not stay out of the leadership arena based on some global and self-defeating generalization such as "I am not the leader type." Experiment and take a few risks with different leadership roles. This will help you appreciate new facets of yourself as well as broaden your leadership self-image.

Summary

This chapter reviews several major points regarding how leadership can be developed through both formal education and experience. One way to get more out of your leadership courses and experiences is through the application of the action-observation-reflection model. This model provides a framework for better understanding of leadership situations. In addition, being aware of the role perception plays in leadership development is also important, as it affects what you observe, how you interpret your observations, and what actions you take as a leader. Finally, it is important to remember that both education and experience can contribute to your development as a leader by enhancing your ability to reflect on and analyze leadership situations. Exposure to formal leadership education programs can help you to develop thinking frames or multiple perspectives to analyze leadership situations, and the people you work with and the task itself can also provide you with insights on how to be a better leader. However, what you gain from any leadership program or experience is a function of what you make of it. Successful leaders are those who have "an extraordinary tenacity in extracting something worthwhile from their experience and in seeking experiences rich in opportunities for growth" (McCall, Lombardo, & Morrison, 1988, p. 122). If you want to become a better leader, then you must seek challenges and try to get all you can from any leadership situation or opportunity.

Key Terms

action-observation-reflection model
executive coaching
spiral of experience
perceptual set
attribution
fundamental attribution error
actor/observer difference
self-fulfilling prophecy
single-loop learning
double-loop learning
thinking frames

mentor
individualized feedback
case studies
role playing
simulations
self-serving bias
games
in-basket exercises
leaderless group discussions
action learning

Discussion Questions

1. Not all effective leaders seem to be reflective by nature. How do you reconcile that with the concept of the spiral of experience and its role in leadership development?

2. Explain how you can use knowledge about each of the following to enrich the benefits of your own present leadership experiences:
   a. The action-observation-reflection model.
   b. The people you interact and work with.
   c. The activities you're involved in.

3. Using the role of teacher as a specific instance of leadership, discuss how a teacher's perceptual set, expectations of students, and attributions may affect student motivation and performance. Do you think some teachers could become more effective by becoming more aware of these processes? Would that be true for leaders in general?

4. If you were to design the perfect leadership development experience for yourself, how would you do so and what would it include? How would you know it was effective?

5. Do you think people have a need for growth and development?

6. One important aspect of learning from experience is observing the consequences of one's actions. Sometimes, however, the most significant consequences of a leader's actions do not occur for several years (e.g., the ultimate impact of certain personnel decisions or a strategic decision to change a product line). If that is so, then is there any way individuals can learn from the consequences of those actions in a way to modify their behavior? If consequences are so delayed, is there a danger they might draw the wrong lessons from their experiences?

5　Assessing Leadership and Measuring Its Effects

Chapter Outline

Introduction

In the 1980s George Bush served as vice president of the United States under Ronald Reagan, and in 1988 he won election as president himself. In the early 1990s, at the height of Operation Desert Shield and Desert Storm, Bush's approval ratings were over 80 percent, some of the highest public approval ratings of any modern U.S. president. In 1992, however, Bush lost the presidential election to Bill Clinton.

How could someone with 12 years of experience as one of the top leaders in the United States and such high popularity fall out of favor so quickly? Although many political observers have offered opinions as to why Bush fell out of favor, the truth is that no one can say definitively what caused Bush to lose the 1992 election.

The study of why Bush succeeded in 1988 yet failed to be reelected president in 1992 is one example of leadership research, and it highlights some of the challenges to improving the state of leadership today. One of those challenges is that leadership *practitioners* often want fast answers about how to be more effective or successful (or win elections). Even before Bush lost the election, scores of observers from the media, consultants to other campaigns, and so on were dissecting the lessons of Bush's slide. Paradoxically, another challenge is that high-quality leadership research is difficult, expensive, and time-consuming to conduct. For example, it often takes five years or more for a leadership study to be conducted and published (Fiedler, 1995). Obviously, leadership practitioners cannot wait this long for answers.

This tension between discovering the truth about a leadership question and being able to apply what is learned is what we call the **practice-research gap**. Leadership practitioners often seek information about how to improve their leadership skills, but typically find little help in the work of leadership researchers, whose studies may seem untimely or to have little practical value. Hogan, Curphy, and Hogan (1994) pointed out that the knowledge accumulated from 80 years of leadership research is of tremendous value, yet scientists have paid little attention to the ultimate consumers of their work—leaders and leaders to be. As a result, real leaders understandably turn to popular books and articles that *appear* to provide timely answers to their practical concerns. Unfortunately, however, the claims in the popular literature are rarely based on sound research. They oversimplify the complexities of the leadership process, and many times offer bad advice. Relatively little weight is given to well-researched leadership studies primarily because the arcane requirements of publishing articles in scholarly journals make their content virtually unreadable (and certainly uninteresting) to actual leadership practitioners.

One key objective of this book is to make the results of leadership research more usable to leaders and leaders to be. This chapter is specifically designed to help readers better understand how leadership research is conducted, gain an appreciation for some of the practical applications of this research, and sharpen critical thinking skills about leadership and leadership research.

At the same time, however, we should stress that this book is *not* intended to be a guide for conducting leadership research; it is a guide to help leadership students and budding practitioners *be* better leaders by helping them understand the complex relationships among many factors affecting leadership. It provides a framework for conceptualizing leadership so that individuals may maximize what they learn from experience. In that context, there are two main reasons we cover this material in this chapter. First, the findings of leadership research will be emphasized throughout the book, and so it will be helpful for you to be familiar with the ways leadership and its effects are typically measured. Second, it may be helpful for you as a leadership practitioner to be aware of the limitations of personal opinions as the primary basis for assessing leadership effectiveness. Understanding that leadership effectiveness can be measured in multiple ways will, we hope, encourage you to pay attention to alternative indicators of leadership impact (also see Highlight 5–1).

Highlight 5–1

Leadership Quotes, Chapter 5

As you go through life, brother
Whatever be your goal,
Keep your eye on the doughnut
And not upon the hole.

> Mayflower coffee shop slogan

If you can't measure it, you can't manage it.

> Peter Drucker

If you're worried about that last at-bat, you're going to be miserable, you're only going to get depressed; but if you put a picture in your mind that you're going to get a base hit off him the next time, now how do you feel? I try to put positive pictures into the minds of my players.

> Tommy Lasorda

Half the CEOs of the world are below average.

> David Campbell

Trust men and they will be true to you; treat them greatly and they will show themselves to be great.

> Ralph Waldo Emerson

By and large, executives make poor promotion and staffing decisions. By all accounts, their batting average is no better than .333. At most, one-third of such decisions turn out right, one-third are minimally effective, and one-third are outright failures. In no other area would we put up with such miserable performance; indeed, we need not and should not. Managers making people decisions will never be perfect, of course, but they should come pretty close to batting 1.000.

> Peter Drucker

Everything you do at work counts.

> Mike Watkins

When a doctor makes a poor diagnosis, their patient dies. When a lawyer fails to present a good case, their client goes to jail. But when a manager makes a poor hiring decision, they have to face the consequences of that decision every single day.

> Pete Ramstad

A fish stinks from the head down.

> Bruce Berg

As an overview, this chapter first reviews the major techniques leadership researchers have used to assess or measure leadership. When assessing leadership, researchers are looking at the ways in which leaders are different from followers or for ways successful leaders differ from unsuccessful leaders in terms of variables such as their values, personality traits, intelligence, job knowledge, experience, or behavior. Next, the chapter discusses the major indicators used to measure leadership effectiveness. After that, we look at several methodologies used to study leadership. This section explores the empirical foundations of studying the *relationship* between leadership and other variables—in other words, the relationship between what leaders do and what happens as a result.

Assessing Leadership

Because this chapter is about assessing leadership, it seems appropriate to begin with an example from research. The research in this case deals with leadership in commercial airline crews. Many airline crews consist of three positions with very distinct responsibilities. The aircraft captain is the final authority for all decisions regarding the aircraft and is ultimately responsible for the safety of the passengers and crew. The copilot helps the captain fly the aircraft, and the flight engineer is primarily responsible for the aircraft's preflight inspections and operation of systems (electrical, hydraulic, fuel, communication, etc.). Since airline crews must work together as a coordinated team in order to successfully complete a flight, one of the authors (Ginnett, 1988) of this text studied factors affecting crew coordination. As a part of this project, he flew with a number of different airline crews and recorded conversations between crew members. The following is an excerpt of an interview between a first officer and the researcher:

> *Researcher:* Are all the captains you fly with pretty much the same?
> *Aircrew member:* Oh no. Some guys are the greatest guys in the world to fly with. I mean they may not have the greatest hands in the world but that doesn't matter. When you fly with them, you feel like you can work together to get the job done. You really want to do a good job for them. Some other captains are just the opposite . . . you just can't stand to work with them. That doesn't mean you'll do anything that's unsafe or dangerous but you won't go out of your way to keep him or her out of trouble either. So you'll just sit back and do what you have to and just hope he or she screws up.
> *Researcher:* How can you tell which kind of captain you're working with?
> *Aircrew member:* Oh, you can tell.
> *Researcher:* How?
> *Aircrew member:* I don't know how you tell but it doesn't take very long. Just a couple of minutes and you'll know.

The above conversation details many of the main points in this section. Although it was the airline pilot's personal opinion that it was relatively easy to recognize good captains, scientists use more systematic ways to assess leadership, which in this case is precisely the project Ginnett undertook. Scientists use these more systematic techniques because personal opinions can vary substantially across individuals. But if leadership researchers do not rely on personal opinions to determine which traits, abilities, or behaviors are necessary for effective leadership, then just how do they assess leaders? Generally speaking, leadership researchers have used observations, interviews, and paper-and-pencil measures to assess leadership empirically. For example, leadership researchers could interview airline captains about their leadership styles, administer personality tests to captains to measure their personality traits, or observe captains giving orders and interacting with other crew members. Each of these techniques would give a different perspective about each captain and the type of leader he or she may be. Because leadership is playing an increasingly important role in the success of the organization, leadership assessment is rapidly becoming a big business. Many organizations are using the techniques described in this section to select entry level managers, and even more sophisticated assessment techniques to select senior leaders.

There are many factors to consider when assessing leadership, but two of the most important are the researcher's own definition of leadership and the general assessment technique used. The following is a more complete discussion of the relationship between leadership definitions and leadership assessment.

The Importance of Leadership Definitions

By far the most important factor influencing what aspects of leadership will be assessed in any study is the individual researcher's own definition or theory of leadership. If a researcher defines leadership as a certain set of behaviors, then she is apt to assess only those behaviors she feels are important and probably will not assess other behaviors, abilities, or values. And because there are many different theories and definitions of leadership, researchers have assessed a variety of leadership behaviors and attributes. Over time, researchers have systematically assessed leaders' behaviors (Komacki, 1986; Hazucha, 1992), charismatic potential and rhetorical skills (Bass & Yammarino, 1988; Curphy, 1991; Shamir, Arthur, & House, 1994), use of influence tactics (Hinkin & Schreisheim, 1989; Yukl & Falbe, 1991; Yukl, Lepsinger, & Lucia, 1992), intelligence levels (Gibson, 1992; Lord, DeVader, & Allinger, 1986), personality traits (Hogan, Curphy, & Hogan, 1994; Zaccaro, Foti, & Kenny, 1991), and experience levels (Fiedler & Garcia, 1987; Gibson, 1992). Given a group of leaders, researchers could potentially assess any or all of these characteristics. Because leadership research often has a fairly narrow focus, however, how a researcher defines leadership will largely dictate what will be assessed in any given study.

Leadership definitions do not just affect leadership researchers and what they study. They also affect leadership practitioners. Much like researchers, leadership practitioners have their own biases and preferences for what makes up successful and unsuccessful leadership. For example, Genghis Khan was identified as the leader a group of new Japanese civil servants would most like to work for (*Denver Post*, September 26, 1997). In many organizations these preferences for certain leadership behaviors have been formalized to form **competency models**. A competency model is a set of desired skills, values, or behaviors the organization feels its leaders need in order to successfully meet current and future business challenges. Competency models often drive performance appraisal, compensation, training, succession planning, and selection systems, and as such have a tremendous impact on who gets hired, rewarded, and promoted in a company. For example, if a company were opening new manufacturing or retail facilities in South America, then some of the competencies their leaders might need would include a high level of drive, stress tolerance, interpersonal skills, independence, resourcefulness, problem solving skills, cultural sensitivity, and the ability to speak Spanish or Portuguese. These competencies would in turn be used to design a selection system to hire leaders for these facilities. Whether you get hired for a particular company may depend to a large extent on its competency model; you may get offered a job with a company whose competencies match your strengths and may be less likely to get an offer when there is less of a match.

Although competency modeling has a number of positive attributes and is very popular these days (Curphy, 1998), this technique may also have several drawbacks. Perhaps their biggest advantage is that they help to align all of the human resource processes and systems in an organization. In other words, the skills and behaviors used to determine whether someone gets hired into a leadership position are the same skills and behaviors that get rewarded, compensated, trained, and promoted on the job. You may think that organizations do not need a competency model to do this, but often there is considerable misalignment between the skills and behaviors used to evaluate candidates and the behaviors that help someone get promoted or rewarded in an organization. On the downside, organizations must take care that their competency models help to meet strategic business needs and are inherently free of bias. It may be that the skills and behaviors identified in a competency model are more likely to be exhibited by a particular gender or ethnic group, the end result being an underrepresentation of other gender or ethnic groups, who in reality do have the skills necessary to be effective leaders in the organization (Alimo-Metcalfe, 1994).

This underrepresentation at the executive level may be a potential explanation for the **glass ceiling effect**. In corporate America, females seem to run into significantly more barriers than men in reaching the top rungs of the organization. For example, females make up over 40 percent of the workforce, but only 10 percent of the executive positions in Fortune 500 companies are female. Moreover, only 2 percent of females hold one of the top five jobs in these organizations and about 100 of the Fortune 500 companies have no females in top positions (Jackson, 1996). Minorities do not fare much better with respect to executive representation. However, research has shown that there are few developmental differences between male and female executives, and at least at the middle management level there seem to be few practical differences in performance between males and females and among ethnic groups (Baisden, Chung, Hezlett, & Ronnkvist, 1996; Lyness & Thompson, 1997). So if there are few performance and developmental differences between men and women and among racial groups at the mid-management level, then why aren't a higher percentage of underrepresented groups filling executive positions? It may well be that top executives have implicit competency models which tend to exclude underrepresented groups. Leaders tend to hire people in their own image, and if that image is one of a white male, then it is likely white males will be chosen to become their successors. Perhaps the first step in breaking this cycle is to develop explicit, unbiased leadership competency models. An unbiased leadership competency model will reveal few practical performance differences between various groups. If there are few performance differences at the mid-management level, and if executive successors are coming primarily from the mid-management ranks, then over time a higher percentage of females and minorities should reach the executive level.

Methods Used to Assess Leadership

How would you go about determining a leader's values, personality, skills, intellect, or behaviors? Although *what* can be assessed is fairly broad, *how* these assessments are accomplished tends to be more limited. Probably the three most common assessment techniques are interviews, observations, and paper-and-pencil measures. These three techniques can be used to assess any of the attributes listed in the previous section, but some assessment techniques are better suited than others to studying certain aspects of leadership. For example, it is relatively difficult to accurately assess a leader's personality through interviews. Instead, a researcher may ask leaders to complete a personality test in order to more accurately assess their personalities. And because different personality tests measure different traits, the definition or theory of leadership underlying the research might even dictate which personality test will be best for a given study.

Different assessment techniques also can be used to investigate the same phenomenon. For example, Curtis, Smith, and Smoll (1979) used trained observers, interviews, and questionnaires to assess the leadership behaviors of Little League coaches. Because such diverse measures typically portray many different facets of leaders, this study led to a broader understanding of coaching through the use of a combination of assessment techniques.

Perhaps one of the most common techniques used to assess various leadership attributes is the interview. In **structured interviews**, the interviewer asks the leader a predetermined set of questions, whereas in **unstructured interviews** the interviewer does not follow a predetermined set of questions (Campion, Palmer, & Campion, 1997; Saal & Knight, 1988). In an unstructured format, the interviewer has the latitude to allow the interview to proceed in whatever direction seems appropriate. The researcher–aircrew member conversation at the beginning of this chapter is an excerpt from an unstructured interview. Although unstructured interviews can provide interesting insights into the leadership process, it is difficult to compare the results of interviews from different leaders. Structured interviews, with their common set of questions and rating scales, usually make it much easier to compare different leaders' attitudes and feelings (see Highlights 5–2, 5–3, and 5–4).

Interviewing: The Good, the Bad, and the Ugly

The Good: Structured Interviews

Hiring managers make much better hiring decisions if they use structured interviews. Structured interviews are based on two premises, which are that *past behavior is the best predictor of future behavior,* and that *recent behavior is a better predictor than distant past behavior.* Thus, the interviewer is using questions which ask applicants to describe situations similar to those they may encounter on the job, how they reacted or behaved in those situations, and what the impact of those behaviors was. Moreover, good interviewers probe for examples from the recent past. Some of the structured interview questions an applicant for a management position would be asked might include:

(Motivation): Describe the toughest obstacle you ever had to overcome. Describe the situation, what you did, and the outcome of those behaviors.

(Interpersonal Skills). Describe the last time you had to resolve a conflict between you and one of your peers. What was the situation, what did you do, and what were the consequences of those behaviors?

(Leadership Skills). Describe the last time you had to deal with a performance problem with a subordinate. What was the situation, how did you handle the problem, and how was the problem actually resolved?

As you might imagine, it takes considerable training to be a good structured interviewer. However, this investment in time can have a big payoff. Research has shown that skilled structured interviewers make substantially better hiring decisions than unskilled unstructured interviewers (see Table 5–1, page 113).

So far we have discussed the interviewer's perspective. You may be wondering what are the best practices for interviewees? In other words, what can you do to improve the odds that you will get offered a position as the result of an interview? The are several practical steps you can take to improve your interviewing performance, which include:

1. *Learn as much as you can about the company prior to the interview.* Most companies have Web pages on the Internet. If they do not, then call the company and ask for a copy of its latest annual report. You need to know why the company exists, its history, products and services, financial status, and so on.
2. *Conduct a personal talent audit.* According to Bill Byham of Development Dimensions International, organizations are looking for people who have a history of continous learning and growth, teamwork, communication skills, decision-making savvy, and initiative. You should practice describing how your school and work experiences relate to these factors.
3. *Project a professional appearance.* Most hiring decisions are made early in the interview. People who dress unprofessionally or act inappropriately during the interview have less chance in being hired (see Highlight 5–4 for examples of inappropriate behaviors in an interview).
4. *Be yourself.* One of the biggest mistakes interviewees make is to be someone they are not. Many times these behaviors are not well practiced and come across poorly under the high stress of an interview.

Highlight 5–3

Interviewing: The Good, the Bad, and the Ugly

The Bad: Unstructured Interviews

Perhaps the most prevalent selection technique is the unstructured interview. In this situation each different applicant may be asked entirely different questions by the person or committee doing the hiring. Simple and logical as it must seem, there are nonetheless several problems with this technique. First, Department of Labor research shows that up to 80 percent of the hiring managers using unstructured interviews make selection decisions during the first five minutes of the interview. As it is virtually impossible to know anything about an applicant's skills, knowledge, or experience within the first five minutes of the interview, hiring managers instead seem to focus on largely irrelevant information such as dress, personal mannerisms, or tone and pitch of speech. Second, some people, particularly at the more senior levels, are very good at self-presentation. They have been interviewed so many times that they know how to say all the right buzzwords and are very good at endearing themselves to the interviewer. The impact of self-presentation skills is substantially greater in unstructured interviews; skilled interviewees can guide the interview in such a way that all their strengths shine through and their weaknesses remain uncovered. The best defense against self-presentation is to use a structured interview. Having the interviewee describe specific details of his or her past behaviors and the circumstances surrounding these behaviors will help the interviewer both to better control the interview and to gather more accurate data about the interviewee.

Some problems are shared by both structured and unstructured interviews. Interviews of both sorts are time-consuming, which typically limits the number of individuals who can be interviewed in any study. Also, beyond the question of how many leaders can be interviewed is the question of which leaders should be interviewed. Some authors, such as Tichy and Devanna (1986), Bennis and Nanus (1985), and Astin and Leland (1991), conducted interviews only with individuals they perceived to be successful leaders. Because these studies included no interviews with unsuccessful leaders to serve as a comparison, it is impossible to discern whether successful leaders are really doing anything differently (or, more pertinently, are *saying* anything differently) than unsuccessful leaders; by interviewing only successful leaders, these studies limit the confidence we have in using interviews as a basis for gaining insight about effective leadership. The latter problem is not limited to interviews, but can affect all of the techniques used to assess leadership. It is important to *keep the size and representativeness of the sample in mind* whenever reading the results of leadership research.

Observation is another common technique used to assess leaders. Like interviews, observation also can be structured or unstructured. With the former,

---

Highlight 5–4

Interviewing: The Good, the Bad, and the Ugly

The Ugly: Top 10 Stupid Interviewing Tricks

A survey of some of the top personnel executives in corporate America yielded the following stupid interviewing tricks:

1. She wore a Walkman and said she could listen to me and the music at the same time.
2. The candidate announced that she hadn't eaten lunch and proceeded to eat a hamburger and french fries during the interview.
3. The interviewee said he was so well qualified that if he didn't get the job, it would prove that the company's management was incompetent.
4. The applicant wore a jogging suit for a Financial Vice President position.
5. The candidate interrupted the interview so that he could phone his therapist for advice on answering questions.
6. During the interview, an alarm clock went off from inside the candidate's briefcase. He took it out, shut it off, apologized, and said he had to leave for another interview.
7. During the interview he took off his right shoe and sock and sprinkled medicated foot powder on his foot. While he was putting his shoe back on, he mentioned that he had to use the powder four times a day, and this was one of these times.
8. The interviewee asked who the lovely babe was, pointing at the picture on the interviewer's desk. When the interviewer said it was his wife, the interviewee asked if she was home right now and wanted her phone number.
9. The interviewee asked the interviewer if she wanted any cocaine before starting the interview.
10. The candidate threw up on my desk and immediately started asking questions about the job, like nothing had happened.

Sources: V. Arnold, "Management and Executive Assessment," paper presented at Personnel Decisions International, Denver, CO, September 1997; B. Byham, *Landing the Job You Want: How to Have the Best Job Interview of Your Life* (Pittsburgh: DDI Press, 1997); T. Janz, L. W. Hellervik, & D. C. Gilmore, *Behavior Description Interviewing* (Boston: Allyn and Bacon, Inc., 1986).

---

observers are trained to categorize different behaviors into a predetermined set of dimensions. For example, the observers in the Little League study had to categorize the different behaviors manifested by the coaches into 12 categories such as technical instruction, punishment, goal setting, and positive reward (Curtis, Smith, & Smoll, 1979). Mintzberg (1973), on the other hand, used unstructured observations to record the activities of five executives over a one-month period.

TABLE 5–1   Typical Correlations between Different Assessment Techniques and Job Performance

Assessment Technique	Correlation	U.S. Companies Using This Technique
Work sample/skill test	.54	15–20%
Mental abilities test	.53	15–20%
Assessment center/job simulation	.50	Unknown
Peer evaluation	.49	Unknown
Behavioral consistency experience rating	.49	Unknown
Job knowledge test	.48	Unknown
Miniature training and evaluation	.48	Unknown
Job tryout	.44	Unknown
Biographical questionnaire	.40	10–15%
Structured interview	.40	Unknown
Academic performance	.20	Unknown
Unstructured interview	.20	90%+
Reference check	.14	80%+
Training and experience rating	.13	Unknown
Application blank	.10	90%+
Personality/interest test[a]	.10	10–20%

[a]When the proper steps are taken, research has shown that personality traits correlate in the .3–.6 range with job performance. Some of these steps are described in Chapter 7.

Source: K. Pearlman, "Validity Generalization: From Theory to Application," paper presented at the Center for Human Resources Programs, Institute of Industrial Relations, University of California–Berkeley, 1985.

Mintzberg used only a stopwatch and a notepad to record all the different activities his subjects performed. After collecting the data, Mintzberg then categorized the activities the managers performed into 10 different leadership roles, such as negotiator, leader, figurehead, or disturbance handler. Thus, the biggest difference between structured and unstructured observation is not so much that one involves categorizing behavior and the other does not; rather, they differ with regard to *when* the categorization occurs. With structured observation the behavior dimensions are predetermined, but with unstructured observation the dimensions are developed after data are collected.

Observations can provide detailed information about what leaders actually do, but several cautions are in order when observations are used to assess leadership. First, as with interviews, observations take considerable time and effort, and so the number of leaders actually assessed tends to be small. Second, recording and categorizing behaviors via structured observations is not as simple as it sounds (Martinko & Gardner, 1985). For example, if a leader asks a subordinate to develop a plan for introducing a new product into the marketplace, should the leader's behavior be categorized as motivating subordinates, developing subordinates, or as planning? Some of these problems can be overcome through training and the use of videotape, but it is relatively costly to train observers. Third, it is important to recognize that observations measure only overt behavior. This assessment technique cannot measure cognitive activities, such as problem solving or strategy development, that are an important aspect of leadership and management. Despite such cautions, however, observation is a viable technique for assessing what managers actually do, and we agree with Campbell (1977) that more leadership studies should use this technique.

Paper-and-pencil measures are often used to assess leaders and include personality inventories, intelligence tests, preference inventories, and behavioral questionnaires. Although these will be discussed in more detail in Chapters 6 through 11, two aspects of questionnaires need elaboration. First, it is worth noting that not all personality, intelligence, or behavioral questionnaires are alike. Paper-and-pencil measures that assess personality can and do differ greatly. For example, the traits assessed by one personality inventory are often different from those assessed by another inventory. The same holds true for intelligence tests and behavioral questionnaires. Second, researchers often get different pictures of a leader's behavior depending on *who* completes a particular paper-and-pencil measure. Suppose you wanted to assess a professor's leadership in one of your courses. Even if you use the same questionnaire, you might get different impressions depending on whether you examined the department chairperson's ratings, the instructor's self-ratings, or students' ratings. With research results, it is helpful to keep in mind who completed any questionnaires and whether or not similar results would have been obtained if a different group had provided the ratings of the leader.

Practical Applications of Leadership Assessment

After reading the preceding section, many of you may well be saying something like this to yourself: "There are a number of leadership attributes or behaviors that can be assessed, what gets assessed will depend on one's theory or definition of leadership, and there are three major ways to conduct these assessments. But so what? I never plan on doing leadership research, so this section really has little personal relevance."

Although you may never conduct leadership research, this material is likely much more relevant to you than may first appear. Many of the assessment techniques developed by researchers have found their way into schools, businesses, and government institutions. For example, it is very likely that you took either the SAT or ACT as part of the college admission process. These paper-and-pencil measures were developed to assess potential college success, just as other measures have been developed to assess potential leadership success. When applying for a management position, you will likely have to complete some type of paper-and-pencil measure (such as a background form or application blank) and undergo at least one if not several interviews. Institutions using more sophisticated assessment techniques for hiring managers may require candidates to go through an **in-depth managerial assessment** or an **assessment center**. Because these two types of assessments are becoming more and more prevalent, they are worth discussing in more detail.

One of the leaders in in-depth managerial assessments has been Personnel Decisions International (PDI). PDI is an international management consulting firm that has conducted over 30,000 in-depth managerial assessments. These assessments are often used when an organization has several possible internal and external candidates for a supervisory, a management, or an executive position. Suppose four candidates applied for the superintendent position for a medium sized school district, and the school board opted to use in-depth management assessments to determine each candidate's level of motivation, thinking skills, management (i.e., administrative) skills, leadership skills, ability to tolerate stress, and overall fit with the job. The in-depth managerial assessment process begins by having candidates complete four to six hours of prework, which usually consists of a background form for assessing educational and work history and several personality tests. Upon completion of the pre-work, each candidate then goes through a one-day assessment at PDI. After a brief orientation meeting, the assessment begins with two hours of intelligence testing. Next, each candidate is asked to complete an in-basket exercise. An **in-basket exercise** is a work simulation which requires candidates to go through the articles, notes, letters, messages, and memos found in a typical superintendent's in-basket. Candidates are first given a brief summary of the situation at the school district and organizational charts, and then are given two hours to indicate what they would do with each of the memos, letters, and the rest. Upon completion of the in-basket exercise, candidates then participate in a **role play** work simulation. In this particular role play, candidates are asked to conduct a 30-minute meeting with a school principal having several performance problems. Candidates are given 30 minutes to read material about the school principal and the situation prior to the meeting; the principal is played by a PDI assessor. The assessor is trained in behavioral observation techniques, acts in a certain manner during the role play, and watches (and later records) how candidates reacted to their behaviors. The assessment concludes with a one-and-one-half hour structured interview with a psychologist.

After the assessment process has been completed, the school board would get a report that described each candidate's level of motivation, leadership skills, thinking skills, and so on. The report would be written by a psychologist who considers the requirements of the position and compares each candidate's performance to the 30,000 managers in the PDI norm group. It is important to note that in-depth management assessments use all three assessment techniques to identify the relative strengths and weaknesses of candidates, and some techniques work better than others for assessing different attributes. For example, the in-basket exercise is particularly good for assessing management skills; the interview, personality tests, and role play work well for assessing interpersonal skills; and intelligence tests and the in-basket exercise are good indicators of thinking skills. Although the results of an in-depth management assessment are only one component of the hiring process, this assessment technique levels the playing field for the applicants and helps improve the quality of selection decisions.

Assessment centers probably represent the most sophisticated and expensive method for assessing leadership (or at least leadership potential). They were first used in Europe in the 1920s to select officers for the German military (Simoneit, 1944) and civil servants and foreign service officers for the British government (Garforth, 1945). In the United States, assessment centers were first used to select special agents and spies for the Office of Strategic Services, now known as the Central Intelligence Agency (Murray & MacKinnon, 1946). The purpose of modern-day assessment centers is to assess, identify, and develop leadership potential, and well over 200 institutions utilize this process (Spychalski, Quinones, Gaugler, & Pohley, 1997). To this end, all the techniques previously discussed in this section are used. Over the course of several days, subjects attending an assessment center go through a "virtual reality" experience specifically designed for managers. In other words, attendees spend two to three days in a simulated company and are put in a number of difficult, complex situations where their behaviors are recorded by highly trained observers. They have to make difficult business decisions based on sketchy information, face ethical or legal dilemmas, make oral presentations, coordinate activities with other managers going through the center, write letters and reports, negotiate contracts, resolve conflicts between subordinates, and deal with poorly performing subordinates (who are played by trained assessors). Prior to the assessment, candidates complete a number of questionnaires, personality inventories, and intelligence tests. Assessors use the input from these measures and the work simulations to write a report on the relative strengths and weaknesses of the candidate.

Although assessment centers were originally designed for personnel selection, more and more organizations are using them for management development (Spychalski, Quinones, Gaugler, & Pohley, 1997). For example, a center may be designed around what the organization feels its managers will need to be able to do five years in the future. Placing managers in this type of work simulation enables them to get feedback on where they are with respect to the skills they will need to have in the future. This way they can work toward developing these skills *before* they may need them. And because assessment centers do a pretty good job of assessing and developing leadership potential (Gaugler, Rosenthal, Thornton, & Benson, 1987; Hunter & Hunter, 1984), it is entirely possible that someday you may participate in one, particularly if you are trying to get a job with a large corporation.

Although you may never go through an in-depth management assessment or assessment center, you should know that organizations are paying increasing attention to their selection processes and procedures. Many organizations are discovering that they can save considerable training time and money and see substantial increases in productivity by hiring the right people in the first place. Thus, organizations are opting to use more sophisticated assessment techniques for hiring both leaders *and* followers. Readers should not be surprised if they are asked to go through some type of assessment when applying for a job; additionally, it will be useful for readers to understand that different assessment techniques can

Highlight 5–5

Résumé Screening and Testing

A common technique many organizations use to hire new employees is résumé screening. A **résumé** is a brief summary of a candidate's work and educational experiences, and it is very likely that you will be asked to submit your résumé when applying for a job. Hiring managers or human resource representatives screen candidates' résumés to determine who should be tested or interviewed for the position. Because résumés often represent the first step in the hiring process and are an opportunity for candidates to put their best foot forward, you would think that they would be closely edited before they are submitted. However, some errors seem to get through the editing process. Excerpts of some of the more hilarious mistakes found on résumés include:

1. "Instrumental for ruining the entire operation of a Midwest chain store."
2. "Note: Please don't misconstrue my 14 jobs as 'job hopping.' I have never quit a job."
3. "The company made me a scapegoat, just like my three previous employers."
4. "Am a perfectionist and rarely if if ever forget details."
5. "I have lurnt Word Perfect 6.0, computer and spreadsheat progroms."
6. "References: None. I've left a path of destruction behind me."

Source: A. Fisher, "Stupid Resume Tricks: How to Avoid Getting Hired," *Fortune*, July 21, 1997.

provide useful information about people applying *to* them for positions. Part of being a good leader is making savvy staffing decisions, and wise leaders understand how they can use different assessment techniques to assemble the best team possible (see Highlights 5–5 and 5–6).

Measuring the Effects of Leadership

After a company invests time, energy, and money in developing and implementing a sophisticated hiring system, the key question is whether the leaders who are hired have any positive impact on the organization. Do good leaders differ from bad leaders with respect to the effect they have on subordinates? Do they really make a difference in others' lives or do the groups they lead achieve better results? How could you tell? What would you use to differentiate successful from unsuccessful leaders? Just as various techniques are used to assess leaders, there also are various ways to measure their *effects* on subordinates or organizations. But just what do we mean here by effects on subordinates? A useful way to think about this is in terms of the ways in which we typically define

Highlight 5–6

Selection Practices in Europe

Americans alone cannot be blamed for making poor selection decisions. Europeans seem to fall into many of the same traps. For example, consider the assessment techniques used by the following European executive selection consultancies:

	Percent Usage			
Assessment Technique	*France*	*Germany*	*Italy*	*United Kingdom*
Interviews	100.0	93.3	100.0	100.0
References	56.6	60.0	75.0	87.8
Psychological testing	34.8	40.0	37.5	40.0
Graphology (handwriting analysis)	47.8	13.3	6.3	2.6

Unfortunately for the French, there has yet to be a single shred of evidence to support the notion that how one writes (i.e., graphology) has anything to do with managerial competence. Another way to think about this is to use an American example—which occupation in America has the worst handwriting? A good guess here may be the smartest of all occupational groups, medical doctors. Although being a good doctor does not mean one will be a good manager, these two groups do share some common skills.

Source: Kerr-Brown PDI, "European Head Hunting," *Update 12,* (Spring 1994).

leadership success. We usually do not differentiate between successful and unsuccessful leaders by the behaviors they exhibit or the attributes they possess; rather, we are more likely to consider whether their followers are productive or satisfied. For example, we could make judgments about the success of a leader by looking at a coach's win–loss record, a college professor's end-of-course student ratings, or the production or quality rates for a production manager's work unit. Although a leader's behavior or personality traits may play a key role in these indices, when making judgments about the relative success of a leader we are examining the *consequences* or *impact* of these behaviors and not the behaviors per se. The material in this section describes how researchers typically measure leadership impact and their respective strengths and limitations.

Common Measures of Successful and Unsuccessful Leadership

In reality, a vast number of measures are available to judge successful and unsuccessful leaders (see, for example, Highlight 5–7). Some of the more commonly used measures include a superior's effectiveness or promotion ratings, subordinates' ratings of their job satisfaction and morale or of their leader's effectiveness,

---

Highlight 5–7

Measures for Evaluating
School Principal Effectiveness

It is becoming increasingly clear that good schools are led by good principals. It is also clear that certain performance dimensions, or competencies, distinguish between a really good principal and an average or poor one. A competency model for school principals, which could also be used to create a performance appraisal form, might include:

Communicate a vision of school goals and priorities to students, teachers, and the community.

Build parent and community support for the school.

Assure a safe, secure, and orderly school setting.

Build a school climate and culture conducive to learning.

Develop a curriculum and instructional objectives related to school goals.

Are instructional experts sought out by their staffs.

Obtain needed teaching resources for their staffs.

Monitor teacher, student, and school performance.

Are visible presences in their schools.

Given the development of this form, who would you think would be in the best position to rate a principal's performance on these dimensions—students, parents, superintendents, school board members, or teachers? Each constituency sees the principal in a unique way. Moreover, some constituencies may be in a position to make more accurate judgments about the principal's performance on certain dimensions than others. Given these unique perspectives, researchers may create different versions of the rating forms for these different constituencies.

Sources: R. E. Blum, J. A. Butler, and N. L. Olson, "Leadership for Excellence: Research-Based Training for Principals," *Educational Leadership 45 (1)*, (1987), pp. 25–29; R. Brandt, "On Leadership and Student Achievement: A Conversation with Richard Andrews," *Educational Leadership 45 (1)*, (1987), pp. 9–16; and M. Sashkin and G. Huddle, "Recruit Top Principals." *School Administrator 45 (2)*, (1988), pp. 8–15.

---

and various work-unit performance indices. We will discuss each of these in further detail below.

Superiors' Effectiveness and Performance Ratings.   One way to judge a leader's success is in terms of her past performance appraisal ratings. Most performance appraisals are accomplished by a leader's superior and include ratings of performance on several relevant dimensions, as well as a recommendation (or not) for promotion. For example, Bass and Yammarino (1988) used superiors' overall performance ratings and promotion recommendations as criteria for judging the leadership effectiveness of navy surface fleet officers.

Because almost all organizations use some type of performance appraisal system, it may be worthwhile to briefly describe a typical performance appraisal form. The better performance appraisal forms typically include several features. First, superiors use some type of scale to rate how well a target leader accomplished several key objectives. Superiors also rate the leader on several key dimensions the organization believes are important—integrity, leadership, administrative skills, communication impact, and the like. Finally, superiors then rate the overall performance and/or the promotability of the leader.

Although performance appraisal ratings are frequently available, it turns out that many times these ratings may not be an accurate reflection of a leader's true impact on her followers or the organization. Sometimes superiors simply do not take the time to provide accurate and comprehensive performance appraisal ratings; at other times superiors may be largely unaware of, or unfamiliar with, a target leader's performance. This latter phenomenon is becoming more prevalent as organizations downsize, eliminate layers of management, and increase the number of people any one superior may supervise. Some superiors have difficulties dealing with conflict and would rather give average ratings than have to deal with the emotions and distress associated with unflattering ratings. In addition, friendships, perceptual sets, and attribution errors can bias superiors' ratings of a leader's true performance. Some performance appraisal systems do such a poor job of measuring a leader's true impact that superiors find them to be virtually useless when making promotion or compensation decisions.

Subordinates' Ratings of Satisfaction, Organizational Climate, Morale, Motivation, and Leadership Effectiveness.   If leadership is defined partly in the eyes of followers, then perhaps a better way to judge leadership success is to ask subordinates to rate their level of satisfaction or the effectiveness of their leader. Subordinates may be relatively satisfied or dissatisfied, may be motivated or unmotivated, may feel their team is cohesive or in conflict, or may believe their leader is relatively effective or ineffective.

Fostering a sense of motivation, cohesiveness, cooperation, and morale among unit members is a goal toward which most leaders will strive, yet several cautions may be in order when using subordinates' motivation or cohesiveness ratings to judge a leader's effectiveness. For one thing, some subordinates may be relatively unmotivated toward work no matter what the leader does. For example, it may be relatively difficult for a leader to motivate assembly-line workers, given the inherent boredom of many assembly-line jobs. For another, success in instilling a strong sense of motivation and cohesiveness in subordinates does not guarantee effective performance. It often is also necessary, for example, to ensure that subordinates are adequately trained and have the necessary equipment and resources to do the job. Without training and equipment, subordinates' performance still might be relatively low even if the subordinates are motivated. In addition, subordinates may be performing at a low level yet rate their leader as being relatively effective because he or she does not make them work very hard. Conversely, some subordinates may rate the leader as relatively ineffective if he or she does make them work hard.

Despite these cautions, there are two reasons why followers' ratings may be a more accurate reflection of a leader's impact than superiors' ratings. First, followers are often in a better position to make these judgments; they see their boss's leadership behaviors, often on a day-to-day basis. Second, although subordinates' ratings can also suffer from distortion or bias, such effects tend to cancel each other out when multiple raters are used.

Unit Performance Indices.   Rather than use ratings to judge a leader's effectiveness, we could examine what impact leaders have on their organizations' bottom lines. In other words, we could make judgments about leadership success by examining unit sales, profit margins, the number of defective products returned, the number of on-time deliveries, crime rates, high school graduation rates, the dollar amount of charitable contributions collected, win–loss records, or lost days due to accidents. Like the other measures described earlier, none of these measures are perfect. The biggest qualification to remember in using them as measures of leadership is that these measures are often affected by factors beyond a leader's control. For example, many different factors can affect yearly sales figures for the manager of a car dealership. These can include having an inventory of lower-quality cars or trying to sell cars during difficult economic times. Conceivably, a sales manager could do all the right things yet still sell fewer cars from one year to the next, primarily due to circumstances beyond his or her control. Conversely, a sales manager may make a number of mistakes but may work in a dealership that sells a greater number of cars due to a decrease in interest rates and the release of a hot-selling car. Leadership practitioners need to remember that unit performance indices often are affected by several factors, some of which have more impact than anything a leader might do. It is important to estimate how much a leader's behavior might affect a particular unit performance index before using that index to judge the leader's effectiveness.

Practical Implications Concerning Leadership Success Measures

Right about now you may be wondering if it is even possible to develop accurate measures of leadership success. Superiors' and subordinates' ratings have their inherent problems, as do unit performance indices. Despite these problems, these measures generally yield useful information about a leader's effectiveness. Moreover, these measures get at different aspects of effectiveness. It is entirely possible for leaders to get strong ratings from their superiors but poor ratings from subordinates. This may be the case if a leader was brought in to turn around a poorly performing unit or if the leader has spent a considerable amount of time engaging in "strategic sucking up." On the other hand, leaders could have poor relationships with their bosses and great relationships with their subordinates, and such relationships would be reflected in the ratings they get from these two groups. Practitioners need to understand the advantages and problems associated with the different measures, and that multiple measures often yield the best information about leadership success.

Practitioners also need to think critically about how their behavior affects the measures used to judge their leadership success. A leader may perform relatively poorly on several unit performance indices yet also realize that performance on these indices is both relatively insensitive to her behavior and largely a function of, say, local economic conditions or inadequate resources. Leaders instead may choose to focus on improving their effectiveness in terms of criteria more sensitive to their actions, such as improving subordinates' perceptions of motivation, climate, or satisfaction.

Another concern for leadership practitioners might be the degree to which leadership success measures are biased. A study of over a million performance appraisals from the British National Health Service revealed that females received significantly lower performance appraisal evaluations than males (Alimo-Metcalfe, 1994). Females receive less pay for the same job as their male counterparts in both the United Kingdom and the United States (Alimo-Metcalfe, 1994; Jackson, 1996), and minority female managers only make 57 percent of the pay of their white male counterparts in the United States (*Denver Post*, October 23, 1997). These results imply that females receive lower performance appraisal ratings across most jobs in these two countries. Because males make up the majority of managers in these two countries, it may be some time before both genders receive the same level of effectiveness and performance ratings from their superiors. It is important to remember that not all male managers automatically give all female subordinates lower performance appraisal ratings, however. The research cited above indicates overall trends; individual male managers may or may not give female subordinates lower performance or effectiveness ratings.

Methodologies Used to Study Leadership

So far we have discussed the techniques used to assess a leader's personality traits or behaviors. We have also gone over the measures commonly used to evaluate a leader's success. What we have not discussed is whether there is a *relationship* between a leader's personality traits, behaviors, or values and subordinates' level of satisfaction, win–loss records, sales results, percentage of on-time takeoffs, and so forth. Do leaders who are more outgoing, better problem solvers, and good listeners, or who can handle stress well really have happier and more productive subordinates? The nature and strength of the relationships between various leadership attributes and performance or effectiveness measures is of primary importance to researchers and practitioners alike. If there is little or no relationship between a leader's personality traits or behaviors and subordinates' satisfaction levels, then organizations would be wasting their time and money to assess these values and traits as part of their hiring or promotion processes. However, there is a large body of research which shows that certain leadership attributes can be reliably assessed and are related to a number of positive leadership outcomes. But how do leadership researchers

A Case Study of a Middle School Principal

The following is a description of a principal, written by a teacher from the same school:

In a staff meeting, the principal, a former football coach, was advising us on the procedure if a kid was caught smoking in the bathroom. He was asked what to do in the case of marijuana. He stated, "There was no marijuana at Smithville Middle School." He went on to say he wouldn't even know what it smelled like. Several of us offered to educate him, and suggested he walk through the south stairwell after third lunch. He never did take our advice, and in the three years I taught there we never dealt with a kid under the influence of marijuana on an official basis. I did get to know the schedule of a few of my students and established a warning system with the shop teacher to keep certain students away from band saws and drills on certain days.

Staff meetings were held infrequently (about three a year), and departmental meetings were nonexistent. The building had been built with an open classroom architectural concept, but no in-servicing was done to provide teachers with the methodology to develop curriculum and classes within that concept. Instead, bookcases were installed blocking out ventilation and light to try to keep the classrooms isolated. "Do your own thing" was the operational motto. This included the alcoholic teacher with the bottle in the locked file cabinet, the principal who was only seen when doing evaluations (of teachers) or when granting personal leave, and the homosexual who kept his private life very private until we had a staff party at his house. It was only when it was too late did we learn that one of the English teachers had an inoperable brain tumor which accounted for her rather bizarre disorientation at times.

This principal did little to adjust class size to make teaching possible. He did not even acknowledge a teacher giving up lunch and planning time in order to split two large classes into smaller ones. Nor did he show any compassion when that same teacher succumbed to mononucleosis. He still didn't figure out that the problem was the numbers and the schedule when the sub had to call in sick! He avoided anything personal such as illness or injury. He was more concerned with order and discipline. He yelled at a teacher in front of the class because the children were not sitting in chairs. The name of the game in that setting was containment first, education second.

systematically determine whether there is a relationship? Three of the more common techniques include case studies, correlational studies, and experiments.

Case Studies

A **case study** consists of an in-depth analysis of a particular leader's activities. A common form of the case study is the biography. Biographies usually provide detailed descriptions of the various situations facing the leader, the actions taken in response to these situations, and the results of the leader's actions (see Highlight 5–8). Case studies can provide leadership practitioners with valuable ideas on what to do in different leadership situations, particularly if the situations facing the practitioner are similar to those described in a biography or case study. However, there is no objective way to determine whether the actions taken actually caused the results described. Often factors beyond the leader's actions have a greater role in determining outcomes. Because of these problems, caution should always be used when trying to apply lessons discerned from a case study or biography; they may not fit your particular leadership style or may not apply to your leadership situation. Nevertheless, case studies often provide interesting and valuable reading, and offer leadership practitioners alternative perspectives for analyzing leadership situations.

Correlational Studies

Correlational studies are used to determine the statistical relationship between leaders' traits, mental abilities, or behaviors and various measures of leadership effectiveness such as subordinates' satisfaction or climate ratings. An example of a correlational study would be to identify some group of leaders (e.g., fire station chiefs in a large urban area), collect their scores on some type of paper-and-pencil test (an intelligence test), and also collect satisfaction ratings from their respective subordinates (e.g., their firemen). A **correlation coefficient** would then be calculated between the intelligence test scores and subordinates' satisfaction ratings. Correlation coefficients can range between -1.00 and $+1.00$. If the correlation coefficient were close to $+1.00$, then it would indicate that leaders with the highest IQs also had the most satisfied subordinates and that leaders with the lowest IQs had the least satisfied subordinates. A correlation coefficient of -1.00 would signify a perfect inverse relationship between these two sets of scores (i.e., leaders with the highest IQs had the least satisfied subordinates). If the correlation coefficient were zero, then we could conclude a leader's mental abilities and subordinates' satisfaction ratings were unrelated. In real life, sets of data like these are rarely, if ever, perfectly correlated, and correlation coefficients between $+1.00$ and -1.00 reflect degrees of statistical relationship between the sets; the greater the absolute value of the coefficient, the stronger the relationship. Table 5–1 (page 113) provides some of the typical correlations obtained between various types of assessment techniques and superiors' ratings of job performance.

A good example of a correlation study was recently published (Dorfman, Howell, Hibino, Lee, Tate, & Bautista (1997). It examined whether directive, supportive, contingent-reward, contingent-punishment, charismatic, and participative leadership behaviors had the same relationship with subordinates' satisfaction levels in the United States, Mexico, Japan, South Korea, and Taiwan. Looking at subordinates' ratings of a large number of managers in all five countries, they found that leaders who exhibited higher levels of supportive, contingent-reward, and charismatic behaviors had more-satisfied and more-motivated subordinates across all five cultures (correlations were in the .3–.6 range). These three leadership behaviors appeared to have universal effects; followers reported being happier and working harder for leaders who displayed these behaviors in any of the five countries. Directive behaviors had little relationship to followers' satisfaction levels in the United States, Japan, or South Korea (correlations averaged about .2), but were more positively related to followers' satisfaction levels in Taiwan and Mexico (correlations averaged about .5). Leaders' participative and contingent punishment behaviors had the strongest link to followers' satisfaction levels in the United States; there were generally only weak relationships between these behaviors and followers' satisfaction levels in the other four countries. The Dorfman et al. (1997) results show that leaders acting in a particular manner may be more or less effective depending on the country they are in; thus, culture and context must always be taken into account when examining relationships between leadership behaviors and effectiveness.

Correlational studies are among the most common methods used to study leadership. Both the ease of data collection and the ability of correlational studies to illuminate relationships between leader characteristics and effectiveness measures are two major advantages of these studies. However, they do have one major drawback. It is usually difficult (though it is often tempting) to make **causal inferences** based on correlational data. A causal inference occurs when leadership researchers can definitely say that certain leadership behaviors or attributes *cause* various kinds of leadership outcomes. Although correlational studies help researchers to determine the relationship between leadership attributes and outcomes, they cannot be used to make causal inferences. Researchers cannot tell whether the leadership behaviors or attributes that were assessed "caused" the effectiveness outcome of interest or vice-versa. For example, the researchers in the Little League study described earlier discovered a modest negative relationship between a coach's punitive behaviors and the number of games the team won (Curtis, Smith, & Smoll, 1979). In other words, the more a coach used punishment, the fewer games his Little League team won. Some people may conclude that a coach's use of punishment caused the team to lose more games, but an equally plausible alternative put forth by the researchers was that the losing teams had less talent, and thus their coaches had many more opportunities to use punishment than did the coaches of the winning teams. The team's relative lack of talent, not the coach's use of punishment, may have been the primary reason for the team's poor performance. Thus the researchers could not definitively tell whether punishment caused poorer team performance or if poorer team performance caused higher levels of punishment to occur. Leadership practitioners should be aware that the existence of a statistical relationship between two variables does not necessarily mean there is a cause-and-effect relationship between them. In fact, some of the most common erroneous reasoning from research results involves inferring causal relationships between variables when only a correlational relationship has been established.

Experiments

Experiments allow researchers to make causal inferences about leadership, and experimental designs are often based on the results of earlier case and correlational studies. Experiments generally consist of both **independent** and **dependent**

variables. The independent variable is what the researcher manipulates or varies to test the hypothesis; it causes change in the dependent variable. In leadership research, the independent variable is often some type of leadership behavior and the dependent variable is usually some measure of leadership effectiveness, such as work-unit performance or subordinates' satisfaction ratings.

A description of a laboratory experiment on leadership may help make the distinction between independent and dependent variables a bit clearer. Howell and Frost (1988) were interested in determining whether charismatic leaders caused subordinates to perform at a higher level than supportive or directive leaders. These researchers trained two actresses to manifest either charismatic, directive, or supportive leadership styles. Thus, the style of leadership exhibited by the actress-leader for different groups of subordinates was the independent variable in this experiment; with some groups the actress-leaders exhibited charismatic behaviors, with others they exhibited only supportive or directive behaviors. The dependent variable was subordinates' performance, which in this case was measured by the number of memos subordinates successfully completed during a 45-minute in-basket exercise. As you can see, the researchers manipulated or changed the independent variable (the actresses' leadership styles varied across different groups of subordinates), but they merely recorded the subordinates' performance on the dependent variable (the number of memos successfully completed) at the end of each 45-minute session. The researchers reported that subordinates' performance levels were highest when leaders exhibited charismatic behaviors and as a result concluded that these leadership behaviors caused subordinates to perform at the highest levels.

Although experiments allow us to make causal inferences about leadership, experiments have drawbacks of their own. One is that the effects obtained in many laboratory experiments are stronger than the effects obtained when the same experiments are conducted in organizations. This is primarily due to the fact that laboratory experiments are run under tightly controlled conditions, whereas experiments in organizations cannot be so tightly controlled. Extraneous influences often minimize or distort the effects of the independent variable on the dependent variable when the experiment is conducted in an organizational setting. Another problem concerns the subjects used in many laboratory experiments. Many times, college undergraduates are used as subjects in leadership experiments, and these individuals may have little leadership or followership experience. For such reasons it becomes legitimate to ask how much the results of any particular laboratory experiment can be generalized to actual organizations.

Maxims and Theories of Leadership

Most of what people read about leadership amounts to little more than someone else's opinion about it. Often, such material is both anecdotal and

Highlight 5–9

Some of Colin Powell's Lessons of Experience

- It ain't as bad as you think. It will look better in the morning.
- It can be done!
- Be careful what you choose. You may get it.
- Don't let adverse facts stand in the way of a good decision.
- Check small things.
- Share credit.
- Remain calm. Be kind.
- Have a vision. Be demanding.

Source: C. Powell and J. E. Persico, *My American Journey* (New York: Random House, 1995).

prescriptive: anecdotal in the sense it reflects just one leader's views, and prescriptive in advising others how to be more effective. For example, although Colin Powell is an outstanding leader whose rules make intuitive sense (see Highlight 5–9), it is nonetheless uncertain whether his maxims would apply equally well for very different leaders in very different situations. It is important to be mindful of the difference between this kind of literature about leadership and more scientific or empirical approaches to understanding it. The latter are represented by data-based studies and theories reported in this book. Although both approaches have legitimate purposes, it is vital to understand the differences between them.

The scientific alternative to leadership maxims is leadership theory. A leadership **theory** is a framework for conceptualizing relationships between variables and guiding research toward a fuller understanding of phenomena. With a theory a researcher makes public predictions about how certain leadership attributes or behaviors will systematically impact certain leadership effectiveness measures. Then the researcher collects the leadership assessment and effectiveness data prescribed by the theory, and conducts statistical analyses to determine whether her predictions are supported or refuted. For example, say a researcher predicted that the personality traits of dominance (wanting to be in charge of others) and dependability (being a reliable, trustworthy, and hardworking employee) were positively related to sales results in the computer retail industry. The researcher could use a paper-and-pencil measure of personality to assess store managers' standings on the traits of dominance and dependability. The researcher could then collect annual sales results (a unit performance index) for each store and conduct a correlational study to determine the nature and strength of the relationships between these three variables. The researcher might then publish the results of her findings in a scientific journal so that other researchers could replicate, support, or refute the original theory and findings.

The public predictions of how leadership variables are interrelated, the systematic gathering and analysis of data, and the peer review of results are what make theories so central to scientific research. Theories are often modified to take new findings into account as peers collect, analyze, and publish their findings about the theory. For example, other researchers may find that store managers' intelligence levels also are related to store performance. The original theory would then need to be modified so that dominance, dependability, and intelligence could all be used to predict sales managers' success. These findings could in turn be used to develop a competency model and selection system for future store managers in the computer retail industry.

The essence of theories of leadership, then, is to provide a reasonably coherent conceptual structure of how critical variables interact, involving ideas that can be put to the test and revised as new data accumulate. Simply put, theories of leadership involve testable ideas, whereas prescriptive approaches to leadership involve no such intended testability. Although both leadership maxims and theories are useful for understanding leadership situations, in general only leadership theories add to the body of knowledge concerning the science of leadership and help in the development of universal laws of leadership. It is also important to understand that theory building is hard, painstaking work. It is fairly easy to state one's opinions on how one should act as a leader; it is an entirely different matter to design a study, collect and analyze data, and finally publish the results.

An actual example might help to further clarify how theories are formulated and tested, and build our knowledge base about leadership. One of the preeminent leadership theorists today is Fred Fiedler. Fiedler has been conducting leadership research and developing leadership theories for well over 40 years. A number of years ago, Fiedler was conducting small-group research and observed that some groups led by seasoned, experienced leaders did not perform problem-solving tasks as well as groups led by relatively young and inexperienced leaders. In other problem-solving situations, however, the most experienced leaders had the highest performing problem-solving groups. Fiedler was puzzled by these findings—why would leadership experience appear to boost group performance in some situations but seem to interfere with it in others? Moreover, because we often hire leaders explicitly because of their experience, could it be that we had been assessing the wrong leadership characteristics for making hiring decisions?

Upon reviewing his group problem-solving data, Fiedler noted two trends. First, experienced leaders seemed to have higher-performing groups when their groups faced highly stressful situations. Second, smart but inexperienced leaders seemed to have higher-performing groups in situations involving little or no stress. This led Fiedler to formulate two **hypotheses**. Hypotheses are specific predictions designed to be tested using either correlational studies or experiments. Fiedler's first hypothesis posited that groups having to solve problems in highly stressful situations will perform at a higher level when led by experienced rather than inexperienced leaders. Fiedler's second hypothesis posited that groups having to solve problems in low-stress situations will perform at a higher level when led by more-intelligent but less-experienced leaders than when led by experienced leaders.

Fiedler then conducted a series of experiments in order to test these two hypotheses. He assessed group leaders' intelligence levels through the use of various paper-and-pencil measures and also assessed their level of experience (in terms of years of leadership experience). He then placed either highly experienced or highly intelligent (but inexperienced) leaders in charge of one of two problem-solving groups. One group had to solve novel, complex problems under low-stress conditions, and the other group had to solve novel, complex problems under highly stressful conditions. Fiedler then compared the number of problems successfully solved by groups led by both types of leaders under both the stressful and nonstressful conditions.

The two independent variables in his experiments were (1) the level of experience/intelligence of the leaders and (2) the degree of stress experienced by the problem solving group. The dependent variable was the number of problems successfully solved by each group. These experiments confirmed the two original hypotheses; experienced leaders have higher-performing problem-solving groups in high-stress conditions, but lower-performing groups in low-stress situations. Intelligent but inexperienced leaders had higher-performing problem-solving groups in the low-stress condition, but these groups did substantially poorer than the groups led by experienced leaders in the high-stress condition. Fiedler and his associates then conducted a number of other experiments to verify these original findings and to further explore whether these predictions held up in groups performing other tasks, in other situations, and so on. Fiedler used these findings to develop his Cognitive Resources Theory (Fiedler, 1995; Fiedler & Garcia, 1987), a leadership theory that makes very specific predictions about the relationships between a leader's intelligence, experience, a group's ability to solve problems, and the degree of stress in the situation (more about this theory can be found in Chapter 7).

As stated earlier, one of the distinct advantages of a theory is that others can design and conduct experiments that test and extend the theory. For example, Gibson (1992) conducted experiments to see what happened when both highly intelligent *and* highly experienced leaders were in charge of problem-solving groups in high- versus low-stress conditions. He found that leaders who had both of these characteristics had highly successful problem-solving groups under both high- and low-stress conditions. His findings further added to the Cognitive Resources Theory and to our collective knowledge of leadership. As stated earlier, maxims can provide useful, practical advice for being a better

The Top Five Critical-Thinking Questions Practitioners Should Ask When Reading about Leadership

1. *Who is in the sample?*

   How big is the sample?

   Is the sample representative of most leaders?

   How similar are the leaders to you?

2. *What is the situation?*

   What challenges and opportunities do the leaders face?

   If you are reading about an experiment, then how generalizable to the real world are the conditions?

   What situational factors could affect the results of the experiment?

   Is the situation similar to the one you currently face?

3. *What leadership qualities, characteristics, or behaviors are being assessed?*

   Are the right attributes being assessed?

   Are the best assessment techniques being used?

4. *How is leadership success being determined?*

   Via superiors' ratings, subordinates' ratings, or unit performance indices?

   Are the best measures being used, or would alternative measures paint a different picture?

   How might these measures be affected by factors beyond the leader's control?

5. *How do the writers link leadership assessment to success?*

   Via case studies, correlational studies, or experiments?

   Are the right conclusions being drawn?

   Are there any other plausible alternative explanations?

   Did the writers acknowledge these alternative explanations?

leader, but we gain the most useful knowledge by systematically exploring the relationships between various leader characteristics and leadership effectiveness measures and developing theories that can help explain these relationships (see Highlight 5–10).

Despite all of the advantages of conducting systematic research around the topic of leadership, there remains the question of why case studies and maxims carry so much weight among leadership practitioners. Academicians may be prompted to wonder why books such as *The 7 Habits of Highly Effective People*

(Covey, 1990), *The Female Advantage* (Helgesen, 1995), or *My American Journey* (Powell & Persico, 1995) are so popular among practitioners. Perhaps the more central question, however, is why research-based articles in leadership and management journals are not more popular themselves. One reason is probably that the very format of research articles, with their emphasis on statistical results and so forth, is fairly dull and inaccessible to anyone but university professors and graduate students. However, we also suspect that leadership researchers themselves sometimes forget that other academicians should not be their only important audience. Leadership researchers need to do a better job of making the findings from their studies more relevant and accessible to practicing managers and leaders.

Summary

Although this chapter focused on leadership research, there are several reasons it is relevant for leadership practitioners even though they are unlikely to actually conduct leadership research themselves. First, organizations can and do use a number of techniques to assess the values, personality, intelligence, and behaviors for any applicant pool. Although none of these techniques is perfect, they can help hiring managers make substantially better staffing decisions, and many organizations are using fairly sophisticated assessment techniques to improve the odds of hiring good leaders. In all likelihood most of the people applying for any type of management position will go through one or more of the assessment techniques described in this chapter.

Second, practitioners need to understand that there are multiple ways to measure success. Additionally, superiors' ratings, subordinates' ratings, and unit performance measures can many times paint different pictures about the relative success of a leader. Practitioners need to understand which of these measures are the most important to their long-term success, which are the most sensitive to their efforts, and which may be more strongly influenced by factors beyond their control.

Third, practitioners also should know that there are three methods commonly used to study the linkage between what leaders do with different success measures. Case studies have the advantage of helping practitioners better understand the context in which a leader acts. However, they usually only describe the actions of one leader in one situation, and the generalizability of their findings to the reader may be questionable. Correlational studies have the advantage of using larger sample sizes and describing the statistical relationships between the results of different assessment techniques and success measures. These studies cannot tell us much about cause-and-effect relationships, however. Leadership experiments do yield valuable information about the cause-and-effect relationships between independent and dependent variables. Thus, experiments can tell us how different leadership behaviors affect group performance, subordinates' satisfaction levels, and the like. But experiments are hard to conduct in field settings, and most laboratory experiments about leadership use college students as subjects. The generalizability of the findings for these latter experiments is always questionable.

Finally, leadership practitioners should understand the difference between maxims and theories of leadership. Maxims are personal opinions that can give leaders valuable advice about leadership. However, since they amount to little more than personal opinion, different sets of maxims sometimes give conflicting advice, and by their very nature there is no systematic way to test maxims. Theories, on the other hand, are a collection of testable predictions about the relationships between certain variables. Theories are developed based on observations, and their corresponding hypotheses are tested and refined via correlational and experimental studies. Theories are useful in that they guide research and make predictions about how different variables interact. Theories add to our collective leadership knowledge, whereas maxims do not. Because we will describe a number of different leadership theories throughout this book, practitioners need to be able to think critically about leadership theories and to determine how these theories can help them be better leaders.

Key Terms

practice-research gap	subordinates' ratings of effectiveness
competency model	unit performance indices
glass ceiling effect	case studies
structured interviews	correlational studies
unstructured interviews	correlation coefficient
observation	causal inferences
paper-and-pencil measures	experiments
in-depth managerial assessment	independent variable
in-basket exercise	dependent variable
role play simulation	maxims
assessment center	theories
résumé	hypotheses
superiors' performance ratings	

Discussion Questions

1. How do you react to the phrase *assessing leadership?* What positive and negative connotations does it have for you?

2. Some organizations are using graphology, or handwriting analysis, to make selection decisions. What do you think about this technique?

3. What are some of the measures you could use to judge a coach's performance? A teacher's? A student's? What are the advantages and disadvantages with each of these measures?

4. Given the results depicted in Table 5–1, what impact do you think research has had on hiring practices in the United States?

5. How could you design a correlational study or an experiment to test one of

Colin Powell's Rules in Highlight 5–9?

6. What is the single best thing you have ever read about leadership or being a leader? What does that book or article say about assessing leadership, measuring leadership effectiveness, methods used to study leadership, or leadership maxims and theories?

II   FOCUS ON THE LEADER

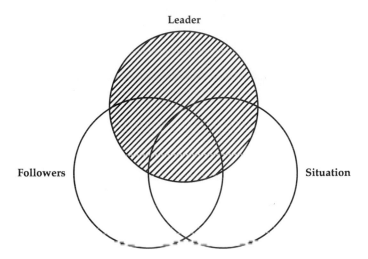

Part II focuses on the leader. The effectiveness of leadership, good or bad, is typically attributed to the leader much more than to the other elements of the framework. Sometimes the leader is the only element of leadership we even think of. One great leader's views were clear enough about the relative importance of leaders and followers:

> *Men are nothing; it is the man who is everything   It was not the Roman army that conquered Gaul, but Caesar; it was not the Carthaginian army that made Rome tremble in her gates, but Hannibal; it was not the Macedonian army that reached the Indus, but Alexander.*

Napoleon

Because the leader plays such an important role in the leadership process, the next six chapters of this book review research related to the characteristics of leaders, and what makes leaders effective. Part II begins with a chapter on power and influence since those concepts provide the most fundamental way to understand the process of leadership. Chapter 7 then looks at the closely related issues of ethics, values, and attitudes. In Chapter 8 we consider what aspects of personality are related to leadership, and in Chapter 9 we explore how leadership is affected by a leader's intelligence and creativity. Chapter 10 examines how all these preceding variables are manifested in effective or ineffective leader behavior. Part II concludes with a chapter on charisma and transformational leadership, setting the stage for Part III and its focus on the followers.

6 POWER AND INFLUENCE

Chapter Outline

Introduction

We begin this part, called "Focus on the Leader," by examining the phenomenon of power. Some of history's earliest characterizations of leaders concerned their use of power. Shakespeare's plays were concerned with the acquisition and failing of power (Hill, 1985), and Machiavelli's *The Prince* has been described as the "classic handbook on power politics" (Donno, 1966). Current scholars have also emphasized the need to conceptualize leadership as a power phenomenon (Gardner, 1986; Hinkin & Schriesheim, 1989). Power may be the single most important concept in all the social sciences (Burns, 1978), though scholars today disagree on precisely how to define power or influence. But it's not just scholars who have different ideas about power. The concept of power is so pervasive and complex that each one of us probably thinks about it a little differently (see Highlight 6–1).

What comes to *your* mind when *you* think about power? Do you think of a person wielding enormous authority over others? Do you think of high office? Do you think of making others do things against their will? Is power ethically

---

Highlight 6-1

Leadership Quotes, Chapter Six

You do not lead by hitting people over the head—that's assault, not leadership.

Dwight D. Eisenhower

He who has great power should use it lightly.

Seneca

Don't threaten. I know it's done by some of our people, but I don't go for it. If people are running scared, they're not going to make the right decisions. They'll make decisions to please the boss rather than recommend what has to be done.

Charles Pilliod

And when we think we lead, we are most led.

Lord Byron

All forms of tampering with human beings, getting at them, shaping them against their will to your own pattern, all thought control and conditioning, is, therefore, a denial of that in men which makes them men and their values ultimate.

A. A. Berle, Jr.

The true leader must submerge himself in the fountain of the people.

V. I. Lenin

Unreviewable power is the most likely to self-indulge itself and the least likely to engage in dispassionate self-analysis.

Warren E. Burger

Power in an organization is the capacity generated by relationships.

Margaret A. Wheatley

neutral, or is it inherently dangerous as Lord Acton said? ("Power corrupts, and absolute power corrupts absolutely.") Do you think a leader's real power is always obvious to others? What sorts of things might enhance or detract from a leader's power? What are the pros and cons of different ways of trying to influence people? These are the kinds of issues we will explore in this chapter.

Some Important Distinctions

Power has been defined as the capacity to produce effects on others (House, 1984), or the potential to influence others (Bass, 1990). While we usually think of power belonging to the leader, it is actually a function of the leader, the followers, and the situation. Leaders have the potential to influence their followers' behaviors and attitudes. However, followers also can affect the leader's behavior and attitudes. Even the situation itself can affect a leader's capacity to influence his followers (and vice versa). For example, leaders who can reward and punish followers may have a greater capacity to influence followers than those leaders who cannot use rewards or punishments. Similarly, follower or situational characteristics may diminish a leader's potential to influence followers, as when the latter belong to a strong, active union.

Several other aspects of power also are worth noting. Gardner (1986) made an important point about the exercise of power and its effects. He stated that "power does not need to be exercised in order to have its effect—as any hold-up man can tell you" (Gardner, 1986, p. 5). Thus, merely having the capacity to exert influence can often bring about intended effects, even though the leader may not take any action to influence his or her followers. For example, some months after the end of his term, Eisenhower was asked if leaving the White House had affected his golf game. "Yes," he replied, "a lot more people beat me now." Alternatively, power represents an inference or attribution made on the basis of an agent's observable acts of influence (Schriesheim & Hinkin, 1990). Power is never directly observed but rather attributed to others on the basis and frequency of influence tactics they use and on their outcomes.

Many people use the the terms *power, influence, and influence tactics* synonymously (Bass, 1990), but it is useful to distinguish between them. **Influence** can be defined as the change in a target agent's attitudes, values, beliefs, or behaviors as the result of influence tactics. **Influence tactics** refer to one person's actual behaviors designed to change another person's attitudes, beliefs, values, or behaviors. Although these concepts are typically examined from the leader's perspective (e.g., how a leader influences followers), we should remember that followers can also wield power and influence over leaders as well as over each other. Leadership practitioners can improve their effectiveness by reflecting on the types of power they and their followers have and the types of influence tactics that they may use or that may be used *on* them.

Whereas power is the *capacity* to cause change, influence is the degree of *actual change* in a target person's attitudes, values, beliefs, or behaviors. Influence can be measured by the behaviors or attitudes manifested by followers as the result of a leader's *influence tactics*. For example, a leader may ask a follower to accomplish a particular task, and whether or not the task is accomplished is partly a function of the leader's request. (The follower's ability and skill as well as access to the necessary equipment and resources are also important factors.) Such things as subordinates' satisfaction or motivation, group cohesiveness and climate, or unit performance indices can be used to measure the effectiveness of leaders' influence attempts. The degree to which leaders can change the level of satisfaction, motivation, or cohesiveness among followers is a function of the amount of power available to both leaders and followers. On the one hand, leaders with relatively high amounts of power can cause fairly substantial changes in subordinates' attitudes and behaviors; for example, a new and respected leader who uses rewards and punishments judiciously may cause a dramatic change in followers' perceptions about organizational climate and the amount of time followers spend on work-related behaviors. On the other hand, the amount of power followers have in work situations can also vary dramatically, and in some situations particular followers may exert relatively more influence over the rest of the group than the leader does. For example, a follower with a high level of knowledge and experience may have more influence on the attitudes, opinions, and behaviors of the rest of the followers than a brand-new leader. Thus, the amount of change in the attitudes or behaviors of the targets of influence is a function of the agent's capacity to exert influence and the targets' capacity to resist this influence.

Leaders and followers typically use a variety of tactics to influence each other's attitudes or behaviors (see Highlight 6-2 for a description of some nonverbal power cues common to humans). Influence tactics are the overt behaviors exhibited by one person to influence another. They range from emotional appeals, to the exchange of favors, to threats. The particular tactic used in a leadership situation is probably a function of the power possessed by both parties. Individuals with a relatively large amount of power may successfully employ a wider variety of influence tactics than individuals with little power. For example, a well-respected leader could make an emotional appeal, a rational appeal, a personal appeal, a legitimate request, or a threat to try to modify a follower's behavior. The follower in this situation may only be able to use ingratiation or personal appeals in order to change the leader's attitude or behavior.

At the same time, because the formal leader is not always the person who possesses the most power in a leadership situation, followers often can use a wider variety of influence tactics than the leader to modify the attitudes and behaviors of others. This would be the case if a new leader were brought into an organization in which one of his or her subordinates was extremely well liked and respected. In this situation, the subordinate may be able to make personal appeals, emotional appeals, or even threats to change the attitudes or behaviors of the leader, whereas the new leader may be limited to making only legitimate requests to change the attitudes and behaviors of the followers.

Power and Leadership

We began this chapter by noting how an understanding of power has long been seen as an integral part of leadership. Several perspectives and theories have been developed to explain the acquisition and exercise of power. In this section we will first examine various *sources* of power. Then we will look at how individuals vary in their personal *need* for power.

Sources of Leader Power

Where does a leader's power come from? Do leaders *have* it, or do followers *give* it to them? As we shall see, the answer may be both . . . and more.

Gestures of Power and Dominance

We can often get clues about relative power just by paying attention to behaviors between two people. There are a number of nonverbal cues we might want to pay attention to.

The phrase **pecking order** refers to the status differential between members of a group. It reminds us that many aspects of human social organization have roots, or at least parallels, in the behavior of other species. The animal kingdom presents diverse and fascinating examples of stylized behaviors by which one member of a species shows its relative dominance or submissiveness to another. There is adaptive significance to such behavioral mechanisms since they tend to minimize actual physical struggle and maintain a stable social order. For example, lower-ranking baboons step aside to let a higher-status male pass; they become nervous if he stares at them. The highest-status male can choose where he wants to sleep and whom he wants to mate with. Baboons "know their place." As with humans, rank has its privileges.

Our own stylized power rituals are usually so second-nature we aren't conscious of them. Yet there is a "dance" of power relations among humans just as among other animals. The following are some of the ways power is expressed nonverbally in humans.

Staring. In American society, it is disrespectful for a person of lower status to stare at a superior, though superiors are not bound by a similar restriction. Children, for example, are taught not to stare at parents. And it's an interesting comment on the power relationship between sexes that women are more likely to avert their gaze from men than vice versa.

Pointing. Children are also taught it's not nice to point. However, adults rarely correct each other for pointing because more than mere etiquette, pointing seems to be a behavior that is acceptable for high-status figures or those attempting to assert dominance. An angry boss may point an index finger accusingly at an employee; few employees who wanted to keep their jobs would respond in kind. The same restrictions apply to frowning.

Touching. Invading another person's space by touching the person without invitation is acceptable when one is of superior status but not when one is of subordinate status. It's acceptable, for example, for bosses or teachers to put a hand on an employee's or a student's shoulder, but not vice versa. The disparity also applies to socioeconomic status; someone with higher socioeconomic status is more likely to touch a person of lower socioeconomic status than vice versa.

Interrupting. Virtually all of us have interrupted others, and we have all been interrupted ourselves. Again, however, the issue is who was interrupting whom? Higher-power or -status persons interrupt; lower-power or -status persons are interrupted. A vast difference in frequency of behaviors also exists between the sexes in American society. Men interrupt much more frequently than women do.

Source: D. A. Karp and W. C. Yoels, *Symbols, Selves, and Society* (New York: Lippincott, 1979).

Something as seemingly trivial as the arrangement of furniture in an office can affect perceptions of another person's power. One vivid example comes from John Ehrlichman's (1982) book, *Witness to Power*. Ehrlichman described his first visit to J. Edgar Hoover's office at the Department of Justice. The legendary director of the FBI had long been one of the most powerful men in Washington, D.C., and as Ehrlichman's impressions reveal, Hoover took every opportunity to reinforce that image. Ehrlichman was first led through double doors into a room replete with plaques, citations, trophies, medals, and certificates jamming every wall. He was then led through a second room, similarly decorated, then into a third trophy room, and finally to a large but bare desk backed by several flags and still no J. Edgar Hoover. The guide opened a door behind the desk, and Ehrlichman went into a smaller office, which Hoover dominated from an impressive chair and desk that stood on a dais about six inches high. Erhlichman was instructed to take a seat on a lower couch, and Mr. Hoover peered down on Ehrlichman from his own loftier and intimidating place.

On a more mundane level, many people have experienced a time when they were called in to talk to a boss and left standing while the boss sat behind the desk. Probably few people in that situation misunderstand the power messages there. In addition to the factors just described, other aspects of office arrangements also can affect a leader's or follower's power. One factor is the shape of the table used for meetings. Individuals sitting at the ends of rectangular tables often wield more power, whereas circular tables facilitate communication and minimize status differentials. However, specific seating arrangements even at circular tables can affect participants' interactions; often individuals belonging to the same cliques and coalitions will sit next to each other. By sitting next to each other, members of the same coalition may exert more power as a collective group than they would sitting apart from each other. Also, having a private or more open office may not only *reflect* but also *affect* power differentials between people. Individuals with private offices can dictate to a greater degree when they want to interact with others by opening or closing their doors or by giving instructions about interruptions. Individuals with more open offices have much less power to control access to them. By being aware of dynamics like these, leaders can somewhat influence others' perceptions of their power relationship.

Prominently displaying symbols like diplomas, awards, and titles also can increase one's power. This was shown in an experiment in a college setting where a guest lecturer to several different classes was introduced in a different way to each. To one group he was introduced as a student; to other groups he was introduced as a lecturer, senior lecturer, or professor, respectively. After the presentation, when he was no longer in the room, the class estimated his height. Interestingly, the same man was perceived by different groups as increasingly taller with each increase in academic status. The "professor" was remembered as being several inches taller than the "student" (Wilson, 1968).

This finding demonstrates the generalized impact a seemingly minor matter like one's title can have on others. Another study points out more dramatically how dangerous it can be when followers are overly responsive to the *appearances* of title and authority. This study took place in a medical setting and arose from concern among medical staff that nurses were responding mechanically to doctors' orders. A researcher made telephone calls to nurses' stations on numerous different medical wards. In each, he identified himself as a hospital physician and directed the nurse answering the phone to prescribe a particular medication for a patient on that ward. Many nurses complied with the request despite the fact it was against hospital policy to transmit prescriptions by phone. Many did so despite never even having talked to the particular "physician" before the call—and despite the fact that the prescribed medication was dangerously excessive, not to mention unauthorized. In fact, 95 percent of the nurses complied with the request made by the most easily falsifiable symbol of authority, a bare title (Cialdini, 1984). (Also see Highlight 6–3.)

Even choice of clothing can affect one's power and influence. Uniforms and other specialized clothing have long been associated with authority and status, including their use by the military, police, hospital staffs, clergy, and so on. In one experiment, people walking along a city sidewalk were stopped by someone dressed either in regular clothes or in the uniform of a security guard and told this: "You see that guy over there by the meter? He's overparked but doesn't have any change. Give him a dime!" Whereas fewer than half complied when the requestor was dressed in regular clothes, over 90 percent did when he was in uniform (Bickman, 1974). This same rationale is given for having personnel in certain occupations (e.g., airline crew members) wear uniforms. Besides more easily identifying them to others, the uniforms increase the likelihood that in emergency situations their instructions will be followed. Similarly, even the presence of something as trivial as tattoos can affect the amount of power wielded in a group. One of the authors of this text had a friend named Del who was a manager in an international book-publishing company. Del was a former merchant marine whose forearms were adorned with tattoos. Del would often take off his suit coat and roll up his sleeves when meetings were not going his way, and he often exerted considerably more influence by merely exposing his tattoos to the rest of the group.

A final situational factor that can affect one's potential to influence others is the presence or absence of a crisis. Leaders usually can exert more power during a crisis than during periods of relative calm. Perhaps this is because during a crisis leaders are willing to draw on bases of power they normally forgo. For example, a leader who has developed close interpersonal relationships with followers generally uses her referent power to influence them. During crises or emergency situations, however, leaders may be more apt to draw on their legitimate and coercive bases of power to influence subordinates. That was precisely the finding in a study of bank managers' actions; the bank managers were more apt to use legitimate and coercive power during crises than during noncrisis situations (Mulder, de Jong, Koppelar, & Verhage,

The Milgram Studies

One intriguing way to understand power, influence, and influence tactics is to read a synopsis of Stanley Milgram's classic work on obedience and to think about how this work relates to the concepts and theories discussed in the present chapter. Milgram's research explored how far people will go when directed by an authority figure to do something that might injure another person. More specifically, Milgram wanted to know what happens when the dictates of authority and the dictates of one's conscience seem incompatible.

The participants were men from the communities surrounding Yale University. They were led to believe they were helping in a study concerning the effect of punishment on learning; the study's legitimacy was certainly enhanced by being conducted on the Yale campus itself. Two subjects at a time participated in the study, one as a teacher and the other as learner. The roles apparently were assigned randomly. The teacher's task was to help the learner memorize a set of word pairs by providing electric shocks whenever the learner (who would be in an adjacent room) made a mistake.

A stern experimenter described procedures and showed participants the equipment for administering punishment. This "shock generator" looked ominous, with rows of switches, lights, and warnings labeled in 15-volt increments all the way to 450 volts. Various points along the array were marked with increasingly dire warnings such as *extreme intensity* and *danger: severe*. The switch at the highest level of shock simply was marked XXX. Every time the learner made a mistake, the teacher was ordered by the experimenter to administer the next higher level of electric shock.

In actuality, there was only one true subject in the experiment—the teacher. The learner was really a confederate of the experimenter. The supposed random assignment of participants to teacher and learner conditions had been rigged in advance. The real purpose of the experiment was to assess how much electric shock the teachers would administer to the learners in the face of the latter's increasingly adamant protestations to stop. This included numerous realistic cries of agony and complaints of a heart condition, all standardized, predetermined, tape-recorded messages delivered via the intercom from the learner's to the teacher's room. If the subject (i.e., the teacher) refused to deliver any further shocks, the experimenter prodded him with comments such as "The experiment requires that you go on" and "You have no other choice; you must go on."

Before Milgram conducted his experiment, he asked mental health professionals what proportion of the subjects would administer apparently dangerous levels of shock. The consensus was that only a negligible percentage would do so, perhaps 1 or 2 percent of the population. Milgram's actual results were dramatically inconsistent with what any of the experts had predicted. Fully 70 percent of the subjects carried through with their orders, albeit sometimes with great personal anguish, and delivered the maximum shock possible—450 volts!

Source: S. Milgram, "Behavioral Study of Obedience;" *Journal of Abnormal and Social Psychology* 67 (1963), pp. 371–78.

Figure 6–1

*Sources of
Leader Power in
the Leader-
Follower-
Situation
Framework*

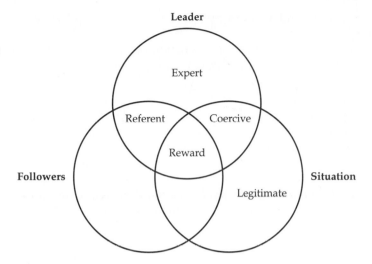

1986). This same phenomenon is observable in many dramatizations. In the television series "Star Trek, the Next Generation," for example, Captain Picard normally uses his referent and expert power to influence subordinates. During emergencies, however, he will often rely on his legitimate and coercive power. Another factor may be that during crises followers are more willing to accept greater direction, control, and structure from leaders, whatever power base may be involved.

A Taxonomy of Social Power.   French and Raven (1959) identified five sources, or bases, of power by which an individual can potentially influence others. As seen in Figure 6–1, these five sources include one that is primarily a function of the leader; one that is a function of the relationship between leaders and followers; one that is primarily a function of the leader and the situation; one that is primarily a function of the situation; and finally, one that involves aspects of all three elements. Understanding these bases of power can give leadership practitioners greater insight about the predictable effects—positive or negative—of various sorts of influence attempts. Following is a more detailed discussion of French and Raven's (1959) five bases of social power.

Expert Power.   Expert power is the power of knowledge. Some people are able to influence others through their relative expertise in particular areas. A surgeon may wield considerable influence in a hospital because others depend on her knowledge, skill, and judgment, even though she may not have any formal authority over them. A mechanic may be influential among his peers because he is widely recognized as the best in the city. A longtime employee may be influential because his corporate memory provides a useful historical perspective to newer personnel. Legislators who are expert in the intricacies of parliamentary procedure, athletes who have played in championship games, and soldiers who have been in combat before are valued for the lessons learned and wisdom they can share with others.

Because expert power is a function of the amount of knowledge one possesses relative to the rest of the members of the group, it is possible for followers to have considerably more expert power than leaders in certain situations. For example, new leaders often possess less knowledge of the jobs and tasks performed in a particular work unit than the followers do, and in this case the followers can potentially wield considerable influence when decisions are made regarding work procedures, new equipment, or the hiring of additional workers. Probably the best advice for leaders in this situation is to ask a lot of questions and perhaps seek additional training to help fill this knowledge gap. So long as different followers have considerably greater amounts of expert power, it will be difficult for a leader to influence the work unit on the basis of expert power alone.

Referent Power. One way to counteract the problems stemming from a lack of expertise is to build strong interpersonal ties with subordinates. Referent power refers to the potential influence one has due to the strength of the relationship between the leader and the followers. When people admire a leader and see her as a role model, we say she has referent power. For example, students may respond positively to advice or requests from teachers who are well liked and respected, while the same students might be unresponsive to less-popular teachers. This relative degree of responsiveness is primarily a function of the strength of the relationship between the students and the different teachers. We knew one young lieutenant who had enormous referent power with the military security guards working for him due to his selfless concern for them, evident in such habits as bringing them hot chocolate and homemade cookies on their late-night shifts. The guards, sometimes taken for granted by other superiors, understood and valued the extra effort and sacrifice this young supervisor put forth for them. When Buddy Ryan was fired as head coach of the Philadelphia Eagles football team, many of the players expressed fierce loyalty to him. One said, "We'd do things for Buddy that we wouldn't do for another coach. I'd sell my body for Buddy" (Associated Press, January 9, 1991). That is referent power.

Another way to look at referent power is in terms of the role friendships play in making things happen. It is frequently said, for example, that many people get jobs based on who they know, not what they know. The fact is, there is some truth to that. But we think the best perspective on this issue was offered by David Campbell, who said, "It's not who you know that counts. It's what who you know *knows about you* that counts!" (personal communication).

Referent power often takes time to develop. Furthermore, it can have a downside in that a desire to *maintain* referent power may limit a leader's actions in particular situations. For example, a leader who has developed a strong relationship with a follower may be reluctant to discipline the follower for poor work or chronic tardiness, as these actions could disrupt the nature of the relationship between the leader and the follower. Thus, referent power is a two-way street; the stronger the relationship, the more influence leaders and followers exert over each other. Moreover, just as it is possible for leaders to develop strong relationships with followers and, in turn, acquire more referent power, it is also possible for followers to develop strong relationships with other followers and acquire more referent power. Followers with relatively more referent power than their peers are often the spokespersons for their work units and generally have more latitude to deviate from work-unit norms. Followers with little referent power have little opportunity to deviate from group norms. For example, in an episode of the television show "The Simpsons," Homer Simpson was fired for wearing a pink shirt to work (everybody else at the Springfield nuclear power plant had always worn white shirts). Homer was fired partly because he "was not popular enough to be different."

Legitimate Power.   Legitimate power depends on a person's organizational role. It can be thought of as one's formal or official authority. Some people make things happen because they have the power or authority to do so. The boss can assign projects; the coach can decide who plays; the colonel can order compliance with uniform standards; the teacher assigns the homework and awards the grades. Individuals with legitimate power exert influence through requests or demands deemed appropriate by virtue of their role and position. In other words, legitimate power means a leader has authority because he or she has been assigned a particular role in an organization (and the leader has this authority only as long as he or she occupies that position and operates within the proper bounds of that role).

It is important to note that legitimate authority and leadership are not the same thing. Holding a position and being a leader are not synonymous, despite the relatively common practice of calling position holders in bureaucracies the leaders. The head of an organization may be a true leader, but he also may not be. Effective leaders often intuitively realize they need more than legitimate power to be successful. Before he became president, Dwight Eisenhower commanded all Allied troops in Europe during World War II. In a meeting with his staff before the Normandy invasion, Eisenhower pulled a string across a table to make a point about leadership. He was demonstrating that just as you can pull a string, not push it, officers must lead soldiers and not push them from the rear.

It is also possible for followers to use their legitimate power to influence leaders. In these cases, followers can actively resist a leader's influence attempt by only doing work specifically prescribed in job descriptions, bureaucratic rules, or union policies. For example, many organizations have job descriptions that limit both the time spent at work and the types of tasks and activities performed. Similarly, bureaucratic rules and union policies can be invoked by followers to resist a leader's influence attempts. Often the leader will need to change the nature of his or her request or find another way to resolve the problem if these rules and policies are invoked by followers. If this is the case, then the followers will have successfully used legitimate power to influence their leader.

Reward Power.   Reward power involves the potential to influence others due to one's control over desired resources. This can include the power to give raises, bonuses, and promotions; to grant tenure; to select people for special assignments or desirable activities; to distribute desired resources like computers, offices, parking places, or travel money; to intercede positively on another's behalf; to recognize with awards and praise; and so on. Many corporations use rewards extensively to motivate employees. At McDonald's, for example, there is great status accorded the All-American Hamburger Maker, the cook who makes the fastest, highest-quality hamburgers in the country. At individual fast-food restaurants, managers may reward salespersons who handle the most customers during rush periods. Tupperware holds rallies for its salespeople. Almost everyone wins something, ranging from pins and badges to lucrative prizes for top performers (Peters & Waterman, 1982). Schools pick teachers of the year and professional athletes are rewarded by selection to all-star teams for their superior performance.

The potential to influence others through the ability to administer rewards is a joint function of the leader, the followers, and the situation. Leaders vary considerably in the types and frequency in which they mete out rewards, but the position they fill also helps to determine the frequency and types of rewards administered. For example, employees of the month at Kentucky Fried Chicken are not given new cars; the managers of these franchises do not have the resources to offer such awards. Similarly, leaders in other organizations are limited to some extent in the types of and frequency with which they can administer awards. Nevertheless, leadership practitioners can enhance their reward power by spending some time reflecting on the followers and the situation. Often a number of alternative or innovative rewards can be created, and these rewards, along with ample doses of praise, can help a leader overcome the constraints his or her position puts on reward power.

Although using the power to administer rewards can be an effective way to change the attitudes and behaviors of others, there are several situations where a leader's use of reward power can be problematic. For example, the perception that a company's monetary bonus policy is handled equitably may be as important in motivating good work (or avoiding morale problems) as the amount of the bonus itself. Moreover, a superior may mistakenly assume that a particular reward is valued when it is not. This would be the case if a particular subordinate were publicly recognized for her good work when she actually dislikes public recognition. Leadership practitioners can avoid the latter problem by developing good relationships with subordinates and administering rewards that they, not the leader, value. Another potential problem with reward power is that it may produce compliance but not other desirable outcomes like commitment (Yukl, 1989). In other words, subordinates may perform only at the level necessary to receive a reward and may not be willing to put forth the extra effort needed to make the organization better. An overemphasis on rewards as payoff for performance may also lead to resentment and feelings by workers of being manipulated, especially if it occurs in the context of relatively cold and

Reprinted with special permission of King Features Syndicate

distant superior-subordinate relationships. Extrinsic rewards like praise, compensation, promotion, privileges, and time off may not have the same effects on behavior as intrinsic rewards such as feelings of accomplishment, personal growth, and development. There is evidence that under some conditions extrinsic rewards can decrease intrinsic motivation toward a task and make the desired behavior less likely to persist when extrinsic rewards are not available (Deci, 1972; Ryan, Mims, & Koestner, 1983). Overemphasis on extrinsic rewards may instill an essentially contractual or economic relationship between superiors and subordinates, diluting important aspects of the relationship like mutual loyalty or shared commitment to higher ideals (Wakin, 1981).

All these cautions about reward power should not cloud its usefulness and effectiveness, which is very real. As noted previously, top organizations make extensive use of both tangible and symbolic rewards in motivating their workers. Furthermore, some of the most important rewards are readily available to all leaders—sincere praise and thanks to others for their loyalty and work. The bottom line is that leadership practitioners can enhance their ability to influence others based on reward power if they (*a*) determine what rewards are available, (*b*) determine what rewards are valued by their subordinates, and (*c*) establish clear policies for the equitable and consistent administration of rewards for good performance.

Finally, because reward power is partly determined by one's position in the organization, some people may believe followers have little, if any, reward power. This may not be the case. If followers have control over scarce resources, then they may use the administration of these resources as a way of getting leaders to act in the manner they want. Moreover, followers may reward their leader by putting out a high level of effort when they feel their leader is doing a good job, and they may put forth less effort when they feel their leader is doing a poor job. By modifying their level of effort, followers may in turn modify a leader's attitudes and behaviors. And when followers compliment their leader (e.g., for running a constructive meeting), it is no less an example of reward power than when a leader compliments a follower. Thus, leadership practitioners should be aware that followers can also use reward power to influence leaders.

Coercive Power.   Coercive power, the opposite of reward power, is the potential to influence others through the administration of negative sanctions or the removal of positive events. In other words, it is the ability to control others through the fear of punishment or the loss of valued outcomes. Like reward power, coercive power is partly a function of the leader, but the situation often limits the coercive actions a leader can take. Examples of coercive power include policemen giving tickets for speeding, the army court-martialing AWOL soldiers, a teacher detaining disruptive students after school, employers firing lazy workers, and parents spanking children (Klein, 1991). Even presidents resort to their coercive powers. Historian Arthur Schlesinger, Jr., for example, described Lyndon Johnson as having a "devastating instinct for the weaknesses of others." Lyndon Johnson was familiar and comfortable with the use of coercion; he once told a White House staff member, "Just you remember this. There's only two kinds at the White House. There's elephants and there's ants. And I'm the only elephant" (Barnes, 1989).

Coercive power, like reward power, can be used appropriately or inappropriately. It is carried to its extreme in harsh and repressive totalitarian societies. One of the most tragic instances of coercive power was in the cult led by Jim Jones, which tragically and unbelievably self-exterminated in an incident known as the Jonestown massacre (Conway & Siegelman, 1979). Virtually all of the 912 who died there drank, at Jones's direction, from large vats of a flavored drink containing cyanide. The submissiveness and suicidal obedience of Jones's followers during the massacre were due largely to the long history of rule by fear Jones had practiced. For example, teenagers caught holding hands were beaten, and adults judged slacking in their work were forced to box for hours in marathon public matches against as many as three or four bigger and stronger opponents. Jim Jones ruled by fear, and his followers became self-destructively compliant.

Perhaps the preceding example is so extreme that we can dismiss its relevance to our own lives and leadership activities. On the other hand, it does provide a dramatic reminder that reliance on coercive power has inherent limitations and drawbacks. This is not to say the willingness to use disciplinary sanctions is never necessary. Sometimes it is. Informal coercion, as opposed to the threat of formal punishment, can also be used to change the attitudes and behaviors of others. Informal coercion is usually expressed implicitly, and often nonverbally, rather than explicitly. It may be the pressure employees feel to donate to the boss's favorite charity, or it may be his glare when they bring up an unpopular idea. One of the most common forms of coercion is simply a superior's temperamental outbursts. The intimidation caused by a leader's poorly controlled anger is usually, in its long-term effects, a dysfunctional style of behavior for leaders.

It is also possible for followers to use coercive power to influence their leader's behavior. For example, a leader may be hesitant to take disciplinary action against a large, emotionally unstable follower. Followers can threaten leaders with physical assaults, industrial sabotage, or work slowdowns and strikes, and these threats can serve to modify a leader's behavior. In all likelihood, followers will be more likely to use coercive power to change their leader's behavior if they have a relatively high amount of referent power with their fellow co-workers. This may be particularly true if threats of work slowdowns or strikes are used to influence a leader's behavior.

Concluding Thoughts about French and Raven's Power Taxonomy.   Based on all this, can we reach any conclusions about what base of power is best for a leader to use? As you might have anticipated, we must say that's an unanswerable question without knowing more facts about a particular situation. For example, consider the single factor of whether or not a group is facing a crisis. This might affect the leader's exercise of power simply because leaders usually can exert *more* power during crises than during periods of relative calm. Perhaps this is because during a crisis leaders are willing to draw on bases of power they normally forgo. For example, a leader who has developed close interpersonal relationships with followers generally uses her referent power to influence them, but during crises or emergency situations leaders may be more apt to draw on their legitimate and coercive bases of power to influence subordinates. That was precisely the finding in a study of bank managers' actions; the bank managers were more apt to use legitimate and coercive power during crises than during noncrisis situations (Mulder, de Jong, Koppelar, & Verhage, 1986). Furthermore, it may be that during crises followers are more *eager* to receive direction and control from leaders.

But can't we make *any* generalizations about using various sources of power? Actually, there has been considerable research looking at French and Raven's ideas, and generally the findings indicate that leaders who relied primarily on referent and expert power had subordinates who were more motivated and satisfied, were absent less, and performed better (Yukl, 1981). However, Yukl (1981) and Podsakoff and Schriesheim (1985) have criticized these findings, and much of their criticism centers on the instrument used to assess a leader's bases of power. Recently, Hinkin and Schriesheim (1989) have developed an instrument that overcomes many of the criticisms, and future research should more clearly delineate the relationship between the five bases of power and various leadership effectiveness criteria.

Even though much of the research to date about the five bases of power may be flawed, four generalizations about power and influence still seem warranted. First, effective leaders typically take advantage of *all* their sources of power. Effective leaders understand the relative advantages and disadvantages of different sources of power, and they selectively emphasize one or another depending on their particular objectives in a given situation. Second, whereas leaders in well-functioning organizations have strong influence over their subordinates, *they are also open to being influenced by them*. High degrees of reciprocal influence between leaders and followers characterize the most effective organizations (Yukl, 1989). Third, leaders vary in the extent to which they share power with subordinates. Some leaders seem to view their power as a fixed resource that, when shared with others (like cutting a pie into pieces), reduces their own portion. They see power in zero-sum terms. Other leaders see power as an expandable pie. They see the possibility of increasing a subordinate's power without reducing their own. Needless to say, which view a leader subscribes to can have a major impact on the leader's support for power-sharing activities like delegation and participative management. A leader's support for power-sharing activities (or, in today's popular language, *empowerment*) is also affected by the practice of holding leaders responsible for subordinates' decisions and actions as well as their own. It is, after all, the coach or manager who often gets fired when the team loses (Hollander & Offermann, 1990; Pfeffer, 1977). Fourth, effective leaders generally work to *increase* their various power bases (i.e., whether expert, referent, reward, or

---
Highlight 6–4

The Limits of Power

A humorous story is told of the Jimmy Carter's presidency which illustrates that even the most powerful individual in the world may face limits to his power.

This incident involved a mouse that had died after it had gotten inside a wall of the Oval Office. The dead mouse's odor became intolerable just about the time President Carter was about to greet a foreign dignitary. A hurried call was made to the General Service Administration (which oversees federal property), but the agency refused to act; it insisted it already had exterminated all the mice in the White House. GSA officials argued that the dead mouse must have entered from *outside* the White House, and therefore was actually the responsibility of the Department of the Interior. Officials at the Department of the Interior, however, were unwilling to provide any assistance arguing that the mouse was now *inside* the White House. Exasperated that the president of the United States could not get a dead mouse removed from the White House, Carter demanded to see officials from both agencies in his office. Facing them both in a room where world-changing decisions are made, he complained, "I can't even get a damn mouse out of my office. . . ." A special task force including personnel from both agencies was created to solve the problem.

legitimate) or become more willing to *use* their coercive power. As Highlight 6–4 humorously points out, however, even that is not always enough.

Leader Motives

Thus far we have been looking at how different *sources* of power can affect others, but that's only one perspective. Another way of looking at the relationship between power and leadership involves focusing on the individual leader's personality. We will look most closely at the role personality plays in leadership in an upcoming chapter, but it will be nonetheless useful now to briefly examine how all people (including leaders) vary in their personal motivation to have or wield power.

People vary in their motivation to influence or control others. McClelland (1975) called this the **need for power**, and individuals with a high need for power derive psychological satisfaction from influencing others. They seek positions where they can influence others, and they are often involved concurrently in influencing people in many different organizations or decision-making bodies. In such activities they readily offer ideas, suggestions, and opinions, and also seek information they can use in influencing others. They are often astute at building trusting relationships and assessing power networks, though they can also be quite outspoken and forceful. They value the tangible signs of their authority and status as well as the more intangible indications of others' defer-ence to them. Two different ways of expressing the need for power have been identified: **personalized power** and **socialized power**. Individuals who have a high need for personalized power are relatively selfish, impulsive, uninhibited, and lacking in self-control. These individuals exercise power for their own self-centered needs, not for the good of the group or the organization. Socialized power, on the other hand, implies a more emotionally mature expression of the motive. Socialized power is exercised in the service of higher goals to others or organizations and often involves self-sacrifice toward those ends. It often involves an empowering, rather than an autocratic, style of management and leadership.

Although the need for power has been measured using questionnaires and more traditional personality inventories, McClelland and his associates have used the Thematic Apperception Test (TAT) to assess need for power. The TAT is a **projective personality** test consisting of pictures such as a woman staring out a window or a boy holding a violin. Subjects are asked to make up a story about each picture, and the stories are then interpreted in terms of the strengths of various needs imputed to the characters, one of which is the need for power. Since the pictures are somewhat ambiguous, the sorts of needs projected onto the characters are presumed to reflect needs (perhaps at an unconscious level) of the storyteller. Stories concerned with influencing or controlling others would receive high scores for the need for power.

The need for power has been found to be positively related to various lead-ership effectiveness criteria. For example, McClelland and Boyatzis (1982) found the need for power to be positively related to success for nontechnical managers at AT&T, and Stahl (1983) found that the need for power was positively related to managers' performance ratings and promotion rates. In addition, Fodor (1987) reported that small groups of ROTC students were more likely to suc-cessfully solve a subarctic survival situation if their leader had a strong need for power. Although these findings appear promising, several cautions should be kept in mind. First, McClelland and Boyatzis (1982) also reported that the need for power was unrelated to the success of technical managers at AT&T. Apparently, the level of knowledge (i.e., expert power) played a more important role in the success of the technical managers versus the nontechnical managers. Second, McClelland (1985) concluded that although some need for power was necessary for leadership potential, successful leaders also have the ability to inhibit their manifestation of this need. Leaders who are relatively uninhibited in their need for power will act like a dictator; such individuals use power impulsively, to manipulate or control others, or to achieve at another's expense. Leaders with a high need for power but low activity inhibition may be success-ful in the short term, but their followers, as well as the remainder of the organi-zation, may pay high costs for this success. Some of these costs may include perceptions by fellow members of the organization that they are untrustworthy, uncooperative, overly competitive, and looking out primarily for themselves. Finally, it may be worth pointing out that some followers have a high need for power too. This can lead to tension between leader and follower when a follower with a high need for power is directed to do something.

Individuals vary in their motivation to manage, just as in their need for power. Miner (1974) described **motivation to manage** in terms of six composites:

- Maintaining good relationships with authority figures.
- Wanting to compete for recognition and advancement.
- Being active and assertive.
- Wanting to exercise influence over subordinates.
- Being visibly different from followers.
- Being willing to do routine administrative tasks.

Like McClelland, Miner also used a projective test to measure a person's motivation to manage. Miner's Sentence Completion Scale (MSCS) consists of a series of incomplete sentences dealing with the six components described above (e.g., "My relationship with my boss . . ."). Respondents are asked to complete the sentences, which are then scored according to established criteria. The overall composite MSCS score (though not component scores) has consistently been found to predict leadership success in hierarchical or bureaucratic organizations (Miner, 1978). Thus, individuals who maintained respect for authority figures, wanted to be recognized, acted assertively, actively influenced subordinates, maintained "psychological distance" between themselves and their followers, and readily took on routine administrative tasks were more apt to be successful in bureaucratic organizations. However, Miner also claimed that different qualities were needed in flatter, nonbureaucratic organizations, and his (1978) review of the MSCS supports this view. We might wonder how much continuing trends in downsizing, decentralization, and the like may further reduce the relevance of this particular individual difference variable.

Findings concerning both the need for power and the motivation to manage have several implications for leadership practitioners. First, not all individuals like being leaders. One reason may be that some have a relatively low need for power or motivation to manage. Because these scores are relatively stable and fairly difficult to change, leaders who do not enjoy their role may want to seek positions where they have fewer supervisory responsibilities.

Second, a high need for power or motivation to manage does not guarantee leadership success. The situation can play a crucial role in determining whether the need for power or the motivation to manage is related to leadership success. For example, McClelland and Boyatzis (1982) found the need for power to be related to leadership success for nontechnical managers only, and Miner (1978) found motivation to manage was related to leadership success only in hierarchical or bureaucratic organizations.

Third, in order to be successful in the long term, leaders may have to have both a high need for socialized power and a high level of activity inhibition. Leaders who impulsively exercise power merely to satisfy their own selfish needs will probably be ineffective in the long term. Finally, it is important to remember that followers, as well as leaders, differ in the need for power, activity inhibition, and motivation to manage. Certain followers may have stronger needs or motives in this area. Leaders may need to behave differently toward these followers than they might toward followers having a low need for power or motivation to manage.

Influence Tactics

Whereas power is the capacity or potential to influence others, influence tactics are the actual behaviors used by an agent to change the attitudes, opinions, or behaviors of a target person. Kipnis and his associates accomplished much of the early work on the types of influence tactics one person uses to influence another (Kipnis & Schmidt, 1982). Various instruments have been developed to study influence tactics, but the Influence Behavior Questionnaire, or IBQ (Yukl, Lepsinger, & Lucia, 1992), seems to be the most promising. Here is a detailed discussion of the different influence tactics assessed by the IBQ.

Types of Influence Tactics

The IBQ is designed to assess nine types of influence tactics, and its scales provide us with a convenient overview of various methods of influencing others. **Rational persuasion** occurs when an agent uses logical arguments or factual evidence to influence others. An example of rational persuasion would be when a politician's advisor explains how demographic changes in the politician's district make it important for the politician to spend relatively more time in the district seeing constituents than she has needed to in the recent past. Agents make **inspirational appeals** when they make a request or proposal designed to arouse enthusiasm or emotions in targets. An example here might be when a minister makes an impassioned plea to members of his congregation about the good works which could be accomplished if a proposed addition to the church were built. **Consultation** occurs when agents ask targets to participate in planning an activity. An example of consultation would be if the minister in the preceding example established a committee of church members to help plan the layout and uses of that new church addition. In this case the consultative work might not only lead to a better building plan but also *strengthen member commitment* to the very idea of a new addition. **Ingratiation** occurs when the agent attempts to get you in a good mood before making a request. A familiar example here would be a salesperson's good natured or flattering banter with you before you make a decision about purchasing a product. Agents use **personal appeals** when they ask another to do a favor out of friendship. A sentence that opens with, "Bill, we've known each other a long time and I've never asked anything of you before" represents the beginning of a personal appeal, whereas influencing a target through the exchange of favors is labeled **exchange.** If two politicians agree to vote for each other's pet legislation despite minor misgivings about each other's bills, that is exchange.

Coalition tactics are different from consultation in that they are used when agents seek the aid or support of others to influence the target. A dramatic example of coalition tactics occurs when several key significant people in an alcoholic's life (e.g., spouse, children, employer, neighbor) agree to confront the alcoholic in unison about the many dimensions of his problem. Threats or persistent reminders used to influence targets are known as **pressure tactics.** A judge who gives a convicted prisoner a suspended sentence but tells him to consider the suspension a "sword hanging over your head" if he breaks the law again is using pressure tactics. Finally, **legitimizing tactics** occur when agents make requests based on their position or authority. A principal may ask a teacher to be on the school's curriculum committee, and the teacher may accede to the request despite reservations just because it is the principal's prerogative to appoint any teacher to that role. In practice, of course, actual tactics often reflect combinations of these different approaches. Rarely, for example, is an effective appeal purely inspirational, without any rational elements at all.

Influence Tactics and Power

As alluded to throughout this chapter, a strong relationship exists between the relative power of agents and targets and the types of influence tactics used. Because leaders with relatively high amounts of referent power have built up close relationships with followers, they may be more able to use a wide variety of influence tactics to modify the attitudes and behaviors of their followers. For example, leaders with a lot of referent power could use inspirational appeals, consultations, ingratiation, personal appeals, exchanges, and even coalition tactics to increase the amount of time a particular follower spends doing work-related activities. Note, however, that leaders with high referent power generally do not use legitimizing or pressure tactics to influence followers since by threatening followers, leaders risk some loss of referent power. Leaders who have only coercive or legitimate power may be able to use only coalition, legitimizing, or pressure tactics to influence followers.

Other factors also can affect the choice of influence tactics (Kipnis & Schmidt, 1985). People typically use hard tactics (i.e., legitimizing or pressure tactics) when an influencer has the upper hand, when she anticipates resistance, or when the other person's behavior violates important norms. People typically use soft tactics (e.g., ingratiation) when they are at a disadvantage, when they expect resistance, or when they will personally benefit if the attempt is successful. People typically use rational tactics (i.e., the exchange and rational appeal) when parties are relatively equal in power, when resistance is not anticipated, and when the benefits are organizational as well as personal.

Other studies, too, have shown that influence attempts based on factual, logical analyses are the most frequently reported method by which middle managers exert lateral influence (Keys, Case, Miller, Curran, & Jones, 1987) and upward influence (Case, Dosier, Murkison, & Keys, 1988). Other important components of successful influence of one's superiors include thoroughly preparing beforehand, involving others for support (i.e., coalition tactics), and persisting through a combination of approaches (Case, Dosier, Murkison, & Keys, 1988).

Findings about who uses different tactics, and when, provide interesting insights into the influence process. It is clear that one's influence tactic of choice depends on many factors, including intended outcomes and one's power relative to the target person. Whereas it may not be very surprising that people select influence tactics as a function of their power relationship with another person, it is striking that the relationship holds true so universally across different social domains. The relationship holds true for business executives, for parents and children, and for spouses. There is a strong tendency for people to resort to hard tactics whenever they have an advantage in clout if other tactics fail to get results (Kipnis & Schmidt, 1985). As the bank robber Willie Sutton once said, "A gun and a smile are more effective than a smile by itself." This sentiment is apparently familiar to bank managers, too. The latter reported greater satisfaction in handling subordinates' poor performance when they were relatively more punishing (Green, Fairhurst, & Snavely, 1986). Highlight 6-5 offers thoughts on how men and women managers sometimes use different techniques in "managing upward."

Although hard tactics can be effective, relying on them can change the way we see others. This was demonstrated in an experiment wherein leaders' perceptions and evaluations of subordinates were assessed after they exercised different sorts of authority over the subordinates (Kipnis, 1984). Several hundred business students acted as managers of small work groups assembling model cars. Some of the students were told to act in an authoritarian manner, exercising complete control over the group's work; others were told to act as democratic leaders, letting group members participate fully in decisions about the work. As expected, authoritarian leaders used more hard tactics, whereas democratic leaders influenced subordinates more through rational methods. More interesting was the finding that subordinates were evaluated by the two types of leaders in dramatically different ways even though the subordinates of both types did equally good work. Authoritarian leaders judged their subordinates as less motivated, less skilled, and less suited for promotion. Apparently, bosses who use hard tactics to control others' behavior tend not to attribute any resultant good performance to the subordinates themselves. Ironically, the act of using hard tactics leads to negative attributions about others, which, in turn, tend to corroborate the use of hard tactics in the first place.

Finally, we should remember that using influence tactics can be thought of as a social skill. Choosing the right tactic to use may not always be enough to ensure good results; the behavior must be *skillfully executed*. We are not encouraging deviousness or a manipulative attitude toward others, merely recognizing the obvious fact that clumsy attempts to influence do, in fact, often come across as phoney. They may be counterproductive in the end. See Highlight 6-6 for some interesting ways skills are applied in the political arena.

Highlight 6–5

Gender Differences in Managing Upward: How Male and Female Managers Get Their Way

Both male and female managers in a Fortune 100 company were interviewed and completed surveys about how they influence upward—how they influence their own bosses. The results generally supported the idea that female managers' influence attempts showed greater concern for others, while male managers' influence attempts showed greater concern for self. Female managers were more likely to act with the organization's broad interests in mind, consider how others felt about the influence attempt, involve others in planning, and focus on both the task and interpersonal aspects of the situation. Male managers, on the other hand, were more likely to act out of self-interest, show less consideration for how others might feel about the influence attempt, work alone in developing their strategy, and focus primarily on the task alone.

One of the most surprising findings of the study was that, contrary to prediction, female managers were less likely than male managers to compromise or negotiate during their influence attempts. The female managers were actually more likely to persist in trying to persuade their superiors, even to the point of open opposition. At first this may seem inconsistent with the idea that the female managers' influence style involved greater concern for their relatedness to others. However, it does seem consistent with the higher value placed by the women managers on involvement. Perhaps female managers demonstrate more commitment to their issue, and greater self-confidence that they are doing the "right thing," precisely because they have interacted with others in the organization more already and know they have others' support.

While male and female managers emphasized different influence techniques, it is important to note neither group overall was more effective than the other. Nonetheless, there may be significant implications of the various techniques for a manager's career advancement. At increasingly higher management levels in an organization, effectiveness may be defined primarily by its fit with the organization's own norms and values. Managers whose style matches most closely that of their superior's may have an advantage in evaluations and promotion decisions. This may be a significant factor for women, given the highly skewed representation of males in the most senior executive ranks.

Source: K. E. Lauterbach and B. J. Weiner, "Dynamics of Upward Influence: How Male and Female Managers Get Their Way," *Leadership Quarterly* 7, no. 1 (1996), pp. 87–107.

A Concluding Thought about Influence Tactics.   In the above discussion, an implicit lesson for leaders is the value of being conscious of what influence tactics one uses and what effects are typically associated with each tactic. Knowledge of such effects can help a leader make better decisions about her

---

Highlight 6–6

To Be or Not to Be . . . a Porcupine

We said before that there are no simple recipes for leadership. This is perfectly evident in the various ways power and influence are exercised in the halls of Congress. In *The Power Game*, author Hedrick Smith offers numerous examples of how Washington, D.C., actually works. For example, it is true that interpersonal relationships play a key part in one's effectiveness, but there are many paths to interpersonal power and influence in government, as the following anecdotes point out.

Barney Frank, a Democratic congressman from Massachusetts, likens success in the House of Representatives to high school. Nobody in the House can give any other member an order, not even the Speaker of the House. Neither can anyone be fired except by their own constituencies. That means, therefore, that those in Congress become influential by persuading people and having others respect but not resent you. In that sense it's like high school.

Sometimes, however, it may pay to be *unlikable*, at least in some situations. Former senator (and later secretary of state) Ed Muskie had a reputation for being a "porcupine," for being difficult in the conference committees where final versions of legislation were hammered out. A former staff member said Muskie was the best porcupine of them all because nobody wanted to tangle with him. Muskie will "be gross. He'll smoke a god-awful cigar. He'll just be difficult, cantankerous." One of the reasons Muskie was so successful as a legislator was precisely because he could be nearly impossible to deal with. People would rather ignore him, try to avoid fights or confrontations with his notorious temper. Muskie knew how to be a porcupine, and he used that behavior to advantage in authoring critical legislation.

Source: H. Smith, The Power Game (New York: Random House, 1988).

---

manner of influencing others. It might also be helpful for leaders to think more carefully about why they believe a particular influence tactic might be effective. Research indicates that some reasons for selecting among various possible influence tactics lead to successful outcomes more frequently than others. More specifically, thinking an act would improve an employee's self-esteem or morale was frequently associated with successful influence attempts. On the other hand, choosing an influence tactic because it followed company policy and choosing one because it was a way to put a subordinate in his place were frequently mentioned as reasons for unsuccessful influence attempts (Dosier, Case, & Keys, 1988). In a nutshell, these results suggest that leaders should pay attention not only to the actual influence tactics they use—to *how* they are influencing others—but also to *why* they believe such methods are called for. It is perhaps an obvious but nonetheless important conclusion to reach from these results that influence efforts intended to build others up more frequently lead to positive outcomes than influence efforts intended to put others down.

Summary

This chapter has defined power as the capacity or potential to exert influence, influence tactics as the behaviors used by one person to modify the attitudes and behaviors of another, and influence as the degree of change in a person's attitudes, values, or behaviors as the result of another's influence tactic. Because power, influence, and influence tactics play such an important role in the leadership process, this chapter provides ideas to help leaders improve their effectiveness. By reflecting on their different bases of power, leaders may better understand how they can affect followers and even expand their power. The five bases of power also offer clues as to why subordinates are able to influence leaders and successfully resist leaders' influence attempts.

Leaders also may gain insight into why they may not enjoy certain aspects of their responsibilities by reflecting on their own need for power or motivation to manage; they may also better understand why some leaders exercise power selfishly by considering McClelland's concepts of personalized power and activity inhibition. Leaders can improve their effectiveness by finding ways to enhance their idiosyncratic credit and not permitting in-group and out-group rivalries to develop in the work unit.

Although power is an extremely important concept, having power is relatively meaningless unless a leader is willing to exercise it. The exercise of power occurs primarily through the influence tactics leaders and followers use to modify the attitudes and behaviors of each other. The type of influence tactics used seems to depend on the amount of different types of power possessed, the degree of resistance expected, and the rationale behind the different influence tactics. Because influence tactics designed to build up others are generally more successful than those that tear down others, leadership practitioners should always consider why they are using a particular influence attempt before they actually use it. By carefully considering the rationale behind the tactic, leaders may be able to avoid using pressure and legitimizing tactics and to find ways to influence followers that build them up rather than tear them down. Being able to use influence tactics that modify followers' attitudes and behaviors in the desired direction at the same time they build up followers' self-esteem and self-confidence should be a skill all leaders strive to master.

Key Terms and Concepts

power	need for power
influence	personalized power
influence tactics	socialized power
expert power	projective personality test
referent power	motivation to manage
legitimate power	legitimizing tactics
reward power	pecking order
coercive power	rational persuasion

inspirational appeals
consultation
ingratiation
personal appeals

exchange
coalition tactics
pressure tactics

Discussion Questions

1. The following questions all pertain to the Milgram studies (Highlight 6-3):

   a. What bases of power were available to the experimenter, and what bases of power were available to the subjects?

   b. Do you think subjects with a low need for power would act differently from those subjects with a high need for power? What about subjects with differing levels of the motivation to manage?

   c. What situational factors contributed to the experimenter's power?

   d. What influence tactics did the experimenter use to change the behavior of the subjects, and how were these tactics related to the experimenter's power base?

   e. What actually was influenced? In other words, if influence is the change in another's attitudes, values, or behaviors as the result of an influence tactic, then what changes occurred in the subject as the result of the experimenter's influence tactics?

   f. Many people have criticized the Milgram study on ethical grounds. Assuming that some socially useful information was gained from the studies, do you believe this experiment could or should be replicated today?

2. Some definitions of leadership exclude reliance on formal authority or coercion (i.e., certain actions by a person in authority may work but should not be considered leadership). What are the pros and cons of such a view?

3. Does power, as Lord Acton suggested, tend to "corrupt" the power holder? If so, what are some of the ways it happens? Is it also possible subordinates are corrupted by a superior's power? How? Or is it even possible that superiors can be corrupted by a subordinate's power?

4. Some people say it dilutes a leader's authority if subordinates are allowed to give feedback to the leader concerning their perceptions of the leader's performance. Do you agree?

5. Is leadership just another word for influence? Can you think of some examples of influence that you would *not* consider leadership?

7 ETHICS, VALUES, AND ATTITUDES

Chapter Outline

Introduction

In the previous chapter, we examined many different facets of power and its use in leadership. The topics in this chapter—ethics, values, and attitudes—go hand in hand with understanding the role of power in leadership. That is because leaders can use power for good or ill, and the leader's personal code of ethics may be one of the most important determinants of how power is exercised or constrained. For example, a political leader may be able to stir a group into a frenzy (and become even more popular) by identifying a scapegoat to blame for a community's or nation's problems, but would it be right? A business executive may be able to earn her company millions of dollars by selling unsafe drugs to patients desperate for something to cure their malady, but would it be right?

But perhaps you find those examples too obvious and simplistic. Therefore, let us slightly modify them. Is it *ever* right for a political leader to stir a populace into a frenzy? And what standards should govern the application of such power? In the second example, because a drug may not yet have passed the strict and lengthy requirements of (say) U.S. Federal Drug Administration approval, should it also be withheld from use in other countries which—facing very different medical challenges than the U.S.—seek its availability? These are more difficult questions to answer, but the general point should be clear: The mere possession of power, of any kind, leads inevitably to ethical questions about how that power should and should not be used. The challenge of leadership becomes even more complex when we consider how individuals of different backgrounds, cultures and nationalities may hold quite different values yet be thrown into increasingly closer interaction with each other as our world becomes both smaller and more diverse. This chapter will explore these fascinating and important aspects of leadership (see Highlight 7–1).

Ethics and Values

Leaders face ethical dilemmas at all levels, and the best leaders recognize and face them with a commitment to doing what is right, not just what is expedient. Of course, the phrase *doing what is right* sounds deceptively simple. Sometimes it will take great moral courage to do what is right, even when the right action seems clear. At other times, though, leaders face ethically complex issues that lack simple black-and-white answers. Whichever the case, leaders set a moral example to others that becomes the model for an entire group or organization, for good or bad. Leaders who themselves do not honor truth do not inspire it in others. Leaders mostly concerned with their own advancement do not inspire selflessness in others. Leaders should internalize a strong set of **ethics**, principles of right conduct or a system of moral values.

Both Gardner (1990) and Burns (1978) have stressed the centrality and importance of the moral dimension of leadership. Gardner said leaders ultimately must be judged on the basis of a framework of values, not just in terms of their effectiveness. He put the question of a leader's relations with his or her followers or constituents on the moral plane, arguing (with the philosopher Immanuel Kant) that leaders should always treat others as ends in themselves, not as objects or mere means to the leader's ends (which, however, does not necessarily imply that leaders need to be gentle in interpersonal demeanor or "democratic" in style). Burns (1978) took an even more extreme view regarding the moral dimension of leadership, maintaining that leaders who do not behave ethically do not demonstrate true leadership.

Highlight 7–1

Leadership Quotes, Chapter 7

Beware of the man who had no regard to his own reputation, since it is not likely he should have any for yours.

George Shelley

I have often thought that the best way to define a man's character would be to seek out the particular mental or moral attitude in which, when it came upon him, he felt himself most deeply and intensively active and alive. At such moments, there is a voice inside which speaks and says, "This is the real me."

William James

Only mediocrities rise to the top in a system that won't tolerate wave making.

Lawrence J. Peter

So near is a falsehood to truth that a wise man would do well not to trust himself on the narrow edge.

Cicero

Subordinates cannot be left to speculate as to the values of the organization. Top leadership must give forth clear and explicit signals, lest any confusion or uncertainty exist over what is and is not permissible conduct. To do otherwise allows informal and potentially subversive "codes of conduct" to be transmitted with a wink and a nod, and encourages an inferior ethical system based on "going along to get along" or the notion that "everybody's doing it."

Richard Thornburgh

Neither shall you allege the example of the many as an excuse for doing wrong.

Exodus 23:2

It's important that people know what you stand for. It's equally important that they know what you won't stand for.

Mary Waldrop

Leadership cannot just go along to get along. . . . Leadership must meet the moral challenge of the day.

Jesse Jackson

One behavior common to many good leaders is that they tend to align the values of their followers with those of the organization or movement; they make the links between the two sets more explicit. But just what are values? How do values and ethical behavior develop? Is one person's set of standards better or higher than another's? These are the sorts of questions we will address in this section.

TABLE 7–1   People Vary in the Relative Importance They Place on Values Like the Following

Terminal Values	Instrumental Values
An exciting life	Being courageous
A sense of accomplishment	Being helpful
Family security	Being honest
Inner harmony	Being imaginative
Social recognition	Being logical
Friendship	Being responsible

Source: Adapted from M. Rokeach, *The Nature of Human Values* (New York: The Free Press, 1973).

What Are Values?

Values are "constructs representing generalized behaviors or states of affairs that are considered by the individual to be important" (Gordon, 1975, p. 2). When Patrick Henry said, "Give me liberty, or give me death," he was expressing the value he placed upon political freedom. The opportunity to constantly study and learn may be the fundamental value or "state of affairs" leading a person to pursue a career in academia. Someone who values personal integrity may be forced to resign from an unethical company. Thus, values play a fairly central role in one's overall psychological makeup and can affect behavior in a variety of situations. In work settings, values can affect decisions about joining an organization, organizational commitment, relationships with co-workers, and decisions about leaving an organization (Boyatzis & Skelly, 1989). It is important for leaders to realize that individuals in the same work unit can have considerably different values, especially since we cannot see values directly. We can only make inferences about people's values based on their behavior.

Some of the major values that may be considered important by individuals in an organization are listed in Table 7–1. The instrumental values found in Table 7–1 refer to modes of behavior, and the terminal values refer to desired end states (Rokeach, 1973). For example, some individuals value equality, freedom, and having a comfortable life above all else; others may believe that family security and salvation are important goals to strive for. In terms of instrumental values, such individuals may think that it is important always to act in an ambitious, capable, and honest manner, whereas others may think it is important only to be ambitious and capable. We should add that the instrumental and terminal values in Table 7–1 are only a few of those Rokeach has identified.

FIGURE 7–1

*Some Influences
on the
Development of
Personal Values*

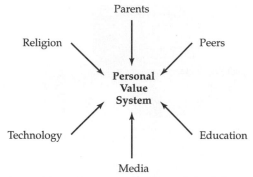

Source: Adapted from M. Massey, *The People Puzzle* (Reston, VA.: Reston Publishing, 1979).

How Do Values Develop?

According to Massey (1979), each person's values reflect the contributions of diverse inputs, including family, peers, the educational system, religion, the media, science and technology, geography, and current events (see Figure 7–1). Although one's values can change throughout one's life, they are relatively firmly established by young adulthood. Figure 7–2 represents the building blocks of leadership skills as a pyramid, and you can see that values are on the bottom of the pyramid (along with interests, motives, lifelong goals, personality traits and preferences, and intelligence). All of the attributes in that bottom row are relatively enduring and permanent; they serve as a foundation to other attributes of leadership that are less enduring and thus more modifiable. At the top of the pyramid are leadership skills and competencies that can be developed through practice.

Massey used the term **value programming** to highlight the extent to which forces outside the individual shape and mold personal values. He analyzed changes in the value-programming inputs that characterized each of the decades since the 1920s and related them to dominant and distinctive values held among people who were value-programmed during those respective periods. For example, he said the monumental event of the 1930s, the Great Depression, programmed people growing up then to especially value economic security. People growing up in the 1960s, however, were value-programmed quite differently. Dramatic shifts and changes in American society occurred during the 1960s. There were violent social protests, experimentation with new lifestyles, and pervasive questioning of establishment values.

Boyatzis and Skelly (1989), Maccoby (1983), and Massey (1979) have all said that the pervasive influence of broad forces like these tend to create common value systems among people growing up at a particular time that distinguish them from people who grow up at different times. There are, of course, significant differences among individuals *within* any generational group, but these authors emphasized differences *between* groups. For example, people who grew up prior to World War II valued authority, job security, and stability; people who grew up in the 1960s

Figure 7–2

*The Building
Blocks of Skills*

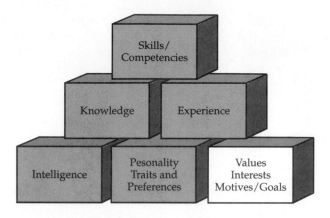

valued participation, informality, and personal growth; and those who grew up in the 1980s valued competitiveness, entrepreneurialism, and cost-effectiveness. These authors attributed much of the misunderstanding between older leaders and younger followers to the fact that their basic value systems were formulated during quite different social and cultural conditions, and these analyses offer a helpful perspective for understanding how differences in values can add tension to the interaction between some leaders and followers. Do you think there are any basic differences in values between the "Baby Boomer" generation (now in their forties) and "Generation X" which might affect the leadership process?

Lest we overemphasize the significance of intergenerational differences, however, we should consider the results of a recent scientific sampling of over 1,000 people living in the United States (Ladd, 1994) which found *little* evidence of a generation gap in basic values. In fact, the director of one of the largest polling organizations in the world called the results some of the most powerful he had seen in 30 years of public-opinion research. They showed, he said, "that even though young people buy different CDs and clothes, they do *not* buy into a set of values different from their elders" (Ladd, p. 50).

Thus, while it's true that experiences unique to particular generations help explain certain values characteristic of people in one generation, people from different generations still share many of the same values. But what might explain value differences *within* a given age group? Actually, they're the same factors depicted in Figure 7–1 which Massey used to explain value differences *across* generations. There may be significant differences in the value-programming experiences of teen-agers from the same generation based on factors like their family's religious affiliation and involvement, the norms of the particular peer group they associate with, their formal education, and so on.

Up to this point the discussion has focused on the *content* of a person's values. Equally important, however, is the question of how one *thinks about* value-laden issues or ethical dilemmas. **Moral reasoning** refers to the process leaders use to make decisions about ethical and unethical behaviors. Moral reasoning does not refer to the morality of individuals per se, or their espoused values, but rather to the *manner by which they solve moral problems*. Values play a key role in the moral reasoning process, since value differences among individuals often result in different judgments regarding ethical and unethical behavior.

Kohlberg (1969) theorized that people progress through a series of *developmental stages* in their moral reasoning. Each stage reflects a more cognitively complex way of analyzing moral situations than the preceding one, and the sequence of stages is fixed, or invariant. Moral reasoning is assessed using ethical dilemmas such as whether a man is morally justified in stealing an overpriced drug to save his dying wife, and an individual's stage of moral reasoning is based on the *way the answer is explained* rather than the particular answer they give. Two individuals, for example, may each argue that the husband was morally wrong to steal the drug—even in those extenuating circumstances—yet offer qualitatively different kinds of reasons as to *why* the action was wrong. Similarly, two individuals may each argue the husband was morally justified in stealing the drug, yet offer different reasons as to why it was justifiable. The focus is on the reasoning process rather than on the decision per se. You may find it interesting to reflect on the moral issues raised in Highlight 7–2. Obviously, different individuals may have quite different points of view on these ethical questions.

That distinction may be clearer by looking in greater detail at different ways of evaluating the husband's behavior. Table 7–2 outlines Kohlberg's six stages of moral development, as well as how a person at each stage might evaluate the husband's behavior. Note that the six stages themselves are organized into three higher-order levels: the **preconventional level**, in which a person's criteria for moral behavior are based primarily on *self-interest* such as avoiding punishment or being rewarded; the **conventional level**, in which the criteria for moral behavior are based primarily on *gaining others' approval* and behaving (as the name implies) *conventionally*; and the **postconventional level**, in which the criteria are based on universal, abstract principles which may even transcend the laws of a particular society. Finally, to say moral development progresses in invariant stages does not imply that all individuals actually achieve the highest stages. Few adults, in fact, actually do. How do you think, in that regard, a political leader at the conventional level may differ in behavior (e.g., in the "stands" he or she takes on issues) from one at the postconventional level?

But what is it that actually *moves* an individual from one level to the next? In summarizing several decades of research on moral judgment, Rest (1993) highlighted fundamental, dramatic, and extensive changes which occur in young adulthood (the 20s and 30s) in how people define what is morally right or wrong. Rest noted that formal education is strongly correlated with these, though no specific academic or personal experiences proved pivotal. Moral judgment is part of each person's *general* personal and social development, and those individuals whose moral judgment develop most are those who "love to learn, seek new challenges, who enjoy intellectually stimulating environments, who are reflective, who make plans and set goals, who take risks, who see themselves in the larger social contexts of history and institutions, and who take responsibility for themselves and their environs" (p. 209). At the same time, deliberate curricular attempts to affect moral judgment have been shown to be

Highlight 7–2

What Would You Do?

Here are several situations having ethical dimensions. How would you act in each one, and by what principles or reasoning process do you reach each decision?

- Would you vote for a political candidate who was honest, competent, and agreed with you on most issues if you also knew that person was alcoholic, sexually promiscuous, and twice divorced?

- Assume that as a teenager you smoked marijuana once or twice, but that was years ago. Would you answer truthfully on an employment questionnaire if it asked whether you had ever used marijuana?

- Your military unit has been ambushed by enemy soldiers and suffered heavy casualties. Several of your soldiers have been captured, but you also captured one of the enemy soldiers. Would you torture the captured enemy soldier if that were the only way of saving the lives of your own soldiers?

- Terrorists have captured a planeload of tourists and threatened to kill them unless ransom demands are met. You believe that meeting the ransom demands is likely to lead to the safe release of those passengers, but also likely to inspire future terrorist acts. Would you meet the terrorists' demands (and probably save the hostages) or refuse to meet the terrorists' demands (and reduce the likelihood of future incidents).

- If you were an elementary school principal, would you feel it was part of your school's responsibility to teach moral values, or just academic subject matter?

- Assume that you have been elected to your state's legislature, and that you are about to cast the deciding vote in determining whether abortions will be legally available to women in your state. What would you do if your own strong personal convictions on this issue were contrary to the views of the majority of the people you represent?

Source: Adapted from Stock (1991).

effective. Interestingly, though, some of the largest gains from formal moral education programs have occurred with participants in their 20s and 30s rather than with more traditionally school-age students. This should not be surprising. It may be beneficial to have struggled with certain life experiences before the lessons of moral education make complete sense.

Values and Leadership

How Values Affect Leadership.   According to England and Lee (1974), values can affect leaders in six different ways. First, values affect leaders' perceptions of situations and the problems at hand. Leaders who value occupational success

TABLE 7–2   Developmental Levels and Stages of Moral Reasoning

Description of Stages	Examples of Moral Reasoning in Support of Stealing the Drug	Examples of Moral Reasoning against Stealing the Drug
Preconventional Level Stage 1: "Bad" behavior is that which is punished Stage 2: "Good" behavior is that which is concretely rewarded	"If you let your wife die you will get in trouble." "If you do happen to get caught, you could give the drug back and not get much of a sentence."	"If you steal the drug you will get in trouble." "Even if you were caught and didn't get much of a sentence, your wife would probably die while you were in jail and it wouldn't do you much good."
Conventional Level Stage 3: "Good" behavior is that which is approved by others; "bad" behavior is that which is disapproved by others Stage 4: "Good" behavior conforms to standards set by social institutions; transgressions lead to feelings of guilt or dishonor	"If you don't steal the drug you'll never be able to look anyone in the face again." "If you have any sense of honor, you'd do your duty as a husband and steal the drug."	"Everyone would know you are a thief." "If you stole the drug, however desperate you felt, you'd never be able to look at yourself in the mirror again."
Postconventional Level Stage 5: "Good" behavior conforms to community standards set through democratic participation; concern with maintaining self-respect and the respect of equals Stage 6: "Good" behavior is a matter of individual conscience based on responsibly chosen commitments to ethical principles.	"If you don't steal the drug you'd lose your own respect and everyone else's too." "If you didn't steal it, you might have satisfied the letter of the law, but you wouldn't have lived up to your own standards of conscience."	"We've all agreed to live by common rules, and any form of stealing breaks that bond." "Maybe others would have approved of your behavior, but stealing the drug would still have violated your own conscience and standards of honesty."

Source: Adapted from Kohlberg (1984).

above all else may see a work-related problem as an obstacle to their achievement, whereas leaders who value helping others may see a work-related problem as an opportunity to help a subordinate or another work unit. Second, leaders' values affect the solutions generated and the decisions reached about problems. If leaders believe being courageous and standing up for one's beliefs are important, then they may be more likely to generate solutions or make decisions not considered politically correct in their organizations. Third, values play an extremely important role in interpersonal relationships; they influence how leaders perceive different individuals and groups. For example, leaders who value self-control may have a difficult time dealing with followers who are very emotionally demonstrative and, in turn, may choose to have fairly distant relationships with these followers. Fourth, values often influence leaders' perceptions of individual and organizational successes as well as the manner in which these successes are to be achieved. Leaders who primarily value competitiveness, independence, and imagination may assess leadership effectiveness differently from leaders who value helpfulness, logic, and cheerfulness. Fifth, values provide a basis for leaders to differentiate between right and wrong, and between ethical and unethical behavior. Sixth, values also may affect the extent to which leaders accept or reject organizational pressures and goals. Leaders who place a premium on being obedient may never question the goals of the organization. However, leaders who believe being independent is important may often question and even actively resist the implementation of some organizational goals in their work units.

Some of the values and beliefs articulated by a great sports leader are presented in Highlight 7–3. But values may be expressed by whole organizations too. Many organizations are adopting and disseminating formal statements of their corporate core values in order to assure their widespread understanding and practice. One example of this is seen in Highlight 7–4. Not all organizations, however, embrace such lofty aspirations. What role do you think shared values play in the membership and leadership of extremist groups such as the assorted "patriot" or militia movements in the United States? Of skinheads? Of religious terrorist groups? Of cults like Heaven's Gate, whose members committed mass suicide in 1996 in the belief they would be transported to an alien spacecraft? Of the Jonestown commune described in the preceding chapter?

Empirical Studies of the Ethical Dimension of Leadership.   Empirical studies of the ethical dimension of leadership have looked at factors affecting moral reasoning and ethical versus unethical behavior, the frequency or prevalence of unethical behaviors in the workplace, the relationship between values and leadership success, and tolerating unethical conduct in others.

Several researchers have reported that individuals with strong value systems tend to behave more ethically, which at first may seem like a classic case of discovering the obvious. However, certain kinds of situations increased the likelihood of unethical behavior from people regardless of their value systems. Such situations tended to be highly competitive and unsupervised. Unethical behavior also was more likely to occur when there was no formal ethics policy governing behavior, when there was no threat of punishment for unethical behavior, or when unethical behavior actually was rewarded (Hegarty & Sims, 1978, 1979; Malinkowski & Smith, 1985; Trevino & Youngblood, 1990).

Studies exploring opinions about unethical behaviors or practices in the workplace have yielded fairly disturbing results. For example, a 1988 Harris poll reported that 89 percent of the 1,200 workers and managers surveyed believed it was important for leaders to be upright, honest, and ethical in their dealings. However, only 41 percent indicated their current supervisor had these characteristics. Another Harris poll conducted in 1989 reported that many individuals believed businesses would purposely sell unsafe products, risk employee health and safety, and harm the environment (see Figure 7–3). In addition, Pitt (1985) asked middle and senior managers in South Africa to rate the corruptness of various business practices and then indicate how frequently they believed colleagues and friends engaged in such acts. A representative finding was that

John Wooden, on Staying Power

The following advertisement by Panhandle Eastern Corporation appeared in many newspapers in 1986. It conveys many of John Wooden's values. Coach Wooden is arguably the greatest college basketball coach of all time.

John Wooden on Staying Power

John Wooden is the only man ever enshrined in the basketball Hall of Fame as both player and coach. He retired after 40 years of coaching, leaving a record unparalleled in American sport.

During his 27 years as coach of UCLA, his teams never had a losing season. In his last 12 years there, they won 10 national championships, 7 of those in succession, and still hold the world's record for the longest winning streak in any major sport—88 games bridging four seasons.

Although retired now, he still conducts coaching clinics and basketball camps, and lectures widely.

"Like most coaches, my program revolved around fundamentals, conditioning, and teamwork. But I differed radically in several respects. I never talked about winning."

Peaks Create Valleys

"I believe that for every artificial peak you create, you also create valleys. When you get too high for anything, emotion takes over and consistency of performance is lost and you will be unduly affected when adversity comes. I emphasized constant improvement and steady performance.

"I have often said, 'The mark of a true champion is to always perform near your own level of competency.' We were able to do that by never being satisfied with the past and always planning for what was to come. I believe that failure to prepare is preparing to fail. This constant focus on the future is one reason we continued staying near the top once we got there."

Develop Yourself, Don't Worry about Opponents

"I probably scouted opponents less than any coach in the country. Less than most high school coaches. I don't need to know that this forward likes to drive the outside. You're not supposed to give the outside to any forward whenever he tries it. Sound offensive and defensive principles apply to any style of play.

"Rather than having my teams prepare to play a certain team each week, I prepared to play anybody. I didn't want my players worrying about the other fellows. I wanted them executing the sound offensive and defensive principles we taught in practice."

There's No Pillow as Soft as a Clear Conscience

"To me success isn't outscoring someone, it's the peace of mind that comes from self-satisfaction in knowing you did your best. That's something each individual must determine for himself. You can fool others but you can't fool yourself.

"Many people are surprised to learn that in 27 years at UCLA, I never once talked about winning. Instead I would tell my players before games, 'When it's over, I want your head up. And there's only one way your head can be up, that's for you to know, not me, that you gave the best effort of which you're capable. If you do that, then the score doesn't really matter, although I have a feeling that if you do that, the score will be to your liking.' I honestly, deeply believe that in not stressing winning as such, we won more than we would have if I'd stressed outscoring opponents."

> *Why Do So Many People Dread Adversity,*
> *When It's Only through Adversity that We Grow Stronger?*
>
> "There's no great fun, satisfaction, or joy derived from doing something that's easy. Failure is never fatal, but failure to change might be.
>
> "Your strength as an individual depends on, and will be in direct proportion to, how you react to both praise and criticism. If you become too concerned about either, the effect on you is certain to be adverse."
>
> *The Main Ingredient of Stardom*
>
> "I always taught players that the main ingredient of stardom is the rest of the team. It's amazing how much can be accomplished if no one cares who gets the credit. That's why I was as concerned with a player's character as I was with his ability.
>
> "While it may be possible to reach the top of one's profession on sheer ability, it is impossible to stay there without hard work and character. One's character may be quite different from one's reputation.
>
> "Your character is what you really are. Your reputation is only what others think you are. I made a determined effort to evaluate character. I looked for young men who would play the game hard, but clean, and who would always be trying to improve themselves to help the team. Then, if their ability warranted it, the championships would take care of themselves."
>
> Source: Reprinted with permission of the Panhandle Eastern Corporation.

although approximately 95 percent of the respondents said taking a large bribe was definitely wrong, they believed one-third of their friends and colleagues would do so. Furthermore, even in the case of such a clearly corrupt act as bribery, only one-third of the respondents said they believed legal action against the individual afterward would be appropriate. Among other things, data like these suggest that ethical practices do not receive a high enough priority in many organizations. On the contrary, there are numerous examples of organizations that have been financially rewarded for unethical behavior (e.g., bribes to secure lucrative contracts, defense industries padding contracts with the government).

Other studies also have examined how leaders' values are related to leadership style or success. Some have shown that men and women differ in the values they emphasize in moral reasoning; men are more concerned about equity and justice, whereas women show more care for others and social responsibility in their moral reasoning (Brockner & Adsit, 1986; Gilligan, 1982; Powell, Posner, & Schmidt, 1984). In addition, Schmidt and Posner (1986) reported that both public and private administrators were relatively more concerned with their obligations to their organizations than with their obligations to society, and Weber (1989) reported that managers often used majority opinion rather than universal principles of justice when making decisions with ethical implications. Despite the cynicism that exists about the ethical practices of people in some leadership positions, managers with a strong sense of right and wrong do appear to be better leaders. Both Ghiselli (1968) and Gordon (1975) reported that leaders' personal values correlated positively with leadership effectiveness.

Highlight 7–4

Levi Strauss—A Values-Based Company

Levi Strauss & Co. is guided by a set of corporate aspirations written by its top management and most strongly endorsed by its CEO, Robert D. Haas (the great-great-grandnephew of founder Levi Strauss). Many companies today are extolling the virtues of diversity and empowerment, but few so explicitly and consistently as Levi Strauss.

This is what Levi's aspires to:

New Behaviors: Management must exemplify "directness, openness to influence, commitment to the success of others, and willingness to acknowledge their own contributions to problems."

Diversity: Levi's "values a diverse workforce (age, sex, ethnic group, etc.) at all levels of the organization. . . . Differing points of view will be sought; diversity will be valued and honestly rewarded, not suppressed."

Recognition: Levi's will "provide greater recognition—both financial and psychic—for individuals and teams that contribute to our success."

Ethical Management Practices: Management should epitomize "the stated standards of ethical behavior. We must provide clarity about our expectations and must enforce these standards throughout the corporation."

Communications: Management must be "clear about company, unit, and individual goals and performance. People must know what is expected of them and receive timely, honest feedback."

Empowerment: Management must "increase the authority and responsibility of those closest to our products and customers. By actively pushing the responsibility, trust, and recognition into the organization, we can harness and release the capabilities of all our people."

Source: *Business Week*, August 1, 1994, pp. 46–52.

A slightly different question than behaving unethically oneself is that of tolerating unethical behavior in others. It seems that reporting or confronting individuals whose behavior violated ethical or organizational norms depends on at least two situational variables: the seriousness of the infraction and the emotional relationship of the violator (Curphy, Gibson, Macomber, Calhoun, Wilbanks, & Burger, 1995). Individuals appear less likely to blow the whistle on another's ethical infraction if the violation did not seem serious and if the offender was a close friend of the potential whistleblower.

Group and Organizational Dimensions of Moral Reasoning and Ethical Conduct.
From a leadership perspective, we might well ask what happens when you combine individuals from different levels of development together into one group:

FIGURE 7–3

*Perceptions of
Unethical
Business
Practices—
Percent of People
Expressing
Belief Business
Would . . .*

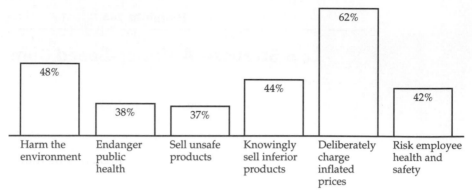

Source: Harris Poll, reported in *Business Week,* May 29, 1989, p. 29.

What level does the group as a whole manifest? Researchers have found that group decisions about ethical dilemmas can be at lower levels of moral reasoning than the decisions made by individual members if the leader of the group is a less-principled moral reasoner (Dukerich, Nichols, Elm, & Vollrath, 1990). This finding has significant implications for what a group's collective morality may be when the leader is relatively unprincipled. What, for example, is likely to happen to a group's collective behavior if its leader is intelligent, quite domineering, and supremely unprincipled? Do you know of any leaders like that?

Even whole organizations may have characteristic levels of "moral sense" analogous to levels of personal moral development in individuals (Stevens, 1981; Petrick & Manning, 1990). Organizationally speaking, the preconventional level of moral development refers to organizations characterized by rampant fear and manipulation among organization members; life is a moral jungle where all that counts is surviving, even if through treachery, manipulation, or deceit. In organizations at the conventional level of moral development, good behavior is defined by satisfying others, complying with proper authority, and following the rules. The highest level of ethical climate in organizations (i.e., the postconventional level) is characterized by norms of principled and open decision making, including "respect for justice and the minority rights of productive and creative individuals: searching for consensus rather than relying on majority vote" (Petrick & Manning, 1990, p. 15). Bill O'Brien (1994), the former CEO of a major insurance company, likened an organization's poor ethical climate to a bad odor one gets used to:

> Organizations oriented to power, I realized, also have strong smells, and even if people are too inured to notice, that smell has implications. It affects performance, productivity, and innovation. The worse aspect of this environment is that it stunts the growth of personality and character of everyone who works there. (p. 306)

And just as we asked what moves individuals from one level of moral reasoning to the next, we might also ask what moves *organizations* from one level to the next. One approach suggests five concerted steps. (1) Improve the quality of the leader–follower relationship so that genuine support for ethical conduct and initiative is provided. (2) Have explicit ethical guidelines and systems in place to deal quickly with unethical conduct. (3) Have an organizational ombudsmen appointed to address ethical conflicts. (4) Have a formal ethics education program for all organizational members. (5) Most importantly, ensure that both formal and informal leaders model high standards of ethical conduct (Petrick & Manning, 1990). Recommendations like these reflect increasing recognition that ethical behavior is an organizational responsibility, not just an individual responsibility; and that standards of ethical conduct are not synonymous with standards of legal conduct, they are higher. Something can be unethical even though it is legal, so no leader should be content merely to ensure organizational members avoid breaking the law. Here are just a few examples of the kinds of actions which may be legal yet clearly unethical (Brumback, 1991):

- Scapegoating personal failures.
- Shirking unpleasant responsibilities.
- Knowingly making unreasonable demands of others.
- Breaking promises.
- Slacking off.
- Favoring friends for desirable assignments when others are more qualified.

Others, too, are calling attention to the organizational dimensions of ethical behavior. It seems clear that ethical behavior within an organization (or *by* it) is not simply the sum of the collective moralities of its members. Covey (1990), for example, has developed and popularized an approach called **principle-centered leadership**. This approach postulates a fundamental interdependence between the personal, the interpersonal, the managerial, and the organizational levels of leadership. The unique role of each level may be thought of like this:

Personal: The first imperative is to be a trustworthy person, and that depends on both one's character *and* competence. Only if one is trustworthy can one have trusting relationships with others.

Interpersonal: Relationships that lack trust are characterized by self-protective efforts to control and verify each other's behavior.

Managerial: Only in the context of trusting relationships will a manager risk empowering others to make full use of their talents and energies. But even with an empowering style, leading a high-performing group depends on skills such as team building, delegation, communication, negotiation, and self-management.

Organizational: An organization will be most creative and productive when its structure, systems (e.g., training, communication, reward), strategy, and vision are aligned and mutually supportive. Put differently, certain organizational alignments are more likely to nurture and reinforce ethical behavior among its members than others.

When Good People Do Bad Things.   An important aspect of ethical conduct involves the mental gymnastics by which people can dissociate their moral thinking from their moral acting. One's ability to reason about hypothetical moral issues, after all, does not assure that one will *act* morally. Furthermore, one's moral actions may not always be consistent with one's espoused values. Bandura (1986, 1990), in particular, has pointed out several ways people with firm moral principles nonetheless may behave badly without feeling guilt or remorse over their behavior. We should look at each of these.

Moral justification involves reinterpreting otherwise immoral behavior in terms of a higher purpose. This is most dramatically revealed in the behavior of combatants in war.

> Moral reconstrual of killing is dramatically illustrated by the case of Sergeant York, one of the phenomenal fighters in the history of modern warfare. Because of his deep religious convictions, Sergeant York registered as a conscientious objector, but his numerous appeals were denied. At camp, his battalion commander quoted chapter and verse from the Bible to persuade him that under appropriate conditions it was Christian to fight and kill. A marathon mountainside prayer finally convinced him that he could serve both God and country by becoming a dedicated fighter. (Bandura, 1990, p. 164)

Another way to dissociate behavior from one's espoused moral principles is through **euphemistic labeling**. This involves using "cosmetic" words to defuse or disguise the offensiveness of otherwise morally repugnant or distasteful behavior. Terrorists, for example, may call themselves "freedom fighters," and firing someone may be referred to as "letting him go." **Advantageous comparison** lets one avoid self-contempt for one's behavior by comparing it to even more heinous behavior by others ("If you think *we're* insensitive to subordinates' needs, you should see what it's like working for *Acme*"). Through **displacement of responsibility** people may violate personal moral standards by attributing responsibility to others. Nazi concentration camp guards, for example, attempted to avoid moral responsibility for their behavior by claiming they were merely "carrying out orders."

A related mechanism is **diffusion of responsibility**, whereby reprehensible behavior becomes easier to engage in and live with if others are behaving the same way. When everyone is responsible, it seems, no one is responsible. This way of minimizing individual moral responsibility for collective action can be one negative effect of group decision making. Through **disregard or distortion of consequences**, people minimize the harm caused by their behavior. This can be a problem in bureaucracies when decision-makers are relatively insulated by their position from directly observing the consequences of their decisions. **Dehumanization** is still another way of avoiding the moral consequences of one's behavior. It is easier to treat others badly when they are dehumanized, as evidenced in epithets like "gooks" or "satan-worshippers." Finally, people sometimes try to justify immoral behavior by claiming it was caused by someone else's actions. This is known as **attribution of blame**.

How widespread are such methods of minimizing personal moral responsibility? When people behave badly, Bandura (1977) said, it is *not* typically because of a basic character flaw; rather, it is because they use methods like these to construe their behavior in a self-protective way.

Darley (1994) suggested still another way people justify seemingly unethical conduct, and his observations illuminate certain common leadership practices. Darley said *ethical problems are almost inherent in systems designed to measure performance.*

> The more any quantitative performance measure is used to determine a group's or an individual's rewards and punishments, the more subject it will be to corruption pressures and the more apt it will be to distort and corrupt the action patterns and thoughts of the group or individual it is intended to monitor. . . . The criterial control system unleashes enormous human ingenuity. People will maximize the criteria set. However, they may do so in ways that are not anticipated by the criterion setters, in ways that destroy the validity of the criteria. The people "make their numbers" but the numbers no longer mean what you thought they did. (Darley, 1994)

This has been called **Darley's law**, and it is exemplified in a story from Joseph Heller's novel *Catch-22*. You can read about it in Highlight 7–5, though Darley's law is not limited to fiction. Halberstam (1986) described another organization in which the "numbers game" had a corrupting effect. In this case, it was in the Ford Motor Company. In the eyes of those who worked in Ford plants around the country in the 1950s, Detroit "number crunchers" like Robert McNamara (later a secretary of defense during the Vietnam war) did not want to know the truth. McNamara and his people in Detroit were the ones who kept making liberal agreements with the unions and at the same time setting higher and higher levels of production while always demanding increased quality. They talked about quality, but they did not give the plant managers the means for quality; what they really wanted was production. So the plant managers were giving them what they wanted, numbers, while playing lip service to quality. Years later in Vietnam, some American officers, knowing McNamara's love of numbers, cleverly juggled the numbers and played games with body counts in order to make a stalemated war look more successful than it was. They did this not because they were dishonest, but because they thought if Washington really wanted the truth it would have sought the truth in an honest way. In doing so they were the spiritual descendants of the Ford factory managers of the fifties (p. 220).

Darley described three general problems that can arise when performance measurement systems are put in place. A person might cheat on the measurement system by exploiting its weaknesses either in hopes of advancement or through fear of falling behind. Or, even with the best will in the world, a person might act in a way that optimizes his or her performance measurements without realizing that this outcome was not what the system really intended. Finally, a person may even have the best interests of the system in mind and yet manipulate the performance measurement system to allow continuation of the actions that best fulfill his or her reading of the system goals. One major disadvantage of this particular approach is that it "takes underground" constructive dialogue about system goals or modifications in system measurements.

Highlight 7–5

Catch 22

This story is about Yossarian, the central character of Joseph Heller's novel *Catch 22*. It demonstrates how a performance measurement system can create forces that morally corrupt the individuals functioning within that system.

During World War II, the allied high command needed some measure of when each bomber crew flying over Germany had "done enough." The answer they came up with was simply to count the number of bombing missions each crew had flown. It seemed to demand a commensurate risk among all concerned, and also seemed correlated with other primary objectives like the number of enemy factories destroyed. After flying a certain number of missions, crews expected to be rotated back to the states.

What was Yossarian's story? Terrified of flying the dangerous combat missions assigned to him, he flew his B-29 on different and infinitely safer routes over the open ocean. He simply dropped the plane's entire payload of bombs there over water. *From the point of view of the military indicator of missions flown, these were successful missions* which even earned Yossarian points toward a safe follow-on assignment. Driven by fear, Yossarian had corrupted the indicator from one that was correlated with organizational success to one that was arguably negatively correlated with organizational success.

You might wonder whether this proves the indicator was inherently flawed. Wasn't the bomber command justified in designing the measurement system without consideration of this particular possibility? Was it not entitled to assume American soldiers would not commit acts of treasonous cowardice? The intriguing point of Heller's novel is that *Yossarian's act was a perfectly normal response to the particular dynamics in which it arose.* In Heller's novel, *Yossarian's commanders were cheating on the system themselves!* Some, for example, were trying to gain promotion by raising the number of missions required to go home while not flying any missions themselves. Other commanders let friends and favorites accumulate missions by flying "milk runs" in which little enemy opposition was experienced. Still other leaders tried to get credit for bombing missions even though, in fact, they had not flown any. The leadership itself, in other words, destroyed any possibility that pilots like Yossarian would see any moral barriers to cheating. *Corruption is contagious*, and Darley suggests that performance measurement systems inherently invite widespread corruption.

Souce: Adapted from Darley (1994).

What, ethically, should one do when one is part of a performance measurement system? Darley suggested "that the time for the individual to raise the moral issue is when he or she feels the pressure to substitute accountability for morality, to act wrongly, because that is what the system requires. And that intervention might then be directed at the system, by honorably protesting its design." For those who are governed by a performance measurement system, a constant moral vigilance is necessary—it is needed most of all by those in leadership positions.

Attitudes

What Are Attitudes?

An **attitude** "refers to a general and enduring positive or negative feeling about some person, object, or issue" (Petty & Cacioppo, 1981, p. 7). Attitudes have three components: ideational, affective, and behavioral. The **ideational component** concerns *what* the attitude is about, and the **affective component** concerns the feelings one has about those ideas. For example, a leader may dislike the administrative aspects of her responsibilities. Her attitude has both a feeling dimension (she *detests* filling out seemingly endless forms) and a cognitive dimension (administrative tasks at work).

Attitudes also have a **behavioral component,** which means that attitudes dispose people to act in certain ways. For example, our leader above may tend to procrastinate on paperwork and underemphasize the importance of documentation and filling out forms properly. Students with positive attitudes about school tend to do more homework, turn in assignments on time, and ask more questions than students with negative attitudes about school. Similarly, workers with negative attitudes toward their employer are more likely to change jobs if given the opportunity. Like traits and values, however, attitudes do not *always* predict behavior. Fishbein and Azjen (1975) have shown that some attitudes are so general they tell us very little about how people actually act and that attitudes best predict behavior when they specifically pertain to relevant behaviors. For example, knowing only that a person has the attitude "democracy is good" will not help predict this person's vote in a presidential election. However, knowing this person has a strong attitude about a particular political candidate will be a more accurate predictor of his voting behavior. Attitudes do not always predict specific behavior because behavior is influenced by more factors than just attitudes. For example, a supervisor may be forced to terminate a subordinate's employment because of forced company downsizing despite having very positive attitudes about the person's work. Still, although many factors can affect a leader's behavior, a leader's attitudes can reveal useful insights about her approach to her role.

Attitudes share certain properties with values, but they are also different from values in fundamental ways. Both are unseen constructs that can affect behavior, both are inferred from one's behavior, and both are typically measured using paper-and-pencil measures. Nevertheless, values occupy a more central role in one's overall psychological makeup than attitudes do (Rokeach, 1973). Although the number of basic values anyone holds is relatively small, the number of attitudes anyone holds may be in the thousands, as they refer to diverse opinions about people, activities, or things. Despite these differences, values and attitudes are intimately linked: Values serve to organize our attitudes, and our attitudes are derived from and reflect our more basic values. For example, a person may embrace compassion toward others as one of his fundamental values. His attitudes toward specific charities, government programs, religious groups, and so on, would be rooted in his more general value of compassion.

Leaders' Attitudes about Subordinates

A leader's interaction with subordinates depends in part on his or her implicit views of human nature. As Covey (1990) wrote, "Ultimately the leadership style one adopts springs from one's core ideas and feelings about the nature of man" (p. 69). A leader's basic attitudes about what motivates others, about whether people generally can be trusted or not, and about the extent to which individuals can grow and develop all influence how a leader interacts with others in both overt and subtle ways. Several decades ago, Douglas McGregor (1966) explained different styles of managerial behavior on the basis of their implicit attitudes about human nature, and his work remains quite influential today. McGregor identified two contrasting sets of assumptions people make about human nature, calling these **Theory X** and **Theory Y.** These represent two different sets of attitudes, or belief systems, about ways to effectively influence subordinates. In the long run, any manager's approach to subordinates generally reflects such underlying assumptions and tendencies. Moreover, managers often are not consciously aware of their assumptions; they act as though their views are obviously true.

In the simplest sense, Theory X reflects a traditional and somewhat pessimistic view of others. Managers with this orientation rely heavily on coercive, external-control methods to motivate workers, such as pay, disciplinary techniques, punishments, and threats. They assume people are not naturally industrious or motivated to work. Hence, it is the manager's job to minimize the harmful effects of workers' natural laziness and irresponsibility by closely overseeing their work and creating external incentives to do well and disincentives that prevent slacking off. Theory Y, on the other hand, reflects a view that most people are intrinsically motivated by their work. Rather than needing to be coaxed or coerced to work productively, most people value a sense of achievement, personal growth, pride in contributing to their organization, and respect for a job well done. Managers ascribing to a Theory Y attitude believe followers value the opportunity to take on tasks of greater responsibility and autonomy independently of whether there may be greater tangible rewards for doing so. The generally optimistic view of human nature implicit in Theory Y is reflected in a remark by former Supreme Court Justice Tom Clark, who said, "I'm convinced that every boy, in his heart, would rather steal second base than an automobile."

Hall and Donnell (1979) reported findings of five separate studies involving over 12,000 managers that explored the relationship between managerial achievement and attitudes toward subordinates. Their criterion of managerial achievement was an objective index calculated on the basis of each manager's career progress in the context of chronological age and upward movement in an organizational hierarchy. These objective scores were transformed into standard scores that were the basis for categorizing three levels of managerial achievement—high, average, and low. The average-achieving group comprised essentially the middle two-thirds of the distribution. Hall and Donnell compared the personal beliefs of high-, average-, and low-achieving managers and reasoned that managers with a Theory Y philosophy would better accomplish organizational objectives and better tap the potential of subordinates. Managers ascribing to a Theory X philosophy were predicted to restrict subordinate growth and limit organizational potential. In fact, managers who strongly subscribed to Theory X beliefs were far more likely to be in Hall and Donnell's low-achieving group.

Leaders' Attitudes about Themselves

We have seen that a leader's attitudes about others can have a substantial impact on his effectiveness. Another important factor in a leader's effectiveness concerns his attitudes about himself. The concept of self is one of the oldest and most central concepts in psychology. Some of the most important psychological concepts for understanding individuals are self-concept and self-esteem. Each of these deals with particular attitudes one has about oneself, and each plays a significant part in how we respond to events and to other people.

Self-concept is a construct from phenomenological personality theory (Kelly, 1955) and refers to the collection of attitudes we have about ourselves. One source of these attitudes involves the various experiences a person has had and the roles a person currently occupies, such as spouse, parent, supervisor, friend, athlete, or committee member. For example, if we asked the question, "Who are you?" a particular leader might respond that she is a college-educated mother of two who is married and supervises 14 salespeople in a computer retail firm. **Self-esteem** refers to the overall positiveness or negativeness of a person's feelings about these experiences and roles. Individuals with high self-esteem generally see themselves in a positive light; individuals with low self-esteem generally see themselves in a negative light. Thus, if the leader above had high self-esteem, she may be likely to perceive that she is well loved by her children and husband and respected at work by her subordinates, peers, and superiors. Another way to think about self-esteem is in terms of the congruence or divergence between one's actual self and one's ideal self. In that sense, a person has high self-esteem if she perceives herself as being relatively close to the way she ideally would like to be; a person has low self-esteem if he perceives himself as being very unlike the way he ideally would like to be. Because self-esteem involves perceptions and feelings, it does not necessarily reflect an objective assessment of one's strengths and accomplishments. One can be extremely accomplished or hold a high position and yet have relatively low self-esteem. Let's return to our leader above, supposing her children consistently have been on the school honor role, she had just celebrated her 20th wedding anniversary, and she had received a bonus at work. Even in the face of such outward success, the person could have low self-esteem if she expected even more of herself.

FIGURE 7–4

The Interactions between Attitudes toward Self and Attitudes toward Others

Theory Y	*Theory X*
Positive Self-Concept	
High self-esteem	High self-esteem
Respects others	Overbearing
Self-confident	Bossy
Accepts positive feedback	Highly evaluative of others
Gives positive feedback	Impatient
Expects others to succeed	Hostile
Nonjudgmental	Task-oriented
Nondefensive	
Seeks win-win solutions	
Negative Self-Concept	
Low self-esteem	Low self-esteem
Difficulty accepting positive feedback	Feelings of helplessness and hopelessness
Unassertive	Blames others and world
Worrisome	Nothing matters
Assumes own fault	Expects to fail

Attitude and Leadership Style

To briefly summarize the two foregoing sections, leaders can have positive or negative attitudes about themselves, and they can have positive or negative attitudes about others. An even simpler way of putting this is to say leaders can feel relatively positive or negative about themselves, and relatively positive or negative about others. These possibilities create four different attitudinal "positions." As seen in Figure 7–4, a leader's attitudes about himself or herself and others interact to produce four quite different leadership styles. Leaders who have a positive self-concept and ascribe to a Theory Y philosophy typically give and accept positive feedback, expect others to succeed, and give others autonomy in completing tasks. Leaders with a positive self-concept and a Theory X philosophy tend to be bossy, pushy, and impatient; they also generally take on a dictatorial leadership style. Leaders with a negative self-concept and a Theory Y philosophy may seem afraid to make decisions, unassertive, and self-blaming. Finally, leaders with a negative self-concept and a Theory X philosophy blame others for the work unit's problems, are pessimistic about the possibility of resolving personal or organizational problems, and generally promote feelings of hopelessness among followers.

The Impact of Sex Role Stereotypes on Leadership

Leadership Emergence among Women and Men

Gaining entry to and investing in a career are the first steps in the leadership development process. The most typical route to occupational leadership for women and men involves starting at an entry level in a formal organization (often in a technical or specialized function), then moving up to manage others

FIGURE 7–5

Women's Membership in Parliaments

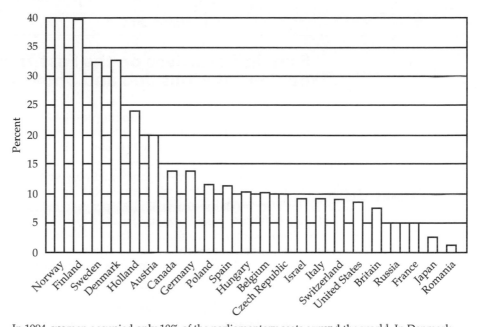

In 1994, women occupied only 10% of the parliamentary seats around the world. In Denmark, Sweden, Finland, and Norway, however, they occupied more than one-third of the seats. What is different about these countries? It's not just their views toward women; they all have proportional representation, a rule that provides party representation in parliamentary bodies based on the proportion of total votes the party receives (different, for example, from the "winner take all" rule practiced in U.S. congressional elections). Women have done much more poorly in countries without proportional representation, including Japan, Britain, and the United States.

Source: *The Economist*, November 19, 1994.

in the function, then managing managers of the function, and finally becoming a general manager of the groups of functions that form the business. It does appear that women are increasingly in the "pipeline" for becoming leaders in the world of work. In 1992, for example, it was estimated that 40 percent of midlevel managers and 2.9 percent of senior-level managers in Fortune 1,000 companies were women. In many countries there are also significant numbers of women in government roles (see Figure 7–5). Nonetheless, there still are obstacles ahead for women moving into leadership roles even as we see women entering law, medicine, sciences, the arts, and commerce in numbers equal to, if not greater than, white males (also see Highlight 7–6). What problems still exist?

In a classic study of sex roles, Schein (1973, 1975) demonstrated how bias in sex role stereotypes created problems for women moving up through these managerial roles. Schein asked male ($n = 300$) and female ($n = 167$) middle managers to complete a survey on which they rated various items on a 5-point scale in terms of how characteristic they were of (*a*) men in general, (*b*) women in general, or (*c*) successful managers. Schein found a high correlation between the ways both male and female respondents perceived "males" and "managers," but no correlation between the ways the respondents perceived "females" and "managers." It was as though being a manager was defined by attributes

Highlight 7–6

Female Executives on the Fast Track: You Can Take This Job and Shove It . . .

Although a higher percentage of females are filling positions in the executive suite, many of the best and brightest female managers are choosing to leave their parent organizations. Many are doing so because they have seen less-qualified males get promoted ahead of them, were frustrated with the slow pace of advancement, or had finally moved to a position where they could observe the top level of management and did not like what they saw. Few left their organizations for monetary reasons (many were making well over $150,000 per year) but instead left the comfort and security of their parent organizations in order to form their own small businesses. These females had all the requisite skills needed to be successful in the corporate world, but many of these skills were also precisely those needed to start up and maintain a small business. Many of these businesses have been phenomenal success stories, not only in terms of the bottom-line results but also as places where people prefer to work. These companies were often modeled after the values of their leaders—competitive and ambitious but also collaborative, affiliative, and supportive. Although these women are playing a key role in the American economy (over 70 percent of all workers are employed in companies with less than 50 people), one wonders how much more successful large organizations would be if they could stem the hemorrhaging of this talent. Moreover, because there is a real shortage of good leaders in our companies and institutions, organizations can ill afford to lose this talent.

Source: L. Baum, "Corporate Women: What It Takes to Get to the Top," *Business Week,* June 22, 1987, pp. 72–78.

thought of as masculine. Furthermore, it does not appear that the situation has changed much over the past two decades. In 1990, management students in the United States, Germany and Great Britain, for example, still perceived successful middle managers in terms of characteristics more commonly ascribed to men than to women (Schein & Mueller, 1990). One area where views *do* seem to have changed over time involves women's perceptions of their own roles. In contrast to the earlier studies, women today see as much similarity between "female" and "manager" as between "male" and "manager" (Brenner, Tomkiewicz, & Schein, 1989). To women, at least, being a woman and being a manager is not a contradiction in terms.

There also have been many other studies of the role of women in management. In one of these, *Breaking the Glass Ceiling* (Morrison, White, & Van Velsor, 1987), researchers documented the lives and careers of 78 of the highest-level women in corporate America. A few years later the researchers followed up with a small sample of those women to discuss any changes that had taken place in their leadership paths. The researchers were struck by the fact that the women were much like the senior men they had worked with in other studies. Qualitatively, they had the same fears: They wanted the best for themselves and for their families. They wanted their company to succeed. And, not surprisingly, they still had a drive to succeed. In some cases (also true for the men) they were beginning to ask questions about life balance—was all the sacrifice and hard work worth it? Were 60-hour workweeks worth the cost to family and self?

Looking more quantitatively, however, the researchers expected to find significant differences between the women who had broken the glass ceiling and the men who were already there. After all, the popular literature and some social scientific literature had conditioned them to expect that there is a feminine versus a masculine style of leadership, the feminine style being an outgrowth of a consensus/team oriented leadership approach. Women, in this view, are depicted as leaders who, when compared to men, are better listeners, more empathic, less analytical, more people oriented, and less aggressive in pursuit of goals.

In examining women in leadership positions, the researchers collected behavioral data, including ratings by both self and others, assessment center data (gathered from leadership development programs at the Center for Creative Leadership), and their scores on the California Psychological Inventory. Contrary to the stereotypes and popular views, however, there were no statistically significant differences between men's and women's leadership styles. Women and men were equally analytical, people oriented, forceful, goal oriented, empathic, and skilled at listening. There were other differences between the men and women, however, beyond the question of leadership styles. The researchers did find (and these results must be interpreted cautiously because of the relatively small numbers involved) that women had significantly lower well being scores, their commitment to the organizations they worked for was more guarded than that of their male counterparts, and the women were much more likely to be willing to take career risks associated with going to new or unfamiliar areas of the company where women had not been before.

Continued work with women in corporate leadership positions has both reinforced and somewhat clarified these findings. For example, the lower scores for women with regard to their ratings of general well-being may reflect the inadequacy of their support system for dealing with day-to-day issues of living. This is tied to the reality for many women that in addition to having roles in their companies they remain chief caretakers for their families. Further, there may be additional pressures of being visibly identified as proof that the organization has women at the top.

Other types of differences—those particularly around "people issues"—are still not evident. In fact, the hypothesis is that such supposed differences may hinder the opportunities for leadership development of women in the future. For example, turning around a business that is in trouble or starting a new business are two of the most exciting opportunities a developing leader has to test her leadership abilities. If we apply the "women are different" hypothesis, then the type of leadership skills needed for successful completion of either of these assignments may well leave women off the list of candidates. However, if we accept the hypothesis that women and men are more alike as leaders than they are different, then women will be found in equal numbers on the candidate list.

FIGURE 7–6

*The Narrow
Band of
Acceptable
Behavior*

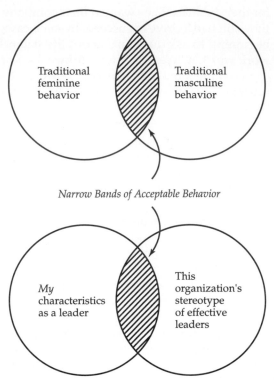

Narrow Bands of Acceptable Behavior

Source: Adapted from A. M. Morrison, R. P. White, and E. Van Velsor, *Breaking the Glass Ceiling* (Reading, MA: Addison-Wesley, 1987).

The Narrow Band of Acceptable Behavior

One of the most important factors which seems to impede the advance of women and other minorities into leadership roles is bias, a bias that might be labeled the **narrow band of acceptable behavior** (Morrison, White, & Van Velsor, 1987a &1987b). The narrow band of acceptable behavior is depicted in Figure 7–6. The characteristics and behaviors in the right-hand circle are those associated with traditional masculine behavior, and the characteristics and behaviors in the left-hand circle are those associated with traditional feminine behavior. The narrow band of overlap between the two circles can be thought of as a "hoop" women executives needed to pass through. Women executives in the *Glass Ceiling* project

> had to show their toughness and independence and at the same time count on others. It was essential that they contradict the stereotypes that their male executives and coworkers had about women—they had to be seen as different, "better than women" as a group. But they couldn't go too far, to forfeit all traces of femininity, because that would make them too alien to their superiors and colleagues. In essence, their mission was to do what *wasn't* expected of them as women to gain acceptance. The capacity to combine the two consistently, to stay within a narrow band of acceptable behavior, is the real key to success.

"That's what they all say, honey."

The concept of a narrow band of acceptable behavior is not limited to women. It may be applied to any individual's deviation from organizationally defined standards. The more a person looks like, acts like, dresses like, and talks like other leaders in the organization, the wider the band of acceptable behavior (the greater the overlap of the two circles). The less one looks like, acts like, dresses like, and talks like others—some of which, like gender, race, or nationality are beyond a person's control—the narrower the band of acceptable behavior. One implication of this view is that an individual who differs in obvious ways from the prototypical image of leader (as with gender) has less "wiggle room" available; it's as though there are already one or two strikes against that person. To put it differently, a narrower band of acceptable behavior is like walking a tightrope. The tightrope for the women executives in the *Glass Ceiling* study, for example, involved balancing the following inherently contradictory sets of expectations:

- Taking risks, but being consistently outstanding.
- Being tough but not macho.
- Being ambitious, but knowing you will not receive equal treatment.
- Taking responsibility, but following others' advice.

Even today, this active bias—some would call it a comfort factor of having leaders in the organization sharing common modes of behavior, values, looks, and attitudes—is still the basis for excluding women and other minorities from leadership ranks and from development opportunities. But is such bias inevitable? Must all women leaders pass the narrow band of acceptable behavior? Maybe not.

Research on second-generation managerial women suggest many of them appear to be succeeding *because of* characteristics heretofore considered too feminine for effective leadership (Rosener, 1990). Rosener's survey research identified several differences in how men and women described their leadership experiences. Men tended to describe themselves in somewhat transactional terms, viewing leadership as an exchange with subordinates for services rendered. They influenced others primarily through their organizational position and authority. The women, on the other hand, tended to describe themselves in transformational terms. They helped subordinates develop commitment for broader goals than their own self-interest, and described their influence more in terms of personal characteristics like charisma and interpersonal skill than mere organizational position.

According to Rosener such women leaders encouraged participation and shared power and information, but went far beyond what is commonly thought of as participative management. She called it **interactive leadership**. Their leadership self-descriptions reflected an approach based on enhancing others' self-worth and believing that the best performance results when people are excited about their work and feel good about themselves.

How did this interactive leadership style develop? Rosener concluded it was due to these women's socialization experiences and career paths. As we indicated above, the social role expected of women has emphasized they be cooperative, supportive, understanding, gentle, and service-oriented. As they entered the business world, they still found themselves in roles emphasizing these same behaviors. They found themselves in staff, rather than line, positions, and in roles lacking formal authority over others such that they had to accomplish their work without reliance on formal power. What they had to do, in other words, was employ their socially acceptable behavioral repertoire in order to survive organizationally.

> What came easily to women turned out to be a survival tactic. Although leaders often begin their careers doing what comes naturally and what fits within the constraints of the job, they also develop their skills and styles over time. The women's use of interactive leadership has its roots in socialization, and the women interviewees firmly believe that it benefits their organizations. Through the course of their careers, they have gained conviction that their style is effective. In fact, for some it was their own success that caused them to formulate their philosophies about what motivates people, how to make good decisions, and what it takes to maximize business performance. (p. 124)

Such women's success, however, does not mean the narrow band of acceptable behavior has disappeared. The women in the survey were for the most part *not* from large, traditional companies, like those in the *Glass Ceiling* project. Rosener called for organizations to expand their definitions of effective leadership—to create a *wider* band of acceptable behavior so that both men and women will be

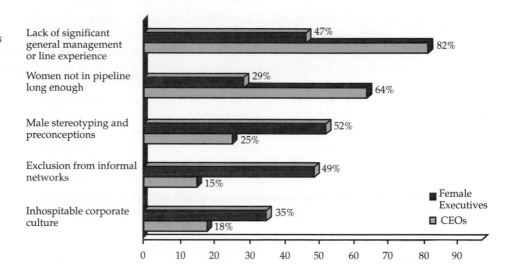

FIGURE 7–7

What Prevents Women from Advancing to Corporate Leadership?

freer to lead in ways which take advantage of their true talents (see Highlight 7–6 on page 186). The extent of the problem is suggested by data from a recent study looking at how CEOs, almost all male, and senior female executives explained the paucity of women in corporate leadership roles. Figure 7–7 compares the percentages of CEOs versus female executives who endorsed various possible explanations of the situation. It is clear that the CEOs attributed it primarily to inadequacies in the quantity and quality of experience of potential women candidates for the top spots, while the females themselves attributed it to various forms of stereotyping and bias.

Leading Across Cultures

A rather common problem for office managers in the United States is controlling the use of the office copier. Frequently, office managers publish policies and procedures to govern use of the machines, and hence control administrative costs. When a U.S. manager of a water resources project in Indonesia did the same thing, however, an action he considered routine, he was accused of insensitivity to Indonesian ways—in fact, accused not just of unfriendliness but of unethical behavior. After a series of similar incidents, he lost his job. Leading across cultures requires an appreciation of the sometimes profound differences in the value systems of other cultures.

What Is Culture?

A good starting place for understanding differences in cultural value systems is with the concept of culture itself. **Culture** refers to those learned behaviors characterizing the total way of life of members within any given society. Cultures differ from one another just as individuals differ from one another. To outsiders, the most salient aspect of any culture typically involves behavior—the distinctive actions, mannerisms, and gestures characteristic of that culture. Americans visiting Thailand, for example, may find it curious and even bothersome to see male Thais hold hands with each other in public. They may react negatively to such behavior since it is untypical to *them*, and laden with *North American* meaning (e.g., "It's okay for women to hold hands in public, but men just shouldn't do that!"). Salient as such behaviors are, however, they are also just the tip of the iceberg. The "mass" of culture is *not* so readily visible, just as most of an iceberg lies beneath the water. Hidden from view are the beliefs, values, and myths that provide context to manifest behaviors (Kohls, 1984). A clear implication for business leaders in the global context, therefore, is the need to become aware and respectful of cultural differences and cultural perspectives. Barnum (1992) pointed out the importance of being able to look at one's own culture through the eyes of another:

> Consciously or unconsciously they will be using their own beliefs as the yardsticks for judging you, so know how to compare those yardsticks by ferreting out their values and noting where they differ the least and most from yours. For example, if their belief in fatalism outweighs your belief in accountability, there will be conflicts down the road. This is a severe problem in the Middle East, for instance, and affects management styles in companies and even the ability to market life insurance, which is frowned upon in communities where Muslim observances are strong. (p. 153)

A Framework for Understanding Cultural Differences

Thus, it can be helpful to see one's own culture through the eyes of another; just as it also can be helpful to see other cultures through eyes unbiased (or at least less biased) by one's own filters. Researchers at the *Center for Creative Leadership* have developed a tool for doing just that, a conceptual framework for analyzing cultural differences (Wilson, Hoppe, & Sayles, 1996). In the world of work, especially, they suggest that there are seven fundamental dilemmas that people of all cultures face. Let us look at each of these seven dilemmas in greater detail.

Source of Identity: Individual–Collective. This deals with the degree to which individuals should pursue their own interests and goals versus contribute to a larger group, whether extended family, ethnic group, or company.

Goals and Means of Achievement: Tough–Tender. This deals with how success is defined in a culture. Is it defined by tangible rewards like financial success and material well-being or by intangible rewards such as good relationships with others or spiritual satisfaction?

Orientation to Authority: Equal–Unequal. How should people of different status, authority, or power behave toward each other—as equals or unequals?

Response to Ambiguity: Dynamic–Stable. To what extent is uncertainty accepted or tolerated? In running an organization, are tight controls and structure imposed to ensure certainty, or is greater tolerance for ambiguity and uncertainty evident via loose or nonexistent control systems?

Means of Knowledge Acquisition: Active–Reflective. Is action or reflection more valued as a means of acquiring information and knowledge?

Perspective on Time: Scarce–Plentiful. Is the sense or experience of time urgent or relaxed?

Outlook on Life: Doing–Being. Which is more preferred—mastery over nature or living in harmony with nature? Is the outcome of life more dependent upon human effort or on the expression of divine will?

You probably can see how misunderstandings and slights can occur when people from different cultures are working together, but let us look at two specific applications of this scheme. First, consider the historic U.S. emphasis on individualism (e.g., the focus on *self*-confidence, *self*-control, *self*-concept, *self*-expression, or the way rugged individualists are heroically portrayed in film, television, and literature) and how it might impact work. Given an individualist perspective, certain management practices and expectations seem self-evident, such as the idea of individual accountability for work. When individual accountability is valued, for example, decision-making authority tends to be delegated to individual managers. What's more, those same managers may be inclined to take personal credit when the job is well done. A different norm, however, applies in industrialized Japan. Decision making is often very time-consuming, to assure that everyone who will be impacted by a decision has input on it beforehand. (Highlight 7–7 examines other differences between Japanese and American management practices.) Another "self-evident" principle to the U.S. mind is that individual career progress is desirable and "good." In some other cultures, however, managers resist competing with peers for rewards or promotions so as not to disturb the harmony of the group or appear self-interested.

Another example of potential conflict or misunderstanding can be seen in the case of orientation to authority, how people should handle power and authority relationships with others. The United States is a relatively young and mobile country, populated mostly by immigrants. Relative to other countries, there is little concern with family origin or class background. There is a belief that success should come through an individual's hard work and talent, not by birthright or class standing. This all leads to a relative informality at work, even among individuals of strikingly different position within a company. Subordinates expect their bosses to be accessible, even responsive in some ways to their subordinates. In some other cultures, however, higher status in a company confers nearly unchallengeable authority, and as well an expectation that most decisions will be referred *up* to them (as distinguished from delegated down to others). You can see even from just these two examples that the seven dimensions of cultural values create quite an array of possible tensions between people from different cultures working together.

Implications for Leadership Practitioners

The perspectives and findings presented in this chapter have significant implications for leadership practitioners. Perhaps most importantly, leadership practitioners should *expect* to face a variety of challenges to their own system of ethics, values, or attitudes during their careers. Additionally, values

Highlight 7–7

Japanese and American Management Practices

Working in a manufacturing plant located in the United States but owned by a Japanese parent company can require adapting to a very different management style than one is accustomed to. Here are some common Japanese management practices and philosophies that may require getting used to on the part of U.S. workers and managers.

- Emphasis on team cooperation and group harmony.
- Shallow organizational hierarchies and vague job descriptions.
- Mandatory morning exercise for all employees.
- Company uniforms.
- Morning pep talks by supervisors.
- Emphasis on company loyalty.
- No direct orders from supervisors to employees.
- Extensive lateral communication.
- Bottom-up, consensual decision making.
- After-work socializing with fellow employees to foster cohesiveness and company loyalty.

Would you feel comfortable adapting to such practices at work? Do you feel you should need to? Is it your choice (or any worker's) whether you adapt to them or not?

often are a source of interpersonal conflict. Although we sometimes say two people don't get along because of a personality conflict, often these conflicts are due to differences in value systems, not personality traits. Often, people on either side of an issue see *only* themselves and their own side as morally justifiable. Nonetheless, people holding seemingly antithetical values may still need to work together, and dealing with diverse and divergent values will be an increasingly common challenge for leaders. As noted earlier, interacting with individuals and groups holding divergent and conflicting values will be an inevitable fact of life for future leaders (see Highlight 7–8). This does not mean, however, that increased levels of interpersonal conflict are inevitable. Both leaders and followers might be well advised to minimize the conflict and tension often associated with value differences. Leaders in particular have a responsibility not to let their own personal values interfere with professional leader–subordinate relationships unless the conflicts pertain to issues clearly relevant to the work and the organization. (See Highlight 7–9 for a perspective on how subordinates' values may or may not affect the evaluation of a leader.)

Highlight 7–8

Louis Farrakhan and the Million Man March

Louis Farrakhan, leader of the Nation of Islam, assembled the largest black audience ever in America for his Million Man March in 1995. Farrakhan is a highly visible yet unsettling figure in contemporary America. After all, what should people make of a religious leader who calls those of other faiths "bloodsuckers," and is implicated by rumor in the assassination of Malcolm X, his predecessor? Without question, Farrakhan evokes strikingly different reactions in others.

To some extent, perceptions of Louis Farrakhan are skewed by race, much as perceptions of O. J. Simpson's guilt or innocence are skewed by race. In a *Time* magazine poll, for example, 48 percent of whites (compared to 36 percent of blacks) believed the phrase "a bigot and racist" accurately applied to Farrakhan. Forty-eight percent of blacks said the phrase did not apply at all to Farrakhan, whereas only 12 percent of whites said it did not apply. Even within the black community, however, there are widely divergent views of Farrakhan. Eldridge Cleaver, for example, a black leader who gained notoriety as a radical in the 1960s, said that after Malcolm X's murder, "Farrakhan gravitated to the top of the heap as the slime-ball, scheming, renegade bandwagoner that he is."

Sometimes Farrakhan seems paranoid as well as racist. For example, he believes that Jewish financiers manipulate world events. And he was infuriated by television reports that claimed the actual attendance at his Million Man March fell far short of the number he claimed were there. Such deceitful media reports, he said, were a racist plot. Despite such wild claims, however, Farrakhan did make the Million Man March a reality. Although he has been criticized by other black leaders for his failure to use the march as a stimulus for corrective political action, perhaps no other contemporary black leader could have orchestrated the march at all, Jesse Jackson and Colin Powell included.

The comparison between Farrakhan and Powell is an interesting one. There are several parallels between them. Both were born in New York in the 1930s to West Indian immigrants. Both were raised in the Episcopal church. Both are extremely intelligent, articulate, and recognizable. But they followed different paths to prominence: Powell sought success in white society via the integrated U.S. Army, Farrakhan among the troops of racial separatism.

It remains to be seen which of them will have the greater long-term impact on the country.

Sources: H. L. Gates, Jr., "The Charmer," *The New Yorker*, April 29, 1996, pp.116–131; H. Fineman and V. E. Smith, "An Angry Charmer," *Newsweek*, October 30, 1995, pp. 32–37; S. Monroe, "The Mirage of Farrakhan," *Time*, October 30, 1995, p. 52.

Summary

This chapter reviews evidence regarding the relationships between ethics, values, attitudes, and leadership success. Values are constructs that represent general sets of behaviors or states of affairs that individuals consider to be

Does Character Count?

Does one's character make a difference in the kind of leader one will be? Decades ago, Richard Nixon's critics frequently asked, "Would you buy a used car from this man?" The obvious implication was whether a person who seemed shifty was suited for high political office.

Once again, as this book goes to press, the United States is confronting the relationship between private and public character, and the answers are anything but clear. Despite being embroiled in one of the more notorious scandals in recent American political history, President Clinton's approval ratings have remained high. For example, a *Time*/CNN survey in March 1998 indicated an approval rating of 67 percent, just a point below his own all time high. This, even while a majority (52 percent) also expressed the belief that he has engaged in a pattern of sexual misconduct while president. On the surface, it would seem that "mere" sexual misconduct is not enough to tarnish a president's job performance. On a more fundamental level, however, do these results really imply that people do not care whether their leaders demonstrate integrity and trustworthiness?

We gain some insight into this issue by examining the polling data in further detail. The 67 percent who approved of Clinton's job performance despite accusations of his sexual misconduct explained their rationale in the following ways (percentages represent those who said reasons were "extremely" or "very" important factors in their judgment):

- A president is a human being, with all the temptations the rest of us have (68 percent).
- A president's private life has no bearing on his suitability for the job (37 percent).
- His performance in running the country is so good that I'm willing to put up with his failings (52 percent).
- While lying is seldom acceptable, lying about sex is something that most of us do (40 percent).

In reviewing the public sentiment on this issue, many of us seem to find that we have drastically lowered our expectations that leaders should exemplify outstanding character. Others, though, might counter that we are finally becoming realistic in our expectations of leaders.

What do *you* think? Rather than focusing on the fairly distant world of presidential politics, however, answer the following questions with reference to *your own boss (or professor!)*:

- If you found this person had lied to you about something in his or her personal life, would it have no impact whatsoever on your estimation of him or her as a leader?
- If this person had a pattern of sexual misconduct with very junior members of the staff (or students), would that seem "harmless" to you, and irrelevant to his or her leadership effectiveness?

Source: *Time*, March 30, 1998, pp. 21–25.

important, and they play a central part of a leader's psychological makeup. Values are an important component of the moral reasoning process, which is the process people use to resolve moral or ethical dilemmas. This is important since leaders undoubtedly will face a variety of ethical dilemmas during their careers. Values also serve to organize attitudes, which are general and enduring positive or negative feelings about some person, object, or issue. People typically have only a few strongly held values, but they can have literally thousands of different attitudes. Although leaders can have a variety of attitudes, their attitudes about themselves and about others play particularly important roles in leadership behaviors. Finally, despite the significant progress women have made in moving into managerial and leadership ranks in their organizations, sex role stereotypes still adversely impact the opportunity of women—and other minority groups too—to exercise the full range of their talents and behavioral repertoire and be rewarded for it.

Key Terms

values	postconventional level
value programming	affective component
moral reasoning	Darley's law
attitude	principle-centered leadership
ideational component	narrow band of acceptable behavior
behavioral component	culture
Theory X	moral justification
Theory Y	euphemistic labeling
ethics	advantageous comparison
interactive leadership	displacement of responsibility
self-concept	diffusion of responsibility
self-esteem	distortion of consequences
preconventional level	dehumanization
conventional level	attribution of blame

Discussion Questions

1. Do you think it always must be "lonely at the top" (or that if it is not, you are doing something wrong)?

2. How do you believe one's basic philosophy of human nature affects one's approach to leadership?

3. Identify several values you think might be the basis of conflict or misunderstanding between leaders and followers.

4. Can a leader's public and private morality be distinguished? Should they be?

5. Can a bad person be a good leader?

6. Are there any leadership roles men and women should not have equal opportunity to compete for?

8 PERSONALITY

Chapter Outline

Introduction

It is natural for people to think about leadership mostly in terms of the personal qualities of leaders (see Highlight 8–1). Perhaps the earliest theory of leadership was the **Great Man theory** (Stogdill, 1974). This theory, popular in the early 1900s, held that leaders and followers were fundamentally different. More specifically, this theory was based on the premise that, compared to followers, leaders were more capable and possessed a qualitatively different set of personality traits. And because leaders were thought to possess a different set of personality traits, it was also believed that they acted in ways that differed fundamentally from those of followers. Although the Great Man theory generated a considerable amount of research, the general conclusion from it all was that leaders and followers were not fundamentally different. This lack of

Leadership Quotes, Chapter 8

The question, "Who ought to be boss?" is like asking, "Who ought to be the tenor in the quartet?" Obviously, the man who can sing tenor.

Henry Ford

There is an optical illusion about every person we ever meet. In truth, they are all creatures of a given temperament, which will appear in a given character, whose boundaries they will never pass: but we look at them, they seem alive, and we presume there is impulse in them. In the moment, it seems like impulse, in the year, in the lifetime, it turns out to be a certain uniform tune, which the revolving barrel of the musicbox must play.

Ralph Waldo Emerson

You'll get hired for your intelligence, but you'll get fired for your personality.

Gordy Curphy

Being entirely honest with oneself is a good exercise.

Sigmund Freud

If a man be gloomy, let him keep to himself. No one has a right to go croaking about society, or what is worse, looking as if he stifled grief.

Benjamin Disraeli

*O wad some Power the giftie gie us
to see ourselves as others see us!*

Robert Burns

When reviewing personality feedback, I am always amazed at people's capacity to be infinitely interested in themselves.

Gordy Curphy

support for the Great Man theory was due primarily to the diversity of successful leaders: Some leaders were outgoing and others were more introspective, some were planful and organized and others were more impulsive and spontaneous, and some were stoic and approachable and others temperamental and distant. Nevertheless, this and more recent research clearly shows that possessing certain personality traits generally helps leaders (and in many cases followers) to be more successful, but that personality traits alone are no guarantee for success.

As an overview, this chapter begins by reviewing some common definitions of personality and then provides a model for organizing personality traits. The next sections describe ways personality traits are typically assessed, the dark side of personality, and the implications of personality assessment and research results for leadership practitioners. After reviewing what we know about personality traits and leadership, we discuss an alternative model for describing personality: types. The chapter concludes with a discussion of a popular personality typology based on psychological preferences and its implications for leadership.

Personality Traits and Leadership

What Is Personality?

Despite its common usage, Robert Hogan (1991) notes that the term **personality** is fairly ambiguous, and has at least two quite different meanings. One meaning refers to the impression a person makes on others. This view of personality emphasizes a person's *social reputation* and reflects not only a description but also an evaluation of the person in the eyes of others. From the standpoint of leadership, this view of personality addresses two distinct issues: "What kind of leader or person is this?" and "Is this somebody I would like to work for or be associated with?" When we say one person is aloof but another is warm and outgoing, we are making judgments about their social reputations. This definition of personality concerns public information that can be easily verified, and research has shown observers tend to have high levels of agreement when describing another's typical behavior patterns (Curphy, 1998b; Curphy & Osten, 1993; J. Hogan, 1992; Nilsen, 1995). In other words, social impressions are fairly universal; people tend to use the same terms when describing another's public reputation.

In a practical sense, this view of personality comes into play whenever you describe someone to a roommate or friend. For example, you might describe a classmate as pushy, honest, outgoing, neat, impulsive, decisive, friendly, arrogant, and independent. Furthermore, whatever impression this person made on you, chances are others would use many of the same terms to describe him or her. In that same vein, many people would probably say that Colin Powell is self-confident, friendly, conventional, outgoing, and achievement-oriented, and that he handles pressure well.

As noted earlier, however, this all pertains to just one meaning of personality. Its second meaning emphasizes the underlying, unseen structures and processes inside a person that explain why we behave the way we do; why each person's behavior tends to be relatively *similar across different situations*, yet also *different from another person's behavior*. Over the years psychologists have developed many theories to explain how such unseen structures may cause individuals to act in their characteristic manner. For example, Sigmund Freud (1913) believed that the intrapsychic tensions among the id, ego, and superego caused one to behave in characteristic ways even if the real motives behind the behaviors were unknown (i.e., unconscious) to the person. Although useful insights about personality have come from many different theories, most of the research addressing the relationship between personality and leadership success has been based on the **trait approach**, and that emphasis is most appropriate here.

"**Traits** refer to recurring regularities or trends in a person's behavior" (R. Hogan, 1991, p. 875), and the trait approach to personality maintains that people behave the way they do because of the strengths of the traits they possess. Although traits cannot be seen, they can be inferred from consistent patterns of behavior and reliably measured by paper-and-pencil tests. For example, the personality trait of dependability differentiates people who tend to be hardworking and rule abiding from those who do not like to work hard and are more prone to break rules. People getting higher scores on the trait of dependability on a personality test would be more likely to come to work on time, do a thorough job in completing work assignments, and rarely leave work early. We would also infer that people getting lower scores on the trait of dependability would be late to work more often or fail to turn in assignments more frequently.

Personality traits are useful concepts for explaining why people act fairly consistently from one situation to the next. This cross-situational consistency in behavior may be thought of as analogous to the seasonal weather patterns in different cities (Hogan, Hogan, & Roberts, 1996; Roberts, 1996). We know that it is extremely cold and dry in Minneapolis in January, and hot and humid in Hong Kong in August. Therefore, we can do a pretty good job of predicting what the weather will generally be like in Minneapolis in January, even though our predictions for any particular day will not be perfect. Although the average temperature in Minneapolis hovers around 20°F, the temperature ranges from −30°F to 30°F on any single day in January.

Similarly, knowing how two people differ on a particular personality trait can help us predict more accurately how they will tend to act in a variety of situations. Even if one person is generally more outgoing and gregarious whereas the other is generally more shy and introspective, it is difficult to predict how either individual will act in any specific situation (e.g., a particular staff meeting at work). As we will see later in this chapter, effective leaders generally act somewhat similarly across situations, but how they might act in any particular situation is never absolutely certain.

Just as various climate factors can affect the temperature on any single day, so can external factors affect a leader's behavior in any given situation. The trait approach maintains that a leader's behavior reflects an interaction between her personality traits and various situational factors (see, for example, Highlights 8–2 and 8–3). Traits play a particularly important role in determining how people behave in unfamiliar, ambiguous, or what we might call **weak situations**. On the other hand, situations that are governed by clearly specified rules, demands, or organizational policies—**strong situations**—often minimize the effects traits have on behavior (Curphy, 1997a, c; 1996b).

Here is an example of how a personality trait may exert greater or lesser influence on a person's behavior depending on the strength of the situation. Suppose two people differ on the personality traits of dominance and steadiness (e.g., the first is interpersonally very competitive and sensitive to stress, whereas

---

Highlight 8–2

Personality and the Presidency, I

Traits are unseen dispositions that can affect the way people act. Their existence can be inferred by a person's consistent pattern of behaviors. One way of examining a person's standing on the trait of achievement-orientation is to examine one's achievements and accomplishments over the life span. People with higher levels of achievement-orientation tend to set high personal goals and are persistent in the pursuit of these goals. When considering the following leader's achievements and accomplishments, think about this person's standing on this personality trait, and try to guess who this person might be:

Age 23: lost a job.
Age 23: was defeated in bid for state legislature.
Age 24: failed in business venture.
Age 25: was elected to legislature.
Age 26: sweetheart died.
Age 27: experienced several emotional problems.
Age 27: was defeated in bid to be speaker of the house.
Age 34: was defeated for nomination to Congress.
Age 37: was elected to Congress.
Age 39: lost renomination to Congress.
Age 40: was defeated in bid for land office.
Age 45: was defeated in bid for U.S. Senate.
Age 47: was defeated for nomination to be vice president.
Age 49: was defeated in bid for Senate a second time.
Age 51: was elected president of the United States.

The person was Abraham Lincoln.

---

the other is interpersonally very cooperative and calm). Might these two people act differently while driving their car? The answer is, it would depend a lot on whether a particular traffic situation is weak or strong. Some situations, like waiting at a red light or being followed by a police car, are so strong that the two individuals are likely to behave quite similarly whatever their personality traits may be (i.e., both would wait until the light turns green or avoid speeding). In weaker traffic situations, however, like driving behind a car going very slowly in the fast lane, we might expect the driver's behavior to reflect his personality traits to a much greater degree. The first driver might be more likely to behave in such ways as cursing out loud, honking the horn, or making unwelcome gestures at the car ahead. In a similar fashion, traits typically have the greatest impact on leadership behavior in relatively weak situations—for example, in situations where there are few policies, procedures, guidelines, or norms to govern behavior.

Personality and the Presidency, II: The Toughness of Harry Truman

Historians consider Harry Truman one of the greatest American presidents, and many older Americans consider him one of their favorites. However, he also was an unexpected president in two different ways. He first assumed the presidency when Franklin Delano Roosevelt died, and he won election to the presidency in his own right very unexpectedly in 1948. When Harry Truman defeated Thomas Dewey, the highly favored Republican candidate, it was the upset of the century. In the final weeks of the campaign, a poll of 50 political experts indicated that every one of them predicted a GOP landslide (Clifford, 1991). You may have seen the famous pictures of Truman grinning and holding a newspaper with the premature and embarrassingly erroneous headline "Dewey Defeats Truman."

Clark Clifford, a key advisor to Truman during that campaign, and to numerous presidents since then, saw one reason for Truman's victory that transcended all others—the man himself. Truman's tenacity and unwillingness to give up when few others held out any hope made the difference. This is one example of how personality made a significant difference in national leadership. Following are a few of Harry Truman's more famous quotations, which convey his toughness.

I told them I knew they had been making trouble for the previous commanders. I said: "I didn't come over here to get along with you. You've got to get along with me. And if there are any of you who can't, speak up and I'll bust you right back." We got along.

> Captain Harry S Truman
> On taking command of a field artillery battalion, 1918

If you need a friend in Washington, get a dog.

A president who's any damn good at all makes enemies, makes a lot of them. I made a few myself and I wouldn't be without them.

The buck stops here.
(A sign on his desk)

In December 1950, President Truman's daughter, Margaret, gave a public singing recital in Washington, which was unenthusiastically received by Paul Hume, music critic of the Washington Post. He characterized her voice as having "little size and fair quality," said she sang flat much of the time, and complained that there were "few moments . . . when one can relax and feel confident that she will make her goal, which is the end of the song." In response to the review Truman penned the following letter:

> *I have just read your lousy review buried in the back pages. You sound like a frustrated old man who never made a success, an eight-ulcer man on a four-ulcer job, and all four ulcers working. I have never met you, but if I do you'll need a new nose and plenty of beefsteak and perhaps a supporter below. Westbrook Pegler, a gutter-snipe, is a gentleman compared to you. You can take that as more of an insult than as a reflection on your ancestry.*

> This letter was made public and caused a considerable furor, but most Americans seem generally to have approved Truman's fatherly readiness to leap to his daughter's defense.
>
> Sources: Adapted from Clifton Fadiman, ed., *The Little, Brown Book of Anecdotes* (Boston: Little, Brown, 1985); and William Safir and Leonard Safir, eds., *Leadership* (New York: Simon & Schuster, 1990).

The Big Five Model of Personality

Although personality traits provide a useful approach to describing distinctive, cross-situational behavioral patterns, one potential problem is the sheer number of traitlike terms available to describe another's stereotypical behaviors. As early as 1936 Allport and Odbert identified over 18,000 trait-related adjectives in a standard English dictionary. Despite this large number of adjectives, research has shown that most of the traitlike terms people use to describe others' behavioral patterns could be reliably categorized into five broad personality dimensions. Historically, this five-dimension model was first identified by Webb in 1915 (Deary, 1996) and independently verified by Thurstone (1934), but over the years a number of researchers using very diverse samples and assessment instruments have noted similar results (see Hogan, Curphy, & Hogan, 1994). Given the robustness of the findings, there appears to be a compelling body of evidence to support these five dimensions of personality. These dimensions are referred to in the personality literature as the **"Big Five" model of personality**, and most modern personality researchers endorse some version of this model (Azar, 1995; Barrick & Mount, 1996; Curphy, 1998b; Hogan, 1991; Hogan, Hogan, & Roberts, 1996).

At its core, the Big Five model of personality is a categorization scheme. Most, if not all, of the personality traits that you would use to describe someone else could be reliably categorized into one of the Big Five personality dimensions. A diagram and description of the model can be found in Table 8–1. The

TABLE 8–1   The Big Five Model of Personality

Big Five Dimensions	Traits	Behaviors/Items
Surgency	*Dominance*	I like having responsibility for others.
	Extroversion	I like to tell jokes and stories at parties.
Agreeableness	*Compassion*	I am a sympathetic person.
	Warmth	I am usually in a good mood.
	Sociability	I have a large group of friends.
Dependability	*Organization*	I usually make "to do" lists.
	Credibility	I practice what I preach.
	Conformity	I rarely get into trouble.
	Achievement orientation	I am a high achiever.
Adjustment	*Steadiness*	I remain calm in pressure situations.
	Self-acceptance	I take personal criticism well.
Intellectance		I like traveling to foreign countries.

five major dimensions include surgency, dependability, agreeableness, adjustment, and intellectance. Perhaps the easiest way to understand this categorization scheme is to describe how different people would fall into each of the Big Five categories. The lead characters from several popular television series and movies might prove useful for explaining the different personality dimensions of the Big Five model.

Surgency (also referred to as dominance, self-confidence, the need for power, or dynamic) involves patterns of behavior often exhibited in group settings and generally concerned with getting ahead in life (Michel & Hogan 1996). Such behavioral patterns often appear when someone is trying to influencing others. Individuals higher in surgency like to be around others and enjoy influencing and competing with them. Individuals lower in surgency prefer to work by themselves and have relatively little interest in influencing or competing with others. Surgency is made up of two highly related personality traits, *dominance* and *extroversion*. Dominance is the extent to which a person likes or needs to control or influence others; individuals higher in dominance seek out positions of authority, like to lead others, and tend to be competitive whereas leaders lower in dominance tend to be more deferential and collaborative. Individuals higher in extroversion are relatively outgoing and gregarious whereas leaders lower in extroversion are less apt to initiate conversations (but are often seen as good listeners). Given her competitive and outspoken nature, Mimi from the "Drew Carey" show might be a good example of someone who is relatively high in dominance and extroversion. Jerry Seinfeld, on the other hand, seems to be much less competitive and talkative (in his everyday behavior on the show, not as stand up comedian), and may be lower in both dominance and extroversion.

Another Big Five personality dimension is **agreeableness** (also known as empathy, collegiality, or the need for affiliation). Unlike surgency, however, this personality dimension concerns how one gets along with, as opposed to getting ahead of, others (Michel & Hogan, 1996). Individuals high in agreeableness tend to be empathetic and approachable, and to have a large circle of friends; those lower in agreeableness are more apt to appear insensitive and distant, and to have fewer friends. Agreeableness is made up of three related personality traits. Individuals who are sensitive to, and concerned with, others' feelings and problems tend to be higher in *compassion*, whereas those lower in compassion may be seen as insensitive. People who are higher in *warmth* tend to be easygoing, optimistic, and friendly, whereas those who are lower on this trait may seem cold, pessimistic, and difficult to approach. Those who make friends easily tend to be high in *sociability*; those lower in the trait of sociability tend to develop fewer relationships. Because he comes across as insensitive and pessimistic, and has a small group of friends, George Costanza on "Seinfeld" would probably have scores close to the bottom of the scale on all three personality traits. George and Jerry's friend Kramer, however, seems more sensitive to others' problems and more optimistic, and he has a larger circle of friends; Kramer would probably have higher scores on all three traits.

Dependability (also known as conscientiousness or the need for achievement) does not involve interacting with others but rather concerns those behavioral patterns related to work itself. People who are higher in dependability tend to be planful and hardworking, follow through with their commitments, and rarely get into trouble. Those who are lower in dependability tend to be more spontaneous and less concerned with getting a job done or following through with commitments. Dependability is made up of four related traits: *organization, credibility, conformity,* and *achievement orientation.* Individuals high in the trait of organization tend to be methodical and detail oriented. Those higher in the trait of credibility are more apt to keep promises and "walk their talk," whereas those lower in credibility are more likely, for example, to miss deadlines. Individuals higher in the trait of conformity are less likely to break rules, whereas those lower in conformity are more likely to question policies and break rules. The trait of achievement orientation differentiates individuals who set high personal goals and willingly put in extra time and effort in order to accomplish them from those who set lower personal goals and are less willing to make these sacrifices. Given his fastidious, studious nature and tendency to not break promises, Niles Crane of "Frasier" might score at the top of all four of the personality traits associated with dependability. Kramer, George Costanzo, and Bart Simpson seem to set low personal goals and come across as spontaneous and willing to break rules and promises for personal benefit, and as a result would have lower scores on all four traits.

Adjustment (also known as emotional stability or self-control) is concerned with how people react to stress, failure, or personal criticism. Individuals higher in adjustment tend to be calm and tend not to take mistakes or failures personally, whereas those lower in adjustment may become tense, anxious, or exhibit emotional outbursts when stressed or criticized. Like the other personality dimensions, adjustment is made up of related personality traits, which in this case are *steadiness* and *self-acceptance.* Individuals who are higher in emotional stability typically appear to be on an even keel temperamentally and may even seem to thrive on pressure; those lower in steadiness may more frequently complain about a problem situation, criticize others, or exhibit emotional outbursts. Those higher in self-acceptance are comfortable with themselves and can tolerate personal criticism. People lower in self-acceptance are often more thin-skinned and may dwell on their own personal mistakes or failures. Because of their thin-skinned and temperamental natures, both Elaine and George from "Seinfeld" are probably lower in the trait of adjustment. With her ability to stay cool under pressure, Ripley in the *Aliens* movie series would be a good example of someone considerably higher in adjustment.

Those behavioral patterns dealing with how one reacts to new experiences are related to the personality dimension of **intellectance** (also known as openness to experience). Individuals higher in intellectance tend to be imaginative, broad-minded, and curious; they seek out new experiences via traveling, the arts, movies, sports, reading, going to new restaurants, or learning about new cultures. Individuals lower in intellectance tend to be more practical and have narrower interests; they like doing things the tried-and-true way rather than experimenting with new ways. Given their interests in theater, art, music, and food, both Niles and Frasier Crane are good examples of people high in the trait of intellectance. Marty Crane (their father), who sits in the same chair to watch a standard regimen of television programs (mostly sports), is probably much lower in intellectance.

Another way to differentiate between people receiving higher and lower scores on intellectance is to look at the choices they make when scheduling classes. People with higher intellectance like taking courses in diverse subjects, whereas those lower in intellectance are more likely to stick to elective courses within their major area to the extent possible. As a final point, it is important to note that intellectance is not the same thing as intelligence—smart people are not necessarily intellectually curious.

Advantages and Disadvantages of the Big Five Model

The trait approach and the Big Five model provide leadership researchers and practitioners with several useful tools and insights. For one, personality traits provide researchers and practitioners with an explanation for leaders' and followers' tendencies to act in consistent ways over time. They help us to understand why some leaders are dominant versus deferent, outspoken versus quiet, planful versus spontaneous, warm versus cold, and so forth. It is also important to note that the behavioral manifestations of personality traits are often exhibited automatically and without much conscious thought. People high in dominance and extroversion, for example, will often maneuver to influence or lead whatever groups or teams they are a part of without even thinking about it. However, although our personality traits predispose us to act in certain ways, we can nonetheless learn to modify our behaviors through experience, feedback, and reflection.

As seen in Figure 8–1, personality traits are one of the key components of behavior and are relatively difficult to change. Moreover, because personality traits tend to be stable over the years and the behavioral manifestations of traits occur somewhat automatically, it is extremely important for leaders, and leaders to be, to have insight into their personalities. For example, consider a leader who is relatively low in the trait of adjustment, but also is deciding whether to accept a high-stress/high-visibility job. On the basis of his personality trait scores alone, we might predict that this leader could be especially sensitive to criticism, as well as moody and prone to emotional outbursts. If the leader understood that he may have issues dealing with stress and criticism, then he could choose not to take the position, modify the situation to reduce the level of stress, or learn techniques for effectively dealing with these issues. A leader who lacked this self-insight would probably make poorer choices and have more difficulties coping with the demands of this position (Curphy, 1996a).

FIGURE 8–1

*The Building
Blocks of Skills*

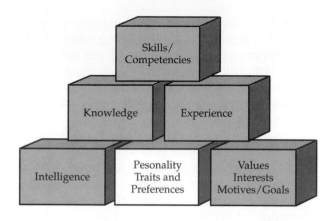

The Big Five model has proved to be very useful in several different ways. It is fairly robust, and most personality researchers currently embrace some form of the Big Five model (Azar, 1995; Barrick & Mount, 1996; Curphy, 1998b; Hogan, Hogan, & Roberts, 1996; Howard & Howard, 1995). Furthermore, the model has proved to be a very useful categorization scheme. For example, one of the problems with the personality-leadership performance research of the past was that different researchers would use different trait labels to refer to essentially the same patterns of behavior. One researcher might label a particular behavioral pattern as dominance, whereas others might label the same pattern as control, surgency, self-confidence, assertiveness, or the need for power. This labeling dilemma made it almost impossible to find consistent relationships between personality and leadership *even when they really existed*; researchers might only look at those studies including measures of dominance and overlook those examining control, surgency, or assertiveness. Although there was some evidence showing that personality was related to leadership, Hogan, Curphy, and Hogan (1994) were the first to use the Big Five model to summarize the past 70 years of personality and leadership research, and to show that four of the Big Five dimensions were consistently related to leadership success. The implications of personality and the Big Five model for leaders can be found later in this chapter, and answers to some common questions about personality are found in Highlight 8–4.

Another advantage of the Big Five model is that it is a useful method for categorizing or profiling people. For example, Heckman and Roberts (1997) showed that engineers and accountants tended to be lower in the trait of surgency but higher in the trait of dependability. They seemed to be more deferent and soft-spoken but were also achievement oriented, planful, and rule abiding. On the other hand, marketing and sales place a premium on creativity and on influencing others, and people in these occupations tended to be higher in surgency but lower in dependability. In a similar vein, Blake (1996) reported some

Common Questions About Personality

How Stable Is Personality?

As measured by personality tests, personality becomes remarkably stable by age 30. For example, people who are optimistic and outgoing at 30 will likely be optimistic and outgoing at 70; the same is true for people who are cold and aloof. However, scores for agreeableness and dependability do slightly increase, and scores for extroversion and intellectance fall slightly over time. Although the results of a personality test may not always predict how one will act at any given moment, they do predict fairly accurately how one tends to act over time. And because personality is relatively stable, life becomes more predictable for all of us (Costa & McCrae, 1994; Howard & Howard, 1995).

Is One's Personality Caused by Heredity or by the Environment?

Your personality appears to be a function of both heredity and environment. Studies of identical twins reared together or apart (i.e., adopted and separated at birth) show that at least part of one's personality is inherited. However, the data also indicate that heredity plays a relatively small role in personality (McCue & Bouchard, 1990; Tellegen et al., 1988).

Are People Really Accurate in Describing Their Own Personalities?

Often, but not always. Researchers have traditionally relied on self-ratings of personality to determine one's characteristic behavior patterns. However, research has shown that some people do not have good insight about their own behavior patterns or how they come across to others (Funder, 1987). Because of this lack of self-insight, self-rated personality inventories may yield *inaccurate* information about characteristic behavior patterns for some people. To get around this dilemma, researchers have started asking acquaintances to also rate an individual's personality. Research has shown that "other-rated" personality inventories are substantially better predictors of leadership success than self-rated inventories (Campbell, 1991; Curphy & Nilsen, 1995; Curphy & Osten, 1993; Mount, Barrick, & Strauss, 1994; Nilsen, 1995).

interesting findings for military cadets who were higher in agreeableness and surgency. His research indicated that higher agreeableness was positively related to performance ratings during the freshman and sophomore years but that higher surgency was more strongly related to performance ratings over the last two years at the U.S. Coast Guard Academy. Apparently getting along with others and developing strong social supports are very important during the first two years of a military cadet's life, but getting ahead becomes more important over the last two years. It may be that it takes a couple of years to develop strong social networks and supports, and once they have been established, other personality traits, such as surgency, become more important.

A final advantage of the Big Five model is that it appears universally applicable across cultures (Curphy, 1997a, 1996b; Hogan, Hogan, & Roberts, 1996; Salgado, 1997). People from Asian, Western European, Middle Eastern, Eastern European, or South American cultures seem to use the same five personality dimensions to categorize, profile, or describe others.

While the categorization schemes seem to be the same, however, some cultures do place varying importance on different personality dimensions. For example, Barrick and Mount (1996) reported that dependability was positively related to job performance across *all* jobs in the United States. No matter what the job, it seems that people who are more planful, rule abiding, goal oriented, and reliable are generally higher performers than people who lack these attributes. These same findings for dependability hold true for employees in European countries, but in Europe higher performing employees also had higher adjustment scores (Salgado, 1997).

Despite these advantages of the Big Five model, it still suffers from two general criticisms. The first criticism concerns its comprehensiveness. Some argue that five factors or dimensions are not enough to adequately encompass all the different personality traits (Brinkmeyer & Hogan, 1997; Cellar, Miller, Doverspike, & Klawsky, 1996; Curphy, 1997c). Many of these arguments center on the fact the Big Five model focuses on the positive, or bright, side of personality, and does a poor job of addressing the negative, or dark, side of personality traits. More about the bright and dark side of personality can be found later in this chapter.

Another criticism of the Big Five model concerns the usefulness of the five dimensions in predicting job performance. Research clearly shows that personality traits such as dominance, extroversion, and achievement orientation have higher correlations with job performance than the broader personality dimensions of surgency and dependability (Curphy, 1997a, 1998b; Tett, Jackson, & Rothstein, 1991). The Big Five personality dimensions tend to be fairly heterogeneous internally. For example, the dimension of dependability is made up of four different personality traits. It is entirely possible for someone to be high in conformity and organization yet low in credibility and achievement orientation. Such a person would behave quite differently than one who is relatively low in conformity and organization while high in credibility and achievement orientation, yet their overall surgency scores could be the same. A person with these scores would be very different than someone who scored in the midrange for all four traits. The heterogeneity of the Big Five dimensions does make them relatively poor predictors of job performance as compared to personality traits.

Assessing Personality Traits

Personality assessment, of course, is something that we are all involved in, not just researchers. For example, you might have found yourself thinking about how some of your own acquaintances fit into the higher or lower categories for various traits while you were reading the trait descriptions. Although there is some mystique surrounding formal personality assessment, the reality is that professionals simply use more systematic methods for determining a person's standing on different personality traits, and then use the resulting scores to make inferences about that person's likely future behavior and its consequences.

Although some of you may never have taken a personality inventory before, it is worth noting that such inventories often play a significant role in the selection process (see Highlight 8–5). Some instruments have become so prevalent that they have been translated into 45 different languages (Gough, 1987)! Why do many organizations use personality inventories so pervasively? The answer is quite simple. They do a reasonable job of describing a job candidate's day-to-day behavior patterns, and predicting leadership or occupational success; better, for example, than job interviews typically do. Furthermore, members of work teams sometimes take personality inventories to better understand their own and other team members' behavior, and improve their interactions. Many managers and executives also take these tests as part of their own personal and professional development (Curphy, 1997b; 1996a; Curphy, Osten, & Voetberg, 1996).

This is not to say that a valid and reliable assessment of personality is easy. In fact, it's somewhat trickier than assessing intelligence or knowledge. As opposed to tests of *maximal performance* (e.g., intelligence tests or final exams), personality tests are designed to assess *typical* behavior (Campbell, Dunnette, Lawler, & Weick, 1970). There are basically two types of tests used to assess personality traits. One type, **projective personality tests,** was described in Chapter 6. The other type, **objective personality tests,** typically consists of a standard set of items such as adjectives, statements, or questions. Subjects are asked to indicate the extent to which such items are descriptive of them. Usually, the strength of any trait is a function of the number and strength of the ratings for adjectives or items endorsed. For example, there are seven items assessing dominance on the Leadership Personality Survey, and the extent to which an individual agrees or disagrees that these items describe their own day-to-day behaviors determines their score for dominance. Examples of objective personality tests are the Adjective Check List (Gough & Heilbrun, 1987), Campbell Leadership Index (Campbell, 1991), Leadership Personality Survey (Curphy, 1998b; Curphy & Osten, 1993), Hogan Personality Inventory (Hogan, 1986), California Psychological Inventory (Gough, 1987), and NEO-PI (Costa & McCrae, 1985).

Leadership researchers investigating the relationship between personality traits and leadership success generally administer objective personality

Highlight 8–5

The Use of Personality Tests in the NFL

Of all the different businesses in the United States, perhaps none dwells on its hiring decisions more than professional sports teams. As described in Chapter 5, most organizations hire leaders and followers through a combination of interviews and résumé screens. Professional sports teams, however, often put their candidates through extensive physical fitness tests, training camps, and preseason games to determine who will make the final team roster or the season. Because many of the players coming out of the college ranks demand multi-million-dollar contracts before ever playing a professional game, professional sports teams are using all the assessment techniques available to help make good drafting decisions. Most recently, a number of NFL teams adopted intelligence and personality tests as part of the selection process. Because offenses and defenses are becoming much more complicated these days, intelligence test scores help coaches to determine who among the draftees will be the quickest learners and who will best be able to apply their knowledge to new situations. According to George Young, general manager for the New York Giants, "The character of your players has always been just as important as how high he can jump and how fast he can run. We can see the guys run and jump. We use personality tests to see what kind of people they are and if there are any red flags."

So what kind of personality is the NFL looking for? It appears that different teams look for different qualities in their players, and as such look for different combinations of personality trait scores. The New York Giants look at overall character; the San Francisco 49ers look for respect for authority, toughness, and competitiveness; and the Miami Dolphins want players who "eat nails and spit bullets."

Source: T. W. Smith, "Punt, Pass, and Ponder the Questions: In the NFL, Personality Tests Help Teams Judge the Draftees," *New York Times*, April 20, 1997.

inventories to subjects and then collect data about their performance or effectiveness as a leader. For example, if you want to investigate whether personality is related to effectiveness in managing restaurants, then you can administer a personality inventory to a large number of restaurant managers and then collect data about the financial performance, customer satisfaction ratings, or job performance ratings for those same managers. You could then look at the correlations between various personality dimensions and traits and the different performance indices.

Organizations using personality inventories as one basis of hiring decisions take a similar approach. They analyze a position in question to determine the relevant personality traits related to success, administer personality inventories to prospective candidates, collect job performance ratings for the candidates hired, and finally examine the correlations between personality trait scores and job performance ratings to ensure the personality inventory is a valid and useful predictor of job performance.

The Dark Side of Personality

It goes without saying that not all leaders are successful, and some fail miserably. Why do leaders fail? Failure can occur for a variety of reasons, some of which are beyond the leader's or anyone else's control. Sometimes, however, leaders fail for personal, rather than situational, reasons—they may simply lack the abilities or experience needed to be successful. At other times, they may possess these assets but still fail. When this happens it is often because the leaders have been promoted to positions where they can no longer rely on themselves to do all the work but must instead succeed through others. Such leaders generally lack the ability to form cohesive, goal-oriented teams, and this deficit can be the result of one or more dark-side personality traits. **Dark-side personality traits** are irritating or counterproductive behavioral tendencies that interfere with a leader's ability to form cohesive teams and that cause followers to exert less effort toward goal accomplishment. Several aspects of dark-side traits are worth noting. First, typical measures of personality are designed to detect bright-side traits, and dark-side traits are usually not assessed or detected with interviews, personality tests, or assessment center techniques. Thus, people can have relatively high scores on many Big Five personality dimensions and traits and still possess one or more dark-side traits (Brown, 1997; Curphy, 1997d; Curphy, Gibson, Asiu, Horn, & Macomber, 1994; Hogan, Curphy, & Hogan, 1994; Rybicki & Klippel, 1997). Second, these counterproductive tendencies typically become apparent only after a leader has been in the position for some period of time. Candidates possessing dark side traits may do very well in interviews but be poor performers once on the job. Here are descriptions of some of the more common dark-side traits:

Argumentative. This trait identifies leaders who are suspicious, are overly sensitive to criticism, and expect to be mistreated. Individuals possessing this trait do not take personal criticism well and are apt to start arguments and have a hard time ending them.

Interpersonal Insensitivity. Leaders possessing this trait tend to be aloof and unaware of how they come across to others, and to have difficulties putting themselves in "other peoples' shoes."

Narcissism. Leaders with this trait tend to be overly self-confident, self-centered, and extremely ambitious. They grossly overestimate their abilities, have a strong sense of entitlement, and often hold others in contempt. Extremely arrogant, they are always right and not afraid to tell you so. Such individuals often exploit followers for their own self-aggrandizement.

Fear of Failure. These individuals make poor leaders because they dread being criticized. As a result, they tend to be overly cautious and reluctant decision makers. When forced to make decisions, they often impose old solutions to problems even when it is obvious that they will not work.

Perfectionism. This dark-side trait identifies individuals who are conscientious and methodical but also attend so closely to details that they have trouble setting and maintaining priorities. They maintain extremely high standards for themselves and their followers, and their inflexibility, nit-picking, and micromanaging tendencies can be extremely irritating.

Impulsivity. As leaders, these individuals are hedonistic and often ignore the feelings of followers when in pursuit of their own pleasure. They enjoy testing limits, may fail to keep promises and commitments, and often neglect to consider the consequences of their actions.

The behaviors associated with dark-side traits can occur anywhere in an organization. Many times organizations put up with these tendencies because an individual is smart, is experienced, or possesses unique skills. Nevertheless, leaders manifesting dark-side traits tend to leave a longer and longer trail of bruised people, and it is often only a matter of time before these tendencies catch up with them. As seen in Highlight 8–6, these tendencies can and often do have tragic consequences. See if you can pick out which dark-side traits these two individuals exhibited.

Implications for Leaders

What more should the practitioner understand about personality and leadership? Perhaps most importantly, leadership practitioners should gain an appreciation for the many ways in which leaders and followers can differ. Few people, if any, have high scores on all of the traits found in Table 8–1 (page 204). It is in the nature of personality trait measures that different people will have different profiles of scores across all the traits. The picture becomes even more complicated when leaders' intelligence, values, preferences, and attitudes are also considered (see Highlight 8–7). Nevertheless, personality inventory results can help leaders gain considerable insight into their own day-to-day behavioral patterns, including their interactions with others and the ways they approach various tasks and challenges. Personality inventory results can also help leaders make better choices when selecting followers, as these instruments provide clues to the day-to-day behavioral patterns of different candidates. Personality inventory results should never be used as the sole hiring criteria, but when combined with additional selection information, they can be a valid and cost-effective predictor of job performance.

Two Examples of Dark-Side Personality Traits

The Case of the Commuter Airline Pilot

Given the recent spate of accidents, the commuter airline industry has been under considerable scrutiny. Although some of these accidents seem to be aircraft related, others point to pilot error. Because these pilots work longer hours in less-sophisticated aircraft, it would seem likely that the airlines would pay considerable attention to hiring commuter pilots. However, it turns out that it is easier to get hired as a commuter pilot than as a pilot for a larger airline. The subject in this case was a former charter pilot and flight instructor who spent time in the U.S. Navy as a reactor officer in nuclear submarines and had flown for a commuter airline for over five years. Colleagues who had flown with the individual were almost unanimous in their description of him. They said he was abusive to his copilots—one officer said he was even punched in the headset during a flight. At least six others indicated they were intimidated by the subject because he was headstrong and argumentative—he always thought he was right. Others said the pilot would be deliberately rough on flight controls when he was angry with the company, and he once stated that "some might consider him sloppy, but he just didn't care."

One morning in 1993 the subject was called in to fly on a scheduled day off. The pilot was visibly angry with the decision—he argued with the ramp service agent before taking off and chewed out his copilot for doing an exterior preflight checklist wrong. The flight proved to be the subject's last. Approximately one hour after takeoff, the plane crashed and killed all on board. Although the cause of the crash still remains unknown, one has to wonder whether his behavior contributed to the 18 fatalities. More importantly, if the pilot had the reputation for this type of behavior, then why did the company put up with it?

The Case of the Corporate CEO

The subject in this case is a CEO of a $2 billion book publishing company who was recently dismissed as part of a corporate buyout. The individual started his career with the company as a book salesman over 30 years ago and reigned as the CEO for over 15 years. His leadership credo was "business is conflict. . . . You don't get excellence by saying yes. You get love, but you don't get excellence. This company has raised the hurdles of excellence every bloody day."

According to his staff, the subject ruled by intimidation and fear. His profane harangues were an industry legend. Scores of former employees tell of meetings at which he publicly threatened to lop off people's hands or private body parts or tear out their throats for failure to perform. Whenever something went wrong or a goal wasn't achieved, the subject always saw it as a personal matter rather than the result of the business situation. As a result, the subject always placed personal blame for failure and the staff quickly learned not to come forward with problems.

He rarely went through a single meeting without going after someone, and people saw his use of degradation and humiliation as a way of controlling his staff.

Many of his staff saw the buyout as the only way to get rid of the CEO. He had been in place for over 15 years and played a key role in making the company a multi-billion-dollar organization. Nevertheless, after the buyout the parent organization faced the specter of mass resignations if the subject was allowed to remain as CEO. As a result of his discontented staff, the CEO was asked to resign. Unfortunately, even to this day the CEO has no idea on why he was let go and seems genuinely despondent over the decision. When confronted with stories of abuse and intimidation, he either denies that they ever took place or claims that they were blown out of all proportion.

Source: R. T. Hogan, G. J. Curphy, and J. Hogan, "What Do We Know about Leadership: Effectiveness and Personality," *American Psychologist 49* (1994) pp. 493–504.

Second, there is a compelling body of evidence showing the Big Five dimensions of surgency, dependability, agreeableness, and adjustment are all related to leadership success (Curphy, 1998b; Hogan, Curphy, & Hogan, 1994). These findings imply that individuals with higher scores on these four dimensions generally make better leaders. People who are more decisive, outgoing, planful, achievement oriented, rule abiding, friendly, sensitive, stoic, and thick-skinned tend to make better leaders than those scoring at the opposite end on these traits. The findings for intellectance are less consistent; for some jobs higher scores are better, but in other jobs intellectance scores do not seem to matter. It is important to note that only a few leaders have high scores across all of the Big Five personality dimensions, yet many more are successful.

There are several reasons why higher scores on the relevant Big Five dimensions are not always predictive of leadership success. One reason is that personality inventories do not provide relevant information about a person's intelligence, knowledge, values, or experience, and these are important aspects of leadership success too. Another reason is that some of the dimensions and traits associated with leadership success may be detrimental when one is in a follower role. For example, leaders with high dominance scores are usually willing to take charge, exercise authority, and give directions; however, they may not like being told what to do. In reality, however, almost all leaders spend more time as a follower than as a leader, and exhibiting negative reactions when being given guidance can have an adverse impact on the boss, that follower, and others as well.

It is important to remember that any trait's impact on behavior will vary with the situation. Some situations are fairly constrained, and the formal and informal expectations governing behavior may play a larger role in determining how a leader acts than her traits. A highly visible leader at a military academy may have low conformity scores, yet control his inclination to be nonconforming because of the demands of the situation. Furthermore, situational factors

Highlight 8–7

Is There a Military Mind?

To many, the word *leadership* is synonymous with military authority. It evokes images of uniforms, salutes, rank and insignia, and discipline. To some it suggests positive associations like the chain of command's clear lines of authority and responsibility, decisiveness, respect for authority, camaraderie, selfless commitment to a higher mission, and good discipline. Even individuals who never served in the military themselves may think of it as epitomizing good leaders and good leadership. Others, however, do not have such a positive view. They may agree with Groucho Marx that military intelligence is a contradiction in terms. They may think of military leadership in mostly negative terms, promoting the sort of mindless inefficiency captured in this familiar soldier's adage:

If it moves, salute it.
If it doesn't move, pick it up.
If you can't pick it up, paint it!

What are military leaders really like? For more than a decade, all newly promoted generals in the U.S. Army have attended a special leadership development course at the Center for Creative Leadership. It included a significant emphasis on individual psychological feedback to the generals based on a comprehensive battery of psychological tests. Psychologist David Campbell has extensively analyzed these test results, and his conclusions provide perhaps the best answers to questions about the psychological characteristics of military leaders. Campbell's analysis examined how military generals compared to both people in the general population and civilian leaders on various intelligence, personality, and vocational preferences tests as well as on behavioral assessments during group exercises. His study is a good example of how personality trait, ability, and preference measures all can be used in profiling commonalities among leaders in a particular sphere of activity.

Generals proved to be an extremely bright group, averaging at the 95th percentile of IQ for the general population. They scored higher, in fact, than a sample of corporate CEOs. In terms of personality, they are have extremely high dependability scores; they are socially mature, alert to ethical and moral issues, and more conventional (i.e., less innovative) in their approach to problem solving than other executive groups, but they still score right at the average for the overall population. The generals also attained very high dominance and achievement orientation scores. In considering data from all sources, Campbell identified a common personality profile among the generals, which he termed "The Aggressive Adventurer." This profile describes dominant, competitive, action-oriented, patriotic men drawn to physically adventurous activities.

Source: D. P. Campbell, "The Psychological Test Profiles of Brigadier Generals: Warmongers or Decisive Warriors?" Invited address presented to Division 14 of the American Psychological Association, New York, 1987.

also play a large role in determining which traits are important for leadership success. Depending on the leadership position, some of the dimensions and traits found in Table 8–1 (page 204) may be unrelated to leadership success. For example, extraversion may have little relevance for head librarians but may have a lot of relevance for public relations executives.

It is also important to remember that it is relatively difficult to change a person's personality. We point this out since considerable money is invested each year by companies sending managers to programs which seem to be aimed at changing some of the most basic patterns of interpersonal behavior. Although all behavior is volitional and can be changed, it is much more difficult to teach someone skills that do not come naturally or are not a part of their personality makeup. Extroverted leaders can learn to be good listeners, dominant leaders can learn to be more collaborative, and insensitive leaders can learn to take others' feelings into account, but chances are it will take more than a relatively short training program for these skills to become part of *those* individuals' day-to-day behavioral patterns.

The issue has several additional implications for leaders and followers. As described earlier in this chapter, many people exhibit both their bright- and dark-side day-to-day behavioral patterns without much conscious thought. It is almost as if they are on autopilot; they speak up in groups, react negatively to criticism, or tidy up their desk almost automatically. And because many of these behaviors are rewarded and reinforced over the years, they are precisely the same behaviors people fall back on when placed in new or stressful situations. More importantly, many people may not be aware of the impact these behavioral patterns have on others. For example, one executive was unaware of her tendencies to be extremely dominant and narcissistic, and to show little compassion toward others. When presented with the results of various personality inventories, she consistently told the psychologist that the results were inaccurate. A short time later she literally yanked the psychologist's handwritten notes from his hands in order to "ensure that I am getting all of the right messages." She did not ask the psychologist if she could see his notes, nor did she realize that this behavior was a perfect manifestation of the very traits she was denying she had. Unfortunately for this leader (and her followers), she frequently exhibited the same kinds of behavior in the workplace.

Personality Types and Leadership

The Differences between Traits and Types

Traits are not the only way to describe personality. An alternative way to describe how people differ in their day-to-day behavioral patterns is through **types**, or in terms of a **personality typology**. Superficially, there may appear to be little difference between traits and types. Even some of the same words are used to name them. Extroversion, for example, may be the name of a trait in one theory, but another theory may talk about extroverted *types*. And, as it turns out, the differences here are more than skin-deep. We will only emphasize one aspect of the differences, the one we believe is most fundamental conceptually. Each trait (e.g., dominance) is conceptualized as a *continuum* along which people vary, typically in a bell-curve distribution. A person may be relatively lower or relatively higher on that trait, and the differences in behavioral patterns between any two people may be thought of as roughly proportional to how close or far apart their scores fall on the scale. Types, on the other hand, are usually thought of as relatively *discrete categories*.

This distinction may be clearer with an example. Let us take the trait of dominance, and compare it with a hypothetical construct we will call a "dominant type." Psychological typologies are often expressed in terms of polar opposites, so let us further suppose that our typology also refers to the bipolar opposite of dominant types, which we'll call submissive types. Importantly, people are considered to be *one or the other*, just as everyone is either male or female. If you are a dominant type you are considered to be more like all other dominant types than you are like any submissive type; if you are a submissive type you are considered to be more like every other submissive type than you are like any dominant type. In other words, typologies tend to put people into discrete psychological categories and emphasize the *similarities* among all people in the same category regardless of actual score (as long as it is in the right "direction"). Furthermore, typologies tend to emphasize *differences* between people of different types (e.g., between dominant and submissive types) regardless of actual score.

This point may become even clearer by looking at Figure 8–2. The upper line refers to the continuum of the trait defined at one end by submissiveness and at the other end by dominance. The trait scores of four different individuals—Jim, John, Joe, and Jack—are indicated on the scale. You can infer from their relative positions on the scale that John is more like Joe than he is like either Jim or Jack. But now look at the lower line. This refers to a typology of submissive types and dominant types. The theory behind personality types suggests that John is more like Jim than Joe, and Joe is more like Jack than John.

Psychological Preferences as a Personality Typology

One very popular personality typology involves psychological preferences, or what me might call "mental habits." Like traits, our **preferences** play a role in the characteristic and unique ways we behave from day to day. According to Jung (1971), preferences influence our choice of careers, ways of thinking, relationships, and work habits. Nearly 2 million people take the Myers-Briggs Type Indicator (MBTI) every year (Myers, 1976, 1977, 1980; Myers

FIGURE 8–2

Traits and Types

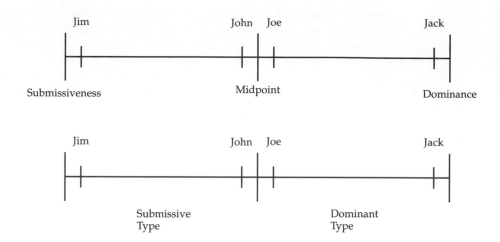

& Briggs, 1943/1962; Myers & McCaulley, 1985), which not only is the most popular measure of preferences but also one of the most popular psychological tests around (Quast & Hansen, 1996; Thayer, 1988). The MBTI is often used in college-level leadership and adult education courses, formal leadership training programs, organizational personnel programs, and by consultants as a part of various organizational interventions. Moreover, numerous books and articles have been published about how the MBTI can be used to better understand one-self, co-workers, partners in intimate relationships, children, and educational or occupational preferences. Because of the overall popularity of the preferences and the MBTI, we believe it is worthwhile to review this theory and its most popular assessment instrument in some detail.

Somewhat paradoxically, one reason knowledge about our psychological preferences is important is precisely because it is so easy to forget about them. It is easy to forget how subjective and idiosyncratic preferences really are; we easily confuse our *preferences* with *the way things are, or ought to be.* For example, those who value being organized may prefer *everyone* to be organized. They may get annoyed when working with others who are less organized than they are. In other words, it is easy to let preferences affect judgments of others (e.g., people "should" be organized; therefore, not being well-organized is a deficiency). Many people are unaware of the extent to which their preferences shape their perceptions of reality.

According to Myers and McCaulley (1985), there are four basic preference dimensions in which people can differ. These four dimensions are **extraversion–introversion, sensing–intuition, thinking–feeling,** and **judging–perceiving.** The four dimensions are bipolar, meaning that individuals generally prefer being either, say, extraverted or introverted. A more in-depth description of the day-to-day behavioral patterns of these four dimensions can be found below.

The *extraversion-and-introversion* dimension is fundamentally concerned with where people get their energy. Some leaders are naturally gregarious and outgoing. Their spontaneous sociability makes it easy for them to strike up conversations with anyone about almost anything. Not surprisingly, such extraverts have a breadth of interests and a large circle of acquaintances. They are energized by being around others, but their tendency to "think out loud" and speak whatever is on their mind can sometimes get them into trouble. Other leaders are more comfortable alone, or with just a few others. Introverts can interact effectively with others, but they are fundamentally both more reserved and more deliberate than extraverts. Introverted leaders prefer to think things through and only announce their final decisions, and followers may have a difficult time understanding the process the leader used to reach his or her conclusions. Because introverts find being around others to be draining, they may come across as less approachable than extraverts. This preference dimension can easily be seen at parties or social gatherings. Extraverts work the crowd and are often the last to leave; introverts keep to themselves or talk to a small group of friends and leave early. Of course, everyone needs to act in both extraverted and introverted ways at various times; however, some of us are more comfortable with one than the other.

The *sensing-and-intuition* dimension is concerned with how people look at data. Leaders who prefer their sensing mode like facts and details; the focus of information gathering concerns the real, the actual, the literal, the specific, and the present. Hence, sensing leaders tend to be practical, orderly, and down-to-earth decision makers. By contrast, leaders who rely on their intuition look for the big picture beyond particular facts or details; information is most meaningful for its pattern, framework, figurative meaning, and future possibilities. Intuitive leaders tend to be innovative and conceptual (though sometimes impractical), and are more comfortable with their hunches and inspirations. This preference dimension can often be seen in presentations. A sensing leader will use a relatively large number of overheads in order to explain all of the facts leading up to a practical decision. An intuiting leader will use a few overheads that summarize key trends and focus on the possible implications of these trends. Intuitive leaders sitting through a sensor's presentation will often get bored with the details and will think this follower "just doesn't get it." Sensing leaders sitting through an intuitive's presentation will wonder, "Where's the beef?" and ask lots of questions about the facts and assumptions underlying the implications of the data.

Whereas the sensing-and-intuition dimension is concerned with how leaders and followers look at data, the *thinking-and-feeling* dimension is concerned with the considerations leaders prefer when making decisions. Thinking leaders like to analyze, criticize, and approach decisions impersonally and objectively. They use their heads to adopt a relatively detached stance toward decisions and pay more attention to operational, bottom-line considerations. Feeling leaders naturally empathize and appreciate, and prefer to approach decisions personally and subjectively. They value humaneness and social harmony and use their hearts to weigh the impact of any decision on particular people. As an example, say a thinking leader was the head of a customer service support center, and his feeling follower just got a call that her child was sick at school and she needed to go pick her up. The leader's first thoughts might be "How will I be able to field customer calls in my follower's absence?" whereas the follower's first thought might be "I hope my child is okay." Similarly, the CEO of a large home improvement retail organization was a strong thinker, and one of his division presidents was a feeler. The CEO would look at the monthly financial trends and make decisions that he thought would help increase shareholder value. The division president would look at these decisions and immediately think about how they would affect his 26,000 employees. Both the CEO and the division president looked at the same data; they just approached their decisions differently based on their preferences.

The *judging-and-perceiving* dimension has to do with the amount of information a leader needs before feeling comfortable making a decision. Judging leaders strive for closure; they like things to be settled and come across as decisive, methodical, and organized. Judgers get nervous *before* decisions are made and only want a minimal amount of information when making decisions. Although they make up their minds quickly, they may not have all relevant facts and as a result make poorer decisions. Perceiving leaders like to keep their options open; they are curious, spontaneous, and flexible. Perceivers prefer to collect as much information as possible before making a decision or a commitment. Perceivers often get nervous *after* a decision is made, as they may not feel that enough information was collected or data was analyzed. Although perceivers are good at gathering and analyzing additional data, they sometimes are accused of suffering from "analysis-paralysis." This personality preference can be readily seen in meetings. Judging leaders prefer to have an agenda, stick to the agenda, and make as many decisions as possible in the meeting. Perceivers dislike agendas, do not mind going off on tangents, and may or may not make any decisions in the meeting. They also have no problems revisiting a decision made in an earlier meeting if some new information comes to light. Judging followers can often get frustrated working for perceiving leaders and vice versa over these meeting and decision-making issues.

As with personality traits, many leaders and followers exhibit the behaviors associated with their preference dimension almost automatically, particularly in weak or stressful situations. However, it is important to note that people are not locked into exhibiting only those behaviors associated with their preferences. Leaders can and do exhibit those behaviors associated with the opposite side of any preference dimension, but it takes personal insight and conscious energy and effort to do so. Moreover, the more extreme the preference score, the more likely the associated behavioral patterns will be exhibited, and the more focused will be the effort needed to exhibit nonpreference behaviors.

Highlight 8–8

Personality Preferences and Types for Mutual Fund Managers

The portfolio managers for mutual funds often control billions of dollars of assets. These individuals and their staffs closely scrutinize different companies' financial reports, industry and business trends, local and global economic indicators, political and governmental activity, technological advances, and so on, to determine which stocks or bonds their mutual fund should invest in, hold, or sell. Obviously, most mutual fund managers are very bright and good with numbers, but what kind of personality preferences are associated with successful mutual fund managers? It turns out that most mutual fund managers are ISTJs. They are introverted, which means that they are introspective and tend to keep to themselves. Mutual fund managers are also strong sensors; they are data driven and not driven to acting on hunches that are contradicted by information. As thinkers their decisions are not swayed by emotion and have a strong bottom-line focus. And as judgers they are likely to focus on and reach closure on one issue before moving to the next. Psychologists who have used the MBTI to assess mutual fund managers also report that many mutual fund managers are ineffective team players—they are loners and consummate individual contributors. So even though they may make very good financial decisions, they may not be a whole lot of fun to work with or for. Unless, of course, you also happen to be an ISTJ.

Source: B. O'Reilly, "Does Your Fund Manager Play the Piano?" *Fortune*, December 29, 1997, pp. 139–44.

Based on the descriptions provided above, you could make judgments about whether you are an extravert versus introvert, sensor versus intuitor, thinker versus feeler, or judger versus perceiver. The predominant preference scores for each of the four dimensions can be used to create one of 16 **psychological types.** For example, someone with high preferences for introversion, sensing, thinking, and judging would be categorized as an ISTJ (see Highlight 8–8 for a more in-depth description). Myers and McCaulley (1985) and Hirsh and Kummerow (1990) maintained that individuals within a particular type were more similar to each other than they were to individuals of a different type. Thus, ESTJ leaders are more like other ESTJ leaders than they are like INTJ or ESFP leaders.

Implications for Leaders: Types and Preferences

As stated earlier, the preference scores for the four basic dimensions are combined to form 1 of 16 different types. Kroeger and Thuesen (1988) maintained that no one type was necessarily better than another in terms of leadership success, and that each type had unique strengths and potential weaknesses. Although there appears to be little published evidence to support this claim, there is evidence to show that leaders are disproportionately represented by certain types far more than others. A majority of leaders preferred thinking and judging activities over feeling and perceiving activities. Leaders were more likely to be ISTJs, INTJs, ESTJs, or ENTJs than any of the other 12 types (McCaulley, 1988). We should add, however, that this finding may be a more accurate generalization for adults whose vocational choices and organizational socialization already are relatively well established. It may not be a valid generalization for leaders who are of college age or younger (Cummings, 1992).

Although more research is needed concerning how preferences affect leadership, it seems reasonable that awareness and appreciation of them can enhance any leader's effectiveness. In the following paragraphs, we will highlight several implications of knowing your preference type for leaders.

• *Knowing about your type increases awareness of both your own and others' behavior.* Greater self-understanding reduces personal blind spots and helps anyone perceive leadership situations (including one's own behavior) more accurately. Leaders have a difficult time changing behavior if they are not aware of how they are acting, and some behaviors are difficult to change precisely because they have become so automatic. Knowledge of type can help leaders better understand their behavioral patterns at work and see how they might be able to avoid being prisoners of their own preferences. It can also help leaders see others in new ways, with greater insight and tolerance.

• *Knowledge of one's type helps broaden one's behavioral repertoire, which is helpful because leaders face a great diversity of situations.* Sometimes leaders must inspire a group about a vision of the future; sometimes they just need to listen to someone else's ideas about how to do things differently. Sometimes leaders must take a stand that will displease and maybe hurt others; sometimes leaders need to make group morale a primary concern. Because different followers may be very different types, they may react very differently to a leader's behavior. Leaders may be more successful if they are able to adjust their behavior according to followers' types.

• *People of different types are often motivated in different ways.* There's a lot of truth to the saying "Different strokes for different folks." All leaders need to remember that followers of different types appreciate different things. For example, introverts prefer working alone, sensors like facts, feelers hate impersonal treatments, perceivers like doing things their own way, and judgers want closure. Leaders need to take stock of their followers' preferences and determine whether the behaviors associated with their own preferences are helping or hindering the morale or motivation of their work group.

• *Working with people of different types can be difficult.* Some difficulties with others at work are due to differences in preferences. For example, introverts may feel that an extravert they share an office with is obnoxious and loudmouthed; extraverts may become frustrated when they find out an introvert they are working with on a project had a great idea but did not mention it because no one asked him directly for his opinion. Understanding that office conflicts may be due to differences in type can give leadership practitioners some insight on how to resolve these conflicts.

• *Working with people of different types can also be potentially more productive.* People say two heads are better than one, but that is not always true. If two heads have exactly the same thoughts, then one of them is redundant! In a sense, two people of different types provide greater differences of opinion and talent than do two people of exactly the same type. Lee Iacocca (1984) wrote about the importance of diverse interests and outlooks in organizations:

> By their very nature, financial analysts tend to be defensive, conservative, and pes-
> simistic. On the other side of the fence are the guys in sales and marketing—aggres-
> sive, speculative, and optimistic. They're always saying, "Let's do it," while the bean
> counters are always cautioning you on why you shouldn't do it. In any company you
> need both sides of the equation, because the natural tension between the two groups
> creates its own system of checks and balances. (p. 43)

Despite the potential advantages of a knowledge of type, leaders also should be aware of several cautions with regard to "typing." Although the MBTI is an extremely popular and potentially useful instrument, leadership practitioners need to be aware of its limitations and possible misuses. The four preference dimensions can provide useful insights about oneself and others, but the fundamental concept of being a type is problematic. First, types are not completely stable over time. Some research indicates at least one letter in the four-letter type may change in half the people taking the test in as little as five weeks (McCauley & Carskadon, 1983; Myers & McCaulley, 1985). There also are data showing major developmental changes in distribution of types with age (Cummings, 1992). It is difficult to see how one should select individuals for teams or provide career guidance to others based on types if the types (or at least type scores) change, in some cases seemingly quickly. Furthermore, since the behavior of two people of the same type may vary as greatly as that of people of different types, the utility of typing systems remains uncertain.

But perhaps the most serious problem of all in using typologies concerns the way they are sometimes *misused* (Gibson & Curphy, 1996). Unfortunately, some people become so enamored with simple systems of classifying human behavior that they begin to see *everything* through "type" glasses. Some people habitually categorize their friends, spouses, and co-workers into types. Knowledge of type should be a basis for appreciating the richness and diversity of behavior, and the capabilities in others and ourselves. It is not meant to be a system of categorization that oversimplifies our own and others' behavior by seemingly putting people into neat and tidy little boxes (i.e., types). Believing someone is a particular type (e.g., "He's an ISTJ") can become a sort of perceptual filter that keeps us from actually recognizing when that person is acting in a manner contrary to that type's characteristic style. Another misuse occurs when someone uses "knowledge" of type as an excuse or a rationalization for his own counterproductive behaviors ("I know I'm talking on and on and dominating the conversation, but after all, I'm an extravert!"). In this case, the misuse of type can become a self-fulfilling prophecy that may make it very difficult for a leader to change a follower's behavior. Millions of people apparently believe the MBTI is a useful tool in enhancing awareness of self and others, but leadership practitioners need to understand that, like any tool, it can be misused too.

Summary

Although the term *personality* has many different meanings, we use the term to describe one's typical or characteristic patterns of behavior. There are several different theories to describe why people act in characteristic ways, but the trait approach to personality has been the most thoroughly researched, and as such plays a key role in the chapter. Many personality traits have been found related to leadership success. However, one of the problems surrounding personality traits is that, historically, researchers have used different terms, or labels, to describe similar patterns of behavior. This inconsistency in labeling made it difficult to determine personality trait–leadership relationships. The adoption of the Big Five model of personality has helped to clarify these relationships, and researchers have noted that leadership success is positively correlated with the Big Five personality dimensions of surgency, dependability, agreeableness, and adjustment.

Although exhibiting high levels of these four dimensions increases the likelihood that one will be an effective leader, personality alone is no guarantee of leadership success. The strength of the relationship between personality and leadership depends to a large extent on the particular situation. Moreover, because one's personality tends to change very slowly, it can be quite difficult to try to change a leader's personality after she has already been placed in a particular role.

Personality types are another way of looking at distinctive behavioral patterns. The most popular test of types is the Myers-Briggs Type Indicator (MBTI), which measures a person's preferences on four major dimensions. Individuals' scores for these four dimensions are typically combined to define a psychological type.

Key Terms

Great Man theory	projective personality test
personality	objective personality test
trait approach	dark side of personality traits
traits	Myers-Briggs Type Indicator (MBTI)
weak situations	personality typology

strong situations
Big Five model of personality
surgency
agreeableness
dependability
adjustment
intellectance

preferences
extraversion–introversion
sensing–intuiting
thinking–feeling
judging–perceiving
psychological types

Discussion Questions

1. Do you think personality changes over time? Do you think certain aspects of personality might change over time due to experience in leadership roles?

2. What Big Five and dark-side personality traits and personality dimensions do you think would help professional sports players be more successful? Would successful coaches need the same or different personality traits and preferences? Would successful players and coaches need different traits and preferences for different sports?

3. A theme of this book is that leaders will be more effective to the extent they can adapt their behavior to the needs of particular circumstances. Do you believe adjustment or adaptability in a leader is valuable? What, to you, is the difference between "behavioral flexibility" or adaptability, and "personality change"? (This is an issue we will revisit in a later chapter.)

4. Do you think personality is a helpful dimension for understanding the effectiveness of political leaders? Does this question necessarily imply that successful political leaders have good personalities, and unsuccessful ones bad personalities? (Hint: explore this issue by considering both the bright and the dark side of personality.)

5. Do you think Abraham Lincoln could be elected president today? Why or why not?

6. Describe the situational factors that constrain or limit your behavior. Describe the situational factors that constrain or limit the effects personality has on some specific leader's behavior.

7. Do you think persons of every preference type can be effective leaders?

9 INTELLIGENCE AND CREATIVITY

Chapter Outline

Introduction

Virtually every institution in our society today faces dynamic and complex challenges. It is no wonder then, that organizations of all sorts are placing an ever greater premium on hiring smart and innovative leaders. It is certainly easy to think of particular leaders who are known for their superior intellect. In the political arena, for example, both former Senator Bill Bradley and President Bill Clinton were Rhodes Scholars, one indication of high intelligence. You may also think of *other* contemporary political leaders, however, who do not strike you as highly intelligent, despite holding positions of significant influence and power. Therefore, we might ask just what *is* the relationship between intelligence and leadership? Is the brightest person in any group always the best person to be the leader? In this chap-

Highlight 9–1

Leadership Quotes, Chapter 9

Literate cultures everywhere and throughout history have had words for saying that some people are smarter than others. Given the survival value of intelligence, the concept must be still older than that.

Richard Herrnstein and Charles Murray, *The Bell Curve*

If the blind lead the blind, both shall fall into the ditch.

Matt. 15:14

A little learning is not a dangerous thing to one who does not mistake it for a great deal.

William Allen White

Everyone is ignorant, only on different subjects.

Will Rogers

The first method for estimating the intelligence of a ruler is to look at the men he has around him.

Machiavelli

The best way to have a good idea is to have a lot of ideas.

Dr. Linus Pauling

Creativeness often consists of merely turning up what is already there. Did you know that right and left shoes were thought up only a little more than a century ago?

Bernice Fitz-Gibbon

Creativity is so delicate a flower that praise tends to make it bloom, while discouragement often nips it in the bud. Any of us will put out more and better ideas if our efforts are appreciated.

Alex F. Osborn

Creative minds always have been known to survive any kind of bad training.

Anna Freud

Genius, in truth, means little more than the faculty of perceiving in an unhabitual way.

William James

---

ter we will review research regarding the relationship between intelligence and leadership, starting with an examination of the nature of intelligence itself. We will also examine the relationship between leadership and creativity, another mental talent, including a look at the components of creativity, potential blocks to creativity, and ways to better foster creativity among subordinates (see also Highlight 9–1).

Intelligence and Leadership

What Is Intelligence?

"Perhaps no concept in the history of psychology has had or continues to have as great an impact on everyday life in the Western world as that of general intelligence" (Scarr, 1989, p. 75). Overwhelming evidence exists to support the notion that general intelligence plays a substantial role in human affairs (Arvey et al., 1994; Humphreys, 1984; Neisser et al., 1996; Ree & Earles, 1992, 1993; Schmidt & Hunter, 1992; Sternberg, 1997). Still, intelligence and intelligence testing are among the most controversial topics in the social sciences today. There is contentious debate over questions like how heredity and the environment affect intelligence, whether intelligence tests should be used in public schools, and whether ethnic groups differ in average intelligence test scores. For the most part, however, we will bypass such controversies here. Our focus will be on the relationship between intelligence and leadership. (See Arvey et al., 1994; Azar, 1995; Brody, 1992; Cronbach, 1984; Humphreys, 1984; Linn, 1989; Neisser et al., 1996; and Sternberg, 1997, for reviews of these controversies.)

We define **intelligence** as a person's all-around effectiveness in activities directed by thought (Arvey et al., 1994; Cronbach, 1984). On a practical level, this definition implies that leaders and followers with higher levels of intelligence are faster learners; can more easily see connections between issues or patterns in data; make better assumptions, deductions, and inferences; better understand the implications of their decisions; and are quick on their feet. Therefore, leaders and followers with higher levels of intelligence tend to be better problem solvers, a skill that has strong links to our definition of leadership described in Chapter 1.

As seen in Figure 9–1, intelligence is relatively difficult to change. It is also an unseen quality. Intelligence is not as easily measured as a person's height or weight, and can only be inferred by observing behavior. Moreover, intelligence does not affect behavior equally across all situations. Some activities, such as following simple routines, put less of a premium on intelligence than others. Finally, we should point out that our definition of intelligence does not imply that intelligence is a fixed quantity. Although heredity plays a role, intelligence can be and is modified through education and experience (Arvey et al., 1994; Brody, 1997; Cronbach, 1984; Humphreys, 1989; Neisser et al., 1996; Rushton, 1997).

A Brief History of Intelligence Testing

You can think of intelligence testing as a kind of technology, and like many other technologies it was originally developed to solve an important social problem. Intelligence tests were initially developed in order to select the best people possible to lead and run a society. While this may sound like a relatively modern approach, you may be surprised to learn that intelligence testing was first begun

FIGURE 9–1

*The Building
Blocks of Skills*

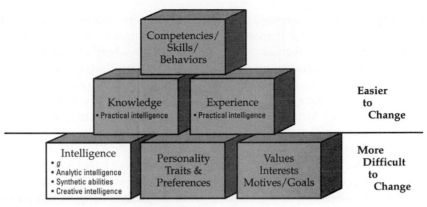

Source: © Personnel Decisions International, 1997.

around 1115 B.C. in China. From then until the early 1900s, China was run by a series of monarchies, or dynasties. However, the membership of any particular royal family was relatively small in comparison with the whole society, so the monarchy was faced with the task of identifying competent leaders to run their bureaucracies. The Chinese developed a series of standardized tests that measured the characteristics needed to successfully lead their institutions. The characteristics considered important included knowledge and skill in music, archery, horsemanship, writing, arithmetic, and the rites and ceremonies of public and social life. The competition in these tests was extremely intense, as test scores dictated which jobs candidates would fill, and they were the only way to advance in Chinese society. Literally millions of men would prepare for the tests. In any region of the dynasty, only 100 men out of the 10,000 taking the test would be asked to compete at the next level. The next level of competition was just as intense—only one out of 100 regional finalists would be asked to compete further. This highly selective process continued until the top candidate in the empire was identified, who was then given a premier role in one of the Chinese bureaucracies (Dubois, 1964).

The history of intelligence testing in Western society is much briefer, but the same general issues underlay the development and use of tests in nineteenth-century Europe. Alfred Binet is credited with developing the modern intelligence test in the late 1800s. At that time France had passed a compulsory education law, and the French government asked Binet to develop a technique to fairly identify students likely to do best in either a public or special education environment. Before the development of the test, decisions about who should or should not attend public schools were based on teacher recommendations. French lawmakers, however, were concerned that teacher recommendations were arbitrary at best. Binet's intelligence test was designed to make the recommendation process more objective and to *mitigate* the adverse impact of teachers' ratings. Binet's test met with great success and the test was brought to the United States by Louis Terman.

Terman worked at Stanford University, and he both translated and added to the Binet test (hence the name, the Stanford-Binet Intelligence Test). As Binet had done, Terman used his test to help schools make better educational decisions. However, intelligence testing in the United States did not receive widespread use until World War I. The manpower requirements of World War I made it necessary for the War Department to identify which draftees would be the fastest learners and best problem solvers, and intelligence tests proved to be the best predictor of military officer success. Literally everyone who joined the military in World War I took either the Army's Alpha test or its Beta test (one test was in English and the other for non-English speakers), and scores on these tests largely dictated whether draftees became enlistees or officers.

Because of the success of intelligence testing in World War I, commercial intelligence testing evolved from a cottage industry into a big business between the wars. Literally millions of Americans were seeking admission to colleges or applying for jobs, and a large number of them took these tests. The tests were administered in group settings using procedures similar to those developed in ancient China. The tests were fair, objective, and efficient, thanks to the advent of machine scoring systems. The onset of World War II once again saw the widespread use of intelligence testing for determining enlisted or officer status in the military. Also during this time, tests were developed to assess specific abilities, such as aptitude for flying. Mental-abilities testing played a pervasive and relatively uncontroversial role in American society until the 1960s, a time of great societal turmoil and change. In the 1960s, for the first time in American history, intelligence testing was seriously questioned.

In the field of psychology, intelligence testing was challenged by new theories of learning. A school of psychology known as behaviorism held that essentially all behavior was learned, even what we call intelligence (or intelligent behavior). Emphasis was placed on the modifiability of behavior by controlling environment rather than on the pursuit of measuring through testing how much fixed intelligence an individual possessed.

In the society at large, political and social pressures were growing to assure equality and social justice for all citizens. In that milieu, intelligence tests were seen by some as devices for maintaining an unjust status quo. Perhaps the key work articulating opposition to intelligence was the best seller, *The Mismeasure of Man* (Gould, 1981). However, the publication of books advocating the importance of intelligence and intelligence testing, such as *The Bell Curve* (Herrnstein & Murray, 1994), make it unlikely this debate will end anytime soon.

Although intelligence testing remains a contentious public issue, much of the debate among scientists who study the issue has abated. Some of the most widely accepted findings among scientific experts in the field are presented in Highlight 9–2. Perhaps the most important conclusion is that intelligence test scores do predict a number of socially relevant criteria, and in all likelihood everyone reading this book has taken at least one (and probably several) of these tests over the years. Other, more specific implications for leaders can be found later in this chapter.

Highlight 9–2

Mainstream Science on Intelligence

As stated earlier, intelligence is one of the most controversial subjects in Western society, and the publication of *The Bell Curve* (Herrnstein & Murray, 1994) only added fuel to the fire. One of the problems with intelligence is that many social and political commentators either know very little about the concept or are unwilling to let the data affect their opinions. As a result, many comments are either misguided or clearly unsupported by data. In order to add some clarity to this controversy, some of the most prominent scientists in the field have summarized what we know about intelligence and intelligence testing. Here are some of their conclusions:

1. Intelligence is a very general trait of mental capacity that, among other things, involves the ability to reason, plan, solve problems, think abstractly, comprehend complex ideas, learn quickly, and learn from experience. It is not merely book learning, a narrow academic skill, or test-taking smarts. Rather, it reflects a broader and deeper capability for comprehending our surroundings—"catching on," "making sense" of things, or "figuring out what to do."

2. Intelligence, so defined, can be measured, and intelligence tests measure it well. They are among the most accurate (in technical terms, reliable and valid) of all psychological tests and assessments. They do not measure creativity, character, personality, or other important differences among individuals, nor are they intended to.

3. The spread of people along the IQ continuum, from low to high, can be represented well by the bell curve. Most people cluster around the average (IQ = 100). Few are very bright or very dull: About 3 percent of Americans score above 130 (often considered the threshold for "giftedness") with about the same percentage scoring below 70 (often considered the threshold for mental retardation).

4. A high IQ is an advantage in life because virtually all activities require some reasoning and decision making. Conversely, a low IQ is often a disadvantage, especially in disorganized environments. Of course, a high IQ no more guarantees success than a low IQ guarantees failure in life. There are many exceptions, but the odds for success in our society greatly favor individuals with higher IQs.

5. Intelligence tests are not culturally biased against American blacks or other native-born, English-speaking peoples in the United States. Rather, IQ scores predict accurately for all such Americans, regardless of race or social class. Individuals who do not understand English well can be given either a nonverbal test or one in their native language.

6. Individuals differ in their intelligence due to differences in both their environments and genetic heritage. Heritability estimates range from 0.4 to 0.8 (on a scale of 0 to 1), indicating that genetics plays a prominent role in creating IQ differences in individuals. Nevertheless, members of the same family

> tend to differ substantially in intelligence (by an average of 12 points). These differences are due to genetics (brothers and sisters share only half their genes) and differences in family upbringing (e.g., birth order).
> 7. Certain personality traits, special talents, aptitudes, physical abilities, experience, and the like, are important (sometimes essential) for successful performance in many jobs, but they have narrower "transferability" across tasks, jobs, and situations when compared with general intelligence.
>
> Sources: R. D. Arvey et al., "Mainstream Science on Intelligence," *The Wall Street Journal*, December 13, 1994; U. Neisser, G. Boodoo, T. J. Bouchard, A. W. Boykin, N. Brody, S. J. Ceci, D. F. Halpern, J. C. Loehlin, R. Perloff, R. J. Sternberg, and S. Urbina, "Intelligence: Knowns and Unknowns," *American Psychologist* 51, no. 2 (1996).

Three Views of Intelligence

Although the debate about intelligence testing has abated among psychologists, there is still an ongoing debate about the nature of intelligence. Many psychologists have tried to determine the structure of intelligence; is intelligence a unitary ability, or does it involve a collection of related mental abilities (Azar, 1995; Gardner, 1983; Herrnstein & Murray, 1994)? Other psychologists have said that the *process* by which people do complex mental work is much more important than determining the number of mental abilities (Sternberg, 1985, 1997). These three views about the nature of intelligence differ not only in the way they assess intelligence. More importantly for our purposes, they differ in how intelligence might be understood to impact leadership.

The unitary view is founded on findings early in this century that individuals' scores on different types of such tests were all positively correlated—a person doing well on a vocabulary test was likely to do well on a memory or numeric reasoning test and vice versa. Therefore, Spearman (1904) hypothesized that a unitary mental ability, which he designated as g, was the underlying basis of this consistency in mental test scores and can be defined as the general ability to solve complex mental problems. On a practical level, higher levels of g imply greater problem solving ability, so that people doing well on mental-abilities tests would likely be faster learners and better problem solvers on the job. Because there is a considerable amount of evidence showing that g is the best single predictor of job performance across virtually all jobs (Neisser et al., 1996; Ree & Earles, 1992, 1993), measures of g are often used by organizations making hiring decisions. In line with this kind of reasoning, *leaders with higher g would be predicted to do well in learning and problem solving across diverse situations.*

There are many, however, who do not accept the validity of g, or unitary intelligence. Another school of thought maintains that instead we all possess **multiple intelligences**. These include: linguistic, musical, logical-mathematical, spatial, bodily-kinesthetic, intrapersonal, and interpersonal intelligence (Gardner, 1983). This view is based on common observations of people. For example, why do some mentally retarded individuals possess incredible memories (think of Dustin Hoffman in the movie *Rain Man*)? Gardner, a proponent of this view, reasoned if there truly were a unitary mental ability such as g, then we should never see examples where someone does poorly on a standardized intelligence tests but exhibits extraordinary musical or memory skills. Although this theory is intriguing, there is little empirical evidence thus far to support it.

Perhaps the most comprehensive and compelling theory of intelligence developed and tested over the past fifteen years is Sternberg's (1985, 1997) **triarchic theory of intelligence**. It also offers some of the most significant implications for leadership. The triarchic theory focuses on what a person *does* when solving complex mental problems, such as how information is combined and synthesized when solving problems, what assumptions and errors are made, and the like. According to this theory, there are three basic types of intelligence. **Analytic intelligence** is similar to g and can be assessed using the same standardized mental abilities tests described earlier. Like those with high levels of g, leaders and followers with higher levels of analytic intelligence tend to be quick learners; do well in school; have a good fund of general knowledge; and have the ability to make accurate deductions, assumptions, and inferences with relatively unfamiliar information.

There is still much, however, that g does not explain. There are a number of people who do well on standardized tests but not in life (Sternberg, Wagner, Williams, & Horvath, 1995). At the same time, some people do relatively poorly on standardized intelligence tests but often develop ingenious solutions to practical problems. For example, Sternberg and his associates described a situation where students in a school for the mentally retarded did very poorly on standardized tests yet consistently found ways to defeat the school's elaborate security system. In this situation the students possessed a relatively high level of **practical intelligence,** or "street smarts." People with street smarts know how to adapt to, shape, or select new situations in order to get their needs met better than people lacking street smarts (e.g., think of a stereotypical computer nerd and an inner-city kid both lost in downtown New York). In other words, practical intelligence involves knowing how things get done and how to do them. For students, it might be knowing how to apply for the best scholarships or loans or how to "game" the registration system in order to get the best classes and schedules. For leaders, practical intelligence involves knowing what to do and how to do it when confronted with a particular leadership situation, such as dealing with a poorly performing subordinate or leading large groups of employees.

Because of its potential importance to leadership effectiveness, there are several other aspects of practical intelligence worth noting. First, practical intelligence is much more concerned with knowledge and experience than analytic intelligence (see Figure 9–1, page 231). Leaders can build their practical intelligence by building their leadership knowledge and experience. Thus, textbooks such as this one can help you to build your practical intelligence. Getting a variety of leadership experiences, and perhaps more importantly, reflecting on these experiences, will also help you to build practical intelligence. Second, practical intelligence is *domain specific*. A leader who has a lot of knowledge and experience in leading a pharmaceutical research team may feel like a duck out of water when asked to lead a major fund-raising effort for a charitable institution. As another example, one of the authors recently worked with a highly successful retail company having over 100,000 employees. All of the key leaders had over 20 years of retail operations and merchandising experience, but they also did very poorly on standardized intelligence tests. The company had successfully expanded in the United States (which capitalized on their practical intelligence), but their attempt to expand to foreign markets was a failure. This failure was due in part to the leaders' inability to learn, appreciate, or understand the intricacies of other cultures (analytic intelligence), their lack of knowledge and experience in foreign markets (practical intelligence), and in turn their development of inappropriate strategies for running the business in other countries (a combination of analytic and practical intelligence). Thus, practical intelligence is extremely useful when leading in familiar situations, but analytic intelligence may play a more important role when leaders are facing new or novel situations.

Third, this example points out the importance of having both types of intelligence. Organizations today are looking for leaders and followers who have the necessary knowledge and skills to succeed (practical intelligence) and the ability to learn (analytic intelligence) (Stamps, 1996). Fourth, it may be that high levels of practical intelligence may compensate for lower levels of analytic intelligence. Leaders having lower analytic abilities may still be able to solve complex work problems or make good decisions provided they have plenty of job-relevant knowledge or experience. Fifth, Sternberg and his associates have developed a test of managerial street smarts; sample items from the test can be found in Highlight 9–3. Other tests of practical intelligence or street smarts are the in-basket and role play exercises described in Chapter 5. In such exercises leaders are asked to indicate what they would do to solve a variety of practical leadership problems. Sternberg's research has shown that scores on his test of managerial street smarts are relatively unrelated to scores on standardized intelligence tests. Performance on Sternberg's test or on an in-basket exercise will depend much more on one's practical leadership knowledge and experience than on one's analytic intelligence. Nevertheless, because people who do well on standardized tests tend to be quicker learners, all things being equal, it may be that these individuals develop their street smarts more quickly than people who do less well on these tests. Analytic intelligence may play a lesser role once a domain of knowledge is mastered, but a more important role when encountering new situations.

The third component of the triarchic theory of intelligence is **creative intelligence**. Creative intelligence is the ability to produce work that is both novel and useful (Sternberg, 1997; Sternberg & Lubart, 1996). Using *both* criteria (novel and useful) as components of creative intelligence helps to eliminate many of the more outlandish solutions to a potential problem by ensuring that adopted solutions can be realistically implemented or have some type of practical payoff. A more complete description of creative intelligence can be found later in this chapter.

Highlight 9–3

Typical Items Found on Intelligence Tests

An Example Item of Managerial "Street Smarts"

You are responsible for selecting a contractor to renovate several large buildings. You have narrowed the choice to two contractors on the basis of their bids, and after further consideration, you are considering awarding the contract to Wilson & Sons Company. Rank order the importance of the following pieces of information in making your decision to award the contract to Wilson & Sons.

_____ The company has provided letters from satisfied former customers.

_____ The Better Business Bureau reports no major complaints about the company

_____ Wilson & Sons has done good work for your company in the past.

_____ Wilson & Sons' bid was $2,000 less than the other contractor's (approximate total cost of the renovation was $325,000)

_____ Former customers whom you have contacted strongly recommend Wilson and Sons for the job.

Source: Adapted from Sternberg & Wagner, 1993.

Example Items from Typical Speed Tests of Intelligence

Vocabulary: Choose the word most similar in meaning:

Dogma   A. Canine   B. Religion   C. Doctrine   D. Dower

Verbal Reasoning: Pick out one word in each column to make the sentence true and sensible:

_____ is to noon as breakfast is to _____

1. Flow   A. Include
2. Lunch   B. Morning
3. Supper   C. Coffee
4. Door   D. Corner

Numerical Reasoning: Choose the number which best completes the pattern:

4 6 8 5 7 9 6 ___   A. 5   B. 6   C. 7   D. 8   E. 9

(A typical speed test consists of 20 to 30 items, and test takers are only given five minutes to answer as many items as possible.)

The three types of intelligence in Sternberg's theory correspond nicely with the three leaders identified in Chapter 1. Although all three leaders probably possess high levels of all three types of intelligence, it may be that Madeline Albright has particularly strong analytic intelligence. She not only has her doctorate, but she is known for her ability to learn new information, see connections between various world events, and think through the implications of foreign policy decisions. Colin Powell has highly developed practical intelligence for leading in the military. He has commanded a number of large and small military units and held line and staff positions during times of peace and war. An open question is how relevant his extensive military knowledge and experience would be if he were ever elected president, however. Konosuke Matsushita may have the most developed creative intelligence, as he and his company are known for developing new and useful consumer products.

Finally, it is important to note that of the three views of intelligence, the bulk of the evidence currently supports the existence of g, or analytic intelligence. Because analytic intelligence has been shown to be a consistent predictor of job performance, it is not likely that mental-abilities testing as we currently know it will change anytime soon. Nevertheless, some researchers are beginning to demonstrate that other characteristics, such as personality traits, values, job knowledge, practical intelligence, and creativity, may play as great a role as g in job performance—or even greater (Fiedler, 1995; Hogan, Curphy, & Hogan, 1994; McClelland, 1993; Schmidt & Hunter, 1993; Sternberg, 1997). This may be particularly true in leadership, if we assume that most of the candidates applying for a leadership position have roughly the same level of g. If that is so, standardized intelligence testing would not do a good job of differentiating the best from the poorest performers in the candidate pool. It is more likely that the candidates would differ in their values, personality, and job-relevant experience, and assessing these characteristics may prove to be more useful in predicting leadership success.

Assessment and Research Results

It is easy to underestimate the impact intelligence testing has had on the fields of education and business in the United States. If you include achievement tests, such as the Iowa Basics, PSAT, SAT, ACT, GMAT, LSAT, or GRE as part of intelligence testing (these tests correlate around .8 with intelligence tests and essentially measure the same thing), then perhaps up to 40,000,000 Americans are tested annually. Psychologists typically use paper-and-pencil tests to assess intelligence, although oral and computer-administered techniques are also used. Many different intelligence tests have been developed, partly because psychologists do not agree on a common definition of intelligence. Nevertheless, these tests can be roughly divided into two major categories. The assumption underlying **speed tests** is that smarter people solve problems more quickly than people who are not as smart. A typical speed test may consist of 29–30 items, and candidates are given five minutes to complete as many items as possible (see

FIGURE 9–2

The Bell or Normal Curve

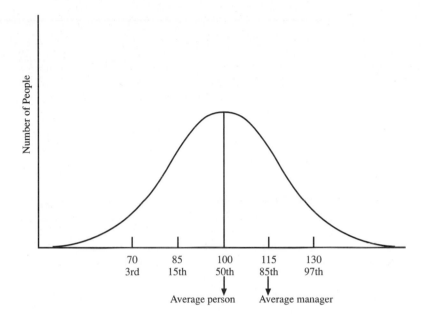

Highlight 9–3). In all likelihood most people would get virtually all of the problems on a speed test right if they had plenty of time. However, most people only get about half of the items right in the five-minute time frame. **Power tests** are not time-limited, but the problems become progressively more difficult throughout the test. The assumption behind power tests is that smarter people can solve more difficult problems than people who are not as smart.

Scores from both speed or power tests can be used to calculate a person's **intelligence quotient (IQ)**, which is often used to signify his or her general level of intelligence. By definition, the average person has an IQ of 100, and only 3 percent of the population have scores above 130, with an equal percentage below 70 (see Figure 9–2). Although some researchers have argued that intelligence tests primarily measure thinking in terms of white, middle-class values (Kincheloe, 1996), there is overwhelming evidence showing that IQ scores are useful predictors of a number of socially significant phenomena (Humphreys, 1984). IQ scores are often associated with level of education achieved, success in school, occupational choice, income levels, and performance within an occupation (Arvey et al., 1994; Brody, 1997; Ceci & Williams, 1997; Neisser et al., 1996; Ree & Earles, 1992; Scarr, 1989; Schmidt & Hunter, 1992;). Graphic evidence to support some of these propositions can be found in Figures 9–3 and 9–4. Figure 9–3 depicts the average power test scores for people at four management levels.

As you can see, people who have the most authority and make the most money (i.e., executives) have the highest test scores (and IQs). Similarly, Bray, Campbell, and Grant (1974) and Bray and Howard (1983) reported that people with higher IQs received more promotions, earned higher salaries, and reached

FIGURE 9–3

*Average
Intelligence Test
Scores by
Management
Level*

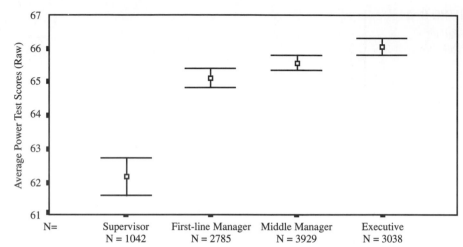

Source: N. Kuncel, "Personality and Cognitive Differences among Management Levels" (Unpublished manuscript, Personnel Decisions International, Minneapolis, 1996).

higher organizational levels over 20 years at AT&T than people with lower IQs. Figure 9–4 looks at job performance within a particular technical occupation. People with the highest IQs have the best overall job performance. Moreover, in their first year people with the highest IQs were already performing at a level it took people with the lowest IQs three years to achieve.

There have been 200 separate studies that have examined the relationship between intelligence test scores and leadership effectiveness or emergence, and these studies have been the topic of major reviews by Stogdill (1948); Mann (1959); Ghiselli (1963); Stogdill (1974); Bray, Campbell, and Grant (1974); Cornwell (1983); Bray and Howard (1983); Lord, DeVader, and Allinger (1986); Bass (1990); and Fiedler (1992). Most of these reviews reported the relationship between intelligence and leadership to be in the $r = .3$ range. However, Lord, DeVader, and Allinger (1986) used advanced statistical techniques to estimate the true correlation between intelligence and leadership emergence to be $r = .5$. Thus, the 10 reviews listed above provide overwhelming support for the idea that leadership effectiveness or emergence is positively correlated with intelligence.

Implications for Leaders

What do all these different views and findings about intelligence and intelligence testing mean for the typical leadership practitioner? First, candidates applying for management or executive positions in many organizations may well need to take some type of intelligence test as part of the selection process. Second, people in managerial positions tend to be smarter than the general population. As seen in Figure 9–3, the average manager often scores around the 80th percentile of the general population. Moreover, Figure 9–4 shows that leaders

FIGURE 9–4

An Example of How Intelligence Test Scores Are Related to Job Performance Over Time

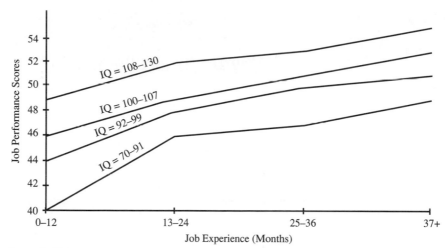

Source: D. H. Born, "Preservice Arrest History: Another Indicator of Recruit Quality," in W. Sellman (Chair), "Moral Character Screening: Sorting Good and Bad Apples" (Symposium presented at the 105th Annual Meeting of the American Psychological Association, Chicago, August 1997).

higher in the organization are generally smarter than leaders lower in the organization. These findings make sense, as the problem-solving demands of managers and executives are often greater and more complex than those found for many other occupations.

Third, it is nonetheless important to recognize that the correlation between intelligence and leadership success is far from perfect. The smartest people are not always the best leaders. Moreover, the magnitude of the correlation between intelligence and leadership effectiveness may depend on the situation. Leadership situations that are relatively routine and unchanging may place more importance on experience and less importance on intelligence than dynamic and ever changing situations. Similarly, intelligence may be a better predictor of success in certain leadership roles than in others. Having a high level of intelligence may be very important at the top levels of the organization, where leaders must be able to detect themes and patterns in seemingly unrelated information, make accurate assumptions about market conditions, or make wise merger and acquisition decisions. However, research also shows that intelligence alone does not guarantee leadership success (see Highlight 9–4 and Highlight 9–5).

Fourth, it is relatively difficult for leaders to improve their level of *g*, analytic intelligence, or IQ. Although researchers have shown that it is possible to raise the IQ of children by putting them through relatively long and intense developmental interventions (Perkins & Grotzer, 1997), these interventions are probably impractical for adults. Then again, it is important to realize that the relationship between intelligence test scores and leadership effectiveness is not perfect. It is possible for leaders to compensate for a relative lack of analytic intelligence by building their leadership knowledge and experience (i.e., practical intelligence), effectively using power and influence tactics (see Chapter 6),

Highlight 9–4

Why Do Smart People Fail?

Intelligent people do not always make successful leaders and sometimes can make quite a mess out of their lives. In his book, *Intelligence Applied*, Sternberg (1986) described some of the reasons why smart people fail, which include:

1. Lack of motivation.
2. Lack of impulse control.
3. Lack of perseverance.
4. Fear of failure.
5. Inability to translate thought into action.
6. Inability to see the forest for the trees.
7. Distractibility and lack of concentration.
8. Indecision.
9. Procrastination.
10. Inability to complete tasks.
11. Spreading oneself too thick or thin.
12. Too little or too much self-confidence.

You will probably see many of these reasons rear their heads if you are in (or choose to enter) graduate school. You may also see evidence for these factors at your 5- or 10-year high school reunion—some of the smartest people in your school may not have achieved the occupational status you and everyone else thought they would. Interestingly enough, many of these reasons have more to do with personality than with intelligence.

developing a solid set of values and good leadership attitudes (see Chapter 7), capitalizing on their personality traits (see Chapter 8), demonstrating effective leadership or charismatic leadership behaviors (see Chapters 10 and 11), or leveraging a high level of achievement motivation (see Chapter 14). Leadership is a very complex picture, and intelligence alone is far from the whole story.

In fact, intelligence often has a *curvilinear* relationship with leadership effectiveness (Ghiselli, 1963; Stogdill, 1974). It is possible for leaders to be too smart; leaders who are substantially smarter than their followers may not be as effective as leaders who are just slightly smarter than their followers. When differences in intelligence between leader and followers are too great, communication can be impaired; a leader's intelligence can become an impediment to being understood by subordinates (Bass, 1990).

An alternative explanation for the curvilinear relationship between intelligence and leadership effectiveness may have to do with how stress affects leader–subordinate interactions. It may be that some studies in which *more intel-*

Highlight 9–5

Emotional Quotient (EQ): Fact or Fiction?

More and more has been written about the positive attributes of a leader's emotional quotient, or EQ. The term has become so popular that the American Dialect Society voted EQ as the most useful phrase of 1995. But what is EQ, and does it relate to the concept of personality or the three types of intelligence described in this chapter? To answer these questions, we provide a brief historical overview of the concept.

As described in Chapters 6 through 8, a considerable amount of research has shown that attributes other than intelligence, such as power, influence tactics, values, and personality traits, are related to leadership success, and that in some situations these characteristics have even stronger relationships with leadership effectiveness than intelligence. Two psychologists, Peter Salovey and John Mayer, studied why some bright people fail to be successful, and discovered that many of them ran into trouble due to their lack of interpersonal sensitivity and skills. Daniel Goleman, a science writer for the *New York Times,* summarized some of this work in his book *Emotional Intelligence.* Goleman argued that success in life is based more on one's self-motivation, persistence in the face of frustration, mood management, ability to adapt, and ability to empathize and get along with others than on one's analytic intelligence, or IQ. The term *EQ* joined the pop culture with the publication of an "EQ Quiz" in a 1995 edition of *USA Today.*

Two other aspects of EQ led the business community to embrace it. First, many human resource professionals believed that EQ justified certain training programs which emphasized "softer" interpersonal skills over "harder" financial or business analysis skills. Second, many of the attributes associated with EQ, such as oral communication skills, interpersonal skills, and the ability to adapt to new situations, are just the kind of attributes employers are currently looking for in their new hires. But is EQ really something new, or just a repackaging of old ideas and findings? Leaders do benefit from good interpersonal skills, achievement motivation, and emotional self-control. But is this a new insight? Not at all.

Sources: D. Goleman, *Emotional Intelligence* (New York: Bantam Books, 1995); D. Stamps, "Are We Too Smart for Our Jobs?" *Training*, April 1996; H. Weisinger, *Emotional Intelligence at Work* (New York: Jossey-Bass, 1997).

ligent leaders were *less effective* primarily involved leadership challenges that were highly stressful. In that regard, Fiedler (1992) and Gibson (1992) found that smart, but inexperienced, leaders were less effective in stressful situations than less intelligent, experienced leaders. An example of this finding was clearly demonstrated in the movie *Platoon.* In one frantic scene, an American platoon is ambushed by the Vietcong, and an inexperienced, college-educated lieutenant calls for artillery support from friendly units. He calls in the wrong coordinates, however, and as a result artillery shells are dropped on his own platoon's, rather than the enemy's, position. The situation comes under control only after an experienced sergeant sizes up the situation and tells the artillery unit to cease firing. These notions are explored further in the next section.

Leaders and Stress: Cognitive Resources Theory

In the preceding section we noted that intelligence may be a more important quality for leaders in some situations than others. You may be surprised to learn, however, that recent research actually suggests there are times when intelligence may be a disadvantage. A key variable affecting this paradoxical finding seems to be whether or not the leader is in a stressful situation. Recent research suggests that stress plays a key role in determining just how a leader's intelligence affects his or her effectiveness. While it is not surprising that stress affects behavior in various ways, Fiedler and Garcia (1987) developed the **cognitive resources theory** (CRT) to explain the interesting relationships between leader intelligence and experience levels, and group performance in stressful versus non stressful conditions.

As first described in Chapter 5, CRT consists of several key concepts. Certainly one of these is intelligence. Fiedler and Garcia (1987) and Fiedler (1995) defined intelligence as we have earlier—it is one's all-around effectiveness in activities directed by thought and is typically measured using standardized intelligence tests. Another key concept is experience, which represents the habitual behavior patterns, overlearned knowledge, and skills acquired for effectively dealing with task-related problems. Although experience is often gained under stressful and unpleasant conditions, experience also provides a "crash plan" to revert back to when under stress (Fiedler, 1992, 1995). As Fiedler observed, people often act differently when stressed, and the crash plan describes this change in behavior patterns. For most of the CRT studies, experience has been defined as time in the job or organization. A third key concept in CRT is stress. Stress is often defined as the result of conflicts with superiors or the apprehension associated with performance evaluation (Fiedler, 1995; Gibson, 1992). This interpersonal stress is believed to be emotionally disturbing and can divert attention from problem-solving activities (Sarason, 1986). In other words, people can get so concerned about how their performance is being evaluated that they may fail to perform at an optimal level. In sum, cognitive resource theory provides a conceptual scheme for explaining how leader behavior changes under stress levels to impact group performance.

Cognitive resources theory makes two major predictions with respect to intelligence, experience, stress, and group performance. First, because experienced leaders have a greater repertoire of behaviors to fall back on, leaders with greater experience but lower intelligence are hypothesized to have higher-performing groups under conditions of high stress. Experienced leaders have "been there before" and better know what to do and how to get it done when faced with high-stress situations. Leaders' experience levels can interfere with performance under low-stress conditions, however.

That leads to a second hypothesis. Because experience leads to habitual behavior patterns, leaders with high levels of experience will have a tendency to misapply old solutions to problems when creative solutions are called for (Fiedler, 1992, 1995). Experienced leaders overrely on the tried and true when faced with new problems, even when under relatively low periods of stress. Thus, leaders with higher levels of intelligence but less experience are not constrained by previously acquired behavior patterns and should have higher-performing groups under low-stress conditions. In other words, experience is helpful when one is under stress but is often a hindrance to performance in the absence of stress.

These two major predictions of CRT can be readily seen in everyday life. For the most part, it is not the most intelligent but the most experienced members of sporting teams, marching bands, acting troops, or volunteer organizations who are selected to be leaders. These leaders are often chosen because other members recognize their ability to perform well under the high levels of stress associated with sporting events and public performances. In addition, research with combat troops, firefighters, senior executives, and students has provided reasonably strong support for the two major tenets of CRT (Fiedler & Garcia, 1987; Fiedler, 1992, 1995; Gibson, 1992).

Despite this initial empirical support, one problem with CRT concerns the apparent dichotomy between intelligence and experience. Fiedler and Garcia's (1987) initial investigations of CRT did not examine the possibility that leaders could be both intelligent and experienced. Subsequent research by Gibson (1992) showed not only that many leaders were both intelligent and experienced, but also that these leaders would fall back on their experience in stressful situations and use their intelligence to solve group problems in less-stressful situations.

Another issue with CRT concerns the leader's ability to tolerate stress. As Schonpflug (1995) and Zaccaro (1995) correctly pointed out, some leaders may be better able to tolerate high levels of stress than others. Some leaders may have personalities characterized by considerable emotional stability or adjustment, and it may be that such leaders may do well in high-stress situations even when they lack experience because of their inherent ability to handle stress. Further research on this issue seems warranted.

In general, Fiedler and his colleagues have provided solid evidence to support the major tenets of CRT. Because of this research, CRT has several important implications for leaders. First, Sternberg (1995) has commented that intelligence and experience have strong parallels to analytic and practical intelligence in his triarchic theory or intelligence. As stated earlier, it may be that the best leaders are often smart *and* experienced. Although intelligence tests are good indicators of raw mental horsepower, it is just as important for leaders to broaden their leadership knowledge and experience if they want to be successful in high-stress situations. This latter point may be very important today, where the additional stress of organizational downsizing and "delayering" may cause the performance of leaders to be scrutinized even more closely than in the past. In fact, this additional scrutiny may well cause leaders who were previously successful to perform rather poorly in this high-stress environment.

Second, leaders may not be aware of the degree to which they are causing stress in their followers. If followers perceive that their performance is being closely watched, then they are likely to revert to their crash plans in order to perform. If the situation calls for new and novel solutions to problems, however, the leaders' behavior may be counterproductive. A key point here is that leaders may be unaware of their impact on followers. For example, they may want to more closely review their followers' work in order to be helpful, but followers may not perceive it this way.

Third, the level of stress inherent in the position needs to be understood before selection of leaders. Those doing the selection to fill high-stress leadership positions can either look for experienced leaders or reduce the stress in the situation so that more-intelligent leaders can be more successful (Levy-Leboyer, 1995). Another alternative could be to hire more-intelligent leaders and put them through some type of stress management program so that the effects of stress are minimized (Fielder, 1995). It is also possible that experienced leaders may get bored if placed into low-stress positions.

Creativity and Leadership

Suppose you were asked to pick a new manager for your organization. Assume that many of the candidates' characteristics were the same, but that they differed on these three points:

Candidate A is a very quick learner and has a good memory for facts.
Candidate B gets along extremely well with others.
Candidate C can develop new and useful solutions to problems.

Did you pick candidate C, who seems to have considerable creative intelligence? Creativity is a vitally important topic in business today. The development of intellectual capital and innovative products and services can be so important to the survival of some companies that they base a large part of their business strategies around creativity. For example, in 1991 Toyota set a goal for employees to put forth eight suggestions a month for improving their car-manufacturing processes. That year over 98 percent of the 2,000,000 suggestions forwarded were adopted. Similarly, one of 3M's corporate strategies is to have 25 percent of their worldwide revenue coming from products less than five years old. The Center for Creative Leadership's very mission emphasizes the close association between creativity and leadership (see Highlight 9–6).

Interestingly, despite creativity's importance, relatively little research has been devoted to it. Sternberg and Lubert's (1996) review of the literature showed that less than two-tenths of 1 percent of the psychologically based journal articles published over the past 20 years were dedicated to the study of creativity. Even so, there are some general points worth noting dealing with both the leader's own creativity and (perhaps more importantly) the leader's ability to stimulate creativity in others. The latter point is important because innovative products, services, and procedures are much more likely to be formulated and

HIGHLIGHT 9–6

The Center for Creative Leadership

One of the premier leadership development organizations in the world is the Center for Creative Leadership, with headquarters in Greensboro, North Carolina. It is an international, nonprofit institution committed to enhancing the understanding and effectiveness of leadership in an increasingly complex and demanding world. It is a resource for organizations and individuals seeking not simply to weather change, but to guide it—and thrive on it.

The phrase *creative leadership* in its title underscores the nearly inseparable relationship it sees between creativity and effective leadership. This linkage extends to virtually any domain of activity one can imagine: in education, in government, in entertainment and sports, and the like. Even many religious leaders today are searching for—and finding—creative solutions to problems such as dwindling attendance at traditional services.

How does the Center stimulate creative leadership? One of the most important ways is through week-long training programs which enhance the individual leader's self-awareness. Participants receive feedback about their personalities, their cognitive styles, their psychological preferences, their vocational interests, how others perceive their effectiveness in their real life jobs, how they are perceived by other participants in the program (based on various group problem solving challenges), and so on. A common theme in Center programs is learning to value the contributions of people whose personalities and cognitive styles differ from one's own.

developed at the working level than in management ranks (Amabile & Conti, 1995; Hogan & Morrison, 1993; Keller, 1989; Oldham & Cummings, 1996).

To be able to foster creativity in others, it is important to begin with an appreciation of what creativity is and the psychological and organizational factors that block or stifle creativity. In the latter case, creativity can be impeded by perceptual blocks (e.g., failing to see that one thing can be used as something else) and emotional blocks (e.g., fear of failure). Additionally, part of the leader's challenge is appreciating the nature of group interaction and organizational dynamics in the creative process. For example, creativity can be impeded by uncooperativeness and mistrust among co-workers.

What Is Creativity?

Before describing the factors that can facilitate or impede creativity, we must first define what creativity is. According to Cronbach (1984), **creativity,** or **divergent thinking,** is one's adeptness in making fresh observations and ideas. Creativity is the ability to see something in a new way. Sternberg and Lubart (1996) expanded this definition somewhat by adding an evaluative component to the mix.

According to the triarchic theory of intelligence, **creative intelligence** involves developing both novel and useful solutions to problems. When Newton discovered gravity, for example, his great insight was recognizing an essential similarity between a falling apple and the orbiting moon (Koestler, 1964). The inventor of Velcro got his idea while picking countless thistles out of his socks; he realized that the same principle that produced his frustration might be translated into a useful fastener. The inventor of 3M's Post-it notes was frustrated because bookmarks in his church hymnal were continually sliding out of place, and he saw a solution in a low-tack adhesive discovered by a fellow 3M scientist. To the latter scientist, the low-tack glue represented a failure since he had been trying to develop a new superglue. To the Post-it inventor, however, it was a step toward a bookmark that would attach to a page and come off without damaging the printing. The scientists who designed the Pathfinder mission to Mars were given a budget that was one-tenth that of the previous mission to Mars, the Viking Lander. Yet the scientists were challenged to develop a spacecraft that had more capabilities than the Viking Lander. Their efforts with Pathfinder were a resounding success, due in part to some of the novel solutions used both to land the spacecraft (an inflatable balloon system) and to explore the surrounding area (the Sojourner rover). As described by Cronbach, all these insights involved looking at one thing and seeing something else. However, as in Sternberg and Lubart's analysis, these novel ideas were also accompanied by some level of critical thinking or evaluation—novel ideas alone may not be very helpful in solving a problem. Moreover, it is important to note that a person's creativity seems to be specific to certain fields and subfields: Most composers are not architects, and most writers are not mathematicians (Cronbach, 1984; Sternberg & Lubart, 1996).

Two of the more-interesting questions surrounding creativity and divergent thinking concern the role of intelligence and the assessment of creative ability. Guilford (1967) said that divergent thinking was related to intelligence but still a separate ability. Barron and Harrington (1981) maintained that intelligence was a necessary but not a sufficient condition for creativity. More recent research by Sternberg and Lubart (1996) shows that g, or analytic intelligence, correlates at about the .5 level with creative intelligence. Thus, the best research available indicates that intelligence and creativity are related, but the relationship is far from perfect. Some level of intelligence seems necessary for creativity, but having a high level of intelligence is no guarantee that someone will be creative.

In addition, actually assessing creativity is no simple matter. Tests of creativity, or divergent thinking, are very different from tests that assess **convergent thinking**. Tests of convergent thinking usually have a single best answer; good examples here are most intelligence and aptitude tests. Conversely, tests of creativity or divergent thinking have many possible answers (see Highlight 9–7). Moreover, because creativity is field-specific, it is not clear whether generating as many uses for a common object as possible is at all related to creativity in painting, sculpting, writing music, or solving technical production problems. Although Sternberg and Lubart (1996) show that it is possible to reliably judge the relative creativity of different responses, the fact remains that judging cre-

---

Highlight 9–7

Typical Tests of Divergent Thinking

Product improvement. Individuals are given a drawing of a typical household product and are asked to modify the drawing in any way that would improve the usefulness of the product.

Unusual uses. These tests ask individuals to come up with as many uses as possible for common products, such as paper clips or bricks.

Clever plot titles. In these tests, people are given a short story to read and are asked to come up with a clever title.

Source: Adapted from L. J. Cronbach, *Essentials of Psychological Testing*, 4th ed. (San Francisco: Harper & Row, 1984).

---

ativity is more difficult than scoring convergent tests. For example, there are no set answers or standards for determining whether the title for a short story is truly creative. Another difficulty in assessing creativity is that it may wax and wane over time; many of the most creative people seem to have occasional dry spells or writer's block. This is very different from analytic intelligence, where performance on mental abilities tests remains fairly constant over time.

Creativity may be more difficult to measure, but creative people do seem to act differently than others. Children with high creativity test scores tend to be expansive and spontaneous, whereas less-creative children tend to be more cautious and insecure (Wallach & Kogan, 1965). Adults seen as creative tend to gravitate into certain occupations, such as music, art, drama, or architecture (Campbell, Hyne, & Nilsen, 1992). Nevertheless, people vary considerably in creativity within any occupation. For example, peers characterized creative female mathematicians as being rebellious and nonconforming, having unconventional thought processes, and being thorough and patient in research. Less-creative female mathematicians were characterized by their peers as grasping others' ideas quickly, favoring conservative values, and having an active and well-organized mind (Helson, 1971). Creativity has also been found to be related to leadership effectiveness, although the strength of this relationship may vary depending on level of authority. Rusmore (1984) and Rusmore and Baker (1987) showed that general intelligence was more highly related to lower-level managers' success and that creativity was more important for upper-level managers' success.

The Components of Creativity

So far we have discussed creativity as a unitary ability. However, recent research suggests that creativity appears to be made up of seven components: *synthetic ability, analytic intelligence, practical intelligence, thinking style, personality factors, intrinsic motivation,* and *environmental factors* (Amabile & Conti, 1995; Kohn, 1987; Oldham & Cummings, 1996; Sternberg, 1985; Sternberg & Grigorenko, 1997; Sternberg & Lubart, 1996). **Synthetic ability** is what we traditionally view as creativity; these skills help people see things in new ways or recognize novel patterns or connections. Analytic intelligence helps people to evaluate solutions, and practical intelligence provides the knowledge and experience base from which novel solutions are developed. According to Sternberg and Lubart, these first three components are very important to the creative process, and leaders lacking in any one of them will be less creative than those possessing all three.

Thinking style is somewhat related to synthetic ability. Thinking styles are not abilities per se, but rather are the preferred ways for using the abilities one has (Sternberg & Grigorenko, 1997). For example, some people seem to prefer improving or adapting already existing products or processes. A first-line supervisor in a manufacturing facility may be very adept at modifying existing production schedules or equipment in order to better meet customers' needs. Other people seem to prefer developing completely new products. A team leader tasked with developing a new ad campaign for a major brewer might come up with a series of promotional ads using novel attention-getting devices, such as frogs or chameleons. According to Kirton (1987), these two examples illustrate the difference between **adaptive** and **innovative thinking styles**. Adaptors prefer to modify or change existing products or processes; innovators prefer to create entirely new processes or products. Adaptors and innovators may have the same level of synthetic ability, but they just seem to use this ability in different ways. It is important to note that U.S. companies seem particularly adept at developing new technology (i.e., innovation), whereas Japanese industries are very good at improving the technology and finding efficient ways to bring it to the marketplace (i.e., adaptation).

Several personality factors also seem to play a role in creativity. More specifically, people having higher levels of self-confidence, energy, risk-taking, independence, impulsiveness, and intellectance seem to be more creative than people who lack self-confidence, are more conforming, and are less open to new and novel experiences (Amabile & Gryskiewicz, 1987; Hogan & Morrison, 1993; Oldham & Cummings, 1996; Sternberg & Lubart, 1996). People will also be more creative when they are intrinsically motivated or feel challenged by the subject matter or problem itself (Amabile & Hennessey, 1988). Creative people are more likely to focus attention on solving the problem at hand, not on the need to meet deadlines, make money, or impress others.

Finally, several situational or environmental factors appear related to creativity. People who have more-complex or challenging jobs and who have supportive, noncontrolling leaders seem to be more creative than people in uninteresting jobs who also have highly controlling supervisors (Oldham & Cummings, 1996). Several aspects of work groups also seem to affect creativity. Although the size of the group did not seem to matter, teams that were given clear goals, stayed task focused, and provided mutual support and participation often developed more innovative solutions than teams lacking these qualities (West & Anderson, 1996).

Team stability also seems to play a role in creativity. Amabile and Conti (1995) studied a Fortune 500 company before, during, and after going through a large downsizing, and reported that teams that remained relatively intact during this process were substantially more creative in terms of patent applications than teams that were broken up. These authors also reported that an organization's support for creativity, in terms of time and resources, was a key factor in the creativity of individual employees.

The story of Chester Carlson provides a good example of how some of the seven components play important roles in developing a creative and useful solution to a problem. Chester Carlson invented the photocopy duplicating process, which revolutionized office work. Duplicating machines are relied on so much today that most people probably assume the invention was met with instant acceptance. That was not the case, however. Most people do not realize that it was 22 years from the time Carlson got the idea to the time his product became commercially available—or that refining and "selling" his concept was an uphill battle primarily because of the existence of carbon paper. (With carbon paper, people thought, why would you need anything else?) His solution for making copies of documents was certainly imaginative, but it was also derived from his considerable technical expertise. Moreover, his persistence in developing and persuading others of the potential of his process is a testament to the importance of intrinsic motivation in creativity.

Creative thinking is not an entirely rational or conscious process. Many times we do our most imaginative thinking unconsciously; people often gain sudden insights to an old problem out of the blue. There are interesting anecdotal accounts of how different creative thinkers recognized and even harnessed these unconscious processes. Einstein, for example, once remarked that he got his best ideas in the morning when he was shaving. The great inventor Thomas Edison reportedly developed a technique to awaken himself and capture the typically unusual imagery and mental activity occurring as one falls asleep. These thinkers recognized the mind's fertility during its resting periods. Einstein's and Edison's receptivity to ideas emerging from their nonlogical mental processes was surely an important part of their genius. They were able to harness their unconscious rather than censor it, as many of us may do by suppressing or discounting mental activity that seems purposeless, nonsensical, or threatening.

Implications for Leaders

Perhaps the most-important point leaders should remember is that their primary role is not so much to be creative themselves as to build an environment where others can be creative. This is not to say that leaders should be uncreative, but rather that most innovations have their roots in ideas developed by people closest to a problem or opportunity (i.e., the workers). Leaders can boost the creativity throughout their groups or organizations in many ways, but particularly through selecting creative people in the first place, and providing opportunities for others to develop their creativity, and through broader interventions like making sure the motivation or incentives for others are conducive to creativity and providing at least some guidance or vision about what the creative product or output should look like.

There are several things leaders can do to improve the group and organizational factors affecting creativity. Leaders should be mindful of the effect various sorts of incentives or rewards can have on creativity; certain types of motivation to work are more conducive to creativity than others. Research has shown that people tend to generate more-creative solutions when they are told to focus on their intrinsic motivation for doing so (i.e., the pleasure of solving the task itself) rather than focusing on the extrinsic motivation (i.e., public recognition or pay) (Amabile, 1985; Amabile & Hennessey, 1988). When they need to foster creativity, leaders may find it more effective to select followers who truly enjoy working on the task at hand (i.e., are intrinsically motivated) rather than relying on rewards (i.e., extrinsic motivation) to foster creativity.

It is also helpful to remember that synthetic abilities can also be hindered if people believe that their ideas will be evaluated. Amabile's (1983, 1987) experiments showed that students who were told their projects were to be judged by experts produced less creative projects than students who were not told their projects would be judged. A similar sort of phenomenon can occur in groups. Even when a group knows its work must ultimately be evaluated, there is a pronounced tendency for members to be evaluative and judgmental too early in the solution-generating process. This tends to reduce the number of creative solutions generated, perhaps because of a generally shared belief in the value of critical thinking (and in some groups the norm seems to be the more criticism the better) and of subjecting ideas to intense scrutiny and evaluation. When members of a group judge ideas as soon as they are offered, two dysfunctional things can happen. People in the group may censor themselves (i.e., not share all their ideas with the group), as even mild rejection or criticism has a significant dampening effect (Prince, 1972), or they may prematurely reject others' ideas through negativistic focus on an idea's flaws rather than its possibilities. Given these findings, leaders may want to hold off on evaluating new ideas until they are all on the table, and should also encourage their followers to so the same.

Finally, leaders who need to develop new products and services should try to minimize the level of turnover in their teams and provide them with clear goals. Teams having unclear goals may successfully develop new or novel products, but these products may have low marketability or usefulness. Two examples might help illustrate this point. In the 1980s Texas Instruments decided to delve into the personal computer business. Texas Instruments (TI) had a reputation for technical excellence, and one of the best managers in the company was asked to head up the project. The manager did not have a clear sense of what customers wanted or what a personal computer should be able to do. This lack of clarity had some fairly dramatic effects. As more and more engineers were added to the project, more and more innovative hardware ideas were added to the computer design. These additions caused the project to take much longer and cost a lot more than planned, but the TI personal computer ended up winning a number of major engineering awards. Unfortunately, it was also a business disaster, as the product ultimately failed to meet customer needs. Although Compaq computers arose from the ashes of TI's failure, the TI project serves as a good example for a concept called **creeping elegance**. Leaders not having a clear vision of what a final project should look like may end up with something that fails to meet customer needs. Leaders need to provide enough room for creativity to flourish, but enough direction for effort to be focused.

One industry that places a premium on creativity is the motion picture industry. Because creativity is so important to the commercial success of a movie, it is relatively easy for a movie to succumb to creeping elegance. But how do movie directors successfully avoid creeping elegance when dealing with highly creative people having huge egos? Part of the answer may be in the approach of two of Hollywood's most successful directors. Steven Speilberg and Ron Howard said before they ever shot a scene that they first had a very clear picture of it in their own minds. If they did not have a clear picture, then they sat down with the relevant parties and worked it out. Both situations point out the importance of having a clear vision when managing creativity. Still further ideas about the relationship between leadership and creativity can be found in Highlight 9–8.

Summary

This chapter examined the relationships between intelligence, creativity, and leadership success. Intelligence and intelligence testing are somewhat controversial subjects in society today, but given the general usefulness of the concept it appears that intelligence testing will not be fading away anytime soon. The most recent theory for understanding intelligence divides it into three related components: analytic intelligence, practical intelligence, and creative intelligence. All three components are interrelated. Most research shows that leaders possess higher levels of analytic intelligence than the general population, and that more-intelligent leaders often make better leaders. Analytic intelligence appears to confer two primary benefits upon leaders. First, leaders who are smarter seem to be better problem solvers. Second, and perhaps more importantly, smarter leaders seem to profit more from experience.

The roles of practical and creative intelligence in leadership are receiving increasing attention. Practical intelligence, or one's relevant job knowledge or experience, is proving to be extremely important for leaders. Leaders with higher levels of practical intelligence seem to be better at solving problems under stress and may be able to develop more-creative and useful solutions. Moreover, practical intelligence seems to be the easiest of the three components to change. This implies that leaders should use techniques such as the action-observation-reflection model, described in Chapter 2, to extract the most learning from their experiences.

Highlight 9–8

Managing Creativity

Hogan and Morrison (1993) maintained that people who are seen as more creative tend to have several distinguishing personality characteristics. In general, creative people are more open to information and experience, have high energy, can be personally assertive and even domineering, react emotionally to events, are impulsive, are more interested in music and art than in hunting and sports, and finally are very motivated to prove themselves (i.e., are concerned with personal adequacy). Thus, creative people tend to be independent, willful, impractical, unconcerned with money, idealistic, and nonconforming. Given that these tendencies may not make them ideal followers, the interesting question raised by Hogan and Morrison is, How does one lead or manage creative individuals? This question becomes even more interesting when considering the qualities of successful leaders or managers. As discussed in Chapter 7, successful leaders tend to be intelligent, dominant, conscientious, stable, calm, goal oriented, outgoing, and somewhat conventional. Thus, one might think that the personalities of creative followers and successful leaders might be the source of considerable conflict and make them natural enemies in organizational settings. Because many organizations depend on creativity to grow and prosper, being able to successfully lead creative individuals may be a crucial aspect of success for these organizations. Given that creative people already possess technical expertise, imaginative thinking skills, and intrinsic motivation, Hogan and Morrison suggested that leaders take the following steps to successfully lead creative followers:

1. *Set goals.* Because creative people value freedom and independence, this step will be best accomplished if leaders use a high level of participation in the goal-setting process. Leaders should ask followers what they can accomplish in a particular time frame.

2. *Provide adequate resources.* Followers will be much more creative if they have the proper equipment to work with, as they can devote their time to resolving the problem rather than spending time finding the equipment to get the job done.

3. *Reduce time pressures, but keep followers on track.* Try to set realistic milestones when setting goals, and make organizational rewards contingent on reaching these milestones. Moreover, leaders need to be well organized to acquire necessary resources and to keep the project on track.

4. *Consider nonmonetary as well as monetary rewards.* Creative people often gain satisfaction from resolving the problem at hand, not from monetary rewards. Thus, feedback should be aimed at enhancing their feelings of personal adequacy. Monetary rewards perceived to be controlling may decrease, rather than increase, motivation toward the task.

5. *Recognize that creativity is evolutionary, not revolutionary.* Although followers can create truly novel products (such as the Xerox machine), often the key to creativity is continuous product improvement. Making next year's product

faster, lighter, cheaper, or more efficient requires minor modifications that can, over time, culminate in major revolutions. Thus, it may be helpful if leaders think of creativity more in terms of small innovations, not major breakthroughs.

Source: R. T. Hogan and J. Morrison, "Managing Creativity," in *Create & Be Free: Essays in Honor of Frank Barron*, ed. A. Montouri: (Amsterdam: J. C. Gieben, 1993).

Creative intelligence involves developing new and useful products and processes, and creativity is extremely important to the success of many businesses today. Creativity consists of seven components, including synthetic abilities, analytic intelligence, practical intelligence, thinking skills, relevant personality traits, intrinsic motivation, and several environmental factors. Understanding the seven components of creativity is important as the factors can give leaders ideas about how to improve their own and their followers' creativity. It is important that leaders learn how to successfully stimulate and manage creativity, even more than being creative themselves.

Key Terms

intelligence	intelligence quotient (IQ)
g	cognitive resources theory (CRT)
multiple intelligences	emotional intelligence
triarchic theory of intelligence	divergent thinking
analytic intelligence	convergent thinking
practical intelligence	synthetic ability
creative intelligence	adaptive thinking style
speed tests	innovative thinking style
power tests	creeping elegance

Discussion Questions

1. Individuals may well be attracted to, selected for, or successful in leadership roles early in their lives and careers based on their analytic intelligence. But what happens over time and with experience? Do you think *wisdom*, for example, is just another word for intelligence, or is it something else?

2. One psychologist recently issued a challenge to his colleagues—are there any jobs where less-intelligent people perform better than more-intelligent people? Can you think of any examples?

3. Is there really any difference between an intelligent versus a creative response to a problem?

4. We usually think of creativity as a characteristic of individuals, but might some organizations be more creative than others? What factors do you think might affect an organization's level of creativity?

5. Is creativity needed for all jobs? What jobs would place more emphasis on creativity than others?

6. Have you ever experienced creeping elegance on a school or work project?

10 LEADERSHIP BEHAVIOR

Chapter Outline

Introduction

In the preceding chapters of Part II, we examined the relationships between leadership success and variables such as a leader's intelligence, personality traits and types, values, and attitudes. Important as they may be, however, variables like these may have only an indirect relationship with leadership effectiveness. Their effect presumably comes from the impact they have on leader behavior, which appears to have a more direct relationship with leadership success (see Highlight 10–1).

One advantage of looking at leaders in terms of behavior instead of, say, personality is that behavior is often easier to measure; leadership behaviors can be observed whereas personality traits, values, or intelligence must be inferred from behavior or measured with tests. Another advantage of looking at leader behavior is that many people are less defensive about, and feel in more control

---

Highlight 10–1

Leadership Quotes, Chapter 10

Always be tactful and well mannered and teach your subordinates to be the same. Avoid excessive sharpness or harshness of voice, which usually indicates the man who has shortcomings of his own to hide.

Field Marshall Erwin Rommel

For every person who's a manager and wants to know how to manage people, there are 10 people who are being managed and would like to figure out how to make it stop.

Scott Adams, the creator of "Dilbert"

If I had to sum up in one word what makes a good manager, I'd say decisiveness. You can use the fanciest computers to gather the numbers, but in the end you have to set a timetable and act.

Lee Iacocca

A human being should be able to change a diaper, plan an invasion, butcher a hog, conn a ship, design a building, write a sonnet, balance accounts, build a wall, set a bone, comfort the dying, take orders, give orders, cooperate, act alone, pitch manure, solve equations, analyze a new problem, program a computer, cook a tasty meal, fight efficiently, die gallantly. Specialization is for insects.

Robert A. Heinlein, *The Note Book of Lazarus Long*

Muerto el perro, se feron las pulgas. Translation: When the dog is dead, the fleas are gone.

Puerto Rican folk saying

Organizations don't change; people change. If you want your organization to do something differently, then you'll have to figure out how to get people to change their behavior.

David B. Peterson

---

of, specific behaviors than they do about their personalities or intelligence. This point has significant implications for developing leadership skills, a topic we will take up in detail at the end of this book.

Leaders with certain traits, values, or attitudes may find it easier to effectively perform some leadership behaviors than others. For example, leaders with higher agreeableness scores (as defined in Chapter 8) may find it relatively easy to show concern and support for followers but may also find it difficult to discipline followers. Leaders on a committee who are judgers and prefer planning out activities may have a difficult time learning to tolerate team members who feel that plans tie them down (i.e., perceivers). Leaders can learn new behaviors, but it may take practice to develop ease and competence in performing them in new situations.

This chapter begins with a discussion on why it is important to study leadership behavior. We then review some of the early research on leader behavior, and discuss several ways to categorize or conceptualize different leadership behaviors. Next, we briefly summarize what is currently known about an increasingly common leadership behavior assessment technique, the 360-degree, or multirater, feedback questionnaire. The last section provides both a research perspective and some practical advice on behavioral change. It includes such topics as development planning, coaching, and mentoring.

Studies of Leader Behavior

Why Study Leadership Behavior?

Thus far, we have reviewed research on a number of key variables affecting leadership behavior, but we have not directly examined whether, fundamentally, leaders behave differently than followers. It is appropriate, therefore, to turn our attention to leader behavior itself, for if we could identify how successful versus unsuccessful leaders actually act, then we could design systems that would allow us to hire, develop, and promote the skills necessary for organizations to succeed in the future. Unfortunately, given the success of the Dilbert comic strip and the explosive growth of management consulting firms, it appears that there are a number of leaders (or persons in positions of leadership) who either do not know what to do and how to do it, or do not realize how their behavior is affecting the people who work for them (Curphy, 1996a, 1998a).

Before we go into the different ways to categorize leadership behaviors, it might be good to review what we know so far about leadership skills and behaviors. As seen in Figure 10–1, leadership behaviors (which include skills and competencies) are a function of intelligence, personality traits and preferences, values, attitudes, interests, knowledge, and experience. The factors in the bottom layer of blocks are relatively difficult to change, and they predispose a leader to act in distinctive ways. As described in Chapter 8, one's personality traits and preferences are pervasive and almost automatic, occurring typically without much conscious attention. The same could be said about how values, attitudes, and intelligence affect behaviors. Over time, however, leaders (hopefully) learn and discern which behaviors are more appropriate and effective than others. In addition, it is always useful to remember the pivotal roles individual difference and situational variables can play in a leader's actions (see Highlight 10–2).

FIGURE 10–1

*The Building
Blocks of Skills*

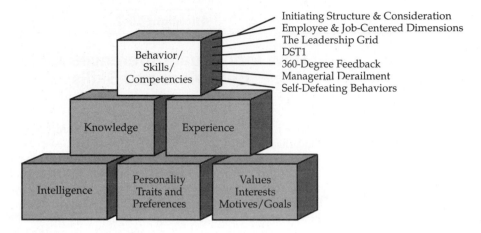

Behavior/
Skills/
Competencies

Initiating Structure & Consideration
Employee & Job-Centered Dimensions
The Leadership Grid
DST1
360-Degree Feedback
Managerial Derailment
Self-Defeating Behaviors

Knowledge   Experience

Intelligence   Personality
Traits and
Preferences   Values
Interests
Motives/Goals

The Early Studies

If you were asked how to study and identify the behaviors that best differentiated effective from ineffective leaders, how would you do it? According to Chapter 5, observation and paper-and-pencil techniques (e.g., questionnaires) would seem to be the most likely approaches. You could either follow the leaders around to see how they actually behave, or administer questionnaires to ask them and those they work with how often the leaders exhibited certain behaviors. Both of these approaches have been used in past and present leadership research.

As we noted previously, the earliest data-based approaches to studying leaders focused on their personality traits. The change in focus from the trait approach to the behavioral approach occurred for two primary reasons. The first involved a widespread overreaction to the conclusions of a comprehensive review of the trait research literature. Stogdill (1948) concluded in his review that certain individual-difference variables *do* indeed appear related to leadership success. He also noted, however, that having particular personality traits was no guarantee of success. Unfortunately, many other leadership researchers focused only on Stogdill's latter point and mistakenly concluded that traits were unrelated to leadership success.

A second factor in the shift from studying leader traits to studying leader behaviors involved a trend taking over the entire field of psychology. As described in Chapter 9, psychologists were initially interested in how behavior could be explained in terms of differences between people on certain stable, measurable dimensions (i.e., individual differences). In the 1940s and 1950s, however, the behavioral school in psychology was gaining ascendance. More emphasis was placed on how the situational factors (e.g., rewards and punishments) systematically affected overt behavior. Because of the disillusionment with the trait approach in general, the misunderstanding of Stogdill's work, and the paradigm shift away from traits and intelligence, leadership research in the 1940s and 1950s shifted toward the study of leader behaviors.

Highlight 10–2

How Individual Differences Affect Behaviors and Skills

Leadership behaviors are somewhat different from leadership skills. A leadership behavior concerns a specific action, whereas a leadership skill consists of three components, which include a well-defined body of knowledge, a set of related behaviors, and clear criteria of competent performance. Perhaps leadership skills may be better understood by using an analogy from basketball. People differ considerably in their basketball skills; good basketball players know when to pass and when to shoot, and are adept at making lay-ups, shots from the field, and free throws. Knowing when to pass and when to shoot is an example of the knowledge component, and hitting lay-ups and free throws is an example of the behavioral component of skills. In addition, shooting percentages can be used as one criterion for evaluating basketball skills. Leadership skills, such as delegating, can be seen much the same way. Good leaders know when and to whom a particular task should be delegated (i.e., knowledge), they effectively communicate their expectations concerning a delegated task (i.e., behavior), and they check to see whether the task was accomplished in a satisfactory manner (i.e., criteria). Thus, a skill is knowing when to act, acting in an manner appropriate to the situation, and acting in such a way that it helps the leader accomplish team goals.

Just as basketball skills can improve with practice, so too can leadership skills improve with practice. For example, shooting 200 free throws a day should improve a player's free throw shooting percentages in games, and taking advantage of public-speaking opportunities can improve a leader's public-speaking skills. The degree of practice needed to develop proficiency in a skill will, of course, vary from person to person. Almost everyone can learn the skill of solving algebraic problems. However, people with relatively greater quantitative ability will learn how to solve more-difficult algebraic problems, will solve them faster, and will be more likely to apply them in novel situations than people with weaker quantitative ability. Similarly, leaders with higher dominance, sociability, and emotional-stability scores may benefit more from a relatively brief public-speaking course than introverted leaders who do not have a strong desire to influence others. This does not mean the latter cannot benefit from a public-speaking course, only that they may need to work longer at developing the skill than others. Thus, just as natural athleticism can make learning a new sport more or less difficult, so too can traits, cognitive abilities, values, or preferences help or hinder the development of a new leadership skill. Both initial individual differences and practice play important roles in the acquisition and development of leadership skills.

Much of the initial leader behavior research was conducted at Ohio State University and the University of Michigan. Collectively, the Ohio State University studies developed a series of questionnaires to measure different leader behaviors in work settings. Hemphill (1949) began this development effort by collecting over 1,800 questionnaire items that described different types of leadership behaviors. These items were collapsed into 150 statements, and these statements were then used to develop a questionnaire called the **Leader Behavior Description Questionnaire (LBDQ)** (Hemphill & Coons, 1957). In order to obtain information about a particular leader's behavior, subordinates were asked to rate the extent to which their leader performed behaviors like the following:

> He lets subordinates know when they've done a good job.
>
> He sets clear expectations about performance.
>
> He shows concern for subordinates as individuals.
>
> He makes subordinates feel at ease.

In analyzing the questionnaires from thousands of subordinates, the statistical pattern of responses to all the different items indicated leaders could be described in terms of two independent dimensions of behavior called consideration and initiating structure (Fleishman, 1973; Halpin & Winer, 1957). **Consideration** refers to how much a leader is friendly and supportive toward subordinates. Leaders high in consideration engage in many different behaviors that show supportiveness and concern, such as speaking up for subordinates' interests, caring about their personal situations, and showing appreciation for their work. **Initiating structure** refers to how much a leader emphasizes meeting work goals and accomplishing tasks. Leaders high in initiating structure engage in many different task-related behaviors, such as assigning deadlines, establishing performance standards, and monitoring performance levels.

The LBDQ was not the only leadership questionnaire developed by the Ohio State researchers. They also developed, for example, the Supervisory Descriptive Behavior Questionnaire (SBDQ), which measured the extent to which leaders in industrial settings exhibited consideration and initiating structure behaviors (Fleishman, 1972). The Leadership Opinion Questionnaire (LOQ) asked leaders to indicate the extent to which they believed different consideration and initiating behaviors were important to leadership success (Fleishman, 1989). The LBDQ-XII was developed to assess 10 other categories of leadership behaviors in addition to consideration and initiating structure (Stogdill, 1959). Some of the additional leadership behaviors assessed by the LBDQ-XII included acting as a representative for the group, being able to tolerate uncertainty, emphasizing production, and reconciling conflicting organizational demands.

Rather than trying to describe the variety of behaviors leaders exhibit in work settings, the researchers at the University of Michigan sought to identify leader behaviors that contributed to effective group performance (Likert, 1961). They concluded that four categories of leadership behaviors are related to effective group performance: leader support, interaction facilitation, goal emphasis, and work facilitation (Bowers & Seashore, 1966).

Both goal emphasis and work facilitation are **job-centered dimensions** of behavior similar to the initiating structure behaviors described earlier. **Goal**

emphasis behaviors are concerned with motivating subordinates to accomplish the task at hand, and **work facilitation** behaviors are concerned with clarifying roles, acquiring and allocating resources, and reconciling organizational conflicts. Leader support and interaction facilitation are **employee-centered dimensions** of behavior similar to the consideration dimension of the various Ohio State questionnaires. **Leader support** includes behaviors where the leader shows concern for subordinates; **interaction facilitation** includes those behaviors where leaders act to smooth over and minimize conflicts among followers. Like the researchers at Ohio State, those at the University of Michigan also developed a questionnaire, the Survey of Organizations, to assess the degree to which leaders exhibit these four dimensions of leadership behaviors (Bowers & Seashore, 1966).

Although the behaviors composing the task-oriented and people-oriented leadership dimensions were similar across the two research programs, there was a fundamental difference in assumption underlying the work at the University of Michigan and that at Ohio State. Researchers at the University of Michigan considered job-centered and employee-centered behaviors to be at *opposite ends of a single continuum of leadership behavior*. Leaders could theoretically manifest either strong employee *or* job-centered behaviors, but not both. On the other hand, researchers at Ohio State believed that consideration and initiating structure were *independent continuums*. Thus, leaders could be high in both initiating structure and consideration, low in both dimensions, or high in one and low in the other.

The key assumption underlying both research programs was that certain behaviors could be identified that are universally associated with leadership success. Here are the kinds of questions researchers were interested in:

> Who were the more-effective leaders, those who exhibited higher initiating structure or those who exhibited more-job-centered behaviors?
>
> Is leadership effectiveness really only dependent upon leaders getting along with and supporting direct reports (i.e., consideration)?
>
> What role do situational factors play in leadership effectiveness? Might certain behaviors be particularly effective in some situations, but unrelated to leadership success in other situations?

The answers to these questions have several practical implications. If leaders need to exhibit only job- or employee-centered behaviors, then selection and training systems need to focus only on these behaviors. But if situational factors play a role, then researchers need to identify which variables are the most important, and to train leaders how to modify their behavior accordingly.

As you might suspect, the answer to all of these questions is, "It depends." In general, researchers have reported that leaders exhibiting a high level of consideration or employee-centered behaviors had more satisfied subordinates. Leaders who exhibited high role and task clarification (i.e., initiating structure or job-centered) behaviors often had higher-performing work units if the group faced relatively ambiguous or ill-defined tasks (Bass, 1990). At the same time, however, leaders whose behavior was highly autocratic (an aspect of initiating structure) were more likely to have relatively dissatisfied subordinates (Bass, 1990). Findings like these suggest that *there is no universal set of leader behaviors always associated with leadership success*. Often the degree to which leaders need to exhibit task- or people-oriented behaviors depends upon the situation, and it is precisely this finding that prompted the research underlying the contingency theories of leadership first described in Chapter 3. If you go back and review these theories, you will see strong links to the job- and employee-centered behaviors identified 40 years ago.

Alternative Conceptualizations of Leadership Behaviors

The Ohio State and University of Michigan studies were a good first step in describing what leaders actually do. Other researchers have extended these findings into more user-friendly formats or developed different schemes for categorizing leadership behaviors. Like the earlier research, these alternative conceptualizations are generally concerned with: (*a*) identifying key leadership behaviors, (*b*) determining whether these behaviors have positive relationships with leadership success, and (*c*) developing those behaviors related to leadership success. One popular conceptualization of leadership is really an extension of the findings reported by the University of Michigan and Ohio State leadership researchers. The **Leadership Grid®** profiles leader behavior on two dimensions, called **concern for people** and **concern for production** (Blake & McCanse, 1991; Blake & Mouton, 1964). The word *concern* reflects how a leader's underlying assumptions about people at work and the importance of the bottom line affect leadership style. In that sense, then, the Leadership Grid deals with more than just behavior. Nonetheless, it is included in this chapter because it is such a direct descendant of earlier behavioral studies.

As Figure 10–2 shows, leaders can get scores ranging from 1 to 9 on both concern for people and concern for production depending on their responses to a leadership questionnaire. These two scores are then plotted on the Leadership Grid, and the two score combinations represent different leadership orientations. Each orientation reflects a "unique set of assumptions for using power and authority to link people to production" (Blake & McCanse, 1991, p. 29). Amid the different leadership styles, the most-effective leaders are claimed to have both high concern for people and high concern for production, and Leadership Grid training programs are designed to move leaders to a 9,9 leadership style. Whereas this objective seems intuitively appealing, where do you think Madeline Albright, Colin Powell, or Konosuke Matsushita score on these two dimensions? Do all three of them show a high concern for production and people? Are there differences between the three leaders, or are all three 9,9 leaders?

Although the Leadership Grid can be useful for describing or categorizing different leaders, we should note that the evidence to support the assertion that 9,9 leaders are the most effective comes primarily from Blake, Mouton, and their

FIGURE 10–2

*The Leadership
Grid Figure*

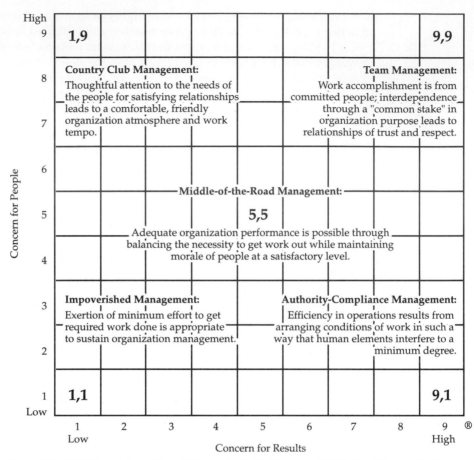

Source: Robert R. Blake and Anne Adams McCanse; *Leadership Dilemmas—Grid Solutions* (Houston: Gulf
Publishing Company, 1991), p. 29. Copyright 1991, by Scientific Methods, Inc. Reproduced by permission of the
owners.

associates. However, some more recent research might shed some light on
whether 9,9 leaders are really the most effective. Johnson (in press) used a much
more comprehensive measure of leadership behavior to categorize leaders
exhibiting the same behaviors into one of three different leadership types. The
sample in this study included approximately 500 midlevel managers from 80
different companies across the United States. Johnson's Type I leaders frequently
exhibited behaviors associated with accomplishing goals and solving problems
but displayed few behaviors associated with building rapport or getting along
with others. Type I leaders were technically competent but interpersonally aus-
tere; they were essentially high initiating structure and low consideration, or 9,1
leaders. Type II leaders were just the opposite; they displayed high consideration but low initiating structure behaviors (i.e., 1,9 leaders). Type III leaders displayed both high initiating structure and consideration behaviors but lacked the
quantitative and financial skills of the Type I leader. In the Leadership Grid

framework, these individuals could be categorized as 9,9 leaders. Johnson (in press) reported that Type I and III leaders were equally successful and significantly more successful than Type II leaders. In this study, it appeared that getting results (i.e., a concern for production or initiating structure) was more related to leadership effectiveness than getting along with, and providing support for, others. Thus the notion that 9,9 leaders are always the most effective is somewhat questionable, given the results of this recent study.

Two other conceptualizations of leadership behaviors are not prescriptive in the sense that the Leadership Grid is, but rather provide more extensive taxonomies of the different types of behaviors leaders perform. The Coaching Behavior Assessment System (CBAS) was designed to be used by observers to help them assess the frequency with which coaches exhibit different leadership behaviors (Curtis, Smith & Smoll, 1979). The CBAS consists of 12 behavior dimensions, including reinforcement, encouragement after mistakes, technical instruction after mistakes, punishment, and organization. Another leadership taxonomy involved an applied behavioral analysis framework for categorizing leaders' behaviors. **Applied behavioral analysis** is concerned with identifying the factors that preceded a particular behavior and identifying the rewards and punishments administered as a consequence of a particular behavior. Thus, several of the dimensions of the Operant Supervisory Taxonomy and Index (OSTI) categorized different leadership behaviors as antecedents, monitoring, or consequences of subordinates' behaviors (Komacki, 1986; Komacki, Zlotnik, & Jensen, 1986).

Both the CBAS and OSTI systems assess what a leader does to *change or modify* his or her direct reports' behavior. With the CBAS, researchers are examining the different types of coaching behaviors exhibited by leaders. With the OSTI, researchers are looking at how certain situational variables or subordinates' behaviors may trigger different behaviors or responses in leaders. Although both conceptualizations provide ideas about what leaders specifically do to successfully (or unsuccessfully) change others' behaviors, leadership is more than just changing others' behaviors. As such, these two conceptualizations are somewhat limited in describing all the different things leaders do.

So far in this section we have described a number of ways to categorize leaders or leadership behaviors, but what are the implications of this research for leadership practitioners? Believe it or not, you can see the practical application of this leadership behavior research in just about every Fortune 500 company in the United States, and with many of the major businesses in Europe and Asia. As first discussed in Chapter 5, competency models describe the behaviors and skills managers need to exhibit if an organization is to be successful. Just as leaders in different countries may need to exhibit behaviors uniquely appropriate to that setting in order to be successful, different businesses and industries within any one country often emphasize different leadership behaviors. Therefore, it is not unusual to see different organizations having distinct competency models depending upon the nature and size of the business, its level of globalization, or the role of technology or teams in the business. An

FIGURE 10–3

*An Example of a
Management
Competency
Model for a
Fortune 500
High-Tech Firm*

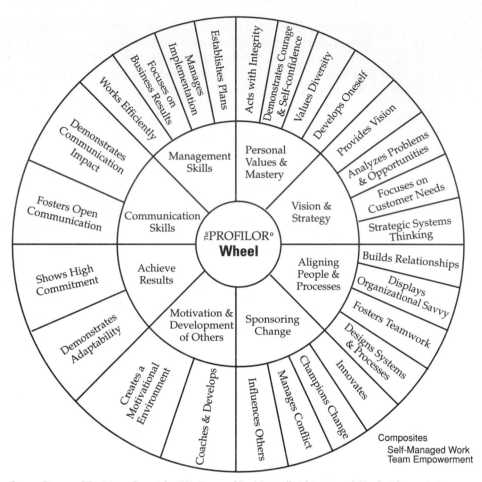

Source: Personnel Decisions. Copyright 1991, *Personnel Decisions*. All rights reserved. Used with permission.

example of a competency model for a major high-tech firm can be found in Figure 10–3. The inside wheel represents the general competencies, and the outside wheel represents the more specific skills managers in this company need to successfully lead it into the 21st century.

Competency models can be developed for most jobs, and may be used to identify the best predictors of initial management performance. For example, college recruiters use competency models to determine what types of tests they need to administer, or interview questions they should ask applicants. Management competency models are also used to develop midlevel management and executive selection systems, training and development programs, performance appraisal systems, succession planning programs, and to even help make outplacement decisions (Bracken, 1994; Gebelein, 1994, 1996). Given that many human resource systems are driven by these models, it is no wonder that organizations place considerable time and energy into competency modeling.

Assessing Leadership Behaviors: Multirater Feedback Instruments

One way to improve leadership effectiveness is to provide leadership practitioners with feedback regarding the frequency and skill with which they perform various types of leadership behaviors. Unfortunately, both the CBAS and OSTI are difficult to use in a practical sense, as both require a set of highly trained observers who need to watch leaders over a fairly lengthy period of time before their results could be used to provide meaningful feedback. Nevertheless, many organizations feel that managers need to get feedback about their work behaviors, and a $100 million industry has developed over the past decade to meet this need. This is the **360-degree**, or **multirater feedback**, instrument industry, and it is difficult to overestimate the importance it has had on management development both in the United States and overseas. Jack Welsh, the CEO of GE, has stated that these tools have been critical to GE's success (Gebelein, 1994; Tichy & Cohen, 1997). Practically all of the Fortune 500 companies are using some type of multirater feedback instrument for managers and key individual contributors (Bracken, 1994; Campbell, Curphy, & Tuggle, 1995; Gebelein, 1994, 1996; Lepsinger & Lucia, 1997; O'Reilly, 1994); some instruments have already been translated into 12 languages (PDI, 1992). Because of the pervasiveness of multirater feedback in both the public and private sectors, it will be useful to examine some of the issues surrounding these instruments.

Gebelein (1994) pointed out that many managers and human resource professionals have assumed that a manager's self-appraisal was the most accurate source of information regarding leadership strengths and weaknesses. This view has changed, however, with the introduction of multirater feedback instruments. These tools show that a variety of perspectives about one's behavior paint a more accurate picture than self-appraisals alone (see Figure 10–4). Because leadership truly exists (or not) in the eyes of others, self-perceptions of behavior are not nearly as important as the perceptions of others. Prior to the introduction of 360 degree instruments, it was difficult for managers to get accurate information about how others perceived their on-the-job behaviors since the feedback they received from others in face-to-face meetings tended to be adulterated or watered down (Campbell, Curphy, & Tuggle, 1995). Moreover, as described in Chapter 8, many of the most-frequent behaviors exhibited by leaders occur almost automatically, and many leaders do not understand or appreciate their impact on others. As a result, for a long time it was difficult for managers to determine how to leverage leadership strengths and overcome behavioral deficits. Today, most organizations use 360-degree tools for management development, as a part of a training or coaching program, in succession planning, or even as a part of the performance appraisal process (Gebelein, 1994, 1996; Lepsinger & Lucia, 1997). To be more specific, subordinates in some organizations actually have a say in their leaders' promotions and pay. Some common questions about 360-degree feedback are answered in Highlight 10–3.

FIGURE 10–4

Sources for 360-Degree Feedback

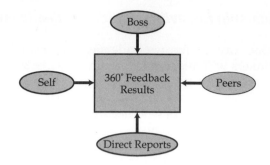

Given the pervasive role 360-degree feedback plays in many organizations today, it is interesting to note that research has lagged far behind the use of these tools. There are two primary reasons for this scarcity of research. First, most 360-degree feedback instruments are relatively expensive, often running $300–$400 per target manager for the questionnaires and feedback report; many leadership researchers simply do not have adequate funds to use these instruments in their studies. Second, because the instruments are not based on theory, some researchers have discounted the accuracy or usefulness of 360-degree feedback (Curphy, 1996b, 1997c).

The 360-degree feedback research conducted to date has yielded interesting, but somewhat inconsistent, results. The main themes of this research have been whether self-insight really matters, whether 360-degree ratings change over time, and whether managers in different ethnic groups receive the same ratings.

With regard to whether self-insight really matters, some researchers (Fleenor, McCauley, & Brutus, 1996) reported that self-insight was not related to job performance. Leaders with large self-observer gaps could be just as effective as those with smaller gaps. The key to effectiveness seemed to be the level of observers' ratings. Leaders with higher observer ratings were more effective than those with lower ratings. On the other hand, Church (1997) reported that managers identified as high-potential candidates generally had smaller self-observer gaps (i.e., greater self-insight) than average-performing managers. This apparent difference in research findings may be due to how these two studies were conducted. Fleenor and his associates did not look at high-potential candidates per se, and it may well be that the highest-performing managers (i.e., high-potential candidates) are those with higher observers' ratings and relatively small self-observer gaps. A tentative conclusion from this research for practitioners is that they should work on building good relationships with co-workers and developing their skills, and get feedback in order to increase their self-insight.

A second line of research has examined whether perceptual gaps shrink over time. In general, observers' ratings do increase and self-observer gaps decrease over time (Atwater, Roush, & Fischthal, 1995; London & Smither, 1995; Smither, London, Vasilopoulos, Reilly, Millsap, & Salvemini, 1995). In other words, leaders seem to improve with feedback; they are more accurate in appraising their

---

Highlight 10–3

Common Questions and Straight Answers about 360-Degree Feedback

1. **What groups have 360-degree feedback instruments been designed for and used?**

   Although 360-degree feedback instruments are primarily used for midlevel managers, different versions have been designed for individual contributors, internal consultants, attorneys, sales, first-line supervisors, senior executives, and teams across a wide variety of organizations and countries.

2. **Are there any gender differences for 360-degree feedback results?**

   Research indicates that there are some gender differences, though these differences tend to be slight. Female managers tend to get higher ratings on the majority of skills, yet their male counterparts are generally perceived as having higher advancement potential. There does not appear to be any same-sex bias in 360-degree feedback ratings, and female managers tend to be lower self-raters. Male managers tend to have less accurate self-insight and a higher number of blind spots when compared to their female counterparts.

3. **Which rating groups provide the highest or lowest average ratings?**

   In general, the highest ratings on a 360-degree feedback instrument tend to come from self-raters. This is usually due to the fact that most of the feedback a target manager has received to date is positive. Research also shows that the higher in the organization a person goes, the less likely he or she is to get constructive feedback. Bosses are often the next highest raters. Direct reports are the next, followed finally by peers. Peers may give lower ratings because they are often less familiar with target manager's day-to-day behavior or because they see the target manager as a potential competitor for the next promotion.

Source: *Feedback on Feedback* (Minneapolis: Personnel Decisions International, Winter 1995), pp. 2–3.

---

own behaviors and do a better job improving their skills after receiving feedback. These findings imply that leadership practitioners are likely to improve both their skill level and their level of self-insight if given 360-degree feedback. Since 360-degree feedback instruments are relatively cheap when compared to multiday management-training programs, these instruments may be a very cost-effective way for leadership practitioners to improve their skills.

The third line of research has examined whether there are racial differences in 360-degree feedback ratings. For example, do white subordinates give white leaders higher ratings? Or do black leaders give black subordinates lower ratings? A comprehensive study by Mount, Sytsma, Hazucha, and Holt (1997) looked at the pattern of responses from bosses, peers, and subordinates for over 20,000 managers from a variety of U.S. companies. In general, these researchers reported that blacks tended to give higher ratings to other blacks, irrespective of whether they were asked to provide peer, subordinate, or boss ratings. However, the overall size of this effect was rather small. White peers and subordinates generally gave about the same level of ratings for both black and white peers and bosses. This was not the case for white bosses, however, who tended to give significantly higher ratings to white direct reports. These findings imply that black leaders are likely to advance at a slower pace than their white counterparts, as 80–90 percent of salary, bonus, and promotion decisions are made solely by bosses (Bernardin & Beatty, 1984). As Mount et al. (1997) aptly point out, we still do not know whether the white-boss ratings are evidence of adverse impact or whether there are true performance differences between black and white leaders. In sum, more research is needed before we can definitively answer this question (see Highlight 10–4).

Managerial Derailment and Self-Defeating Behaviors

So far we have talked about what leaders can do in order to improve their effectiveness. The first lesson might be to determine which behaviors are most closely aligned with success, perhaps by identifying key behaviors via a competency model. Another lesson might be to get 360-degree feedback on these key behaviors. This feedback helps identify strengths and potential development needs. Not all leaders, however, truly learn such lessons. It might behoove us to look not just at how leaders develop, but at the complementary question: why some leaders *fail*? We can learn valuable lessons about what *not* to do as a leader by studying them.

There is a growing body of research that indicates that somewhere between 30 and 50 percent of managers and executives fail (Hogan, Curphy, & Hogan, 1994; Sloane, Hezlett, Kuncel, & Sytsma, 1996). These figures imply that up to half of the leaders in any organization are not going to be able to build cohesive teams or achieve business results, which unfortunately lends some weight to Scott Adams's quote in Highlight 10–1. Initial research on managerial derailment was conducted in the early 1980s by researchers at the Center for Creative Leadership. The researchers went to the human resource departments in a number of Fortune 100 companies seeking lists of their "high-potential" managers. McCall and Lombardo (1983) defined high potentials as those individuals who had been identified as eventually becoming either the CEO/president or one of his or her direct reports sometime in the future. They waited for three years and then returned to these organizations to ask what had happened to the people on the lists. They discovered that roughly a quarter of the high potentials had in fact been promoted to one of the top two levels in the organization, and an equal percentage had not yet been promoted but would be as soon as a position became available. Another 25 percent had left the company; some had quit to form their own company and others were given a better offer somewhere else. Finally, about a quarter of the people on the list were no longer being considered for promotion. If they were still with the company, then they had been moved to a

Highlight 10–4

The Invisible Barrier—What Precludes Black Managers from Advancement?

Herdie Baisden, a black general manager and vice president of a management consulting firm has investigated why black managers failed to advance in many organizations. Working with a variety of psychological assessment instruments as well as 360-degree feedback tools, Baisden noted that black managers tended to react differently to negative feedback than white managers. Baisden stated that blacks tended to dismiss this information as a product of racism rather than viewing it as a springboard for improvement. Blacks also tended to avoid feedback because they felt they needed to be exceptionally competent to succeed and wanted to project an image that "everything is under control and I don't need any help." When black managers did seek feedback from others, they often turned to others they could trust—other blacks. Blacks make up only 6 percent of management but they turned to blacks 22 percent of the time when soliciting feedback. These reactions often resulted in distorted 360-degree feedback ratings for black managers. These individuals tended to overrate their own performance and have bigger self-boss rating gaps when compared to white managers.

Baisden stated that some of these protective behaviors may be natural outgrowths of the work situations facing black managers. If a black manager perceives that a work environment is nonsupportive at best or hostile at worst, then these behaviors make sense. Unfortunately, these reactions ultimately become self-defeating behaviors, as they prevent black managers from getting the feedback they need in order to improve. Baisden maintains that blacks wishing to advance need to be receptive to feedback from others. This not only provides them with developmental ideas, it also tells the organization that the manager is willing to take risks and grow.

Source: H. Baisden, *PDI Indicator: The Rise of Black Managers* (Minneapolis: Personnel Decisions. 1993).

less-influential and -visible position. Many others had been asked to leave the company. These individuals represented **managerial derailment** cases—at one time they were on the fast track, but their careers had derailed.

Several other researchers have investigated the managerial derailment phenomenon (Hazucha, 1992; Lombardo, Ruderman, & McCauley, 1987; Peterson, 1993a, 1993b; Van Velsor & Leslie, 1995). This more recent research used much larger samples (Peterson examined over 600 derailed managers), European samples, and more-sophisticated assessment tools (i.e., 360-degree feedback instruments). Moreover, a substantially higher percentage of women and minorities were represented in this more-recent research, as the initial high-potential list was dominated by white males. As Van Veslor and Leslie (1995) pointed out, this research focused on identifying those factors which helped derailment

---

TABLE 10–1   Themes in Derailment Research

Four Enduring Themes	McCall & Lombardo (1983)	Morrison et al. (1987)	Lombardo & McCauley (1988)	United States (1993–94)	Europe (1993–94)
Problems with interpersonal relationships	Insensitive to others; cold, aloof, arrogant; overly ambitious	Poor relationships, too ambitious	Problems with interpersonal relationships, isolates self	Poor working relations	Poor working relations, organizational isolation, authoritarian, too ambitious
Failure to meet business objectives	Betrayal of trust; poor performance	Performance problems	Lack of follow-through	Too ambitious, lack of hard work	Too ambitious, poor performance
Inability to build and lead a team	Failing to staff effectively	Can't manage subordinates	Difficulty molding a staff	Inability to build and lead a team	Inability to build and lead a team
Inability to develop or adapt	Unable to adapt to a boss with a different style, unable to think strategically	Unable to adapt to a boss or culture, not strategic	Strategic differences with management, difficulty making strategic transitions	Unable to develop or adapt, conflict with upper management	Unable to develop or adapt
Emergent themes	—	Too narrow business experience	—	Not prepared for promotion, narrow functional orientation	Not prepared for promotion, narrow functional orientation
Disappearing themes	Overdependent on advocate or mentor	—	Overdependence	—	—

Source: E. Van Velsor and J. B. Leslie, "Why Executives Derail: Perspectives across Time and Cultures," *Academy of Management Executive* 9, no. 4 (1995), pp. 62–71.

candidates get initially identified as high potentials, as well as on those factors contributing to their ultimate professional demise. Although these studies varied in many ways, there are many consistent findings across them. Both groups were smart, ambitious, willing to do whatever it took to get the job done, and had considerable technical expertise. In other words, all of the high-potential candidates had impressive track records in their organizations.

On the other hand, the derailed candidates exhibited one or more behavioral patterns not evident in the high potentials who succeeded. The derailment themes can be found in Table 10–1 and are described in more detail below. It is important to note that four of the derailment themes included in Table 10–1 have been consistently reported in the research both in the United States and Europe, and that apparently a new theme is emerging and another is disappearing over time. The first derailment pattern has to do with an **inability to**

build relationships with co-workers. The derailed managers exhibiting this pattern of behavior were very insensitive to the needs and plights of their followers and co-workers, and were often overly competitive, demanding, and domineering. They embraced the "my way or the highway" school of management. Many were also extremely arrogant and truly believed no one in their organizations were as good as they were, and they let their co-workers know it every chance they could. Some of these derailed managers also did whatever they felt necessary to get the job done, even if it meant stepping on a few toes in the process. Unfortunately, this is not one of the recommended techniques for winning friends and influencing people. It's better to remember the old adage that you should be careful whom you step on going up the ladder, because you may meet them again on your way down. Many of these managers left a trail of bruised people who were just waiting for the right opportunity to bring these leaders down.

According to Van Velsor and Leslie (1995), approximately two-thirds of European and one-third of American derailment candidates fall into this pattern. For example, a female vice president of marketing and sales for a cellular phone company was fired from her $200,000 job for exhibiting many of the behaviors just listed. She was very bright, had an excellent technical background (she was an engineer by training), had already been the CEO for several smaller organizations, and worked very long hours. Her in-depth managerial assessment results (Chapter 5) indicated that she also had a strong leaderlike personality, with higher scores in surgency and dependability and average scores in agreeableness and adjustment. This assessment also indicated she had extremely high narcissism scores, and at work this dark-side trait would manifest itself by her talking down to people, quickly identifying and capitalizing on others' faults, constantly commenting on their incompetence, running over her peers when she needed resources or support, promoting infighting among her peers and subordinates, and expecting to be pampered. Interestingly, she had no idea she was having such a debilitating effect on those she worked with until she received her 360-degree feedback. Had she received this feedback sooner, she might have been able to stop her career from derailing.

Another derailment pattern identified in Table 10–1 is a **failure to meet business objectives**. Although both successful and derailed managers experience business downturns, the groups handled setbacks quite differently. Successful managers took personal responsibility for their mistakes and sought ways to solve the problem. Derailed managers tended to engage in finger pointing and blaming others for the downturn. *But as long as things were going well*, it was difficult to differentiate these two groups on this factor. Some of these managers were also untrustworthy. They either blatantly lied about business results or failed to keep promises, commitments, or deadlines. A head of a governmental affairs division for an oil and gas company is a good example of this derailment theme. This leader constantly told his bosses he was busy lobbying the state legislature for regulatory relief or helping to craft new bills when in reality he was spending most of his time either at home or at his favorite bar. Over time, it became obvious that the bills and regulatory relief were not forthcoming, and the individual was dismissed from the position.

The third derailment pattern identified by Van Velsor and Leslie (1995) was **an inability to lead and build a team.** Some managers derailed because they hired staff who were just like themselves, which in turn only served to magnify their own strengths and weaknesses. Others wanted to stay in the limelight and hired staff less capable than they were. Still others micromanaged their staffs, even when not expert themselves in the tasks (not that it's ever recommended). These bosses wanted their followers to "check their brains at the door" before coming to work. By the way, one thing that often underlies this pattern is a lack of trust and high perfectionism scores (Chapter 8).

Another derailment profile has to do with a leader's **inability to adapt** to new bosses, businesses, cultures, or structures. As pointed out earlier in this chapter, many business situations require different leadership behaviors and skills, and some derailed managers could not adapt or adjust their styles to changing bosses, followers, and situations. They persisted in acting the same way, even when it was no longer appropriate to new circumstances. When solving problems, they often imposed past solutions that were no longer viable. For example, a first-line supervisor for an electronics firm that built video poker machines was having a very difficult time transitioning from his old job as a missile guidance repairman in the U.S. Air Force. He thought he should lead his subordinates the way he led others when he was in the military: his staff should be willing to work long hours and over the weekends without being told, and to travel for extended periods of time with short notice. Their thoughts or opinions on ways to improve work processes did not matter to him, and he expected everyone to maintain cool and professional attitudes at work. After half of his staff quit as a direct result of his supervision, he was demoted and replaced by one of his subordinates.

In the past, organizations could afford to take their time in identifying and developing leadership talent. Many of the best organizations today have strong programs for systematically developing leadership bench strength (Curphy, 1998a; Tichy & Cohen, 1997). However, more and more organizations today are under increasing pressure to find good leaders quickly, and they are increasingly asking their own high-potential but inexperienced leadership talent to step up to the plate and fill these key roles. Although these new leaders are bright and motivated, however, they often have narrow technical backgrounds and lack the leadership breadth and depth necessary for the new positions. The unfortunate result is that many of these leaders leave the organization because of **inadequate preparation for promotion.**

For example, a relatively young female attorney was promoted to be the vice president of human resources in a large telecommunications firm. Although she was extremely bright and ambitious, it soon became apparent that she lacked much of the necessary skill or knowledge. Although she tried very hard to be successful, she made a number of poor decisions and failed to earn the respect of her staff. After six months she was given a generous separation package and

---

TABLE 10–2 Common Self-Defeating Behaviors

Procrastination	Suspiciousness
Defensiveness	Overcommitted
Worrying	Overly critical
Alienating	Rigidity
Hostility	Overcontrolling
Perfectionism	Inability to trust others

Source: M. R. Cudney and R. E. Hardy, *Self-Defeating Behaviors* (San Francisco: Harper Collins. 1993).

asked to leave the company. According to Van Velsor and Leslie (1995), this is a relatively new derailment theme. Given the contributing factors, it is also a theme that is likely to be more prevalent in the future.

Most derailed managers manifested several of these themes; the presence of only one of these behavioral patterns was usually not enough for derailment. The only exception to this rule was a failure to meet business objectives. Managers who did not follow through with commitments, broke promises, lied, were unethical, and did not get results did not stay on the high-potential list for long. Although this research has not identified any unique derailment patterns for minorities, some male–female differences have been noted. Females were more likely to derail because of their inability to deal with broader and more-complex organizational issues or to lead people from different technical backgrounds than their own. Males were more likely to derail because of their arrogance, inflexibility, or abrasive interpersonal style.

One might think that most managers exhibiting derailment behavioral patterns would be aware of the negative impact they have on others. Unfortunately, this is not always so. Many managers on the path to derailment are simply unaware of the way they come across to others. Recent research on self-defeating behaviors may explain how these counterproductive behavior patterns develop and why some managers lack insight into their behavior. According to Cudney and Hardy (1993), **a self-defeating behavior** is an action or attitude that once helped an individual cope with a stressful experience but interferes with the individual's ability to cope in new situations.

A list of some of the more common self-defeating behaviors can be found in Table 10–2. You can also see that the behaviors in Table 10–2 are similar to the derailment themes and the dark-side personality traits previously identified in Chapter 8. Like the behaviors associated with dark-side personality traits, a big part of the problem with self-defeating behaviors is that they are highly practiced and often performed automatically, with little conscious thought. Furthermore, a person may rationalize the appropriateness of a self-defeating behavior by recalling some particular situation where the behavior *was* adaptive (or seemed so). But problems may occur when such behaviors get generalized from *unusual* circumstances to *most* circumstances. For example, everyone worries about *some* things *sometimes* (e.g., how an interview is going to go; whether your presentation made a good impression on the audience, whom to select for an important assignment, whether to major in this subject or that). Worrying becomes a problem, however, when it becomes habitual and consuming—when it keeps you from *doing* anything else or from actually *making* a decision. It may never be particularly helpful, but that's when it becomes truly self-defeating.

How could such a seemingly irrational and counterproductive behavior ever become a habit for some people? Strange as it may seem, it can happen through reinforcement. The head of a management consulting firm was asked to open a new office in a large U.S. city. He worked an average of 70–80 hours a week, identifying and building relationships with and delivering products and services to key clients. These efforts paid off, and in less than three years the office had grown from 1 to 15 people and from $50,000 to $2,500,000 in annual revenue. As staff and revenues grew, the head of the firm was reinforced though bonus and salary increases to continue to build relationships with, and deliver services to, clients. Unfortunately, this leader failed to acknowledge the importance of supporting, coaching, and developing his people—he was a classic task-focused, 9,1 leader. Although this style of leadership was effective for opening the office, his overcommitment to task performance began to have a debilitating affect on the morale of the office. The leader in this case was fortunate enough to recognize the impact of his self-defeating behaviors, and was able to utilize some of the techniques in the next section to change these behaviors, improve morale, and continue to obtain good business results.

Changing Behavior

Why Change Behavior?

The material covered so far can help leadership practitioners better understand the key behaviors associated with success; how successful leadership behaviors may vary depending on the country, culture, or business; what kind of behaviors could get them into trouble; and how to get feedback on these behaviors. But the fact of the matter is that knowing this information is not enough. Ultimately, some of the leader's behavior needs to *change*. But changing behavior, especially long-standing patterns of behavior, can be quite difficult.

How many times have you asked yourself how you could possibly change your own or another's behavior? Learning how to change your own and others' behaviors is a key leadership skill, given that situations, technology, organizational structure, followers, bosses, products, rules and regulations, and competitors seem to be in a constant state of flux. Just as the head of the management consulting firm learned to add more supportive or employee-centered behaviors to his repertoire, so must you learn how to adapt your behavior to meet the changing demands of the situation. But learning how to change your own behavior is often not enough. Good leaders also know how to change and modify the behaviors of their followers so that they can be more effective team members and better achieve team goals. In the next section we discuss research surrounding three common methods of behavioral change: development planning, coaching, and mentoring. While this section is primarily research focused, practical tips on how to change behavior through development planning and coaching can be found in Part V of this book.

Development Planning

How many times have you made a resolution to change a habit, only to discover two months later that you are still exhibiting the same behaviors? This is often the fate of well-intentioned New Year's resolutions. Most people do not even make such resolutions since the failure rate is so high. Given this track record, you might wonder if it is even possible to change one's behavior, particularly if it has been reinforced over time and is exhibited almost automatically. Fortunately, however, it *is* possible to change behavior, even long-standing habits. For example, many people permanently quit smoking or drinking without going through any type of formal program (Miller & Rollnick, 1991). Others may change after they gain insight into how their behavior affects others. Some will need support to maintain a behavioral change over time, while still others seem destined to never change.

Managers seem to fall into the same categories; some managers change once they gain insight, others change with support, and others may not ever change (Hazucha, Hezlett, & Schneider, 1993; Hezlett & Koonce, 1995; Peterson & Hicks, 1995). But do people just fall into one of these groups by accident? Is there any way to stack the odds in favor of maintaining desired changes? The results from several studies indicate there *are* ways of increasing the likelihood of translating helpful information into relatively permanent behavior change.

The managers in these studies were working for either a public utility company or a large grocery distributor in the Midwest. Managers in one study (Hazucha, Hezlett, & Schneider, 1993) received the results of a 360-degree feedback instrument during a two-hour feedback session with a consultant. Approximately two years later a number of these managers participated in another round of 360-degree feedbacks. The managers had not gone through any type of formalized training or coaching program in the interim. The researchers wanted to see whether leadership behaviors changed over time and whether people who changed the most did anything different than those who did not change. Results indicated that both self and others' ratings of skills on the 360-degree instrument showed a significant positive change over the two-year period. Thus, just gaining insight after receiving 360-degree feedback was enough for some managers to change their behavior. However, the managers who changed the *most* had done several further things in common.

First, they had *written development plans* for the behaviors they intended to change. Plans that were not actually written down tended to be forgotten or were more likely to be pushed aside by competing priorities. These managers also had a very clear picture of the behaviors they wanted to change, and limited their plans to only two or three behavioral objectives. Second, they *reviewed drafts of their development plans with their boss.* Reviewing plans with the boss helped the boss to look for opportunities to provide resources, learning experiences, feedback, and coaching, as well as increasing the manager's commitment to the plan. Third, the development plans *capitalized on on-the-job experiences* rather than on attending seminars or reading books. Although most plans capitalize on books and seminars, most managers feel that they are not particularly helpful in building skills (Hezlett & Koonce, 1995). This may be due to the fact that most behaviors and skills are developed on the job (McCauley, Ruderman, Ohlott, & Morrow, 1994; Peterson & Hicks, 1996). Fourth, they periodically *sought feedback* about progress on their plans from others. Sometimes this feedback was from the boss, and at other times it was from peers, followers, or customers. The source of the feedback was not nearly as important as its frequency. And finally, managers who changed the most were also in situations where *their boss was held accountable for the manager's development.*

Although approximately 25 percent of the sample changed without doing any type of developmental planning, about 50 percent of the managers took at least one of the steps above and noted some change over time. What's more, managers who took more of the steps changed the most. In other words, managers who developed plans, reviewed them with their boss, and sought periodic feedback tended to change more than managers who only drafted plans. About 25 percent of the managers did not take any of the development steps and did not change over time.

The other study (Hezlett and Koonce, 1995) looked at how managers developed after receiving feedback from an in-depth assessment (Chapter 5), and reported similar results. Only 25 percent of the managers in this study built a development plan after receiving feedback, but those who did build a plan and utilized the techniques described in the previous paragraph changed the most. This research points out why it is important for organizations to put some type of formalized development system in place.

Although the development plan itself is fairly straightforward, it is important to realize that **development planning** is more than a plan—it is really a process (Peterson & Hicks, 1995). **Development plans** should be specific and time-bound, should focus on on-the-job experiences, and should specify how the manager will get feedback or support. This later point is extremely important, as managers will often lose interest in development if they get no encouragement or feedback from others. Finally, the development plan should include opportunities for reflection and revision. Good development plans are constantly being revised as new skills are learned or new opportunities become available. Plans that have not been revised over a three-month period are apt to be forgotten (Peterson & Hicks, 1995).

Coaching and Mentoring

Development plans tend to be self-focused; leaders and followers use them as a road map for changing their own behaviors. When trying to change the behavior of followers, however, leaders can often do more than review a follower's development plan, provide on-going feedback, or review plans periodically with followers. The next step in followers' development often involves coaching. Coaching is a popular topic these days, but it is also a frequently misunderstood one. It is hoped that the material in this section will help to clarify what coaching is, and identify some best-coaching practices. Like coaching, mentoring is also becoming popular in many organizations today. Mentoring is a relationship between a mentor and a protege, and there are usually two or more organizational levels between these individuals. Both mentoring and coaching are designed to change another's behavior, but they go about it in somewhat different ways.

Coaching is the "process of equipping people with the tools, knowledge, and opportunities they need to develop themselves and become more successful" (Peterson & Hicks, 1996, p. 14). In general, there are two types of coaching, informal and formal coaching. **Informal coaching** can occur anywhere in an organization, and occurs whenever a leader helps followers to change their behaviors. According to Peterson and Hicks (1996), informal coaching generally consists of five steps. In *forging a partnership*, leaders build a trusting relationship with their followers, identify followers' career goals and motivators, and learn how their followers view the organization and their situation. If a leader fails to build a relationship based on mutual trust with a follower, then chances are the follower will not heed the leader's guidance and advice. Therefore, the first step in coaching is to *determine the level of mutual trust*, and then to improve the relationship if necessary before targeting development needs or providing feedback and advice. Too many inexperienced coaches either fail to build trust, or take the relationship for granted, with the long-term end result being little, if any, behavioral change, and a frustrated leader and follower.

Once a solid, trusting relationship has been built, then leaders need to *inspire commitment*. In this step leaders work closely with followers to gather and analyze data to determine development needs. A leader and a follower may review appraisals of past performance, feedback from peers or former bosses, project reports, 360-degree feedback reports, and any organizational standards that pertain to the follower's career goals. By reviewing this data, the leader and the follower should be able to identify and prioritize those development needs most closely aligned with career goals.

The next step in the coaching process involves *growing skills*. Followers use their prioritized development needs to create a development plan, and leaders in turn develop a **coaching plan** that precisely spells out what they will do to support the followers' development plan. Leaders and followers then review and discuss the development and coaching plans, make necessary adjustments, and execute the plans.

Just because a plan is developed does not mean it will be executed flawlessly. Learning often is a series of fits and starts, and sometimes followers either get distracted by operational requirements or get into developmental ruts. In the step called *promote persistence,* leaders help followers to manage the mundane, day-to-day aspects of development. Leaders can help followers refocus on their development by capitalizing on opportunities to give followers relevant, on-the-spot feedback. Once the new behavior has been practiced a number of times and becomes part of the follower's behavioral repertoire, then leaders help followers to *transfer the skills to new environments* by applying the skills in new settings and revising their development plans. In this step leaders need to also ask themselves how they themselves are role modeling development and whether they are creating an environment that fosters individual development.

There are several points about informal coaching worth additional comment. First, the five-step process identified by Peterson and Hicks (1996) can be used by leadership practitioners to diagnose why behavioral change is *not* occurring and what can be done about it. Second, informal coaching can and does occur anywhere in the organization. Senior executives use this model to develop their staffs, peers can use it to help each other, and so forth. Third, this process is just as effective for high-performing followers as it is for low-performing followers. Leadership practitioners have a tendency to forget to coach their solid or top followers, yet these individuals are often making the greatest contributions to team or organizational success. Moreover, research has shown that the top performers in a job often produce 20–50 percent more than the average performer, depending on the complexity of the job (Hunter, Schmidt, & Judiesch, 1990). So if leaders would focus on moving their solid performers into the highest-performing ranks and making their top performers even better, chances are their teams might be substantially more effective than if they only focused on coaching those doing most poorly (see Figure 10–5).

Leadership practitioners also need to realize that some individuals may be resistant to coaching. If a follower does not believe a particular behavioral change is in his best interest, then the prognosis for permanent behavioral change is poor. Similarly, some behaviors may be so ingrained that they will take considerably more effort on the part of the follower and the leader to change. Change will require more persistence, more practice, and more feedback. Finally, both "remote" coaching of people and coaching of individuals from other cultures can be particularly difficult (Curphy, 1996a; Peterson & Hicks, 1996, 1997). It is more difficult for leaders to build trusting relationships with followers when they are physically separated by great distances. The same may be true with followers from other cultures—what may be important to, say, a Kenyan follower and how this person views the world may be very different from what his or her Dutch or Singaporean leader believes.

The kinds of behaviors that need to be developed can also vary considerably by culture. For example, one senior executive for a high-tech firm was coaching one of his Japanese direct reports on how to do better presentations to superiors. The follower's style was formal, stiff, and somewhat wooden, and the leader wanted the follower to add some humor and informality to his presentations. However, the follower said that by doing so he would lose the respect of his Japanese colleagues, so his commitment to this change was understandably low. What was agreed upon was that his style was very effective in Japan, but that it needed to change when he was giving presentations in the United States.

FIGURE 10–5

What Were the Most Useful Factors in the Coaching You Received?

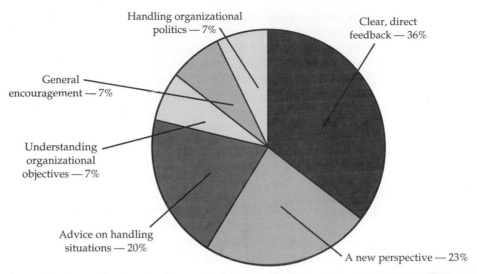

Handling organizational politics — 7%

Clear, direct feedback — 36%

General encouragement — 7%

Understanding organizational objectives — 7%

Advice on handling situations — 20%

A new perspective — 23%

Source: "The Business Leader as Development Coach," *PDI Portfolio*, Winter 1996, p. 6.

Most people are familiar with the idea of a personal fitness trainer, a person who helps design a fitness program tailored to a specific individual's needs and goals. **Formal coaching** programs provide a similar kind of service for executives and managers in leadership positions (Curphy, 1996a; Peterson, 1996; Witherspoon & White, 1996, 1997). Coaching programs are quite individualized by their very nature, but several common features deserve mention. There is a one-on-one relationship between the manager and the coach (i.e., consultant) which lasts from six months to more than a year. The process usually begins with the manager's completion of an extensive battery of personality, intelligence, interests, value, and 360-degree feedback instruments, as well as with interviews by the coach of other individuals in the manager's world of work. As the result of the assessment phase of this process, both the manager and the coach have a clear picture of development needs and how the different components of the building-block model interact and affect these needs. The coach and the manager meet regularly (roughly monthly) to review the results of the feedback instruments and work on building skills and practicing target behaviors. Role plays and videotape are used extensively during these sessions, and coaches provide immediate feedback to clients practicing new behaviors in realistic work situations. Another valuable outcome of coaching programs can involve clarification of managers' values, and identification of discrepancies between their espoused values and their actual behaviors and devising strategies to better align their behaviors with their values.

Approximately 3,000 managers and executives have been through one of the coaching programs designed by Peterson and his associates (Peterson, 1993a, 1993b, 1996; Peterson & Hicks, 1996). Some were derailment candidates, but many were not. Some were high potentials with a few rough edges, and others were successful managers and executives who needed leadership or skill training in one or two key areas. This large sample and PDI's commitment to research have produced some interesting findings.

A formal coaching program can cost more than $30,000 (Smith, 1993; Curphy, 1996a), and it is reasonable to ask, Is it worth it? The answer seems to be at least sometimes yes. A solid body of research shows that well-designed and well-executed coaching programs result in permanent behavioral change (Peterson, 1993a,1993b, 1996; Witherspoon & White, 1997). Such changes can be particularly important if the person making them—that is, the leader being coached—is in a highly placed or very responsible position. Most coaching candidates have hundreds, if not thousands, of subordinates, and usually oversee multi-million- or multi-billion-dollar budgets. Thus, the money spent on a coaching program can be relatively small in comparison to the budgets and resources the candidates control. Many organizations believe if a coaching program helps a leader better utilize resources or get higher productivity from workers, then it is likely that they will see a high return on investment from a coaching program.

Mentoring is a "structure and series of processes designed to create effective mentoring relationships, guide the desired behavior change of those involved, and evaluate the results for proteges, the mentors, and the organization with the primary purpose of systematically developing the skills and leadership abilities of the less-experienced members of an organization" (Murray & Owen, 1991, p. 5). (Note that this perspective on mentoring emphasizes a more-formal and more-structured approach than the more-informal view presented in Chapter 4). Given this definition, mentoring appears to be both similar to, and different from, informal and formal coaching. It is similar to informal coaching in that mentoring involves two people in the same organization, and the focus is on behavioral change. It is similar to formal coaching in that a mentor is assigned to a protege much like a coach is formally assigned to a manager. Like formal coaching, the mentor and protege also get together about once a month to discuss problems, upcoming projects, organizational politics, business strategies, and the like. Mentoring is different in that the mentor is not the protege's immediate supervisor but is often someone two or three levels higher in the organization. Moreover, the program may or may not focus on formal behavioral change. Sometimes mentoring programs consist of the mentor's imparting knowledge or advice or creating high-visibility promotion opportunities; at other times the mentor has the necessary skills and time to create permanent behavioral change in proteges. More often than not, however, behavioral change is assumed to occur as the result of advice, guidance, and feedback from the mentor. The research concerning development plans and coaching shows that very often more than advice is needed for behavior change to take place. In addition, mentor programs can create feelings of jealousy or inequity among those not in the program, and can also jeopardize immediate leader–follower relationships. On the other hand, followers who are given the opportunity to rub shoulders with senior executives often have a better understanding of how the organization works, where the organization is going, who the key players and competitors are, and so on.

Whether mentoring programs really work is still an open question. However, it may be that the best mentoring programs are those that incorporate many of the techniques already described in this book. They use good assessment techniques to pinpoint development needs; mentors and proteges are matched based on development needs; the individual, leader, and mentor create integrated development, coaching, and mentoring plans; and then these individuals meet on a regular basis to discuss progress, reflect on learning, and revise plans.

Summary

Leaders can benefit from the leadership behavior research in several ways. First, the behavioral approach has served the important purpose of directing attention to identifying types of leadership behavior critical to success. Second, the behavioral approach allows leadership practitioners to focus on concrete and specific examples of leader behavior. Third, an outgrowth of the behavioral approach has been the development of competency models and 360-degree feedback instruments. The 360-degree feedback instruments can be used to provide valuable feedback to leadership practitioners, and often play important roles in many training, coaching, and succession-planning programs.

Research has also helped to identify factors that can cause high-potential managers to fail. This research on managerial derailment has identified "fatal flaws," including such counterproductive leadership behaviors as arrogance, insensitivity, or untrustworthiness. Another body of research indicates that many of these derailment factors may be self-defeating behaviors, behaviors that developed as a way of coping with a stressful situation but are misapplied in other situations.

The chapter also examined the process of behavior change. Research shows that some managers seem to be able to change on their own after gaining insight on how their behavior affects others. This insight is often gained through reflection, in-depth assessments, or 360-degree feedback. Nevertheless, more managers will change if some formal system or process of behavioral change is put into place, and these systems include development planning, informal and formal coaching programs, and mentorships. Development planning is the process of pinpointing development needs, creating development plans, implementing plans, and reflecting on and revising plans on a regular bases. A development plan is a written document which specifies strategies and tactics for exploiting behavioral strengths and overcoming weaknesses. Good action plans are specific and timebound, they capitalize on on-the-job experiences, and they specify sources of feedback. Organizations with formal development systems are likely to realize greater behavioral changes from a greater number of managers than organizations having no system or only an informal one.

Leaders can create development plans for themselves, and they can also help their followers with behavioral change through coaching or mentoring programs. Informal coaching programs often consist of a series of steps designed to create permanent behavioral changes in followers, and both leaders and followers play active roles in informal coaching programs. Mentoring programs have many of the same objectives as coaching programs but take place between an individual (the protege) and a leader several levels higher in the organization (the mentor).

Key Terms

Leader Behavior Description Questionnare (LBDQ)
consideration
initiating structure
job-centered dimensions
goal emphasis
work facilitation
employee-centered dimensions
leader support
interaction facilitation
Leadership Grid
concern for people
concern for production
applied behavioral analysis
360-degree or multirater feedback

perceptual gaps or blindspots
managerial derailment
inability to build relationships
failure to meet business objectives
inability to lead and build a team
inability to adapt
inadequate preparation for promotion
self-defeating behavior
development planning
development plan
coaching
informal coaching
coaching plan
formal coaching
mentoring

Discussion Questions

1. Do you think broad behavioral categories like "employee-centered" and "job-centered" mean the same thing to people with different personality traits?

2. Could you create a competency model for college professors? For college students? If you used these competency models to create 360-degree feedback tools, who would be in the best position to give professors and students feedback?

3. What do you think are the advantages and disadvantages of 360-degree feedback to leaders?

4. Do you know anyone who has derailed from a leadership position? What did

this person do? Use the leader-follower-situation model to better understand why this individual derailed.

5. Can you identify any self-defeating behaviors in yourself ? In what situations are these behaviors likely to be exhibited? How could you ensure these behaviors are not misapplied?

6. What would a development plan for students look like? How could you capitalize on school experiences as part of a development plan?

7. What would a leadership coaching program for students look like? How could you tell whether the program worked?

11 CHARISMA AND TRANSFORMATIONAL LEADERSHIP

Chapter Outline

Introduction

We hope that after reading this far in the text you will have a better appreciation of the myriad leader, follower, and situational factors that affect the leadership process. However, few people actually spend time deconstructing the leadership process into factors such as intelligence, power bases, values, behaviors, or personality traits, as we have done here. Most people believe they know leadership when they see it, and if asked to identify their "ideal leader," they often think about those political, religious, military, and business leaders whose personal magnetism, spellbinding powers, and heroic qualities have unusually strong effects on followers, societies, or organizations. These larger-than-life leaders might include such figures as Alexander the Great, Jesus Christ, Joan of Arc, Mahatma Gandhi, Adolph Hitler, Winston Churchill, the Ayatollah Khomeini, President John F. Kennedy, and Martin Luther King, Jr. Although these leaders differ in a number of important ways, one distinct characteristic they all share is charisma. Charismatic leaders are passionate, driven individuals who are able to paint a compelling vision of the future. Through this vision they are able to generate high levels of excitement among followers and build particularly strong emotional attachments with them. The combination of a compelling vision, heightened emotional levels, and strong personal attachments often compels followers to put forth greater effort to meet organizational or societal challenges. The enthusiasm and passion generated by charismatic leaders seems to be a dual-edged sword, however. Some charismatic movements can result in positive and relatively peaceful organizational or societal changes; some recent examples might include Bill McCartney's Promise Keepers, Louis Farrakhan's Million Man March, or Gloria Steinem's feminist movement. On the down side, when this passion is used for selfish or personal gains, history mournfully suggests it can have an equally devastating effect on society. Examples here might include the Heaven's Gate suicides, David Koresh of Waco infamy, or Adolph Hitler.

So what is it about charismatic leadership that causes followers to get so excited about future possibilities that they may willingly give up their lives for a cause? Even though many people conjure up images of charismatic individuals when thinking about leadership, the systematic investigation of charismatic leadership is relatively recent. This chapter reviews research findings on charismatic leadership research, describes the distinguishing characteristics of charismatic leadership, and reviews two of the more-popular transformational leadership theories. The chapter concludes by exploring several questions such as whether charismatic leadership is always desirable and whether charisma is something that can be developed (see Highlight 11–1).

Charismatic Leadership: A Historical Review

Until relatively recently (the past 25 years or so), charismatic leadership was studied primarily by historians, political scientists, and sociologists. Of this early research, probably the single most important work was written by Max Weber (1947). Weber was a sociologist primarily interested in how authority, religion, and economic forces between societies differed and changed over time. Weber maintained that societies could be identified in terms of one of three types of authority systems: traditional, legal-rational, and charismatic.

In the **traditional authority system**, the traditions and unwritten laws of the society dictate who has authority and how this authority can be used. The transfer of authority in such systems is based on traditions such as the passing of power to the first-born son of a king after a king dies. Historical examples would

Highlight 11–1

Leadership Quotes, Chapter 11

Setting an example is not the main means of influencing another, it is the only means.

Albert Einstein

The desire to understand the world and the desire to reform it are the two great engines of progress, without which human society would stand still or retrogress.

Bertrand Russell

A prime function of a leader is to keep hope alive.

John W. Gardner

Nothing great was ever achieved without enthusiasm.

Ralph Waldo Emerson

Vision is only a dream if it does not have commitment and support from the people involved.

Lou Quast and David Lee

There can be no leadership without vision.

Manfred Kets de Vries

There are many paths in the dark woods, but few are brave enough to walk them. Fewer still are those who believe so deeply in their own vision . . . that they risk saying "Follow me," as they begin the journey.

Robert Richardson and Katherine Thayer

The devil that you know is better than the one you do not know.

Old folk saying

We few, we happy few, we band of brothers;
for he to-day that sheds his blood with me
Shall be my brother; be he ne're so vile
This day shall gentle his condition
And gentlemen in England now a-bed
Shall think themselves accurs'd they were not here.
And hold their manhoods cheap whiles any speaks
That fought with us upon Saint Crispians day.

Shakespeare, *Henry V*

include the monarchies of England from the 1400s to the1600s or the dynasties of China from 3000 B.C. to the 1700s. In both examples the power to rule the kingdom or dynasty was generally transferred to the first-born son immediately after the death of the king. As noted by Shakespeare, this method of transferring power and authority often led to some interesting family dynamics. On societal and historical levels, it is important to note that the traditional authority system has been quite widespread but is fairly uncommon today. Although Thailand, the United Kingdom, Spain, Sweden, and a number of other countries maintain monarchies, for the most part these entities play more of a figurehead role, with true governing power lying elsewhere. However, this authority system is very prevalent among many privately held or small businesses across the world, as sons are often chosen to take over the business when the owner (often the father) retires. Examples here might include Peter Coors and August Busch IV taking over the Coors and Anheuser-Busch breweries from their fathers.

The most prevalent authority system in both society and business today is the **legal-rational authority system**. Authority in the legal-rational system derives from society's belief in the laws that govern it. In this system, a person possesses authority not because of tradition or his or her special qualities, but because of the laws that govern the position occupied. For example, elected government officials are legally empowered to take certain actions because of the positions they occupy. The same could be said for people in managerial positions. They typically have authority to make certain decisions about resources by virtue of holding that management position. A distinctive societal characteristic of legal-rational system is the bureaucracy, which exists solely to enforce existing laws and to maintain stability in society.

The basis of authority in the **charismatic authority system** comes from society's belief in the exemplary characteristics of the leader. Charismatic leaders are thought to possess superhuman qualities or powers of divine origin which set them apart from ordinary mortals. The locus of authority in this system rests with the individual possessing these unusual qualities; it is not derived from a society's traditions or laws. Examples might include the Ayatollah Khomeini and Mahatma Gandhi. These individuals wielded a considerable amount of power in Iran and India because of *who* they were, not because they were the first-born sons or had occupied a position that allowed them to wield power.

According to Weber, charismatic individuals come from the margins of society and emerge as leaders during times of great social crisis. These leaders serve to focus society both on the problems it faces and on the revolutionary solutions proposed by the leader. Thus, charismatic authority systems are usually the result of a revolution against traditional or legal-rational authority systems. For example, the Ayatollah Khomeini was able to mobilize the people of Iran to oust the Shah (a traditional authority system) and occupy the U.S. embassy in Tehran for over 400 days. Similarly, Gandhi was able to paint a compelling vision of what a self-governed India could be, and was able to mobilize both the Muslims and Hindus of India to use nonviolence to end British rule (a legal-rational system).

Although these revolutions are associated with a high degree of identification, attachment, and emotional appeal for the charismatic leader, charismatic authority systems tend to be relatively short-lived. Charismatic leaders must project an image of success in order for followers to continue believing they possess superhuman qualities. Any failures to accomplish the proposed changes to society will cause followers to question the divine qualities of the leader and, in turn, seriously erode the leader's authority.

A number of historians, political scientists, and sociologists have commented on various aspects of Weber's conceptualization of charismatic authority systems. Of all of these comments, however, probably the biggest controversy surrounding Weber's theory concerns the locus of charismatic leadership. Is charisma primarily the result of the situation or social context facing the leader, the leader's extraordinary qualities, or the strong relationships between charismatic leaders and followers? A number of authors have argued that charismatic movements could not take place unless the society was in a crisis (Blau, 1963; Chinoy, 1961; Wolpe, 1968). Along these lines, Friedland (1964), Gerth and Mills (1946), and Kanter (1972) argued that before a leader with extraordinary qualities would be perceived as charismatic, the social situation must be such that followers would recognize the relevance of the leader's qualities. In the examples described earlier, both Iran and India were in the throes of crises. These authors would argue that neither Khomeini nor Gandhi would have emerged as a charismatic leader to take over his respective country without this high level of societal turmoil.

Others have argued that charismatic leadership is primarily a function of the leader's extraordinary qualities, not the situation. According to Tucker (1968), these qualities include having extraordinary powers of vision, the rhetorical skills to communicate this vision, a sense of mission, high self-confidence and intelligence, and high expectations for followers. Dow's (1969) review of a number of historical crises lends support to this argument, as he reported that a number of crises were resolved using noncharismatic solutions. Thus, according to Dow's findings, a leader's qualities were the key to charismatic leadership, as a crisis alone was not enough for charismatic leader emergence. Both Khomeini and Gandhi possessed these leadership qualities, and Tucker and Dow would argue that if they did not have these skills and characteristics, then they never would have emerged as leaders of their respective countries.

Finally, several have argued that the litmus test for charismatic leadership does not depend on the leader's qualities or the presence of a crisis, but rather on followers' reactions to their leader (Clark, 1972; Deveraux, 1955; Downton, 1973; Marcus, 1961; Shils, 1965). According to this argument, charisma is attributed only to those leaders who can develop particularly strong emotional attachments with followers. Leaders with extraordinary qualities who fail to develop these strong emotional bonds would not be considered charismatic leaders. People were willing to die for both Khomeini and Gandhi, and this willingness for self-sacrifice was at least partly due to the emotional bonds between these leaders and their followers.

As you will see below, scholars continue to explore many of these same questions and perspectives about charismatic leadership.

Burns's (1978) Theory of Transformational and Transactional Leadership

The debate surrounding the locus of charismatic leadership remained primarily an academic exercise until the publication of the book *Leadership* (Burns, 1978). James MacGregor Burns was a prominent political scientist who had spent a career studying leadership in the national political arena. He reviewed much of what had previously been written about leadership and synthesized these findings with his own observations and thoughts. He focused on the differences between power versus leadership and charismatic versus noncharismatic leadership. His book helped bridge the science-practitioner gap, was a best seller, and brought the topic of leadership into the national limelight.

Burns maintained that power and leadership were two distinct entities. **Power-wielders** were those individuals who marshaled resources and influenced followers to behave in such a way as to accomplish their own (i.e., the power-wielder's) personal goals or satisfy personal needs. These personal goals and needs are usually different from followers' goals, and power-wielders tended to see followers as things or objects to be manipulated, rather than as individuals. Thus, power-wielders often saw followers as a means to an end and treated them accordingly. Examples of power-wielders might include David Koresh or Adolph Hitler; they used their followers to pursue their own selfish needs of power, control, and self-aggrandizement. Leaders, on the other hand, mobilized institutional, social, or political resources in order to arouse and satisfy followers' motives. According to Burns, leadership is inseparable from followers' needs and goals. Using Burns's definition, it would appear that both Khomeini and Gandhi were leaders; they mobilized followers in order to satisfy followers' needs to create a better society. From his perspective, all leaders were power-wielders, but not all power-wielders were leaders. The fundamental difference between the two concerned whose needs and goals were being satisfied; power-wielders rallied followers for personal gain, whereas leaders marshaled resources for their followers' benefit.

Burns also believed that leadership could take one of two forms. **Transactional leadership** occurred when leaders and followers were in some type of exchange relationship in order to get needs met. The exchange could be economic, political, or psychological in nature, and examples might include exchanging money for work, votes for votes, loyalty for consideration, and so on. An example of transactional leadership occurs when supervisors give rewards to salespersons for exceeding their monthly sales quotas or to machinists for exceeding quality standards. Two important aspects of transactional leadership are that it is very common and that it tends to be transitory, in that there may be no enduring purpose to hold parties together once a transaction is made. Thus, people will stay in this type of relationship only as long as it is mutually beneficial and the modal values of honesty, fairness, and fulfilling commitments are being met. **Modal values** are those surrounding the exchange process, and as such play a key role in transactional leadership. Also, Burns noted that while this type of leadership could be quite effective, it did not result in organizational or societal change and instead tended to perpetuate and legitimize the status quo.

The second form of leadership is transformational leadership. **Transformational leadership** serves to change the status quo by appealing to followers' values and their sense of higher purpose. Transformational leaders articulate the problems in the current system and have a compelling vision of what a new society or organization could be. This new vision of society is intimately linked to both the leader's and followers' values; it is an ideal that is congruent with their value systems. According to Burns, transformational leadership is ultimately a moral exercise in that it serves to raise the standard of human conduct. This implies that the acid test for transformational leadership might be the answer to the question, "Do these changes advance or hinder the development of the organization or society?"

Transformational leaders are not only good at appealing to followers' values, but they are also adept at **reframing** issues so that they are aligned with the leader's vision and followers' values, teaching followers how to become leaders in their own right, and inciting them to play active roles in the change movement. With reframing, leaders show how issues can be linked to leader's and followers' value systems.

Related to reframing is the idea that transformational leaders tend to operate at a higher stage of moral development than their followers, and their vision often appeals to followers' end values. **End values** are the ideals by which a society or organization should strive to live, and include justice, liberty, freedom, equality, and brotherhood. Burns believed Gandhi was a classic example of a transformational leader who consistently reframed issues and appealed to followers' end values (see Highlight 11–2).

Burns stated that transformational leadership was both common and uncommon. Transformational leadership is *common* in that it can occur at any level of society. Coaches, teachers, principals, religious figures, leaders of volunteer organizations, and business, civic, and political leaders were all capable of transformational leadership. Anyone who articulated a compelling vision of the future; tied this vision to followers' values; worked to raise followers' standard of conduct; and ultimately caused change in a society, an organization, or an institution was capable of being a transformational leader. This phenomenon is *uncommon* nonetheless, because so many leaders fail to meet the three criteria for transformational leadership. According to Burns, only leaders who manifest modal values and advance the standards of good conduct for humankind, work to achieve end values, and have a positive impact on the people whose lives they touch should be judged as transformational. Leaders not meeting all three of these criteria are either power-wielders or transactional leaders.

It is important to note that all transformational leaders are charismatic, but not all charismatic leaders are transformational. Transformational leaders are

Highlight 11–2

The Humility of Gandhi

Gandhi was one of the great leaders in world history. No less an intellect than Albert Einstein wrote this of him: "Generations to come, it may be, will scarce believe that such a one as this ever in flesh and blood walked upon this earth." Viscount Louis Mountbatten, the last Viceroy of India, compared him to the Buddha and to Christ. As a young journalist, William L. Shirer chronicled Gandhi's rebellion against British colonialism in India and described his first meeting with Gandhi. In reading it, think about what aspects of Gandhi's personality, behavior, and vision made him such a charismatic leader.

Gandhi was squatting on the floor in the corner of the verandah, spinning. He greeted me warmly, with a smile that lit up his face and made his lively eyes twinkle. The welcome was so disarming, his manner so friendly and radiant, that my nervousness evaporated before I could say a word. . . .

As our talk began I tried to take in not only what Gandhi was saying but how he looked. I had seen many photographs of him but I was nevertheless somewhat surprised at his actual appearance. His face at first glance did not convey at all the stature of the man, his obvious greatness. It was not one you would have especially noticed in a crowd. It struck me as not ugly, as some had said—indeed it radiated a certain beauty—but it was not uncommon either. Age—he was 61—and fasting, and Indian sun and the strain of years in prison, of long, hard, nervous work, had obviously taken their toll, turned the nose down, widened it at the nostrils, sunk in his mouth just a little so that the lower lip protruded, and teeth were missing—I could see only two. His hair was closely cropped, giving an effect of baldness. His large ears spread out, rabbit-like. His gray eyes lit up and sharpened when they peered at you through his steel-rimmed spectacles and then they softened when he lapsed, as he frequently did, into a mood of almost puckish humor. I was almost taken aback by the gaiety in them. This was a man inwardly secure, who, despite the burdens he carried, the hardships he had endured, could chuckle at man's foibles, including his own.

He seemed terribly frail, all skin and bones, though I knew that this appearance was deceptive, for he kept to a frugal but carefully planned diet that kept him fit, and for exercise he walked four or five miles each morning at a pace so brisk, as I would learn later when he invited me to accompany him, that I, at 27 and in fair shape from skiing and hiking in the Alps below Vienna, could scarcely keep up. Over his skin and bones was a loosely wrapped dhoti, and in the chilliness of a north Indian winter he draped a coarsely spun white shawl over his bony shoulders. His skinny legs were bare, his feet in wooden sandals.

As he began to talk, his voice seemed high-pitched, but his words were spoken slowly and deliberately and with emphasis when he seemed intent on stressing a point, and gradually, as he warmed up, the tone lowered. His slightly accented English flowed rhythmically, like a poet's at times, and always, except for an occasional homespun cliche, it was concise, homely, forceful.

For so towering a figure, his humble manner at first almost disconcerted me. Most of the political greats I had brushed up against in Europe and at home had seemed intent on impressing you with the forcefulness of their personalities and the boldness of their minds, not being bashful at all in hiding their immense egos. But here was the most gentle and unassuming of men, speaking softly and kindly, without egotism, without the slightest pretense of trying to impress his rather awed listener.

> How could so humble a man, I wondered, spinning away with his nimble fingers on a crude wheel as he talked, have begun almost single-handedly to rock the foundations of the British Empire, aroused a third of a billion people to rebellion against foreign rule, and taught them the technique of a new revolutionary method—nonviolent civil disobedience—against which Western guns and Eastern lathis were proving of not much worth. That was what I had come to India to find out.
>
> Source: W. L. Shirer, *Gandhi* (New York: Simon & Schuster, 1979), pp. 27–29. Reprinted with permission.

charismatic in that they are able to articulate a compelling vision of the future and form strong emotional attachments with followers. However, this vision and these relationships are aligned with followers' value systems and help followers to get their needs met. Charismatic leaders who are *not* transformational can convey a vision and form strong emotional bonds, but they do so in order to get their own needs met. Although both charismatic and transformational leaders strive for organizational or societal change, the difference is whether the changes are for the benefit of the leader or the followers. This distinction can be appreciated more fully by reading Highlight 11–3. In addition, transformational leadership is usually not an overnight process—it takes time for leaders to formulate and articulate a vision and for followers to become emotionally attached to the cause and their leader. It also takes time before any organizational or social change becomes truly permanent. Thus, spending one minute a day with an individual follower, as advocated by Blanchard, Zigami, and Zigami (1985) in *Leadership: The One Minute Manager*, will probably *not* result in transformational leadership. This style of leadership is more along the lines of transactional leadership, which nonetheless can be quite effective. Finally, transformational leaders are always controversial. Charismatic leadership almost inherently raises conflicts over values or definitions of the social good. Controversy also arises in that the people with the most to lose in any existing system will put up the most resistance to a transformational change initiative. The emotional levels of those resisting the transformational leadership movement are often just as great as those who embrace it, and this may be the underlying cause for the violent ends of Martin Luther King, John Kennedy, Mahatma Gandhi, Joan of Arc, or Jesus Christ. Burns stated that transformational leadership always involves conflict and change, and transformational leaders must be willing to embrace conflict, make enemies, exhibit a high level of self-sacrifice, and be thick-skinned and focused in order to perpetuate the cause.

What Are the Common Characteristics of Charismatic and Transformational Leadership?

Many social scientists conducting the early research on charismatic leadership identified characteristics which differentiated charismatic and noncharismatic leaders. More recently, these characteristics have been further elaborated by a number of researchers, including Berlew (1974), House (1977), Bass (1985, 1997),

Highlight 11–3

The Bright and Dark Sides of Charismatic Leadership

Some leaders use their charisma in order to improve the lives of their fellow man, others use it for their own selfish purposes. Often leaders in both camps face similar situations—the organization or society is in middle of a crisis and followers are looking for salvation. The key differentiator between the bright and the dark sides of charisma seems to be the leader's personal value system—does the leader take action in order to meet followers' needs or her or his own? The following two biographical sketches can make these points clearer.

Nelson Mandela

For much of the past 200 years, South Africa was ruled by a white-minority government. Although blacks made up over 75 percent of the populace, whites owned most of the property, ran most of the businesses, and controlled virtually all of the country's resources. Moreover, blacks did not have the right to vote and often worked under horrible conditions for little or no pay. Seeing the frustration of his people, Nelson Mandela spent 50 years working to overturn white-minority rule. His started this movement by organizing the African National Congress, a nonviolent organization that protested white rule through work stoppages, strikes, and riots. Several whites were killed in the early riots, and in 1960 the police killed or injured over 250 blacks in Sharpeville. Unrest over the Sharpeville incident caused 95 percent of the black workforce to go on strike for two weeks, and the country declared a state of emergency. Mandela then set up a separate organization which used acts of sabotage to further pressure the South African government to change. The organization targeted installations and took special care to ensure no lives were lost in the bombing campaign. Mandela was arrested in 1962 and spent the next 27 years in prison. While in prison he continued to promote civil unrest and majority rule, and his cause eventually gained international recognition. He was offered, but turned down, a conditional release from prison in 1985. After enormous international and internal pressure, South African president F.W. de Klerk "unbanned" the ANC and unconditionally released Nelson Mandela from prison. South Africa remained in turmoil, and 4 million workers went on strike in 1992 to protest white rule. Because of this pressure, Mandela forced President de Klerk to sign a document outlining multiparty elections. Mandela won the 1994 national election and is currently the president of the country. His campaign themes were dignity, equality, and fairness, and his government reflects these themes and the racial mix of South Africa.

David Koresh

In April 1993 approximately 85 people died at a religious compound outside of Waco, Texas. Many of them died from a fire that consumed the compound, but others had been killed by a single shot in the head. Twenty-five of the deceased were children. How did this happen? The story of David Koresh is a classic example of what can go wrong when the situational, follower, and leadership elements necessary for charismatic leadership are in place but the leader exploits followers for his own selfish purposes. By all accounts, David Koresh (nee Vernon Wayne Howell) had a miserable childhood. His mother was only 14 when David was born, and went through two divorces before she was 20. As a child David's nickname was Sputnik—he was smart, inquisitive, energetic, but also had a strong need for security. This latter need might have been the result of four years of physical and sexual abuse he received from a male family member, but it was also a need that shaped much of the rest of his life. When David turned 9 his mother decided to attend the local Seventh Day Adventist church. Apparently David loved church and religion—he would be spellbound during sermons and would spend hours listening to religious programs on the radio. He memorized large portions of scripture and could effortlessly recite numerous passages. It was in the church that David found comfort and security. However, in his later teen years David began to have a falling out with the church. David questioned why the church believed in modern day prophets, despite the fact it had been a very long time since the last prophet had walked the earth. David also had questions about a number of other biblical interpretations and often disagreed with those given by church elders. David had a strong need to be the center of attention and spent time convincing others that he was special and worthwhile. He attracted attention by reciting long passages of scripture during church meetings and by telling others that God was talking to him. He became so disruptive that he was eventually asked to leave the church.

He left the Seventh Day Adventists angry and dazed—his source of security was gone and he was no closer to finding the answers to his religious questions. He eventually joined the Branch Davidians, a splinter group of the Seventh Day Adventists. At that time the Branch Davidians were led by Lois Roden, a self-proclaimed prophetess. The Branch Davidians not only believed in modern day prophets, but they also believed in Armageddon. Lois had been leading the Branch Davidians for 25 years, but her sermons were getting redundant and boring, and the world did not seem any closer to Armageddon than it was 25 years earlier. The Branch needed new blood, and David would become the answer.

At the age of 24 David took over the Branch by becoming intimate with the 67-year-old Lois. However, David secretly married one of the 14 year olds in the Branch, and upon finding out what happened, Lois kicked David and his new wife out of the Branch. Lois berated and abused many of the members of her sect for allowing the marriage to happen, and as a result many left to join the new chapter David had formed outside of Waco. Over the next four years David consolidated his hold on leadership, and convinced his fellow sect members that he was a living prophet and that Armageddon truly was at hand. In order to meet the challenge of Armageddon, he and fellow Branch members acquired a large cache of handguns, assault weapons, and explosives.

During this time David's behavior became increasingly temperamental and violent. He made fellow members watch violent war movies and listen to his rock and roll sessions, and he put them through long fasts and strange diets. David would start by abiding by his own rules, such as no food, beer, or sodas, but eventually (he claimed) God would tell David that it was all right for David, and David alone, to violate these rules. David took a number of wives, all of whom were under 15. He

(continued)

(*concluded*)

eventually told the males in the Branch that all of the females were to become his wives and that their existing marriages were no longer valid. This bizarre behavior continued until the raid by the Bureau of Alcohol, Tobacco, and Firearms in February 1993.

Sources: M. Fatima, *Higher than Hope:The Authorized Biography of Nelson Mandela* (New York: Harper & Row, 1990); S. Clark, *Nelson Mandela Speaks: Forming a Democratic, Nonracist South Africa* (New York: Pathfinder Press, 1993); K. R. Samples, E. M. deCastro, R. Abanes, and R. Lyle, *Prophets of the Apocalypse: David Koresh and Other American Messiah*s (Grand Rapids, MI: Baker Books. 1994).

Conger and Kanungo (1988), Kets de Vries (1993), Bass and Avolio (1994), and Hogan, Curphy, and Hogan (1994). Many of these researchers either did not differentiate between charismatic and transformational leadership, or viewed charisma as an important component of transformational leadership. Almost all of the characteristics described below pertain to both charismatic and transformational leaders as defined by Burns. As such, we will use the two terms somewhat interchangeably in the next section, although we acknowledge the fundamental difference between these two types of leadership. As seen in Figure 11–1, the unique characteristics of charismatic and transformational leadership fit in nicely with the leader-follower-situation framework used throughout this text. Like the past debates surrounding charismatic leadership, modern researchers are divided on whether charismatic leadership is due to the leader's superhuman qualities, to a special relationship between leaders and followers, or to the situation.

Leader Characteristics

Some scholars argue that the leader's personal qualities are the key to charismatic or transformational leadership (Boal & Bryson, 1987; C. W. Hill, 1984, Kets de Vries, 1977, 1993; Sashkin, 1988; Zeleznik, 1974). Although we do not believe the leader's qualities are the sole key to charismatic leadership, we do acknowledge several common threads in the behavior and style of both charismatic and transformational leaders. We believe these leaders can be distinguished by their vision and values, their rhetorical skills, their ability to build a particular kind of image in the hearts and minds of their followers, and their personalized style of leadership.

Vision. Both transformational and charismatic leadership are inherently future-oriented. They involve helping a group move "from here to there." Leaders differ, however, in how they define or perceive the here and there. For some, the voyage between here and there is relatively routine, like driving on a familiar road. Others, however, see the need to chart a new course toward unexplored territory. Charismatic leaders perceive fundamental discrepancies between the ways things are and the way things can (or should) be. They recognize the shortcomings of a present order and offer an imaginative vision to overcome them. In Conger's (1989) words, they "see beyond current realities."

FIGURE 11–1

*Factors
Pertaining to
Charismatic
Leadership and
the Interactional
Framework*

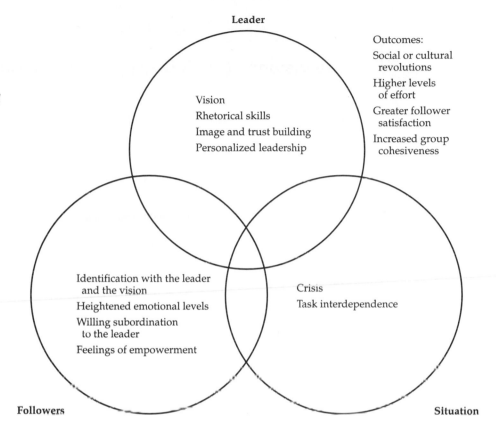

Leader

Vision
Rhetorical skills
Image and trust building
Personalized leadership

Outcomes:

Social or cultural
  revolutions

Higher levels
  of effort

Greater follower
  satisfaction

Increased group
  cohesiveness

Identification with the leader
  and the vision
Heightened emotional levels
Willing subordination
  to the leader
Feelings of empowerment

Crisis
Task interdependence

Followers

Situation

It needs to be pointed out that the importance of vision is not limited to grand social movements; it can apply to commonplace business situations too. For example, the human resources department for a large telecommunications company was completely demoralized by recent events. Many of the staff had lost their positions, and their boss had been asked to resign. The new department head recognized that creating a world-class human resources department was the only way the company could hire and develop the leaders and employees needed to successfully compete in the marketplace. This vision of a better future provided a despondent staff with a glimmer of hope, and pointed a path to success, as every member of the department wanted to be seen as a valued member of the company. The leader's vision gave the staff a direction and sense of purpose, saved the department, and provided the company with the staffing and development services it needed in order to survive (see Highlight 11–4 for other examples of vision).

Several additional aspects of vision are worth elaborating. First, both Bennis and Nanus (1985) and Tichy and Devanna (1986) reported that the leader's vision of the future is often a collaborative effort; the genius of the leader is her ability to synthesize seemingly disparate issues and problems and develop a vision that

Highlight 11–4

The Visions of Walt Disney and Anita Roddick

Walt Disney's motivation to create what eventually became Disneyland grew from visits to amusement parks with his own daughters. He observed the parks' run-down squalor, litter, and unfriendly employees, and the boredom of the parents. Furthermore, he sensed a need among tourists for something to see when they visited Hollywood. In a 1948 memo, he sketched out plans for what he tentatively called Mickey Mouse Park:

> The Main Village, which includes the Railroad Station, is built around a village green or informal park. In the park will be benches, a bandstand, drinking fountain, trees and shrubs. It will be a place for people to sit and rest; mothers and grandmothers can watch over small children at play. I want it to be very relaxing, cool and inviting. (Thomas, 1976, p. 218)

Anita Roddick founded The Body Shop as a small cosmetic company in Brighton, England, in 1976. Since that time, the company has grown to over 1,300 shops in 44 countries and has an estimated market value of $750,000,000. Roddick founded the company because of her disappointment with the regular cosmetic markets' use of animals in testing, excessive packaging, and false advertising. These values run through many of The Body Shop's marketing campaigns, which include "Against Animal Testing," "Reuse, Refill, & Recycle," and "The Body Shop in the Community." The following is an excerpt from a speech she gave at a Women in Business conference in September 1994:

> What we do well at The Body Shop is communicate with passion because passion persuades. We also know that in this decade, to educate and communicate you have to be daring, enlivening, and different. We go onto the highway with our messages, our lorries are like moving billboards. I believe in promoting our products through global culture and linking them to political and social messages. The anecdotes have a dramatic effect because people feel they are part of the planet. I believe that boldness will be The Body Shop's pre-eminent advantage in this slow-growth decade, which as yet has no style or character. When the herd-instinct of our competitors is merely to tinker while waiting for demand to pick up, smart companies like us, are engaged in organizational revolution, altering radically how work is done and how we communicate that with our stakeholders. We see an empty space as an opportunity to create an atmosphere, deliver a message, make a point. Allow me to leave you with a favorite ethos on a T-shirt, given to members of my staff: "Head in the clouds, feet on the ground, heart in the business."

Sources: B. Thomas, *Walt Disney* (New York: Simon & Schuster, 1976), and D. N. Den Hartog and R. M. Verburg, "Charisma and Rhetoric: Communicative Techniques of International Business Leaders," *The Leadership Quarterly 8, no.4,* (1997), pp. 355–92.

---

ties all of these concerns together. In the previous example, the head of human resources built his vision after lengthy discussions to determine the sources of discontent with his staff and internal customers. Second, values play a key role in the leader's vision, and serve as a moral compass for aligning leaders' and

FIGURE 11–2

*A Leader's
Vision of the
Future Can
Align Efforts
and Help Groups
Accomplish
More*

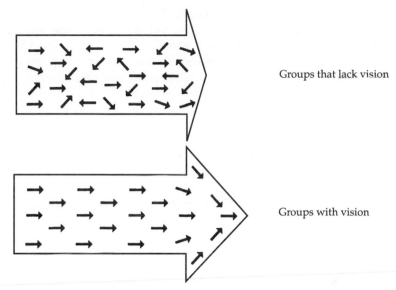

Groups that lack vision

Groups with vision

Source: Adapted from P. M. Senge, *The Fifth Discipline* (New York:Doubleday, 1990).

followers' actions with change initiatives (Ket de Vries, 1993; Shamir, Arthur, & House, 1994; Shamir, House, & Arthur, 1993). In fact, as noted previously, this is one way transformational leaders differ from merely charismatic leaders: the former build a vision based on *followers'* values, whereas the latters' visions are based solely on their *own* values. The head of human resources built his vision on what his followers believed to be important—to be seen as valued business partners. Third, the leader's vision helps followers interpret events and actions in terms of a common perceptual framework (Wofford & Goodwin, 1994). The head of human resources reframed issues so that they were aligned with the vision of the department. For example, instead of merely assigning a task team to develop and implement a new selection system for managers, the head of human resources repeatedly pointed out how this new system would be world class and be a way to be seen as valued business partners in the company. Fourth, Berlew (1974, 1992) maintained that the charismatic leader's vision had both a stimulating and a unifying effect on followers' efforts. Along these lines, Kets de Vries (1993) noted how identifying "enemies" of the vision or movement helped to focus followers' efforts. As seen in Figure 11–2, these effects often result in higher performance levels by followers. In the case of the head of human resources, the enemies were the external consulting firms who were doing many of the higher-visibility activities he wanted his department to perform. The leader consistently pointed out to his staff why they needed to reassume these activities and responsibilities if they were going to survive as a department. Berlew (1974) also maintained that a charismatic leader's vision can arouse followers' emotions only when it is *orally* articulated. Visions usually lose their emotional appeal (and consequently result in lower follower commitment to the vision) when they become "documents."

Recent research (Kirkpatrick & Locke, 1996) sheds additional light on the role vision plays in motivation and performance. These researchers conducted a laboratory experiment where actors systematically varied their vision, vision implementation, and charismatic communication styles, and noted how these variables affected the attitudes, satisfaction, and performance levels of groups of upper-level business students. It was found that the leader's vision affected followers' attitudes about motivation—followers felt more motivated after hearing a compelling versus a noncompelling vision. But they also found that neither vision nor a charismatic communication style had any direct effects on performance in this study. However, vision implementation did have a direct effect on group performance. Apparently, articulating a vision of the future is not enough; leaders also need to demonstrate what followers need to do to implement the vision and provide feedback on their progress if performance is to improve and the vision is to become reality. On a real-world level, the head of human resources in the preceding example also spent a considerable amount of time on vision implementation by demonstrating what he wanted human resource project plans to look like, and providing ample feedback on those project plans developed by his staff.

So what should a leadership practitioner take from all of this research on visioning? First, leaders need to determine the sources of discontent and the key values of their constituents (or staffs, stakeholders, etc.), as their vision must be linked to followers' values and paint a compelling picture of the future. This means that leaders may also have to elaborate on the problems in the current situation and identify enemies for followers to rally against (e.g., competitor groups, social problems). This also means that leaders must have a very clear picture of the vision and be passionate about it. It is difficult to imagine followers' being motivated toward a vision that is unclear or presented by a leader who does not seem to really care about it. Finally, as noted above, the leader should demonstrate how to implement the vision.

Rhetorical Skills.   In addition to *having* vision, charismatic leaders are gifted in *sharing* their vision. As discussed earlier, charismatic and transformational leaders have superb rhetorical skills that heighten followers' emotional levels and inspire them to embrace the vision. These leaders stir dissatisfaction with the present while they build support for their picture of a new future. It should be no surprise, then, that rhetorical skills are one of the most important tools in charismatic leadership. As it turns out, both the content of a transformational leader's speeches and the way the speeches are delivered are vitally important.

Conger (1989); Holladay and Coombs (1994); Shamir, Arthur, and House (1994); and Den Hartog and Verburg (1997) have described some of the rhetorical techniques used by charismatic leaders. Charismatic leaders make extensive use of metaphors, analogies, and stories rather than abstract and colorless rational discourse to make their points. Moreover, these stories and metaphors

Highlight 11–5

"I Have a Dream"

This will be the day when all of God's children will be able to sing with new meaning—"my country 'tis of thee, sweet land of liberty, of thee I sing; land where my fathers died, land of the pilgrim's pride; from every mountain side, let freedom ring"—and if America is to be a great nation, this must become true. So let freedom ring from the prodigious hilltops of New Hampshire. Let freedom ring from the mighty mountains of New York. Let freedom ring from the snow-capped Rockies of Colorado. Let freedom ring from the curvaceous slopes of California. But not only that. Let freedom ring from Stone Mountain of Georgia. Let freedom ring from Lookout Mountain of Tennessee. Let freedom ring from every hill and molehill of Mississippi, from every mountainside, let freedom ring. And when we allow freedom to ring, when we let it ring from every village and every hamlet, from every state and every city, we will be able to speed up that day when all of God's children—Black and White men, Jews and Gentiles, Protestants and Catholics—will be able to join hands and to sing in the words of the old Negro spiritual: "Free at last, free at last; thank God Almighty, we are free at last. "

Source: Martin Luther King, Jr. , ``I Have a Dream. "

---

can be particularly effective when they invoke potent cultural symbols and elicit strong emotions. Transformational leaders are adept at tailoring their language to particular groups, thereby better engaging them mentally and emotionally. Many transformational or charismatic religious and political leaders effectively use speech techniques like repetition, rhythm, balance, and alliteration to strengthen the impact of their messages. According to Holladay and Coombs (1994) and Den Hartog and Verburg (1997), charismatic leaders use stories, analogies, metaphors as a way to reframe issues, and often the delivery of the speech was even more important than the content itself. Poor delivery can detract from compelling content; Adolph Hitler mastered his delivery techniques so well that his speeches can have a hypnotizing power even to people who do not understand German (Willner, 1984). Similarly, many people consider the "I Have a Dream" speech of Martin Luther King, Jr., to be one of the most moving speeches they have ever heard. Note his use of different speech techniques and his masterful evocation of patriotic and cultural themes in the excerpt presented in Highlight 11–5.

From a developmental perspective, it is entirely possible to improve one's rhetorical skills. A case in point may be Vice President Al Gore. During the 1992 and 1996 vice presidential debates he was frequently criticized as a wooden speaker. His messages were usually clear and well supported by statistics, but they lacked compelling stories or metaphors and his delivery was stilted and uninspiring. Since 1997, however, there has been a dramatic change in his speaking style. Vice President Gore has added stories and metaphors to his speeches, and his delivery is more impassioned. His case is a good example of how it is possible to develop one's rhetorical skills. Leaders might be well advised to review their speech content to see if it contains metaphors and stories, and even to videotape occasional presentations to review their delivery and use of elements such as repetition, rhythm, and alliteration.

Image and Trust Building.   Transformational leaders build trust in their leadership and the attainability of their goals through seemingly unshakable self-confidence, strength of moral conviction, personal example and sacrifice, and unconventional tactics or behavior (House, 1977; Conger, 1989; Bass & Avolio, 1994; Bass, 1997). They are perceived to have unusual insight and ability, typically are more experienced and knowledgeable than their followers, and act in a manner consistent with their vision and values. Anita Roddick of The Body Shop and Herb Kelleher of Southwest Airlines are business leaders possessing these characteristics. The head of human resources for the telecommunications company also possessed these characteristics—he put in incredibly long hours, preached the cause, had 25 years of experience with the company, and followed through with his commitments to his staff and customers. Some charismatic leaders even seem to place more importance on creating the *appearance* of success than on success per se (House, 1977). Whereas transformational leaders build support by showing commitment to followers' needs over self-interest, some charismatic leaders are not beyond taking credit for others' accomplishments or exaggerating their expertise (Conger, 1989). Some seemingly charismatic political leaders have conveyed an impression of profound intellect merely by using a good memory to impress others (Willner, 1984).

Personalized Leadership.   One of the most important aspects of charismatic and transformational leadership is the personal nature of the leader's power. It is intensely relational and based almost entirely upon referent power (Chapter 6), even when the leader occupies a formal organizational role. Transformational leadership involves emotionalized relationships with followers. This does not mean that transformational leaders are necessarily friendly with their followers, just that followers of transformational leaders become relatively dependent on the leader's personal approval for their own self-worth. Thus, doing well in the eyes of a charismatic leader can be tremendously uplifting, but letting a charismatic leader down can be psychologically devastating (Conger, 1989). Along these lines, Atwater, Camobreco, Dionne, Avolio, and Lau (1997) showed that leaders who provided unconditional and ongoing praise and support, and followed through with deserved punishments were generally seen as more charismatic than leaders who gave praise based only on followers' performance, or punished followers indiscriminately.

It is this personalized style that seems to be responsible for the feelings of empowerment notable among followers of charismatic or transformational leaders, and it has two important components. First, charismatic leaders tend to be emotionally expressive, especially through such nonverbal channels as their eye contact, posture, movement, gestures, tone of voice, and facial expressions (Bass, 1990; Den Hartog & Verburg, 1997). It is partly through their nonverbal behaviors that some people are perceived to have a magnetic personality. Second, transformational leaders empower followers by building their self-efficacy. They do this by giving followers tasks that lead to successively greater success experiences and heightened self-confidence, thus persuading followers of their capabilities and creating an environment of heightened excitement and positive emotions, and by their own role-modeling as a visible symbol of the group's purpose (Bass, 1997; Bass & Avolio, 1994; Conger, 1989; Kets de Vries, 1993; Rost, 1991).

Charismatic leaders understand that they alone cannot make the vision a reality; they need their followers' help and support to create organizational or societal changes. To increase perceptions as a charismatic leader requires empowering followers by role-modeling and coaching followers on what they should (and should not) be doing, providing feedback and encouragement, and persuading followers to take on more responsibilities as their skills and self-confidence grow. This series of leadership actions is just what the head of human resources did to transform the department and empower his employees. He role-modeled how to be more proactive with the top leadership in the company, coached his staff on the new skills and activities for which they would be held accountable, provided on-going feedback on his staff's performance in line with these new activities, chided them when they fell back into old habits or blamed others for their situation, and encouraged them when they took on greater leadership roles themselves. Over the course of 18 months the self-confidence, skills, and effectiveness of the entire department increased dramatically.

Follower Characteristics

If charismatic leadership were defined solely by a leader's characteristics, then it would be relatively easy to identify individuals with good visioning, rhetorical, and impression-management skills, and place them in leadership positions. Over time we would expect that a high percentage of followers would embrace and act on the leader's vision. However, it appears that a number of leaders possess these attributes but are not seen as charismatic. They may be good, competent leaders in their own right, but they seem unable to evoke strong feelings in followers or to get followers to do more than they thought possible. In reality, charisma is probably more a function of the followers' reactions to a leader than of the leader's personal characteristics. If followers do not accept the leader's vision or become emotionally attached to the leader, then the leader simply will not be perceived to be charismatic or transformational. Thus, **charisma** is in the eyes and heart of the beholder—it is a particularly strong emotional reaction to, identification with, and belief in some leaders by some followers. It is important to note that this definition is value-free—leaders seen as charismatic may or may not share the same values as their followers or meet

Burns's criteria for transformational leadership. Many of the more-popular conceptualizations of charisma and charismatic leadership today also define charisma in terms of followers' reactions to the leader (Bass, 1985, 1997; Bass & Avolio, 1994; Conger & Kanungo, 1988; House, 1977; Howell, 1988; Willner, 1984). Since we have defined charisma as a reaction followers have to leaders, let us turn our attention to the four unique characteristics of these reactions.

Identification with the Leader and the Vision.   Two of the effects House (1977) associated with charismatic leadership included a strong affection for the leader and a similarity between follower beliefs and those of the leader. These effects describe a sort of bonding or identification with the leader personally, and a parallel psychological investment in a goal or activity (a "cause") bigger than oneself. Followers' identities or self-concepts become defined in terms of the leader. Being like the leader or being approved by the leader becomes an important part of one's self-worth. Effects like these go well beyond what might be expected from the typical contractual or exchange relationships between most supervisors and subordinates.

Followers often bond with a leader because they see the implementation of the vision as a solution to all of their problems. Followers may be intensely dissatisfied with the status quo but unsuccessful in developing a satisfactory solution on their own. Charismatic leaders capitalize on this dissatisfaction and on the fact that most people want to belong to something bigger than themselves and they want to make a difference in their organizations or society. Thus, part of the appeal of a charismatic or transformational leader is the ability to articulate a simple vision that focuses followers on their plight and provides compelling ideas on how they can improve it. However, it is often the case that, paradoxically, the more complicated the problem, the more may people be drawn to simplistic solutions.

The vision also helps followers interpret external events and find purpose in their actions—they will align their behaviors to the tenets of the vision. This is exactly what happened in Iran in late 1970s. The Iranian people were extremely dissatisfied with the Shah and his government. The Ayatollah Khomeini articulated a vision of the future, which in this case was a Muslim fundamentalist state that promised to alleviate many ills of the Iranian people. The Iranian people identified with, became committed to, and acted according to this vision. More recently, Bill McCartney's Promise Keepers and Louis Farrakhan's Million Man March are examples where large groups of followers were genuinely dissatisfied with the direction cultural, religious, educational, legal, and societal institutions were headed in the United States. In both cases, followers saw these two causes as solutions to many of their own and society's problems, enthusiastically embraced these causes, emulated the values and actions espoused by McCartney or Farrakhan, and believed their participation was a way to better themselves and society. Although followers' identification with the leader can result in positive societal changes, the Heaven's Gate and Jonestown suicides show these strong emotional attachments can also lead to disaster.

Heightened Emotional Levels.   House (1977), Bass and Avolio (1994), Yammarino and Dubrinsky (1994), and Bass (1997) maintained that followers of charismatic leaders also had heightened emotional levels. Charismatic leaders stir followers' feelings, perhaps more intensely than many people suppose. Experimental studies have confirmed greater physiological arousal among subjects listening to inspirational speeches than to travel lectures (Steele, 1977; Stewart & Winger, 1976). Moreover, House (1977), Kets de Vries (1993), and Bass (1985, 1997) have maintained that the result of this heightened emotional state was that increased levels of effort were devoted to accomplishing the vision, which in turn resulted in increased performance levels.

Emotions are often the fuel driving large-scale change initiatives, and charismatic leaders will often do all they can to maintain them, including getting followers to think about their dissatisfaction with the status quo, pointing out real or imaginary enemies to the vision, or making impassioned appeals directly to followers. Emotions are a dual-edged sword, however. The people alienated by a charismatic leader and the movement can have emotions which are just as intense as those of the followers of the vision. This polarizing effect of charismatic leaders may be one reason why they tend to have violent deaths— those who are alienated by a charismatic leader are just as likely to act on their emotions as are the followers within the movement (House, Woycke, & Fodor, 1988).

Specific situations may make heightened emotional arousal more or less appropriate, even in the corporate world. For example, Hewlett-Packard is a very successful company seen by many as a very good place to work. It is also a very consensus-driven organization where everyone is supposed to get along and not show either overly positive or overly negative emotions at work. In such a corporate environment, it may be relatively difficult for a charismatic leader to emerge and succeed, as the level of satisfaction among employees and organizational norms may prevent such leaders from successfully raising the emotions of their followers. On the other hand, at the Home Depot, another very successful company, the open display of emotions is not only welcomed but encouraged. The company's senior leaders are seen as very charismatic people who can raise the emotional levels of their staffs and motivate them to get more done than they thought possible. Part of the phenomenal success of the company has been due to top leadership's ability to raise and channel followers' emotions toward the vision of the company, which is to be the top home improvement retail chain in North America.

Willing Subordination to the Leader.   House (1977) identified three other effects of charismatic leadership: unquestioning acceptance of the leader by followers, willing obedience to the leader and trust in the correctness of the leader's beliefs. Whereas the preceding factor dealt with followers' emotional and psychological closeness to the leader, this factor involves their deference to his authority. Charismatic leaders often seem imbued with superhuman qualities. As a result, followers often willingly submit to the leader's apparently natural authority and superiority. Because followers volitionally submit to a charismatic leader's authority, Willner (1984) used the term **spellbinders** to describe the group of charismatic political leaders she studied who were larger than life in the minds of their followers. The spellbinding qualities of Louis Farrakhan and Bill McCartney would be readily apparent if you had attended the Million Man March or a Promise Keeper event.

Feelings of Empowerment.   House (1977) noted one final effect of charismatic leadership: followers' heightened expectations of themselves. Followers of charismatic leaders are moved to expect more of themselves, and they work harder to achieve these higher goals. Charismatic leaders capitalize on the **Pygmalion effect**: they set high expectations while boosting the self-confidence of followers by expressing confidence in their abilities and providing on-going encouragement and support (Bass & Avolio, 1994; Kets de Vries, 1993). On a more practical level, charismatic leaders empower followers by utilizing many of the techniques used by the head of human resources at the telecommunications company. He set high expectations, provided on-going coaching and feedback on progress toward these expectations, expressed confidence in their ability to turn the department around, and was a constant source of praise and encouragement for his staff. As a result, the staff of the human resources department did have stronger skills and self-confidence, but they still deferred to the leader for guidance on any significant human resource decision. Somewhat paradoxically, then, followers feel stronger and more powerful at the very same time they willingly subordinate themselves to the charismatic leader. Charismatic leaders are able to make their followers feel more powerful without any diminution or threat to their own status. These feelings of empowerment, when combined with heightened emotional levels and a leader's vision of the future, often result in increases in organizational, group, or team performance or significant social change.

Situational Characteristics

We have seen how charismatic leadership can be understood in terms of characteristics of leaders and their relationships with followers, but some scholars have argued that *situational* factors really determine whether a leader will be perceived as charismatic (Bradley, 1987; Roberts & Bradley, 1988; Westley & Mintzberg, 1988). These authors have shown that individuals possessing the qualities of charismatic leaders were perceived to be charismatic *only when confronting certain types of situations*. Because the situation may play an important role in the attribution of charisma, it will be useful to review some of the situational factors believed to affect charismatic leadership.

Crises.   The most important situational factor which contributes to charismatic leadership is probably the presence or absence of a crisis. Followers content with the status quo are relatively unlikely to perceive a need for a charismatic leader or to be willing to devote great effort to attempt fundamental changes to an organization or a society. On the other hand, a crisis—whether reflected by the failure of traditional social institutions or a corporation's imminent financial failure—often creates a sort "charisma hunger" in followers—they are looking for a leader to alleviate or resolve their crisis (Madsen & Snow, 1983; Trice & Beyer, 1986). Because the presence of a crisis seems to play such a key role in the emergence of charismatic leaders, Pawar and Eastman (1997), Avolio and Bass (1988), Boal and Bryson (1987), and Kets de Vries (1977) have all maintained that some leaders actually purposely create crises in order to foster desire among followers for a charismatic leader to appear.

Helping followers focus on a real or an imagined enemy is one way to foment a crisis (Kets de Vries, 1993). For example, some foreign governments routinely claim U. S. threats to their countries in order to remain in power. In the corporate world, leaders often use competitive threats in the marketplace to institute change—Lee Iacocca used threats imposed by Ford, GM, and Japanese automakers as a way to change Chrysler. Even local leaders often identify supposed civic enemies or dangers to mobilize support for their own position. Local politicians may decry how this group or that poses a threat to, for instance, family values; individuals running for school boards may warn of threats to education from enemies, whether other politicians, teachers unions, or dangerously misguided educational innovations. Although a crisis situation does not necessarily make every leader look charismatic, such a situation may set the stage for particular kinds of leader behaviors to be effective.

Interestingly enough, recent research has shown that corporate CEOs tend to manifest more of a transactional style than a transformational style when faced with a crisis (Scully, Sims, Olian, Schneell, & Smith, 1994). Corporate CEOs were more directive, more apt to use reprimands, and focused on shorter-term outcomes when faced with financial crises. However, research has shown that transformational leadership is almost always more effective than transactional leadership, particularly in high-stress situations (Bass, 1985, 1997; Bass & Avolio, 1994; Curphy, 1991a, 1992a; Lowe, Kroeck, & Sivasubramaniam, 1996). It appears that some corporate CEOs may be exhibiting previously successful behaviors in situations where they may be less appropriate (perhaps a form of self-defeating behavior, as described in Chapter 10).

Other corporate CEOs, however, can be quite transformational. Many new companies are the result of a transformational leader's vision. Such leaders often have spent time working in very large companies, and leave because their personal values were not in line with those of the company. These individuals have a strong vision of what their new company will be like, and they attract followers whose own values are in line with this vision.

Task Interdependence.   Another situational characteristic which can affect followers' perceptions of charisma is the level of interdependent effort required to accomplish a task. It may be easier for leaders to be seen as charismatic when the tasks performed by their followers require a high level of interdependent effort. Because team sports such as soccer, basketball, football, and hockey often require self-sacrifice, extra effort, and cooperation among team members for success, coaches of these teams may be more likely to be perceived as charismatic than coaches of individual sports (e. g. , gymnastics) with lower levels of interdependent effort (Curphy, 1991a, 1992a).

Other Situational Characteristics.   There are still other situational characteristics that may help or hinder the emergence of a charismatic leader. Howell and Avolio (1993) found that organizations placing a premium on innovation were much more supportive of transformational leadership than those less committed to innovation. Pawar and Eastman (1997) noted that organizations more receptive to change were more conducive to transformational leadership emergence. Another situational factor that may affect charismatic leadership is organizational downsizing. In many peoples' minds, downsizing has destroyed the implicit contract between employer and employee, and left many employees disillusioned with corporate life (Church, 1994). As a result, many talented managers have left large organizations to form their own companies. These small, entrepreneurial organizations are often led by charismatic leaders who wanted to work in companies that were better aligned with their own personal values. Examples might include The Body Shop, Southwest Airlines, Ben & Jerry's, Dell Computers, Boston Market, or many of the microbreweries cropping up across North America. Employees join these smaller organizations precisely because the company's vision is consistent with their own personal values. However, it is important to note that transformational leadership alone did not make these companies successful. Over 70 percent of new companies fail, and one of the primary reasons for this high failure rate is the leader's inability to build the systems and processes necessary for repeatable excellence and continued growth. The companies above were founded and continue to be led by transformational leaders, but these leaders also had the savvy to build the marketing, sales, customer service, distribution, finance, and human resource systems necessary to sustain continued growth. These systems also help to reduce the workload on employees, as the challenge of working in a new company or for a transformational leader can very stressful.

Concluding Thoughts about the Characteristics of Charismatic and Transformational Leadership

Several final points about the characteristics of charismatic leadership need to be made. First, although we defined charisma as a quality attributed to certain leaders based on the relationships they share with followers, charismatic leadership is most fully understood when we also consider how leader and situational factors affect this attribution process. The special relationships charismatic leaders share with followers do not happen by accident; rather, they are often the result of interaction between the leader's qualities, leader and follower values, and the presence of certain situational factors.

Second, it seems unlikely that all the characteristics of charismatic leadership need to be present before charisma is attributed to a leader. For example, some leaders may have the ability to develop particularly strong relationships with followers in the absence of a vision or a crisis. In this regard, we might ask the following question: If high-task and high-relationship leaders (9,9 leaders) also develop strong emotional bonds with followers, then is charisma nothing more than being a 9,9 leader (see Figure 10–1)? The bottom line for charisma seems to be the relationships certain leaders share with followers, and there may be a variety of ways in which these relationships can develop. This also implies that charisma may be more of a continuum than an all-or-nothing phenomenon. Some leaders may be able to form particularly strong bonds with a majority of followers, others with a few followers. Still others may get along with most followers but not form particularly strong bonds with any of them.

Third, given that there are a number of ways to develop strong emotional attachments with followers, one important question is whether it is possible to attribute charisma to an individual based solely on her position or celebrity status (Etzioni, 1961; Hollander, 1978; Bass, 1990). Some individuals in positions of high public visibility and esteem—such as film stars, musicians, athletes, television evangelists, and politicians—can develop (even cultivate) charismatic images among their fans and admirers. In these cases, it is helpful to recognize that charismatic leadership is a two-way street. Not only do followers develop strong emotional bonds with leaders, but leaders also develop strong emotional bonds with followers and are concerned with follower development (Burns, 1978). It is difficult to see how the one-way communication channels of radio and television can foster these two-way relationships or enhance follower growth. Thus, although we sometimes view certain individuals as charismatic based on media manipulation and hype, this is not transformational leadership in the truest sense.

Fourth, it is important to remember that charismatic leadership does not happen overnight; it takes time for the strong emotional bonds between charismatic leaders and followers to develop. Furthermore, these bonds not only form on the world stage, but they can also be seen on the smaller stages of leadership. For example, charismatic leaders exist in such commonplace environments as college campuses and military-training squadrons. Students identify some professors as more charismatic than others (Labak, 1973), and cadets identify certain military superiors as more inspirational than others (Adams, Prince, Instone, & Rice, 1984; Clover, 1990; Curphy, 1991a). Thus, charismatic leadership is not the exclusive charter of world, societal, or religious leaders but can occur in any type of group, team, or organizational setting (Bass, 1997).

Are Charismatic and Transformational Leadership Universal Concepts?

Two unanswered questions about charismatic leadership are whether it is a universal or global concept, and whether males or females are more likely to be seen as charismatic leaders. Fortunately, independent lines of research over the past 10 years can help to answer these questions. With respect to whether transformational leadership is universal, Bass's (1997) recent work indicates that it is universal across just about all countries, institutions, and hierarchical levels. When individuals in any country or company are asked to identify characteristics of their ideal leader, they invariably describe characteristics associated with transformational or charismatic leadership. Bass (1997) reported that transformational leadership can be found in India, Canada, the Dominican Republic, China, Austria, South Africa, Japan, Israel, Italy, Sweden, Spain, New Zealand, Germany, Mexico, Indonesia, Singapore, and the Roman Catholic clergy. It has been found on every continent except Antarctica, and is particularly prevalent in countries possessing more collectivistic versus individualistic societies (Jung, Bass, & Sosik, 1995).

Along these same lines, Kanungo and Mendonca (1996) have argued that transformational leadership is precisely what developing countries need in order to change their current situation and advance to the next level. Transformational leaders challenge the status quo and get followers to do more than they thought possible, whereas transactional leaders maintain the status quo and are limited by the rewards they can administer. Transactional leadership can also have differing effects across countries; performance is closely tied to rewards in the West, but performing at a higher level than one's peers can cause a loss of face in Japan, and Egypt has a highly structured bureaucracy that allows little latitude for reward (Bass, 1997).

Accumulating research is shedding light on whether men or women are more likely to be seen as transformational or charismatic leaders. Various researchers have reported that females were much more likely to exhibit an "interpersonal leadership style" than men (Eagly, 1987; Eagly, Makhijani, & Klonsky, 1992; Eagly, Karau, & Makhijani, 1995). Some of the attributes associated with this style include friendliness, unselfishness, concern for others, emotional expressiveness, cooperativeness, and participation. These attributes are very similar to those associated with transformational leaders (see Highlights 11–6 and 11–7). Although females exhibiting this style were often more effective than their male counterparts, it also appears that these females were more likely to experience bias or downgraded performance review ratings when working in more male dominated roles. Fortunately, additional research suggests female managers appear to be succeeding *because of* characteristics heretofore considered too "feminine" for effective leadership (Rosener, 1990). Rosener's survey research identified several differences in how men and women described their leadership experiences. Men tended to describe themselves in somewhat "transactional" terms, viewing leadership as an exchange with subordinates for services rendered. They influenced others primarily through their organizational position and authority. The women, on the other hand, tended to describe themselves in "transformational" terms. They helped subordinates develop commitment for broader goals than their own self-interest, and described their influence more in terms of personal characteristics like charisma and interpersonal skill than as mere organizational position.

Highlight 11–6

An Example of a Female Transformational Leader

Dr. Jodi Taylor is a Vice President of The Center For Creative Leadership, and was the founding director of its Colorado Springs branch. She has been extremely successful in that role and is regarded by most who know her as a charismatic leader. We asked her to reflect on her own development as a leader, her feelings about how she is perceived by others, and her vision for her organization.

Charisma and leadership are words that describe a person's impact on others: describing results of behavior rather than motivation or intent. I doubt if anyone plans to grow up to become a charismatic leader. One is a charismatic leader as a result of who one is and what one is about. So I am always surprised when people refer to me as a charismatic leader. Since I feel rather ordinary myself, I am left with the question "What is it about me, or anyone for that matter, that causes them to appear to others as a charismatic leader?"

Growing up in a small West Texas town in the middle of oil and wheat country, life was very stable for me. Both my parents worked, so expectations of achievement and hard work seemed perfectly normal. Additionally, people have always described me as a person with restless energy and focus. By the age of nine, I was reading a book a day. By the age of 14, I had my first job working in a factory. As a senior in high school I worked two after-school jobs while continuing to be an honor student body officer, wrote a column for the school newspaper, served on both the annual and school magazine staffs. Again, that all seemed quite ordinary to me.

A fascination with people was another theme in my early life. My grandmother always drove my handicapped aunt downtown each Saturday afternoon to park on the main street and watch the people shopping. I often joined them and developed a lifelong curiosity about the differences among people.

Always propelled by a strong future orientation, by the age of 13 I was worried about what I would be when I grew up, so I read the encyclopedia of occupations. When I discovered "psychologist," it immediately connected with my interest in people and I began focusing on that career, completing my Ph.D. by the age of 24. My background in psychology, with its emphasis on people, combined with my strong need to create, has led me to organizational settings. By combining focus, energy, interest in people, and the need to create, I have been able to facilitate an organizational structure that enables people to grow and allows us collectively to make the world a better place. This sense of mission, personal growth, and commitment to the team in turn gives us new energy, focus, and vision to be more creative so that the end result is an upward spiral. It's that upward spiral that leadership is all about.

Perhaps *upward spiral* is the best term to describe what has happened at CCL Colorado Springs over the last five years. When I became director (part-time) in 1987, we had no full-time employees and were conducting only 13 courses a year. We did, however, have a solid basis formed by CCL's reputation and a viable product. My mission for the branch was to build on that basis so we could leverage our impact on organizations. We wanted to "really make a difference" in organizations by working with a "critical mass" of people in the organization, not just one or two people at a time, as we do in our public courses. At the same time, we also focused our energies on working with senior executives. I wanted the image of CCL, Colorado Springs, and the mountains to be inextricably linked whenever people from anywhere in the world thought of senior leadership. To

(continued)

(*concluded*)

> achieve that vision, I set out to hire the best people I could find in the area of leadership training and build them into a team and an intellectual community. We could achieve our vision only if we practiced what we preached—by being a high-functioning team, constantly searching for new ideas about leadership and looking for ways to share them.
>
> So far, we are succeeding (although you are never complete when trying to achieve a vision). Our revenues and staff have increased significantly over the past decade, and we have embarked on an ambitious building project to create our own training campus. This building will then enable us to fulfill our mission even better, as we can offer more courses, have more space for research, and then impact more people. We are in that delicious stage of the life cycle of an organization when we believe anything is possible.
>
> Again, it is that upward spiral. Today, with a strong high-functioning team, we have even more leverage to build toward that vision of using our knowledge and research to make the world a better place by tapping the leadership potential in everyone we work with.

According to Rosener, such women leaders encouraged participation and shared power and information, but went far beyond what is commonly thought of as participative management. She called it **interactive leadership**. Their leadership self-descriptions reflected an approach based on enhancing others' self-worth, believing that the best performance results when people are excited about their work and feel good about themselves.

How did this interactive leadership style develop? Rosener concluded it was due to these women's socialization experiences and career paths. As we indicated above, the social roles expected of women have emphasized that they should be cooperative, supportive, understanding, gentle, and service oriented. As they entered the business world, they still found themselves in roles emphasizing these same behaviors. They found themselves in staff, rather than line, positions, and in roles lacking formal authority over others; and they had to accomplish their work without reliance on formal power. What they had to do, in other words, was employ their socially acceptable behavioral repertoire in order to survive organizationally.

> What came easily to women turned out to be a survival tactic. Although leaders often begin their careers doing what comes naturally and what fits within the constraints of the job, they also develop their skills and styles over time. The women's use of interactive leadership has its roots in socialization, and the women interviewees firmly believe that it benefits their organizations. Through the course of their careers, they have gained conviction that their style is effective. In fact, for some it was their own success that caused them to formulate their philosophies about what motivates people, how to make good decisions, and what it takes to maximize business performance. (p. 124)

Although Eagly and Rosener did not directly address the transformational versus transactional leadership differences between men and women, this research does shed some light on the topic. Researchers who have focused on answering this question more directly include Druskat (1994); Bycio, Hackett, and Allen (1995); Bass, Avolio, and Atwater (1996); and Yammarino, Dubrinsky,

---

Highlight 11–7

Pat Summitt, the Wizard of Knoxville

She has been called the best basketball coach since famed John Wooden. Just some of her credentials include winning the first-ever Olympic gold medal in U.S. women's basketball history; six national championships, surpassed only by Wooden's record; an . 814 winning percentage, fifth among all coaches in college basketball history; and so many trips to basketball's Final Four that her record in all likelihood will never be equaled. Her 1997–98 University of Tennessee team finished the regular season 30 and 0, and won its third consecutive national title.

Beyond coaching records, however, what is Summitt like as a person? Among other things, she is intense and authoritative. When she walks into a room, she has erect carriage, a confident smile, a direct manner of speaking, and a piercing gaze. Her calendar documents her pressured schedule: appointments are noted at five- or ten-minute intervals, arrows point to annotated reminders of other obligations, key meetings are underlined, and the most important ones conclude with multiple exclamation points!!!! But she is also a deeply caring person, appropriate for a farm daughter who grew up imitating her mother's selfless generosity in visiting the sick or taking a home-cooked dinner to anyone in need.

Summitt clearly has many extraordinary qualities as a coach, but perhaps most striking is the nature of the relationship she develops with her players. Journalist Gary Smith described a player's perspective on sitting in the coach's office:

> How does she do it? How could a woman be transformed that completely, so that when you sit in her office, she leans toward you to connect with you, the flesh around those piercing eyes wrinkling in concentration, and invariably asks what you think the team needs, and then, as you're getting ready to leave, asks if you think her beige shoes go with her white skirt. Not to con you or charm you, because you would eventually sniff that out. She asks so intently that it seems the two of you are the only ones in the universe, so honestly that you smell the unsure girl beneath the awe-inducing coach. (p. 97)

Source: Gary Smith, "Eyes of the Storm," *Sports Illustrated*, March 2, 1998, pp 89–106.

Comer, and Jolson (1997). In general, this research shows that females receive higher ratings on transformational leadership than their male counterparts, irrespective of whether the ratings come from male or female followers. However, these differences were not particularly large and do not appear to have much practical significance. Some have suggested these higher ratings were due to the unique one-on-one relationships female leaders build with their followers (Yammarino et al., 1997; Bass, Avolio, & Atwater, 1996). Females spend more time focusing on improving relationships in order to achieve business results; males focus on setting goals and task accomplishment (i. e, transactional leadership) in order to achieve business results.

Perhaps the most disturbing theme from this research is that many male-dominated organizations do not embrace or tolerate different approaches to getting results. Because of this lack of appreciation for a more interactive or transformational leadership style, female leaders appear to cope with this situation by taking one of two actions. Some females leave the organization to start companies which are more aligned with their own values and style of leadership (Bass, Avolio, & Atwater, 1996), and others change their style in order to better fit with organizational expectations. For example, Druskat (1994) reported that women tended to show more of a transactional leadership style in male-dominated organizations, and more of a transformational style in non-traditional, female-dominated organizations. She also pointed out that organizations that are male dominated (most, in other words) often fail to capitalize on the transformational potential of their female managers.

Are Charismatic Leaders Always Good?

Just as charismatic leaders can be seductive, the very topic of charismatic leadership can be seductive, too. It is all too easy in reading about the personal magnetism, vision, and empowering style of charismatics to conclude that they are the best leaders and that theirs is a style all leaders should emulate. It is worth reminding ourselves, therefore, that not all charismatic leaders are necessarily good leaders. Precisely because charismatic leaders' effects can be more emotional than rational, many observers have warned of the dangers charismatic leaders can pose.

Followers of charismatic leaders can be so zealous that they are blind to things they don't want to see, a bit like the children who followed the Pied Piper of Hamelin (Newman, 1983) (also see Highlight 11–8). At their best, charismatic leaders can positively transform and empower their followers, and researchers have reported that some charismatic U.S. presidents, social leaders, and organizational leaders were the underlying cause of many positive social and organizational changes (Deluga, 1997; House, Spangler, & Woycke, 1991; House, Woycke, & Fodor, 1988; O'Connor et al., 1995; Tichy & Devanna, 1986; Westley & Mintzberg, 1988; Willner, 1984). At their worst, however, charismatic leaders emotionally manipulate followers and create dysfunctional dependencies for their own self-aggrandizement; they can even wreak havoc on the rest of the world (e. g. , Alexander the Great, Genghis Khan, Attila the Hun, Adolph Hitler, or Saddam Hussein). A tragic example of the negative aspects of charismatic leadership was the Jim Jones cult that self-exterminated in the Jonestown massacre (Conway & Siegelman, 1979). Virtually all of the 912 who died there voluntarily drank from large vats of a flavored drink containing cyanide after Jones said they all must commit "mass suicide for the glory of socialism." As described in Chapter 6, part of that seemingly bizarre behavior probably had been conditioned by Jones's extensive use of punishment as a control technique, but there seems to be little question that he also had a charismatic impact on the group. More recent examples of the dark side of charisma were the 39 Heaven's Gate

Highlight 11–8

Marjoe Gortner

At the age of four, Marjoe Gortner preached at tent revival meetings, billed as "The World's Youngest Ordained Minister." He was well prepared for it, having been coached in dramatic techniques including the right way to shout "Glory" into a microphone. His sermons (with titles such as "Heading for the Last Roundup") were memorized down to each pause and gesture. Gortner's role, in his own view, was to be a sort of conductor, orchestrating and engineering the group frenzy. Cynically recalling his manipulations, Gortner said, "It's the same as at a rock and roll concert . . . You have an opening number with a strong entrance; then you go through a lot of the old standards, building up to your hit song at the end" (Conway & Siegelman, 1979, p. 48). Was Marjoe a charismatic leader? In one sense, because he was able to get followers to form strong emotional bonds with him and to trust in the correctness of his religious beliefs, Marjoe would probably be considered a charismatic leader, using our definition of charisma. However, in another sense, Marjoe would not be considered a charismatic leader. According to Burns (1978), charismatic or transformational leaders also develop strong emotional bonds and are concerned with the development of their followers. Because Marjoe was interested only in developing relationships with followers for his own personal gain and self-aggrandizement, he would not be considered a transformational leader according to Burns's definition.

Source: F. Conway and J. Siegelman, *Snapping* (New York: Delta, 1979).

suicides outside of San Diego in 1997, and the fiery end of the Branch Davidian cult outside of Waco, Texas, in 1993. Like the Jonestown cult, both of these groups were headed by charismatic leaders who also happened to use punishment as a control technique.

Several researchers have offered explanations for why some charismatic leaders have such extreme effects, either tremendously positive or tremendously negative effects, on those around them. Both Kets de Vries (1977, 1993) and Zaleznik (1974) maintained that there are two types of charismatic leaders, one type being psychologically "healthy" and the other type being psychologically "unhealthy." Zaleznik (1974) posited that healthy charismatic leaders have well-developed inner lives and had healthy and significant relationships with their mothers. Because unhealthy leaders are typically overattached to their mothers, they have not resolved their inner conflicts and foster similar overdependent relationships in their followers. Kets de Vries added that unhealthy charismatic leaders are particularly dangerous, as such leaders often have the ability to turn their internal fantasies of power and control into reality.

Howell (1988) maintained that there are both socialized and personalized charismatic leaders. Socialized charismatic leaders express goals that are follower driven, and they work to develop followers into leaders; Burns would define these individuals as transformational leaders. Personalized charismatic leaders pursue leader-driven goals and promote feelings of obedience, dependency, and submission in followers; Burns would define these leaders as power-wielders or charismatics. As pointed out by Burns, however, the differences between these two types of leaders may be due primarily to their values, not their personalities. Martin Luther King, Jr., and Adolph Hitler may have shared certain similarities in ability and personality, and these similarities may have played a major role in allowing them to develop strong emotional bonds with followers and to articulate their visions of the future. However, no one would argue that these two leaders shared the same value systems. Nevertheless, it may also be that socialized and personalized charismatic leaders share the same bright-side personality traits, but they may differ significantly with respect to their standing on various dark-side personality traits (Chapter 8). Deluga (1997) reported that narcissism was related to both socialized and personalized charismatic leadership, and O'Connor et al. (1995) found a positive relationship between narcissism and destructiveness among 20th-century world-class leaders. Thus, the differences between positive and negative charismatic leaders may be due to differences in value systems and dark-side personality traits; negative charismatic leaders may be interested only in their own self-aggrandizement and power, whereas positive charismatic leaders are primarily motivated to improve their followers, organizations, or societies (see Highlight 11–9).

At this point it is important to reemphasize a fundamental theme of this book—there are multiple pathways to leadership success. After reading about the "heroic" qualities of charismatic leaders and their ability to influence followers, you can easily fall into the trap of thinking that leaders can be categorized into one of two groups (those having charisma or those not having charisma), and that it is better to be in one than the other. As we have seen, though, the leadership process is much more complicated than such a simple dichotomy. Some leaders are very effective because they are smart and experienced, others have exemplary administrative skills, and still others have excellent communication and interpersonal skills. None of these leaders may be seen by followers to be charismatic, yet all might be very good at forming cohesive teams and helping groups accomplish goals. Moreover, some charismatic leaders may be viewed as tyrants when the final ledger is written. Although most of us may never be seen as transformational leaders, we all can have a tremendous, positive impact on the lives of our followers and our organizations if we learn to leverage our leadership strengths and continue to work on developmental goals.

Bass's (1985) Theory of Transformational and Transactional Leadership

Although the previous section described several recent conceptualizations of charismatic leadership, the best-known of these has yet to be mentioned: Bass's (1985, 1997) **theory of transformational and transactional leadership**. One strength of Bass's theory, first developed with executives from South Africa in

---

Highlight 11–9

The Destruction of Alexander the Great

Just as some charismatic leaders can have significant positive changes on an organization, a society, or a nation, so can others have an equally strong negative effect on organizations or societies. The story of Alexander the Great provides an excellent example of a famous charismatic leader whose actions and activities were focused solely on his own self-aggrandizement. The following are some of the distinctive accomplishments and characteristics of Alexander the Great.

His accomplishments: Alexander the Great was born in 356 B.C., and 35 years later he had managed to conquer most of the known world. Based in Macedonia (in the southern peninsula of Greece), Alexander's campaigns allowed him to rule lands in Turkey, Lebanon, Israel, Egypt, Syria, Iraq, Iran, Pakistan, Afghanistan, and India.

His vision: Quite simply, Alexander's vision was to rule the world. He viewed his campaign as a Homerian epic and wanted to guarantee himself a place in history.

His intellect: Alexander was an incisive strategist and a brilliant tactician. For example, because the massive Persian fleet was powered by rowers (who needed food and water to power the ships), Alexander correctly assumed that the Persian fleet would be rendered useless if their home ports were captured. Moreover, he learned from his battles and sieges, and applied this knowledge in future battles.

His concern for his followers and personal example: Alexander was a man of tireless energy and an absolutely fearless warrior. He showed a complete disregard for danger in battle—he was often at the front lines leading his troops into the thick of the battle. Because of his leadership style, Alexander had been wounded by swords, spears, darts, stones, clubs, and catapult missiles over the course of his campaigning. Nevertheless, he showed a great deal of compassion toward his troops. He granted many of his troops leave and canceled all of their debts. He made sure they had enough food, visited the wounded after each battle, and conducted elaborate military funerals for his fallen comrades.

His excellent rhetorical and dramatic skills: Alexander was formally schooled in debate and epic poetry by Aristotle. He spoke in a forceful, dramatic style and had the gift of being able to tailor his messages to the situation at hand. Alexander was also very theatrical; he feigned sleep immediately before the battle of Gaugamela. Similarly, when rumors about his wounding and death began circulating among his troops after a particularly fierce battle, he stayed within his tent for three days, allowing the rumors to reach a fever pitch. He waited until he was the subject of concern of all of his troops before he assuaged their fears.

He understood the importance of success: He constantly excelled at war, as he knew failures would cause his troops to question his "supernatural" powers.

The destruction: Although Alexander conquered much of the known world at the time, to what end did this destruction serve? He did not formally develop his troops, nor did he advance Greek society beyond supplying it with the spoils of his campaigns. The destruction of Alexander's campaigns served only to secure his own place in history—he did not create a new and better society for the Macedonians or for the people whose lands he conquered.

Source: J. Keegan, *The Mask of Command* (New York: Penguin Press, 1988).

the early 1980s, is that it has generated considerable research. As a matter of fact, much of the research already cited in this chapter has been based on Bass's theory. Bass believed that transformational leaders possessed those charismatic-leader characteristics described earlier; he used subordinates' perceptions or reactions to determine whether or not a leader was transformational. Thus, transformational leaders possess good visioning, rhetorical, and impression-management skills, and they use these skills to develop strong emotional bonds with followers. According to Bass, transactional leaders do not possess these leader characteristics, nor are they able to develop strong emotional bonds with followers or inspire followers to do more than they thought they could. Instead, transactional leaders were believed to motivate followers by setting goals and promising rewards for desired performance.

The Multifactor Leadership Questionnaire

Like the "initiating structure" and "consideration" behaviors described in Chapter 10, Bass hypothesized that transformational and transactional leadership composed two independent leadership dimensions. Thus, individuals could be high-transformational but low-transactional leaders, low-transformational and low-transactional leaders, and so on. Bass developed a questionnaire, known as the **Multifactor Leadership Questionnaire (MLQ)**, to assess the extent to which leaders exhibited transformational or transactional leadership and the extent to which followers were satisfied with their leader and believed their leader was effective. Before going into the research findings, however, we will describe the various factors comprising transformational and transactional leadership assessed by the MLQ.

Although the original version of MLQ has undergone a number of modifications over the past 15 years, the MLQ basically assesses five transformational and three transactional leadership factors (B. Avolio, personal communication, 4 February 1998; Bass, 1997). The five factors in transformational leadership are idealized attributes, idealized behaviors, inspirational motivation, individualized consideration, and intellectual stimulation. The *idealized-attribute* and *idealized-behavior* factors are essentially measures of charismatic leadership, and assess the degree to which the leader instills pride in others, displays power and confidence, makes personal sacrifices or champions new possibilities, considers the ethical or moral consequences of decisions, and talks about the importance of having a collective sense of mission. The *inspirational-motivation* factor on the MLQ assesses the leader's ability to articulate a compelling vision of the future, as well as the degree to which he or she sets challenging standards and takes a stand on controversial issues. The *individualized-consideration* factor concerns the extent to which leaders treat followers as individuals and how much of a mentoring or coaching orientation leaders have for followers. Items on this factor ask followers to indicate how much their leader gives them personal attention, coaching, personal advice, and opportunities to develop. The last transformational leadership factor is *intellectual stimulation*. Intellectual stimulation concerns the leader's vision and those behaviors that increase followers' understanding of the problems they face. Transformational leaders use intellectual stimulation to point out the problems in the current situation and contrast them with their vision of the future. Followers' heightened emotional reactions and willingness to work toward the accomplishment of the vision are believed to be the result of the leader's ability to demonstrate the behaviors associated with these five factors of the MLQ (Bass, 1997; Bass & Avolio, 1996).

The MLQ also assesses three transactional leadership factors: contingent reward, active management-by-exception, and passive management-by-exception. The *contingent-reward* factor concerns the extent to which leaders set goals, make rewards contingent on performance, obtain necessary resources, and provide rewards when performance goals have been met. Avolio and Bass (1987, 1988) maintained that contingent-reward behaviors could have positive effects on follower satisfaction and performance levels, but they also stated that these behaviors were often underutilized because of time constraints, a lack of leader skills, and a disbelief among leaders that rewards could boost performance. Bass (1997) has also maintained that contingent-reward behaviors only perpetuate the status quo; a leader's use of rewards does not result in the long-term changes associated with transformational leadership. Active and passive management-by-exception make up the other two components of transactional leadership and occur when leaders interact with followers only when standards for performance are not being met. The difference between the two factors is the degree to which leaders monitor followers' performance levels. With *active management-by-exception* leaders closely monitor followers' performance and keep track of mistakes; with *passive management-by-exception* leaders may not even be aware of problems until informed by others and generally fail to intervene until serious problems occur. Moreover, because leaders exhibiting these behaviors only interact with followers during times of substandard performance, these interventions often consist of negative feedback or punishment.

The MLQ also assesses another factor called laissez-faire leadership, which is not associated with either transformational or transactional leadership. Leaders who avoid responsibilities, fail to make decisions, are absent when needed, or fail to follow up on requests would receive higher scores on the laissez-faire leadership factor.

Research Results Using the MLQ

As stated earlier, Bass's theory of transformational and transactional leadership has generated a considerable amount of research. Curphy's (1991a) comprehensive review of this literature showed that most of these studies consisted of administering the MLQ to followers and examining the relationships among the MLQ factors or the relationships between the MLQ factors and followers' satisfaction and leader effectiveness ratings, leaders' promotion rates, or leaders' performance appraisal ratings. In general, Curphy reported that these studies showed the two dimensions of the MLQ, transformational and transactional leadership, were not independent dimensions of leadership. Instead, these two dimensions were highly related; leaders getting high ratings on one dimension tended to get high ratings on the other dimension and vice versa. These research studies also showed that both the transformational factors and the contingent-reward factor of transactional leadership were strongly related to followers' satisfaction and leader effectiveness ratings. The relationships between these leadership factors and leaders' promotion rates and performance appraisal ratings, however, were much lower.

In addition to reviewing the previous research, Curphy (1991a, 1992a) also conducted several studies at the U.S. Air Force Academy that helped to shed additional light on Bass's theory. Curphy's studies were conducted over a two-year period; used much larger sample sizes than previously reported (over 11,500 cadets rated 160 officer leaders); and used unit performance indices, attrition rates, and organizational climate ratings for leadership effectiveness criteria. Like the previous researchers, Curphy also reported that transformational and transactional leadership were not independent but rather were highly interrelated. He also reported both the transformational leadership and contingent-reward factors had strong positive correlations with organizational climate ratings.

Curphy's findings regarding unit performance indices are especially interesting. Curphy found that transformational and contingent-reward leadership had no effect on unit performance indices requiring independent effort but had strong positive effects on those unit performance indices requiring interdependent effort. Moreover, the relationships between those unit performance indices requiring interdependent effort and these leadership factors got stronger over time. Thus, there may be a time lag before one can see the effects of transformational and contingent-reward leadership and performance. Leaders may first have to concentrate on selling their vision, setting goals, developing strong attachments with followers, and administering rewards before they will see any differences in the performance of their work group or team.

More recent research with the MLQ has yielded findings consistent with those reported by Curphy. In terms of performance, Howell and Avolio (1993) found that business unit performance over a one-year period was more related to transformational than to transactional leadership, and Yammarino, Spangler, and Bass (1993) reported that transformational leaders tended to get better performance appraisal ratings later in their careers than transactional leaders. Both studies indicated that it may take time before the effects of transformational leadership are realized. Other researchers have also reported that transformational leadership has higher correlations with subordinate satisfaction levels than transactional leadership (Bass & Avolio, 1994; Yammarino, Spangler, & Bass, 1993).

Perhaps the most comprehensive review of the MLQ to date was done by Lowe, Kroeck, and Sivasubramaniam (1996). They conducted a meta-analysis to determine the statistical robustness of the MLQ and the effects of transformational and transactional leadership on various follower and organizational outcomes. With a **meta-analysis** researchers collect as many published and unpublished studies on the topic of interest as possible, and then use sophisticated statistical techniques to identify themes and trends across studies. This particular meta-analysis looked at approximately 40 studies from a variety of countries, institutions, and organizational levels, and concluded that the MLQ was a valid and reliable measure of transformational, transactional, and laissez-faire leadership.

Some of the other findings were particularly intriguing, however. Transformational leadership was observed in all countries and institutions, and at all organizational levels, but it was more prevalent in public institutions and at lower organizational levels. In other words, there seemed to be more transformational leaders in the lower levels of the military or other public-sector organizations than anywhere else. Furthermore, transformational leadership was a significantly better predictor of followers' ratings of effectiveness and organizational effectiveness indicators than transactional leadership was. Of the transformational leadership factors, idealized attributes and idealized behaviors (i e., charisma) were the best predictors of leadership success across all industries and organizational levels, but were an even better predictor of success in public organizations. Intellectual stimulation and contingent-reward were also particularly good predictors of leadership effectiveness in public organizations. Overall, followers in public organizations tended to give higher transformational and transactional leadership ratings than followers in private organizations, and the authors believed that private companies ought to do more to develop and leverage transformational leadership.

Although these findings are consistent with those reported by Curphy (1991a) and others, they raise some interesting questions for leadership practitioners. For one thing, why is transformational leadership more prevalent in the public sector? Given the public sector's reputation for change, it seems counterintuitive that this type of leadership is more common there. For another, why does transformational leadership occur more frequently among lower-level rather than more senior leaders? Might it be that the more-transformational leaders leave the organization (and thus do not become very senior), or could it be that they "tone down" such behaviors in order to better fit in and get promoted?

Training and Selecting Charismatic Leaders

Given the potential benefits of transformational or charismatic leadership, it is reasonable to wonder whether it is possible to train or select charismatic leaders. In one laboratory experiment that sheds some light on this question, several actresses were trained to exhibit charismatic, directive, or relationship-oriented behaviors as leaders of four-person work groups (Howell & Frost, 1988). For example, actresses exhibiting charismatic behaviors acted confidently and dynamically, expressed high confidence in followers, set high performance expectations, and empathized with the needs of followers. The four-person work groups of charismatic leaders performed at higher levels and had greater levels of satisfaction than the four-person work groups having a directive or relationship-oriented leader. Although some have used these findings to argue that it is possible to train leaders to be more charismatic (Avolio & Gibbons, 1988; Bass, 1988, 1997; Bass & Avolio, 1994; Conger & Kanungo, 1988), this conclusion seems somewhat premature. Because Howell and Frost did not train a leader to exhibit both high-task and high-relationship behaviors, it is uncertain whether the followers of charismatic leaders would have any higher performance or satisfaction levels than followers of 9,9 leaders (Curphy, 1991a; Yukl, 1989).

Two more-recent studies may help to shed light on whether it is possible to train charismatic or transformational leadership. As described earlier in this chapter, Kirkpatrick and Locke (1996) also used actors to demonstrate either visioning, vision implementation, and charismatic communication styles, or the complete opposites of these behaviors. Once again, vision implementation seemed to be the key to enhanced group performance. The fact that it is possible for actors to exhibit certain transformational-leadership behaviors, however, lends support to the notion that these are trainable behaviors.

To test such a notion, Barling, Weber, and Kelloway (1996) looked at the effects of transformational-leadership training on the performance of 20 bank branch managers in Canada. All 20 managers were given the MLQ, and roughly half went through a one-day training program where they were given their MLQ feedback and also participated in four individualized coaching sessions over a four-month period. The other branch managers did not receive their MLQ feedback or go through any training or coaching. When the MLQ was readministered to all 20 branch managers some time later, results showed that the managers who went through the transformational-leadership training and coaching sessions received significantly higher transformational-leadership factor ratings from followers than those managers who did not receive any feedback, training, or coaching. Moreover, the amount of credit card and personal-loan sales was significantly greater for those bank branches whose managers went through the transformational-leadership training.

Although these results are promising, they are certainly not conclusive. It is impossible to pinpoint if it was the MLQ feedback, the one-day training program, or the four coaching sessions that resulted in higher MLQ ratings over time or better financial results. We also cannot tell if the leaders would have obtained the same financial results if they had been given feedback, training, and coaching only on their contingent-reward behaviors. In sum, these initial training results for transformational leadership do look promising, but at present it is not certain such training provides distinct results from other types of systematic leadership feedback and training.

The viability of efforts to train leaders to be more charismatic will probably be limited by the fact that charisma exists ultimately in the eyes of the beholder. Thus, there never could be any guarantee that leaders schooled in the appropriate techniques will be seen as charismatic by followers. Furthermore, while it may be possible to train some leaders to improve their visioning, impression-management, and rhetorical skills, leaders who have relatively low scores on certain personality traits or other individual differences (e.g., intelligence, creativity, surgency, agreeableness, adjustment, and intellectance) may not benefit much from such training. Bass (1985), Curphy (1991a), and Segal (1985) have all stated that a leader's personality is going to have a big effect on whether the leader will be seen as charismatic. Given what we know about individual differences and leadership skills training, a leader's personality will also play a major role in determining whether he or she will benefit from such training. Although some remain firmly convinced that it is possible to train charismatic leaders (Bass, 1988, 1997; Bass & Avolio, 1994; Richardson & Thayer, 1993), this notion at best remains to be demonstrated.

An alternative to training leaders to be more charismatic could be to focus effort toward *selecting* leaders with the individual characteristics associated with charismatic leadership, and then placing them in leadership positions. Unfortunately, there are two difficulties with this strategy. First, we know very little about the personality traits that differentiate charismatic from noncharismatic leaders. A number of researchers have done some preliminary work in this regard, but much more research needs to be accomplished before we can say we have identified those traits consistently associated with charismatic leadership (Hogan, Curphy, & Hogan, 1994; Curphy & Nilsen, 1995; House, Spangler, & Woycke, 1991; House, Woycke, & Fodor, 1988; Ross & Offermann, 1991). Second, the selection of charismatic leaders is particularly difficult because—as we now have noted several times—charisma exists in the eyes of the beholders. In most cases, this means charisma is in the eyes of the followers, yet followers hardly ever play a role in the selection process (in organizations, at least). Again, much more research is needed before we can say with any confidence that we can select or train charismatic leaders.

Summary

Early research by historians, sociologists, and political scientists provided the springboard for many of the questions currently being asked about transformational leadership in organizational settings. We know today that charismatic leadership can occur in any team, group, or organizational setting. We also know transformational or charismatic leadership is more prevalent among women, lower-level leaders, and in the public sector, and that this style of leadership generally has stronger effects on leadership and organizational-effectiveness indicators than transactional or laissez-faire leadership. For example, researchers using Bass's MLQ have shown that transformational leadership is positively related to followers' attitudes toward work and their organizations, and on unit performance indices requiring interdependent effort. Research has also helped to show that values may play a key role in determining whether charismatic leaders have positive or disruptive effects on a group or organization. Charismatic leaders can be particularly disruptive if the leader's vision is in conflict with the goals of the organization or if the leader is only developing strong emotional bonds with followers for his or her own selfish ends. Finally, because charisma is an attribution followers confer upon certain leaders, it may be difficult to select or train leaders to be charismatic. We may be able to improve the odds somewhat by providing appropriate training to individuals with the requisite characteristics, but whether followers will perceive these individuals as charismatic will depend to a large extent on their own needs and expectations.

Key Terms

traditional authority system
legal-rational authority system
charismatic authority system
power-wielders
transactional leadership
modal values
transformational leadership
reframing
end values
vision
rhetorical skills
image and trust building
personalized leadership
charisma

identification with the leader
heightened emotional levels
willing subordination to the leader
spellbinders
feelings of empowerment
pygmalion effect
crises
task interdependence
interactive leadership
Bass's theory of transformational and
   transactional leadership
Multifactor Leadership Questionnaire
   (MLQ)
meta-analysis

Discussion Questions

1. Who, to you, are the most charismatic leaders in the United States today? In the world? How do they differ from noncharismatic national or world leaders?

2. President Bush had some of the highest and lowest presidential approval ratings ever reported for modern U. S. presidents. Do you think most people perceived President Bush to be a charismatic leader during his times of highest ratings (i.e., during the Gulf War)? If so, what role do you think the situation played in people's perceptions of President Bush as a charismatic or noncharismatic leader?

3. Why is it that females are seen as more-transformational leaders yet hold relatively few top leadership positions when compared to men? What, if anything, could you do to change this situation?

4. Research shows that charismatic and transformational leaders need to project an image of success, but muckraking and negativity in political campaigns are at an all-time high. Is it even possible for a political leader today to be seen as charismatic?

5. Can leaders possess the dark-side personality traits described in Chapter 8 and still be seen as charismatic?

III Focus on the Followers

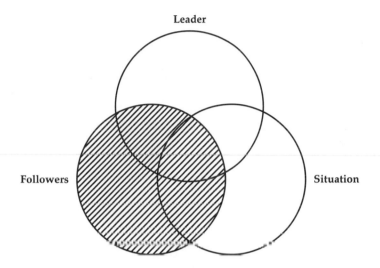

We began Part II with Napoleon's belief that the individual leader is the crucial element of leadership. We begin Part III by qualifying that sentiment. Although the importance of a good leader cannot be denied, followers also play an equally important, if often overlooked, role in the success of any group or organization. It was not, after all, Napoleon by himself who won or lost battles; his soldiers obviously played some part too. In Part III we look at the vital role played by followers in affecting the leadership process.

12 FOLLOWERS AND FOLLOWERSHIP

Introduction

Perhaps no single researcher has studied followers and followership more than Robert Kelley (1988, 1992). According to Kelley's own account, this has not been without considerable misunderstanding, if not ridicule, from others. He recounts a typical conversation from an encounter as he worked on this project while traveling as an airline passenger (1992, pp. 11–12):

"What are you working on?" (asks a fellow passenger).

"Followership," I say.

"What? Run that by me again."

"Followership—the flip side of leadership," I explain.

"Oh, you mean the people who need to be told what to do. The sheep?"

Before we provide Kelley's rejoinder to this statement, you might ask yourself at this point, "How do I view followership?" To make the question a little more personal, ask the question this way: "What would be my parents' reaction if I came home and told them I had been elected the best follower in my class?" To the degree your parents are like many of the adults we (your authors) work with in our roles helping to develop leadership, I expect the response would be less than overwhelming. To take this questioning one step further, you might even be asking yourself right now, "How did these ideas on followership even get into this book? I thought this book was about leaders and leadership." There are several reasons we feel the reader should consider these elements important in the quest for understanding leadership. First of all, there simply is no such thing as leaders without followers. It would be like trying to understand gravity without considering mass. One makes no sense without the other. Second, as we shall see, many of the characteristics of good leadership are also found in highly effective followers. It is also the case that we serve as followers for most of our organizational lives, *even when we may also be serving as leaders.*

Organizational successes and failures often get unfairly attributed to leaders, although followers may have been the true reason for successes and failure (Meindl & Ehrlich, 1987). For example, when professional sports teams are doing well or poorly, the success or failure is often unfairly attributed to the coach. Coaches are often lauded for being the key to a team's successes and are often the first to be dismissed after an abysmal season. However, a team loaded with talented players may have been successful regardless of the coach; conversely, a team with below-average players may be unsuccessful (at winning games) despite having a great coach. Thus, followers play a key role in the fate of an organization, but their contributions are often overlooked or erroneously attributed to leaders.

As we mentioned above, it is important to remember that even when one is identified as a leader, the same person often holds a complementary follower role. Almost all leaders answer to someone else; school coaches answer to athletic directors; principals answer to school superintendents, who in turn answer to school board members; managers answer to directors, who answer to vice presidents, who answer to presidents; colonels answer to generals, and so on. Most individuals will spend more time as followers than as leaders, and it is not at all uncommon to switch between being a leader and being a follower several times over the course of a day. In fact, our research on high performance teams has shown us that in the most successful teams, there is a great deal of role switching among the "followers" concerning who is serving a leadership role at any given time.

Unfortunately, the follower role has been studied very little. Research efforts have focused instead on the characteristics associated with individuals in leadership roles; relatively little research has looked at what makes successful followers. Moreover, there does not appear to be a perfect and direct relationship between good followership and good leadership. Not all good leaders were necessarily good followers, and not all good followers become good leaders. The Center for Creative Leadership has used the term *derailment* to describe what happens to individuals who eventually fail as leaders despite performing well for a long time in followership and junior leadership roles (McCall & Lombardo, 1983). It might be that such individuals fail to reflect sufficiently on their followership experiences and on the potential lessons for their own development.

In sum, because leadership is not a one-way street, and because most individuals are both leaders and followers, this chapter examines the leadership process by focusing on followers. More specifically, this chapter looks at followers from a number of different perspectives: the influence relationships between leaders and followers; effects of followers' individual characteristics on leadership; follower styles, partnering, and SYMLOG analysis of interactions within a team. The chapter concludes with a look ahead to the world of stewardship and the concurrent requirement for courageous followership.

Social Exchange and Leader-Member Relations

Much of the theoretical work on followership has emerged from the influence relationships that develop between leaders and followers. Two of the better-known theories that examine these relationships are Hollander's (1978) **social-exchange theory** and Graen and Scandura's (1987) **leader–member exchange (LMX) theory.** The latter actually emerged from earlier work by Graen and Cashman (1975), known as vertical dyad linkage (VDL) theory. In general, social exchange theory often is used to understand how power is related to the broader relationships that develop in informal, and often leaderless, groups, while leader–member exchange theory typically has been used to examine the different relationships among leaders and followers in formal organizations.

Social-Exchange Theory. When there already exists some hierarchy with appointed leaders and designated followers, such as exists in most organizations, then LMX provides a good framework for examining those relationships. But what happens when no framework exists? How does leadership occur when there are only followers? Social-exchange theory (Hollander, 1978) provides a useful explanation of this phenomenon. Social-exchange theory uses a concept called idiosyncrasy credits to explain why certain individuals emerge as leaders among their peers, or in leaderless groups. Idiosyncrasy credits represent a sort of "psychological bank account" individuals build in the eyes of others through their conformity to group norms and their competence in contributing to group goals. Individuals emerge as leaders and increase their potential to influence others by building their store of idiosyncrasy credits. For example, adolescent gang members gain more idiosyncracy credits (and therefore more power and influence) by wearing gang colors, backing up other gang members during conflicts, and robbing others to get the gang money for alcohol and drugs.

Just as one has greater latitude of financial action when a bank account is sizable, followers gain a greater latitude of action when they have a large store of idiosyncracy credits. A follower's developing leadership status and wealth of idiosyncracy credits can be thought of as "venture capital" with which to take bold action. For example, an emerging leader in a gang with plentiful idiosyncratic credits may risk attacking a strong rival gang. If the attack is successful, the emerging gang leader may wield even more power and influence. This phenomenon can also be seen in work settings where the habitual violation of certain written or unwritten rules (e.g., haircut or dress codes) is tolerated because certain individuals have earned the right to break the rules by virtue of their extraordinary contributions. However, idiosyncratic credits can also be spent by violating group norms or through failures. If the gang has a policy of not associating with members of different races and the leader is discovered secretly dating someone from another race, then the leader may lose all of the idiosyncracy credits he might have previously earned.

Hollander (1978) has generalized the process of influence and counterinfluence among followers in leaderless groups to describe the power and influence leaders have in formal organizations. He called this generalization of social-exchange theory the **transactional approach to leadership**, which has several tenets. First, the leader–follower relationship can be construed partly as an exchange of benefits. Thus, leaders give something to followers (often not tangible or monetary) and also get something from them in return. One of the most important benefits that can be exchanged is social approval. The leader's benefits often include status and the opportunity to exert influence and exercise authority. Some of the important, but subtle, benefits leaders provide to followers include structuring and directing their activities. This includes the leader's "definition of reality," that is, her analysis of the environmental pressures and opportunities the group faces.

Because of the contingencies of these mutual benefits, a sort of "psychological contract" exists between leaders and followers. In some cases, it may be a written contract (e.g., certain labor-management issues), but more often it is not. Whether formal or informal, however, the psychological contract involves the parties' understanding of their mutual rights and obligations, and dictates to a large extent the amount of power leaders can use to change the attitudes and behaviors of followers.

From this perspective, effective leadership exists when everyone perceives a fair exchange of benefits. If leaders receive benefits substantially disproportionate to their (perceived) contributions, followers may feel a sense of injustice. Followers may also feel a sense of inequity in the relationship if they perceive the leader is callous or indifferent to their interests. For example, GM autoworkers were extremely dissatisfied when they heard that former CEO Roger Smith had given himself a $2 million raise while at the same time he was closing several major plants due to falling profits. Moreover, followers may feel frustrated if the leader makes mistakes, especially if the group suffers as a result of the leader's not listening to followers' input or advice. Any of these eventualities may prompt followers to redress perceived inequities in some way. In the corporate sector, for example, this can include threats of work stoppage, industrial sabatoge, or strikes.

Leader–Member Exchange Theory.   Social exchange theory also provides the dominant theoretical basis for LMX (Sparrowe & Liden, 1997). LMX was developed to describe two kinds of relationships that occur among leaders and followers, and how these relationships affect the types of power and influence tactics leaders use (Graen & Cashman, 1975). One type of relationship is characterized by a high degree of mutual influence and attraction between the leader and a limited number of subordinates. These subordinates belong to the **in-group** and can be distinguished by the high degree of loyalty, commitment, and trust they feel toward the leader. Leaders primarily use expert, referent, and reward power to influence members of the in-group. The other subordinates belong to the **out-group**, and leaders typically use reward and legitimate and coercive power to influence them. Leaders have considerably more influence with in-group than with out-group followers. However, this greater degree of influence also has a price. If a leader uses legitimate or coercive power with in-group members, then she risks losing the high levels of loyalty and commitment they feel toward her.

Being a member of the in-group is related to several predictable outcomes. For example, in-group followers receive higher performance ratings than do out-group followers (Liden & Graen, 1980; Scandura, Graen, & Novak, 1986; Dienesch & Liden, 1986; Liden, Sparrowe, & Wayne, 1997). In addition, out-group followers have higher levels of turnover than do in-group followers (Ferris, 1985; Graen, Liden, & Hoel, 1982), and in-group followers have more-positive ratings of organizational climate than do out-group followers (Kozlowski & Doherty, 1989). Finally, it appears that higher levels of job performance by followers are more closely related to strong leader–member relations than they are to strong organizational relations (Wayne, Shore, & Liden, 1997).

Even without resorting to theory, many organizations believe followership is so important to leadership development that they make all members undergo a formalized followership experience prior to holding any type of leadership position. Staff at the U.S. Military Academy, for example, say the first step in developing leadership in new cadets is teaching them to be followers. Though it has been called the *West Point Thesis,* the view that able leaders emerge from the ranks of able followers certainly has applicability well beyond the military academies (Litzinger & Schaefer, 1982). It is also true that able followers may emerge from the ranks of able leaders. One position offering relatively little job security is that of coach of a professional athletic team; in 1991, for example, 17 former National Football League head coaches were working as assistant coaches in the NFL.

Followers as Individuals: Revisiting Characteristics of Leaders

In Chapter 1, we noted how certain myths hinder our understanding of leadership. In a similar fashion, misconceptions about followers limit our understanding of followership. To a large extent, these misconceptions spring from conventions of language that promote a narrow and restrictive understanding of the term *follower*. *Webster's New Collegiate Dictionary* (1979) defines a follower as "one in the service of another; one that follows the opinions or teachings of another; or one that imitates another." At first glance these definitions may well seem reasonable. However, they imply that followers should do nothing until they receive explicit directions from a leader and then proceed to follow those directions in an unquestioning manner. Although sometimes the unquestioning and immediate execution of a leader's directions is important, in many other instances followers need to play a more proactive role in accomplishing a task. Moreover, the definitions above are static; they ignore the fact that individuals often play a variety of leadership and followership roles. These definitions of followership seem to imply a narrower view of the follower role than is actually constructive or realistic (also see Highlight 12–1).

If common definitions are misleading, then what is a good definition of followership? Because individuals are often both leaders and followers over the course of any day, one way to differentiate leadership from followership is to think about the roles individuals play in different work groups. According to Kelley (1988), individuals who are effective in the **follower role** "have the vision to see both the forest and the trees, the social capacity to work well with others, the strength of character to flourish without heroic status, the moral and psychological balance to pursue personal and corporate goals at no cost to either, and, above all, the desire to participate in a team effort for the accomplishment of some greater purpose" (p. 107). Those who successfully fill the **leader role** have the vision to set organizational and work group goals, the interpersonal skills to achieve consensus and develop enthusiasm in others, and a strong desire to lead (Kelley, 1988). Thus, Kelley's (1988) definitions of leader and follower roles take into account both the active nature of followership and the ease with which individuals slip in and out of leadership and followership roles (see Highlights 12–2 and 12–3).

Because leaders are often more visible than followers, the ways in which various leaders differ are often recognized more clearly than the ways various followers differ (to leadership researchers, at least, if not to leadership practitioners). Moreover, because followers are often out of the limelight, it is not uncommon to think of followers as a group of fairly homogeneous or generic individuals. Relatively little of the leadership literature has examined how different follower characteristics affect the nature of leader–follower relationships, yet most leaders are constantly assessing their followers' individual characteristics and adjusting their own behavior accordingly. We think it will be helpful, therefore, to look briefly at followers in light of many of the concepts used to understand leaders as individuals. More specifically, this section uses an

Highlight 12–1

Leadership Quotes, Chapter 12

It does an organization no good when its leader refuses to share his leadership function with his lieutenants. The more centers of leadership you find in a company, the stronger it will become.

David Ogilvey

Commanders should be counseled, chiefly, by persons of known talents, by those who have made an art of war their particular study, and whose knowledge is derived from experience: from those who are present at the scene of action, who see the country, who see the enemy, who see the advantages that occasions offer, and who, like people embarked in the same ship, are sharers of the danger.

Lucius Aemilius Paulus, Roman consul who led victorious campaign against the Macedonians

A nation of sheep begets a government of wolves.

Betrand de Jouvenal

Snowflakes are one of nature's most fragile things, but just look at what they can do when they stick together.

Vesta M. Kelly

Accomplishing the impossible means only that the boss will add it to your regular duties.

Doug Larson

A community is like a ship; everyone ought to be prepared to take the helm.

Henrik Ibsen

The most important political office is that of private citizen.

Louis Brandeis

Question authority, but raise your hand first.

Bob Thaves

I like a little rebellion now and then. It is like a storm in the atmosphere.

Thomas Jefferson

Children are likely to live up to what you believe of them.

Lady Bird Johnson

I am a leader therefore I must follow.

Voltaire

The man who would lift others must be uplifted himself, and he who would command others must learn to obey.

Charles K. Ober

Highlight 12–2

Followership in High Performing Teams

What distinguishes high-performing teams and organizations from more-common-place ones? That is a question the U.S. Navy has explored for many years with the assistance of McBer and Company, a management consulting firm (Whiteside, 1985).

A simple answer to the question is that good organizations have good leaders and good followers. Just a collection of superstars, however, is not enough. This became clear after the McBer researchers conducted more than 750 interviews with ship captains and crews, administered and analyzed surveys, and examined records from numerous different sorts of ships, from aircraft carriers to submarines. They found that what set ships with truly outstanding records of performance apart from others had a lot to do with how the followers on any given ship functioned as a group.

One particularly important group of followers on any navy ship is its young officers. They have significant responsibility but also can include some of the youngest and least-experienced individuals on the entire ship. It is important to bear in mind that the navy's personnel assignment policies tended to equalize the talent among young officers across the different ships. On an individual-by-individual basis, then, one ship could not be judged much better than another, yet some clearly performed much better than the others. The following are some characteristics that distinguished followers on top-performing ships from their cohorts on more average ones:

Cohesion. The young officers on the best ships worked as a team. They interacted a lot in accomplishing their varied tasks, and they also interacted on a personal basis. Although they were not necessarily all friends, they worked effectively despite differences, and they appreciated each other's strengths. They conveyed positive expectations about each other even in the midst of a competitive system of career advancement. Among average units, on the other hand, there was more dysfunctional competition and much less mutual support. There was less communication and less coordination.

Supporting Top Leadership. On the best-performing ships, the young officers adapted to and matched the leadership objectives and style of the ship's captain. They knew and enthusiastically supported the captain's goals and philosophy, showing none of the open criticism found among young officers on more mediocre ships. The best ships were characterized by congruence of leadership at all levels.

Raising Issues with Top Leadership. The superior ships were characterized by a willingness among subordinates to ask questions, raise concerns, and bring both good and bad news to their superiors.

Taking Initiative. On the best ships, younger officers would take the initiative to do what was necessasry without being told, including extra work beyond their normally assigned duties. They also looked for better ways to accomplish their work. On more-average ships, the younger officers tended to be satisfied with just doing their own specific jobs and with the status quo; they were resistant to change and to risk.

Taking Personal Responsibility for Team Performance. On the best ships, the young officers felt a personal responsibility for the performance of their respective work groups.

Highlight 12–3

Meditation on Followership

Ira Chaleff, in his book *The Courageous Follower*, offers the following meditation on followership:

> For me, becoming a courageous follower, like becoming a good human being, is both a daily and a life-long task. Visualizing a desired state helps to realize it. I share this meditation as one visualization of the state I aspire to. You may want to refer to it from time to time.

I am a steward of this group and share responsibility for its success.
I am responsible for adhering to the highest values I can envision.
I am responsible for my successes and failures and for continuing to learn from them.
I am responsible for the attractive and unattractive parts of who I am.
I can empathize with others who are also imperfect.
As an adult, I can relate on a peer basis to other adults who are the group's formal leaders.
I can support leaders and counsel them, and receive support and counsel from them.
Our common purpose is our best guide.
I have the power to help leaders use their power wisely and effectively.
If leaders abuse power, I can help them change their behavior.
If I abuse power, I can learn from others and change my behavior.
If abusive leaders do not change their behavior, I can and will withdraw my support.
By staying true to my values, I can serve others well and fulfill my potential.
Thousands of courageous acts by followers can, one by one, improve the world.
Courage always exists in the present. What can I do today?

individual perspective to review how followers' education and experience, performance, power, influence, and other personality traits may affect the relationships among followers and between leaders and followers.

Follower Education and Experience

Followers vary tremendously in the relevant education and experiences they bring to their roles, and these differences can have a dramatic impact on the relationships among followers, and between leaders and followers. For example, as a junior officer in the U.S. Air Force, one of the authors of this book was responsible for managing the 20 enlisted and civilian personnel in a data processing office. The education and experience of these personnel ranged from green 18-year-olds to 55-year-old World War II veterans with master's degrees.

Needless to say, these differences affected the nature of the relationships among the followers in the office and the manner in which the leader interacted with the various followers. The junior and inexperienced personnel needed almost constant guidance, coaching, and feedback, whereas the senior personnel needed only general guidance and periodic feedback in order to maintain high levels of performance. Moreover, the inexperienced personnel often looked up to and sought out the more senior personnel for guidance on how to improve their performance and for personal advice. Leaders will be more effective if they understand and appreciate their subordinates' backgrounds, training, education, and other relevant experiences.

It also will be important for leaders to understand certain trends in the sort of education and skills needed by followers. Workers today are better educated than ever before. One out of four workers between the ages of 25 and 64 is college educated, twice as many as 20 years ago; 85 percent have at least a high school education. Two implications of these facts for leadership are the greater number of options such workers have and the greater expectations they have concerning what a job should be like. A third implication for leadership involves a move away from the sort of control-oriented supervision of workers common when tasks were relatively routine, when power tended to be centralized in supervisors' hands, and when innovation was discouraged (Naisbitt & Aburdene, 1990).

Although workers are better educated than ever, the need for continuing education and training on the job also will increase. One reason is that the technology of work is rapidly changing, and workers will be regularly updating their knowledge and skill bases to stay proficient with new task requirements. Alvin Toffler (1970) coined the term **future shock** 25 years ago to describe the accelerating rate of change in all aspects of our lives, and the increasing pace of technological change at work is no exception. As just one example, companies now recognize the competitive advantage of reducing the time it takes to get new products to customers (cycle time). General Electric has reduced the time it takes to produce customized circuits from three weeks to three days; Motorola has reduced the time it takes to make electronic pagers from three weeks to two hours (Naisbitt & Aburdene, 1990). Working in an environment of constant change takes a new kind of leadership and a new kind of followership. It will put a premium on what perhaps will be the most-essential followership skill of the future: learning how to learn (Naisbitt & Aburdene, 1985).

Along with requirements to deal with the accelerating rate of technological change, essential follower skills also will change because of a pervasive trend to flatten organizational structures. Middle management is being reduced as much as 40 percent in some organizations (Naisbitt & Aburdene, 1985), and much of the authority previously reserved for that level is being delegated to followers.

Follower Power and Influence

Leaders need to bear in mind that they are not the sole possessors of power and influence in their work units; followers can wield considerable influence both with other followers and with the leader. Popular followers may be able to use referent power, and followers with high levels of education and experience may be able to use their expert power to influence other followers and the leader. However, followers in a leader's in-group may wield considerably more power and influence on the leader than followers in the out-group. Followers may even exercise coercive powers over leaders in certain situations. The practice of "fragging" certain leaders in Vietnam is an extreme example of this phenomenon: Leaders who were deemed to be dangerous or those who were perceived as not looking out for their subordinates would be subjected to having a hand grenade rolled into their tent. Leaders need to be cognizant of how these different bases of power and influence affect leader–follower and interfollower relationships.

Other Follower Characteristics

A variety of studies have shown that higher intelligence is associated with higher performance at work (Hunter & Hunter, 1984; Ree & Earles, 1992; Schmidt, Gast-Rosenberg, & Hunter, 1980). Also, research on followers' personality traits has shown that tolerance of stress, agreeableness, and dependability were related to performance in blue-collar jobs (Hogan, 1991; Tett, Jackson, & Rothstein, 1991).

Other research has suggested that a leader's effectiveness may well depend on the match between the leader's personality and the followers' personalities. This research specifically looked at the personality trait of locus of control. Although not discussed as a trait in Chapter 8, locus of control involves a person's expectations about her ability to influence people and events around her. People who believe they are "masters of their own ship" are said to have an **internal locus of control;** people who believe they are (relatively speaking) "pawns of fate" are said to have an **external locus of control** (Rotter, 1966). A study of more than 1,000 employees of a public utility indicated that subordinates' locus of control influenced their preference for their supervisors' practices. Subordinates with an internal locus of control preferred a participatory management style, but subordinates with an external locus of control preferred a directive style (Mitchell, Smyser, & Weed, 1975). Other findings indicated that supervisors with an external locus of control provide more structure and guidance to subordinates than those with an internal locus (Durand & Nord, 1976). Taken together, these findings suggest that subordinates with an external locus of control prefer the behaviors exhibited by leaders with an external locus of control.

We believe that even more research should be conducted on how leadership effectiveness is affected by follower personality traits, values, and preferences. It will be helpful to understand better how leader–follower and interfollower relationships are affected by characteristics like followers' tolerance to stress, agreeableness, dependability, dominance, and self-confidence. Similarly, some work-group conflicts can be understood as the result of differences in followers' values and preferences. For example, followers with a preference for judging (as assessed with the MBTI) may find themselves in frequent conflict when working on projects with others who have a preference for perceiving, as the latter's relative disinclination to make decisions, plan, structure, and reach closure may frustrate the former.

It also is advisable for leaders to be aware of several trends dealing with changes in follower motivation and values that will impact the leadership process. No longer can we assume—as perhaps we could 20 years ago—that workers feel loyal to their company or are primarily concerned with job security. Today, employees are far less committed to their organizations, especially when leadership is poor. They value balance between their work and personal lives, and seek more from work than just fair pay. This includes having work that is challenging and worthwhile, and having opportunities to be creative and develop personally on the job. They expect increased communication with management, participation in decisions that affect them, and flexibility in options afforded them (Mindell & Gorden, 1981; Naisbitt & Aburdene, 1990).

Followership Styles

Recall the opening dialogue in this chapter between Robert Kelley and a fellow airline passenger. The closing line by the traveler was, "Oh, you mean the people who need to be told what to do. The sheep?" Here now is Kelley's reply:

> No, I mean the people who know what to do without being told—the people who act with intelligence, independence, courage, and a strong sense of ethics. I'm interested in what separates exemplary followers from those who perpetuate the negative stereotypes. I believe the value of followers to any organization is enormous.

With that sense of the value of followers, Kelley has studied followership not as the antithesis of leadership but rather with the view that followers are *collaborators* with leaders in the work of organizations.

Just as the Ohio State University leadership studies categorized leader behaviors into two broad dimensions, it may also be possible to categorize follower behaviors or styles using a two-dimensional taxonomy. Kelly (1992) derived these two dimensions not by culling the journals of academic research but rather by interviewing leaders and followers. One of these dimensions ranges from **independent, critical thinking** at one end to **dependent, uncritical thinking** on the othe rend. "The best followers are individuals who 'think for themselves,' 'give constructive criticism,' 'are their own person,' and are 'innovative and creative.' At the other end of the spectrum, the worst followers 'must be told what to do,' 'can't make it to the bathroom on their own,' and 'don't think.' In between are the typical followers, who 'take direction' and 'don't challenge leader or group'" (p. 93). But independent critical thinking is not enough to capture all of what highly effective followers do.

Kelley's second dimension refers to a follower's degree of active engagement in work. This dimension ranges from **active** to **passive**. According to Kelley, "the best followers 'take initiative,' 'assume ownership,' 'participate actively,' 'are self-starters,' and 'go above and beyond the job.' The worst ones

Figure 12–1

*Followership
Styles*

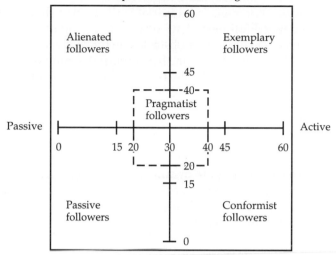

Independent, critical thinking

Source: Figure from Robert E. Kelley, *The Power of Followership* (New York: Doubleday, 1992). © 1992 by Consultants to Executives and Organizations, Ltd. Used by permission of Doubleday, a division of Bantam-Doubleday-Dell, Inc.

are 'passive,' 'lazy,' 'need prodding,' 'require constant supervision,' and 'dodge responsibility.' In between these extremes are the typical followers who 'get the job done without supervision after being told what to do,' 'CYA,' and 'shift with the wind'" (p. 94).

Moreover, because behavior tends to be consistent over time, Kelley (1988, 1992) believed it was possible to use his two-dimensional taxonomy to categorize people as one of five styles of followers (see Figure 12–1). We will discuss each of these styles separately and will conclude with the ideal or exemplary follower.

Alienated Followers

Alienated followers are like festering wounds in their organizations; they are continuing sore spots who are more than happy to point out all the negative aspects of organizational goals, policies, and procedures—and overlook the positive aspects. Kelley says this style is seen in 15 to 25 percent of followers, individuals known to be capable but cynical, frequently holding back their own best efforts, or perhaps displaying disgruntled acquiescence. Interestingly, their own self-image often differs significantly from their image as seen from their leader's perspective. Alienated followers often describe themselves as "mavericks who think for themselves," "having a healthy skepticism," or even as "being the true conscience of the organization." Leaders often see the alienated follower as "troublesome, cynical, negative, headstrong but lacking judgment," "not a team player, "or even "adversarial to the point of being hostile." Kelley believes that alienated followers tend be former exemplary followers who became disgruntled over setbacks or obstacles, so the move to being exemplary followers again may depend much on their own self-examination and reducing their level of negativity through constructive problem solving.

Conformist Followers

Conformist followers are the "yes people" of organizations. They are the active followers who readily carry out orders uncritically. These followers, while very active at doing the organization's work, can be dangerous if their orders contradict societal standards of behavior or organizational policy. Their problem is that they do not critically evaluate the orders they have been given. Historically, this follower style has been associated with horrible events in war. The followers of Lt. William Calley in the Vietnam massacre at My Lai and the Nazi functionaries in World War II concentration camps whose work contributed to the murder of millions of Jews exemplify this pattern. More recently, Oliver North displayed this pattern in his role as a follower when he stated during the Reagan-era Iran Contra hearings that he "was not in the habit of questioning his superiors." Often this style is the result of either the demanding and authoritarian style of the leader or the overly rigid structure of the organization. These considerations will be discussed in more detail in subsequent chapters. It may be the case that many of the 20 to 30 percent of followers who behave according to this style have a personality predisposition to be obsequious and self-deprecating or averse to conflict. As with the alienated follower described above, the conformist follower already possesses one of the valued dimensions of the exemplary follower (albeit the mirror image of the alienated follower). The conformist is already an active participant who is seen as a committed contributor. Conformists also need to recognize, however, that the organization needs their critical views as well. Making this transition will require them to begin to critically evaluate others' ideas (including the leader's), and to gain confidence in their own viewpoints.

Pragmatist Followers

Pragmatist followers are followers who are rarely committed to work-group goals but have learned not to make waves. Because they do not like to stick out, these pragmatists, or survivors, tend to be mediocre performers and clog the arteries of many organizations. Pragmatists, who Kelley said comprise between 25 to 35 percent of the follower force, are those who keep to the center of the road. Because it can be difficult to discern just where they stand on issues, they present an ambiguous image with both positive and negative characteristics. On the positive side, they are sometimes seen as "keeping things in perspective," "knowing how to work the system to get things done," "toeing the middle line so as to keep the organization from going overboard in either direction," or "playing by the rules of the game." Unfortunately, these same behaviors can be interpreted as "playing political games," "bargaining to maximize your own self interest," "being averse to risk and prone to cover your tracks," and "being a bureaucrat who adheres to the letter of the rule rather than the spirit" (Kelley, 1992. p. 116).

Like the other styles, the pragmatist follower may adopt this style as a result of organizational conditions, personal preferences, or some combination of the two. It can be a survivor mode adopted as a coping mechanism in order to "ride out the storm" in an unstable or particularly turbulent organizational environment. Pragmatist followers may become so comfortable in that survivor mode, however, that they remain in that mode even after the storm has passed. Another possibility is that pragmatists are simply averse to taking any risks. A pragmatist may be capable of doing a good job, but be unwilling to do so if it requires him to stick his own neck out. Avoiding failure may be more important than any possible gain from success. In organizational settings, pragmatists may become experts in mastering the bureaucratic rules which can be used to protect them. If they must initiate an action, for example, they may not move until they have signatures from everybody on the "coordination sheet." Pragmatist followers are "stuck in the middle," and to change must decide whether mere organizational survival is sufficiently fulfilling for them. In times of crisis, the answer may well be yes. In more munificent times, however, that may not be enough. If the pragmatist chooses to seek more than organizational survival, he must be willing to stretch along both dimensions of effective followership.

Passive Followers

According to Kelley, only 5 to 10 percent of all followers fall into the style of **passive follower**. These followers display *none* of the characteristics of the exemplary follower. They "look to the leader to do their thinking, and they do not carry out their assignments with enthusiasm. Lacking in initiative and a sense of responsibility, they require constant direction when performing the tasks given them and never venture beyond their assignment" (Kelley, 1992, p. 122). Leaders often see passive followership to be the result of the personality of the follower in that role. They see them as lazy, incompetent, unmotivated, or stupid. While there may be some passive followers who do indeed possess these characteristics, there are likely to be an even greater number who have adopted this style to help them cope with a leader who expects followers to behave that way. Our own research looking at teams has found that team members often behave the way they do in response to the leader and other conditions, not because they are passive by nature (these points will be discussed in much greater detail in the section on the Team Effectiveness Leadership Model, in Chapter 13). In order to improve their effectiveness, passive followers need to change significantly on both dimensions of effective followership, just as pragmatist followers do. They may be served best by leaving the organization.

Exemplary Followers

As opposed to the other styles of followers who present different images depending upon the perspective (e.g., self, leader, co-workers, etc.), the **exemplary follower** seems to present a consistent picture to all who come in contact with him or her. Exemplary followers are seen by co-workers and leaders as independent, innovative, creative, and willing to stand up to superiors. They apply their talents for the benefit of the organization even when confronted with bureaucratic stumbling blocks or passive or pragmatist co-workers. Effective leaders appreciate the value of exemplary followers. When one of the authors was serving in a follower role in a staff position, he was introduced by his leader to a conference as "my favorite subordinate because he's a loyal No-man." This type of description of exemplary followers is not uncommon. Kelley quoted Michael Eisner, the CEO of Walt Disney Co., in describing one of his best followers: "[He] is a great devil's advocate. I mean, he will ask the questions nobody ever thought of, and he will take the opposite side of everything. But he is a deal maker, not a deal breaker and that's very unique" (Kelley, 1992, p. 128). Exemplary followers—high on both critical dimensions of followership—are critical to organizational success. Leaders, therefore, would be well advised to select people who have these characteristics, *and perhaps even more importantly*, to create the conditions that encourage these behaviors.

Kelley noted one other critical benefit to be gained from exemplary followers. They know how to get along with their co-workers and leaders in ways that benefit the organization. Kelley used the analogy of the commons to illustrate this ability. While the term *commons* is familiar to many college students, Kelley (1992) described its origins in a sense that adds meaning to organizational settings as well as college campuses:

> Unlike followers who consistently try to maximize only their own self-interest, the best followers view the organization as a "commons." The term "commons" dates back to pre-industrial England. It refers to the pasture that townspeople shared in "common" with each other for grazing their livestock. The challenge facing the community was to enable everyone to feed their livestock without degrading the commons for future grazing. If one family maximized their feeding at the expense of the community, they gained in the short run. But if everyone followed suit, all the grass would get eaten, destroying the commons for everyone. For all to benefit, each family had to contribute to maintaining the commons by keeping their selfishness in check.
>
> The best followers treat the organization as a commons. Instead of taking a free ride at the organization's expense or focusing solely on their rights, they acknowledge the mutual responsibilities they have with others. Organizational life requires give-and-take if it is going to work. If you are going to drink from the organizational well, you must also help replenish it. (p 149)

Partnering

Since followership is still such a new field of study, it seems appropriate to include mention of some promising work in progress by a team of researchers (Potter, Rosenbach, & Pittman, 1996; Rosenbach, Pittman, & Potter, 1997; Pittman,

Rosenbach & Potter, 1998). These researchers are focusing on an issue they call **partnering**, dealing with the quality of *relationships* between leaders and followers rather than on characteristics of leaders and followers per se. In interviews with effective leaders and followers they have found that the best relationships feel like partnerships. As with any effective partnerships, both partners recognize that they can only be successful in the long term if they share success. Each is flexible and willing to switch between the roles of leader and follower, performing the role that best facilitates achieving the goals of the group or organization.

Rosenbach, Pittman, and Potter began their work making two key assumptions. The first was that followers do not work with an intent to fail—that all workers who *can* survive in the workplace give what they believe will be at least enough effort to keep their jobs. Second, the researchers assumed that leaders do not intend to purposefully alienate the people on whom they depend for their success. Nonetheless, experience and prevailing wisdom have seldom taught followers that anyone who takes the personal initiative to strengthen a relationship with a boss will be more effective. In fact, efforts to build an effective relationship with the boss are more often understood by both parties as ingratiating and advantage-seeking rather than as a sincere effort to build an effective partnership. Consequently, the research team has begun work on an instrument to help followers and leaders develop better partnerships.

Like Kelley's work, the work of this team has developed around these two dimensions: a commitment to high performance and a commitment to develop effective relationships with their partners. Taken together these two dimensions, **performance initiative** and **relationship initiative**, define four types of followers who are familiar to students of the workplace: the **subordinate**, the **valued contributor**, the **politician**, and the **partner**.

The subordinate is the "traditional" follower who does what he or she is told. The subordinate keeps a job and may rise in a seniority-driven organization but demonstrates neither a sensitivity to relationships nor a commitment to high performance. They share much in common with Kelley's "passive follower." The valued contributor behaves in an exemplary way—one who works hard and is known for the quality of her work. Although this person is thorough and creative in obtaining the resources, information, and skills that are needed to do the job, the interpersonal dynamics of the workplace are not of a primary concern. The politician pays more attention to managing relationships than to maximizing performance. This person possesses valuable interpersonal qualities that are often misdirected or misunderstood. Followers such as these are unusually sensitive to interpersonal dynamics and are valuable for their ability to contribute when interpersonal difficulties have arisen or might arise. They can provide valuable assistance to the leader because they are willing and able to give insights into group relationships. However, often these followers neglect the defined aspects of their jobs in favor of the more relationship-oriented or political aspects of their relationship with the boss. This is a particular problem when others rely on them for job performance. The partner is committed to high performance and effective relationships. In fact, the energy given to the development of relationships serves the purpose of gaining the kind of understanding that leads to plans and actions that anticipate new directions and contributions that serve unmet goals.

A significant contribution has also been made by Rosenbach, Pittman and Potter in the instrument they developed to assess these two dimensions. Their **Performance and Relationship Questionnaire (PRQ)** (Rosenbach, Pittman & Potter,1997) allows followers not only to assess their style as described above but also to assess four critical components of each of the two dimensions. The performance initiative considers the extent to which the follower thinks of ways to get his or her assigned job done (**doing the job**), the extent to which the follower treats himself or herself as a valuable resource (**self as resource**), how well the follower works with co-workers (**working with others**), and what view the follower takes toward organizational and environmental change (**embracing change**). Similarly, the relationship initiative considers the extent to which the followers understand and identify with the leader's vision for the organization (**identifying with the leader**), the extent to which the follower actively tries to engender mutual trust with the leader (**building trust**), the extent to which the follower is willing to communicate in a courageous fashion with the leader (**courageous communication**), and how actively the follower works to negotiate differences with the leader (**negotiating differences**).

Finally, Rosenbach, Pittman, & Potter (1998) remind us that while their instrument is quite effective at assessing the follower style currently exhibited, it does not specify the reasons for that style. In order to understand the reasons why a particular follower style is being exhibited, they write, one must "think about the followers, leadership styles, and organizational culture together"—as we have noted in the unifying framework throughout this book.

SYMLOG: A Method for Rating and Graphing Follower Behavior

One obvious similarity in both of the preceding two sections on followership is the idea of two fundamental dimensions of effective followership (or partnerships). In this section we will look at a model which is not limited to just two dimensions.

SYMLOG is an acronym for the <u>SY</u>stematic <u>M</u>ultiple <u>L</u>evel <u>O</u>bservation of <u>G</u>roups. Based upon the lifelong work of Robert F. Bales, it represents an integration of personality theory and group dynamics along with a set of practical methods for measuring and changing behavior. In our work with high-performance teams, we have found it to be an extremely useful tool, especially for helping a group examine the behaviors and underlying values of a leader and the followers in their natural group setting. The model is considerably more complex than we (or you!) would want to cover in this section (Bales has identified 26 behavioral characteristics of importance in group situations), so we will look at just one way of presenting SYMLOG data and focus on its utility for helping followers define and change their behavior to improve effectiveness.

The SYMLOG Field Diagram

Bales described the **field diagram** as a map where the location of each follower (and leader) of the group is shown as a circle labeled with each member's name immediately to the right of their circle. The particular location of each circle in the field is referred to as the "image" of that member. The image is derived from multiple ratings of that person's behavior by other members of the team and is computed as the arithmetical mean of the collective inputs about that particular follower.

The dimensions of the field represent three important bipolar characteristics:

1. Dominance versus submissiveness.
2. Friendliness versus unfriendliness.
3. Acceptance versus nonacceptance of authority.

Because these dimensions are bipolar, each can be thought of as two opposing directions radiating out from the center of the field, which would be the neutral or zero point between the two directions. Unfortunately, Bales developed this multidimensional view of groups and followers before the days of computerized three dimensional graphics. He did, however, come up with an intriguing method for presenting all three dimensions on a flat plane.

Bales uses the second and third dimensions listed above to define the plane in a two dimensional model such as Kelley's. **Friendliness–unfriendliness** represents the horizontal dimension, or "X-axis," of the field, and **acceptance–nonacceptance of authority** represents the vertical dimension, or "Y-axis." These two dimensions intersect at a single point which would be the center of the image circle for any given follower. The first dimension listed above, **dominance–submissiveness**, is derived from the intersection of a plane and a cone, resulting in a circle. The relative size of the circle of the image represents the relative dominance of the particular follower. The metaphor of circle size and relative dominance is a useful mnemonic—the more dominant the follower, the larger the image circle, and, conversely, the smaller the image circle, the more submissive the follower.

A sample field diagram is presented in Figure 12–2. By the relative size of the circles we can see that Tom, Mark, and Mary are larger than other followers. Mark's image circle is the largest, indicating that he is perceived by the group as the most dominant follower. Judy and Bill have the smallest circles, which would tell us that, in the eyes of other followers, they are seen as the most submissive followers in the group.

Sue and Mary are seen as the followers exhibiting the most friendly behaviors while Bill and Charles, whose images are to the left side of the field diagram, are seen as displaying behaviors perceived to be self-interested, individualistic, and self-protective. Sue and Mary are perceived to be most equalitarian, cooperative, and protective of others.

The closer one's image is to the top of the field diagram, the more one is seen as "accepting the task orientation of established authority." This means

FIGURE 12–2

*Sample Field
Diagram*

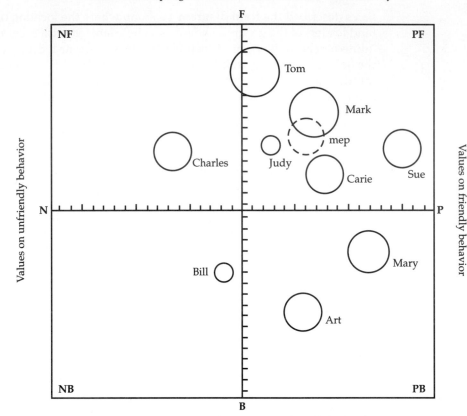

Values on accepting the task-orientation of established authority

Values on opposing the task-orientation of established authority

Source: Used with permission.

that one generally accepts the rules and procedures that have been set up by authorities, both within and external to the group. Again in Figure 12–2, Tom and Mark are most extreme in this dimension, indicating they are seen by the group as having a high commitment to established authority and to the task as defined by authority. At the same time, Mark is seen as more friendly than Tom as well as slightly more dominant. At the other extreme, Mary, Bill, and Art are farthest toward the bottom of the field, indicating that they are perceived by others as unconcerned with the group's task or opposing the task work as defined by authority. Notice also that Mary is seen as more friendly than either Art or Bill, and less opposed to authority than Art. It may well be that Mary is more concerned with interpersonal needs within the group. Indeed, she may be trying to soften the requirements of authority in order to avoid conflict in the group. Because Bill is on the unfriendly side of the field and reasonably in opposition to authority, he is likely seen by other members as the follower most obstructing the progress of the group by focusing attention on himself and disrupting the group's work.

There are many other uses of SYMLOG that go well beyond the scope of this section. But several other aspects are worthy of mention relative to follower images. First note the image designated "mep." This is not a follower but is normative position established by years of research to be the "most effective profile." It is characterized by an orientation that is friendly, accepting of authority, and somewhat more powerful than neutral. We can see that both Mark and Judy are close to the "mep" but that Mark may be overly dominant while Judy appears to be too submissive. By being shown their image relative to the "mep," followers will gain insight into why they treat others as they do and why others may behave in characteristic ways toward them. They will also have the information to make corrections in their behavior that may improve their perceived effectiveness both by leaders and by their peer followers.

If we were to overlay a line from the lower left corner of the field to the upper right (the line referred to by Bales as the "Line of Polarization") and disregarded for the moment the size of the circles (or relative dominance), we would find a remarkable similarity to the work by Kelley and by Rosenbach, Pittman, and Potter in one interesting dimension. Those followers in the upper right quadrant would generally be seen as displaying positive behaviors relative to the team while those in the lower left quadrant would be seen as more negative. The other interesting and useful aspect of SYMLOG relative to this line of polarization is to consider the outliers, or those farthest away from the line. In this sense we would focus our attention on the expected roles for Mary and Charles. Because Mary is not particularly aligned with the task orientation of the group but is seen as quite friendly, she may be a very effective **mediator** for the discrepant views of other followers. Charles is also away from the line of polarization but he also suffers from his image as unfriendly. As a result, in times of group tension, Charles may attract negative feelings from all sides, making him a likely **scapegoat.** Knowing these potentials can be very useful not only for the group as a whole but also for the individual followers. For example, if the above potential was presented to Charles, he might decide that it would be useful for him to pay attention to the image he is presenting to the group. Instead of concentrating on his own project, he might focus some of his attention on how he could contribute to the work of others. He might also take notice of more of the interpersonal factors in everyday group life, and improve his skills in this regard. By moving in a more positive or friendly direction, he would be less likely to assume the scapegoat role for the group. We will discuss group roles more in subsequent chapters.

Stewardship and Courageous Followership

As a way of looking forward to the challenges of followership in the future, we thought it might be appropriate to consider a concept that turns traditional models of leadership thinking on their heads. Such a view is presented by Peter Block

(1993). Block suggests that the traditional models of leadership and management need to be replaced, and that even when organizations have considered such changes, they have been restricted to rhetoric and cosmetic changes. By replacing the traditional management tools of control and consistency with opportunities for partnerships and choices at all levels, individuals will begin to see themselves as stewards of the organization's purpose. This notion of **stewardship** is not solely directed at our views of leadership, although there are certainly critical changes that will need to occur in that venue if the practice is to change. But of importance here is the notion that there will need to be changes made in the behaviors and expectations of the followers as well.

In commenting on this change, Block notes that stewardship requires us to "act on our own account. We cannot be stewards of an institution and expect someone else to take care of us. Regardless of how parental our environment may be, we decide whether to support efforts to treat us like children, which expresses our wish for dependency, or whether to keep deciding that we serve the organization best by creating a place of our own choosing." In support of this but in a larger sense, he suggests that we have paid a price for our top-down, parenting, patriarchal governance system: "Democracy can not survive if we only experience it for a moment of voting every two or four years. If day in and day out we go to a workplace that breeds helplessness and compliance, this becomes our generalized pattern of response to the larger questions of our society, and in fact most other aspects of our lives."

What is most intriguing about these problems associated with patriarchy is that even though we see the costs, and according to Block, "spend half our lives complaining about those above us in the hierarchy, we still think leadership is necessary to organize effort and get work done." Perhaps part of this problem is in the nature of the followers themselves. According to Byham (see Kinni, 1994) about 20 percent of the workforce have been waiting anxiously for empowerment, most of the rest will move slowly into that opportunity when offered, and 5 percent will be completely unable to make the transition to an empowered system. And this is only one of the areas in which the diversity inherent in the legions of followers will make a difference. In the future, diversity of effective workforces will not only include considerations of gender and race but also of wide variations in temperaments, age, personal preferences, knowledge, national origins, life and cultural experiences, capabilities, and world views.

Regardless of one's predisposition to assume the mantle of stewardship, it will require courage to step forward into the future and out of the traditions of the past. In his book on the subject of courageous followership, Chaleff (1995) notes a number of challenges facing tomorrow's effective followers as they move forward. Most notable are the requirements for the courage to assume responsibility, the courage to serve, the courage to challenge, the courage to participate in transformation, and finally (and most fittingly) the courage to leave. While there are numerous examples and descriptions of the ways courage will be required that the reader may wish to examine for more detail, such details seems superfluous at this point. What seems more appropriate here as a way to close this

chapter would be to recognize the fundamental tensions that underlie courageous followership. Chaleff lists a number of these tensions and paradoxes:

- A courageous follower has a clear internal vision of service while being attracted to a leader who articulates and embodies its external manifestation.
- Courageous followers remain fully accountable for their actions while relinquishing some autonomy and conceding certain authority to a leader.
- A central dichotomy of courageous followership is the need to energetically perform two opposite roles: implementer and challenger of the leader's ideas.
- There is inherent tension between the identity a follower derives from group membership and the individuation required to question and creatively challenge the group and its leadership.
- Followers often benefit from the leader as mentor, learning crucial things, yet at the same time must be willing to teach the leader.
- At times, courageous followers need to lead from behind, breathing life into their leader's vision, or even vision into the leader's life.
- Senior followers often are important leaders in their own right and must integrate within themselves the perspective of both leadership and followership.

Summary

The importance of followers seems, somewhat curiously, to have been dramatically undervalued. Followers usually play a key role in organizational successes
and failures, yet these outcomes are often attributed solely to leaders. Followers
have also been relatively unappreciated by leadership researchers; followers
tend to be either ignored completely or considered to be a relatively homogeneous group of individuals in most leadership research studies. Additionally,
we have given too little attention to the fact that many individuals, in larger
organizations at least, are both followers and leaders at the same time. In an
absolute sense, everyone has spent and will spend more time as a follower than
as a leader, and spending time reflecting on follower experiences may be one
important key to leadership success.

Because most people spend so much time as followers, and because followers play such an important role in organizational outcomes, this chapter has
reviewed the theoretical underpinnings of followership, including social-
exchange theory and leader–member exchange theory. We then examined followership from four different perspectives. First, the individual perspective
showed that followers differ in as many ways as leaders do. This should hardly
be surprising. Nevertheless, the myriad ways followers can differ from each
other are often overlooked, and these differences can have a major impact on followers' behaviors.

Second, the characteristic styles of followers and followership based on the work of Robert Kelley were presented. Both by being a critical, independent thinker and by playing an active, constructive role, the follower was most apt to be seen in an exemplary style. In a similar manner, Rosenbach, Pittman, and Potter are investigating ways the follower and leader can partner for their mutual benefit as well as the good of the organization as a whole. Their work indicates that a follower who is most apt to be seen as a partner is one who is simultaneously committed to both high performance and to developing effective relationships with the leader.

The work of Bales and his SYMLOG model were presented as a way to help followers identify the behaviors they are presenting to other team members and to give them direction should they decide to change. Equally important is the notion Bales presents of more than two dimensions as important for followers to be aware of. His concept of images in field space provides a useful way for us to conceptualize these complexities that better represent reality.

In closing, the challenges for followers inherent in a stewardship model were discussed along with the requirements for courageous followers if significant change is to occur in the future.

Key Terms

social-exchange theory
idiosyncracy credits
in-group
follower role
leader role
active
individual perspective
future shock
internal locus of control
external locus of control
passive followers
conformist followers
pragmatist followers
alienated followers
exemplary followers
partnering
performance initiative
scapegoat

leader–member exchange theory
transactional approach to leadership
out-group
independent, critical thinking
dependent, uncritical thinking
passive
relationship initiative
subordinate
valued contributor
politician
partner
SYMLOG
field diagram
friendliness–unfriendliness
acceptance–nonacceptance of authority
dominance–submissiveness
mediator

Discussion Questions

1. Ted Turner, *Time* magazine's Man of the Year for 1991, has a plaque on his desk saying "Lead, follow, or get out of the way." Do you agree with that view? Discuss its implications in the context of leader and follower roles.
2. What qualities do you think characterize the ideal follower? In what ways is this list different, if at all, from one characterizing the ideal leader?
3. Do you think the idea of studying partnerships is different from studying followers and leaders? In what ways?
4. In Figure 12–2 (the SYMLOG Field Diagram), why would the other followers want Bill on their team? What could they do to help him change his behavior?
5. Kelley sees "critical, independent thinking" as an important characteristic of effective followers. Bales places value on "acceptance of the task orientation of authority"? Can these two views be reconciled?
6. What would a stewardship model of a university look like? What responsibilities would be shifted from the faculty and the administration to the students under such a concept? Would it work?

13 GROUPS, TEAMS, AND THEIR LEADERSHIP

Introduction

Understanding the unique characteristics that make individual followers tick is useful to leaders, but not enough. Leaders also need to understand how followers *as a group* represent something that cannot be understood solely in terms of the group members' collective individual characteristics. While both leadership and followership often have been conceptualized in terms of characteristics of individuals, it is interesting to note that a survey of 35 texts on organizational behavior found that in each one, the chapter on leadership is in the section on group behavior, not in the section on individual behavior (Ginnett, 1992). This should not be terribly surprising since groups (even as small as two people) are essential if leaders are to impact anything beyond their own behavior. What may be surprising is that the concept of groups is sometimes omitted entirely from books on leadership. As stated earlier, the whole can be greater than the sum of its parts, and the **group perspective** looks at how different group characteristics can affect relationships both with the leader and among followers (also see Highlight 13–1).

This chapter will begin by examining some of the characteristic of groups that uniquely differentiate them from individual phenomena. Given the high interest in organizational team work, we will move from the group to the team and conclude with a model developed to help leaders design, diagnose, and leverage high-impact factors to create the conditions which foster team effectiveness.

The Nature of Groups

Perhaps we should begin by defining just what a **group** is. A group can be thought of as "two or more persons who are interacting with one another in such a manner that each person influences and is influenced by each other person" (Shaw, 1981). Three aspects of this definition are particularly important to the study of leadership. First, this definition incorporates the concept of reciprocal influence between leaders and followers, an idea considerably different from the one-way nature of influence implicit in the dictionary's definition of followers. Second, group members interact and influence each other. Thus, people waiting at a bus stop would not constitute a group, as there generally is neither interaction nor influence between the various individuals. On the other hand, eight people meeting to plan a school bond election would constitute a group, as there probably would be a high level of mutual interaction among the attendees. Third, the definition does not constrain individuals to only one group. Everyone belongs to a number of different groups; an individual could be a member of various service, production, sports, religious, parent, and volunteer groups simultaneously.

It is important to realize that though people belong to many groups, just as they do to many organizations, groups and organizations are not the same thing (groups, of course, can exist within organizations). Organizations can be so large that most members do not know most of the other people in the organization. In such cases there is relatively little intermember interaction and reciprocal influence. Similarly, organizations typically are just too large and impersonal to have much effect on anyone's feelings, whereas groups are small and immediate enough to impact both feelings and self-image. People often tend to identify more with the groups they belong to than with the organizations they belong to; they are more psychologically "invested" in their groups. Also, certain important psychological needs (e.g., social contact) are better satisfied by groups than by organizations.

Highlight 13–1

Leadership Quotes, Chapter 13

Trying to change individual and/or corporate behavior without addressing the larger organizational context is bound to disappoint. Sooner or later bureaucratic structures will consume even the most determined of collaborative processes. As Woody Allen once said, "The lion and the lamb may lie down together, but the lamb won't get much sleep." What to do? Work on the lion as well as the lamb designing teamwork into the organization. . . . Although the Boston Celtics have won 16 championships, they have never had the league's leading scorer and never paid a player based on his individual statistics. The Celtics understand that virtually every aspect of basketball requires collaboration.

Robert W. Keidel

If you start yelling and becoming obtrusive and beboppin' around, you give the impression of insecurity, and that becomes infectious. It bleeds down into the actors, and they become nervous; then it bleeds down into the crew, and they become nervous, and you don't get much accomplished that way. You have to set a tone and just demand a certain amount of tranquility.

Clint Eastwood on being a film director

He that would be a leader must be a bridge.

Welsh proverb

A committee is an animal with four back legs.

Jean le Carre

Ask not what your country can do for you. Ask what you can do for your country.

John F. Kennedy

We are born for cooperation, as are the feet, the hands, the eyelids, and the upper and lower jaws.

Marcus Aurelius Antonius

Perhaps an example will clarify the distinction between groups and organizations. Consider a church so large that it may fairly be described as an organization: so large that multiple services must be offered on Sunday mornings; so large that dozens of different study classes are offered each week; so large there are numerous different choirs and musical ensembles. In so large a church, the members hardly could be said to interact with or influence each other except on an occasional basis. Such size often presents both advantages and disadvantages to the membership. On the one hand, it makes possible a rich diversity of activities; on the other hand, such size can make the church itself (i.e., the overall organization) seem relatively impersonal. It may be difficult to identity with a large organization other than in name only (e.g., "I belong to First Presbyterian Church"). In such cases many people identify more with particular groups within the church than with the church itself; it may be easier to *feel* a part of some smaller group such as the high school choir or a weekly study group.

Although groups play a pervasive role in society, in general people spend very little time thinking about the factors that affect group processes and intragroup relationships. Therefore, the rest of this section will describe some group characteristics that can affect both leaders and followers. Much of the research on groups goes well beyond the scope of this chapter (see Gibbard, Hartman, & Mann, 1978; Shaw, 1981; Hackman, 1990), but six concepts are so basic to the group perspective that they deserve our attention. These six concepts are group size, stages of group development, roles, norms, communication, and cohesion.

Group Size

The size of any group has implications for both leaders and followers. First, leader emergence is partly a function of group size. The greater number of people in a large versus a small group will affect the probability that any individual is likely to emerge as leader. Second, as groups become larger, **cliques** are more likely to develop (Yukl, 1981). Cliques are subgroups of individuals who often share the same goals, values, and expectations. Because cliques generally wield more influence than individual members, they are likely to exert considerable influence—positively or negatively—on the larger group. Leaders need to identify and deal with cliques within their groups, as many intragroup conflicts are the results of cliques having different values, goals, and expectations.

Third, group size also can affect a leader's behavioral style. Leaders with a large **span of control** tend to be more directive, spend less time with individual subordinates, and use more-impersonal approaches when influencing followers. Leaders with a small span of control tend to display more consideration and use more-personal approaches when influencing followers (Badin, 1974; Goodstadt & Kipnis, 1970; Kipnis, Schmidt, & Wilkinson, 1980; Udell, 1967). Fourth, group size also affects group effectiveness. Whereas some researchers have suggested the optimal number of workers for any task is between five and seven (Bass, 1960; Indik, 1965), it probably is wise to avoid such a simple generalization. The answer to the question of appropriate group size seems to be "just big enough to get the job done." Obviously, the larger the group, the more likely it is that it will involve differentiated skills, values, perceptions, and abilities among its members. Also, there certainly will be more "people power" available to do the work as group size increases.

There are, however, limits to the benefits of size. Consider the question, "If it takes 1 person two minutes to dig a 1-cubic-foot hole, how long will it take 20 people to dig the same size hole?" Actually, it probably will take the larger group considerably *longer*, especially if they all participate at the same time. Beyond the purely physical limitations of certain tasks, there also may be decreasing returns (on a per capita basis) as group size increases. This is true even when the efforts of all group members are combined on what is called an **additive task**. An additive task is one where the group's output simply involves the combination of individual outputs (Steiner, 1972). Such a case may be illustrated by the number of individuals needed to push a stalled truck from an intersection. One individual probably would not be enough—maybe not even two or three. At some point, though, as group size increases in this additive task, there will be enough combined force to move the truck. However, as the group size increases beyond that needed to move the truck, the individual contribution of each member will appear to decrease. Steiner (1972) suggested this may be due to **process loss** resulting from factors such as some members not pushing in the right direction. Process losses can be thought of as the inefficiencies created by more and more people working together.

Group size can affect group effectiveness in a number of other ways. As group size increases, the diminishing returns of larger work groups may be due to **social loafing** (Latan'e, Williams, & Hawkins, 1979). Social loafing refers to the phenomenon of reduced effort by people when they are not individually accountable for their work. Experiments across different sorts of tasks have tended to demonstrate greater effort when every individual's work is monitored than when many individuals' outputs are anonymously pooled into a collective product. Recent evidence, however, suggests the process may be considerably more complicated than initially thought (Porter, Bird, & Wunder, 1991). The performance decrement may be affected more by the level of task complexity or the reward structure (e.g., cooperative versus competitive) than by outcome attribution.

Sometimes, working in the presence of others may actually increase effort or productivity through a phenomenon called **social facilitation.** Social facilitation was first documented in classic experiments at the Hawthorne plant of the Western Electric Company (see Highlight 13–2). However, social facilitation is not limited to research situations. It refers to any time people increase their level of work due to the presence of others. Typically this occurs when the presence of others increases individual accountability for work, in contrast to other occasions when being in a group reinforces individual anonymity and social loafing (Zajonc, 1965).

Developmental Stages of Groups

Just as children go through different stages of development, so do groups. Tuckman's (1965) review of over 60 studies involving leaderless training, experimental, or therapeutic groups revealed that groups generally went through four distinct stages of development. The first stage, **forming,** was characterized by polite conversation, the gathering of superficial information about fellow members, and low trust. The group's rejection of emerging potential leaders with negative characteristics also took place during the forming stage. The second

Social Facilitation and the Hawthorne Effect

Social facilitation was first documented in experiments conducted at the Hawthorne plant of the Western Electric Company during the late 1920s and early 1930s. These classic studies were originally designed to evaluate the impact of different work environments (Mayo, 1933; Roethlisberger & Dickson, 1939). Among other things, researchers varied the levels of illumination in areas where workers were assembling electrical components and found production increased when lighting was increased. When lighting was subsequently decreased, however, production again increased. Faced with these rather confusing data, the researchers turned their attention from physical aspects of the work environment to its social aspects. As it turns out, one reason workers' production increased was simply because someone else (in this case, the researchers) had paid attention to them. The term *Hawthorne effect* is still used today to describe an artificial change in behavior due merely to the fact a person or group is being studied.

stage, **storming**, usually was marked by intragroup conflict, heightened emotional levels, and status differentiation as remaining contenders struggled to build alliances and fulfill the group's leadership role. The clear emergence of a leader and the development of group norms and cohesiveness were the key indicators of the **norming** stage of group development. Finally, groups reached the **performing** stage when group members played functional, interdependent roles that were focused on the performance of group tasks.

The four stages of group development identified by Tuckman (1965) are important for several reasons. First, people are in many more leaderless groups than they may realize. For example, many sports teams, committees, work groups, and clubs start out as leaderless teams. Team or club captains or committee spokespersons are likely to be the emergent leaders from their respective groups. On a larger scale, perhaps even many elected officials initially began their political careers as the emergent leaders of their cliques or groups, and were then able to convince the majority of the remaining members in their constituencies of their viability as candidates.

Another reason it is important to understand stages of group development is the potential relationships between leadership behaviors and group cohesiveness and productivity. Some experts have maintained that leaders need to focus on consideration or group maintenance behaviors during the norming stage to improve group cohesiveness, and on task behaviors during the performing stage in order to improve group productivity (Stogdill, 1972; Terborg, Castore, & DeNinno, 1975). They also have suggested that leaders who reverse these behaviors during the norming and performing stages tend to have less-cohesive and less-productive groups. Thus, being able to recognize stages of group development may enhance the likelihood that one will emerge as a leader as well as increase the cohesiveness and productivity of the group being led.

Group Roles

Group roles are the sets of expected behaviors associated with particular jobs or positions. Most people have multiple roles stemming from the various groups with which they are associated. In addition, it is not uncommon for someone to occupy numerous roles within the same group as situations change. Ginnett (1990) found that members of airline crews have varying roles over the course of a day. Although some behaviors were universally associated with certain roles, effective team members on these airline crews generally were more flexible in changing their behavior as other role demands changed. For example, whereas the captain of an airplane is responsible for the overall operation and decision making during a flight, flight attendants often take over responsibility for planning and carrying out the crew's social activities in the evening (i.e., when the flight is over). One captain in the study, however, continued to make *all* the crew's decisions, including their evening social plans; he was inflexible with regard to the role of decision maker. Not coincidentally, he was seen as a less-effective leader—even during the actual flights—than more flexible captains.

Some roles, like positions on athletic teams, have meaning only in relatively specific contexts. Generally speaking, for example, one only plays a lineman's role during football games (admittedly, one might argue that at many schools being an intercollegiate athlete is a role that extends to aspects of student life outside sports). Other roles are more general in nature, including certain common ones that play a part in making any group work—or not work—well. Highlight 13–3 presents a vivid example of how powerful roles can be as determinants of behavior.

In Chapter 10, leader behavior was characterized initially in terms of two broad functions. One deals with getting the task done (**task role**), and the other with supporting relationships within the work group (**relationship role**). Similarly, roles in groups can be categorized in terms of task and relationship functions (see Highlight 13–4). Many of the roles in Highlight 13–4 are appropriate for followers, not just the official group leader; all of these different roles are part of the leadership process and all contribute to a group's overall effectiveness. Moreover, it is important to recognize that the very distinction between task and relationship roles is somewhat arbitrary. It is sensible enough when looking at the short-term impact of any given behavior, but in another sense relationship roles are task roles. After all, task-oriented behavior may be adequate for accomplishing short-term objectives, but an appropriately cohesive and supportive group increases the potential for long-term effectiveness at future tasks as well as present tasks.

Although the roles in Highlight 13–4 generally contribute to a group's overall effectiveness, several types of problems can occur with group roles that can impede group performance. One type of role problem concerns the **dysfunctional**

Highlight 13–3

The Stanford Prison Experiment

A fascinating demonstration of the power of roles occurred when social psychologist Philip Zimbardo and his colleagues (1973) created a simulated prison environment at Stanford University. From a larger group of volunteers, two dozen male college students were randomly assigned to be either "prisoners" or "guards." The simulation was quite realistic, with actual cells constructed in the basement of one of the university buildings. The guards wore uniforms, and carried nightsticks and whistles; their eyes were covered by sunglasses. The prisoners were "arrested" at their homes by police cars replete with blazing sirens. They were handcuffed, frisked, blindfolded, and brought to the "jail." They were fingerprinted, given prisoner outfits, and assigned numbers by which they would henceforth be addressed.

It did not take long for the students' normal behavior to be overcome by the roles they were playing. The guards became more and more abusive with their power. They held prisoners accountable for strict adherence to arbitrary rules of prison life (which the guards themselves created), and seemed to enjoy punishing them for even minor infractions. They increasingly seemed to think of the prisoners—truly just other college students—as bad people. The emotional stress on the prisoners became profound, and just six days into the two-week episode the experiment was halted. This unexpected outcome basically occurred because participants' roles had become their reality. They were not just students role-playing guards and prisoners; to a disconcerting degree they became guards and prisoners.

What should people conclude from the Stanford prison study? At an abstract level, the study dramatically points out how behavior is partly determined by social role. Additionally, it is clear how just being in the role of leader, especially to the extent it is attended by tangible and symbolic manifestations of power, can affect how leaders think and act toward followers. Still another lesson people might draw involves remembering the volunteers all had many different roles in life than those assigned to them in the study, though being a guard or a prisoner was certainly the salient one for a period of time. Whereas everyone has many roles, the salience of one or another often depends on the situation, and a person's behavior changes as his or her role changes in a group.

Source: P. Zimbardo, C. Haney, W. Banks, and D. Jaffe, "The Mind Is a Formidable Jailer: A Pirandellian Prison," *New York Times Magazine*, April 8, 1973, pp. 38–60.

---

roles, listed in Highlight 13–5. The common denominator among these roles is how the person's behavior primarily serves selfish or egocentric purposes rather than group purposes.

Another role problem is **role conflict**. Role conflict involves receiving contradictory messages about expected behavior and can in turn adversely affect a person's emotional well-being and performance (Jamal, 1984).

Highlight 13–4

Task and Relationship Roles in Groups

Task Roles

Initiating: Defining the problem, suggesting activities, assigning tasks.

Information Seeking: Asking questions, seeking relevant data or views.

Information Sharing: Providing data, offering opinions.

Summarizing: Reviewing and integrating others' points, checking for common understanding and readiness for action.

Evaluating: Assessing validity of assumptions, quality of information, reasonableness of recommendations.

Guiding: Keeping group on track.

Relationship Roles

Harmonizing: Resolving interpersonal conflicts, reducing tension.

Encouraging: Supporting and praising others, showing appreciation for others' contributions, being warm and friendly.

Gatekeeping: Assuring even participation by all group members, making sure that everyone has a chance to be heard and that no individual dominates.

Source: Adapted from K. D. Benne and P. Sheats, "Functional Roles of Group Members," *Journal of Social Issues* 4 (1948), pp. 41–49.

Role conflict can occur in several different ways. Perhaps most common is receiving inconsistent signals about expected behavior from the same person. When the same person sends mixed signals, it is called **intrasender role conflict** ("I need this report back in five minutes, and it had better be perfect"). **Intersender role conflict** occurs when someone receives inconsistent signals from several others about expected behavior. Still another kind of role conflict is based on inconsistencies between different roles a person may have. Professional and family demands, for example, often create role conflicts. **Interrole conflict** occurs when someone is unable to perform all of his roles as well as he would like. A final type occurs when role expectations violate a person's values. This is known as **person-role conflict.** An example of person-role conflict might be when a store manager encourages a salesperson to mislead customers about the quality of the store's products when this behavior is inconsistent with the salesperson's values and beliefs.

A different sort of role problem is called **role ambiguity.** In role conflict, one receives clear messages about expectations, but the messages are not all congruent. With role ambiguity, the problem is lack of clarity about just what the expectations

Highlight 13–5

Dysfunctional Roles

Dominating: Monopolizing group time, forcing views on others.

Blocking: Stubbornly obstructing and impeding group work, persistent negativism.

Attacking: Belittling others, creating a hostile or intimidating environment.

Distracting: Engaging in irrelevant behaviors, distracting others' attention.

Source: Adapted from K. D. Benne and P. Sheats, ``Functional Roles of Group Members,'' *Journal of Social Issues* 4 (1948), pp. 41–49.

---

are (House, Schuler, & Levanoni, 1983; Rizzo, House, & Lirtzman, 1970). There may have been no role expectations established at all, or they may not have been clearly communicated. A person is experiencing role ambiguity if he or she wonders, "Just what am I supposed to be doing?" It is important for leaders to be able to minimize the degree to which dysfunctional roles, role conflict, and role ambiguity occur in their groups, as these problems have been found to have a negative impact on organizational commitment, job involvement, absenteeism, and satisfaction with co-workers and supervisors (Fisher & Gitelson, 1983).

Group Norms

Norms are the informal rules groups adopt to regulate and regularize group members' behaviors. Although norms are only infrequently written down or openly discussed, they nonetheless often have a powerful and consistent influence on behavior (Hackman, 1976). That is because most people are rather good at reading the social cues that inform them about existing norms. For example, most people easily discern the dress code in any new work environment without needing written guidance. People also are apt to notice when a norm is violated, even though they may have been unable to articulate the norm before its violation was apparent. For example, most students have expectations (norms) about creating extra work for other students. Imagine the reaction if a student in some class complained that not enough reading was being assigned each lesson or that the minimum length requirements for the term paper needed to be substantially raised.

Norms do not govern all behaviors, just those a group feels are important. Norms are more likely to be seen as important and apt to be enforced if they (*a*) facilitate group survival; (*b*) simplify, or make more predictable, what behavior is expected of group members; (*c*) help the group avoid embarrassing interpersonal problems; or (*d*) express the central values of the group and clarify what is distinctive about the group's identity (Feldman, 1984).

One irony about norms is that an outsider to a group often is able to learn more about norms than an insider. An outsider, not necessarily being subject to the norms himself, is more apt to notice them. In fact, the more "foreign" an observer is, the more likely it is the norms will be perceived. If a man is accustomed to wearing a tie to work, he is less likely to notice that men in another organization also wear ties to work, but is *more* likely to note that the men in a third organization typically wear sweaters and sweatshirts around the office.

Group Cohesion

Group cohesion is the glue that keeps a group together. It is the sum of forces that attract members to a group, provide resistance to leaving it, and motivate them to be active in it. Highly cohesive groups interact with and influence each other more than do less-cohesive groups. Furthermore, a highly cohesive group may have lower absenteeism and lower turnover than a less-cohesive group, and low absenteeism and turnover often contribute to higher group performance; higher performance can, in turn, contribute to even higher cohesion, thus resulting in an increasingly positive spiral.

However, greater cohesiveness does not always lead to higher performance. A highly cohesive but unskilled team is still an unskilled team, and such teams will often lose to a less-cohesive but more-skilled one. Additionally, a highly cohesive group may sometimes develop goals that are contrary to the larger organization's goals. For example, members of a highly cohesive research team at a particular college committed themselves to working on a problem that seemed inherently interesting to them. Their nearly zealous commitment to the project, however, effectively kept them from asking, or even allowing others to ask, if the research aligned itself well with the college's stated objectives. Their quite narrow and basic research effort deviated significantly from the college's expressed commitment to emphasize applied research. As a result, the college lost some substantial outside financial support.

Other problems also can occur in highly cohesive groups. Researchers (Alderfer, 1977; Ginnett, 1987) have found that some groups can become so cohesive they erect what amount to fences or boundaries between themselves and others. Such **overbounding** can block the use of outside resources that could make them more effective. Competitive product development teams can become so overbounded (often rationalized by security concerns or inordinate fears of "idea thieves") that they will not ask for help from willing and able staff within their own organizations.

One example of this problem was the failed mission to rescue U.S. embassy personnel held hostage in Iran during the Carter presidency. The rescue itself was a rather complicated mission involving many different sorts of U.S. military forces. Some of these forces included sea-based helicopters. The helicopters and their crews were carried on regular naval vessels, though most sailors on the vessels knew nothing of the secret mission. Senior personnel were so concerned that some sailor might leak information, and thus compromise the mission's secrecy, that maintenance crews aboard the ships were not directed to perform increased levels of maintenance on the helicopters immediately before the critical mission.

Symptoms of Groupthink

An illusion of invulnerability, which leads to unwarranted optimism and excessive risk taking by the group.

Unquestioned assumption of the group's morality and therefore an absence of reflection on the ethical consequences of group action.

Collective rationalization to discount negative information or warnings.

Stereotypes of the opposition as evil, weak, or stupid.

Self-censorship by group members from expressing ideas that deviate from the group consensus due to doubts about their validity or importance.

An illusion of unanimity such that greater consensus is perceived than really exists.

Direct pressure on dissenting members, which reinforces the norm that disagreement represents disloyalty to the group.

Mindguards, who protect the group from adverse information.

Source: Adapted from I. L. Janis, *Groupthink*, 2nd ed. (Boston: Houghton Mifflin, 1982).

Even if a helicopter was scheduled for significant maintenance within the next 50 hours of flight time (which would be exceeded in the rescue mission), crews were not told to perform the maintenance. According to knowledgeable sources, this practice did impact the performance of at least one of the failed helicopters, and thus the overall mission.

Janis (1982) discovered still another disadvantage of highly cohesive groups. He found that people in a highly cohesive group often become more concerned with striving for unanimity than in objectively appraising different courses of action. Janis labeled this phenomenon **groupthink** and believed it accounted for a number of historic fiascoes, including Pearl Harbor and the Bay of Pigs invasion. It may have played a role in the *Challenger* disaster, and it also occurs in other cohesive groups ranging from business meetings to air crews, and from therapy groups to school boards.

What is groupthink? Cohesive groups tend to evolve strong informal norms to preserve friendly internal relations. Preserving a comfortable, harmonious group environment becomes a hidden agenda that tends to suppress dissent, conflict, and critical thinking. Unwise decisions may result when concurrence seeking among members overrides their willingness to express or tolerate deviant points of view and think critically. Janis (1982) identified a number of symptoms of groupthink, which can be found in Highlight 13–6.

A policy-making or decision-making group displaying most of the symptoms in Highlight 13–6 runs a big risk of being ineffective. It may do a poor job of clarifying objectives, searching for relevant information, evaluating alternatives, assessing risks, and anticipating the need for contingency plans. Janis (1982) offered the following suggestions as ways of reducing groupthink and thus of improving the quality of a group's input to policies or decisions. First, leaders should encourage all group members to take on the role of critical evaluator. Everyone in the group needs to appreciate the importance of airing doubts and objections. This includes the leader's willingness to listen to criticisms of his or her own ideas. Second, leaders should create a climate of open inquiry through their own impartiality and objectivity. At the outset, leaders should refrain from stating personal preferences or expectations, which may bias group discussion. Third, the risk of groupthink can be reduced if independent groups are established to make recommendations on the same issue. Fourth, at least one member of the group should be assigned the role of devil's advocate, an assignment that should rotate from meeting to meeting.

One final problem with highly cohesive groups may be what Shephard (1991) has called **ollieism**. Ollieism, a variation of groupthink, occurs when illegal actions are taken by overly zealous and loyal subordinates who believe that what they are doing will please their leaders. It derives its name from the actions of Lieutenant-Colonel Oliver North, who among other things admitted he lied to the U.S. Congress about his actions while working on the White House staff during the Iran-Contra affair. Shephard cites the slaying of Thomas à Becket by four of Henry II's knights and the Watergate break-in as other prime examples of ollieism. Ollieism differs from groupthink in that the subordinates' illegal actions usually occur without the explicit knowledge or consent of the leader. Nevertheless, Shephard points out that although the examples cited of ollieism were not officially sanctioned, the responsibility for them still falls squarely on the leader. It is the leader's responsibility to create an ethical climate within the group, and leaders who create highly cohesive yet unethical groups must bear the responsibility for the group's actions. It will be interesting to see if ollieism is a factor in any of the ethical issues surrounding subordinates in the Clinton administration.

After reading about the uncertain relationships between group cohesion and performance, and the problems with overbounding, groupthink, and ollieism, one might think that cohesiveness should be something to avoid. Nothing, however, could be further from the truth. First of all, problems with overly cohesive groups occur relatively infrequently, and in general, leaders will be better off thinking of ways to create and maintain highly cohesive teams than not developing these teams out of concern for potential groupthink or overbounding situations. Second, perhaps the biggest argument for developing cohesive groups is to consider the alternative—groups with little or no cohesiveness. In the latter groups, followers would generally be dissatisfied with each other and the leader, commitment to accomplishing group and organizational goals may be reduced, intragroup communication may occur less frequently, and interdependent task performance may suffer (Robbins, 1986). Because of the problems associated with groups having low cohesiveness, leadership practitioners need to realize that developing functionally cohesive work groups is a goal they all should strive for.

In summary, the group perspective provides a complementary level of analysis to the individual perspective presented earlier in this chapter. A follower's behavior may be due to his or her values, traits, or experience (i.e., the individual perspective), or this behavior may be due to the followers' roles, the group norms, the group's stage of development, or the group's level of cohesiveness (i.e., the group perspective). Thus, the group perspective can also provide both leaders and followers with a number of explanations of why individuals in groups behave in certain ways. Moreover, the six group characteristics just described can give leaders and followers ideas about (*a*) factors that may be affecting their ability to influence other group members and (*b*) what to do to improve their level of influence in the group.

Groups versus Teams: Is There a Difference?

Virtually everyone has been involved in some group or other, often with the sort commonly called teams. But is there a difference between a group and a team? With *teams* and *teamwork* being the buzzwords of the 1990s, it is worth discussing the concept of teams and coordinated group work, or teamwork

As described earlier in this chapter, two identifying characteristics of groups are mutual interaction and reciprocal influence. Members of teams also have mutual interaction and reciprocal influence, but we generally distinguish teams from groups in four other ways. First, team members usually have a stronger sense of identification among themselves than groups members do. Often, both team members and outsiders can readily identify who is and who is not on the team (athletic uniforms are one obvious example); identifying members of a group may be more difficult. Second, teams have common goals or tasks; these may range from the development of a new product to an athletic league championship. Group members, on the other hand, may not have the same degree of consensus about goals as team members do. Group members may belong to the group for a variety of personal reasons, and these may clash with the group's stated objectives. (This phenomenon probably happens with teams, too, although perhaps not to the same extent.)

Third, task interdependence typically is greater with teams than with groups. For example, basketball players usually are unable to take a shot unless other team members set picks or pass the ball to them. On the other hand, group members often can contribute to goal accomplishment by working independently; the

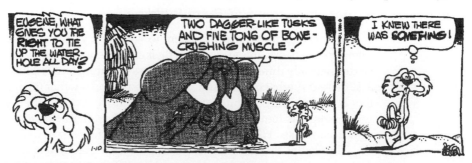

Highlight 13–7

Examples of Effective and Ineffective Teams

Most people can readily think up a number of examples of ineffective and effective teamwork. Consider the relative effectiveness of the teams depicted in the following two true stories:

Ineffective Teamwork: After an airline flight crew failed to get a "nose gear down and locked" indicator light to come on while making a landing approach into Miami, all three crew members became involved in trying to change the burned-out indicator bulb in the cockpit. Nobody was flying the airplane and none of them were monitoring the flight of the L-1011 as it descended into the Everglades and crashed.

Effective Teamwork: The crew of a DC-10, after having lost all capability to control the airplane through flight controls as a result of an engine explosion, realized they needed all the help they could get. Captain Al Haynes discovered another experienced captain was traveling in the passenger cabin and invited him to come up to the cabin to help the regular crew out. Miraculously, their combined abilities enabled the crew—using techniques developed on the spot—to control the plane to within a few feet of the ground. Even though there were fatalities, over 100 people survived a nearly hopeless situation.

successful completion of their assigned tasks may not be contingent on other group members. Of course, task interdependence can vary greatly even across teams. Among athletic teams, for example, softball, football, soccer, and hockey teams have a high level of task interdependence, whereas swimming, cross-country, and track teams have substantially lower levels of task interdependence. Fourth, team members often have more-differentiated and specialized roles than group members. In the preceding section, we noted that group members often play a variety of roles within the group; however, team members often play a single, or primary, role on a team. Finally, it is important to bear in mind that the distinctions we have been highlighting probably reflect only matters of degree. One might consider teams to be highly specialized groups.

Effective Team Characteristics and Team Building

Not only do teams vary in the extent to which they have specialized roles or task interdependence; teams also vary in their effectiveness. Virtually identical teams can be dramatically different in terms of success or failure (see Highlight 13–7). We must ask, therefore, what makes one team successful and another unsuccessful? Although this is an area only recently studied, exploratory work at the Center for Creative Leadership has tentatively identified several key characteristics for effective team performance (see Highlight 13–8 for an astronaut's perspective on teamwork).

The Center for Creative Leadership's research with teams indicated that successful and unsuccessful teams could be differentiated on the basis of eight key

---

Highlight 13–8

Women in Leadership, IV: Teamwork from an Astronaut's Perspective

Dr. Bonnie J. Dunbar is an American astronaut. She has flown on four space shuttle missions. We asked her to share a few personal reflections about the meaning of teamwork and followership to her as she was growing up, as well as presently in her role in the space program. She wrote this during preparation for her flight in June 1992. She was payload commander for that space shuttle mission.

Above all, the success of a space flight depends upon teamwork: within the crew and between the ground controllers and the crew. Teamwork is a valued attribute among currently selected astronauts.

I was very fortunate as a young girl to have been exposed to that concept by my family. With four children and a multitude of chores to be performed, my mother and father impressed upon us our responsibilities within the family unit. Success of the farm (and our future) depended upon our contribution. As the oldest, I was expected to participate in all chores, including driving the tractor and "round-up" by horseback. There were no distinctions in these responsibilities between my brothers and me. Group experiences within the 4-H organization (showing steers, etc.) and playing on baseball, volleyball, and basketball teams reinforced the pride of sharing success together and consoling each other in defeat.

When I attended college, some of that team experience was missed. By virtue of my gender, I was considered an unwelcome minority by many in the engineering college. Therefore, I was never invited to the study groups or participated in group solution of the home work problems. Still, I found an outlet in group activities by belonging to Angel Flight (co-ed auxiliary to Air Force ROTC—I was elected Commander of 50 my junior year) and by continuing to play co-ed baseball. Ironically, my engineering classmates needed my athletic ability as first baseman on the playing field.

I was also supported by three very important individuals during this time: my father, my mother, and the chairman of the Ceramic Engineering Department, Dr. James I. Mueller. My parents always encouraged me to pursue my "dreams" and to be the best person I could be. The fact that I was the first in the family to attend college was a source of pride for them. That I subscribed to their principles of hard work, human compassion, and honesty was probably a source of greater pride. They were proud of my selection as an astronaut but my father was more concerned that I not forget how to get manure on my boots.

In my professional life, the closest I have come to real group esprit de corps has come through my association with the Astronaut Office. Perhaps it was due to the concept of "class training," or the similarity of individuals involved, but I consider those I work with as also my closest friends. Our successes are really those of a family team that extends out to the engineers, managers, and administrative support in the Space Shuttle program.

I am now on my third NASA Space Shuttle crew. As Payload Commander I have tried to convey to the noncareer payload specialists on my next flight the importance of being part of the crew . . . that we will share both the successes and the failures of the flight. It has been an interesting experience to assess others' ability to become "part of the team." I have seen what not being part of the team can do, and in a flight environment that can be highly risky. Not being a team member does more than cause internal friction within the crew; it can be hazardous.

(continued)

(concluded)

> So, what does being "part of the team" mean? It doesn't always mean being the smartest or the fastest. It does mean recognizing the big picture goal and the contribution that each individual brings to the whole. It may not mean being the life of the party, but it does mean being able to get along with people and to tread a fine line . . . knowing when to compromise and knowing when to stand firm. And, in an organization such as ours with competitive individuals used to being on top of the hill, it means knowing when to be a Chief and when to be an Indian. In the astronaut office, mission specialists rotate through technical jobs and different responsibilities during flights. Sometimes they are Indians instead of Chiefs. Those that perform best and appear to be well-regarded can do each equally well.

characteristics, the first six of which are primarily concerned with task accomplishment (Hallam & Campbell, 1992). First, effective teams had a *clear mission* and *high performance standards*. Everyone on the team knew what the team was trying to achieve and how well he or she had to perform in order to achieve the team's mission. Second, leaders of successful teams often *took stock* of their equipment, training facilities and opportunities, and outside resources available to help the team. Leaders of effective teams spent a considerable amount of time *assessing the technical skills* of the team members. After taking stock of available resources and skills, good leaders would work to *secure those resources and equipment* necessary for team effectiveness. Moreover, leaders of effective teams would spend a considerable amount of time *planning* and *organizing* in order to make optimal use of available resources, to select new members with needed technical skills, or to improve needed technical skills of existing members.

The last two characteristics of effective teams were concerned with the group maintenance or interpersonal aspects of teams. Hallam and Campbell's (1992) research indicated that *high levels of communication* were often associated with effective teams. These authors believed this level of communication helped team members to stay focused on the mission and to take better advantage of the skills, knowledge, and resources available to the team. High levels of communication also helped to *minimize interpersonal conflicts* on the team, which often drained energy needed for team success and effectiveness.

The characteristics of effective teams identified in this research provide leadership practitioners with a number of ideas about how they may be able to increase the effectiveness of their work units or teams. Further ideas about how to develop effective teams are offered in the book *Groups That Work (and Those That Don't)* (Hackman, 1990). Hackman has developed a normative model of group effectiveness, based on his research, that identifies several characteristics critical to a team's effectiveness. An expanded revision of Hackman's normative model will be presented later. For now, let us focus on the part of the model that deals with group or team design. The model, as modified by Ginnett (1993), posits four components that help any group get off to a good start, whatever its task. This is important because some groups' failures can be traced to having been set up inappropriately from the beginning. The four variables that need to be in place if a team is going to be able to work effectively and efficiently are the following:

1. *Task structure*: Does the team know what its task is? Is the task reasonably unambiguous and consistent with the mission of the team? Does the team have a meaningful piece of work, sufficient autonomy to perform it, and access to knowledge of its results?

2. *Group boundaries*: Is the collective membership of the team appropriate for the task to be performed? Are there too few or too many members? Do the members collectively have sufficient knowledge and skills to perform the work? In addition to task skills, does the team have sufficient maturity and interpersonal skills to be able to work together and resolve conflicts? Is there an appropriate amount of diversity on the team (e.g., members are not so similar that they do not have differing perspectives and experiences, and yet not so diverse that they cannot communicate or relate to one another)?

3. *Norms*: Does the team share an appropriate set of norms for working as a team? Norms can be acquired by the team in three ways: (*a*) They can be imported from the organization existing outside the team, (*b*) they can be instituted and reinforced by the leader or leaders of the team, or (*c*) they can be developed by the team itself as the situation demands. If the team is to have a strategy that works over time, then it must ensure that conflicting norms do not confuse team members. It also needs to regularly scan and review prevailing norms to ensure they support overall objectives.

4. *Authority:* Has the leader established a climate where her authority can be used in a flexible rather than a rigid manner? Has she, at one end of the authority continuum, established sufficient competence to allow the group to comply when conditions demand (such as in emergencies)? Has she also established a climate such that any member of the team feels empowered to provide expert assistance when appropriate? Do team members feel comfortable in questioning the leader on decisions where there are no clear right answers? In short, have conditions been created where authority can shift to appropriately match the demands of the situation?

As noted above, many of these team design components may be imported from preexisting conditions in the organization within which the team is forming, from the industry in which the organization operates, or even from the environment in which the industry exists. To help team leaders consider these various levels, Hackman and Ginnett (1986, 1993) developed the concept of **organizational shells** (see Figure 13–1). Notice that the four critical factors for team design (task, boundaries, norms, and authority) are necessary for the group to work effectively. In some cases, all the information about one of these critical factors may be input from the industry or organizational shell level. In these cases, the leader need do little else but affirm that condition. In other cases, there may be too little (or even inappropriate) input from the organizational level to allow the team to work effectively. In these cases, the leader needs to

Figure 13–1

Organizational Shells

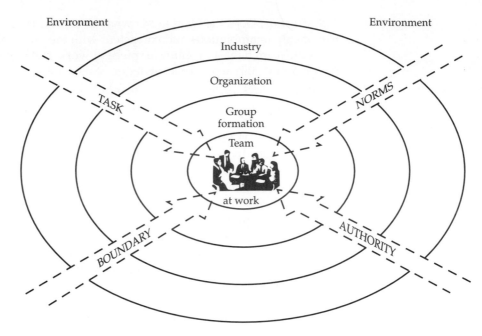

modify the factors for team design. Ideally this is done during the formation process—the final shell before the team actually begins work.

These ideas may require a new way of thinking about the relationship between a leader and followers. In many organizational settings, leaders are assigned. Sometimes, however, the people who create conditions for improved group effectiveness are not the designated leaders at all; they may emerge from the ranks of followers, as described in the previous chapter. In fact, this model has been used to differentiate between effective and ineffective "self-managing work groups"—teams where the followers and leaders were the same people. Moreover, because the model is prescriptive, it also provides a number of suggestions about what ineffective work groups can do in order to be successful. That same purpose underlies the following model as well.

The Team Effectiveness Leadership Model

Since we have emphasized that leadership is a group or team function and have suggested that one measure of leadership effectiveness may be whether the team achieves its objectives, it is reasonable to examine a model specifically designed to help teams perform more effectively: the **Team Effectiveness Leadership Model,** or **TELM** (Ginnett, 1993, 1996). Another way to think of this model is as a mechanism to first identify what a team needs to be effective, and then to point the leader either toward the roadblocks that are hindering the team or toward ways to make the team even more effective than it already is. This approach is similar to McGrath's (1964) description of leadership, which suggested that the

FIGURE 13–2

*General Systems
Theory Applied
to Teams*

leader's main job is to determine what needs the team is faced with and then take care of them. This approach also will require us to think about leadership not as a function of the leader and his or her characteristics but as a function of the team. As the title of the model suggests, team effectiveness is the underlying driver.

We have mentioned this model of group or team effectiveness briefly before, but now we will explore it in greater detail. The original model for examining the "engine of a team" was developed by Richard Hackman and has been the basis for much research on groups and teams over the last 20 years (Hackman, 1990). The model presented here includes modifications by Ginnett and represents an example of a leadership model that has been developed primarily using field research. It provides the underlying structure for the "Leadership and High Performance Teams" course now offered by the Center for Creative Leadership. While there have been controlled experimental studies validating portions of the model (Smith, Salas, & Brannick, 1994), the principle development and validation has been completed using actual high-performance teams operating in their own situational context. Examples of the teams studied in this process include commercial and military air crews in actual line flying operations, surgical teams in operating suites, top management teams, product development and manufacturing teams, and, most recently, teams preparing the Space Shuttle fleet for launch. A complete illustration of the model will be shown later. Because of its complexity, it is easier to understand by starting with a few simpler illustrations.

At the most-basic level, this model (see Figure 13–2) resembles a systems theory approach with inputs on the left (i.e., individual, team, and organizational factors), processes or throughputs in the center (i.e., what one can tell about the team by actually observing team members at work), and outputs on the right (i.e., how well the team did in accomplishing its objectives). We will examine each of these stages. However, we will proceed through the model in reverse order—looking at outputs first, then the process stage, then inputs.

Outputs

What do we mean by outputs? Quite simply, **outputs** (see Figure 13–3) are the results of the team's work. For example, a football team scores 24 points. A production team produces 24 valves in a day. A tank crew hits 24 targets on an artillery range. Such raw data, however, are insufficient for assessing team effectiveness. How do we know if a team's output is good? How do we know if a team is effective? Even though it was possible for the three different teams mentioned

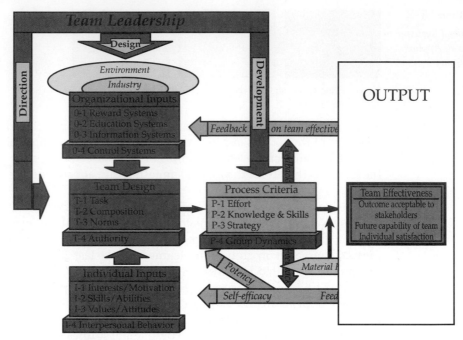

above to measure some aspect of their work, these measurements are not very helpful in determining their effectiveness, either in an absolute sense or in a relative sense. For comparison and research purposes, it is desirable to have some measures of team effectiveness that can be applied across teams and tasks. Hackman (1990) argued that a group is effective if (*a*) the team's productive output (goods, services, decisions) meets the standards of quantity, quality, and timeliness of the people who use it; (*b*) the group process that occurs while the group is performing its task enhances the ability of the members to work as members of a team (either the one they were on or any new teams they may be assigned to) in the future; and (*c*) the group experience enhances the growth and personal well-being of the individuals who compose the team.

Process

It should be obvious why leaders should be concerned with the outputs listed in the preceding section. After all, if a team does not "produce" (output), then it could not be considered effective. But what is process? And why should a leader care about it? Actually, there are several reasons a leader might want to pay attention to the team's process—how the team goes about its work.

Some teams may have such a limited number of products that the leader can ill afford to wait until the product is delivered to assess its acceptability to the client. For example, a team whose task is to build one (and only one) satellite to

FIGURE 13–4

Process Criteria of Team Effectiveness

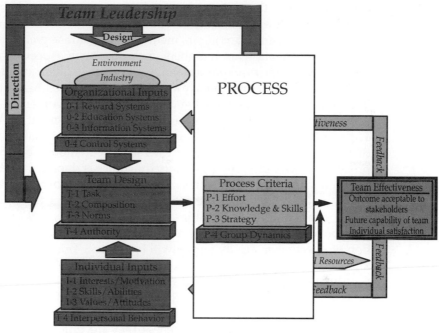

be launched into orbit will have no second chances. There may be no opportunity to correct any problem once the satellite is launched (or, as was the case with the flawed Hubble Space Telescope, correction can be made only after great expense). Therefore, it may be desirable for the leader of such a team to assess his team's work while it is working rather than after the satellite is launched. Other kinds of teams have such high standards for routine work that there simply are not enough critical indicators in the end product to determine effectiveness from outcome measures. As an example of this situation, a team operating a nuclear power plant is surrounded by so many technical backup systems that it may be difficult to determine team effectiveness by looking at "safe operation" as a measurement criterion. But we have evidence that not all teams in nuclear power plants operate equally well (Chernobyl and Three Mile Island are but two examples). It would seem helpful to be able to assess real teams "in process" rather than learn of team problems only following disastrous outcomes. Even leaders of noncritical teams might like to be able to routinely monitor their teams for evidence of effective or ineffective processes. So it turns out that the way teams go about their work can provide some very useful information to the leader.

Since process assessment is so important, let us focus for a moment on the block containing the four process measures of effectiveness in Figure 13–4. These four **process measures** of effectiveness provide criteria by which we can examine the ways in which teams work. If a team is to perform effectively, it must (*a*) work hard enough; (*b*) have sufficient knowledge and skills within the team to perform the task, (*c*) have an appropriate strategy to accomplish its work (or ways to approach the task at hand), and (*d*) have constructive and positive group dynamics among its members. The phrase *group dynamics* refers to interactions among team members, including such aspects as how they communicate with others, express feelings toward each other, and deal with conflict with each other, to name but a few of the characteristics. Assessing and improving group process is no trivial matter, as has been documented extensively in a comprehensive view of group process and its assessment by Wheelan (1994). The process measures are identified in the TELM by the labels P-1 through P-4 (P stands for process) in Figure 13–4. Lastly, it should be apparent that the process measure identified as group dynamics is depicted as the base or foundation for the other process measures. Our research over the last six years has consistently shown that to be precisely the case: effective group dynamics are the foundation upon which other team work proceeds. If the team is ultimately to achieve the three valued outcome measures of effectiveness, a firm foundation of effective group dynamics will be critical. This foundation concept will appear in other sections of the model described later, as well.

What should the leader do if she discovers a problem with one of these four process measures? Paradoxically, the answer is not to focus her attention on that process per se. While the four process measures are fairly good diagnostic measures for a team's ultimate effectiveness, they are, unfortunately, not particularly good leverage points for fixing the problem. An analogy from medicine would be a doctor who diagnoses the symptoms of an infection (a fever) but who then treats the symptoms rather than attacking the true underlying cause (a nail in the patient's foot). Similarly at the team level, rather than trying to correct a lack of effort being applied to the task at hand (perhaps a motivation problem), the team leader would be better advised to discover the underlying problem and fix that than to assume that a motivational speech to the team will do the job. This is not to imply that teams cannot benefit from process help. It merely suggests that the leader should ensure that there are not underlying problems (at the input level) that should be fixed first.

Inputs

In a manufacturing plant, **inputs** are the raw materials that are processed into products for sale. Similarly in team situations, inputs are what is available for teams as they go about their work. However, an important difference between an industrial plant and a team is that for a plant, the inputs are physical resources. Often for team design, we are considering psychological factors. There is a variety of levels of inputs, ranging from the individual level to the environmental level. Some of the inputs provide little opportunity for the leader to have an influence—they are merely givens. Leaders are often put in charge of teams with little or no control over the environment, the industry, or even the organizational conditions. There are other inputs, however, that the leader can directly impact to create the conditions for effective teamwork.

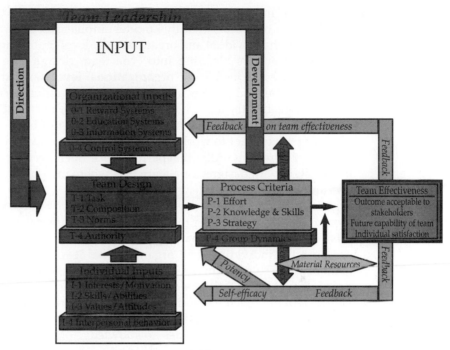

Figure 13–5 shows the multiple levels in the input stage of the model. Note that there are input factors at the individual and organizational levels and that both of these levels affect the team design level, as depicted by the direction of the arrows between these levels. Also note that there is a **leverage point** I(ndividual) 1–4, T(eam) 1–4, and O(rganization) 1–4 corresponding to each of the four process measures of effectiveness (P-1 through P-4). The meaning and importance of these leverage points will be clearer if we look at a few specific examples. Let us assume we have observed a team and discovered that its members are just not working very hard. They seem to be uninterested in the task, frequently wandering off or not even showing up for scheduled team work. We would diagnose this at the process level as a problem of effort (P-1). Rather than just encouraging them to work harder (or threatening them), we should first look at the input level to see if there is some underlying problem. The individual level (I-1, corresponding to a P-1 diagnosis) suggests that we look at the interests and motivations of the individual team members. These are referred to as **individual factors** in the model. If we have built a team to perform a mechanical assembly task but the individuals assigned have little or no interest in mechanical work, and instead prefer the performing arts, they may have little interest in contributing much effort to the team task. Here, using instruments such as the Cambell Interest and Skills Survey to select personnel may help our team's effort level from an individual perspective (D. P. Campbell, Hyne, & Nilsen, 1992).

While it may seem tempting to move to the team-level inputs next, it is important to remember that this model emphasizes the way teams are influenced by both individual and organizational level inputs (again, note the direction of the arrows "leading into" the team design stage in Figure 13–5). Therefore, we will look at the **organizational level** next. At the organizational level (O-1), the model suggests that we should examine the reward system that may be impacting the team. If the individuals have no incentive provided by the organization for putting forth effort, they might not be inclined to work very hard, or perhaps, not to work at all. Similarly, the reward system may be solely structured to reward individual performance. Such a reward structure would be inconsistent with designs for a team task where interdependence and cooperation among members is often an underlying premise. If a professional basketball organization provides rewards for players based only on individual points scored, with no bonuses for team performance (games won or making the playoffs), you can expect little passing, setting picks for teammates, and so on.

Both the individual- and organizational-level variables contribute to the team's ability to perform the task. But there can also be problems at the **team design** level. Here (T-1), a poorly designed task is hypothesized to be unmotivating. (An approach for designing intrinsically rewarding work based on job characteristics will be discussed in the next chapter.) If a job is meaningless, lacks sufficient autonomy, or provides no knowledge of results, we would not expect to see followers putting forth much effort.

Using the model, we found key leverage points at various levels of the input stage that would impact the way the team went about its work (team process). In the example cited, we diagnosed a process-level problem with effort (P-1), so we examined the 1-level variables at the individual, organizational, and team levels as the most likely location for finding input stage problems. By the way, the concept of leverage point does not imply that only factors at corresponding "numbers" should be considered. For example, a team's effort might be affected by an oppressive and authoritarian leader. As we have already seen, this "foundation-level variable" can have a tremendous impact on the other variables. Indeed, so powerful is this component, we should examine the process measure of group dynamics (P-4) and its corresponding leverage points in more detail. Consider the following two examples:

Surgical Team. A surgical team composed of highly experienced members is involved in a surgical procedure that each member has participated in numerous times before. During one portion of the procedure, the surgeon asks for a particular instrument. The scrub nurse looks across the table at the assistant with a questioning gaze and then hands the surgeon the instrument he requested. Recognizing the instrument he has been handed (and asked for) is not correct for the current procedure, he throws it down on the table and curses at the scrub nurse. All members of the surgical team take a half-step back from the table and all casual conversation stops. No one offers any further voluntary assistance to the surgeon.

Commercial Airline Crew. A commercial airline crew is making a routine approach into an uncrowded airport on a clear day. The captain is flying and has declared a visual approach. His final approach to the runway is not good, which greatly complicates the plane's landing, and the landing is poor. After taxiing to the gate, the captain and his entire crew debrief (discuss) the poor approach, and the team members talk about what they could have done individually and collectively to help the captain avoid or improve a poor approach in the future. The captain thanks the members for their help and encourages them to consider how they could implement their suggestions in other situations.

Obviously, the group dynamics are very different in these two cases. In the first example, the surgeon's behavior, coupled with his status, created a condition inappropriate for effective teamwork. The airline captain in the second example, even though not performing the task well, created a team environment where the team was much more likely to perform well in the future. In both of these cases, we would have observed unusual (one negative and one positive) group dynamics while the team was at work. These are examples of the group dynamics at the P-4 level.

Again returning to the model for determining points of leverage, we would check the I-4 variable at the individual level to determine if the team members involved had adequate interpersonal skills to interact appropriately. At the organizational level, the O-4 variable would suggest we check organizational components to determine if there are organizational control systems that inhibit or overly structure the way in which the team can make decisions or control its own fate. Such factors may include organizational design or structure limitations (a subject we will discuss in more detail in Chapter 15), or it may be a rigid computerized control system that specifies every minute detail of the tasks not only of the teams as a whole but of all the individuals composing the team. These excessive controls at the organizational level can inhibit effective teamwork. Finally, at the team design level, the T-4 variable would have us examine authority dynamics created between the leader and the followers. Authority dynamics describe the various ways the team members, including the leader, relate and respond to authority. It is at the team level that the followers have opportunities to relate directly with the team's authority figure, the team leader. The intricacies of how these various authority dynamics can play themselves out in a team's life are more complex than this chapter warrants. Suffice it to say that there is a range of authority relationships that can be created, from autocratic to laissez-faire. For a more detailed explanation of this concept, see Ginnett (1993). But even without further description, it should be no surprise that the varied group dynamics observed in the previous two examples were leveraged by the leaders' use of authority in very different ways.

It would be simple if leaders could identify and specify in advance the ideal type of authority for themselves and their teams, and then work toward that objective. However, teams seldom can operate effectively under one fixed

"Well, guess I did it again, eh guys? Missed a field goal in the final seconds. But, hey, we're a team, right? Right, guys? . . . Guys?"

type of authority over time. The leader might prefer to use his or her favorite style, and the followers might also have an inherent preference for one type of authority or another; but if the team is to be effective, then the authority dynamics they are operating with should complement the demands of the situation. Since situations often change over time, so should the authority dynamics of the team. This idea is very similar to a point made earlier in the book—that effective leaders tend to use all five sources of leader power.

In research on the behavior of leaders in forming their teams, Ginnett (1993) found that highly effective leaders used a variety of authority dynamics in the first few minutes of the team's life. This does not mean that each highly effective leader used a single style that was different from the others (i.e., other leaders). It does mean that each one of the effective leaders used a variety of authority styles. At one point in the first meeting of the team, the leader would behave directively, which enabled him to establish his competence and hence his legitimate authority. At another time, he would engage the team in a very participative process and actively seek participation from each member of the team. By modeling a range of authority behaviors in the early stages of the team's life, the effective leaders laid the groundwork for continuing expectations of shifting authority as the situational demands changed.

Prescriptions of the Model

Having seen two examples of how this model uses team process measures to guide the search for critical input variables (or key leverage points) at the individual, organizational, and team design levels, we are ready to move on to the job of the leader. Following McGrath's (1964) view of the leader's role (the leader's main job is to identify and help satisfy team needs), and using the TELM, it is possible to identify constructive approaches for the leader to pursue. As described earlier in this chapter, what leaders do depends on where a team is in its development. Ideally, leaders will have the opportunity to assume their leadership role at the very beginning of a team's life. With that luxury, the leader can proceed directly through the model from left to right. In this way, she can implement the three critical functions for team leadership: direction, design, and development.

Direction.   Obviously, the team needs to have clear direction. In their book *The Wisdom of Teams* (1994), Katzenbach and Smith suggest that this may be the most important single step in teamwork. If the team has a challenging and demanding goal, teamwork may be necessary to accomplish the task. In highly effective work teams, the leader ensures that the team has a clear vision of where they are going. The communication of a vision frequently involves metaphorical language so that team members actually "paint their own picture" of where the team is headed.

Design.   The importance of the design function of leadership cannot be overstated. Whether in the startup of a team or in the midstream assignment of leaders, designing the team is critical. It is also often the most frequently omitted step. Managers have long been trained to detect deviations and correct them. But what if the deviations are not detectable until the output stage? At their best, managers often detect deviations at the process stage and attempt to fix them "right where they are seen." Far too often, little time or attention is focused at the input level. Senior-level leaders may resist changing the organizational systems for a number of reasons, including having a vested interest in maintaining the status quo (whatever it is, it at least let them rise to their current position!). And while individual team leaders may have little control over the organizational context and systems, they always have the opportunity for making an impact in their own team's design.

This is a luxury few leaders get, however. If a leader takes over the reins of an in-place team, then she should (1) examine the team at work to determine if the process measures indicate potential problems, (2) back up to the appropriate level in the input stage to identify problems that may need to be corrected or redesigned, and (3) take appropriate action.

Development.   If the leader finds that the team has a clear sense of direction and vision, and the input variables at the individual, organizational, and team levels are contributing positively to team effectiveness (i.e., the design portion of the leader's job has been taken care of), then she can turn her attention to the development level. Development is the ongoing work done with the team at the process level to continue to find ways to improve an already well designed team. Given our individualistic culture, we have identified many teams in organizations that are apparently well designed and supported at the input level, but that have had no training or experience in the concept of teamwork. There are times when effective teamwork is based on very different concepts than effective individual work. For example, for a team to do well, the individuals composing the team must sometimes not maximize their individual effort. Referred to as subsystem nonoptimization, this concept is at first not intuitively obvious to many newly assigned team members. Nevertheless, consider the example of a high school football team that has an extremely fast running back and some very good (but considerably slower) blocking linemen as members of the offense. Often, team members are told they all need to do their absolute best if the team is going to do well. If our running back does his absolute best on a sweep around the end, then he will run as fast as he can. By doing so, he will leave his blocking linemen behind. The team is not likely to gain much yardage on such a play, and the linemen and the back, who have done their individual best, are apt to learn an important experiential lesson about teamwork. Most important, after several such disastrous plays, all of the team members may be inclined to demonstrate poor team process (lower effort, poor strategy, poor use of knowledge, and poor group dynamics represented by intrateam strife). If we assume that all the input stage variables are satisfactorily in place, ongoing coaching may now be appropriate. The coach would get better results if he worked out a better coordination plan between the back and the linemen. In this case, the fast running back needs to slow down (i.e., not perform maximally) to give the slower but excellent blockers a chance to do their work. After they have been given a chance to contribute to the play, the back will have a much better chance to then excel individually, and so will the team as a whole.

We are now in a position to consider the complete model (see Figure 13–6). It has been shown that leaders can influence team effectiveness by (*a*) ensuring the team has a clear sense of purpose and performance expectations; (*b*) designing or redesigning input stage variables at the individual, organizational, and team design levels; and (*c*) improving team performance through ongoing coaching at various stages, but particularly while the team is actually performing its task. These "midcourse corrections" should not only improve the team outcomes but should also help to avoid many of the team-generated problems that can cause less-than-optimal team performance (Steiner, 1972).

Concluding Thoughts about the Team Effectiveness Model

It is helpful to point out the few remaining items depicted in the model which have not been discussed. Note first the box labeled **material resources**. Note that this is a physical requirement, not an issue for the design or coaching of the team itself. Even if a team is well designed, has superior organizational systems

Figure 13–6

Ginnett's Team Effectiveness Leadership Model

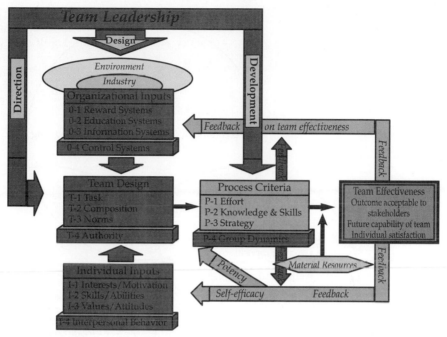

supporting its work, and has access to superior-quality ongoing development, without adequate physical resources it is not likely to do well on the output level. Also note that background shells representing the industry and the environment have been included, as discussed earlier in this chapter. While the team leader may have little opportunity to influence these shells, the shells will certainly have an impact on the team.

Finally, there are several feedback loops which provide information to various levels of the organization. Usually, information is available to the organization as a whole (either formally or informally) about which teams are doing well and which are struggling. Whether leaders have access to this information is largely a function of whether they have created or stifled a safe climate. Feedback at the individual level can influence the perceived efficacy of the individual members of the team (Bandura, 1977; Lindsley, Brass, & Thomas, 1995), while the overall potency of the team is impacted even for tasks which the team has yet to attempt (Guzzo, Yost, Campbell, & Shea, 1993).

Lastly, let us reinforce a limitation noted earlier. For ease of use and guidance, this model has been presented as if it were a machine (e.g., if P-2 breaks, check I-2, O-2, and G-2). As with other models of leadership or other human systems, however, nothing is that simple. There are obviously other variables that impact teams and team effectiveness. There are also complex interactions between the variables described even in this model. But we have considerable evidence that the model can be useful for understanding teams (Hackman,

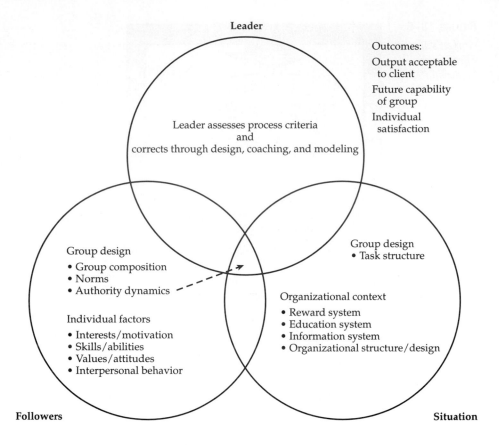

FIGURE 13–7

Factors from the Normative Model of Group Effectiveness and the Interactional Framework

Leader

Outcomes:

Output acceptable to client

Future capability of group

Individual satisfaction

Leader assesses process criteria and corrects through design, coaching, and modeling

Group design
• Group composition
• Norms
• Authority dynamics

Individual factors

• Interests/motivation
• Skills/abilities
• Values/attitudes
• Interpersonal behavior

Group design
• Task structure

Organizational context
• Reward system
• Education system
• Information system
• Organizational structure/design

Followers

Situation

1990), and, in light of the relationship between teams and leadership, we are now using it as an underlying framework in courses to help leaders more effectively lead their teams.

Let us integrate the variables from this model into our L-F-S framework (see Figure 13–7). Clearly, there are variables of importance in each of the three arenas. However, in this model, the characteristics of the leader play a lesser role because the leader's job is to work on what is not being provided for the team in order for it to perform its task. The focus thus has shifted from the leader to the followers and to the situation.

Geographically Dispersed Teams

Just as teams and teamwork have become essential to the accomplishment of work in organizations in the present decade (and as far as we can foresee into the future), so too will be an understanding of teams that are not in a single location. With the movement toward the global marketplace and the resultant globalization of organizations, it is appropriate to briefly consider the difficulties and recommended solutions for leading geographically dispersed teams (GDT), or

What Is the "Global Population" of Your Classroom?

Your authors attended a training session conducted by a major corporation intended for their newly appointed executives. One session was devoted to demonstrating the need for a global perspective in today's environment. To illustrate the key point, the instructor divided the room into unequal groups representing the geographical distribution of the world's population and had each group stand up in turn. As each group stood, she told them the proportion of the global population they represented. The proportions she used are provided below. You might try it in your classroom—it makes the point dramatically.

Australia and New Zealand	2%
North America	5%
Former Soviet Union	5%
Latin America	7%
Western/Eastern European	10%
Africa	12%
Asian	56%

as they are sometimes referred to, virtual teams. There is considerable discussion about the labeling of such teams (Kossler & Prestridge, 1996), but for simplicity we will call them GDT here.

The marketplace is the globe (see Highlight 13–9). Western corporations are recognizing that growth and development opportunities are often much greater in the former Soviet Union, China, Latin America, and Africa than they are in their traditional markets of North America and Europe. But with this realization come new challenges for leading teams that are not only dispersed geographically but are often culturally different as well. Fortunately, information and communication technology is offering some new opportunities, if not solutions, for part of these problems. By the year 2000, personal computer sales are predicted to top 100 million annually, or one PC for every 60 people on the planet; more than 60 million people will use cellular phones; and the Internet and World Wide Web are expanding at approximately 100 percent growth annually (Lipnack & Stamps, 1997). But is the mere opportunity to communicate electronically sufficient to ensure teamwork? Apparently not.

Researchers at the Conference Board (1996) reported that there were five major areas that needed to change if global teams were to work. The five listed were senior management leadership, innovative use of communication technology, adoption of an organization design that enhances global operations, the prevalence of trust among team members, and the ability to capture the strengths of diverse cultures, languages, and people.

Armstrong and Cole (1994) did in-depth studies of GDT and have reported three conclusions which should be considered by leaders of these teams. First, the distance between members of a GDT is multidimensional. "Distance" includes not just geographical distance, but also organizational distance (e.g., different group or department cultures), temporal distance (e.g., different time zones), and differences in national culture. Second, the impact of such distances on the performance of a distributed work group is not directly proportional to objective measures of distance. In fact, Armstrong and Cole suggested that a new measure of distance between group members that reflects the degree of group cohesion and identity, a measure of psychological distance between members, would predict group performance better than geographical distance. Finally, the differences in the effects that distance seems to have on work groups is due at least partially to two intervening variables: (1) integrating practices *within* a GDT, and (2) integrating practices *between* a GDT and its larger host organization.

Finally, there are a number of frameworks under development to help leaders work with GDTs, and there may be specific factors that these frameworks provide which can be useful. However, in our admittedly limited exposure to GDTs in a pure research sense, a number of our clients have reported the TELM (discussed earlier) has been quite useful in considering the process problems that present themselves and in suggesting appropriate leverage points for intervention.

Summary

The group perspective showed that followers' behaviors can be the result of factors somewhat independent of the individual characteristics of followers. Group factors that can affect followers' behaviors include group size, stages of group development, roles, norms, communication networks, and cohesion. Leadership practitioners should use these concepts to better understand followers' behaviors. Leaders should also use a team perspective for understanding follower behavior and group performance. Leadership practitioners need to bear in mind how a team's sense of identity, common goals or tasks, level of task interdependence, and differentiated roles affect functional and dysfunctional follower behavior. Additionally, because effective teams have several readily identifiable characteristics, leadership practitioners may want to use the suggestions provided by Hackman (1990), Ginnett (1992), or Hallam and Campbell (1992) to develop more effective teams.

The Team Effectiveness Leadership Model posited that team effectiveness can best be understood in terms of inputs, processes, and outcomes. The input level consists of the intelligence, skills, personality traits, and values of the followers; the design of the team itself; and various organizational systems which create the context in which the teams will operate. The process level concerns the way in which teams behave while going about their tasks, and the output level concerns whether customers and clients are satisfied with the team's product, whether the team improves and develops as a performing unit, and whether followers are satisfied to be members of the team. By identifying certain process problems in teams, leaders can use the model to diagnose appropriate leverage points for action at the individual, team design, or organizational levels, or for ongoing development at the process level. Although this model is relatively new, leaders concerned with team work in organizational settings have found this framework useful in helping them conceptualize factors affecting team effectiveness and identifying targets for change.

Key Terms

Team Effectiveness Leadership Model	group
outputs	group perspective
process measures	cliques
inputs	span of control
leverage point	additive task
individual factors	social loafing
organizational level	social facilitation
team design	forming
material resources	storming
norming	performing
group roles	task role
relationship role	relationship role
dysfunctional roles	role conflict
intrasender role conflict	intersender role conflict
interrole conflict	interrole conflict
person-role conflict	role ambiguity
norms	group cohesion
overbounding	groupthink
organizational shells	ollieism

Discussion Questions

1. How do the tenets of the Team Effectiveness Leadership Model compare with the components of team performance described earlier?

2. Not all group norms are positive or constructive from the leader's perspective. If a group holds counterproductive norms, what should the leader do?

3. Contrast groupthink with managing agreement (as exemplified in the Abilene paradox described in an earlier chapter). Do both phenomena reflect the same underlying dynamics?

14 MOTIVATION, SATISFACTION, AND PERFORMANCE

Chapter Outline

Introduction

If you go back to Chapter 1, we defined leadership as "the process of influencing an organized group toward accomplishing its goals." Implicit in this definition is the ability to motivate others, and many people believe this may be one of the most important qualities of a good leader. The importance of follower motivation is suggested in findings from diverse work groups that most people believe they could give as much as 15 percent or 20 percent more effort at work than they now do with no one, including their own bosses, recognizing any difference. Perhaps even more startling, these workers also believed they could give 15 percent or 20 percent *less* effort with no one noticing any difference (Kinlaw, 1991). Moreover, variation in work output varies significantly across leaders and followers. Hunter, Schmidt, and Judiesch (1990) estimated the top 15 percent of workers in any particular job produced from 20 to 50 percent more output than the average worker, depending on the complexity of the job. Put another way, the best computer programmers or sales clerks might write up to 50 percent more programs or process 50 percent more customer orders. Might better methods of motivating workers lead to higher productivity from *all* the workers? And are more-motivated workers happier or more-satisfied workers? What can leaders do to increase the motivation and satisfaction levels of their followers?

Creating highly motivated and satisfied followers depends, most of all, on understanding others. Therefore, whereas motivation is an essential part of leadership, it is appropriate to include it in this part of the book, which focuses on the followers. As an overview, this chapter will address three key areas. First, we will examine the links between leadership, satisfaction, motivation, and performance—four closely related concepts. Second, we will review the major theories and research for motivation and satisfaction. Last, and perhaps most importantly, we will discuss what leaders can do to enhance the motivation and satisfaction of their followers if they implement these different theories (see also Highlight 14–1).

Defining Motivation, Satisfaction, and Performance

Motivation, satisfaction, and performance seem clearly related. For example, Colin Powell probably could have pursued a number of different vocations, but was *motivated* to complete ROTC and join the army. He was also motivated to put in extra time, energy, and effort in his various positions in the army, and he was judged or rated by his superiors as being an exceptional performer. His outstanding *performance* as an officer was crucial to his promotion as the head of the Joint Chiefs of Staff during the Reagan and Bush administrations. We could also infer that he was happy or *satisfied* with military life, as he was a career officer in the army. Highlight 14–2 provides another example of motivation, satisfaction, and performance. In this case, Lori seems to have *motivated* her team to work hard and thereby develop a high level of proficiency. By developing this high level of proficiency, her team was able to *perform* well at both the state fair and the international championships. It also seems likely that the team took great pride (i.e., *satisfaction*) in winning these championships. But let's explore each of these concepts a bit more closely.

Most people probably think of motivation as dealing with choices about what we do and how much effort we put into doing it. According to Kanfer (1990), **motivation** is anything that provides *direction, intensity,* and *persistence* to behavior. Another definition considers the term *motivation* a sort of shorthand to describe choosing an activity or task to engage in, establishing the level of effort to put forth on it, and determining the degree of persistence in it over time (Campbell & Pritchard, 1976). Other researchers define motivation as a behavior probability; it is the likelihood an individual will initiate and continue exhibiting certain behaviors (Miller & Rollnick, 1991). Like personality traits and types, motivation is not directly observable; it must be inferred from behavior.

Leadership Quotes, Chapter 14

The body of every organization is structured from four kinds of bones. There are the wishbones, who spend all their time wishing someone would do the work. Then there are the jawbones, who do all the talking, but little else. The knucklebones knock everything anybody else tries to do. Fortunately, in every organization there are also the backbones, who get under the load and do most of the work.

Leo Aikman, *On Bones*

Some players you pat their butts, some players you kick their butts, some players you leave alone.

Pete Rose

The first thing a young officer must do when he joins the Army is to fight a battle, and that battle is for the hearts of his men. If he wins that battle and subsequent similar ones, his men will follow him anywhere; if he loses it, he will never do any real good.

Viscount Montgomery of Alamein

Better debate a question without settling it than settle a question without debating it.

Joseph Joubert

There is no limit to the good one can do if he doesn't care who gets the credit.

George C. Marshall

The beatings will continue until morale improves.

Sign on an executive's desk

Only the mediocre are always at their best.

Jonathan Winters

Be a yardstick of quality. Some people aren't used to an environment where excellence is expected.

Steve Jobs

Work is love made visible.
And if you cannot work with love but only with distaste, it is better that you should leave your work and sit at the gate of the temple and take alms of those who work with joy.
For if you bake bread with indifference, you bake a bitter bread that feeds but half a man's hunger.

Kahlil Gibran

An acre of performance is worth the whole world of promise.

Clark Howell

Highlight 14–2

One Young Leader's Motivation

When Lori graduated from high school, she took a part-time position as coach of the cheerleading team she had just served with. There had been some opposition to offering Lori the job, since she was barely older than the present cheerleaders. However, the need for a coach was great; the school took pride in the caliber of its cheerleaders, and the previous coach had departed. Furthermore, Lori had been a superior cheerleader herself, and she was available for part-time work since she was a freshman at a nearby college. Lori got the job, but it was not all roses. In some ways the concerns about her youth had been justified. It was more difficult for Lori to enforce certain standards (e.g., punctuality at practice) when the perception of some team members was that she hadn't followed all the rules herself when she was a cheerleader. Nonetheless, the confidence in this young woman proved justified. As a result of her dynamic leadership, technical skill, and demanding training, the team proved good enough to win the cheerleading competition at the state fair. It was even invited to go to the international cheerleading championships in Japan. Unfortunately, accepting the invitation seemed unlikely since the trip's total expenses would amount to over $50,000. Lori accepted the invitation, however, believing the team could raise the money. She personally organized numerous fundraisers such as car raffles, candy sales, fashion shows, and so on. She won widespread community support and received significant donations from local businesses. The team went to Japan . . . and placed first! Lori's team was best in the world.

Apply the various approaches to motivation covered in this chapter to Lori and the other members of her team. Which theories or models help explain Lori's level and persistence of effort? Which might help explain the motivation of the other members of the cheerleading team, a group little different from Lori in many ways?

We would infer that one person would be highly motivated to do well in school if she spent a lot of time studying for exams. She could choose to spend her time and energy on socializing, intramurals, or volunteer work, but because she is spending time outlining readings and reviewing class notes we say she is motivated to do well in school. At work, if one person regularly assembles twice as many radios as any other person in his work group—assuming all have the same abilities, skills, and resources—then we likely would say this first person is more motivated than the others. We use the concept of motivation to explain differences we see among people in the energy and direction of their behavior. Thus, the energy and effort Madeleine Albright expended advancing her career in the academic and the diplomatic communities, or Konosuke Matsushita expended to grow his company would be examples of the direction, intensity, and persistence components of motivation.

Performance, on the other hand, concerns those behaviors directed toward the organization's mission or goals, or the products and services resulting from those behaviors. At work or school we can choose to perform a wide variety of

FUNKY WINKERBEAN by Tom Batiuk

Source: Reprinted with special permission of King Features Syndicate.

behaviors, but performance would only include those behaviors related to the production of goods or services or obtaining good grades. Performance differs from **effectiveness**, which generally involves making judgments about the adequacy of behavior with respect to certain criteria such as work-group or organizational goals. Lori's team was motivated (they chose to practice and spent a lot of time practicing), performed those behaviors associated with team success (they focused on practicing the cheerleading movements and maneuvers they would use in competition), and were judged to be effective at the state and international competitions (Campbell, McCloy, Oppler, & Sager, 1992; Hogan, Curphy, & Hogan, 1994). Similarly, Konosuke Matsushita was motivated to start and grow his company and performed those behaviors associated with building successful companies, and many people would judge these behaviors to be effective given the phenomenal growth of his business conglomerate.

Performance is affected by more than a person's motivation. Factors such as intelligence, skill, and the availability of key resources can affect a person's behavior in accomplishing organizational goals (i.e., performance) independently of that person's level of motivation. For example, a salesperson may put considerable effort into establishing and maintaining sales contacts over a two-month period but still fail to make a single sale. In terms of the level and persistence of effort, the salesperson would be seen as highly motivated. However, if she made poor decisions about which contacts to maintain or lacked adequate computer resources to keep track of her clients, then much of her behavior would have been misdirected and her performance would suffer. Moreover, if sales volume was used to judge the salesperson's effectiveness, then that individual would be judged to be ineffective. Thus, an adequate level of motivation may be a necessary but insufficient condition of effective performance.

Job satisfaction is not how *hard* one works or how *well* one works, but rather how much one *likes* a specific kind of job or work activity. Job satisfaction deals with one's attitudes or feelings about the job itself, pay, promotion or educational opportunities, supervision, co-workers, workload, and so on (Saal & Knight, 1988). Various polls over the past half century have consistently shown the vast majority of men and women report liking their jobs (see Campbell & Hyne, 1995; Health, Education, & Welfare Task Force, 1973;

Hoppock, 1935; Smith, Scott, & Hulin, 1977; or Staines & Quinn, 1979). Research has also shown that people who are more satisfied with their jobs are more likely to engage in **organizational citizenship behaviors**—behaviors not directly related to one's job that are helpful to others at work. Organizational citizenship behaviors make for a more supportive workplace. Examples might include volunteering to help another employee with a task or project, or filling in for another employee when asked (Organ & Ryan, 1995). Happier workers tend to be more helpful workers.

Although people generally like the work they do, two related events have caused a recent downturn in job satisfaction levels among employees in the United States. Over the past 10 years, many organizations have downsized or substantially reduced the number of people on the company payroll. For example, Kodak and Digital Equipment Corporation have each eliminated over 25,000 positions, AT&T eliminated 60,000 jobs, and the U.S. military has shrunk by over a million positions since the early 1990s. These positions were eliminated in order to reduce costs and improve profitability, but they also dramatically increased the workload for the remaining workers (i.e., the same amount of work was being performed by fewer people), and severed the implicit contract between workers and employers (i.e., if workers performed at a high level, then employers guaranteed a job for life). The end result is that job dissatisfaction among workers is at an all time high. Although people report being satisfied with what they do for a living, the forced overtime, increased workload, and erosion of trust between employers and employees has significantly lowered levels of job satisfaction (Howard, 1996; Curphy, 1998b). As a result, more workers are leaving their jobs than ever before, and it is has been very difficult to maintain various indices of organizational effectiveness when many of the best and brightest employees are leaving the company. Job satisfaction may not have as direct an effect on the accomplishment of organizational goals as motivation or performance, but the indirect effects of reduced organizational citizenship behaviors or increased turnover are so important that leaders can ill afford to ignore them. The best leaders may well be those who can motivate workers to perform at a high level while maintaining an equally high level of job satisfaction.

Having now defined motivation, performance, and job satisfaction, we can explore their relationships a bit further. We have already noted how motivation does not always assure good performance. If followers lack the necessary skills or resources to accomplish a group task, then trying to "motivate them more" could be unproductive and even frustrating (Campbell, 1977; 1988). For example, no high school basketball team is likely to defeat the Chicago Bulls, however motivated the players may be. The players on the high school team simply lack the abilities and skills of the Bulls players. Higher motivation will usually only affect performance if followers already have the abilities, skills, and resources to get the job done. Motivating others is an important part of leadership, but not all of it; pep talks and rewards are not always enough.

The relationships between motivation and job satisfaction are a bit more straightforward—as a matter of fact, many theories of motivation are also theories of job satisfaction. The implicit link between satisfaction and motivation is that satisfaction increases when people accomplish a task, particularly when the task requires a lot of effort. It might also seem logical that *performance* must be higher among more-satisfied workers, but actually this is not always so (Iaffaldano & Muchinsky, 1985; Podsakoff & Williams, 1986). It is just not true that happy workers are always the most productive ones, nor is it true that unhappy or dissatisfied workers are always the poorest performers. It is entirely possible, for example, for poorly performing workers to be fairly satisfied with their jobs (maybe because they are paid well yet do not have to work very hard, like Homer Simpson in the television show "The Simpsons"). It is also possible for dissatisfied workers to be relatively high performers (they may have a strong work ethic, or they may be trying to improve chances to get out of their current job). Despite the intuitive appeal of believing that satisfied workers usually perform better, it may be that satisfaction has only an indirect effect on performance (Locke & Latham, 1990). Nevertheless, having both satisfied *and* high-performance followers is a goal leaders should usually strive to achieve.

Understanding and Influencing Follower Motivation

Few topics of human behavior have been the subject of so much attention as that of motivation. So much has been written about motivation that a comprehensive review of the subject is beyond the scope of this book. We will, however, survey several major approaches to understanding worker motivation, as well as address the implications of these approaches for follower satisfaction and performance. (See Kanfer, 1990; Campbell & Pritchard, 1976, for more comprehensive reviews.) These motivational theories and approaches provide leadership practitioners with a number of suggestions to get followers to engage in and persist with different behaviors. It is important to understand that some motivational theories are particularly useful in certain situations but are not as applicable in others. Just as a carpenter can successfully build better wooden structures or furniture by having a larger set of tools, so can leadership practitioners solve a greater number of motivational problems among followers by becoming familiar with different motivational theories and approaches. People who have only hammers in their tool kits are more likely to see every problem as a nail needing hammering, and it is not unusual for less-effective leaders to call on a very limited number of approaches to any motivational problem. *Leaders who are knowledgeable about different motivational theories are more likely to choose the right theory for a particular follower and situation, and often have higher-performing and more-satisfied employees as a result.*

Another problem in motivating followers is that leaders—even experienced ones—often *assume* they know what works in motivating others. For example, one of the authors played on a highly successful Division I hockey team. The coach was a two time Olympic medalist, and had over 20 years of coaching experience. He was internationally acknowledged as having one of the best minds in the sport. However, the coach motivated others the same way he was motivated

TABLE 14–1   Ten Motivational Approaches

Category	Theory or Approach	Major Themes or Characteristics
Need	Maslow's hierarchy of needs	Satisfy needs to change behavior.
	Alderfer's ERG theory	Can satisfy multiple needs simultaneously.
	Herzberg's two-factor theory	Hygiene factors result in dissatisfaction; motivators result in satisfaction.
Individual difference	Achievement orientation	Personality trait.
	Intrinsic motivation	People are more motivated to do some activities than others.
Cognitive	Goal setting	Set goals to change behavior.
	Expectancy theory	Motivate others by clarifying links between behaviors, performance, and rewards.
	ProMES	Motivate others by clarifying links between behaviors, performance, evaluations, rewards, and personal needs.
Situational	Job characteristics model	Modify task or job to increase motivation.
	Operant approach	Change rewards and punishments to change behavior.

as a player, which was to dish out plenty of criticism and punishment and give little praise. Many of the players did not like the coach's approach to motivation, but as long as the team was successful they were willing to put up with it. However, after about five years the team started to falter. The talent was there, but many of the players openly started to resent the coach's style. Some very talented players quit the team because of the coach's approach to motivating his players, which in turn caused the team to be even less successful. After several disappointing seasons the coach was eventually asked to retire.

There are three important points in this story. First, the coach's approach to motivation worked with some players but clearly failed with others. Second, although the coach was experienced and knowledgeable in the sport, he did not have a good understanding of different perspectives on motivation. Had he been aware of the different motivational theories, he might have tried different approaches with his players, especially as circumstances changed. Third, this story again highlights the importance of the action-observation-reflection model of Chapter 4. The coach continued acting the same way with his players even though the situation clearly dictated that he needed to do something different. His failure to reflect on his behaviors and their outcomes and adjust his behavior accordingly eventually led to his downfall.

In this section we will discuss the key aspects of 10 different approaches to understanding motivation in a work or leadership context. We have organized the approaches into four broad categories: need theories, individual-difference approaches, cognitive theories, and situational approaches. This categorization seems helpful for explanatory purposes, even though it is admittedly atheoretical. These theories and approaches are listed in Table 14–1, and for illustrative purposes we will also discuss how leadership practitioners could apply these approaches to motivate two fictitious followers, Julie and Ling Ling. Julie is a 21-year-old ski lift operator in Banff, British Columbia. Her primary job is to ensure that people get on and off her ski lift safely. She does periodic equipment safety checks, maintains the lift lines and associated areas, and helps people to get on or off the lifts. Julie works from 7:30 A.M. to 5:00 P.M. five days a week, gets paid a salary, and has a pass that allows her to ski for free whenever she is off work. Ling Ling is a 35-year-old real estate agent in Hong Kong. She works for an agency that locates and rents apartments for people on one- to three-year business assignments for various multinational companies. She works many evenings and weekends showing apartments, and gets paid a salary plus a commission for every apartment she rents. How the nine approaches could be used to motivate Julie and Ling Ling will be discussed periodically throughout this section.

Need Theories

The three major need theories include Maslow's (1954) hierarchy of needs, Alderfer's (1969) existence-relatedness-growth (ERG) theory, and Herzberg's (1964, 1966) two-factor theory. These theories assume that all people share a common set of basic needs; the theories primarily differ in the types of needs that supposedly underlie or drive people's behavior. **Needs** refer to internal states of tension or arousal, or uncomfortable states of deficiency people are motivated to change (Kanfer, 1990). Hunger would be a good example of a need, as people are motivated to eat when they get hungry. Other needs might include the need to live in a safe and secure place, to belong to a group with common interests or social ties, or to do interesting and challenging work. If these needs were not being met, then people would choose to engage in and persist with certain behaviors until they were satisfied. According to these motivational approaches, leadership practitioners can get followers to engage in and persist with certain behaviors by correctly identifying and appeasing their needs.

Maslow's Hierarchy of Needs.   According to Maslow (1954), people are motivated by five basic sorts of needs. These include the need to survive physiologically, the need for security, the need for affiliation with other people (i.e., belongingness), the need for self-esteem, and the need for self-actualization. Maslow's conceptualization of needs is usually represented by a triangle with the five levels of needs arranged in a hierarchy (see Figure 14–1) called, not surprisingly, the **hierarchy of needs.** According to Maslow, any person's behavior can be understood primarily as the effort directed to satisfy one particular level of need in the hierarchy. Which level happens to be motivating a person's behavior at any time depends on whether or not lower needs in the hierarchy have been satisfied. According to Maslow, lower-level needs must be satisfied before the next higher level becomes salient in motivating behavior.

Maslow (1954) said higher-level needs like those for self-esteem or self-actualization would not become salient (even when unfulfilled) until lower

FIGURE 14–1

*Maslow's
Hierarchy of
Needs*

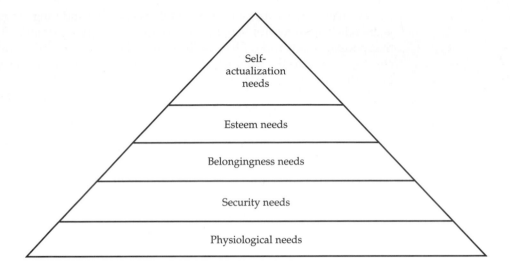

needs were satisfied. Thus, a practical implication of his theory is that leaders may only be successful in motivating follower behavior by taking account of the follower's position on the need hierarchy. Applying Maslow's hierarchy to Julie, it might be relatively inefficient to try to motivate our ski lift operator by appealing to how much pride she could take in a job well done (i.e., to her self-esteem) if she was underdressed for weather conditions. If her boss wanted Julie to do more, then she should first make sure that Julie's physiological (i.e., clothing) needs were met, that she worked and lived in a secure place, and that she had ample opportunities to socialize with other employees. Only after these lower needs have been met should the boss try to increase Julie's self-esteem. Thus, if leadership practitioners want to use Maslow's hierarchy of needs to motivate employees to work harder, then they need to determine where their followers fall on the need hierarchy and ensure all lower-order needs are satisfied before appealing to their followers' self-esteem or self-actualization needs. Leadership practitioners should watch for "mismatches" between their motivational efforts and followers' *lowest* (on the hierarchy) unsatisfied needs.

ERG Theory.   Alderfer's (1969) **existence-relatedness-growth (ERG) theory** is similar to Maslow's hierarchy of needs. In the terms of ERG theory, *existence* needs basically correspond to Maslow's physiological and security needs; *relatedness* needs are like Maslow's social and esteem needs; and *growth* needs are similar to the need for self-actualization. Beyond those similarities, however, are two important differences.

First, Alderfer (1969) reported that people sometimes try to satisfy *more than one need at a time*. For example, even though a follower's existence needs may not be entirely satisfied, she may still be motivated to grow as a person. Second, he claimed *frustration of a higher-level need can lead to efforts to satisfy a lower-level need*. In other words, a follower who is continually frustrated in achieving some need might regress and exert effort to satisfy a lower need that has already been satisfied. For example, if Ling Ling had strong relatedness needs but was unable to build friendships with her co-workers, she might regress to satisfying her existence needs. Some of these behaviors might include moving to an upscale neighborhood; buying a more expensive wardrobe, a new sportscar, or new stereo equipment; or demanding more pay. Alderfer called this the **frustration regression hypothesis.**

The practical implications for motivating followers using ERG theory are threefold. First, leadership practitioners should identify the degree of need for existence, relatedness, and growth for their followers. Followers having relatively unmet existence or relatedness needs will focus their behaviors on satisfying these needs, and leadership practitioners may be able to help with these endeavors. Second, followers having relatively satisfied existence and relatedness needs are more apt to focus on growth needs. Leadership practitioners can get a lot of motivational "mileage" by helping followers satisfy their growth needs, as these followers are more willing to develop and master new skills, apply skills in new situations, look for more responsibility and independence, and strive to achieve greater personal and organizational challenges. Third, leadership practitioners should also be on the lookout for the frustration regression hypothesis among followers. If followers are repeatedly thwarted in satisfying a need, and have shifted their efforts to oversatisfying a lower-level need, then appealing to the need that was thwarted may be relatively fruitless. For instance, trying to motivate Ling Ling to work harder by stating the real estate agency is a team and needs to work together to get results will probably not result in substantial behavioral change for Ling Ling. Instead, the leader may need to work closely with Ling Ling to determine why she has been unable to satisfy her relatedness needs, and coach her on how to build relationships with others in the agency. Only after these relationships are established will the leader be able to motivate Ling Ling to work as a part of a team to get results.

Herzberg's Two-Factor Theory.   Herzberg (1964, 1966) developed the **two-factor theory** from a series of interviews he conducted with accountants and engineers. More specifically, he asked what satisfied them about their work and found that their answers usually could be sorted into five consistent categories. Furthermore, rather than assuming that what dissatisfied people was always just the opposite of what satisfied them, he also specifically asked what *dissatisfied* people about their jobs. Surprisingly, the list of satisfiers and dissatisfiers represented entirely different aspects of work.

Herzberg labeled the factors that led to *satisfaction* at work **motivators,** and he labeled the factors that led to *dissatisfaction* at work **hygiene factors.** The most common motivators and hygiene factors can be found in Table 14–2. According to the two-factor theory, efforts directed toward improving hygiene factors will not increase followers' motivation. No matter how much leaders improve working conditions, pay, or sick-leave policies, for example, followers *will not* exert any additional effort or persist any longer at a task. For example, followers will

TABLE 14–2   Motivators and Hygiene
Factors of the Two-Factor Theory

Hygiene Factors	*Motivators*
Supervision	Achievement
Working conditions	Recognition
Co-workers	The work itself
Pay	Responsibility
Policies/procedures	Advancement and growth
Job security	

Source: Adapted from F. Herzberg, *Work and the Nature of Men*
(Cleveland, OH: World Publishing, 1966).

probably be no more motivated to do a dull and boring job merely by being given pleasant office furniture. On the other hand, followers may be asked to work in conditions so poor as to create dissatisfaction, which can distract them from constructive work.

Given limited resources on the leader's part, the key to increasing followers' effort levels according to two-factor theory is to just adequately satisfy the hygiene factors while maximizing the motivators for a particular job. It is important for working conditions to be adequate, but it is even more important (for enhancing motivation and satisfaction) to provide plenty of recognition, responsibility, and possibilities for advancement (see Figure 14–2). In the words of Fred Herzberg, "If you don't want people to have Mickey Mouse attitudes, then don't give them Mickey Mouse work" (unpublished comments).

Two-factor theory suggests that there are several actions Julie's boss could take if she wanted Julie to work harder as a ski lift operator. Although improving the hygiene factors will not get Julie to work harder, they can serve as demotivators if not adequately addressed. Thus, Julie's boss should first determine how satisfied Julie is with pay, co-workers, working conditions, and her actions as a supervisor, and do all she can to improve these factors. Once these factors are addressed, then Julie's boss should focus on Julie's need to do a good job by getting her some recognition for being one of the best ski lift operators at the resort, increasing her responsibility, or providing her with opportunities for advancement. According to the theory, leaders appealing to motivators before addressing hygiene factors are unlikely to get their followers to exert extra effort toward team or organizational goals.

Although the two-factor theory offers leaders ideas about how to, and how not to, bolster followers' satisfaction, it has received little empirical support beyond Herzberg's (1964) own results. In other words, it just may not be an accurate explanation for job satisfaction despite its apparent grounding in data. We present it here in part because it has become such a well-known approach to work motivation and job satisfaction that the present account would appear incomplete if we ignore it. The problem with two-factor theory, however, seems

FIGURE 14–2

Herzberg's Two-Factor Theory

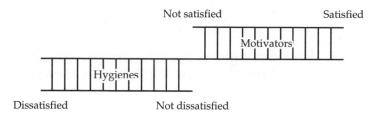

to lie in the very aspect that at first seemed its strength: the original data on which it was based. For one thing, as noted earlier, Herzberg developed his theory after interviewing only accountants and engineers, two groups who are hardly representative of workers in other lines of work or activity. Furthermore, his subjects typically attributed job satisfaction to *their* skill or effort, yet blamed their dissatisfaction on circumstances beyond their control. This sounds suspiciously like the fundamental attribution error described earlier in this book. Despite such limitations, however, Landy (1985) concluded that the two-factor theory has provided useful insight into what followers find satisfying and dissatisfying about work.

Concluding Thoughts on Need Theories.   Although Maslow's, Alderfer's, and Herzberg's theories have played an important historical role in our understanding of motivation, they do have several limitations. For one thing, none of the theories makes specific predictions about what an individual will do to satisfy a particular need (Betz, 1984; Kanfer, 1990). In the example above, Ling Ling may exert considerable effort to establish new friendships at work, try to make friends outside of work, or even spend a lot of money on a new car or stereo equipment (the frustration-regression hypothesis). The theories' lack of specificity and predictive power severely limits their practical applicability in real-life settings. On the other hand, awareness of the general nature of the various sorts of basic human needs described in these theories seems fundamentally useful to leaders. Leaders will have a difficult time getting followers to maintain various work behaviors by emphasizing good relationships with co-workers or appealing to their sense of pride if the job pays only minimum wage and followers are having a difficult time making ends meet. A person may be reluctant to volunteer for a self-actualizing opportunity in support of a political campaign if such participation may risk that person's financial security. Perhaps the greatest insight provided by these three theories is that leadership practitioners may need to address some basic, fundamental areas before their attempts to get followers to expend more effort on work-related behaviors will be successful (see Highlight 14–3).

Another limitation of these three theories is that they are somewhat dated; Maslow developed the hierarchy of needs over 40 years ago, and the other two theories are approximately 30 years old. Although these theories seem to have withstood the test of time, it may be that recent demographic, cultural, or economic trends have altered the profile or salience of needs. Another question is whether

Highlight 14–3

Physiological Needs in the Workplace: The Case of Bathroom Breaks

Physiological or existence needs are not particularly big drivers of behavior in many jobs. Most employers provide offices and cubicles with adequate furniture and lighting, and allow morning, lunch, and afternoon breaks, and many even have on-site cafeterias and exercise facilities. However, extreme cold, dampness, heat, or foul air can be strong drivers of behavior for oil platform workers, coal miners, and paper mill employees. Most oil, coal, and paper companies do all they can to mitigate the effects of these extreme working conditions on employee motivation levels, but some industries seem to have taken a different approach. Apparently, federal and state labor laws do not require employers to guarantee resting periods or bathroom breaks, and some employers used these laws to make their employees work during their entire shift. The poultry processing industry may be among the worst offenders in this area, as these companies put a strong emphasis on production, have few relief workers, often have an inadequate number of bathrooms per employee, and allow few if any breaks during a shift. Moreover, many of the employees are immigrants in need of work and fearful of raising concerns. Could the high accident and disability rates associated with this industry be partly due to the inability to satisfy basic physiological needs for 8- to 12-hour periods? Would worker performance and effectiveness increase if periodic work breaks were built into the shifts? What would it be like to be a leader in one of these facilities?

Source: S. Franklin, "Boss, Give us a Break.," *Denver Post*, March 1, 1998, p. K-8.

there are any gender differences in these needs. Recent research by Gordon and Whelan (1998) indicates that working men and women do in fact have some different needs, and that these needs change over time. As seen in Table 14–3, midlife women seem to have the most complicated set of needs. Although some of the needs listed in Table 14–3 could be easily categorized into one or more of the needs identified in the three theories, other needs, such as work-family balance, may not. Leadership practitioners who are familiar with these newer needs may be able to better motivate employees by finding ways to help them to successfully satisfy these needs.

Individual Differences in Motivation

Maslow's hierarchy of needs, Alderfer's ERG theory, and Herzberg's two-factor theory claimed that all people share certain common fundamental needs. A very different approach to understanding human motivation involves focusing on stable and consistent *differences* between people in the strength of various motives.

TABLE 14–3   Early and Midcareer Gender Differences in Needs*

Needs	Younger Women	Midlife Women	Midlife Men
Child care	Logistical issues of child care dominate	Logistical issues of child care resolved	Typically not a concern
Flexible work hours	Rely on their organizations to create flexibility	Hold sufficiently senior positions to create their own flexibility	Typically not a concern
Career advancement	Strong needs, traditional definitions of success	Strong needs, individual definitions of success	Strong needs; may feel a failure if no traditional career advancement
Reevaluate past experiences and current life structure	Little evaluation occurs	Reevaluation focuses on need for balance	Reevaluation focuses on realizing dreams and career achievement
Face mortality	Typically not a concern	Recognize aging and become aware of mortality of their nuclear family as grown children leave home	Feel old and become aware of their own mortality
Reaffirm dreams or build new ones	Still working on first dreams	Revise definitions of success to focus on personal accomplishment in career and family, not on social definitions of success	Evaluate whether career achieved expectations and add new aspects to life, e.g., greater family or relationship time
Renewed work-family balance	Attempt to meet both career and family needs, through "superwoman" approach, with career needs often dominating	Develop a new perspective about work and family with clear reassessment of priorities within each domain	Spend more time with family that they have neglected for career advancement
More personal time	Unwilling to acknowledge need for personal time over time required by job, spouse, or children	Willing to accept need for personal time and spend time on themselves, rather than on job, spouse, or children	More focus on expanding relationships previously ignored
Continued achievement, accomplishment, perceived value to organization	Beginning to achieve and accomplish, trying to become valuable to their organization	Acknowledge that they have achieved and accomplished but strongly desire to continue and also be perceived as valuable to their organization	Want continued recognition and advancement, but recognize that they may have plateaued
Meet the challenges of the next decade	Present oriented and not focused on future	Begin to acknowledge that they must prepare for different family, career, and personal challenges in the next decade	Primary focus on mortality and needing to accomplish goals immediately

*Based on Hochschild, A. 1997. *The Time Bind: When Work Becomes Home & Home Becomes Work.* New York: Metropolitan Books; Lechner, V., and Creedon, M. 1994. *Managing Work and Family Life.* New York: Springer; *Business Week.* 1988. Work & Family. June 28:88; Mason, J. C. 1993. Working in the Family Way. *Management Review* 82(7), July 1993: 25-28; Hall, D. T., and Richter, J. 1988. Balancing Work Life and Home Life: What Can Organizations Do to Help? *Academy of Management Executive* 2(3):213-223; Moore, L. L. (ed.) 1986. *Not as Far as You Think: The Realities of Working Women.* Lexington, Mass.: Lexington Books; Ehrensaft, D. 1987. *Parenting Together: Men and Women Sharing the Care of the Children.* New York: Free Press; Levinson, D. J. 1977. The Mid-Life Transition: A Period in Adult Psychosocial Development, *Psychiatry* 40:99-112; Levinson, D. J. 1978. *The Seasons of a Man's Life.* New York: Alfred A. Knopf; and the results of this study.

Source: J. R. Gordon and K. S. Whelan, "Successful Professional Women in Midlife: How Organizations Can More Effectively Understand and Respond to the Challenges," *The Academy of Management Executive* 12, no. 1 (1998), pp. 8–27. Reprinted with permission.

Two prominent examples of this approach focus, respectively, on the personality trait of achievement orientation, and on how intrinsically motivating a particular task or activity is for any given person. These two approaches differ from the need theories in that individuals are believed to vary substantially in terms of (1) achievement orientation, and (2) the activities and tasks people enjoy doing. Whereas need theories assume all people have the same needs, the individual-difference approach emphasizes how individuals differ in the strength of various needs.

Achievement Orientation.   Atkinson (1957) proposed that an individual's tendency to exert effort toward task accomplishment depended partly on the strength of her motive to achieve success, or, as Atkinson called it, her **achievement orientation.** McClelland (1975) further developed Atkinson's ideas and said that individuals with a strong achievement orientation (or in McClelland's terms, a strong *need for achievement*) were competitive, liked taking responsibility for solving problems, and strived to accomplish socially acceptable endeavors and activities. These individuals also preferred tasks that provided immediate and ample feedback and were moderately difficult (i.e., tasks that required a considerable amount of effort but were accomplishable). Additionally, individuals with a strong need to achieve felt satisfied when they successfully solved work problems or accomplished job tasks (McClelland, 1975). Individuals with a relatively weak need to achieve were generally *not* as competitive, preferred easier tasks, and did not feel satisfied by solving problems or accomplishing assigned tasks. McClelland (1975) maintained that differences in achievement orientation were a primary reason people differed in the levels of effort they exerted to accomplish assignments, objectives, or goals. Thus, achievement orientation is a bit like "fire in the belly"; people with more achievement orientation are likely to set higher personal and work goals and are more likely to expend the effort needed to accomplish them. People with lower levels of achievement motivation tend to set lower personal and work goals, and are less likely to accomplish them.

Achievement orientation is also a component of the Big Five personality dimension of dependability (see Chapter 8). Like intelligence, dependability has been found to be positively related to performance across virtually all jobs (Barrick & Mount, 1991; Ones, Mount, Barrick, & Hunter, 1994; Tett, Jackson, & Rothstein, 1991; Tett, Jackson, Rothstein, & Reddon, 1994). Achievement orientation has been found to predict success in school (Gough, 1987), in the military (Curphy & Osten, 1993; Hough, 1992), in blue collar and retail workers (Hogan & Hogan, 1992; Paajanen, Hansen, & McLellan, 1993), and in managers (Nilsen, 1995; Curphy, 1998b). Thus, people with higher levels of achievement orientation are likely to do better in school, pursue postgraduate degrees, get promoted more quickly, and get paid higher salaries and bonuses than their lower-scoring counterparts. Achievement orientation can often be a compensating factor for intelligence, and grades in school can provide an example. One individual may get better grades at school than another whose tested IQ score is higher just by capitalizing on higher motivation to achieve.

TABLE 14–4   Women's Career Strategies for Advancing to Senior Management

Strategy	Critical	Fairly Important	Not Important	Did Not Use
Consistently exceed performance expectations	77%	22%	1%	0%
Develop style that men are comfortable with	61%	35%	3%	1%
Seek difficult or high visibility assignments	50%	44%	2%	4%
Have an influential mentor	37%	44%	9%	9%
Network with influential colleagues	28%	56%	9%	6%
Gain line management experience	25%	29%	11%	33%
Move from one functional area to another	23%	34%	20%	22%
Initiate discussion regarding career aspirations	15%	47%	25%	12%
Be able to relocate	14%	22%	17%	45%
Upgrade educational credentials	12%	33%	24%	29%
Change companies	12%	24%	23%	39%
Develop leadership outside office	11%	41%	29%	18%
Gain international experience	5%	19%	24%	51%

Source: B. R. Ragins, B. Townsend, and M. Mattis, "Gender Gap in the Executive Suite: CEOs and Female Executives Report on Breaking the Glass Ceiling," *Academy of Management Executive* 12, no. 1 (1998), pp. 28–42. Reprinted with permission.

Given that individuals with higher achievement orientation scores set high personal goals and put in the time and effort necessary to achieve them, it is hardly surprising that achievement orientation is often a key success factor for people who advance to the highest levels of the organization. For example, achievement orientation appears to be a common theme across many of the career advancement strategies women have used to reach the top levels in Fortune 1000 companies (see Table 14–4).

So, what does achievement orientation imply for the leadership practitioner? Because personality traits do not change much over time, hiring people with high levels of achievement orientation may be the easiest way for leaders to use this approach for assuring motivated followers. Let's look at how achievement orientation might come into play for Julie and Ling Ling. Say the hiring process for both Julie and Ling Ling involved personality testing, and both had high levels of achievement orientation. Given these results, we would expect Ling Ling to work with her boss to set aggressive goals for renting apartments and then work as many nights and weekends as are needed to achieve them. We might also expect Ling Ling to obtain her MBA from Hong Kong University over the next few years. Julie could also be expected to set high personal and work goals, but she may find that her job limits her ability to pursue these goals. Unlike Ling Ling, who can control the number of nights and weekends she wants to work, Julie has no control over the number of people who ride on her lift. The job itself may limit Julie's ability to fulfill her high level of achievement orientation. As a result, she may pursue other activities, such as becoming an expert skier, joining the ski patrol, doing ski racing, looking for additional responsibilities or opportunities for advancement, or finding another job where she has the opportunity to achieve and get rewarded for her efforts. Because Julie will set and work toward high personal goals, a good boss would work closely with Julie to find work-related ways to capitalize on her achievement orientation. Thus, achievement orientation may be a dual-edged sword. Leadership practitioners may be able to hire a group of highly motivated followers, but they also need to provide them with opportunities to set and achieve work-related goals; otherwise they may find different ways to fulfill their high levels of achievement orientation.

Intrinsic Motivation.   Work behavior is motivated by both internal and external factors. In this section, we will focus on the former, although we also will examine how the two factors interact. We use the term **intrinsic motivation** to describe behavior seemingly motivated for its own sake, for the personal satisfaction and increased feelings of competence or control one gets from doing it. In other words, some people are motivated to persist in certain behaviors for the simple reason that they like to do them. Julie or Ling Ling might spend a lot of time operating ski lifts or showing apartments simply because they enjoy these activities. What is intrinsically motivating for one person, however, may not be for someone else. Hobbies, for example, are almost by definition intrinsically motivating, yet they also reflect the diversity of human tastes for different activities. Stamp collecting may be intrinsically motivating to one person, yet exceedingly boring to many others. The key for leadership practitioners is to identify the activities their followers like to perform (within reason), and increase their job opportunities to do them.

Deci (1975) and Dawes (1991) observed that individuals often voluntarily put forth effort toward activities they enjoy doing. If an individual is already engaged in an intrinsically motivating activity, we might ask just what would result if extrinsic rewards were added to the intrinsic reward of just performing the activity. It might seem at first as though the activity would be even further strengthened if external rewards were added to the internal rewards. Sometimes, though, that is not the case. Some research has shown that external rewards or incentives may backfire if they are given to people already intrinsically motivated to perform the tasks. That can result in a *decrease* in the person's intrinsic motivation toward the tasks (Calder & Staw, 1975; Deci, 1972; Kohn, 1993). Further study of this **overjustification effect** has shown that external rewards can result in a decrease in intrinsic motivation when they are perceived to be "controlling"; however, rewards seen as providing "informational" value (e.g., letting a person know how well he or she is doing) or those that are consistent with societal norms concerning pay and benefits typically do not result in a decrease in intrinsic motivation for the task (Deci, 1975; Eisenberger & Cameron, 1996; Fisher, 1973; Lepper, Greene, & Nisbett, 1973). After reviewing the results of approximately 100 studies, Eisenberger and Cameron (1996) go on to say that the overjustification effect is more of a myth than reality; the number of situations where this occurs is so limited and so easily avoided that it rarely, if ever, happens in the real world. Despite this preponderance of evidence, however, many educators and leaders continue to believe in the notion that rewards reduce the intrinsic motivation of tasks.

So how would intrinsic motivation and the overjustification effect work with Julie and Ling Ling? In both cases, the leaders would need to spend time with both individuals to find out what they enjoy doing at work. Not only might the boss learn that Julie really likes to work outdoors; she might also like the social nature of interacting with the crowds waiting in lift lines. This might indicate Julie would particularly enjoy working in the largest and most crowded lifts, something other lift operators may not enjoy so much. Ling Ling might really like sales but hate the paperwork associated with closing leases. Her boss could assign the administrative aspects of Ling Ling's job to an administrative support person, or find other ways (such as using technology) to reduce her administrative workload. Although followers will almost always have to perform activities they may not like, the more a leader aligns her followers' intrinsic interests with their work activities, the more motivated her team is likely to be.

Concluding Thoughts on Individual Differences in Motivation. Because people vary in their achievement orientation and in the tasks they find intrinsically motivating, one way to ensure that followers will exert the effort needed to accomplish their tasks is to select individuals already high in these motives. Although McClelland (1985) has reported successfully training people to be higher in achievement orientation, this can be a relatively expensive and inefficient process; putting more emphasis on selecting the right people for the job in the first place may be a preferable approach for leaders to take.

It is also important to remember that perhaps the most effective way to determine what followers find to be intrinsically motivating is to simply ask them what they like to do. However, many leaders either do not have particularly good relationships with their followers or assume they know what motivates them, so they often fail to ask this simple question. While it may not be possible to completely align tasks with followers' intrinsic interests, leaders may be able reassign or periodically rotate tasks to increase the level of follower motivation. Leaders often assume that jobs and task assignments are static and unchangeable, but most organizations do not care who does the work as long as it gets done. Leaders may be able to get higher-quality work and have more satisfied employees by reassigning work according to intrinsic interests.

Cognitive Theories

The three cognitive theories we will describe here deal primarily with clarifying the conscious thought processes people use when deciding how much effort to exert toward some task or goal. Leadership practitioners using cognitive theories to motivate followers do so by either *setting goals* or clarifying the *links* between level of effort and desirable outcomes.

Goal Setting. One of the most familiar and easiest formal systems of motivation to use with followers is **goal setting**. From the leader's perspective, it involves helping followers see how a goal might be attained by following a systematic

The High-Performance Cycle

According to Locke and Latham (1990), leaders can have both high-performing and highly satisfied workers by implementing the high-performance cycle in their work groups. Leaders start the high-performance cycle by first setting high expectations for followers and giving them specific, difficult goals to achieve. Specific, difficult goals will energize followers to develop task strategies, exert a certain level of effort, and persist on the task. Given this effort, followers will successfully accomplish the goal if they are committed to the goal, are given timely feedback, and have the necessary resources and abilities. Successful goal accomplishment leads to valued rewards, which in turn leads to increased job satisfaction and organizational commitment. Higher organizational commitment will allow leaders to set more difficult goals and to expect higher levels of performance and satisfaction from followers.

plan to achieve it. According to Locke and Latham (1990), goals are the most powerful determinants of task behaviors. Goals serve to direct attention, mobilize effort, help people develop strategies for goal achievement, and help people continue exerting effort until the goal is reached. That leads, in turn, to even higher goals (see Highlight 14–4).

Locke and Latham (1990) reported that nearly 400 studies across individuals, groups, and organizations in eight different countries have provided consistent support for several aspects of goal setting. First, this research showed goals that were both *specific* and *difficult* resulted in consistently higher effort and performance when contrasted to "do your best" goals. Second, *goal commitment* is critical. Merely having goals is not enough. Although follower participation in setting goals is one way to increase commitment, goals set either by leaders unilaterally or through participation with followers can lead to necessary levels of commitment. Commitment to assigned goals was often as high as commitment to goals followers helped to set, provided the leader was perceived to have legitimate authority, expressed confidence in followers, and provided clear standards for performance (Locke & Latham, 1990). Third, followers exerted the greatest effort when goals were accompanied by *feedback*; followers getting goals or feedback alone generally exerted less effort.

Several other aspects of goal setting are also worth noting. First, goals can be set for any aspect of performance, be it reducing costs, improving the quality of services and products, increasing voter registration, or winning a league championship. Nevertheless, leaders need to ensure that they do not set conflicting goals, as followers can only exert so much effort over a given period of time. Second, determining just how challenging to make goals creates a bit of a dilemma for leaders. Successfully completed goals provide followers with a sense of job satisfaction, and easy goals are more likely to be completed than difficult goals. However, easily attainable goals result in lower levels of effort (and, in turn, performance) than do more difficult goals. Locke and Latham (1990) suggested that leaders might motivate followers most effectively by setting moderately difficult goals, recognizing partial goal accomplishment, and making use of a continuous-improvement philosophy by making goals incrementally more difficult (Imai, 1986).

More recent research has shed additional light on goal setting. Locke and Latham's review was primarily focused on the effects goal setting had on individual performance, but goal setting can have the same effects on group performance (O'Leary-Kelly, Martocchio, & Frink, 1994). This research also showed that goal specificity is especially critical for improving group performance. Sagie's (1994) research showed that participation and feedback may have additive effects; leaders with the highest performing groups worked with followers to jointly set goals, and also gave concrete feedback on goal progress. Leaders who only gave feedback or only used participative goal setting had lower performing groups. Leaders with the poorest-performing groups neither provided feedback nor allowed their groups any say in setting goals. Finally, Wagner (1994) noted that although participative goal setting does have positive effects on performance and satisfaction, these effects were not dramatic. If time is limited, it may be more preferable for leaders to set specific and challenging goals and provide ongoing feedback than to use participative goal-setting techniques.

Could leadership practitioners apply goal setting to Julie and Ling Ling in order to increase their motivation levels? Given the research findings just described, Julie and Ling Ling's bosses should work with these two followers to set specific and moderately difficult goals, and provide regular feedback on goal progress. Julie and her boss could look at Julie's past performance or other lift operators' performance as a baseline, and then set specific and measurable goals around the number of hours worked, the number of people who fall off the lift during a shift, customer satisfaction survey ratings from skiers, the length of lift lines, or the number of complaints from customers. Similarly, Ling Ling and her boss could look at some real estate baseline measures and set goals around the number of apartments rented for the year, the total monetary value of these rentals, the time it takes to close a lease and complete the necessary paperwork, customer complaints, and sales expenses. Note that both Ling Ling and Julie's bosses would need to take care that they do not set conflicting goals. For example, if Julie had a goal only for the number of people who fell off the lift, then she might be more likely to run the lift very slowly, resulting in long lift lines and numerous customer complaints. In a similar vein, bosses need to ensure that individual goals do not conflict with team or organizational goals. Ling Ling's boss would need to make sure that Ling Ling's goals did not interfere with those of the other real estate agents in the firm. If Ling Ling's goals did not specify territorial limits, then she might rent properties in other agents' territories, which in turn might cause a high level of interoffice conflict. Both bosses should also take care to set measurable goals; that way they could provide both Julie and Ling Ling with the feedback they need to stay on track. More information on the specific steps of goal setting can be found in Part V of this book.

Expectancy Theory.   The next two cognitive theories are concerned with clarifying the links between what people do and the rewards or outcomes they will obtain. First described by Tolman (1932), **expectancy theory** has been modified for use in work settings (Vroom, 1964; Porter & Lawler, 1968; Lawler, 1973). It involves two fundamental assumptions: (*a*) motivated performance is the result of conscious choice, and (*b*) people will do what they believe will provide them the highest (or surest) rewards. Thus, expectancy theory is a highly *rational* approach to understanding motivation. It assumes that people act in ways that maximize their expectations of attaining valued outcomes, and that reliable predictions of behavior are possible if the factors that influence those expectations can be quantified. In this model, there are three such factors to be quantified. The first two are probability estimates (expectancies), and the third is a vector sum of predicted positive and negative outcomes. Expectancy theory maintains that leadership practitioners will be able to motivate followers if they understand the process followers use to determine whether certain behaviors will lead to valued rewards.

The first probability estimate is the **effort-to-performance expectancy.** Like all probabilities, it ranges from no chance of the event occurring to absolute certainty of it's occurring; or, in decimal form, from 0.0 to 1.0. Here, the follower estimates the likelihood of performing the desired behavior adequately, assuming she puts forth the required effort. The second probability estimate is the **performance-to-outcome expectancy.** In this case, our follower estimates the likelihood of receiving a reward, given that she achieves the desired level of performance. This is a necessary step in the sequence since it is not uncommon for people to actually do good work yet not be rewarded for it (e.g., someone else may be the teacher's pet). Finally, the follower must determine the likely outcomes, assuming that the previous conditions have been met, and determine whether their weighted algebraic sum (**valence**) is sufficiently positive to be worth the time and effort. To put it more simply, expectancy theory says that people will be motivated to do a task if three conditions are met: (1) they can perform the task adequately if they put forth enough effort, (2) they will be rewarded if they do it, and (3) they value the reward (see Figure 14–3).

Applying these three concepts to Ling Ling might be helpful here. Since the Chinese government takeover in 1997 and the collapse of the Asian economy, the real estate rental market has been depressed in Hong Kong. Even though Ling Ling has been working three weekday evenings a week and all day Saturday (showing an average of 12 apartments per week), she is 25 percent behind her sales quota. According to expectancy theory, Ling Ling would first determine if working the additional two weekday evenings a week would enable her to rent more apartments (effort-to-performance expectancy). Second, Ling Ling would

FIGURE 14–3

An Example of Expectancy Theory

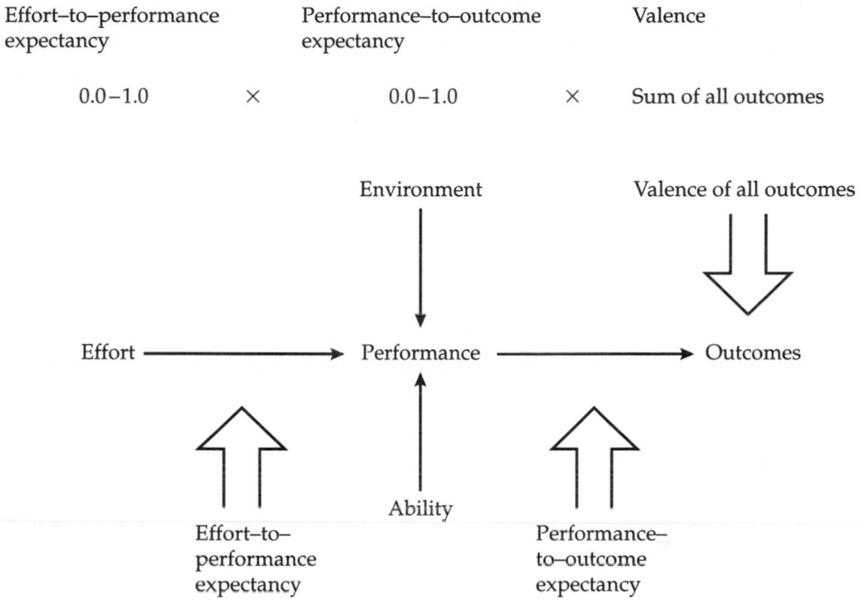

Effort–to–performance expectancy

Performance–to–outcome expectancy

Valence

$$0.0-1.0 \qquad \times \qquad 0.0-1.0 \qquad \times \qquad \text{Sum of all outcomes}$$

Environment

Valence of all outcomes

Effort $\longrightarrow$ Performance $\longrightarrow$ Outcomes

Ability

Effort–to–performance expectancy

Performance–to–outcome expectancy

have to determine if renting these additional apartments would be sufficient to reach her sales quota by the end of the year (performance-to-outcome expectancy). Finally, Ling Ling would have to weigh the advantages of reaching her sales quota (sales bonus, job security,) relative to the disadvantages (stress, loss of free time, loss of sleep, etc.) (valences). Notice that if Ling Ling did not believe that (*a*) working additional weekday evenings would help her to rent more apartments, (*b*) renting these additional apartments would be enough to reach her annual sales quota, or (*c*) the benefits of reaching her sales quota outweighed the costs, then Ling Ling would choose not to put forth the effort to rent additional apartments. She may feel that the real estate market is in such bad shape, or her bonus so low that even if she were to meet her quota, it would not be worth the additional effort. As seen in Figure 14–3, all three components must have a relatively high probability or be favorably weighted in order for Ling Ling to exert further effort in renting additional apartments.

Leadership practitioners using expectancy theory to motivate a follower to do a work project would need to take three steps. First, the leader would have increase effort-to-performance expectancy by clarifying the links between the follower's level of effort and project completion. To do this, the leader and follower might discuss what the follower would need to do, and the amount of time and resources it would take to complete the project. Second, the leader would need to increase the performance-to-reward expectancy by discussing the positive outcomes to the follower and the organization if the project were completed on time and at cost. This might involve such things as a year-end bonus, increased recognition by upper management, or reduced costs or increased market share for the organization. Finally, the leader would need to clarify all of the potential valences for successfully completing the project. This may not be obvious to the follower, so the leader would need to clearly describe both the pros and cons but emphasize the positive aspects of the project.

ProMES.   Another cognitive theory of motivation that can be used with individuals, groups, and organizations is called the **Productivity Measurement and Enhancement System (ProMES)** (Pritchard, Jones, Roth, Stuebing, & Ekeberg, 1988). Like expectancy theory, ProMES takes a very rational approach to motivation, and focuses on the decision-making process followers use when choosing to perform specific behaviors. In this process, followers are more motivated when they see clear links between: (1) the behaviors they exhibit, (2) the products and services they produce, (3) the evaluations they receive, (4) the rewards they earn, and (5) their personal needs. To motivate followers, leaders set goals and provide feedback on followers' behaviors, they clarify and provide feedback on how these behaviors are creating valued products and services for the team or organization, and they describe how these products and services are in turn related to followers' performance evaluations, rewards, and personal needs. According to Pritchard and his colleagues, any break in the motivational sequence will have a dramatic effect on followers' motivational levels. For example, if leaders have not set clear goals, then followers may not see how their behaviors are creating value-added products and services. Similarly, if leaders do not provide feedback on the number or quality of the products and services produced, or have not explained how different performance levels will lead to different evaluations and rewards, then followers are likely to be much less motivated to perform.

ProMES is a very data-driven, metrics-based theory of motivation. Workers must be given regular feedback on the products and services they are producing, and how they are doing with respect to performance evaluations and rewards. To implement a ProMES program, leaders and followers work together to develop measures of productivity, evaluation, and reward for their work groups. This process helps to clarify what tasks followers will need to perform and how well or frequently they need to do them. Identifying the type, frequency, and format of the feedback for each task is also part of this process (feedback is often provided using various graphs or charts). Care is taken so that followers' behaviors are aligned with team or organizational objectives. Pritchard and his colleagues have implemented ProMES in nine different countries at dozens of manufacturing, service, sales, and military organizations, and the results have been very impressive. In almost all cases, ProMES has led to productivity gains that have far outstripped those associated with individual organizational interventions, such as goal setting, training, or personnel selection (Azar, 1997). Pritchard believes these results are due to the fact that ProMES addresses *all* the links in the motivational sequence. Rewards alone may be motivating if rewards are the problem, but they may not be particularly effective in situations where the rewards are not valued or where the links between what people do and what they produce are not clear.

So how might we apply ProMES to increase Julie's level of motivation as a ski lift operator? The first step would be to have Julie and her boss set several areas of goals for various ski lift operator tasks, such as running the lift safely, minimizing lift line lengths, or maintaining a high level of customer service. Next, Julie and her boss would select what metrics to use to provide feedback and measure progress. These might include weekly customer service surveys or the number of times the ski lift was slowed down or stopped for safety reasons. Julie could review her progress using daily lift stoppage charts and weekly graphs for the survey results. Julie and her boss would then need to decide how certain levels of performance would link to various performance evaluation ratings. Having customer satisfaction ratings above 70 percent may be a "4," above 80 percent a "3," above 90 percent a "2," and above 95 percent a "1." Next, Julie and her boss would also decide how different evaluation ratings would result in different rewards. For example, Julie could be eligible for an additional $300 per month if her performance evaluations averaged 1.0–1.5, $150 per month for evaluations averaging 1.5–2.0, and so on. Finally, the boss would need to ensure that these monetary rewards were valued by Julie. It may turn out that Julie would rather have time off, substitute her operator shifts to ski patrol shifts, or be sponsored as a ski racer by the resort. In this case, the boss would have to link Julie's performance evaluations to the more-valued rewards.

Concluding Thoughts on Cognitive Theories of Motivation.   All three of the preceding cognitive theories assume that people make rational, conscious decisions about what to put their energies into. Unfortunately (or fortunately?), human behavior does not always correspond to what rational analysis might predict. Human motivation is often affected by nonrational or emotional considerations as well as by rational ones; behavior does not follow a simple and logical formula. For example, while it may be very logical for Julie to work five days a week, she may nonetheless decide to "blow off" work one day and go skiing at another resort instead. It is worth recalling our earlier discussion about how people always operate in both rational and emotional realms of behavior. Because people make choices to exert effort based on both rational and emotional considerations, predictions based on rational modeling alone are inexact. For example, the highest levels of follower motivation are often noted with charismatic or transformational leaders, and none of these three models can adequately explain why followers are so willing to put forth high levels of energy and effort for these leaders. Still, they may provide leadership practitioners with several useful ideas on how to better motivate followers in a broad variety of situations, and they are more helpful than having no theories at all. Just because rational approaches do not reflect the full complexity of being human does not mean leaders should ignore the insights they offer.

Perhaps more than the other theories and approaches described in this section, the cognitive theories place a strong premium on leader-follower communication. It is hard to imagine how goal setting, expectancy theory, or ProMES would work if the leader did not articulate goals, provide on-going feedback, and continually clarify motivational links with followers. If leader-follower communication is poor, then it is unlikely that leaders will realize the benefits of these three approaches. The research generally shows these theories can effectively increase worker motivation; when they fail it often has more to do with how the theory was implemented than with inadequacy of the theory. Thus, leaders with poor interpersonal communication and feedback skills might have a difficult time using these theories to increase follower motivation levels.

Situational Approaches

As the phrase implies, these approaches emphasize how the *situation* affects motivation. In other words, these approaches emphasize the leader's role in changing various aspects of the situation in order to increase followers' motivation. The two theories that emphasize situational influences in motivation are the job characteristics model and the operant approach.

The Job Characteristics Model.   According to the **job characteristics model,** jobs or tasks having certain kinds of characteristics provide inherently greater motivation and job satisfaction than others. Hackman and Oldham (1976, 1980) said that followers will work harder and be more satisfied if their tasks are meaningful, provide ample feedback, allow considerable latitude in deciding how to accomplish them, and require use of a variety of skills. The Hackman and Oldham model is based on five critical job characteristics: task identity, task significance, feedback, autonomy, and skill variety. Note that while a job high in all these characteristics might seem intrinsically motivating, this model is *not* just another way of looking at intrinsic motivation. *Individuals* differ in their intrinsic motivation, whereas the job characteristics model says some *jobs* are, by their nature, more motivating and satisfying than others.

This is not to say that individual differences are unimportant in the job characteristics model. They actually do play a key role in the model via a concept called **growth-need strength.** This refers to the degree to which an individual is motivated by the need to fulfill herself (in Maslow's terms, to increase her self-esteem or self-actualization). Hackman and Oldham (1976, 1980) said that individuals with high growth-need strength especially desire jobs high on the five characteristics in the model; they are even more motivated and satisfied than others with such jobs, and even less motivated and satisfied than others with jobs very low on those characteristics. Thus, if leaders were to follow the tenets of the job characteristics model to increase followers' satisfaction and motivation, then they would hire followers with high growth-need strength, and they would restructure followers' jobs to have more favorable task characteristics.

Research has provided mixed support for the job characteristics model. The 28 studies reviewed by Loher, Noe, Moeller, and Fitzgerald (1985) provided evidence that strongly confirmed the satisfaction hypothesis. Other research, however, has called into question the satisfaction and motivation predictions of the model. There is even some evidence calling into question the presumed causal relationship between job satisfaction and job characteristics. While Hackman and Oldham (1976, 1980) presumed higher job satisfaction *resulted from* working in a job that had certain characteristics, other research indicated that people may, in fact, rate their job characteristics higher *as a result* of being satisfied in those jobs. For example, one study provided workers who had similar and equally satisfying jobs false satisfaction feedback. Those who were given higher job satisfaction feedback rated their job characteristics higher than workers given lower job feedback (Adler, Skov, & Salvemini, 1985). Moreover, Griffin, Welsh, and Moorhead (1981) reported that there was little evidence to show that workers with favorable job characteristics and high growth-need strength actually exerted more effort or persisted at tasks longer than workers with less favorable job characteristics and lower growth-need strength. Despite these mixed findings, the job characteristics theory does provide an alternative perspective for improving followers' motivation levels and has been used extensively in designing or redesigning jobs.

There are several other aspects of the job characteristics model worthy of comment. First, it is important to remember what work was like when this model was developed. In the mid-1970s, a number of jobs were highly routinized and people were essentially doing a small number of highly repeatable tasks. This was particularly true in the manufacturing and service sectors, where, for example, assembly line workers or phone operators did the same tasks over and over. However, technology and organizational downsizing has changed the nature of work in the United States and many other western countries. Technology has made jobs either more simple or substantially more complex. For example, workers at MacDonald's no longer have to enter the dollar amount of items or calculate change, they now merely push buttons with item or meal symbols, and the register automatically calculates the total amount due and change. On the other hand, many assembly line workers now need to have a much higher level of knowledge of electronics, pneumatics, robotics, and advanced materials in order to successfully perform their jobs. Furthermore, downsizing has required the people remaining in an organization to assume the responsibilities and tasks previously done by those who were let go. More than 85 percent of the Fortune 1000 companies downsized between 1987 and 1991, and over 5 million jobs were eliminated (Xie & Johns, 1995).

These three changes probably have made most jobs more complex, and according to the job characteristics model people should be happier and more productive than they were 20 years ago. Although national statistics report worker productivity is at an all-time high, other research shows that people are much less happy with work now then they have ever been (Kleiman, 1997). Perhaps the biggest reason for this relatively high level of worker dissatisfaction is organizational downsizing and worker burnout. People with higher growth-need strength may welcome these additional responsibilities and duties, but those with lower growth-need strengths may be the most vocal about the changes, and the most susceptible to long-term exhaustion and burnout. Xie and Johns (1995) reported that there is a point where job scope exceeds capabilities, and the total direct and indirect costs of burnout may exceed $100 *billion* per year. Of course, the job characteristics model is not responsible for this high level of burnout. As a matter of fact, if job redesign for the survivors is done according to the model, then it may be possible to boost employee motivation and minimize the debilitating effects of stress associated with most downsizings. Unfortunately, however, top management usually assigns new responsibilities and tasks with little regard to the knowledge, skills, training, or resources needed to successfully carry them out (Bedeian & Armenakis, 1998). Cascio's (1995) longitudinal analysis of approximately 500 organizational downsizings shows that most gain some short-term financial benefits, but fail to boost stock prices over the long haul. This failure to gain long-term benefits may be due to employee burnout. Moreover, as Tom Peters so aptly pointed out, most organizations do not shrink to greatness (Peters, 1997).

Despite the mixed findings, a boss could use the job characteristics model to make Julie's job more motivating. Given that Julie spends most of her working day operating a ski lift, task identity is probably not an issue. Her actions affect the number of people getting on and off the lift. Task significance could be an issue, however, if the boss has not explained how Julie's job is a highly visible and important part of the ski resort. It may be worth the boss's time to point out the importance of Julie's role in ski resort operations and how her actions could impact the reputation and financial well-being of the resort, particularly if a skier got hurt due to an unsafe ski lift. The feedback component of Julie's job could also be lacking, and the boss might implement some of the feedback mechanisms discussed earlier with ProMES to enhance this aspect of Julie's job. In terms of autonomy, however, it may be difficult for the boss to change this aspect of Julie's job to increase her motivation levels. The boss may get the biggest motivational increase by increasing the skill variety of Julie's job. In general, operating a ski lift is fairly routine and monotonous. The boss may be able to increase Julie's skill variety by having her rotate through regular shifts of trail grooming with the snow cat, working in the gift shop, handling customer complaints at the resort, or doing ski patrol duties. Given these possible interventions, the job characteristics model can provide leadership practitioners with another perspective on how to change certain aspects of the situation to increase followers' motivation levels. However, this model also assumes that leaders have some control over situational variables, but in some situations, such as union environments, leaders may be very limited in their ability to restructure work to improve followers' motivation.

The Operant Approach.   One very popular way to change the direction, intensity, or persistence of behavior is through rewards and punishments. It will help at the outset of this discussion of the **operant approach** to define several terms. A **reward** is any consequence that *increases* the likelihood that a particular behavior will be repeated. For example, if a Julie gets a cash award for a suggestion to improve customer service at the ski resort, then she will be more likely to forward additional suggestions. **Punishment** is the administration of an aversive stimulus or the withdrawal of something desirable, each of which *decreases* the likelihood a particular behavior will be repeated (Arvey & Ivancevich, 1980). Thus, if Ling Ling loses her bonus for not getting her paperwork in on time, then she will be less likely to do so again in the future. Both rewards and punishments can be administered in a contingent or noncontingent manner. **Contingent** rewards or punishments are administered as *consequences of a particular behavior*. Giving Julie a medal immediately after she won a skiing race or giving Ling Ling a bonus check for exceeding her sales quota might be good examples here. **Noncontingent** rewards and punishments are not associated with particular behaviors. Monthly paychecks might be an example here, if both Julie and Ling Ling receive the same amount of base pay every month whatever their actual effort or output. Finally, behaviors that are not rewarded will eventually be eliminated through the process of **extinction.**

The operant approach for motivating employees was discussed earlier in the section on transactional leadership in Chapter 11, and research evidence has consistently shown that this approach is an effective way of modifying followers' motivation and performance (Bass, 1997; Bass & Avolio, 1994; Curphy, 1991a; Komacki, Zlotnick, & Jensen, 1986; Luthans & Kreitner, 1985; Pritchard, Hollenback, & DeLeo, 1980). Other evidence has shown that rewards are more strongly related to satisfaction and performance than punishment (Luthans & Kreitner, 1985; Podsakoff, Todor, & Skov, 1982; Sims & Szilagyi, 1975), and that contingent rewards and punishments were more strongly related to satisfaction and performance than noncontingent rewards and punishments (Arvey, Davis, & Nelson, 1984; Pritchard, Hollenback, & DeLeo, 1980; Podsakoff & Todor, 1985). These research results imply that leadership practitioners will be better able to change the direction and intensity of their followers' behavior by using considerably more contingent rewards than punishment.

Although these findings paint an encouraging picture of the practical utility of the operant approach, implementing it correctly in a work setting can be difficult (Saal & Knight, 1988). Using operant principles properly to improve followers' motivation and hence performance requires following several steps. First, *leadership practitioners need to clearly specify what behaviors are important*. This means that Julie's and Ling Ling's leaders will need to specify what they want them to do, how often they should do it, and the level or performance required. Second, *leadership practitioners need to determine if those behaviors are currently being punished, rewarded, or ignored*. Believe it or not, sometimes followers are actually rewarded for behaviors that leaders are trying to extinguish, and punished for behaviors that leaders want to increase. For example, Julie may get considerable positive attention from peers by talking back to her leader or for violating the ski resort dress code. Similarly, Ling Ling may be overly competitive and get promoted ahead of her peers (e.g., by renting apartments in her peers' territories), even when her boss extols the need for cooperation and teamwork. It also may be the case that leaders sometimes just ignore the very behaviors they would like to see strengthened. An example here would be if Julie's boss consistently failed to provide rewards when Julie worked hard to achieve impressive safety and customer service ratings (see Highlights 14–5 and 14–6).

Highlight 14–5

The Folly of Rewarding A While Hoping for B

Steven Kerr has written a compelling article detailing how many of the reward systems found in government, sports, universities, businesses, medicine, and politics often *compel people to act in a manner contrary to that intended.* For example, voters want politicians to provide the specifics of their programs or platform, yet politicians often get punished for doing so. Some constituency is bound to get hurt or offended whenever the specifics of a program are revealed, which in turn will cost the politician votes. If a politician keeps overall goals vague, more voters are likely to agree with the politician, and in turn vote for him or her in the next election. Similarly, many universities maintain that their professors are rewarded for both teaching and research excellence, yet the rewards for research far outweigh those for teaching. As a result, many of the top professors in any field spend most of their time doing research. Often they either do not teach any classes or spend a very limited amount of time with undergraduate students. Moreover, the rewards for being a good teacher are few and far between, and the negative consequences for being a poor teacher, particularly after tenure has been conferred, are virtually nonexistent. This state of affairs has gotten so bad that one of the authors once had a professor who stated, "Being a college professor would be a lot better if there weren't any students."

Businesses, like universities and politicians, often utilize inappropriate reward systems. According to Kerr, the following are some of the more common management reward follies:

We hope for . . .	But we often reward . . .
Long term growth	Quarterly earnings
Teamwork	Individual effort
Downsizing or rightsizing	Adding staff and budget
Commitment to total quality	Shipping on schedule, even with defects
Surfacing bad news	Reporting good news, whether it is true or not
Reduced accident rates	Doing work as quickly as possible

Kerr states that managers who complain about unmotivated workers should consider the possibility that their current reward system is incongruent with the performance they desire. To change this situation, Kerr suggests taking a hard look at the current system—are followers being rewarded for performance? Or is the system rewarding irrelevant behaviors or actually punishing good performance? Not all behavior is caused by a formal rewards and punishment system, but leaders can often see substantial gains in performance by ensuring that this system is aligned with appropriate work behaviors.

Source: S. Kerr, "On the Folly of Rewarding A, while Hoping for B," *Academy of Management Executive* 9, no. 1 (1995), pp. 7–14.

Highlight 14–6

Why Incentive Plans Cannot Work

Alfie Kohn has written a series of articles and books about the failure of reward systems. Kohn maintains that incentive or reward systems fail not because of misalignment or administration factors, but rather due to the inadequacy of the psychological assumptions underlying such programs. Reward systems are based on behaviorist theory, which assumes that people will continue engaging in a certain set of behaviors *as long as they are rewarded for doing so.* According to Kohn, this is the fatal flaw in incentive programs, as leaders get only temporary compliance, rather than long-term commitment, when using these programs to motivate followers. Followers will behave in a certain manner only as long as they continue to be rewarded for these behaviors. Once the rewards stop, so do their efforts. Moreover, incentive programs may promote increasing expectations among followers—what worked as an incentive last year will no longer work the next. Thus, an ever-increasing spiral of expectations and rewards occurs whenever an incentive plan is used to improve performance. Unfortunately, these expectations and rewards eventually have no relationship with performance. For example, a number of studies show that most compensation for executives is unrelated or even negatively related to corporate performance. Kohn stated that incentive plans fail for six reasons:

1. *Pay is not a motivator.* There is no firm basis for saying that money motivates people to work harder in the long run. Although some level of pay is necessary, it does not follow that doubling one's pay will result in a two-fold increase in performance.

2. *Rewards punish.* Rewards are ultimately manipulative and followers can feel like they are being overcontrolled.

3. *Rewards rupture relationships.* Incentive programs often foster dysfunctional competition and stifle collaboration among co-workers.

4. *Rewards ignore reasons.* Relying on incentives to boost performance often ignores the real reasons underlying suboptimal performance. Poor performance is sometimes due to a lack of skills or equipment; rewarding increased performance in these situations really fails to address the real problem.

5. *Rewards discourage risk-taking.* People will do no more or less than they are asked to do in order to get a reward. Thus, some of the first casualties with incentive programs are innovation, creativity, and excellence.

6. *Rewards undermine interest.* Rewards can undermine intrinsic interest in work behaviors.

Kohn did state that incentive plans are very motivating, but that they motivate people to get rewards rather than contribute to the organization.

Source: A. Kohn, "Why Incentive Plans Cannot Work," *Harvard Business Review*, September–October, 1993, pp. 54–63.

Highlight 14–7

Emery Air Freight

Emery Air Freight is one of the most-successful examples of how leaders can change the direction, intensity, and persistence of followers' behaviors through the operant approach. Emery Air Freight discovered that it was using the full capacity of its air freight containers only 45 percent of the time and, because of the highly competitive nature of the air freight shipping business, wanted to reduce costs and increase profits by making better use of its air freight containers. The company initially had given employees detailed instructions on how to better use air freight containers. However, this intervention met with little success, and the senior executives at Emery Air Freight consequently decided to implement an operant motivational strategy.

Emery Air Freight's operant strategy consisted of several different steps. First, checklists for air freight container usage were developed. These checklists consisted of the specific behaviors or actions workers could take when preparing an air container for delivery. Second, workers recorded their performance on the checklists, which provided them with information on their own performance with respect to organizational goals. Third, supervisors were trained to provide positive reinforcement on a contingent basis, and in turn praised and rewarded workers for meeting goals or showing improvement over time. In terms of results, Emery Air Freight credited the operant strategy with $2 million in reduced costs after only three years.

Third, *leadership practitioners need to find out what followers actually find rewarding and punishing*. Leaders should *not* make the mistake of assuming that followers will find the same things rewarding and punishing as they do, nor should they assume that all followers will find the same things to be rewarding and punishing. What may be one follower's punishment may be another follower's reward. For example, Ling Ling may dislike public attention and actually exert less effort after being publicly recognized, yet some of her peers may find public attention to be extremely rewarding. Fourth, *leadership practitioners need to be wary of creating perceptions of inequity when administering individually tailored rewards*. A peer may feel that she got the same results as Ling Ling, yet she received a smaller bonus check for the quarter. Leaders can minimize inequities by being clear and consistent with rewards and punishments. Fifth, *leadership practitioners should not limit themselves to administering organizationally sanctioned rewards and punishments*. Using a bit of ingenuity, leaders can often come up with an array of potential rewards and punishments that are effective and inexpensive, and do not violate organizational norms or policies. Julie might find driving the snow cat to be extremely enjoyable, and her boss could use this reward to maintain or increase Julie's motivation levels for operating the ski lift. Finally, because the administration of noncontingent consequences has relatively little impact, *leadership practitioners should administer rewards and punishments in a contingent manner whenever possible*. Highlight 14–7 is an example of the positive results that can come from implementing the operant approach systematically.

Concluding Thoughts on Situational Approaches to Motivation.   The job characteristics model and the operant approach make an important point that is often overlooked in other theories of motivation: By changing the situation, leaders can enhance followers' motivation, performance, and satisfaction. Unfortunately, many leaders naively assume it is easier to change an *individual* than it is to change the *situation*, but this is often not the case. It is important to remember that the situation is not always fixed, and followers are not the only variable in the performance equation. Leaders can often see positive changes in followers' motivation levels by restructuring work processes and procedures, which in turn can increase task identity and significance or skill variety. Tying these changes with a well-designed and well-implemented reward system can result in further increases in motivation. However, leaders are likely to encounter some resistance whenever they change the processes, procedures, and rewards for work, even if these changes are for the better. As noted by Peterson and Hicks (1996), doing things the old way is easy, as followers know the expectations for performance and usually have developed the skills needed to achieve results. Followers often find that doing things a new way can be frustrating, as expectations may be unclear and they may not have the requisite skills. Leadership practitioners can help followers work through this initial resistance to new processes and procedures by showing support, providing training and coaching on new skills, and capitalizing on opportunities to reward progress. If the processes, procedures, and rewards are properly designed and administered, then in many cases followers will successfully work through their resistance and, over time, wonder how they ever got work done using the old systems. The successful transition to new work processes and procedures will rest squarely on the shoulders of leaders.

Motivation Summary

We hope that, after reading this chapter, you will have a better understanding of the variety of ways both you and your followers are motivated (and demotivated). Moreover, you should be able to start recognizing situations where some theories provide better insights about problems in motivation levels than others. For example, if we go back to the survival situation described in Chapter 1, then we can see that the need theories (Maslow and Alderfer) provide better explanations for the behavior of the survivors than the job characteristics model or intrinsic motivation. On the other hand, if we think about the reasons we might not be doing well in a particular class, then we may see that we have not set specific goals for our grades or that the links between our efforts and our grades are not very clear. Or if we are working in a bureaucratic organization, then we may see that there are few consequences for either substandard or superior performance; thus, there is little reason to exert any extra effort. Perhaps the best strategy for leaders is to be flexible in the types of interventions they consider to affect follower motivation. That will require, of course, familiarity with the strengths and weaknesses of the different theories and approaches presented here. Just as a carpenter can more effectively build a house by using a variety of tools, a leader can be more effective by using a variety of motivational interventions to resolve work problems.

At this point it is also important to note that one of the most important tools for motivating followers has not been addressed in this chapter. As described in Chapter 11, charismatic or transformational leadership is often associated with extraordinarily high levels of follower motivation, yet none of the theories described in this chapter can adequately explain how these leaders can get their followers to do more than they ever thought possible. Perhaps this is due to the fact that the theories in this chapter take a very rational or logical approach to motivation, yet transformational leadership uses emotion as the fuel to drive followers' heightened motivational levels. Just as our needs, thoughts, personality traits, intrinsic interests, and rewards can motivate us to do something different, so can our emotions drive us to engage in and persist with a particular activity. A good example here may be political campaigns. Do people volunteer to work for these campaigns because of some underlying need, personal goals, or their intrinsic interests in politics? Although these are potential reasons for some followers, the emotions generated by political campaigns, particularly where the two lead candidates represent different value systems, often seem to provide a better explanation for the large amount of time and effort people contribute. Leadership practitioners should not overlook the interplay between emotions and motivation, and the better able they are to address and capitalize on emotions when introducing change, the more successful they are likely to be.

A final point concerns the relationship between motivation and performance. Many leadership practitioners equate the two, but as we pointed out earlier in this chapter, they are not the same concepts. Getting followers to put in more time, energy, and effort on certain behaviors will not help the team to be more successful if they are the wrong behaviors to begin with. Similarly, followers may not know how and when to exhibit those behaviors associated with performance. Leadership practitioners must clearly identify those behaviors related to performance, coach and train their followers on how and when to exhibit these behaviors, and then use one or more of the theories described in this chapter to get followers to exhibit and persist with those behaviors associated with higher performance levels.

Understanding and Influencing Follower Satisfaction

As stated earlier, job satisfaction concerns one's attitudes about work, and there are several practical reasons why job satisfaction is an important concept for leaders to think about. According to Locke and Latham (1990), satisfied workers are more likely to continue working for an organization. Satisfied workers are also more likely to engage in organizational citizenship behaviors, behaviors that go beyond job descriptions and role requirements and help reduce the workload or stress of others in the organization (Organ & Ryan, 1995). Dissatisfied workers are more likely to be adversarial in their relations with leadership (e.g., file griev-

---

TABLE 14–5   Why People Leave or Stay with Organizations

Why Do People Leave Organizations?		*Why Do People Stay with Organizations?*	
Limited recognition and praise	34%	Promises of long-term employment	82%
Compensation	29%	Supports training and education	78%
Limited authority	13%	Hires/keeps hard-working, smart people	76%
Personality conflicts	8%	Encourages fun, collegial relationships	74%
Other	16%	Bases job evaluation on innovation	72%

Sources: Pace Communication, Inc., *Hemispheres Magazine*, November 1994, p. 155; and "Keeping Workers Happy," *USA Today*, February 10, 1998, p. 1B.

ances) and engage in diverse other sorts of counterproductive behaviors (e.g., foster dissent). Dissatisfaction is one of the key reasons people leave organizations (Tett & Meyer, 1993), and many of the reasons people are satisfied or dissatisfied with work are within the leader's control (see Table 14–5). Although the total costs of dissatisfaction are difficult to measure, the direct costs of replacing a first-line supervisor or an executive can range from $5,000 to $100,000 per hire, depending on recruiting, relocation, and training fees, and these costs do not include those associated with the productivity lost as a result of unfilled positions (Curphy, 1998a). Employee dissatisfaction can also affect revenue and capital available for organizational expansion and upgrades. A survey of major corporations showed that 40 percent switched to another vendor because of poor customer service (Peters, 1997). Barry Gibbons, the CEO of Burger King, stated that "70–90 percent of the decisions not to repeat purchase of anything are not about product or price. They are about dimensions of service" (McKay, 1998). McKay stated that employees are probably not going to provide world-class service if they are unhappy with their job, boss, or company. The inability to retain customers will directly affect revenues and make investors think twice about buying stock in a company. Relatedly, Schellenbarger (1997) reported that 35 percent of investor decisions are driven by nonfinancial factors. Number 5 on a list of 39 factors investors weighed before buying stock was the company's ability to attract and retain talent. These findings imply that a company's stock price is driven not only by market share and profitability, it is also driven by service and bench strength considerations. Thus, employee satisfaction (or dissatisfaction) can have a major impact on the organization's bottom line.

Of these outcomes, perhaps employee turnover has the most-immediate impact on leadership practitioners. It would be very hard for Julie's or Ling Ling's bosses to achieve results if ski resort or real estate personnel were constantly having to be replaced, and the leader was spending an inordinate amount of time recruiting, hiring, and training replacements. Although some level of **functional turnover** is healthy for an organization (i.e., these followers are retiring, did not fit into the organization, or were substandard performers), dysfunctional turnover is not. **Dysfunctional turnover** occurs when the "best and brightest" in an organization become dissatisfied and leave it. Bedeian and

TABLE 14–6   Typical Items on a Satisfaction Questionnaire

1. Overall, I am satisfied with my job.
2. I feel the workload is about equal for everyone in the organization.
3. My supervisor handles conflict well.
4. My pay and benefits are comparable to those in other organizations.
5. There is a real future for people in this organization if they apply themselves.
6. Exceptional performance is rewarded in this organization.
7. We have a good health care plan in this organization.
8. In general, I am satisfied with my life and where it is going.

These items are often rated on a scale ranging from *strongly disagree* (1) to *strongly agree* (5).

Armenakis (1998) point out that dysfunctional turnover is most likely to occur when downsizing is the response to organizational decline (i.e., increased costs or decreased revenues, marketshare, or earnings). In these situations, dysfunctional turnover may have several devastating effects. First, those individuals in the best position to turn the company around are no longer there. Second, those who remain are even less capable of successfully dealing with the additional workload associated with the downsizings. Compounding this problem is that training budgets also tend to be slashed during downsizings. Third, organizations that downsize have a very difficult time recruiting people with the skills needed to turn the company around. Either competent candidates avoid applying for jobs within the organization because of the uncertainties of job security, or the less-competent managers remaining with the company may decide not to hire anyone who could potentially replace them (Bedeian & Armenakis, 1998). Because leaders can play an important role in followers' satisfaction levels, and because followers' satisfaction levels can have a substantial impact on various organizational outcomes, it is worth going into the topic in greater detail.

Global, Facet, and Life Satisfaction

There are different ways to look at a person's attitudes about work, but researchers usually collect this data using some type of job satisfaction survey (Bracken, 1992). Such surveys typically include items such as those found in Table 14–6, and they are usually sent to a representative sample of employees in the organization. Their responses are collected and tabulated, and the results are usually disseminated throughout the organization. Table 14–6 presents examples of three different types of items typically found on a job satisfaction survey. Item 1 is a **global satisfaction** item, which assesses the overall degree to which employees are satisfied with their organization and their job. Items 2 through 7 are **facet satisfaction** items, which assess the degree to which employees are satisfied with different aspects of work, such as pay, benefits, promotion policies,

---

Highlight 14–8

Work-Life Balance and Job Satisfaction: An International Perspective

One of the facets of job satisfaction receiving more attention among leaders these days is work-life balance. Many leaders are concerned with employee burnout, and want to minimize dysfunctional turnover by introducing programs to restore work-life balance. Although allowing employees to spend more time at home sounds good, the practicality of these programs can and does vary considerably depending on where you work. For example, IBM executives wanted to improve work-life balance among Japanese employees through telecommuting, but the program failed miserably because the Japanese tend to live in small homes with extended families. IBM solved this problem by renting suburban office space, which would help employees to substantially reduce commuting times and increase the time spent with their families. At Motorola's facility outside of Taipei, employees make use of the on-site day care facility to help increase work-life balance. The notion of work-life balance can be tricky water to navigate for many employers, however. When BMW first introduced these programs to employees, many thought the company should focus more on making cars than on caring for babies. Nevertheless, because the retention of intellectual capital is a key success factor in many industries, and because dual career couples are becoming a fact of life in the United States, it is very likely that flexible work schedules, telecommuting, and on-site day care will be even more prevalent in the years to come.

Source: M. Jackson, "Work-Life Balancing Act Trickier for Global Firms," *Denver Post*, March 1, 1998, p. K-5.

---

working hours and conditions, and the like. People may be very happy overall but still dissatisfied with certain aspects of work. For example, one study reported that while managers were highly satisfied overall, their satisfaction with promotion opportunities declined from 1989 to 1990 (PDI, 1991). Moreover, female managers were even less satisfied with their promotion opportunities than their male counterparts during this time period. Highlight 14–8 provides another example of facet satisfaction.

Leadership practitioners should be aware of several other important findings regarding global and facet satisfaction. The first finding is that people generally tend to be very happy with their vocation or occupation. They may not like the pay, benefits, or their boss, but they do seem to be satisfied with what they do for a living (Campbell & Hyne, 1995). This points out the importance of intrinsic motivation, as most people gravitate to tasks or jobs they find interesting and enjoyable. The second finding pertains to the **hierarchy effect**. In general, persons with longer tenure or in higher positions tend to have higher global and facet satisfaction ratings than those new or lower in the organization

(Campbell & Hyne, 1995). Because people higher in the organization are happier at work, they may not understand or appreciate why people at lower levels are less satisfied. From below, leaders at the top can appear somewhat naive and out of touch. From above, the complaints about morale, pay, or resources are often perceived as whining. One of the authors was recently working with a utilities company that had downsized and was suffering from all of the ill effects associated with high levels of dysfunctional turnover. Unfortunately, the executive vice president responsible for attracting and retaining talent and making the company "an employer of choice" stated that he had no idea why employees were complaining, and that things would be a lot better if they just quit whining. Because the executive did not understand or appreciate the sources of employee complaints, the programs to improve employee morale completely missed the mark, and the high levels of dysfunctional turnover continued. The hierarchy effect also implies that it will take a considerable amount of top leaders' focus and energy to increase the satisfaction levels of nonmanagement employees—lip service alone is never enough.

Compensation is another facet of job satisfaction that can have important implications for leadership practitioners. As you might expect, the hierarchy effect is alive and well with pay, with a survey of 3,000,000 employees reporting that 71 percent of senior management, 58 percent of middle management, and only 46 percent of nonmanagers rate their pay as "very good." Of nonmanagers, 33 percent rate their pay as "so-so" and 20 percent rate their pay as "very poor" (Kleiman, 1998). Given the wage gap between males and females, it may be correct to assume that a disproportionate amount of females can be found in these less-satisfied groups. Many of these females may be the highest performers in their positions, and this wage discrepancy, in combination with relatively small annual pay increases over the past few years, may contribute to disproportionately high levels of dysfunctional turnover among females. At more senior levels, Beatty and Zajac (1994) point out that tying executive compensation to company performance can result in lower risk taking among senior executives.

People who are happier with their jobs also tend to have higher life satisfaction ratings (Judge, Boudreau, & Bretz, 1994; Judge & Watanabe, 1993). **Life satisfaction** concerns one's attitudes about life in general, and Item 8 in Table 14–6 is an example of a typical life satisfaction question. Since leaders are often some of the most influential people in their followers' lives, they should never underestimate the impact they have on their followers' overall well-being. Unfortunately, at least some of the increasing violence at home and in the workplace may be exacerbated by poor leadership (Ferlise, 1995; Hogan, Curphy, & Hogan, 1994).

Job satisfaction surveys are used extensively in both public and private institutions. Organizations using these instruments typically administer them every one or two years to assess workers' attitudes about different aspects of work, changes in policies or work procedures, or other initiatives. Such survey results are most useful when they can be compared with those from some **reference group**. The organization's past results can be used as one kind of reference

FIGURE 14–4

Results of a Facet Satisfaction Survey

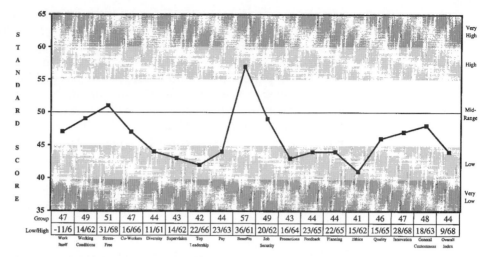

Group	47	49	51	47	44	43	42	44	57	49	43	44	44	41	46	47	48	44
Low/High	-11/6	14/62	31/68	16/66	11/61	14/62	22/66	23/63	36/61	20/62	16/64	23/65	22/65	15/62	15/65	28/68	18/63	9/68

Work Itself / Working Conditions / Stress-Free / Co-Workers / Diversity / Supervision / Top Leadership / Pay / Benefits / Job Security / Promotions / Feedback / Planning / Ethics / Quality / Innovation / General Contentment / Overall Index

Source: D. P. Campbell and S. Hyne, *Manual for the Revised Campbell Organizational Survey* (Minneapolis: National Computing Systems, 1995).

group—are people's ratings of pay, promotion, or overall satisfaction rising or falling over time? Job satisfaction ratings from similar organizations can be another reference group—are satisfaction ratings of leadership and working conditions higher or lower than those in similar organizations?

Figure 14–4 shows the facet and global satisfaction results for approximately 80 employees working at a medium-sized airport in the western United States. Employees completing the survey included the director of aviation and his supervisory staff ($n = 11$), the operations department ($n = 6$), the airfield maintenance department ($n = 15$), the communications department ($n = 6$), the airport facilities staff ($n = 12$), the administration department ($n = 10$), and the custodial staff ($n = 20$). The airport is owned by the city and has seen tremendous growth since the opening of the new terminal in 1995. By 1997 aircraft emplanements had already reached the level projected for the year 2010, and had exceeded the capacity of the new terminal. Unfortunately, staffing had remained at the 1995 levels, and the resulting workload and stress were thought to be adversely affecting morale and job satisfaction. Because of these concerns, the director of aviation decided to do a job satisfaction survey to pinpoint problems areas and develop action plans to resolve them.

Scores above 50 on Figure 14–4 are areas of satisfaction, scores below 50 are areas of dissatisfaction when compared to national norms. Here we see that airport employees are very satisfied with their benefits, are fairly satisfied with the work itself, but are dissatisfied with top leadership, ethics, supervision, feedback, promotion opportunities, and the like. All airport employees got to review these results, and each department discussed the factors underlying the survey results and developed and implemented action plans to address problem areas. Top leadership, in this case the director of aviation, was seen as the biggest source of dissatisfaction by all departments. The director was a genuinely nice person and meant well, but he never articulated his vision for the airport, never explained how employees' actions were related to this mission, failed to set goals for each department, did not provide feedback, never clarified roles or areas of responsibilities for his staff, delegated action items to whomever he happened to see in the hall, often changed his mind with key decisions, and failed to keep his staff informed of airline tenant or city council decisions. When confronted with this information, the director placed the blame on the rapid growth of the airport and the lack of staffing support from the city (the fundamental attribution error in action again). The city manager then gave the director six months to substantially improve employee satisfaction levels. The director did not take the problem very seriously, and not surprisingly the survey results six months later were no different for top leadership. The director was subsequently removed from his position because of his failure to improve the morale at the airport.

It is important to point out that rarely is it enough to merely administer surveys. Leaders must also be willing to take action on the basis of survey results, or risk losing credibility and actually increasing job dissatisfaction. Upon receiving the results of these surveys, leaders with bad results may feel tempted to not share any results with their followers, but this is almost always a mistake. Although the results may not be flattering, the rumors are likely to be much worse than the results themselves. Also, followers will be less than willing to fill out subsequent satisfaction surveys if they see denial of the results, and little if any change to the workplace. Furthermore, leaders feeling defensive about such results and tempted to hide them should remember that the bad results may not be a surprise to anyone but themselves; therefore, what's to hide? On a practical level, leaders should never assess employees' attitudes about work unless they are willing to share the results and take action.

Three Theories of Job Satisfaction

All of the theories of motivation described earlier provide insight into followers' levels of job satisfaction too. For example, it would be difficult for Julie to be satisfied with her job if she was consistently underdressed for weather conditions, or for Ling Ling to be satisfied if her goals were unclear, she was not provided feedback, or she failed to be rewarded for good performance. Nonetheless, several other theories offer even better explanations for job satisfaction.

Affectivity.   Affectivity refers to one's tendency to react to stimuli in a consistent emotional manner (Judge & Hulin, 1993; Judge & Locke, 1993; Judge, Locke, Durham, & Kluger, 1998). People with a disposition for **negative affectivity** consistently react to changes, events, or situations in a negative manner. They tend to be unhappy with themselves and their lives, and are more likely to focus on the downside or disadvantages of a situation. People with a disposition for **positive affectivity** consistently react to changes, events, or situations in a positive manner. They are happy with their lives, and tend to take an upbeat, optimistic approach when faced with new situations. People with a positive affective disposition tend to see a cup as half full; people with a negative affective disposition are more likely to describe a glass as half empty. These two groups of individuals are thought to attend to, process, and recall information differently, and these differences affect both job satisfaction and satisfaction with life itself. Researchers have found that negative affectivity was related to job dissatisfaction, and positive affectivity to job satisfaction (Judge & Hulin, 1993). Of course, such results are hardly surprising—we all know individuals who never seem happy whatever their circumstances, and others who seem to maintain a positive outlook even in the most adverse circumstances.

These findings suggest that leadership initiatives may have little impact on a person's job satisfaction if their affective disposition is either extremely positive or negative. For example, if Ling Ling has a negative affective disposition, she may remain dissatisfied with her pay, working conditions, and so forth, *whatever her leader does*. This is consistent with the findings of a study of identical twins reared apart and together which discovered that affectivity has a strong genetic component (Arvey, Bouchard, Segal, & Abraham, 1989). Given that leaders can do little to change followers' genetic makeup, these findings again highlight the importance of using good selection procedures when hiring employees. Trying to increase followers' job satisfaction is a reasonable goal, but some followers may be hard (impossible?) to please, no matter what the leader does.

From a leader perspective, affectivity can have several implications in the workplace. First and foremost, one's own affectivity can have a strong influence on followers' morale or satisfaction levels. Say you worked for a leader with negative affectivity. Chances are he or she would find fault in your work, and constantly complain about organizational policies, resources, and so on. The opposite might be true if you worked for someone having positive affectivity. Second, leading a high percentage of followers having either positive or negative affectivity would likely result in very different leadership experiences. The positive group may be much more tolerant and willing to put up with organizational changes; the negative group would likely find fault in any change the leader made. Increasing job satisfaction via affectivity means hiring those with positive affectivity. However, few, if any, selection systems address this important workplace variable. Because negative affectivity may not be assessed or even apparent until a follower has been on the job for a period of time, perhaps the best advice for leadership practitioners is that some followers might well have a permanent chip on their shoulders, and there may be little you can do to change it.

Equity Theory.   This cognitive approach assumes that people value fairness in leader–follower exchange relationships (Kanfer, 1990). Followers are said to be most satisfied when they believe that what they put into an activity or a job and what they get out of it are roughly equivalent to what others put into and get out of it (Adams, 1963; Vecchio, 1982). **Equity theory** proposes a very rational model for how followers assess these issues. Followers presumably reach decisions about equitable relationships by assigning values to the four elements in Figure 14–5

FIGURE 14–5

Equity Theory Ratios

$$\frac{\text{Personal outcomes}}{\text{Personal inputs}} = \frac{\text{Reference group outcomes}}{\text{Reference group inputs}}$$

and then comparing the two ratios (Adams, 1963). Regarding the specific elements in each ratio, personal outcomes refer to what one is receiving for one's efforts, such as pay, recognition, job satisfaction, opportunity for advancement, and personal growth. Personal inputs refer to all those things one contributes to an activity or a job, such as time, effort, knowledge, and skills.

A key aspect of equity theory is that Figure 14–5 contains *two* ratios. Judgments of equity are always based on a comparison to some reference group. It is the *relationship between the two ratios* that is important in equity theory, not the absolute value of either one's own or another's outcomes or inputs, considered by themselves. What matters most is the comparison between one's own ratio and that of a reference group such as one's co-workers or workers holding similar jobs in other organizations. For example, one of the authors worked with an investment banker who was making over $400,000 per year but was extremely dissatisfied with her pay. The banker stated that, on the one hand, she got paid a "ridiculously high" amount of money for what she did, but on the other hand, she knew investment bankers who even were making considerably more than she was. Similarly, Ling Ling may make more money than her peers, but she may also work longer hours, have more skills, and rent more apartments. In other words, although her outcomes are greater, so are her inputs, and thus the ratios may still be equal; there is equity.

In essence, equity theory does not try to evaluate equality of inputs or equality of outcomes. It is concerned with fairness of inputs relative to outcomes. The perception of inequity creates a state of tension and an inherent pressure for change. As long as there is general equality between the two ratios, there is no motivation (at least based on inequity) to change anything, and people are reasonably satisfied. If, however, the ratios are significantly different, a follower will be motivated to take action likely to restore the balance. Exactly what the follower will be motivated to do depends on the direction of the inequality. Adams (1965) suggested six ways people might restore balance: (*a*) changing their inputs, (*b*) changing their outcomes, (*c*) altering their self-perceptions, (*d*) altering their perceptions of their reference group, (*e*) changing their reference group, or, if all else fails, (*f*) leaving the situation. Thus, if Julie believed her ratio was lower than her co-worker's, she might reduce her level of effort or seek higher pay elsewhere. She could also change her reference group to that of ski lift operators at other resorts, or even quit. Research has shown that perceptions of underpayment generally resulted in actions in support of the model, but perceptions of overpayment did not. Instead of working harder in an overpayment condition (to make their own ratio more equitable), subjects often rationalized that they really deserved the higher pay (Campbell & Pritchard, 1976). An example of how equity theory might affect some salary negotiations is presented in Highlight 14–9.

Highlight 14–9

Professional Athlete Salary Demands and Equity Theory

It can be difficult for anyone earning a modest income to understand an athlete's justification in demanding an increase from (say) $2 million to $3 million a year. One might argue that no one deserves that much money, much less just for playing a sport. However, the athlete's demands can be better understood by using an equity theory perspective. Whereas it may be difficult in any absolute way to assign the right salary level to athletic performance, it is possible to look at one athlete's salary and compare it to the salary and performance of another athlete. If, for example, one NL pitcher earns a higher salary than another even when the latter has had several more productive years, then this inequity becomes grounds for the latter to demand more money. This is precisely the argument presented during the contract negotiations for many professional athletes. Moreover, these contract negotiations generally result in rising pay schedules for all players. These higher costs for arguably average baseball players was one of the primary reasons behind the 1994–1995 baseball strike.

Organizational Justice.   **Organizational justice** is a cognitive approach based on the premise that people who are treated unfairly are less productive, satisfied, and committed to their organizations. Moreover, these individuals are more likely to initiate collective action and engage in various counterproductive work behaviors (Sheppard, Lewicki, & Minton, 1992). According to Trevino (1992), organizational justice is made up of three related components. **Retributive justice** concerns followers' perceptions of a "just world." Followers are most satisfied when they perceive a compensation or disciplinary system to be unbiased, valid, and fair. **Distributive justice** concerns followers' perceptions of whether the level of reward or punishment is commensurate with an individual's performance or infraction. Dissatisfaction occurs when followers believe someone has received too little or too much reward or punishment. Perceptions of **procedural justice** involve the process in which rewards or punishments are administered. If someone is to be punished, then followers will be more satisfied if the person being punished has been given adequate warnings and has had the opportunity to explain his actions, and if the punishment has been administered in a timely and consistent manner. Research has shown that these different components of organizational justice are, in fact, related to pay, promotion, and job satisfaction (McFarlin & Sweeney, 1992; Sheppard, Lewicki, & Minton, 1992; Trevino, 1992; Moorman, 1991; Brockner & Wisenfeld, 1996; Ployhart & Ryan, 1998).

Summary

This chapter has reviewed research concerning motivation, satisfaction, and performance. Motivation was defined as anything that provides direction, intensity, and persistence to behavior. Although motivation is an important aspect of performance, performance and motivation are not the same thing. Performance is a broader concept than motivation, as abilities, skills, group norms, and the availability of resources can all affect followers' levels of performance. Job satisfaction is a set of attitudes that people have about work. Although a majority of people are generally satisfied with their jobs, people often have varying levels of satisfaction for different aspect of their jobs, such as pay, working conditions, supervisors, or co-workers.

Many of the approaches to understanding motivation have distinct implications for increasing performance and satisfaction. Therefore, several different theories of motivation were reviewed in this chapter. The first three theories, Maslow's (1954) hierarchy of needs, Alderfer's (1969) ERG theory, and Herzberg's (1964, 1966) two-factor theory assume that people are motivated to satisfy a universal set of needs. The next two theories examined motivation in terms of individual differences, emphasizing a person's intrinsic motivation to perform a particular task or a person's general level of achievement orientation. The next set of theories examined motivation from a cognitive perspective. These theories assume that people make rational, conscious choices about the direction, intensity, and persistence of their behaviors, and generally engage in behaviors that maximize payoffs and minimize costs. The last two theories examined motivation from a situational perspective. Leadership practitioners likely will be more effective if they learn to recognize situations where various approaches, or the insights particular to them, may be differentially useful. Just as a carpenter can more effectively build a house by using a variety of tools, a leader can be more effective by using a variety of motivational interventions to enhance work.

Several other theories seem to be more useful for explaining followers' attitudes about work. Some research suggests that individuals vary in the characteristic tenor of their affectivity; some people are generally affectively positive whereas others are generally affectively negative. Such differences may set limits on the extent to which initiatives by leaders will actually impact follower satisfaction. Leaders may also be able to increase satisfaction levels by clarifying followers' perceptions of equity and organizational justice. Followers (and leaders for that matter) are more likely to have positive attitudes about work if they believe that their compensation is similar to that of others and that the reward and disciplinary systems are fair and just.

Key Terms

motivation	growth-need strength
performance	operant approach
effectiveness	reward

job satisfaction
organizational citizenship
  behaviors
needs
hierarchy of needs
existence-relatedness-growth
  (ERG) theory
frustration-regression
  hypothesis
two-factor theory
motivators
hygiene factors
achievement orientation
intrinsic motivation
overjustification effect
goal setting
expectancy theory
effort-to-performance
  expectancy
performance-to-outcome
  expectancy
valence

Productivity Measurement
  and Enhancement System
  (ProMES)
punishment
contingent
noncontingent
extinction
functional turnover
dysfunctional turnover
global satisfaction
facet satisfaction
hierarchy effect
life satisfaction
reference group
negative affectivity
positive affectivity
equity theory
organizational justice
retributive justice
distributive justice
procedural justice

Discussion Questions

1. Why do you think there are so many different theories or approaches to understanding motivation? Shouldn't it be possible to determine which one is best and just use it? Why or why not?

2. Many good leaders are thought of as good motivators. How would you rate Colin Powell, Madeleine Albright, and Konosuke Matsushita in terms of their ability to motivate others?

3. Select any group of followers you are personally familiar with. Analyze their different motivations in terms of the theories or approaches presented in this chapter.

4. Which theory or theories of motivation do you think comes the closest to explaining why followers working for a charismatic or transformational leader put in so much energy and effort?

5. What is your own view of what motivates people to work hard and perform well?

6. Do you know of any examples where reward systems are inconsistent with desired behavior?

7. What do you find personally satisfying or dissatisfying at work or school? For those things you find dissatisfying, how could you make them more satisfying? What theory of job satisfaction best explains your actions?

8. Do you think there might be a relationship between affectivity and Kelley's concept of alienated followers?

IV   FOCUS ON THE SITUATION

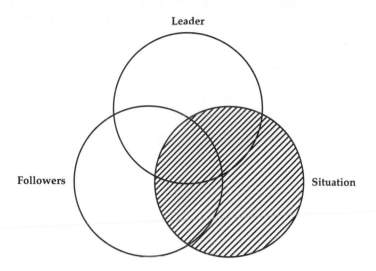

In previous chapters we noted that understanding leaders and followers is much more complicated than many people first think. For example, we examined how leaders' personality characteristics, behaviors, and attitudes affect the leadership process. Similarly, followers' attitudes, experience, personality characteristics, and behaviors, as well as group norms and cohesiveness also affect the leadership process. Despite the complexities of leaders and followers, however, perhaps no factor in the interactional framework is as complex as the situation. Not only do a variety of task, organizational, and environmental factors affect behavior, but the relative salience or strength of these factors varies dramatically across people. What one person perceives to be the key situational factor affecting his or her behavior may be relatively unimportant to another person. Moreover, the relative importance of the situational factors also varies over time. Even in the course of a single soccer game, for example, the situation changes constantly: The lead changes, the time remaining in the game changes, weather conditions change, injuries occur, and so on. Given the dynamic nature of situations, it may be a misnomer to speak of "the" situation in reference to leadership.

Because of the complex and dynamic nature of situations and the substantial role perceptions play in the interpretation of situations, no one has been able to develop a comprehensive taxonomy describing all of the situational variables affecting a person's behavior. In all likelihood, no one ever will. Nevertheless, considerable research about situational influences on leadership has been accomplished. Leadership researchers have examined how different task, organizational, and environmental factors affect both leaders' and followers' behavior, though most have examined only the effects of one or two situational variables on leaders' and followers' behavior. For example, a study might have examined the effects of task difficulty on subordinates' performance yet ignored how broader issues, such as organizational policy or structure, might also affect their performance. This is primarily due to the difficulty of studying the effects of organizational and environmental factors on behavior. As you might imagine, many of these factors, such as market conditions or crisis situations, do not easily lend themselves to realistic laboratory experiments where conditions can be controlled and interactions analyzed. Nonetheless, several consistent findings have emerged. We review them in this part.

15 CHARACTERISTICS OF THE SITUATION

Chapter Outline

Introduction

In a book designed to introduce students to the subject of leadership, a chapter about "the situation" poses some challenging obstacles and dilemmas. The very breadth of the topic is daunting; it could include almost everything else in the world that has not been covered in the previous chapters! To the typical student who has not yet begun a professional career, pondering the magnitude of variables comprising the situation is a formidable request. For one thing, the situation you find yourself in is often seen as completely beyond your control. For example, how many times have you heard someone say, "Hey, I don't make the rules around here. I just follow them." Furthermore, the subject is made more difficult by the fact that most students have limited organizational experience as a frame of reference. So why bother to introduce the material in this chapter? Because the situation we are in often explains far more about what is going on and what kinds of leadership behaviors will be best than any other single variable we have discussed so far!

In this chapter we will try to sort out some of the complexity and magnitude of this admittedly large topic. First, we will review some of the research which has led us to consider these issues. Then, after considering a huge situational change that is now occurring, we will present a model to help in considering key situational variables. Finally, we will take a look forward through one interesting lens. Throughout the chapter, though, our objective will be primarily to increase awareness rather than to prescribe specific courses of leader action.

Background

The appropriateness of a leader's behavior with a group of followers often makes sense only when you look at the situational context in which the behavior occurs. Whereas severely disciplining a follower might seem a poor way to lead, if the follower in question had just committed a safety violation endangering the lives of hundreds of people, then the leader's actions may be exactly right. In a similar fashion, the situation may be the primary reason personality traits, experience, or cognitive abilities are related less consistently to leadership effectiveness than to leadership emergence (R. T. Hogan, J. Hogan, & Curphy, 1992; Yukl, 1989). Most leadership emergence studies have involved leaderless discussion groups, and for the most part the situation is quite similar across such studies. In studies of leadership effectiveness, however, the situation can and does vary dramatically. The personal attributes needed to be an effective leader of a combat unit, chemical research-and-development division, community service organization, or fast-food restaurant may change considerably. Because the situations facing leaders of such groups may be so variable, it is hardly surprising that studies of leader characteristics have yielded inconsistent results when looking at leadership effectiveness across jobs or situations. Thus, the importance of the situation in the leadership process should not be overlooked (also see Highlight 15–1).

Historically, some leadership researchers emphasized the importance of the situation in the leadership process in response to the Great Man theory of leadership. These researchers maintained that the situation, not someone's traits or abilities, plays the most important role in determining who emerges as a leader (Murphy, 1941; Person, 1928; Spiller, 1929). As support for the situational viewpoint, these researchers noted that great leaders typically emerged during economic crises, social upheavals, or revolutions; great leaders were generally not associated with periods of relative calm or quiet. For example, Schneider (1937) noted that the number of individuals identified as great military leaders in the British armed forces during any time period depended on how many conflicts the country was engaged in; the greater the number of conflicts, the greater the number of great military leaders. Moreover, researchers advocating the situa-

---

Highlight 15–1

Leadership Quotes, Chapter 15

If you want to give a man credit, put it in writing. If you want to give him hell, do it on the phone.

Charles Beacham

A man may speak very well in the House of Commons, and fail very complete in the House of Lords. There are two distinct styles requisite.

Benjamin Disraeli

I claim not to have controlled events, but confess plainly that events have controlled me.

Abraham Lincoln

When you've exhausted all possibilities, remember this: you haven't!

Robert H. Schuller

The way of the superior is three-fold, but I am not equal to it. Virtuous, he is free from anxieties; wise, he is free from perplexities; bold, he is free from fear.

Confucius

The brain is a wonderful organ; it begins working the moment you get up in the morning and does not stop until you get to the office.

Robert Frost

---

tional viewpoint believed leaders were made, not born, and that prior leadership experience helped forge effective leaders (Person, 1928). These early situational theories of leadership tended to be very popular in the United States, as they fit more closely with American ideals of equality and meritocracy, and ran counter to the genetic views of leadership that were more popular among European researchers at the time (Bass, 1990). (The fact that many of these European researchers had aristocratic backgrounds probably had something to do with the popularity of the Great Man theory in Europe.)

More recent leadership theories have explored how situational factors affect leaders' behaviors. In **role theory,** for example, a leader's behavior was said to depend on a leader's perceptions of several critical aspects of the situation: rules and regulations governing the job; role expectations of subordinates, peers, and superiors; the nature of the task; and feedback about subordinates' performance (Merton, 1957; Pfeffer & Salancik, 1975). Role theory clarified how these situational demands and constraints could cause role conflict and role ambiguity. Leaders may experience role conflict when subordinates and superiors have conflicting expectations about a leader's behavior or when company policies contradict how superiors expect tasks to be performed. A leader's ability to successfully resolve such conflicts may well determine leadership effectiveness (Tsui, 1984).

Another effort to incorporate situational variables into leadership theory was Hunt and Osborn's (1982) **multiple-influence model.** Hunt and Osborn distinguished between microvariables (e.g., task characteristics) and macrovariables (e.g., the external environment) in the situation. Although most researchers looked at the effects tasks had on leader behaviors, Hunt and Osborn believed macrovariables had a pervasive influence on the ways leaders act. Both role theory and the multiple-influence model highlight a major problem in addressing situational factors, which was noted previously: that situations can vary in countless ways. Because situations can vary in so many ways, it is helpful for leaders to have an abstract scheme for conceptualizing situations. This would be a step in knowing how to identify what may be most salient or critical to pay attention to in any particular instance.

One of the most basic abstractions is **situational levels.** The idea behind situational levels may best be conveyed with an example. Suppose someone asked you, "How are things going at work?" You might respond by commenting on the specific tasks you perform (e.g., "It is still pretty tough. I am under the gun for getting next year's budget prepared, and I have never done that before."). Or, you might respond by commenting on aspects of the overall organization (e.g., "It is really different. There are so many rules you have to follow. My old company was not like that at all."). Or, you might comment on factors affecting the organization itself (e.g., "I've been real worried about keeping my job—you know how many cutbacks there have been in our whole industry recently."). Each response deals with the situation, but each refers to a very different level of abstraction: the task level, the organizational level, and the environmental level. Each of these three levels provides a different perspective with which to examine the leadership process (see Figure 15–1).

These three levels certainly do not exhaust all the ways situations vary. Situations also differ in terms of physical variables like noise and temperature levels, workload demands, and the extent to which work groups interact with other groups. Organizations also have unique "corporate cultures," which define a context for leadership. And there are always even broader economic, social, legal, and technological aspects of situations within which the leadership process occurs. What, amid all this situational complexity, should leaders pay attention to? We will try to provide some insights into this question by presenting a model which considers many of these factors. But first, let us consider an environmental aspect of the situation that is changing for virtually all of us as we move into the new millennium.

From the Industrial Age to the Information Age

All of us have grown up in the age of industry, but perhaps in its waning years. Starting just before the American Civil War and continuing up through the last quarter of the current century, the industrial age supplanted the age of agricul-

FIGURE 15–1

*An Expanded
Leader-
Follower-
Situation Model*

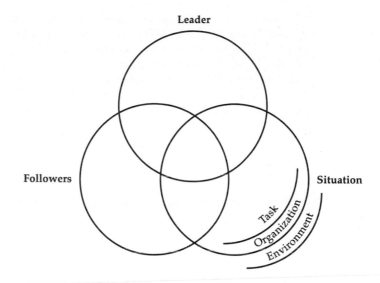

ture. During the industrial age, companies succeeded according to how well they could capture the benefits from "economies of scale and scope" (Chandler, 1990). Technology mattered, but mostly to the extent that companies could increase the efficiencies of mass production. Now a new age is emerging, and in this information age many of the fundamental assumptions of the industrial age are becoming obsolete.

Kaplan and Norton (1996) described a new set of operating assumptions underlying the information age and contrasted them with their predecessors in the industrial age. They described changes in the following ways companies operate:

Cross Functions. Industrial age organizations gained competitive advantage through specialization of functional skills in areas like manufacturing, distribution, marketing, and technology. This specialization yielded substantial benefits, but over time, also led to enormous inefficiencies, and slow response processes. The information age organization operates with integrated business processes that cut across traditional business functions.

Links to Customers and Suppliers. Industrial age companies worked with customers and suppliers via arm's-length transactions. Information technology enables today's organizations to integrate supply, production, and delivery processes and to realize enormous improvements in cost, quality, and response time.

Customer Segmentation. Industrial age companies prospered by offering low-cost but standardized products and services (remember Henry Ford's comment that his customers "can have whatever color they want as long as it is black." Information age companies must learn to offer customized products and services to diverse customer segments.

Global Scale. Information age companies compete against the best companies throughout the entire world. In fact, the large investments required for new products and services may require customers worldwide to provide adequate returns on those costs.

Innovation. Product life cycles continue to shrink. Competitive advantage in one generation of a product's life is no guarantee of success for future generations of that product. Companies operating in an environment of rapid technological innovation must be masters at anticipating customers' future needs, innovating new products and services, and rapidly deploying new technologies into efficient delivery processes.

Knowledge Workers. Industrial companies created sharp distinctions between an intellectual elite on the one hand (especially managers and engineers), and a direct labor work force on the other. The latter group performed tasks and processes under direct supervision of white-collar engineers and managers. This typically involved physical rather than mental capabilities. Now, all employees must contribute value by what they know and by the information they can provide.

One needs only to reflect upon Kaplan and Norton's list of changing operating assumptions to recognize that the situation leaders find themselves in today is different from the situation of 20 years ago. What's more, it is probably changing at an ever increasing rate. In a very real sense, the pace of change today is like trying to navigate white-water rapids; things are changing so rapidly it can be difficult to get one's bearings. Therefore, we believe it is helpful to use a model that identifies some of the key elements of the situation in an organizational setting.

The Congruence Model

Like the Team Effectiveness Leadership Model described in the previous chapter, the Congruence Model, presented most recently by Nadler and Tushman (1997), is a systems model with *inputs*, *processes*, and *outputs*. We will focus on the four factors making up the organizational processes in this chapter, but we should briefly discuss the inputs and outputs first. As can be seen in Figure 15–2, there are three components under inputs: the environment, the resources, and the history. Attention to these components must be kept to a minimum here, but their importance in impacting leaders and followers is nonetheless significant. We already have noted the magnitude of changes resulting from the shift in environment from the industrial age to the information age. Beyond that, *environment* also includes market changes, governmental regulations and laws, competitors, financial institutions and even changes in weather patterns (consider the impact of *El Niño* in 1998). We will return to examine some further ways to specify environmental factors later in the chapter. *Resources* are anything which the organization can use to its benefit, and may include not only material components such as capital or information, but also less-tangible components such as perceptions of quality (e.g., Nikon cameras or Mercedes Benz automobiles). *History of the organization* includes not only the recent past that bears upon today's work but also myths about the organization's origin. For example, when taking important visitors on tours of the facilities at a large manufacturing plant, the guides would always stop and point out a series of visitor parking spots located near the executive wing of the building. The guides explained that the first plant manager and his team had decided to do away with executive

FIGURE 15–2

*A Congruence
Model*

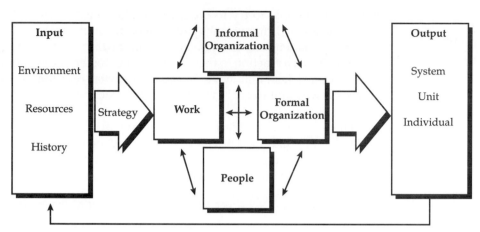

Source: *Competing by Design: The Power of Organizational Architecture,* by David Nadler and Michael Tushman.
Copyright © 1997 Oxford University Press. Used by permission of Oxford University Press, Inc.

parking slots by consensus, and that "consensus decision making was still the
way everyone worked here"—25 years later.

Outputs are evaluated by the impact on the system as a whole, the unit, and
the individual (again, very much like the TELM). At each of these levels, it is
appropriate to ask how well the organization met its objectives, how efficient it
was at achieving those outcomes, and how well the organization has scanned
the horizon for new opportunities and threats. Before moving to the core process
variables of the situation in this model, it is necessary to note that strategy is the
collective set of business decisions about how to allocate scarce resources to
maximize the strengths of the organization, given the external opportunities,
while minimizing the organizational weaknesses, given the external threats.

The core of the Congruence Model has four components: the work, the people, the formal organization, and the informal organization. Note that each component relates to the other three. This is a key component of this model and is
the basis of its name. Based upon a tenet of systems theory, the components of
the model attempt to stay in balance or homeostasis. The better the fit of all the
components, the more "congruence" there is between its various elements. Just
one implication of this idea is that if a leader wanted to make changes in the
outputs of his or her team, the model suggests it would be better to make small
but equal changes in all the subsystems than it would be to make a substantial
change in only one component. If only one element is changed, the other major
components in the model, in trying to achieve homeostasis, would tend to resist
and react to pull the "out-of-balance" element back in line.

The Work

At the most fundamental level, the work is "what is to be done" by the organization and its component parts. Given the variety of tasks people perform, it is

natural for people to try to order and make sense of them. In thinking back across the many different tasks you have performed, you might categorize them as boring, challenging, dangerous, fun, interesting, and so on. However, labeling tasks is just a reaction to them and does not foster understanding about what aspects of any task may have caused a particular reaction. In looking at tasks, therefore, we want to get beyond subjective reactions to more objective ways of analyzing them.

There are several objective ways to categorize tasks performed by leaders and followers. Tasks can be categorized according to their function, the skills or abilities needed to perform them, the equipment needed to perform them, and so on. As seen in an earlier chapter, tasks also can be described in terms of the characteristics of the job itself: skill variety, task identity, task significance, autonomy, and feedback from the job. We will add to those characteristics two other dimensions: task structure and task interdependence.

Job Characteristics.   **Skill variety** and the next four dimensions of tasks are all components of the job characteristics model (Hackman & Oldham, 1976, 1980) described in Chapter 14. Skill variety refers to the degree to which a job involves performing a variety of different activities or skills. For example, if an individual attaches the left taillight to a car on an automobile assembly line by mechanically screwing in the fasteners, there would be increased work but no increased skill variety if he subsequently stepped over the line to the other side to install the right taillight. Skill variety involves using different skills, whether mechanical, cognitive, or physical. We might also add that there is a qualitative dimension to skill variety. In general, jobs requiring greater skill variety are more enjoyable than those requiring lesser skill variety, but it also matters whether any particular individual personally values the skills she performs.

Although satisfaction may also depend on growth-need strength (the individual's psychological need for personal accomplishment, for learning, and for personal development), typically jobs that require a low variety of skills are repetitive, monotonous, boring, and dissatisfying (Bass, 1990; Hackman & Oldham, 1980; House & Desslesr, 1974). And like structured tasks, tasks with low levels of skill variety make it easier for leaders to use directive behaviors but, because followers already know how to do the job, also make directive leadership behavior somewhat redundant (Howell & Dorfman, 1981, 1986; Kerr & Jermier, 1978; Kipnis, 1984). In such situations, leaders might try to restructure a subordinate's job in order to increase the number of (valued) skills needed. If that is not possible, then high levels of support and consideration for followers are helpful (Hackman & Oldham, 1980; House & Dessler, 1974).

Task identity refers to the degree to which a situation or task requires completion of a whole unit of work from beginning to end with a visible outcome. For example, if one works on an assembly line where circuit boards for compact disc (CD) players are being produced, and the task is to solder one wire to one electronic component and then pass the circuit board on to the next assembly worker, then this job would lack task identity. At the other extreme, if one assembled an entire CD player, perhaps involving 30 or 40 different tasks, then the perception of task identity would increase dramatically as one could readily see the final results of one's efforts. Furthermore, the job's skill variety (as discussed above) would increase as well.

Task significance is the degree to which a job substantially impacts others' lives. Consider an individual whose task is to insert a bolt into a nut and tighten it down to a certain specification using a torque wrench. If that bolt is one of several that fasten a fender to other parts of an automobile body on an assembly line, then both skill variety and task identity would probably be very low. Moreover, if the assembly person leaves the entire bolt off, it may cause a squeak or a rattle, but probably would not cause the fender to fall off. In such a job, task significance would be quite low as well. However, if the worker tightens the only bolt securing a critical component of a brake assembly on the space shuttle, then skill variety and task identity would be exactly the same as for our fender installer. However, task significance would be substantially higher.

Autonomy is the degree to which a job provides an individual with some control over what he does and how he does it. Someone with considerable autonomy would have discretion in scheduling work and deciding the procedures used in accomplishing it. Autonomy often covaries with technical expertise, as workers with considerable expertise will be given more latitude, and those with few skills will be given more instruction and coaching when accomplishing tasks (Hersey & Blanchard, 1977, 1984). Moreover, responsibility and job satisfaction often increase when autonomy increases (Hackman & Oldham, 1980).

The last task component in the job characteristics model is **feedback**, which refers to the degree to which a person accomplishing a task receives information about performance *from performing the task itself*. In this context feedback does not refer to feedback received from supervisors but rather to what is intrinsic to the work activity itself. Driving a car is one example of feedback intrinsic to a task. If you are a skilled driver on a road with a number of twists and turns, then you get all the feedback you need about how well you are accomplishing the task merely by observing how the car responds to the inputs you make. This is feedback from the job itself as opposed to feedback from another person (who in this example would be a classic backseat driver). Extending this example to work or team settings, leaders sometimes may want to redesign tasks so that they (the tasks) provide more intrinsic feedback. Although this does not absolve the leader from giving periodic feedback about performance, it can help to free up some of the leader's time for other work-related activities. Additionally, leaders should understand that followers may eventually become dissatisfied if leaders provide high levels of feedback for tasks that already provide intrinsic feedback (House & Dessler, 1974; Howell & Dorfman, 1981; Kerr & Jermier, 1978).

Task Structure.   Perhaps the easiest way to explain **task structure** is by using an example demonstrating the difference between a structured and an unstructured task. Assume the task to be accomplished is solving for x given the formula $3x + 2x = 15$. If that problem were given to a group of people who knew the fundamental rules of algebra, then everyone would arrive at the same answer. In this example there is a known procedure for accomplishing the task; there are rules governing how one goes about it; and if people follow those rules, there is one result. These features characterize a *structured task.*

On the other hand, if the task is to resolve a morale problem on a team, committee, or work group, then there may be no clear-cut method for solving it. There are many different ways, perhaps none of which is obvious or necessarily best for approaching a solution. It may even be that different observers would not see the problem in the same way; they may even have quite different ideas of *what morale is.* Solving a morale problem, therefore, exemplifies an *unstructured task*

People vary in their preferences for, or ability to handle, structured versus unstructured tasks. With the Myers-Briggs Type Indicator (MBTI), for example, perceivers are believed to prefer unstructured situations, whereas judgers prefer activities that are planned and organized (Myers & McCaulley, 1985). Individuals with high tolerance for stress may handle ambiguous and unstructured tasks more easily than people with low tolerance for stress (Bass, 1990). Aside from these differences, however, we might ask whether there are any general rules for how leaders should interact with followers as a function of task structure. One consideration here is that while it is *easier* for a leader or coach to give instruction in structured tasks, it is not necessarily the most helpful thing to do.

We can see that by returning to the algebra problem described earlier. If a student had never seen such an algebra problem before, then it would be relatively easy for the teacher to teach the student the rules needed to solve the problem. Once any student has learned the procedure, however, he can solve similar problems on his own. Extending this to other situations, once a subordinate knows or understands a task, a supervisor's continuing instruction (i.e., initiating structure or directive behavior) may provide superfluous information and eventually become irritating (Ford, 1981; House & Dessler, 1974; Kerr & Jermier, 1978; Yukl, 1989). Subordinates *need* help when a task is unstructured, when they do not know what the desired outcome looks like, and when they do not know how to achieve it. Anything a supervisor or leader can do to increase subordinates' ability to perform unstructured tasks is likely to increase their performance and job satisfaction (Siegall & Cummings, 1986). Paradoxically, though, unstructured tasks are by nature somewhat ill defined. Thus, they often are more difficult for leaders themselves to analyze and provide direction in accomplishing. Nonetheless, reducing the degree of ambiguity inherent in an unstructured situation is a leadership behavior usually appreciated by followers.

Task Interdependence.   **Task interdependence** concerns the degree to which tasks require coordination and synchronization in order for work groups or teams to accomplish desired goals. Task interdependence differs from autonomy in that workers or team members may be able to accomplish their tasks in an autonomous fashion, but the products of their efforts must be coordinated in order for the group or team to be successful. Tasks with high levels of interdependence place a premium on leaders' organizing and planning, directing, and communi-

Highlight 15–2

Golf and the Task Factors of the Situation

Golf provides a convenient skill for illustrating the seven task factors described in this chapter. Golf provides a reasonable amount of *task structure*, as there are basic rules and procedures for properly hitting woods, long irons, and short irons, and for putting.

Skill variety comes into play because golfers use a variety of skills and talents. These include deciding on a club, the method used to swing the club, how hard to swing it, what kind of equipment to use, where to target the ball, how to compensate for wind, when to putt, and so on.

Because one person does all of the driving, pitching, and putting and is solely responsible for his or her score, a round of golf has a high level of *task identity*.

Task significance may be a little more difficult to appreciate in this example. It may not be there at all unless one is a particularly poor golfer (where he or she endangers the lives of other people) or, in the case of the professional golfer, has a family who depends on his or her performance.

Autonomy is certainly present when playing golf. The golfer gets to decide when to do the "work," how to do it, which clubs to use, and what strategies and tactics to use.

Feedback from the job is also apparent. Shortly after a golfer strikes the ball, she receives feedback on how well her swing worked. Whether it slices, hooks, or goes straight down the fairway is a bit of information that tells the golfer immediately how well her work is being accomplished.

Finally, golf generally lacks *task interdependence*. Golfers are not dependent on the other members in their foursome for their own score.

cation skills (Curphy, 1991a, 1992; Galbraith, 1973). In one study, for example, coaches exhibiting high levels of initiating-structure behaviors had better-performing teams for sports requiring relatively interdependent effort, such as football, hockey, lacrosse, rugby, basketball, and volleyball; the same leader behaviors were unrelated to team performance for sports requiring relatively independent effort, such as swimming, track, cross-country, golf, and baseball (Fry, Kerr, & Lee, 1986). Like task structure and skill variety, task interdependence can also dictate which leader behaviors will be effective in a particular situation.

In summary, these seven task dimensions provide a variety of ways in which to categorize or describe tasks. For example, ironing a shirt would probably have high task structure, autonomy, task identification, and feedback, and low skill variety, task significance, and task interdependence. On the other hand, building your own home may garner high ratings on all seven dimensions. Still another familiar activity is evaluated on these dimensions in Highlight 15–2. These seven dimensions can provide leaders with insight about how their behavior and work assignments may either help or hinder followers' satisfaction and performance. At the same time, leaders should remember that these dimensions exist somewhat in the eye of the beholder. What one follower perceives as an unstructured task might be seen by another as fairly structured. Finally, as we have emphasized before, leaders should use their communication and listening skills to assure that they understand subordinates' feelings and beliefs about the work they perform.

The People

We can afford to be very brief here since much of the rest of the book has focused on this topic. Still, it is worth repeating that leaders should look at the followers in terms of skills, knowledge, experience, expectations, needs and preferences. In an increasingly global society, leaders can no longer afford to be parochial in their selection of followers. Compounding the global nature of work is, as noted earlier, the increasing rate of change in the environment. In a stable environment, any species can select a niche and survive for eons. But in a rapidly changing environment, diversity allows the species to sense and adapt more quickly. The same is true in the leadership world as well. Diversity is no longer merely the politically correct facade of leadership—it is essential to quality and survival in a rapidly changing world.

The Formal Organization

As with tasks, there also are a variety of dimensions for conceptualizing the organizational level of situations. This section will address how level of authority, organizational structure, organizational design, lateral interdependence, and organizational culture affect leaders' and followers' behavior.

Level of Authority.   **Level of authority** concerns one's hierarchical level in an organization. The types of behaviors most critical to leadership effectiveness can change substantially as one moves up an organizational ladder. First-line supervisors, lower-level leaders, and coaches spend a considerable amount of time training followers, resolving work-unit or team-performance problems, scheduling practices or arranging work schedules, and implementing policies. Leaders at higher organizational levels have more autonomy and spend relatively more time setting policies, coordinating activities, and making staffing decisions (Blankenship & Miles, 1968; Luthans, Rosenkrantz, & Hennessey, 1985; Mintzberg, 1973; Page & Tornow, 1987). Moreover, leaders at higher organizational levels often perform a greater variety of activities and are more apt to use participation and delegation (Chitayat & Venezia, 1984; Kurke & Aldrich, 1983). A quite different aspect of how level of authority affects leadership is presented in Highlight 15–3.

Organizational Structure.   **Organizational structure** refers to the way an organization's activities are coordinated and controlled, and represents another level of

Highlight 15–3

The Glass Ceiling and the Wall

While the 1990s have been marked by increasing movement of women into leadership positions, it still is a fact that women occupy only a tiny percentage of the highest leadership positions. In Fortune 500 companies, for example, only 1 or 2 percent of the corporate officers are women. Researchers at the Center for Creative Leadership embarked on the Executive Woman Project to understand why (Morrison, White, & Van Velsor, 1987).

They studied 76 women executives in 25 companies who had reached the general-management level or the one just below it. The average woman executive in the sample was 41 and married. More than half had at least one child, and the vast majority were white.

The researchers expected to find evidence of a "glass ceiling," an invisible barrier that keeps women from progressing higher than a certain level in their organizations *because they are women*. One reason the women in this particular sample were interesting was precisely because they had apparently "broken" the glass ceiling, thus entering the top 1 percent of the work force. These women had successfully confronted three different sorts of pressure throughout their careers, a greater challenge than their male counterparts faced. One pressure was that from the job itself, and this was no different for women than for men. A second level of pressure, however, involved being a female executive, with attendant stresses such as being particularly visible, excessively scrutinized, and a role model for other women. A third level of pressure involved the demands of coordinating personal and professional life. It is still most people's expectation that women will take the greater responsibility in a family for managing the household and raising children. And beyond the sheer size of such demands, the roles of women in these two spheres of life are often at odds (e.g., being businesslike and efficient, maybe even tough, at work yet intimate and nurturing at home).

The Center for Creative Leadership researchers described the "lessons for success" of this group of women who had broken through the glass ceiling. They also reported, however, a somewhat unexpected finding. Breaking through the glass ceiling presented women executives with an even tougher obstacle. They "hit a wall" that kept them out of the very top positions. The researchers estimated that only a handful of the women executives in their sample would enter the topmost echelon, called senior management, and that none would become president of their corporation.

the situation in which leaders and followers must operate. Organizational structure is a conceptual or procedural reality, however, not a physical or tangible one. Typically, it is depicted in the form of a chart that clarifies formal authority relationships and patterns of communication within the organization. Most people take organizational structure for granted and fail to realize that structure is really just a tool for getting things done in organizations. Structure is not an end in itself, and different structures might exist for organizations performing similar work, each having unique advantages and disadvantages. There is nothing sacrosanct or permanent about any structure, and leaders may find that having a basic understanding of organizational structure is not only useful but imperative. Leaders may wish to design a structure to enhance the likelihood of attaining a desired outcome, or they may wish to change structure to meet future demands. There are a number of ways to describe organizational structures, but perhaps the simplest way is to think of structure in terms of complexity, formalization, and centralization.

Complexity.   Horizontal, vertical, and spatial elements make up organizational complexity. Concerning an organizational chart, **horizontal complexity** refers to the number of "boxes" at any particular organizational level. The greater the number of boxes at a given level, the greater the horizontal complexity. Typically, greater horizontal complexity is associated with more specialization within subunits and an increased likelihood for communication breakdowns between subunits. **Vertical complexity** refers to the number of hierarchical levels appearing on an organization chart. A vertically simple organization may have only two or three levels from the highest person to the lowest. A vertically complex organization, on the other hand, may have 10 or more. Vertical complexity can affect leadership by impacting other factors such as authority dynamics and communication networks. **Spatial complexity** describes geographical dispersion. An organization that has all of its people in one location is typically less spatially complex than an organization that is dispersed around the country or around the world. Obviously, spatial complexity makes it more difficult for leaders to have face-to-face communication with subordinates in geographically separated locations, and to personally administer rewards or provide support and encouragement. Generally, all three of these elements are partly a function of organizational size. Bigger organizations are more likely to have more-specialized subunits (horizontal complexity) and a greater number of hierarchical levels (vertical complexity), and to have subunits that are geographically dispersed (spatial complexity).

Formalization.   **Formalization** describes the degree of standarization in an organization. Organizations having written job descriptions and standardized operating procedures for each position have a high degree of formalization. The degree of formalization in an organization tends to vary with its size, just as complexity generally increases with size (Robbins, 1986). Formalization also varies with the nature of work performed. Manufacturing organizations, for example, tend to have fairly formalized structures, whereas research-and-development organizations tend to be less formalized. After all, how could there be a detailed job description for developing a nonexistent product or making a scientific discovery?

The degree of formalization in an organization poses both advantages and disadvantages for leaders and followers. Whereas formalizing procedures clarifies methods of operating and interacting, it also may constitute demands and constraints on leaders and followers. Leaders may be constrained in the ways

Are There Substitutes for Leadership?

Are leaders always necessary? Or are certain kinds of leader behaviors, at least, sometimes unnecessary? Kerr and Jermier (1978) proposed that certain situational or follower characteristics may well effectively neutralize or substitute for leaders' task or relationship behaviors. *Neutralizers* are characteristics that reduce or limit the effectiveness of a leader's behaviors. *Substitutes* are characteristics that make a leader's behaviors redundant or unnecessary.

Kerr and Jermier (1978) developed the idea of **substitutes for leadership** after comparing the correlations between leadership behaviors and follower performance and satisfaction with correlations between various situational factors and follower performance and satisfaction. Those subordinate, task, and organizational characteristics having higher correlations with follower performance and satisfaction than the two leadership behaviors were subsequently identified as substitutes or neutralizers. The following are a few examples of the situational factors Kerr and Jermier found to substitute for or neutralize leaders' task or relationship behaviors:

- A subordinate's ability and experience may well substitute for task-oriented leader behavior. A subordinate's indifference toward rewards overall may neutralize a leader's task and relationship behavior.
- Tasks that are routine or structured may substitute for task-oriented leader behavior, as can tasks that provide intrinsic feedback or are intrinsically satisfying.
- High levels of formalization in organizations may substitute for task-oriented leader behavior, and unbending rules and procedures may even neutralize the leader's task behavior. A cohesive work group may provide a substitute for the leader's task and relationship behavior.

Source: S. Kerr and J. M. Jermier, "Substitutes for Leadership: Their Meaning and Measurement," *Organizational Behavior and Human Performance* 22 (1978), pp. 375–403.

they communicate requests, order supplies, or reward or discipline subordinates (Hammer & Turk, 1987; Podsaskoff, 1982). If followers belong to a union, then union rules may dictate work hours, the amount of work accomplished per day, or who will be the first to be laid off (Hammer & Turk, 1987). Other aspects of the impact of formalization and other situational variables on leadership are presented in Highlights 15–4 and 15–5.

Centralization. **Centralization** refers to the diffusion of decision making throughout an organization. An organization that allows decisions to be made by only one person is highly centralized. When decision making is dispersed to

---

Highlight 15–5

A "Soap" Opera

Most of us have a preference for the type of organizational structure we would like to work in. Some people prefer formal structures, while others prefer almost no organizational structure at all. As we have noted, different structures enable certain behaviors better than others. When we mix preferences and structures, we can get some interesting and often humorous results. Such is the case in the following "soap" opera transmitted over an electronic mail network, where we find a man who would prefer a little personal attention in a system designed to apply the same rules to everyone. The setting is a London hotel that supplies free soap.

Dear Maid:

Please do not leave any more of those little bars of soap in my bathroom since I have brought my own bath-sized Dial. Please remove the 6 unopened little bars from the shelf under the medicine chest and another 3 in the shower soap dish. They are in my way.

Thank you, T. Brown

Dear Room 545:

I am not your regular maid. She will be back tomorrow from her day off. I took the 3 hotel soaps out of the shower soap dish as you requested. The 6 bars on your shelf I took out of your way and put on top of your Kleenex dispenser in case you should change your mind. This only leaves 3 bars I left today. My instructions from the management are to leave 3 soaps daily. I hope this is satisfactory.

Kathy, Relief Maid

Dear Maid:

I hope you are my regular maid. Apparently Kathy did not tell you about my note to her concerning the little bars of soap. When I got back to my room this evening I found you had added 3 little Camays to the shelf under my medicine cabinet. I am going to be here in the hotel for two weeks and have brought my own bath-sized Dial, so I won't need those 6 little Camays which are on the shelf. They are in my way when shaving, brushing teeth, etc. Please remove them.

T. Brown

Dear Mr. Brown:

My day off was last Wednesday so the relief maid left 3 hotel soaps which we are instructed by the management. I took the 6 soaps which were in your way on the shelf and put them in the soap dish where your Dial was. I put the Dial in the medicine cabinet for your convenience. I didn't remove the 3 complimentary soaps, which are always placed inside the medicine cabinet for all new check-ins, and which you did not object to when you checked in last Monday. Please let me know if I can be of further assistance.

Your regular maid, Dotty

Dear Mr. Brown:

The assistant manger, Mr. Kensedder, informed me this A.M. that you called him last evening and said you were unhappy with the maid service. I have assigned a new girl to your room. I hope you will accept my apologies for any past inconvenience. If you have any future complaints, please contact me so I can give it my personal attention. Call extension 1108 between 8 A.M. and 5 P.M. Thank you.

Elaine Carmen, Housekeeper

Dear Miss Carmen:

It is impossible to contact you by phone since I leave the hotel for business at 7:45 A.M. and don't get back before 5:30–6:00 P.M. The reason I called Mr. Kensedder last night was because you were off duty. I only asked Mr. Kensedder if he could do anything about those little bars of soap. The new maid you assigned me must have thought I was a new check-in today, since she left another 3 bars of hotel soap in my medicine cabinet along with her regular delivery of 3 bars on the bathroom shelf. In just 5 days here I have accumulated 24 little bars of soap. Why are you doing this to me?

T. Brown

Dear Mr. Brown:

Your maid, Kathy, has been instructed to stop delivering soap to your room and to remove the extra soaps. If I can be of further assistance please call extension 1108 between 8 A.M. and 5 P.M. Thank you.

Elaine Carmen, Housekeeper

Dear Mr. Kensedder:

My bath-sized Dial is missing. Every bar of soap was taken from my room including my own bath-sized Dial. I came in late last night and had to call the bellhop to bring me 4 little Cashmere Bouquets.

T. Brown

Dear Mr. Brown.

I have informed our housekeeper, Elaine Carmen, of your soap problem. I cannot understand why there was no soap in your room since our maids are instructed to leave 3 bars of soap each time they service a room. The situation will be rectified immediately. Please accept my apologies for the inconvenience.

M. L. Kensedder, Asst. Man.

Dear Mrs. Carmen:

Who the hell left 54 little bars of Camay in my room? I came in last night and found 54 bars of soap. I don't want 54 little bars of Camay. I want my 1 damn bar of bath-sized Dial. Do you realize I have 54 bars of soap in here? All I want is my bath-sized Dial. Please give me back my bath-sized Dial.

T. Brown

Dear Mr. Brown:

You complained of too much soap in your room so I had them removed. Then you complained to Mr. Kensedder that all your soap was missing so I personally returned them. The 24 Camays which had been taken and the 3 Camays you are supposed to receive daily. I don't know anything about the 4 Cashmere Bouquets. Obviously your maid, Kathy, did not know I had returned your soaps so she also brought 24 Camays plus the 3 daily Camays. I don't know where you got the idea this hotel issues bath-sized Dial. I was able to locate some bath-sized Ivory which I left in your room.

Elaine Carmen, Housekeeper

Dear Mrs. Carmen:

Just a short note to bring you up-to-date on my latest soap inventory. As of today I possess:

(continued)

(*concluded*)

- on the shelf under medicine cabinet—18 Camay in 4 stacks of 4 and 1 stack of 2
- on the Kleenex dispenser—11 Camay in 2 stacks of 4 and 1 stack of 3
- on the bedroom dresser—1 stack of 3 Cashmere Bouquet, 1 stack of 4 hotel-size, bath-sized Ivory, and 8 Camay in 2 stacks of 4
- in the medicine cabinet—14 Camay in 3 stacks of 4 and 1 stack of 2
- in the shower soap dish—6 Camay, very moist
- on the northeast corner of the tub—1 Cashmere Bouquet, slightly used
- on the northwest corner of the tub—6 Camay in 2 stacks of 3.

Please ask Kathy when she services my room to make sure the stacks are neatly piled and dusted. Also, please advise her that stacks of more than 4 have a tendency to tip. May I suggest that my bedroom windowsill is not in use and will make an excellent spot for future soap deliveries. One more item, I have purchased another bar of bath-sized Dial which I am keeping in the hotel vault in order to avoid future misunderstandings.

T. Brown

Source: The authors do not know of a published source for this episode. It was provided to the authors by Sally Hollar, an acquaintance who works for American Express, who received it over that company's electronic mail network. We were unsuccessful in locating any other source.

---

the lowest levels in the organization, the organization is very decentralized. Advantages of decentralized organizations include increased participation in the decision process and, consequently, greater acceptance and ownership of decision outcomes. These are both desirable outcomes. There are also, however, advantages to centralization, such as uniform policies and procedures (which can increase feelings of equity), and clearer coordination procedures (Bass, 1990). The task of balancing the degree of centralization necessary to achieve coordination and control, on the one hand, and gaining desirable participation and acceptance, on the other, is an ongoing challenge for the leader.

Organizational Design.   In addition to being classified by their degree of complexity, formalization, and centralization, organizations can also be classified into several different kinds of organizational design. Organizational design can be thought of most easily in the following two questions: (1) How do I want to divide up the work? (2) How do I want the divisions to coordinate their work? Three of the most common kinds of **organizational designs** in the traditional (or industrial age) format include functional, product, and matrix organizations.

Functional.   Some organizations have their structures designed around certain important and continuing functions. For example, a manufacturing company with a **functional design** might have its organizational chart include one block for manufacturing, one for sales or marketing, one for research and development, and so on (see Figure 15–3). Advantages of functional organizations include efficient use of scarce resources, skill development for technical personnel, centralized decision making and control, and excellent coordination within each functional department. Disadvantages of functional organizations can include

FIGURE 15-3

A Manufacturing Company with a Functional Design

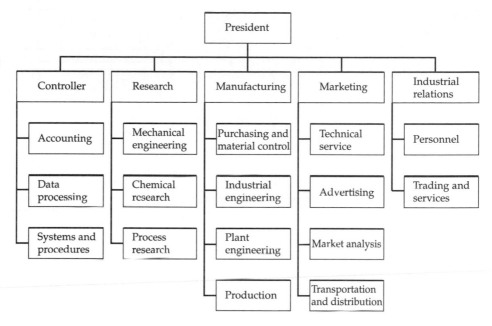

poor coordination across departments, slow responses to change, a piling up of decisions at the top of the hierarchy, and narrow or limited views by employees of overall organizational goals (Austin, Conlon, & Daft, 1986). In organizations structured functionally, in other words, the very commonality within the various functional units can create problems. Functional groups can become so cohesive that they create rigid boundaries and dysfunctional competitiveness between themselves and other groups within the same organization.

Product.   In an organization with a **product design,** the blocks on the organization chart define the various products or services that are delivered ultimately to the consumer. One might consider an automobile organization such as General Motors, where there are the Buick, Oldsmobile, Chevrolet, Cadillac, Saturn, and Pontiac divisions. These are identifiable products, and employees are assigned to these product groupings. A different product design is represented in Figure 15-4. A product organization design overcomes some of the problems associated with functional organizations, as a product organization has better coordination across functional skills, places a premium on organizational goals rather than functional goals, and has better control over diverse products or services. The disadvantages of product organizations include duplication of resources, less in-depth technical expertise, and weak coordination across different product groupings.

Matrix.   The **matrix design** is a combination of the product and functional designs. In this design, both product orientation and functional specialties are

FIGURE 15–4

*A Petroleum
Company with a
Product Design*

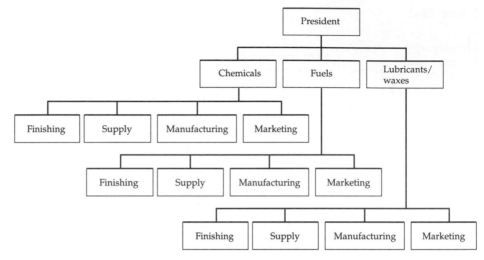

maintained (see Figure 15–5). In a matrix organization, there is a product manager for each product and one of her tasks is to obtain the resources necessary from the functional specialties as requirements demand. If the product will require the services of a computer software engineer, for example, then the product manager must acquire those services from the manager of the engineering function.

The greatest advantage of the matrix is efficient utilization of human resources. Imagine putting together a team to design a new product, and further suppose that a chemical engineer's services are among the team's needs. Also imagine, however, that the chemical engineer is required for only one month's work whereas the total product design phase encompasses a whole year. If our imaginary organization were designed according to a product orientation, the product manager would have to hire a full-time chemical engineer despite needing her services for only one month. In a matrix organization, on the other hand, the chemical engineer could be assigned to the engineering division, and the various product managers could arrange to acquire her time on an as-needed basis. Such an arrangement can create scheduling nightmares, but it also results in more efficient utilization of unusual or scarce resources. Another advantage of the matrix design includes increased lateral communication and coordination.

The greatest disadvantage of the matrix design is that employees end up working for two bosses. Such a dual-authority structure can create confusion and frustration. In the case above, the chemical engineer may have "professional loyalty" to the engineering group (which would dictate the highest-quality engineering possible) and "profitability loyalty" to the product group (which would dictate the most cost-effective engineering). Our chemical engineer might very well experience conflict over which loyalty to serve first. Additionally, matrix designs can lead to conflict and disagreements over the use of shared resources,

FIGURE 15–5

A Manufacturing Company with a Matrix Design

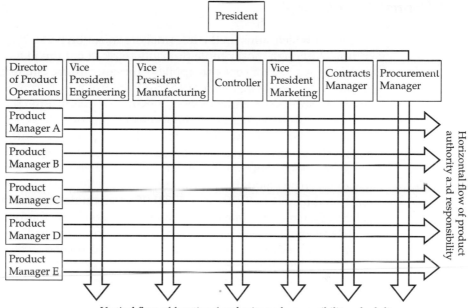

Vertical flow of functional authority and responsibility scheduling

and time is lost through frequent meetings to resolve such issues. Thus, administrative costs are high in matrix organizations. Finally, matrix designs can work well only if managers see the big picture and do not adopt narrow functional or product perspectives.

Lateral Interdependence.   The degree of lateral interdependence in an organization can also affect leaders' and followers' behaviors. Lateral interdependence concerns the degree of coordination or synchronization required between organizational units in order to accomplish work-group or organizational goals. Thus, lateral interdependence is similar to task interdependence but at a higher organizational level; lateral interdependence represents the degree to which a leader's work group is affected by the actions or activities of other subunits within the organization (Bass, 1990; Sayles, 1979). For example, a leader of a final assembly unit for personal computers will be very dependent on the activities of the power supply, cabinet, monitor, mother board, floppy drive, and hard drive manufacturing units in order to successfully meet production goals. On the other hand, the leader of a manufacturing unit that makes all of the products used to assemble backpacks has a much lower degree of lateral interdependence. As lateral interdependence increases, leaders usually spend more time building and maintaining contacts in other work units or on public relations activities (Hammer & Turk, 1987; Kaplan, 1986). Moreover, leaders are more likely to use rational persuasion as an influence tactic when the level of lateral interdependence is high (Kanter, 1982; Kaplan, 1986).

The Informal Organization

One word which sums up the informal organization better than any other is its culture. Although most people probably think of culture in terms of very large social groups, the concept also applies to organizations. **Organizational culture** has been defined as a system of shared backgrounds, norms, values, or beliefs among members of a group (Schein, 1985), and **organizational climate** concerns members' subjective reactions about the organization (Bass, 1990; Kozlowski & Doherty, 1989). These two concepts are distinct in that organizational climate is partly a function of, or reaction to, organizational culture; one's feelings or emotional reactions about an organization are probably affected by the degree to which a person shares the prevailing values, beliefs, and backgrounds of organizational members (Schneider, 1983). If a person does not share the values or beliefs of the majority of members, then in all likelihood this person would have a fairly negative reaction about the organization overall. Thus, organizational climate (and indirectly organizational culture) is related to how well organizational members get along with each other (Bass, 1990; Kozlowski & Doherty, 1989). It is also important to note that organizational climate is narrower in scope but highly related to job satisfaction. Generally, organizational climate has more to do with nontask perceptions of work, such as feelings about co-workers or company policies, whereas job satisfaction usually also includes perceptions of workload and the nature of the tasks performed.

Just as there are many cultures across the world, there are a great number of different cultures across organizations. Members of many military organizations have different norms, background experiences, values, and beliefs, for example, from those of the faculty at many colleges. Similarly, the culture of an investment firm is very different from the culture of a research-and-development firm, a freight hauling company, or a college rugby team. Cultural differences can exist between different organizations even within any of these sectors. The culture of the U.S. Air Force is different from the culture of the U.S. Marine Corps, and Yale has a different culture than the University of Colorado even though they are both fine institutions of higher learning.

One of the more fascinating aspects of organizational culture is that it often takes an outsider to recognize it; organizational culture becomes so second nature to many organizational members that they are unaware of how it affects their behaviors and perceptions (Bass, 1990). Despite this transparency to organizational members, a fairly consistent set of dimensions can be used to differentiate between organizational cultures. For example, Kilmann and Saxton (1983) stated that organizational cultures can be differentiated based on members' responses to questions like those found in Table 15–1. Another way to understand an organization's culture is in terms of myths and stories, symbols, rituals, and language (Schein, 1985). A more-detailed description of the four, key factors identified by Schein can be found in Highlight 15–6.

Here is an example of how stories contribute to organizational culture. A consultant was asked to help a plant that had been having morale and production prob-

---

TABLE 15–1   Some Questions That Define Organizational Culture

---

- What can be talked about or not talked about?
- How do people wield power?
- How does one get ahead or stay out of trouble?
- What are the unwritten rules of the game?
- What are the organization's morality and ethics?
- What stories are told about the organization?

Source: Adapted from R. H. Kilmann and M. J. Saxton, *Organizational Cultures: Their Assessment and Change* (San Francisco: Jossey-Bass, 1983).

lems for years. After talking with several individuals at the plant, the consultant believed he had located the problem. It seems everyone he talked to told him about Sam, the plant manager. He was a giant of a man with a terrible temper. He had demolished unacceptable products with a sledgehammer, stood on the plant roof screaming at workers, and done countless other things sure to intimidate everyone around. The consultant decided he needed to go talk to this plant manager. When he did so, however, he met a very agreeable person named Paul. Sam, it seems, had been dead for nearly a decade, but his legacy lived on (Dumaine, 1990).

It is important for leaders to realize that they can play an active role in changing an organization's culture, not just be influenced by it (Bass, 1985; Kouzes & Posner, 1987; Schein, 1985; Tichy & Devanna, 1986). Leaders can change culture by attending to or ignoring particular issues, problems, or projects. They can modify culture through their reactions to crises, by rewarding new or different kinds of behavior, or by eliminating previous punishments or negative consequences for certain behaviors. Their general personnel policies send messages about the value of employees to the organization (e.g., cutting wages to avoid layoffs). They can use role modeling and self-sacrifice as a way to inspire or motivate others to work more vigorously or interact with each other differently. Finally, leaders can also change culture by the criteria they use to select or dismiss followers.

Changing an organization's culture, of course, takes time and effort, and sometimes it may be extremely difficult. This is especially true in very large organizations or those with strong cultures (see, for example, Highlight 15–7). New organizations, on the other hand, do not have the traditions, stories or myths, or established rites to the same extent that older companies do, and it may be easier for leaders to change culture in these organizations.

Why would a leader *want* to change an organization's culture? It all should depend on whether the culture is having a positive or a negative impact on various desirable outcomes. We remember one organization with a very "polite" culture, an aspect that seemed very positive at first. There were never any potentially destructive emotional outbursts in the organization, and there was an apparent concern for other individuals' feelings in all interactions. However, a darker side

Schein's Four Key Organizational Culture Factors

Myths and stories are the tales about the organization that are passed down over time and communicate a story of the organization's underlying values. Virtually any employee of Wal-Mart can tell you stories about Sam Walton and his behavior—how he rode around in his pickup truck, how he greeted people in the stores, and how he tended to "just show up" at different times. The Center for Creative Leadership has stories about its founder, H. Smith Richardson, who as a young man creatively used the mail to sell products. Sometimes stories and myths are transferred between organizations even though the truth may not lie wholly in either one. A story is told in AT&T about one of its founders and how he trudged miles and miles through a blizzard to repair a faulty component so that a woman living by herself in a rural community could get phone service. Interestingly enough, this same story is also told in MCI.

Symbols and artifacts are objects that can be seen and noticed and that describe various aspects of the culture. In almost any building, for example, symbols and artifacts provide information about the organization's culture. For example, an organization may believe in egalitarian principles, and that might be reflected in virtually everyone having the same-size office. Or there can be indications of opulence, which convey a very different message. Even signs might act as symbols or artifacts of underlying cultural values. At one university that believed students should have first priority for facilities, an interesting sign showed up occasionally to reinforce this value. It was not a road sign, but a sign appearing on computer monitors. When the university's main computer was being overused, the computer was programmed to identify nonstudent users, note the overload, and issue a warning to nonstudent users to sign off. This was a clear artifact, or symbol, underlying the priority placed on students at that school.

Rituals are recurring events or activities that reflect important aspects of the underlying culture. An organization may have spectacular sales meetings for its top performers and spouses every two years. This ritual would be an indication of the value placed on high sales and meeting high quotas. Another kind of ritual is the retirement ceremony. Elaborate or modest retirement ceremonies may signal the importance an organization places on its people.

Language concerns the jargon, or idiosyncratic terms, of an organization and can serve several different purposes relevant to culture. First, the mere fact that some know the language and some do not indicates who is in the culture and who is not. Second, language can also provide information about how people within a culture view others. Third, language can be used to help create a culture. A good example of the power of language in creating culture is in the words employees at Disneyland or Walt Disney World use in referring to themselves and park visitors. Employees—all employees, from the costumed Disney characters to popcorn vendors—are told to think of themselves as members of a cast, and never to be out of character. Everything happening at the park is part of the "show," and those who paid admission to enter the park are not mere tourists, but rather "the audience." Virtually everyone who visits the Disney parks is impressed with the consistently friendly behavior of its staff, a reflection of the power of words in creating culture. (Of course, a strict and strongly enforced policy concerning courtesy toward park guests also helps.)

Highlight 15–7

John Delorean and Counterculture at GM

One of the more interesting stories about organizational culture and the actions taken to change a culture concerns John DeLorean (Martin & Siehl, 1983). DeLorean was a senior executive at GM, an institution with a well-established culture. One of GM's key cultural values was showing deference and respect to authority. For example, subordinates were expected to meet out-of-town superiors at the airport, carry their bags, pay their hotel and meal bills, and chauffeur them around day and night. Additionally, the more senior the executive, the bigger the traveling party would be. Some employees were so eager to please their boss that a group of Chevrolet sales people had a refrigerator put in the hotel room of a visiting senior executive after they had learned he liked to have a few cold beers and to make a sandwich before going to bed. Unfortunately, the door to the suite was too small to accommodate the refrigerator, so the Chevrolet sales personnel went so far as to hire a crane to bring in and later remove the refrigerator through the windows of the suite. A second core value at GM was communicating invisibility by visible cues. Ideal GM employees dressed identically, had the same office decor and layout, were "team players," and could easily fit in without drawing attention to themselves. The last key cultural value at GM was loyalty to one's boss. Loyalty to one's boss was clearly evident in the ritual of the retirement dinner, where a loyal subordinate was given the task of providing a detailed account of the retiree's steady rise through the corporation, counterpointed with allusions to the retiree's charming wife and family.

DeLorean took a number of actions to change the dominant culture at GM. First, DeLorean liked independence and dissent, and he modeled the behavior he wished others to emulate. He wore suits that stood out, and when appointed to head the Chevrolet division, he immediately changed the office furniture, carpeting, and decor and allowed executives to decorate their offices any way they wanted to "within reasonable limits." Second, because DeLorean believed that subordinates were more productive doing work than catering to superiors, he traveled by himself and did not greet his superiors at the airport, nor did he have his subordinates pick him up. Third, he changed the performance appraisal system within his division. Subordinates were to be rewarded on the basis of objective performance data, not subjective data that indicated a willingness to fit in. Although for a time DeLorean managed to maintain a delicate balance between culture and counterculture, his dissent was eventually met with disfavor, and he left GM to form a company of his own. Nevertheless, DeLorean's story provides several insights about the pervasiveness of organizational culture and the actions a leader might take to change culture.

of that culture gradually became apparent. When it was appropriate to give feedback for performance appraisals or employee development, supervisors were hesitant to raise negative aspects of behavior; they interpreted doing so as not being polite. And so the organization continued to be puzzled by employee behavior that tended not to improve; the organization was a victim of its own culture.

Leaders especially need to be sensitive to how their own "brilliant ideas" may adversely impact subtle but important aspects of organizational culture. What may appear to be a major technical innovation (and therefore seemingly desirable) may also be devastating to organizational culture. For example, for hundreds of years in England, coal was mined by teams of three persons each. In England, coal is layered in very narrow seams, most only a few feet high. In the past, the only practical means to get the coal out was to send the three-person teams of miners down into the mines to dig coal from the seam and then haul it to the surface on a tram. These mining teams had extremely high levels of group cohesiveness. A technological development called the long-wall method of coal extraction was to upset these close relationships, however. In the long-wall method, workers were arrayed all along an entire seam of coal rather than in distinct teams, and the method should have resulted in higher productivity among the miners. However, the breakdown of the work teams led to unexpected decreases in productivity, much higher levels of worker dissatisfaction, and even disruption of social life among the miners' families. Although the long-wall method was technically superior to the three-person mining team, the leaders of the coal-mining companies failed to consider the cultural consequences of this technological advancement (Emery & Trist, 1965).

After reading these examples, you may be asking whether it is better for leaders to create cultures that emphasize interpersonal relationships or organizational productivity. We can glean some insights into this question by looking at Mitchell's (1985) study of two groups of successful organizations. Mitchell compared two different groups of organizational cultures: those of organizations considered well managed, and those of organizations considered well liked by people working in the organization. The former group consisted of the 62 organizations identified in I*n Search of Excellence* (Peters & Waterman, 1982), and the latter group included firms identified in *The One Hundred Best Companies to Work for in America* (Levering, Moskowitz, & Katz, 1984).

Interestingly, there was relatively little overlap between the two lists. According to Mitchell, this lack of overlap was due primarily to differences between task- and relationship-oriented organizational cultures. Cultures in the well-liked organizations emphasized making employees feel they were part of a family, reducing social distance, and making the organization a pleasant one to work in. Cultures in the well-managed organizations, on the other hand, were much more manipulative. Those firms had cultures that valued people not for themselves but as instruments of productivity. Although which type of culture is best for an organization is still under debate, it is important to note that the 62 companies deemed excellently managed by Peters and Waterman did not provide any higher returns on investments than less well managed firms (Simpson & Ireland, 1987), and many of these 62 companies and cultures look considerably less excellent today.

An Afterthought on Organizational Issues for Students and Young Leaders.
Let us conclude this section by adding an afterthought about what relevance it

may have for students or others at the early stages of their careers, or at lower levels of leadership within their organizations. It is unlikely that such individuals will be asked soon to redesign their organization's structure or change its culture. As noted earlier, this chapter is not intended as a how-to manual for changing culture. On the other hand, it has been our experience that younger colleagues sometimes develop biased impressions of leaders or have unrealistic expectations about decision making in organizations, based on their lack of familiarity with, and appreciation for, the sorts of organizational dynamics discussed in this section. In other words, one of the primary reasons for being familiar with such organizational variables is the context they provide for understanding the leadership process at your own level in the organization. Finally, we have worked with some senior leaders of huge organizations who have been with their company for their entire career. They have often been unable to identify *any* of the dimensions of their culture because they have never seen anything else. In these cases we were amazed by how junior managers were far better at describing the culture of the large organization. While these junior people may have only had five to eight years of total work experience, if that experience had been obtained in several different organizations, they were much better prepared to describe the characteristics of their new large organization's culture than were the senior executives.

Environmental Characteristics

We mentioned the environment earlier in the chapter as an input variable in the Congruence Model. We now return to a slightly more in-depth analysis of environmental characteristics since not attending to environmental characteristics is the root of extinction, both for the organization and for the population at large. Environmental characteristics concern situational factors outside the task or organization that still affect the leadership process. These include technological, economic, political, social, and legal forces. For example, imagine how changing economic conditions, such as threats of layoffs from a recession or a hostile takeover, would affect leaders' and followers' behavior. These factors often create anxiety, and therefore cause an increase in employees' security needs. They also tend to result in decreased training budgets for workers (Bass, 1990). At this writing, we are still unable to predict the long-term consequences of the monetary instabilities in Asia, but everyone acknowledges that these seemingly distant economic downturns cannot be ignored. Political changes also can have substantial impacts on leaders and followers. Just imagine, for example, how leaders' and followers' behaviors are changing in Eastern Europe as the various countries move from communist systems to private ownership of companies. Legal forces affecting Western organizations include those contributing to the growth of new industries (e.g., industrial waste disposal) or to personnel reductions in other industries due to changes in governmental rules and regulations (Ungson, James, & Spicer, 1985). Finally, technological advances are changing leader-follower relationships. For example, the advent of personal computers, fax machines, and the modem allows people to work at geographically dispersed locations.

Technology and Uncertainty

Technology affects the leadership process in other ways as well. For example, it might determine what design is best for an organization (Woodward, 1965). In environments of low **technological complexity,** workers play a large role and are able to modify their behavior depending on the situation. In environments of high technological complexity, there is a highly predictable work flow.

Examples of organizations in environments of low technological complexity are printing shops, tailor shops, and cabinet makers. In each case, the organization is well suited to meeting specific customer orders. One of the authors of this book recently encountered an organization fitting this mold in trying to find an oak wall unit that would meet his requirements for a stereo system. After much frustrating shopping and finding a number of mass-produced units that would *not* work, he found a shop that had a variety of different units. Some of these came close to what he needed, but even the closest was not quite right. After listening in detail to the requirements, the owner agreed he didn't have anything on the floor that would work. In the next breath, however, he said, "But if you can draw it, we can build it."

A higher level of technological complexity occurs when mass production is the focus and orders are filled from inventory. An example would be furniture purchased from large warehouse stores. As opposed to the individually crafted wall unit described above, most furniture is not specifically designed and built precisely to meet special customer needs. Instead, manufacturers produce large quantities of various pieces of furniture likely to adequately meet the tastes and needs of most customers.

The highest level of technological complexity occurs when a continuous process is mechanized from beginning to end. People don't play much of a role in such organizations at all except to monitor the process flow and detect problems. Oil refining operations, chemical production plants, and nuclear power plants are all examples of continuous-process organizations. In such plants, people are merely observing and monitoring the processes and detecting anomalies that need to be corrected.

The significance of such a range of technological complexity is that different kinds of organizational structures or designs are best suited for different technological environments. An organization is most likely to be successful if the structure fits the technology. If the technological environment is one of moderately high complexity (like large furniture-manufacturing companies), a mechanistic or bureaucratic structure to the organization may be most appropriate. On the other hand, if the technological environment is one of low complexity (like the custom cabinetmaker or printer), setting up a rigid, bureaucratic structure will make it difficult for your organization to produce and "flex" as required by the different specific orders.

In addition to technology, the degree of **environmental uncertainty** also affects optimal organizational design. In stable environments where there is little change, a relatively formalized, centralized, and bureaucratic structure may be desirable. In turbulent environments, on the other hand, structures should be flexible enough to adapt to changing conditions (Burns & Stalker, 1961). In a similar fashion, flat, highly differentiated, and organic structures are most appropriate for very uncertain environments (Lawrence & Lorsch, 1967a, 1967b).

Crises

Another environmental variable that affects the leadership process is the presence or absence of crises. Some researchers believe crises play such an important part in charismastic leadership that certain leaders will purposely create crises in order to be perceived as being charismatic (Bass, 1985; Curphy, 1991; Roberts & Bradley, 1988). Furthermore, the behaviors associated with effective leadership during crises differ from those associated with noncrisis situations. During crises, followers are more likely to look to leaders to identify the problem as well as develop and implement a solution. Thus, work groups facing strong deadlines or crises generally expect their leaders to be more assertive, directive, and decisive (Mulder & Stemerding, 1963). Moreover, leaders are less apt to use participation or consultation during crises (Mulder, de Jong, Koppelaar, & Verhage, 1986; Pfeffer & Salancik, 1975). These findings make sense when contrasting emergency and nonemergency situations. For example, surgeons spend considerable time consulting with colleagues prior to conducting a difficult surgery. However, surgeons do not have time to consult with other specialists when a patient's heart has just stopped during surgery; the doctor must quickly diagnose the reason for the heart failure and coordinate the efforts of the surgical team for the patient to live. Similarly, coaches often spend considerable time consulting with other coaches and staff members when preparing for games, but during particularly close games they may consult with relatively few members of even their own staffs.

Situational Engineering

One of the most important points this chapter can make concerns the idea of situational engineering. Although leaders' and followers' behaviors are affected by a variety of situational factors, all too often leaders and followers completely overlook how changing the situation can help them to change their behavior. Just as a dieter can better stick to a diet by identifying bad eating habits and limiting food cues, so can a leader or follower become more effective by identifying problem areas and restructuring the situation so that these problems become easier to overcome.

Say, for example, a leader attended a leadership development program and received feedback that he did not interact enough with his subordinates. This leader might set a goal and may genuinely make an attempt to increase the level

" . . . *Then it's agreed. As a crowd, we'll be subdued in innings one through seven, then suddenly become a factor in innings eight and nine . . .*"

of interaction with his followers. Because his typical day is hectic and he manages a work group with a high level of lateral interdependence, however, situational demands may more or less force him to revert to his old behaviors. This leader would be likely to realize more success if he also restructured the situation in order to facilitate the accomplishment of this goal.

He could, for example, delegate more activities to subordinates. This would give the leader more opportunities to interact with followers (by mutually setting performance goals and monitoring progress), and it would give the leader more time to engage in other activities. Moreover, the leader could project a more approachable and friendly attitude by rearranging office furniture, keeping his door open as much as possible, and building specific times into his daily schedule to "manage by wandering around."

There are a variety of ways in which leaders and followers can change the task, organizational, and environmental factors affecting their behaviors and attitudes. By asking questions and listening effectively, leaders may be able to redesign work using the suggestions from Hackman and Oldham's (1980) job characteristics model or Herzberg's (1966) two-factor theory in order to improve followers' satisfaction and productivity levels. Similarly, leaders might discover ways to adjust followers' workloads, responsibilities, or levels of task interdependence; rearrange office layouts; establish new or different policies or procedures; or modify reporting relationships and appraisal systems (Yukl, 1989). More senior leaders might be able to change the organization itself or work to influence changes in the environment. Perhaps the most important point regarding situational engineering is to get leaders and followers to understand that the situation is not set in concrete, and to think about how they can change the situation in order for everyone to be more satisfied and productive.

One final example may be useful not only to illustrate the powerful impact of the situational variables but also to link this section to our previous discussion of the Team Effectiveness Leadership Model, introduced in Chapter 13. You may recall that one of the important inputs in the TELM was the organizational level where we identified four types of systems impacting team process. These systems involved rewards, information, education, and control. In one of our research projects we were observing a series of work processes performed by teams in a highly centralized and controlled organization. No work was ever performed without specific directions which were generated by a complex computer program. Engineers, who were not in the buildings where the work was performed, would prepare the working procedures, which were then integrated in the computer system and finally printed out for each task. While engineers could change the procedures, the perception of the workers in the processing facility was that the procedures were "like the bible—and equally difficult to change." In one series of work sequences, a team would prepare a sheet of flexible insulation (according to the printed instructions) for installation by the next team. However, when we followed the insulation, we found that the first thing the installation team would do was to unfold the flexible sheet, and refold it in exactly the opposite manner so that it could be installed. When we asked the preparation team if they were aware that the installation team was having to redo their work, they had no idea that was happening. Even more surprising was that when they did learn of this, both teams decided it was easier to continue their work as described on the computer task sheets than to try to change it! Using the TELM model, we were able to identify at least two systems which were creating problems. First, the interteam information system was inadequate; it should have allowed them to correct inappropriate strategies (e.g., folding it one way only to have that work undone and redone), but it didn't. Of equal impact was the teams' perception of powerlessness because of the oppressive control system in which they operated. Even after problems were discovered, the situation in which the teams operated created conditions which reduced the creative potential of those with direct knowledge of the work flow. Leadership could have changed the way work was done by these teams by improving the information system and modifying the control system. Highlight 15–8 describes one final example of dealing with situations. In this case, a young leader dealt with the stress of being in a new and dangerous situation with a team he'd only just met.

Taking Charge

A critical period for any leader often involves those first few moments and days of assuming command. It is a time when first impressions are formed and expectations are set. It is a crucial time for any leader in any situation, but can be a matter of life or death for a young leader in a combat situation. Here are one young officer's first reactions upon arriving in Southeast Asia to command a platoon.

I was alone. That was my first sensation as a leader. The men were going about the morning's business—breaking out C rations, relieving themselves, shaving, brushing their teeth. They moved among each other comfortably, a word here, a smile there. I could hear snatches of conversation: "A good night's sleep. . . ." "Only ninety days left." Occasionally a man would nod in my direction, or glance at me for a fleeting moment.

I gathered up my belongings—weapon, web gear, and rucksack—and moved toward the command post. I needed a few minutes to gather my thoughts before I made my debut as a platoon leader. I knew it was going to be a tricky business.

I had assumed that I would have a company commander nearby to give me my orders. But I had not even met him yet; I would not meet him for weeks. The fact was, I was totally on my own. What should I do? Whose advice could I ask? The platoon sergeant's? The squad leaders'? In time I would listen to their ideas and incorporate them with my own, but I could hardly begin my tour with "Well what do you think we ought to do, men?" No, I knew that the basic decisions were mine to make.

The first few moments would be crucial. Obviously, I was the object of interest that morning. Everyone was wondering what the new Lieutenant would be like, and I would be telling them with my first words, my gestures, my demeanor, my eyes. I would have no grace period in which to learn my way around. This was a life and death environment. If I began with a blunder, my credibility as a leader would be shot, and so might some of the men.

I decided to begin by giving my attention to tactics. In a military environment, everything is determined by tactical considerations. Where you sleep, when you sleep, where you go, what you do, and in whose company you do it—all are dictated by underlying tactical necessities. I would communicate my style of leadership through my tactical instructions.

As I surveyed the soldiers, the nearby village, the distant rice paddies, the heavy undergrowth, the varied terrain, my mind raced back over the years of tactical training I had received. Conscious of the stares of the men, I hoped to appear composed as I fought back the panic of having to decide, both quickly and correctly.

Source: J. M. McDonough, *Platoon Leader* (San Francisco: Presidio Press, 1985), pp. 30–31. Reprinted with permission.

A Look into the Crystal Ball

Certainly, we do not claim to have a crystal ball with a clear picture of the future situations which will undoubtedly impact leaders and followers. At the same time, we believe that anyone who plans to work in the world of tomorrow needs to pay attention to how the situation might be changing and what the implica-

TABLE 15–2   Differing Worldviews of Second, Third, and Fourth Wave Societies

	Second Wave	Third Wave	Fourth Wave
Relationships	See ourselves as separate and needing to compete	See ourselves as connected and needing to cooperate	See ourselves as one and choose to cocreate
Authority	Externalized; power seen as outside oneself	Begin to question external authority and retain personal locus of authority, take back power	Manifest collaborative systems where authority is fully internalized; power seen as within the person
Values	Rooted in materialism and the supremacy of man	Manifest growing concern for balance and sustainability	Focused on the integration of life and responsibility for the whole
Security	Seen in material terms	Material foundation questioned	Viewed in terms of personal inner trust
Mode of inquiry	Stresses linear thinking	Incorporates intuition and nonrational processes	Moves beyond intuition to tap full range of human abilities
Decision making	Act without awareness from unconscious scripts, rational decision making	Become aware of intentionality and the need for acting with intent	Recognize the centrality of intention

Source: Reprinted with permission of the publisher. From *The Fourth Wave*, copyright 1993 by Maynard & Mehrtens, Berrett-Koehler Publishers, Inc., San Francisco, CA. All rights reserved.

tion of those changes might be. One "crystal ball" that we find reasonably compelling is the work of Maynard and Mehrtens (1993) as presented in *The Fourth Wave*. These authors have adopted Alvin Toffler's concept of waves of change to examine the past and offer a potential insight into the future. We believe the two following tables are reasonably self-explanatory once the reader has a basic understanding of the different "waves." The First Wave was the agricultural revolution. Because it has essentially ended, Maynard and Mehrtens do not address its implications. The Second Wave may be equated with the Industrial Age, and the Third Wave represents much of what is happening now in the Information Age (see the description earlier in this chapter). For want of a better description, we might think of the Fourth Age as the Reality We Choose to Create. With that as background, examine the tables below. Table 15–2 focuses on the world views of societies in the different Waves, and Table 15–3 examines the various corporate roles in the different Waves.

Summary

The situation may well be the most complex factor in the leader-follower-situation framework. Moreover, situations vary not only in complexity but also in strength. Situational factors can play such a pervasive role that they can effectively minimize the effects of personality traits, intelligence, values, and preferences on leaders' and followers' behaviors, attitudes, and relationships. Given the dynamic nature of leadership situations, finding fairly consistent results is a highly encouraging accomplishment for leadership researchers.

TABLE 15–3   Dimensions of the Corporate Role for Second, Third, and Fourth Wave Organizations

	Second Wave	*Third Wave*	*Fourth Wave*
Goals	Maximize profits	Create value	Serve as global steward
Motivation	Make money	Make money and help solve societal problems	Leave valuable legacy for the future
Values	Profit, growth, control	Creating value, trust, learning	Responsibility for the whole service, personal fulfillment
Stakeholders	Owners of business, stockholders	Stockholders, employees, families, suppliers, customers, communities, government	Stockholders, employees, families, suppliers, customers, communities, government, ecosystems, Gaia
Outlook	Self-preservation; business as a way to make a living	Cooperation; business as a way for people to grow and serve	Unity; business as a means to actively promote economic and social justice
Domain	National and local; 5–10 years in future	International; share responsibility for the welfare of local, national, and global communities; decades in future	Global; share leadership in local, national, and global affairs; generations or centuries in future

Source: Reprinted with permission of the publisher. From *The Fourth Wave,* Copyright 1993 by Maynard & Mehrtens, Berrett-Koehler Publishers, San Francisco, CA. All rights reserved.

As an organizing framework, this chapter introduced the Congruence Model as a way to consider many of the situational factors leaders should consider. In terms of work factors, leaders need to be aware of how task interdependence, task structure, and job characteristics can affect both their own and their followers' behaviors, and how they might change these factors in order to improve followers' satisfaction and performance. Research also has shown that organizational factors, such as lateral interdependence, structure, design, and culture play major roles in determining why certain communication problems and conflicts might exist, how work is accomplished, and why some people may be more satisfied in the organization than others. The informal organization or the organizational culture can have a profound impact on the way both leaders and followers behave—and may be the least recognizable since it is the water in the bowl where all the fish are swimming. Factors in the environment, such as legal, political, or economic forces, can also affect leaders' and followers' behaviors. Sometimes these may effectively wipe out any changes a leader may make to improve productivity or satisfaction among work-group members. And finally, we offered a potential crystal ball of what may lie ahead in the situational factors for us all in the 21st century.

Key Terms

role theory
multiple-influence model
situational levels
task structure
skill variety
task identity
task significance
autonomy
feedback
task interdependence
level of authority
organizational structure
lateral interdependence
organizational culture
organizational climate
myths and stories
symbols and artifacts
rituals
technological complexity

horizontal complexity
vertical complexity
spatial complexity
formalization
substitutes for leadership
centralization
organizational design
cognitive resource theory
situational engineering
functional design
product design
matrix design
environmental uncertainty
crises
demands
constraints
choices
language

Discussion Questions

1. The term *bureaucratic* has a pejorative connotation to most people. Can you think of any positive aspects of a bureaucracy?

2. Think of a crisis situation you are familiar with involving a group, team, organization, or country, and analyze it in terms of the leader-follower-situation framework. For example, were the followers looking for a certain kind of behavior from the leader? Did the situation demand it? Did the situation, in fact, contribute to a particular leader's emergence?

3. Can you identify reward systems that impact the level of effort students are likely to put forth in team or group projects? Should these reward systems be different than for individual effort projects?

4. As you look at Tables 15–2 and 15–3, do you agree with the depiction of the past? Where are we today? What does the future look like to you? Do you know of any organizations that are creating a Third or Fourth Wave organization today?

16 A FINAL WORD: LEADERSHIP IN THE FUTURE

Introduction

The purpose of a final chapter is typically twofold: to integrate some of the main ideas presented throughout the book, and to project current trends and issues into the future. We shall try to accomplish both objectives via a hypothetical scenario.

The Challenge

Suppose that some time about the middle of the next century, scientists around the world become increasingly certain of an impending catastrophe predicted to occur just one year in the future. Suppose that anticipated cataclysmic event is such that extraordinary preparation will be required to assure that civilized life can continue and thrive. For our purposes it does not matter just what that event might be. It might be a comet heading toward earth; perhaps it's a series of devastating earthquakes across all the continents, confidently predicted in advance via new seismic technology; or a major alteration to global climate that will change life on the planet as we know it. Whatever it might be, global leaders are united in their estimation of its danger and of the need for a worldwide response.

This is, of course, the stuff of disaster flicks on a colossal scale. It's like *Independence Day* without the aliens, *Deep Impact*, or *Armageddon*. Far-fetched? Perhaps, but as a thought exercise let's assume the scenario is valid, and speculate about its implications for leadership.

In our scenario, global leaders have concluded that the best hope for humankind is to build a giant space station, capable of supporting several thousand men, women, and children for the 50 years before it will be safe to return to earth. The technology exists to build such a station, but the expense will be so great that only one can be built. In reality, though, the challenge ultimately will be less technological than human. The only binding decision at this point is that the space station should include representatives from every nation on earth. Beyond that, however, questions abound. Who from around the world should be selected to populate the ship, and what criteria should be used in their selection? How should life and work on the station be organized—if it is to be organized at all? Who should be the mission's leader? How should he or she be selected? These are just a few of the questions surrounding the mission known as Space Station Earth.

Throughout this chapter we will examine such questions from the perspective of our interactional framework, and in so doing anticipate some of the challenges that leaders and followers *will* experience in the future, whether in such a dramatic fashion as our scenario or not. The reality, of course, is that we all *do* live on an increasingly small and fragile space station. In that regard it may be worth noting how Carl Sagan reflected on the 20th anniversary of man's landing on the moon by observing that "getting to the moon was perhaps not as important as seeing ourselves from it." In a way, that's what we're asking you to do with this exercise: to see yourself—to see ourselves—from a different perspective. In trying to imagine the leadership challenges facing those on Space Station Earth, more questions than answers come to mind (also see Highlight 16–1).

The Leader on Space Station Earth

The Nature of Leadership and Management

In this book's first chapters, we looked at general conceptions (and misconceptions) about leadership. For example, we contrasted common notions of leadership and management. As you think about *Space Station Earth*, do you believe there is a need for an overall mission leader? Would the challenges facing the mission need a leader more than a manager, or vice versa? Or might the mission need two different individuals in overall charge, each playing one of those roles? Or, carrying this a step further, would you prefer "leadership by committee"?

Highlight 16–1

Leadership Quotes, Chapter 16

Risk, gentlemen! That's why we're aboard her.

Captain James T. Kirk, U.S.S. Enterprise

The Chinese use two brush strokes to write the word crisis. One brush strokes stands for danger, the other for opportunity. In a crisis, be aware of the danger—but recognize the opportunity.

Richard M. Nixon

Problems are the price of progress. Don't bring me anything but trouble. Good news weakens me.

Charles Kettering

He who has a why to live for can bear with almost any how.

Nietzsche

For all your days, prepare, and meet them ever alike. When you are the anvil, bear; when you are the hammer, strike.

Edwin Markham

A true test of leadership is not so much based on how much we know, but on how we behave when we don't know what to do.

George Shapiro

Can you even answer these questions without knowing more about who the followers will be and the situation they will face? See Highlight 16–2 for a different perspective on leadership roles for the mission.

Assessing Leadership

If we can assume there would be one overall mission leader, how do you think he or she should be chosen? One possibility might be for an international panel to do the selection. Even then, however, what kind of criteria should the panel use? Do you think there should be any priority given to leader selection based on gender, nationality, or ethnicity? Our guess is that these ideas might strike you as quite biased and inappropriate, that you would think that "the best leader possible" should be selected. However, if the crew itself were to be composed proportionally from among the peoples of the earth, perhaps the leader should be Chinese, or at least Asian. Also, if every country is to be represented, some individuals could be included on the crew whose cultural norms may not

---

Highlight 16–2

What Role Would You Choose?

An interesting way to explore conceptions of leadership is to think of a modern cruise ship, and all the roles associated with making it function. If you had to select just one of them, which best describes your own concept of leadership? Here are a few possibilities.

One obvious choice might be the ship's *captain*, who has overall (but indirect) authority and responsibility for the ship's varied functions.

Another possibility might be the ship's *navigator*. Maybe your conception of leadership emphasizes the importance of making sure your group (or the ship) always knows where it is on the path to success.

Perhaps you see yourself as the *social director*, whose job it is to maximize everyone's enjoyment and sense of well-being.

Or maybe you selected the role of ship's *engineer*, who is invisible to most people on board but plays the critical function of keeping the engines fueled and running efficiently.

There are numerous other roles you might have thought of, too, but we are willing to predict one you *did not* think of: the person who *designed* the ship in the first place. One could argue that person has greater influence over what happens on a ship than anyone else including the captain; the designer establishes the context and structure within which all interactions on a ship occur. In that sense, we are asking you in this chapter to be the designer of Space Station Earth. In this case, however, your task is to design its human systems, not its physical or technical systems.

---

be so gender-fair as you might personally believe proper. Of course, people with such views could be automatically excluded from the mission for having politically incorrect views as judged by certain contemporary western standards. However, that doesn't sound so clearly correct either. By the way, would the person's age play any role in your preferences?

Probably some consideration would be given to a candidate's demonstrated capability for such an important role as evidenced in their public record. For example, the selection panel could review various candidates' past accomplishments and leadership roles. While it may be easy to agree with that general principle, however, it also may be difficult in practice to implement it. For example, what kinds of experiences or credentials should be counted most? What kinds of accomplishments would seem most relevant to you? Political leadership? Scientific leadership? Military leadership? International leadership? Religious leadership? Even recognizing that the prior record likely would be just one factor among several on which final selection would be based, how would you weigh the relative strength of having been an ambassador to the United Nations versus a physician who led a successful "revolution" to improve the health care system of an entire third-world country? Or the CEO of a multinational high-tech company versus a world-respected religious leader who is credited with having helped bring peace to the Middle East? Do some accomplishments count more in your book than others? Are some more relevant for leadership of this mission? Do some sets of leadership skills carry particular weight in your mind?

In selecting the mission leader, would you want to include scientific and systematic methods of assessment in addition to review of public records of accomplishments or the panel's subjective impressions of the candidates' personalities, leadership styles, and so on? Should structured or unstructured interviews be used? What would you ask? Would you use paper-and-pencil measures to assess the candidates' strengths and weaknesses as leaders? To assess what qualities? Would you go so far as to develop an assessment center? What sorts of activities would you want to observe the candidates perform?

Power and Influence

In Chapter 6, we discussed a number of different sources of leader power, including expert power, referent power, legitimate power, reward power, and coercive power. Which of these do you believe will be *most* important for the leader of Space Station Earth to possess? Which one do you believe will be *least* important. With regard to legitimate power, do you envision a succession of people in authority roles? Speaking of power, what kind of "power politics" and influence efforts can you envision taking place on such a long mission?

Finally, what are some of the ways leaders on board Space Station Earth might try to influence others—and be influenced by others? Influence tactics include such approaches as rational persuasion, inspirational appeals, consultation, ingratiation, personal appeals, exchange, coalition tactics, pressure tactics, and legitimizing tactics. Would some of these be less appropriate—or even worse, *inappropriate*—on this mission than they might be in earthbound situations? Which influence tactics do you believe would be most effective on Space Station Earth?

Ethics, Values, and Attitudes

Some of the greatest leadership challenges on Space Station Earth could involve the areas of ethics, values, and attitudes. It is not unlikely that the crew would include representatives from cultures and religions that are not only diverse but even hostile to each other. (Or should we exclude any groups that have a history of antagonistic relations?) Could any leader in such a situation be truly objective and unbiased in dealing with conflicts which might arise?

Of course, one way around that problem would be to exclude any devoutly religious person from the crew; only nonreligious or "vaguely spiritual" crew members might be accepted. On a 50-year mission, however, there is always the possibility that some crew member might peruse on-board computer libraries of religious texts, and experience a conversion. What if that person then tried to proselytize a particular religious faith on board, even recognizing it might offend some? Should such proselytizing be deemed a crime, detrimental to mission safety and public order?

Other Leader Qualities

Another basis for selecting the mission leader could be personality. Maybe candidates for leadership should be assessed on the Big Five personality dimensions and their associated traits. We would want the leader to be intelligent, too, but what *kind* of intelligence do you believe would be most important for the mission leader to have? Merely a high IQ score?

Finally, just to assure that our leader has maximal impact on the whole crew, would you try to select a leader who is fairly charismatic? On the other hand, how would you feel about having others on board who might be even *more* charismatic, and potential rivals to the mission leader for the hearts and minds of the crew? Since crises tend to provide ripe soil for the emergence of creative leaders, the mission of Space Station Earth, based inherently on a crisis, may provide the conditions for charismatic leaders to emerge. Do you think that would be an advantage or a disadvantage?

The Followers on Space Station Earth

Followers, Followership, and Team Effectiveness

Of course, there will be more than one leader on Space Station Earth. While the specific organizational structure and authority system is unknown, surely there would be numerous individuals who serve formally as both leaders and followers (i.e., to different groups), and many more followers will serve as informal leaders. Furthermore, with regard to all of the "middle management" leader-and-follower roles on board our craft, what basis do you believe should be used for assigning them? Who should be placed in the many kinds of authority positions likely to exist? Is there any structure existing today that you think might provide a model for Space Station Earth to copy?

Given the diversity of cultures and nationalities on Space Station Earth, it might seem that some form of cross-national corporation could be copied. Many global companies have proved successful in integrating individuals from many nationalities and cultures into their ranks, and operating effectively amid peoples of different values and perspectives. On the other hand, a business model of any kind seems inappropriate to be a model for this kind of enterprise. As an alternative, maybe international religious organizations would serve as a better model. The Catholic Church, for example, offers a system of values, norms, and authority relationships that transcend international boundaries. But this would seem to fall short of our needs too. While Space Station Earth probably would need to accommodate the spiritual needs of those on the mission, it seems unlikely there would be an official religion for the mission. Perhaps on Space

Station Earth —as today—spiritual authority systems and secular authority systems will need to coexist.

The question of spiritual commitments of mission members raises an even broader issue of loyalty. To whom would members owe allegiance? The mission overall? Their religious faiths? Their ethnic, national, or cultural groups? Should such loyalties be a positive or negative factor in selecting individuals for the mission?

Finally, while stewardship seems an inherent aspect of Space Station Earth's mission—for example, the very high calling of the stewardship of human knowledge and heritage—the emphasis in recent writing about stewardship and courageous followership seem contrary to a social organization primarily favoring order and control. If you were on Space Station Earth, facing the kinds of challenges you anticipate, who would you want to be fellow voyagers with you? Courageous followers, as described by Chaleff? Which of Kelley's follower types would you prefer on the mission? Pragmatists? Exemplary followers? Would the Space Station have no room for conformist followers, or might they be just what it needs? Would you select followers (i.e., general mission members) on the basis of their performance on intelligence tests? Their values?

These are seemingly impossible questions to answer, and when facing such complexities and ambiguities it is often helpful to impose a structure as a basis for sorting through the varied issues. One thing that might be useful here is to use the Team Effectiveness Leadership Model (TELM) for exploring such questions. To the extent teams would be an important part of the mission's work, TELM suggests how to integrate various organizational systems, team design issues, and individual variables to optimize effective team process and effectiveness. See Highlight 16–3 for a different perspective on diversity in space.

Motivation

It might seem superfluous to ask what would motivate the followers on Space Station Earth. The obvious answer might seem to be survival. A moment's thought, however, suggests that that is at best an incomplete, if not inadequate, answer. Surely numerous other complex motives would be operating, and it would behoove the leaders of Space Station Earth to understand and even influence them.

For one thing, it will be critical to understand the basic human needs raised by the mission. Whether you take the perspective of Maslow's hierarchy of needs or Alderfer's ERG theory, it will be critical for the followers' basic physiological and security (or existence) needs to be met. Beyond that, however, will be the emotional significance of being uprooted from one's familiar surroundings and social roots. Psychologically, it might be similar to the situation of a war refugee fleeing to a new land. Since a person may have at most a family member or two accompanying them, there would almost inevitably be few existing communities or social groupings, and perhaps none, from which to

Highlight 16–3

Star Trek and Diversity

The television series "Star Trek" and "Star Trek: The Next Generation" raised some of the same leadership issues which will be faced by those on Space Station Earth. Here is a "Star Trek" perspective on what leaders in the distant future might expect with regard to diversity among their followers.

Even in the original "Star Trek," the crew was international in composition. On the bridge with Captain Kirk, for example, were Lieutenant Uhura, Lieutenant Sulu, and Ensign Chekhov. In fact, the crew was more than just international, it was interplanetary; the science officer Spock was half-human and half-Vulcan. This diversity, however, was nothing compared to that found even later in the 24th century. The crew in "Next Generation" was truly interplanetary, including the Klingon Whorf, and beyond that, not even all were "living." A uniquely valuable member of the crew was Data, the humanoid. Another hopefully prophetic characteristic of the crew was evidenced in the character Geordi LaForge. He was blind, but wore a prosthetic visor for seeing: a reflection of creator Gene Roddenberry's inspiration to include a physically challenged character who could be a full contributor in the 24th century.

And to think it's sometimes difficult today even for Texans and New Yorkers to work together!

have belongingness or relatedness needs met. Finally, there would need to be a variety of mechanisms aboard ship for individuals to have their needs for self-actualization or growth met. At the same time, while needs like these would be fairly universal, there would also be a wide variety of individual differences in motivation (at least there would be unless procedures for selecting voyagers curtailed the range).

A quite different slant on motivation relates to situational approaches of influencing follower motivation. In other words, the leaders of Space Station Earth could design life aboard the space station so as to encourage specific types of behavior. You could get a glimpse into one approach to engineering a community's life in such a way by reading B. F. Skinner's novel *Walden Two*. Skinner was the foremost proponent of the behavioral school of psychology, which held that all behavior was controlled by its consequences. The operant approach, described in Chapter 14, is founded on Skinner's ideas. *Walden Two* describes Skinner's utopian vision of how a community might function if it were based on an enlightened use of rewarding desirable behaviors. Skinner probably would have argued that Space Station Earth also should employ operant procedures to control behavior. On the other hand, you might be able to think of ways a large scale reward system could be abused and become counterproductive to the mission.

The Situation on Space Station Earth

To some extent, we've already been addressing aspects of the situation in the preceding sections. Here, let us consider the situation somewhat more holistically by applying the Congruence Model to Space Station Earth. You may recall that the model has four components: the work itself, the informal organization, the formal organization, and the people themselves. You also may recall that these components remain in a sort of equilibrium with each other. Even small changes in one component can have significant impacts on the other components too. Thus, leaders are well advised to make change efforts in the four components *coherently* rather than arbitrarily in one or another.

This is clear enough with a few possible examples from our hypothetical mission. Whatever formal organization is established will need to be based on an understanding of the kinds of people selected to live and serve on Space Station Earth. And if problems arise six months into the system, it would be risky to change (say) the formal authority system without also taking into consideration the people themselves and informal organizations that have evolved (even over that short time).

Or, what if six months into the mission it becomes evident that certain critical work is not being performed adequately. What would the solution be? Certainly some tasks might need to be redesigned, but that might not be enough. Changes in the other components, too, might be necessary to assure these new critical tasks are accomplished. It would almost certainly not be sufficient to merely change the "job descriptions," and inform the people performing those duties what is expected of them now. What problems could you envision if that happened?

Leadership in the Nearer Future

Undoubtedly you noted—perhaps even with some annoyance or frustration—how we raised more questions than answers about leadership on Space Station Earth. Such an emphasis on questions, however, is appropriate in several ways. For one thing, it would seem foolhardy to be overconfident about such an ill-defined and hypothetical scenario. The purpose of this exercise, after all, was to stimulate thinking, not to suggest there is a right answer to these questions. Furthermore, we unabashedly hope such questioning parallels what is going on in your own minds as you conclude this study of leadership. We can think of few better measures of success at this long endeavor than to find yourself now asking questions about leadership that you hadn't been asking before. We are also confident that good questions come from knowledge and a discernment of complexity that you hadn't possessed before. We are confident, in other words, that asking questions reflects what you have *learned*, not just what you don't know.

In one important sense, though, it would be unfortunate to end this book (at least Parts I through IV) emphasizing the unknown. Let us end, instead, by reminding ourselves of a few things we *do* know about some changing contexts of leadership. There are several related, irreversible trends at work which, if unappreciated, will leave leaders ill-prepared to meet their future challenges. We already have touched on them many times throughout the book. The long-term implications of these trends were suggested *figuratively* in our Space Station Earth scenario, but their effects are already being felt today *in actuality*. In that sense, at least, we are already on Space Station Earth.

The first of these is *diversity*. In some circles, this has unfortunately become a politicized catchword. In its more general sense, however, there can be little question that diversity will increasingly be a part of all our lives. It is part and parcel of the increasing pace of change in our lives. We are coming into increasing contact with individuals who think and act differently than we do, and that will inevitably pose leadership challenges.

Globalization is another irreversible trend impacting nearly every aspect of the world we live in, and hence leadership. For example, the globalization of many organizations has created a need to find alternative ways of organizing work and communicating with each other about it. Increasing numbers of leaders now face the challenge of managing individuals who actually live and work in different countries, even on different continents! Geographically dispersed work teams have become a current hot topic of research, and it wasn't very long ago that it would have been inconceivable to imagine a team existing which couldn't sit down together in the same room or meet on the same playing field.

Finally, our entry into the *information age* is a trend which will dominate the changing nature of leadership in the years and decades ahead. As you've likely noticed, the three trends we've identified are hardly independent. In such manifestations as Internet access to storehouses of information and instant E-mail with people around the world, new technical capabilities emerging in the information age obviously impact both the diversity and globalization trends noted above.

With the context of leadership changing in so many ways, it is fair to say that many organizations today are doing more than merely trying to develop good leaders; they are trying to create a whole new culture of leadership. Some of these changes have to do with the nature and quality of the relationship between leaders and followers. A progressive orientation to leadership would place relatively greater emphasis on Theory Y assumptions about human nature. This might be reflected, in part, by an approach of investing in subordinates through greater use of participative decision making and greater emphasis on subordinate development through education and training programs. Correspondingly, the leader's role becomes one of coach more than boss, and emphasis is placed on empowering subordinates rather than controlling them.

Consistent with this emphasis on empowerment, many organizations are finding it helpful to reduce centralized control over people's actions. Formal structure is being de-emphasized in many organizations, and cross-functional ad hoc work groups are a major mechanism for seeking ever better methods of meeting long-term organizational objectives. Communication is relatively open, both laterally and vertically. Workers are encouraged to use their expertise and

TABLE 16–1 Contrasting Traditional and Progressive Orientations to Leadership in Organizations

Traditional	*Progressive*
Theory X	Theory Y
Bossing	Coaching
Extrinsic motivation	Intrinsic motivation
Authoritarian	Participating
Control	Empowerment
Reactive followers	Active followers
Restricted communication	Open communication
Short-term	Long-term
Centralized	Decentralized
Bureaucracy	More ad hoc groups
Structure	Process
Reward individuals	Reward teams
Competition	Cooperation

creativity in developing better ways to accomplish their work. All this enhances organizational responsiveness to a dynamic social, economic, and technological environment, but it also contributes to another important outcome: It makes work more intrinsically motivating by increasing worker autonomy.

Another factor that is making newer organizational environments motivating to work in is in the nature of co-worker relations. Cooperation among workers is emphasized, rather than competition. One important way this is accomplished is by rewarding teams rather than individuals. Rewards pitting one member against another can be particularly divisive and organizationally dysfunctional. A corporate culture of individualism—a sort of "survival of the fittest" in organizations—is giving way to a corporate culture emphasizing the group or team.

Some of the differences between the leadership culture in traditional organizations and the kind we've been describing are listed in Table 16–1. It is important to appreciate that the various characteristics noted in the table for *either* type of organization should be thought of as an interdependent whole rather than unrelated parts. It should not go unnoticed how emphasis on teams rather than individuals is particularly compatible with cooperative, instead of competitive, practices; how a leader who makes Theory X assumptions may not function well in a participative structure, and a person who makes Theory Y assumptions may not function best in an authoritarian, hierarchical environment; how more open communication is compatible with decentralized authority; and how empowerment increases intrinsic motivation.

None of this is to say that all organizations are moving toward the kind of culture characterized as progressive in Table 16–1, or even that they should be. If leadership needs to be contingent on particular mixtures of leader, follower, and situational characteristics, then there always may be times when the more traditional approach is warranted. Given political, cultural, and technological trends, however, there seems to be a general movement toward what we labeled (primarily for contrast) the progressive orientation. Further, that is *appropriate* for our information age as workers are increasingly diverse, better educated, and face an ever more uncertain and unpredictable future.

Discussion Questions

1. Do you believe it is useful to contrast traditional and progressive approaches to leadership? Do you believe one is better than the other?

2. How have your own views of effective leadership changed after reading the text?

3. What aspect of your own leadership do you most wish to develop?

4. What aspect of your own followership do you most wish to develop?

5. What do you believe are the essential qualities of leadership for Space Station Earth?

V LEADERSHIP SKILLS

One reason any person can improve his or her leadership effectiveness is that part of leadership involves skills, and skills can be practiced and developed. A further advantage of looking at leadership skills is that most people are less defensive about deficits in skills (which can be improved) than about suggested deficits in (say) personality. Our rationale for this final portion of the book is that (1) certain skills do contribute to leadership effectiveness, and (2) they can be learned.

Presenting the skills in this final section does not, however, indicate we believe they should not be covered until the preceding material in the book has been completed. Quite the contrary. We believe it will be most useful to intersperse work on these skills with the other chapters. We also trust that professors and students in a particular course will know better for themselves what order of coverage of the various skills will work best in their unique circumstances. We have taken the liberty, however, of categorizing the skills into two broad groups of basic and more advanced leadership skills. While even this categorization is inherently somewhat arbitrary, it may provide a useful starting point for the reader.

LIST OF SKILLS IN PART V

Basic Leadership Skills

Advanced Leadership Skills

BASIC LEADERSHIP SKILLS

Learning from Experience

Creating Opportunities to Get Feedback
Taking a 10 Percent Stretch
Learning from Others
Keeping a Journal
Having a Developmental Plan

Leadership practitioners can enhance the learning value of their experiences by
(*a*) creating opportunities to get feedback, (*b*) taking a 10 percent stretch,
(*c*) learning from others, (*d*) keeping a journal of daily leadership events, and
(*e*) having a developmental plan.

Creating Opportunities to Get Feedback

It may be difficult for leaders to get relevant feedback, particularly if they occupy
powerful positions in an organization. Yet leaders often need feedback more than
subordinates do. Leaders may not learn much from their leadership experiences if
they get no feedback about how they are doing. Therefore, they may need to create opportunities to get feedback, especially with regard to feedback from those
working for them.

First of all, leaders should not assume they have invited feedback merely by
saying that they have an open-door policy. A mistake some bosses make is pre-
suming that others perceive them as open to discussing things just because they
say they are open to discussing things. How truly open a door is, clearly, is in
the eye of the beholder. In that sense, the key to constructive dialogue (i.e., feedback) is not just expressing a policy but also being perceived as approachable
and sincere in the offer.

Some of the most helpful information for developing your own leadership can come from asking for feedback from others about their perceptions of your behavior and its impact on your group's overall effectiveness. Some of the specific techniques leaders can use to systematically solicit feedback are described in more detail in Chapters 4 and 9. Leaders who take psychological tests and use periodic surveys or questionnaires will have greater access to feedback than leaders who fail to systematically solicit feedback from their followers. Unless leaders ask for feedback, they may not get it.

Taking a 10 Percent Stretch

Learning always involves stretching. Learning involves taking risks and reaching beyond one's comfort zone. This is true of a toddler's first unsteady steps, a student's first serious confrontation with divergent worlds of thought, and leadership development. The phrase *10 percent stretch* conveys the idea of voluntary but determined efforts to improve leadership skills. It is analogous to physical exercise, though in this context stretching implies extending one's behavior, not muscles, just a bit beyond the comfort zone. Examples could include making a point to converse informally with everyone in the office at least once each day, seeking an opportunity to be chairman of a committee, or being quieter than usual at meetings (or more assertive, as the case may be). There is much to be gained from a commitment to such ongoing "exercise" for personal and leadership development.

Several positive outcomes are associated with leaders who regularly practice the 10 percent stretch. First, their apprehension about doing something new or different gradually decreases. Second, leaders will broaden their repertoire of leadership skills. Third, because of this increased repertoire, their effectiveness will likely increase. And finally, leaders regularly taking a 10 percent stretch will model something very valuable to others. Few things will send a better message to others about the importance of their own development than the example of how sincerely a leader takes his or her own development.

One final aspect of the 10 percent stretch is worth mentioning. One reason the phrase is so appealing is that it sounds like a measurable yet manageable change. Many people will not offer serious objection to trying a 10 percent change in some behavior, whereas they might well be resistant (and unsuccessful) if they construe a developmental goal as requiring fundamental change in their personality or interpersonal style. Despite its nonthreatening connotation, though, an actual 10 percent change in behavior can make an enormous difference in effectiveness. In many kinds of endeavor the difference between average performers and exceptional performers is 10 percent. In baseball, for example, many players hit .275, but only the best hit over .300—a difference of about 10 percent.

Learning from Others

Leaders learn from others, first of all, by recognizing they *can* learn from others and, importantly, from *any* others. That may seem self-evident, but in fact people often limit what and whom they pay attention to, and thus what they may learn from. For example, athletes may pay a lot of attention to how coaches handle leadership situations. However, they may fail to realize they could also learn a lot by watching the director of the school play and the band conductor. Leaders should not limit their learning by narrowly defining the sorts of people they pay attention to.

Similarly, leaders also can learn by asking questions and paying attention to everyday situations. An especially important time to ask questions is when leaders are new to a group or activity and have some responsibility for it. When possible, leaders should talk to the person who previously had the position to benefit from her insights, experience, and assessment of the situation. In addition, observant leaders are able to extract meaningful leadership lessons from everyday situations. Something as plain and ordinary as a high school car wash or the activities at a fast-food restaurant may offer an interesting leadership lesson. Leaders can learn a lot by actively observing how others react to and handle different challenges and situations, even very common ones.

Keeping a Journal

Another way leaders can mine experiences for their richness and preserve their learning is by keeping a journal (Csikszentmihalyi, 1990). Journals are similar to diaries, but they are not just accounts of a day's events. A journal should include entries that address some aspect of leaders or leadership. Journal entries may include comments about insightful or interesting quotes, anecdotes, newspaper articles, or even humorous cartoons about leadership. They may also include reflections on personal events, such as interactions with bosses, coaches, teachers, students, employees, players, teammates, roommates, and so on. Such entries can emphasize a good (or bad) way somebody handled something, a problem in the making, the differences between people in their reactions to situations, or people in the news, a book, or a film. Leaders should also use their journals to "think on paper" about leadership readings from textbooks or formal leadership programs or to describe examples from their own experience of a concept presented in a reading.

There are at least three good reasons for keeping a journal. First, the very process of writing increases the likelihood that leaders will be able to look at an event from a different perspective or feel differently about it. Putting an experience into words can be a step toward taking a more objective look at it. Second, leaders can (and should) reread earlier entries. Earlier entries provide an interesting and valuable autobiography of a leader's evolving thinking about leadership and about particular events in his or her life. Third, journal entries provide a repository of ideas that leaders may later want to use more formally for papers, pep talks, or speeches. As seen in Highlight LFE–1, good journal entries provide leaders with a wealth of examples that they may use in speeches, presentations, and so on.

Having a Developmental Plan

Leadership development almost certainly occurs in ways and on paths that are not completely anticipated or controlled. That is no reason, however, for leaders to avoid actively directing some aspects of their own development. A systematic plan outlining self-improvement goals and strategies will help leaders take advantage of opportunities they otherwise might overlook. Developing a sys-

Sample Journal Entries

I went skiing this weekend and saw the perfect example of a leader adapting her leadership style to her followers and situation. While putting on my skis I saw a ski instructor teaching little kids to ski. She did it using the game "red light, green light." The kids loved it and seemed to be doing very well. Later that same day, as I was going to the lodge for lunch, she was teaching adults, and she did more demonstrating than talking. But when she talked she was always sure to encourage them so they did not feel intimidated when some little kid whizzed by. She would say to the adults that it's easier for children, or that smaller skis are easier. She made the children laugh and learn, and made the adults less self-conscious to help them learn too. . . .

Today may not exactly be a topic on leadership, but I thought it would be interesting to discuss. I attended the football game this afternoon and could not help but notice our cheerleaders. I was just thinking of their name in general, and found them to be a good example (of leadership). Everyone gets rowdy at a football game, but without the direction of the cheerleaders there would be mayhem. They do a good job of getting the crowd organized and the adrenaline pumping (though of course the game is most important in that too!). It's just amazing to see them generate so much interest that all of the crowd gets into the cheering. We even chant their stupid-sounding cheers! You might not know any of them personally, but their enthusiasm invites you to try to be even louder than them. I must give the cheerleaders a round of applause. . . .

I've been thinking about how I used to view/understand leadership, trying to find out how my present attitudes were developed. It's hard to remember past freshman year, even harder to go past high school. Overall, I think my father has been the single most important influence on my leadership development—long before I even realized it. Dad is a strong "Type A" person. He drives himself hard and demands a great deal from everyone around him, especially his family and especially his only son and oldest child. He was always pushing me to study, practice whatever sport I was involved in at the time, get ahead of everybody else in every way possible.

tematic plan also will help leaders prioritize the importance of different goals so that their efforts can be put into areas with the greatest relative payoffs. Leaders who carefully choose which seminars and conferences to attend may help themselves maximize their contribution to their personal developmental goals. Leaders should look for opportunities on the job or in volunteer work for responsibilities that may further their growth. Leaders should recognize, however, that they may experience conflict—both internal and external—between doing more of what they already do well and stretching developmentally.

The following is an example of such a conflict. Suppose Sheila is an accountant who has just joined the board of a local charity. Because handling financial records is something many people do not enjoy, and because Sheila has a demonstrable knack for and interest in it, others on the board may well ask her to become the treasurer. Almost certainly Sheila would do as good a job as anyone else on the board. But suppose Sheila's personal goals included developing her public speaking skills. In such a case, doing what she does best (and what others want her to do) might stand in the way of growth in another area.

Sheila has several alternatives. She could refuse the job of treasurer because she has had her fill of accounting. Alternatively, she could accept the job of treasurer and look for yet another activity in which to develop her public speaking skills. Unfortunately, both of these options may present their own problems. Still another alternative would be to negotiate to expand the role of treasurer to allow greater opportunity to blend the role with her own developmental goals. For example, Sheila might choose to make regular oral reports to the board instead of submitting solely written reports. Additionally, she might take on a larger share of speaking at local service clubs for the purpose of public education about the charity and her own expert view of its needs with regard to fund-raising and financial support. The point here is that leaders simply need to be deliberate in seeking opportunities to put their personal development plans into action. Leaders should exercise control over events to the extent they can; they should not let events exercise a counterproductive control over them.

A leader's first step in exercising control over his personal development is to identify what his goals actually are. The example above presumed Sheila already had identified public speaking as a skill she wanted to improve. But what if a leader is uncertain about what he needs to improve? As described earlier, leaders should systematically collect information from a number of different sources. One place a leader can get information about where to improve is through a review of his or her current job performance, if that is applicable. Ideally, leaders will have had feedback sessions with their own superiors, which should help them identify areas of relative strength and weakness. Leaders should treat this feedback as a helpful perspective on their developmental needs. Leaders also should look at their interactions with peers as a source of ideas about what they might work on. Leaders should especially take notice if the same kind of problem comes up in their interactions with different individuals in separate situations. Leaders need to look at their own role in such instances as objectively as they can; there might be clues about what behavioral changes might facilitate better working relationships with others. Still another way to identify developmental objectives is to look ahead to what new skills are needed to function effectively at a higher level in the organization, or in a different role than the leader now has. Finally, leaders can use formal psychological tests and questionnaires to determine what their relative strengths and weaknesses as a leader may be.

On a concluding note, there is one activity leaders should put in their developmental plans whatever else might be included in them: a program of personal reading to broaden their perspectives on leadership. This reading can include the classics as well as contemporary fiction, biographies and autobiographies of successful leaders, essays on ethics and social responsibility, and assorted self-improvement books on various leadership and management issues. A vital part of leadership development is intellectual stimulation and reflection, and an active reading program is indispensable to that. Leaders might even want to join (or form) a discussion group that regularly meets to exchange ideas about a book everyone has read.

Communication

Know What Your Purpose Is
Choose an Appropriate Context and Medium
Send Clear Signals
Actively Ensure that Others Understand the Message

Bass (1990) defined communication effectiveness as the degree to which someone tells others something and ensures they understand what was said. In an even more general sense, **effective communication** involves the ability to transmit and receive information with a high probability that the intended message is passed from sender to receiver. Few skills are more vital to leadership. Studies show that good leaders communicate feelings and ideas, actively solicit new ideas from others, and effectively articulate arguments, advocate positions, and persuade others (Bennis & Nanus, 1985; Kanter, 1983; Parks, 1985). It seems likely the same can be said of good followers, though far less study has gone into that question. Moreover, the quality of a leader's communication is positively correlated with subordinate satisfaction (Klimoski & Haynes, 1980) as well as with productivity and quality of services rendered (Snyder & Morris, 1984). Effective communication skills are also important because they provide leaders and followers with greater access to information relevant to important organizational decisions (Fiechtner & Krayer, 1986).

A systems view of communication is depicted in Figure C–1. Communication is best understood as a process beginning with an intention to exchange certain information with others. That intention eventually takes form in some particular expression, which may or may not adequately convey what was intended. The next stage is reception. Just as with a weak or garbled radio signal or malfunctioning antenna, what is received is not always what was sent. Reception is followed by interpretation. If a driver asks, "Do I turn here?" and a passenger answers, "Right," did the passenger mean *yes* or *turn right?* Finally, it is not enough merely to receive and interpret information; others' interpretations may or may not be consistent with what was intended at the outset. Therefore, it always helps to have a feedback loop to assess any communication's overall effectiveness.

We also can use the scheme in Figure C–1 to think about the knowledge, behaviors, and criteria used to evaluate communication skills. According to this

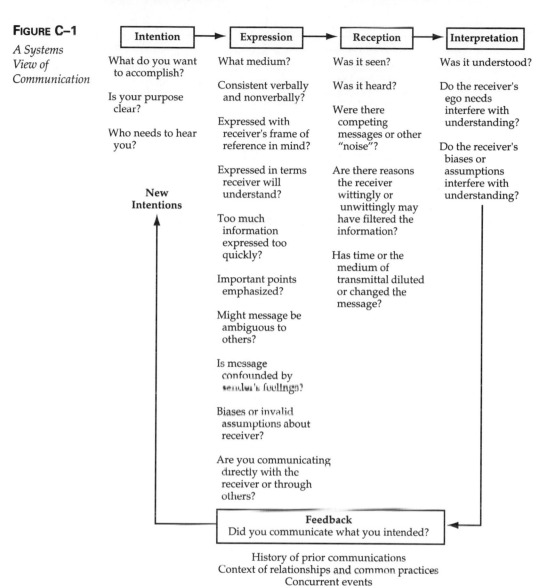

FIGURE C–1

A Systems View of Communication

Intention →	Expression →	Reception →	Interpretation
What do you want to accomplish?	What medium?	Was it seen?	Was it understood?
Is your purpose clear?	Consistent verbally and nonverbally?	Was it heard?	Do the receiver's ego needs interfere with understanding?
Who needs to hear you?	Expressed with receiver's frame of reference in mind?	Were there competing messages or other "noise"?	Do the receiver's biases or assumptions interfere with understanding?
	Expressed in terms receiver will understand?	Are there reasons the receiver wittingly or unwittingly may have filtered the information?	
	Too much information expressed too quickly?	Has time or the medium of transmittal diluted or changed the message?	
	Important points emphasized?		
	Might message be ambiguous to others?		
	Is message confounded by sender's feelings?		
	Biases or invalid assumptions about receiver?		
	Are you communicating directly with the receiver or through others?		

New Intentions

Feedback
Did you communicate what you intended?

History of prior communications
Context of relationships and common practices
Concurrent events

model, the knowledge component of communication skills concerns the intentions of the leader, knowing what medium is most effective, and knowing whether the message was heard and understood. The behavioral component of communication skills concerns the behaviors associated with communicating verbally and nonverbally. Feedback concerning whether or not the message was understood by the receiver comprises the evaluative component of communication skills. An important aspect regarding feedback is that it is an outcome of the previous steps in the communication process. In reality, the effectiveness of

FIGURE C–2

Breakdowns in Communication Sometimes Lead to Finger Pointing

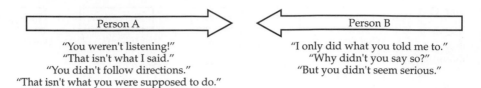

Person A

"You weren't listening!"
"That isn't what I said."
"You didn't follow directions."
"That isn't what you were supposed to do."

Person B

"I only did what you told me to."
"Why didn't you say so?"
"But you didn't seem serious."

the communication process depends on the successful integration of all of the steps in the communication process. Effectiveness in just one step (e.g., speaking ability) is not enough. Successful communication needs to be judged in terms of the effective operation of the whole system.

The model also suggests a number of reasons why communication breakdowns might occur. For example, communication breakdowns can occur because the purpose of the message was unclear, the leader's or follower's verbal and nonverbal behaviors were inconsistent, the message was not heard by the receiver, or because someone may have misinterpreted another's message. Most people see themselves as effective communicators, and senders and receivers of messages often seem disposed to believe communication breakdowns are the other person's fault. Communication breakdowns often lead to blaming someone else for the problem, or "finger pointing" (see Figure C–2). One way to avoid the finger pointing associated with communication breakdowns is to think of communication as a process, not as a set of discrete individual acts (i.e., giving instructions to someone). By using the communication model, leadership practitioners can minimize the conflict typically associated with communication breakdowns.

The model in Figure C–1 can provide leadership practitioners with many ideas about how to improve communication skills. They can do so by (*a*) determining the purpose of their communication before speaking, (*b*) choosing an appropriate context and medium for the message, (*c*) sending clear signals, and (*d*) actively ensuring that others understand the message. The following is a more-detailed discussion of some of the different ways in which leaders can improve their communication skills.

Know What Your Purpose Is

One will communicate more effectively with others if one is clear about what one intends to communicate. By knowing his purpose, a leader or follower can better decide whether to communicate publicly or privately, orally or in writing, and so on. These decisions may seem trivial, but often the specific content of a message will be enhanced or diminished by how and where it is communicated.

Choose an Appropriate Context and Medium

There is a rule of thumb that says leaders should praise followers in public and punish them in private. It points out the importance of selecting physical and social settings that will enhance the effectiveness of any communication. If the leader has an office, for example, then how much of her communication with subordinates should occur in her office and how much in the followers' workplace?

Sometimes, of course, an office is the best place to talk. Even that decision, however, is not all a leader needs to consider. The arrangement of office furniture can enhance or interfere with effective communication. Informal, personal communications are enhanced when two people sit at a 90-degree angle and are relatively close to each other; more formal communication is enhanced when the follower remains standing when the leader is sitting or if the leader communicates across his desk to followers.

Additionally, a leader's communications often take place in a whole organizational context involving broader existing practices, policies, and procedures. Leaders need to take care that their words and deeds do not inadvertently undercut or contradict such broader organizational communications, including their own bosses. Organizational factors also help determine whether any particular communication is most appropriately expressed orally or in writing. Oral communication is the most immediate, the most personal, the most dynamic, and often the most impactive; it is ideal when communication needs to be two-way or when the personalized aspect is especially important. At the other extreme, a more permanent modality is probably most appropriate when the leader needs a record of the communication or when something needs to be expressed in a particular way to different people, at different times, in different settings.

Send Clear Signals

Leaders and followers can enhance the clarity of their communications in several ways. First, it is helpful to be mindful of others' level of expertise, values, experiences, and expectations and how these characteristics affect their **frames of reference**. For example, the leader may brief a new organizational policy to followers, and they may come up with different interpretations of this policy based on different values and expectations. By being sensitive to followers' frames of reference and modifying messages accordingly, leaders can minimize communication breakdowns. Another way to clarify messages is to create a common frame of reference for followers before communicating a message. For example, consider the following passage:

> With hocked gems financing him, our hero bravely defied all scornful laughter that tried to prevent his scheme. "Your eyes deceive," he had said. "An egg, not a table, correctly typifies this unexplored planet." Now, three sisters sought sturdy proof. Forging along, sometimes through calm vastness, yet more often over turbulent peaks and valleys, days became weeks as many doubters spread fearful rumors about the edge. At last, welcome winged creatures appeared signifying momentous success. (Sanford & Garrod, 1981)

Many are slow to recognize that the passage is about Christopher Columbus. Once the correct frame of reference is known, however, the previously confusing elements become sensible. Followers more readily understand new or ambiguous material when leaders paint a common frame of reference prior to introducing new material.

Another way to send clear signals is to use familiar terms, jargon, and concepts. This can serve to clarify and abbreviate messages when receivers are familiar with the terms. However, messages containing jargon can also be confusing to receivers unfamiliar with those terms. For example, a freshman cadet at the United States Air Force Academy might say to another, "I hope we get an ONP this weekend, because after three GRs, a PCE, and a SAMI, I'll need it." Because the second cadet understands this organizational jargon, he or she would have no difficulty understanding what was said. However, a person unfamiliar with the Air Force Academy would not have the slightest idea what this conversation meant. Leaders should make sure followers understand any jargon they use—especially if the followers are relatively inexperienced. (In case you were wondering, the cadet said, "I hope we get a pass to go downtown this weekend, because after three academic tests, a military test, and a room inspection, I'll need it.")

Two other ways to improve the clarity of messages are to use unambiguous, concrete terms and to send congruent verbal and nonverbal signals. For example, a leader who tells a follower, "Your monthly sales were down 22 percent last month" will more effectively communicate her concerns and cause less follower defensiveness than a leader who states, "Your performance has been poor." Thus, the more specific the message, the less likely receivers will be confused over what it means. In addition, leaders will be more effective communicators if their nonverbal signals match the content of the message. Followers, like everyone, can get confused, and tend to believe nonverbal signals when leaders send mixed verbal and nonverbal messages (Remland, 1981). Similarly, followers may send mixed messages to leaders; communication goes both ways.

One particularly destructive form of incongruent verbal and nonverbal signals is sarcasm. It is not the anger of the message per se but rather the implicit message conveyed by dishonest words that drives a wedge in the trust between leaders and followers. It is *not* a wise idea for leaders to always share their transitory feelings with subordinates, but if the leader *is* going to share his or her feelings, it is important to do so in a congruent manner. Similarly, it can be just as unwise for followers to share transitory feelings with leaders; but if it's done, it's important for verbal and nonverbal behaviors to be congruent.

Actively Ensure that Others Understand the Message

Leaders and followers can ensure that others understand their messages by practicing two-way communication and by paying attention to the others' emotional responses. Effective leaders and followers tend to actively engage in two-way communication (though this usually is more under the control of the leader than the follower). They can do so in many ways: by seeking feedback, by mingling in each other's work areas, and by being sincere about having an open-door policy (in the case of leaders) (Luthans & Larsen, 1986).

Although such steps appear to be straightforward, leaders typically believe they utilize two-way communication more frequently than their followers perceive them to be using it (Sadler & Hofstede, 1972). Leaders can get clues about the clarity of their messages by paying attention to the nonverbal signals sent by their followers. When followers' verbal and nonverbal messages seem to be incongruent, it may be because the message sent to them was unclear. For example, followers may look confused when they verbally acknowledge that they understand a particular task. In this case, leaders may find it useful to address the mixed signals directly in order to clear up such confusion.

Listening

Demonstrate Nonverbally that You Are Listening
Actively Interpret the Sender's Message
Attend to the Sender's Nonverbal Behavior
Avoid Becoming Defensive

Our systems view of communication emphasized that effectiveness depends upon both *transmitting and receiving* information. It may seem inconsistent, therefore, to distinguish the topic of listening from the more general topic of communication. Isn't listening *part* of communication, you may ask? Of course, and we do not intend to imply it's not. Our separate treatment of listening is simply for emphasis. It seems to us most discussions of communication emphasize the transmission side and neglect the receiving side. Good leaders and followers recognize the value of two-way communication. Listening to others is just as important as expressing oneself clearly to them. People in leadership roles are only as good as the information they have, and much of their information comes from watching and listening to what goes on around them.

At first, it may seem strange to describe listening as a skill. Listening may seem like an automatic response to things being said, not something one practices to improve, like free throws. However, the best listeners are **active listeners**, not passive listeners (Davis, Hellervik, & Sheard, 1989). In passive listening, someone may be speaking but the receiver is not focused on understanding the speaker. Instead, the receiver may be thinking about the next thing he will say or how bored he is in listening to the speaker. In either case, the receiver is not paying attention to what the sender is saying. To truly get the fullest meaning out of what someone else says, one needs to practice active listening. Individuals who are listening actively exhibit a certain pattern of nonverbal behaviors, do not disrupt the sender's message, try to put the sender's message into their own words, and scan the sender for various nonverbal signals. Knowing what nonverbal signals to send and correctly interpreting the sender's nonverbal signals are the knowledge component of listening skills. One's nonverbal signals are the behavioral component, and how well one can paraphrase a sender's message makes up the evaluative component of listening skills.

In addition to helping one understand others better, active listening is a way to visibly demonstrate that one respects others. Often, people, particularly those with high self-monitoring scores, can sense when others are not truly paying attention to what they are saying. Followers will quickly decide it is not worth their time to give their leader information if they perceive they are not being listened to. Leaders may do the same. To avoid turning off others, leaders and followers can improve their active listening skills in a number of ways. Some of these tips include learning to (*a*) model nonverbal signals associated with active listening, (*b*) actively interpret the sender's message, (*c*) be aware of the sender's nonverbal behaviors, and (*d*) avoid becoming defensive. The following is a more detailed discussion of these four ways to improve active listening skills.

Demonstrate Nonverbally that You Are Listening

Make sure your nonverbal behaviors show that you have turned your attention entirely to the speaker. Many people mistakenly assume that listening is a one-way process. Although it seems plausible to think of information flowing only from the sender to the receiver, the essence of active listening is to see all communication, even listening, as a two-way process. Listeners show they are paying attention to the speaker with their own body movements. They put aside, both mentally and physically, other work they may have been engaged in. Individuals who are actively listening establish eye contact with the speaker, and they do not doodle, shoot rubber bands, or look away at other things. They show they are genuinely interested in what the speaker has to say.

Actively Interpret the Sender's Message

The essence of active listening is trying to understand what the sender truly means. It is not enough merely to be (even if you could) a perfect human tape recorder. One must look for the meaning behind someone else's words. In the first place, this means one needs to keep one's mind open to the sender's ideas. This, in turn, implies not interrupting the speaker and not planning what to say while the speaker is delivering the message. In addition, good listeners withhold judgment about the sender's ideas until they have heard the entire message. This way, they avoid sending the message that their mind is made up and avoid jumping to conclusions about what the sender is going to say. Another reason to avoid sending a closed-minded message is that it may lead others to *not* bring up things one definitely needs to hear.

Another valuable way to actively interpret what the sender is saying is to **paraphrase** the sender's message. By putting the speaker's thoughts into their own words, leaders can better ensure that they fully understand what their followers are saying, and vice versa. The value of paraphrasing even a simple idea is apparent in the following dialogue:

Communication Leads for Paraphrasing and Assuring Mutual Understanding

From your point of view . . . .
It seems you . . . .
As you see it . . . .
You think . . . .
What I hear you saying is . . . .
Do you mean . . . ?
I'm not sure I understand what you mean; is it . . . ?
I get the impression . . . .
You appear to be feeling . . . .
Correct me if I'm wrong, but . . . .

> *Sarah:* "Jim should never have become a teacher."
> *Fred:* "You mean he doesn't like working with kids? Do you think he's too impatient?"
> *Sarah:* "No, neither of those things. I just think his tastes are so expensive he's frustrated with a teacher's salary."

In this example, Fred indicated what he thought Sarah meant, which prompted her to clarify her meaning. If he had merely said, "I know what you mean," Fred and Sarah mistakenly would have concluded they agreed when their ideas were really far apart. Paraphrasing also actively communicates your interest in what the other person is saying. Highlight L–1 offers various "communication leads" that may help in paraphrasing others' messages to improve your listening skills.

Attend to the Sender's Nonverbal Behavior

People should use all the tools at their disposal to understand what someone else is saying. This includes paraphrasing senders' messages, and being astute at picking up on senders' nonverbal signals. Much of the social meaning in messages is conveyed nonverbally, and when verbal and nonverbal signals conflict, people often tend to trust the nonverbal signals. Thus, no one can be an effective listener without paying attention to nonverbal signals. This requires listening to more than just the speaker's words themselves; it requires listening for feelings expressed via the speaker's loudness, tone of voice, and pace of speech as well as watching the speaker's facial expressions, posture, gestures, and so on. These behaviors convey a wealth of information that is immensely richer in meaning than the purely verbal content of a message, just as it is richer to watch actors in a stage play rather than merely read their script (Robbins, 1989). Although there may not be any simple codebook of nonverbal cues with which one can decipher what a sender "really" feels, listeners should explore what a sender is trying to say whenever they sense mixed signals between the sender's verbal and nonverbal behaviors.

Avoid Becoming Defensive

Defensive behavior is most likely to occur when someone feels threatened (Gibb, 1961). Although it may seem natural to become defensive when criticized, defensiveness lessens a person's ability to constructively make use of the information. Acting defensively may also decrease followers' subsequent willingness to pass additional unpleasant information on to the leader or other followers, or even the leader's willingness to give feedback to followers. Defensiveness on the part of the leader can also hurt the entire team or organization, as it includes a tendency to place blame, categorize others as morally good or bad, and generally question others' motives. Such behaviors on a leader's part hardly build a positive work or team climate.

Leaders can reduce their defensiveness when listening to complaints by trying to put themselves in the other person's shoes. Leaders have an advantage if they can empathize with how they and their policies are seen by others; they can better change their behaviors and policies if they know how others perceive them. Leaders need to avoid the temptation to explain how the other person is wrong and should instead just try to understand how he perceives things. A useful warning sign that a leader may be behaving defensively (or perhaps closed-mindedly) is if he begins a conversation saying, "Yes, but. . . ."

Assertiveness

Use "I" Statements

Speak Up for What You Need

Learn to Say No

Monitor Your Inner Dialogue

Be Persistent

What is **assertive behavior**, and what are assertiveness skills? Basically, individuals exhibiting assertive behavior are able to stand up for their own rights (or their group's rights) in a way that also recognizes the concurrent right of others to do the same (see Highlight A–1). Like the skills already discussed, assertiveness skills also have knowledge, behavioral, and evaluative components. The behavioral component of assertiveness skills was mentioned already—it involves standing up for one's own or the group's rights in a constructive, nonhostile way. The knowledge component of assertiveness skills concerns knowing where and when not to behave assertively. People who are overly assertive may be perceived as aggressive and often may "win the battle but lose the war."

Highlight A–1

Assertiveness Questionnaire

Do you let someone know when you think he or she is being unfair to you?

Can you criticize someone else's ideas openly?

Are you able to speak up in a meeting?

Can you ask others for small favors or help?

Is it easy for you to compliment others?

Can you tell someone else you don't like what he or she is doing?

When you are complimented, do you really accept the compliment without inwardly discounting it in your own mind?

Can you look others in the eye when you talk to them?

If you could answer most of these questions affirmatively for most situations, then you do behave assertively.

Source: Adapted from R. E. Alberti, and M. L. Emmons, *Your Perfect Right* (San Luis Obispo, CA: Impact, 1974).

Finally, the evaluative component comes into play when individuals are successful (or unsuccessful) in standing up for their own or their group's rights and continually working in an effective manner with others.

Perhaps the best way to understand assertiveness is to distinguish it from two other styles people have for dealing with conflict: acquiescence (nonassertiveness) and aggression (Alberti & Emmons, 1974). **Acquiescence** is avoiding interpersonal conflict entirely either by giving up and giving in or by expressing one's needs in an apologetic, self-effacing way. Acquiescence is *not* synonymous with politeness or helpfulness, though it is sometimes rationalized as such. People who are acquiescent, or nonassertive, back down easily when challenged. By not speaking up for themselves, they abdicate power to others and, in the process, get trampled on. Besides the practical outcome of not attaining one's goals, an acquiescent style typically leads to many negative feelings such as guilt, resentment, and self-blame, as well as a low self-image. Sometimes people justify their nonassertiveness to themselves with the idea that acquiescing to others is being polite or helpful, but this often is just a rationalization.

Aggression, on the other hand, is an effort to attain objectives by attacking or hurting others. Aggressive people trample on others, and their aggressiveness can take such direct forms as threats, verbal attacks, physical intimidation, emotional outbursts, explosiveness, bullying, and hostility—and such indirect forms as nagging, passive-aggressive uncooperativeness, guilt arousal, and other behaviors that undermine an adversary's autonomy. It is important to understand that aggressiveness is not just an emotionally strong form of assertiveness.

Figure A–1

*Relationships
between
Assertiveness,
Acquiescence,
and Aggression*

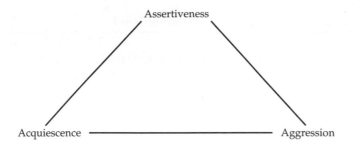

Aggressiveness tends to be reactive, and it tends to spring from feelings of vulnerability and a lack of self-confidence. Aggressive people inwardly doubt their ability to resolve issues constructively through the give-and-take of direct confrontation between mutually respecting equals. Aggressiveness is a form of interpersonal manipulation in which one tries to put oneself in a "top dog" role and others in a "bottom dog" role (Shostrom, 1967). Additionally, aggressive people have difficulty expressing positive feelings.

Assertiveness is different from both acquiescence and aggression; it is not merely a compromise between them or a midpoint on a continuum. Assertiveness involves direct and frank statements of one's own goals and feelings, and a willingness to address the interests of others in the spirit of mutual problem solving and a belief that openness is preferable to secretiveness and hidden agendas. Assertiveness is the behavioral opposite of both acquiescence and aggression, as depicted in Figure A–1. The qualitative differences between these three styles are like the differences between fleeing (acquiescence), fighting (aggression), and problem solving (assertiveness).

It may seem axiomatic that leaders need to behave assertively with subordinates. Sometimes, however, leaders also need to be assertive with their own bosses. Followers often need to be assertive with other followers and even with their leaders sometimes. For example, middle-level supervisors need to communicate performance expectations clearly and directly to subordinates, and they need to be strong advocates for their subordinates' interests with senior supervisors. Likewise, leaders sometimes need to give their own superiors bad news, and it is best to do so directly rather than hesitantly and guardedly. Followers may sometimes need to be assertive with a peer whose poor work habits are adversely impacting the work group. In addition, leaders sometimes need to be assertive with representatives of other power-holding or special-interest groups. For example, the leader of a community group seeking a new elementary school in a residential area may need to take a very assertive stand with local school board officials.

It is important to note that sometimes the hardest people to be assertive with are friends, family, and peers. Leaders who fail to be assertive with friends and peers run the risk of becoming victims of the Abilene paradox (see Highlight A–2). The **Abilene paradox** (Harvey, 1974) occurs when someone suggests that the group engage in a particular activity or course of action, and no one in the

---

Highlight A–2

The Abilene Paradox

That July afternoon in Coleman, Texas (population 5,607), was particularly hot—104 degrees according to the Rexall's thermometer. In addition, the wind was blowing fine-grained West Texas topsoil through the house. But the afternoon was still tolerable—even potentially enjoyable. A fan was stirring the air on the back porch; there was cold lemonade; and finally, there was entertainment. Dominoes. Perfect for the conditions. The game requires little more physical exertion than an occasional mumbled comment, "Shuffle 'em," and an unhurried movement of the arm to place the tiles in their appropriate positions on the table. All in all, it had the makings of an agreeable Sunday afternoon in Coleman. That is, until my father-in-law suddenly said, "Let's get in the car and go to Abilene and have dinner at the cafeteria."

I thought, "What, go to Abilene? Fifty-three miles? In this dust storm and heat? And in an unairconditioned 1958 Buick?"

But my wife chimed in with, "Sounds like a great idea. I'd like to go. How about you, Jerry?" Since my own preferences were obviously out of step with the rest, I replied, "Sounds good to me," and added, "I just hope your mother wants to go."

"Of course I want to go," said my mother-in-law. "I haven't been to Abilene in a long time."

So into the car and off to Abilene we went. My predictions were fulfilled. The heat was brutal. Perspiration had cemented a fine layer of dust to our skin by the time we arrived. The cafeteria's food could serve as a first-rate prop in an antacid commercial.

Some four hours and 106 miles later, we returned to Coleman, hot and exhausted. We silently sat in front of the fan for a long time. Then, to be sociable and to break the silence, I dishonestly said, "It was a great trip, wasn't it?"

No one spoke.

Finally, my mother-in-law said, with some irritation, "Well, to tell the truth, I really didn't enjoy it much and would rather have stayed here. I just went along because the three of you were so enthusiastic about going. I wouldn't have gone if you all hadn't pressured me into it."

I couldn't believe it. "What do you mean 'you all'?" I said. "Don't put me in the 'you all' group. I was delighted to be doing what we were doing. I didn't want to go. I only went to satisfy the rest of you. You're the culprits."

My wife looked shocked. "Don't call me a culprit. You and Daddy and Mama were the ones who wanted to go. I just went along to keep you happy. I would have had to be crazy to want to go out in heat like that."

Her father entered the conversation with one word. "Shee-it." He then expanded on what was already absolutely clear: "Listen, I never wanted to go to Abilene. I just thought you might be bored. You visit so seldom I wanted to be sure you enjoyed it. I would have preferred to play another game of dominoes and eat the leftovers in the icebox."

After the outburst of recrimination, we all sat back in silence. Here we were, four reasonably sensible people who—of our own volition—had just taken a 106-mile trip across a godforsaken desert in furnace-like heat and a dust storm to eat unpalatable food at a hole-in-the-wall cafeteria in Abilene, when none of us had really wanted to go. To be concise, we'd done just the opposite of what we wanted to do. The whole situation simply didn't make sense.

At least it didn't make sense at the time. But since that day in Coleman, I have observed, consulted with, and been a part of more than one organization that has been caught in the same situation. As a result, the organizations have either taken side trips or, occasionally, terminal journeys to Abilene, when Dallas or Houston or Tokyo was where they really wanted to go. And for most of those organizations, the negative consequences of such trips, measured in terms of both human misery and economic loss, have been much greater than for our little Abilene group.

I now call the tendency for groups to embark on excursions that no group member wants "the Abilene paradox." Stated simply, when organizations blunder into the Abilene paradox, they take actions in contradiction to what they really want to do and therefore defeat the very purpose they are trying to achieve. Business theorists typically believe that managing conflict is one of the greatest challenges faced by an organization, but a corollary of the Abilene paradox states that the inability to manage agreement may be the major source of organization dysfunction.

Source: Jerry B. Harvey, "The Abilene Paradox: The Management of Agreement," *Organizational Dynamics*, Summer 1974. Reprinted by permission of the publisher. American Management Association New York. http:www.amanet.org. All rights reserved.

group really wants to do the activity (including the person who made the suggestion). However, because of the false belief that everyone else in the group wants to do the activity, no one behaves assertively and voices an honest opinion about it. Only after the activity is over does anyone voice an opinion (and it is usually negative). For example, someone in your group of friends may suggest that the group go to a particular movie on a Friday night. No one in the group really wants to go, yet because of the false belief everyone else is interested, no one points out the movie is not supposed to be very good and the group should do something else instead. If group members' true opinions surface only *after* the movie, then the group has fallen victim to the Abilene paradox. Leaders can avoid the Abilene paradox by being assertive when suggestions about group decisions and activities are first made.

There are several things everyone can do to help themselves behave more assertively. These things include (*a*) using "I" statements, (*b*) speaking up for what you need, (*c*) learning to say no, (*d*) monitoring your inner dialogue, and (*e*) being persistent. The following is a more detailed discussion of these assertiveness tips.

Use "I" Statements

Assertive people take responsibility for what they say. They are clear in their own minds and with others about what they believe and what they want. One of the easiest ways to do this is to use first-person pronouns when you speak. Highlight A–3 provides examples of how to be more assertive by using first-person pronouns.

Highlight A–3

Tips for Being Assertive

Examples of Good and Bad "I" Statements

Bad: Some people may not like having to maintain those new forms.
Good: I don't think these new forms are any good. I don't think they're worth the effort.
Bad: Maybe that candidate doesn't have all the qualifications we're looking for.
Good: I think his academic record looks fine, but we agreed only to consider candidates with at least five years' experience. I think we should keep looking.

Tips for Speaking Up for What You Need

Do not apologize too much or justify yourself for needing help or assistance (e.g., "I just hate to ask you, and I normally wouldn't need to, but . . .").
At the same time, giving a brief reason for your request often helps.
Be direct. Do not beat around the bush, hinting at what you need and hoping others get the message.
Do not play on someone's friendship.
Do not take a refusal personally.

Tips for Saying No

Keep your reply short and polite. Avoid a long, rambling justification.
Do not invent excuses.
Do not go overboard in apologizing because you cannot do it.
Be up-front about your limitations and about options you could support.
Ask for time to consider it if you need to.

Source: Adapted from K. Back and K. Back, *Assertiveness at Work* (London: McGraw-Hill, 1982).

Speak Up for What You Need

No one has all of the skills, knowledge, time, or resources needed to do all of the taskings assigned to their work group. Virtually everyone will need to ask superiors, peers, or subordinates for help at some time. Both effective leaders and effective followers ask for help from others when they need it. Highlight A–3 also provides guidelines when making requests for help.

Learn to Say No

No one can be all things to all people, but it takes assertiveness to say no to others. Leaders, for example, may need to say no to their own superiors at times to stand up for their subordinates' or organization's rights and to keep from spreading themselves too thin and detracting from other priorities. Additionally, people who cannot (i.e., who *do not*) say no often build up a reservoir of negative emotions, such as those associated with the feeling of being taken advantage of. Tips for assertively refusing to do something also can be found in Highlight A–3.

Monitor Your Inner Dialogue

Most of us talk to ourselves, though not out loud. Such self-talk is natural and common, though not everyone is aware of how much it occurs or how powerful an influence on behavior it can be. Assertive people have self-talk that is positive and affirming. Nonassertive people have self-talk that is negative, doubtful, and questioning. Learning to say no is a good example of the role self-talk plays in assertiveness. Suppose that someone was asked to serve on a volunteer committee he simply does not have time for and that he *wants* to say no. In order to behave assertively, the person would need to talk to himself positively. He would need to ensure that he is not defeated by his own self-talk. It would hardly help the person's resolve, for example, to have an inner dialogue that says, "They'll think I'm selfish if I don't say yes," or "If they can make time for this committee, I should be able to make time for it, too." In learning to behave more assertively, therefore, it is necessary for leaders to become more aware of their own counterproductive self-talk, confront it, and change it.

Be Persistent

Assertive individuals stick to their guns without becoming irritated, angry, or loud. They persistently seek their objectives, even in the face of another person's excuses or objections. Exchanging merchandise can provide a good occasion for assertive persistence. Suppose someone had purchased a shirt at a department store, had worn it once, and then noticed the seam was poorly sewn. A person acting assertively might have an exchange much like that found in Highlight A–4. An assertive person is similarly persistent in standing up for his own or his group's rights.

Providing Constructive Feedback

Make It Helpful
Be Specific
Be Descriptive
Be Timely
Be Flexible
Give Positive as Well as Negative Feedback
Avoid Blame or Embarrassment

Example Exchange between a Buyer and a Clerk

Buyer: "I bought this shirt last week, and it's poorly made."
Clerk: "It looks like you've worn it. We don't exchange garments that already have been worn."
Buyer: "I understand that is your policy, but it's not that I don't like the shirt. It is obviously defective. I didn't know it had these defects when I wore it."
Clerk: "Maybe this seam came loose because of the way you wore it."
Buyer: "I didn't do anything unusual. It is defective. I want it exchanged."
Clerk: "I'm sorry, but you should have returned it earlier. We can't take it back now."
Buyer: "I understand your point, but I didn't get what I paid for. You need to return my money or give me a new shirt."
Clerk: "It's beyond my authority to do that. I don't make the policies, I just have to follow them."
Buyer: "I understand you don't think you have the authority to change the policy. But your boss does. Please tell her I'd like to see her right now."

Giving constructive feedback involves sharing information or perceptions with another about the nature, quality, or impact of that person's behavior. It can range from giving feedback pertaining specifically to a person's work (i.e., performance feedback) to impressions of how aspects of that person's interpersonal behavior may be pervasively affecting relationships with others. Our use of the term *feedback* here is somewhat different from its use in the systems view of communication (Figure C–1). In the communication model, the feedback loop begins with actively checking the receiver's *interpretation* of one's own message, and then initiating or modifying subsequent communications as necessary. A simple example of that meaning of feedback might be noting another person's quizzical expression when you try to explain a complicated point, thereby realizing that you'd better say it differently. The skill of giving constructive feedback, however, inherently involves *actively giving feedback to someone else.*

Getting helpful feedback is essential to a subordinate's performance and development. Without feedback, a subordinate will not be able to tell whether she's doing a good job or whether or not her abrasiveness is turning people off and hurting her chances for promotion. And it's not just subordinates who need constructive feedback to learn and grow. Peers may seek feedback from peers, and leaders may seek feedback from subordinates. Besides fostering growth, effective supervisory feedback also plays a major role in building morale.

In many ways, the development of good feedback skills is an outgrowth of developing good communication, listening, and assertiveness skills. Giving good feedback depends on being clear about the purpose of the feedback and on choosing an appropriate context and medium for giving it. Giving good feedback also depends on sending the proper nonverbal signals and trying to detect emotional signals from whoever may be receiving the feedback. In addition, giving good feedback depends on being somewhat assertive in providing it, even when it may be critical of a person's performance or behavior. Although feedback skills are related to communication, listening, and assertiveness skills, they are not the same thing. Someone may have good communication, listening, and assertiveness skills but poor feedback skills. Perhaps this distinction can be made clearer by examining the knowledge, behavior, and evaluative components of feedback skills.

The knowledge component of feedback concerns knowing when, where, and what feedback is to be given. For example, knowing when, where, and how to give positive feedback may be very different from knowing when, where, and how to give negative feedback. The behavioral component of feedback concerns how feedback actually is delivered (as contrasted with knowing how it should be delivered). Good feedback is specific, descriptive, direct, and helpful; poor feedback is often too watered down to be useful to the recipient. Finally, one way to evaluate feedback is to examine whether recipients actually modify their behavior accordingly after receiving it. Of course, this should not be the only way to evaluate feedback skills. Even when feedback is accurate in content and delivered skillfully, a recipient may fail to acknowledge it or do anything about it.

Although most leaders probably believe that feedback is an important skill, research has shown that leaders also believe they give more feedback than their subordinates think they do (Greller, 1980). There are many reasons leaders may be reluctant to give feedback. Leaders may be reluctant to give positive feedback because of time pressures, doubts about the efficacy of feedback, or lack of feedback skills (Komacki, 1982). Sometimes supervisors are hesitant to use positive feedback because they believe subordinates may see it as politically manipulative, ingratiating, or insincere (Bass, 1990). Leaders also may give positive feedback infrequently if they rarely leave their desks, if their personal standards are too high, or if they believe good performance is expected and should not be recognized at all (Deep & Sussman, 1990). Other reasons may explain the failure to give negative feedback (Larson, 1986), such as fears of disrupting leader-follower relations (Harrison, 1982) or fear of employee retaliation (Parsons, Herold, & Leatherwood, 1985).

Although there are a number of reasons why leaders are hesitant to provide both positive and negative feedback, leaders need to keep in mind that followers, committee members, or team members will perform at a higher level if they are given accurate and frequent feedback. It is difficult to imagine how workgroup or team performance could improve without feedback. Positive feedback is necessary to tell followers they should keep doing what they are doing well, and negative feedback is needed to give followers or team members ideas on how to change other behavior to improve their performance. Although accurate and frequent feedback is necessary, there are several other aspects of feedback that everyone can work on to improve their feedback skills, including (*a*) making sure it's helpful, (*b*) being direct, (*c*) being specific, (*d*) being descriptive, (*e*) being timely, (*f*) being flexible, (*g*) giving both positive and negative feedback, and (*h*) avoiding blame and embarrassment when giving feedback. Highlight F–1 gives examples of each of these different aspects of feedback, and the following is a more-complete description of ways leaders can improve their feedback skills.

Make It Helpful

The purpose of feedback is to provide others with information they can use to change their behavior. Being clear about the intent and purpose is important because giving feedback sometimes can become emotional for both the person giving it and the person receiving it. If the person giving feedback is in an emotional state (e.g., angry), she may say things that make her temporarily feel better but that only alienate the receiver. In order to be helpful, individuals need to be clear and unemotional when giving feedback, and should give feedback only about behaviors actually under the other person's control.

People can improve the impact of the feedback they give when it is addressed to a specific individual. A common mistake in giving feedback is addressing it to "people at large" rather than to a specific individual. In this case, the individuals for whom the feedback was intended may not believe the feedback pertained to them. In order to maximize the impact of the feedback, people should try to provide it to specific individuals, not large groups.

Be Specific

Feedback is most helpful when it specifies particular behaviors that are positive or negative. One of the best illustrations of the value of specific feedback is in compositions or term papers written for school. If someone turned in a draft of a paper to the instructor for constructive comments and the instructor's comments about the paper were "Good start, but needs work in several areas," then the person would have a difficult time knowing just what to change or correct. More helpful feedback from the instructor would be specific comments like "This paragraph does not logically follow the preceding one" or "Cite an example here." The same is true of feedback in work situations. The more specifically leaders can point out which behaviors to change, the more clearly they let the other person know what to do.

Be Descriptive

In giving feedback, it is good to stick to the facts as much as possible, being sure to distinguish them from inferences or attributions. A behavior description reports actions that others can see, about which there could be little question

Tips for Improving Feedback Skills

Being Helpful

Do not: "I got better scores when I was going through this program than you just did."
Do: "This seems to be a difficult area for you. What can I do to help you master it better?"

Being Direct

Do not: "It's important that we all speak loud enough to be heard in meetings."
Do: "I had a difficult time hearing you in the meeting because you were speaking in such a soft voice."

Being Specific

Do not: "Since you came to work for us, your work has been good."
Do: "I really like the initiative and resourcefulness you showed in solving our scheduling problem."

Being Descriptive

Do not: "I'm getting tired of your rudeness and disinterest when others are talking."
Do: "You weren't looking at anyone else when they were talking, which gave the impression you were bored. Is that how you were feeling?"

Being Timely

Do not: "Joe, I think I need to tell you about an impression you made on me in the staff meeting last month."
Do: "Joe, do you have a minute? I was confused by something you said in the meeting this morning."

Being Flexible

Do not (while a person is crying, or while they are turning beet-red with clenched teeth in apparent anger): "There's another thing I want to tell you about your presentation yesterday. . . ."
Do: When a person's rising defenses or emotionality get in the way of their really listening, deal with those feelings first, or wait until later to finish your feedback. Do not continue giving information.

Highlight F–2

Types of Criteria to Use for Evaluative Feedback

1. Compare behavior with others' measured performance. With this method, the subordinate's behavior is compared with that of her peers or co-workers; also called norm-referenced appraisal. For example, a subordinate may be told her counseling load is the lightest of all 10 counselors working at the center.
2. Compare behavior with an accepted standard. An example of this method would be where a counselor was told her workload was substantially below the standard of acceptable performance set at 30 cases per week. This is known as criterion-referenced appraisal.
3. Compare behavior with an a priori goal. With this method, the subordinate must participate in and agree with a goal. This is a form of criterion-referenced appraisal, with the subordinate's "ownership" and acceptance of the goal before the fact critical to the feedback procedure.
4. Compare behavior with past performance.

Source: Adapted from A. C. Filley and L. A. Pace, "Making Judgments Descriptive," In J. E. Jones and J. W. Pfeiffer, eds, *The 1976 Annual Handbook for Group Facilitators* (La Jolla, CA: University Associates Press, 1976), pp. 129–31.

---

or disagreement. Such descriptions must be distinguished from inferences about someone else's feelings, attitudes, character, motives, or traits. It is a behavior description, for example, to say that Sally stood up and walked out of a meeting while someone else was talking. It is an inference, though, to say she walked out because she was angry. However, sometimes it is helpful to describe both the behavior itself as well as corresponding impressions when giving feedback. This is particularly true if the feedback giver believes that the other person does not realize how the behavior negatively affects others' impressions.

Another reason to make feedback descriptive is to distinguish it from evaluation. When a person gives feedback based mostly on inferences, he often conveys evaluations of the "goodness" or "badness" of behavior as well. For example, saying "You were too shy" has a more negative connotation than saying "You had little to say." In the former case, the person's behavior was evaluated unfavorably, and by apparently subjective criteria. Yet evaluation is often an intrinsic part of a supervisor's responsibilities, and good performance feedback may necessitate conveying evaluative information to a subordinate. In such cases, leaders are better off providing evaluative feedback when clear criteria for performance have been established. Filley and Pace (1976) described criteria that can be used to provide evaluative feedback; some are listed in Highlight F–2.

An issue related to impressions and evaluative feedback concerns the distinction between job-related (i.e., performance feedback) and more personal or discretionary feedback. Although leaders have a right to expect followers to listen to their performance feedback, that is not necessarily true concerning feedback about other behaviors. It may well be that sharing perceptions of the person's behavior could be very helpful to that person even when the behavior doesn't pertain specifically to his formal responsibilities; in such cases, however, it is the follower's choice whether to hear it or, if he hears it, whether to act on it or not.

Be Timely

Feedback usually is most effective when it is given soon after the behavior occurs. The context and relevant details of more recent events or behaviors are more readily available to everyone involved, thus facilitating more descriptive and helpful feedback.

Be Flexible

Although feedback is best when it is timely, sometimes waiting is preferable to giving feedback at the very earliest opportunity. In general, everyone should remember that the primary purpose of feedback is to be helpful. Feedback sessions should be scheduled with that in mind. For example, a subordinate's schedule may preclude conveniently giving him feedback right away, and it may not be appropriate to give him feedback when it will distract him from another more immediate and pressing task. Furthermore, it may not be constructive to give someone else feedback when the person receiving it is in a very emotional state (whether about the behavior in question or other matters entirely). Moreover, it is important to be attentive to the other person's emotional responses while giving feedback and to be ready to adjust one's own behavior accordingly.

A final important part of being flexible is to give feedback in manageable amounts. In giving feedback, one does not need to cover every single point at one time, as doing so would only overload the other person with information. Instead, anyone who needs to give a lot of feedback to someone else may want to spread out the feedback sessions and focus on covering only one or two points in each session.

Give Positive as Well as Negative Feedback

Giving *both* positive and negative feedback is more helpful than giving only positive or negative feedback alone. Positive feedback tells the other person or the group only what they are doing right, and negative feedback tells the other person or group only what they are doing wrong. Providing both kinds of feedback is best.

Avoid Blame or Embarrassment

Because the purpose of feedback is to give useful information to other people to help them develop, talking to them in a way merely intended (or likely) to demean or make them feel bad is not a helpful part of the development process. Followers tend to be more likely to believe feedback if it comes from leaders who have had the opportunity to observe the behavior and are perceived to be credible, competent, and trustworthy (Coye, 1982; Quaglieri & Carnazza, 1985; Stone, Guetal, & MacIntosh, 1984). Bass (1990) points out that followers will continue to seek feedback even if their leaders are not competent or trustworthy—though they will not seek it from their leaders. They will seek it from others they do trust, such as peers or other superiors.

Guidelines for Effective Stress Management

Monitor Your Own and Your Followers' Stress Levels
Identify What Is Causing the Stress
Practice a Healthy Lifestyle
Learn to Relax
Develop Supportive Relationships
Keep Things in Perspective
The A-B-C Model

People use the term *stress* in a number of different ways. Sometimes people use the term to describe particular sorts of events or *environmental conditions*. For example, fans might speculate that a professional football coach's heart attack was caused by the *pressures* of his profession. Other examples might include receiving a failing grade on a physics exam, or arriving noticeably late to an important meeting, or playing a sudden-death overtime in hockey. We would acknowledge, for example, that walking in late to a meeting could be very embarrassing (i.e., stressful). Likewise for working at the service counter of a major department store on the day after Christmas; it's a *stressful job*. In each of these instances, stress refers to *characteristics of the environment*. But people also use the term in a quite different way. Sometimes it refers to the *effects* of those environments. The phrase, "I'm feeling a lot of stress" might refer to various *symptoms* a person is experiencing, such as muscular tension or difficulty concentrating. Before we proceed further, therefore, it will be useful to agree upon some conventions of terminology.

We will define stress as the whole process by which we appraise and respond to events that challenge or threaten us (Myers, 1989). These responses usually include increased levels of emotional arousal and changes in physiological symptoms, such as increases in perspiration and heart rates, cholesterol levels, or blood pressure. Stress often occurs in situations that are overly complex, demanding, or unclear. Stressors are those specific characteristics in individuals,

Highlight S–1

Stress Symptoms

Are you behaving "unlike" yourself?

Has your mood become negative, hostile, or depressed?

Do you have difficulty sleeping?

Are you defensive or touchy?

Are your relationships suffering?

Have you made more mistakes or bad decisions lately?

Have you lost interest in normally enjoyable activities?

Are you using alcohol or other drugs?

Do you seem to have little energy?

Do you worry a lot?

Are you nervous much of the time?

Have you been undereating or overeating?

Have you had an increase in headaches or back pains?

This checklist can also be used to help determine the level of stress in followers.

tasks, organizations, or the environment that pose some degree of threat or challenge to people (see Highlight S–1). Although all the factors in Highlight S–1 probably have an adverse impact on people, the degree of stress associated with each of them depends on one's overall level of stress tolerance and previous experience with the stressor in question (Benner, 1984). Similarly, it is important to realize that stress is in the eye of the beholder—what one person may see as challenging and potentially rewarding, another may see as threatening and distressful (McCauley, 1987; Staw, 1984).

Who do you think typically experiences greater stress—leaders or followers? In one sense, the answer is the same as that for much psychological research: it depends. The role of leader certainly can be quite stressful. Leaders face at least one major stressful event at least once a month (Ivancevich, Schweiger, & Ragan, 1986). Followers' stress levels, on the other hand, often depend on their leaders. Leaders can help followers cope with stress or, alternatively, actually increase their followers' stress levels. Many leaders recognize when followers are under a lot of stress and will give them time off, try to reduce their workload, or take other actions to help followers cope. On the other hand, about two out of three workers say their bosses play a bigger part in creating their stress than any other personal, organizational, or environmental factor (R. T. Hogan & Morrison, 1991; Shipper & Wilson, 1992). Similarly, McCormick and Powell (1988) reported that working for a tyrannical boss was the most frequently cited

Highlight S–2

Stress on a TV Game Show

The television game show "Wheel of Fortune" pits contestants against each other in trying to identify common sayings. By spinning a wheel, contestants determine varying dollar amounts to be added to their potential winnings.

The game is similar to the game of "Hangman" you may have played as a child. It begins with spaces indicating the number of words in a saying and the number of letters in each word. One player spins the wheel, which determines prize money, and then guesses a letter. If the letter appears somewhere in the saying, then the player spins the wheel again, guesses another letter, and so on. The letters are "filled in" as they are correctly identified. A player may try to guess the saying after naming a correct letter.

If a player names a letter which does not appear in the saying, then that prize money is not added to the contestant's potential winnings and play moves on to another contestant.

One day a contestant was playing for over $50,000 to solve the puzzle below. Perhaps because of the stress of being on television and playing for so much money, the contestant could not accurately name a letter for one of the four remaining spaces. Most people, not experiencing such stress, easily solve the problem. Can you? For the answer, see the bottom of the box.

T	H	E		T	H	R	I	__
O	F	__	I	__	T	O	R	Y
	A	N	D	T	H	E		
	A	G	O	N	Y	O	F	
	D	E	F	E	A	T		

Answer: The Thrill of Victory and the Agony of Defeat

---

source of stress among workers. It is clear that leaders play a substantial role in how stressful their followers' work experience is, for good or ill.

Stress can either facilitate or inhibit performance, depending on the situation. Too much stress can take a toll on individuals and organizations that includes decreased health and emotional well-being, reduced job performance, and decreased organizational effectiveness (see Highlight S–2 for an example of how too much stress impaired one person's performance).

In order to understand the effects of stress, an analogy might be helpful. Kites need an optimal amount of wind to fly; they will not fly on windless days, and the string may break on a day that is too windy. You can think of stress as like the wind for a kite: There is a certain level that is optimal, neither too little nor too much. Another analogy is your car. Just as an automobile engine operates optimally within a certain range of revolutions per minute (RPM), most people function best at certain levels of stress. A certain amount of stress or arousal is helpful in increasing motivation and performance, but too much stress can be counterproductive. For example, it is common and probably helpful to feel a little anxiety before giving a speech, but being too nervous can destroy one's effectiveness.

The optimal level of stress depends on a number of factors. One is the level of physical activity actually demanded by the task. Another is the perceived difficulty of the task. Performance often suffers when difficult tasks are performed under stressful situations. For example, think how one's performance might differ when learning to first drive a car with an instructor who is quiet and reserved rather than one who yells a lot. Chances are, performance will be much better with the first instructor than with the second.

It is important to note that task difficulty is generally a function of experience; the more experience one has with a task, the less difficult it becomes. Thus, the more driving experience one has, the easier the task becomes. Moreover, not only do people cope with stress more readily when performing easier tasks; people often need higher levels of stress for performing them optimally. One underlying purpose behind any type of practice, be it football, marching band, soccer, or drama, is to reduce task difficulty and help members or players to perform at an even higher level when faced with the stress of key performances and games.

Although stress can have positive effects, research has focused on the negative implications of too much stress on health and work. In terms of health, stress has been linked to heart disease (Friedman & Ulmer, 1984), immune system deficiencies (Pomerleau & Rodin, 1986), and the growth rates of tumors (Justice, 1985). In terms of work behaviors, both Latack (1986) and Quayle (1983) reported that work-related stress has caused a dramatic increase in drug and alcohol use in the workplace, and Jamal (1984) found that stress was positively related to absenteeism, intentions to quit, and turnover. Relatedly, Quayle (1983) and Albrecht (1979) estimated the economic impact of stress to companies in the Unites States to be somewhere between $70 billion and $150 billion annually. Stress can also affect the decision-making process. Although leaders need to act decisively in stressful situations (i.e., crises), they may not make good decisions under stress (Fiedler, 1992; Gibson, 1992; Mulder, de Jong, Koppelaar, & Verhage, 1986). According to Weschler (1955) and Tjosvold (1985), people make poor decisions when under stress because they revert to their intuition rather than think rationally about problems.

As we have noted, too much stress can take a toll on individuals and their organizations. For individuals, the toll can be in terms of their health, mental and emotional well-being, job performance, or interpersonal relationships. For organizations, the toll includes decreased productivity and increased employee absenteeism, turnover, and medical costs. It stands to reason, then, that leaders in any activity should know something about stress. Leaders should understand the nature of stress because the leadership role itself can be stressful and because leaders' stress can impair the performance and well-being of followers. To prevent stress from becoming so excessive that it takes a toll in some important dimension of your own or your followers' lives, the following guidelines for effective stress management are provided.

Monitor Your Own and Your Followers' Stress Levels

One of the most important steps in managing stress is to *monitor your own and your followers' stress levels.* Although this seems straightforward, a seemingly paradoxical fact about stress is that it often takes a toll without one's conscious awareness. A person experiencing excessive stress might manifest various symptoms apparent to everyone but him or her. For that reason, it is useful to develop the habit of regularly attending to some of the warning signs that your stress level may be getting too high. Some of the warning signs of stress are in Highlight S–1. If you answered yes to any of these questions, then your own or your followers' stress levels may be getting too high and it would probably be a good idea to put some of the following stress management strategies into practice right away. On the other hand, answering some of the questions affirmatively does not necessarily mean your stress level is too high. There could, for example, be some other physiological explanation.

Identify What Is Causing the Stress

Monitoring your stress will reduce the chances that it will build to an unhealthy level before you take action, but monitoring is not enough. Leaders also need to *identify what is causing the stress.* It may seem at first that the causes of stress always will be obvious, but that is not true. Sometimes the problems are clear enough even if the solutions are not (e.g., family finances or working in a job with a high workload and lots of deadlines). At other times, however, it may be difficult to identify the root problem. For example, a coach may attribute his anger to the losing record of his team, not recognizing that a bigger cause of his emotional distress may be the problems he is having at home with his teenage son. A worker may feel frustrated because her boss overloads her with work, not realizing that her own unassertiveness keeps her from expressing her feelings to her boss. Problem solving can be applied constructively to managing stress, but only if the problem is identified properly in the first place. Once the problem is identified, then a plan for minimizing stress or the effects of the stressor can be developed.

Practice a Healthy Lifestyle

Practicing a healthy lifestyle is one of the best ways to minimize stress. There are no substitutes for balanced nutrition, regular exercise, adequate sleep, abstention from tobacco products, and drinking only moderate amounts of alcohol (if at all) as keys to a healthy life. A long-term study of the lifestyles of nearly 7,000 adults confirmed these as independent factors contributing to wellness and the absence of stress symptoms (Wiley & Camacho, 1980). Insufficient sleep saps energy, interferes with alertness and judgment, increases irritability, and lowers resistance to illness. Exercise, besides being a valuable part of any long-term health strategy, is also an excellent way to reduce tension.

Learn How to Relax

Believe it or not, some people just do not know how to relax. Although physical exercise is a good relaxation technique, sometimes you will need to relax but not have an opportunity to get a workout. Having practiced other relaxation techniques will come in handy when the situation prevents strenuous exercise. Also, of course, some people simply prefer alternative relaxation techniques to exercise. *Deep-breathing techniques, progressive muscle relaxation, and thinking of calming words and images* can be powerful on-the-spot calming techniques to reduce arousal level. They are applicable in stressful situations ranging from job interviews to sports. The effectiveness of these techniques is somewhat a matter of personal preference, and no single one is best for all purposes or all people.

Develop Supportive Relationships

Another powerful antidote to stress is having a *network of close and supportive relationships* with others (Berkman & Syme, 1979). People who have close ties to others through marriage, church membership, or other groups tend to be healthier than those with weaker social ties. Also, social supports of various kinds (e.g., the supportiveness of one's spouse, co-workers, or boss) can buffer the impact of job stress (Cummings, 1990; Jayaratne, Himle, & Chess, 1988), and unit cohesion is believed to be a critical element of soldiers' ability to withstand even the extreme physical and psychological stresses of combat (West Point Associates, 1988). Leaders can play a constructive role in developing mutual supportiveness and cohesiveness among subordinates, and their own open and frank communication with subordinates is especially important when a situation is ambiguous as well as stressful.

Keep Things in Perspective

As we noted earlier, the stressfulness of any event depends partly on the way one interprets it, not just on the event itself. For example, a poor grade on an examination may be more stressful for one student than for another, just as a rebuke from a boss may be more stressful for one worker than for another. This is partly due, of course, to the fact individuals invest themselves in activities to different degrees because they value different things. A problem in an area of heavy personal investment is more stressful than one in an area of little personal investment. It goes deeper than that, however. Managing stress effectively depends on *keeping things in perspective*. This is difficult for some people because they have a style of interpreting events that aggravates their felt stress.

Individuals who have relatively complex self-concepts, as measured by the number of different ways they describe or see themselves, are less susceptible to common stress-related complaints than are people with lesser degrees of "self-complexity" (Linville, 1987). Take, for example, someone who has suffered a setback at work, such as having lost out to a colleague for a desired promotion. Someone low in self-complexity (e.g., a person whose self-concept is defined solely in terms of professional success) could be devastated by the event. Low self-complexity implies a lack of resilience to threats to one's ego. Consider, on the other hand, someone with high self-complexity facing the same setback. The person could understandably feel disappointed and perhaps dejected about work, but if she were high in self-complexity, then the event's impact would be buffered by the existence of relatively uncontaminated areas of positive self-image. For example, she might base her feelings of professional success on more criteria than just getting (or not getting) a promotion. Other criteria, such as being highly respected by peers, may be even more important bases for her feelings of professional success. Furthermore, other dimensions of her life (e.g., her leadership in the local Democratic party, support to her family) may provide more areas of positive self-image.

The A-B-C Model

Unfortunately, because there are no shortcuts to developing self-complexity, it is not really a viable stress management strategy. There are other cognitive approaches to stress management, however, that can produce more immediate results. These approaches have the common goal of changing a person's self-talk about stressful events. One of the simplest of these to apply is called the A-B-C model (Ellis & Harper, 1975; Steinmetz, Blankenship, Brown, Hall, & Miller, 1980).

To appreciate the usefulness of the A-B-C model, it is helpful to consider the chain of events that precedes feelings of stress. Sometimes people think of this as a two-step sequence. Something external happens (i.e., a stressful event), and then something *internal* follows (i.e., symptoms of stress). We can depict the sequence like this:

    A. Triggering Event

       (e.g., knocking your boss's coffee onto his lap)

    C. Feelings and Behaviors

       (e.g., anxiety, fear, embarrassment, perspiration)

In other words, many people think their feelings and behaviors result directly from external events. Such a view, however, leaves out the critical role played by our thoughts, or self-talk. The actual sequence looks like this:

    A. Triggering Event

       (knocking your boss's coffee onto his lap)

    B. Your Thinking

       ("He must think I'm a real jerk.")

C. Feelings and Behaviors

(anxiety, fear, embarrassment, perspiration)

From this perspective you can see the causal role played by inner dialogue, or self-talk, in contributing to feelings of stress. Such inner dialogue can be rational or irrational, constructive or destructive—and which it will be is under the individual's control. People gain considerable freedom from stress when they realize that by changing their own self-talk, they can control their emotional responses to events around them. Consider a different sequence for our scenario:

A. Triggering Event

(knocking your boss's coffee onto his lap)

B. Your Thinking

("Darn it! But it was just an accident.")

C. Feelings and Behavior

(apologizing and helping clean up)

Thus, a particular incident can be interpreted in several different ways, some likely to increase feelings of stress and distress, and others likely to maintain self-esteem and positive coping. You will become better at coping with stress as you practice listening to your inner dialogue and changing destructive self-talk to constructive self-talk. Even this is not a simple change to make, however. Changing self-talk is more difficult than you might think, especially in emotionalized situations. Because self-talk is covert, spontaneous, fleeting, and reflexive (McKay, Davis, & Fanning, 1981), it, like any bad habit, can be difficult to change. Nevertheless, precisely because self-talk is just a habit, you can change it.

Finally, leaders need to recognize their role in their followers' stress levels. A leader in a stressful situation who is visibly manifesting some of the symptoms found in Highlight S–1 is not going to set much of an example for followers. On the contrary, because followers look to leaders for guidance and support, these behaviors and symptoms could become contagious and may serve to increase followers' stress levels. Leaders need to recognize the importance of role modeling in reducing (or increasing) followers' stress levels. Leaders also need to make sure their style of interacting with subordinates does not make the leaders "stress carriers."

Building Technical Competence

Determining How the Job Contributes to the Overall Mission
Becoming an Expert in the Job
Seeking Opportunities to Broaden Experiences

Technical competence concerns the knowledge and repertoire of behaviors one can bring to bear to successfully complete a task. For example, a highly skilled surgeon possesses vast knowledge of human anatomy and surgical techniques and can perform an extensive set of highly practiced surgical procedures; a highly skilled volleyball player has a thorough understanding of the rules, tactics, and strategies of volleyball and can set, block, and serve effectively. Individuals usually acquire technical competence through formal education or training in specialized topics (i.e., law, medicine, accounting, welding, carpentry), on-the-job training, or experience (Yukl, 1989), and many studies have documented the importance of technical competence to a person's success and effectiveness as both a leader and a follower. This section describes why technical competence is important to followers and leaders; it also provides readers with ideas about how to increase their own technical competence.

There are many reasons why followers need to have a high level of technical competence. First, performance is often a function of technical competence (Borman, Hanson, Oppler, & Pulakos, in press; Schmidt & Hunter, 1992). Relatedly, research has shown that technical expertise plays a key role in supervisors' performance appraisal ratings of subordinates (Borman, White, Pulakos, & Oppler, 1991; J. Hogan, 1992b). Second, followers with high levels of technical competence have a lot of expert power, and at times can wield more influence in their groups than the leader does (Bugental, 1964; Farris, 1971). Third, individuals with high levels of technical competence may be more likely to be a member of a leader's in-group (Duchon, Green, & Taber, 1986). Relatedly, followers with high levels of technical competence are more likely to be delegated tasks and asked to participate in the decision-making process. Conversely, supervisors are more likely to use a close, directive leadership style when interacting with subordinates with poor technical skills (Dewhirst, Metts, & Ladd, 1987; Leana, 1987; Lowin & Craig, 1968; Rosen & Jerdee, 1977). Similarly, Blau (1968) noted that organizations with relatively high numbers of technically competent members tended to have a flatter organizational structure; organizations with relatively fewer qualified members tended to be more centralized and autocratic. Thus, if followers wish to earn greater rewards, exert more influence in their groups, and have greater say in the decision-making process, then they should do all they can to enhance their technical competence.

There are also many reasons why it benefits leaders to have high levels of technical competence. First, technical competence has been found to be consistently related to managerial promotion rates. Managers having higher levels of technical competence were much more likely to rise to the top managerial levels at AT&T than managers with lower levels of technical competence (Howard, 1986; Howard & Bray, 1989). Second, having a high level of technical competence is important because many leaders, particularly first-line supervisors, often spend considerable time training followers (Wexley & Latham, 1981). Perhaps nowhere is the importance of technical competence in training more readily apparent than in coaching; little is as frustrating as having a coach who knows less about the game than the team members. Third, leaders with high levels of technical competence seem to be able to reduce the level of role ambiguity and conflict in their groups (Podsakoff, Todor, & Schuler, 1983; Walker,

1976), and followers are generally more satisfied with leaders who have high rather then average levels of technical competence (Bass, 1985; Penner, Malone, Coughlin, & Herz, 1973). Finally, leaders who have a high level of technical competence may be able to stimulate followers to think about problems and issues in new ways, which in turn has been found to be strongly related to organizational climate ratings and followers' motivation to succeed (Avolio & Bass, 1988; Curphy, 1991a). Given these findings for both leaders and followers, below is some practical advice for improving technical competence.

Determining How the Job Contributes to the Overall Mission

The first step in building technical competence is to determine how one's job contributes to the overall success of the organization. By taking this step, individuals can better determine what technical knowledge and which behaviors are most strongly related to job and organizational success. Next, people should evaluate their current level of technical skills by seeking verbal feedback from peers and superiors, reviewing past performance appraisal results, or reviewing objective performance data (e.g., golf scores, team statistics, the number of products rejected for poor quality). These actions will help individuals get a better handle on their own strengths and weaknesses, and in turn can help people be certain that any formal education or training program they pursue is best suited to meet their needs.

Becoming an Expert in the Job

Becoming an expert in one's primary field is often the springboard for further developmental opportunities. There are a number of ways in which individuals can become experts in their field, and these include enrolling in formalized education and training programs, watching others, asking questions, and teaching others. Attending pertinent education and training courses is one way to acquire technical skills, and many companies often pay the tuition and fees associated with these courses. Another way to increase expertise in one's field is by being a keen observer of human behavior. Individuals can learn a lot by observing how others handle work-coordination problems, achieve production goals, discipline team members, or develop team members with poor skills. Merely observing how others do things is not nearly as effective as observing and reflecting about how others do things, however. One method of reflection is trying to explain others' behaviors in terms of the concepts or theories described in this book. Observers should look for concepts that cast light on both variations and regularities in how others act and think about the reasons why a person might have acted a certain way. Additionally, observers can develop by trying to think of as many different criteria as possible for evaluating another person's actions.

It is also important to ask questions. Because everyone makes inferences regarding the motives, expectations, values, or rationale underlying another person's actions, it is vital to ask questions and seek information likely to verify the accuracy of one's inferences. By asking questions, observers can better understand why team practices are conducted in a particular way, what work procedures have been implemented in the past, or what really caused someone to quit a volunteer organization. Finally, perhaps nothing can help a person become a technical expert more than having to teach someone else about the equipment, procedures, strategies, problems, resources, and contacts associated with a job, club, sport, or activity. Teachers must have a thorough understanding of the job or position in order to effectively teach someone else. By seeking opportunities to teach others, individuals enhance their own technical expertise as well as that of others.

Seeking Opportunities to Broaden Experiences

Individuals can improve their technical competence by seeking opportunities to broaden their experiences. Just as a person should try to play a variety of positions in order to better appreciate the contributions of other team members, so should a person try to perform the tasks associated with the other positions in his or her work group in order to better appreciate how the work contributes to organizational success. Similarly, people should visit other parts of the organization in order to gain an understanding of its whole operation. Moreover, by working on team projects, people get a chance to interact with members of other work units and often get the opportunity to develop new skills. Additionally, volunteering to support school, political, or community activities is another way to increase one's organization and planning, public speaking, fund-raising, and public relations skills, all of which may be important aspects of technical competence for certain jobs.

Building Effective Relationships with Superiors

Understanding the Superior's World
Adapting to the Superior's Style

As defined here, superiors are those individuals with relatively more power and authority than the other members of the group. Thus, superiors could be teachers, band directors, coaches, team captains, heads of committees, or first-line supervisors. Needless to say, there are a number of advantages to having a good working relationship with superiors. First, superiors and followers sharing the same values, approaches, and attitudes will experience less conflict, provide higher levels of mutual support, and be more satisfied with superior–follower relationships than superiors and followers having poor working relationships (Duchon, Green, & Taber, 1986; Porter, 1992). Relatedly, individuals having good superior–follower relationships are often in the superior's in-group and thus are more likely to have a say in the decision-making process, be delegated interesting tasks, and have the superior's support for career advancement (Yukl, 1989).

Second, followers are often less satisfied with their supervisor and receive lower performance appraisal ratings when superior–follower relationships are poor (Pulakos & Wexley, 1983; Weiss, 1977).

Although the advantages of having a good working relationship with superiors seem clear, one might mistakenly think that followers have little, if any, say in the quality of the relationship. In other words, followers might believe their relationships with superiors are a matter of luck; either the follower has a good superior or a bad one, or the superior just happens to like or dislike the follower, and there is little if anything the follower can do about it. However, the quality of a working relationship is not determined solely by the superior, and effective subordinates do not limit themselves to a passive stance toward superiors. Effective subordinates have learned how to take active steps to strengthen the relationship and enhance the support they provide their superior and the organization (Gabarro & Kotter, 1980; Kelley, 1988).

Wherever a person is positioned in an organization, an important aspect of that person's work is to help his superior be successful, just as an important part of the superior's work is to help followers be successful. This does not mean that followers should become apple-polishers, play politics, or distort information just to make superiors look good. It does mean, however, that followers should think of their own and their superior's success as interdependent. It means that followers are players on their superior's team and should be evaluated on the basis of the team's success, not just their own. If the team succeeds, then both the coach and the team members should benefit; if the team fails, then the blame should fall on both the coach and the team members. Because team, club, or organizational outcomes depend to some extent on good superior–follower relationships, understanding how superiors view the world and adapting to superiors' styles are two things followers can do to increase the likelihood their actions will have positive results for themselves, their superiors, and their organizations (Gabarro & Kotter, 1980).

Understanding the Superior's World

There are a number of things followers can do to better understand their superior's world. First, they should try to get a handle on their superior's personal and organizational objectives. Loyalty and support are a two-way street, and just as a superior can help subordinates attain their personal goals most readily by knowing what they are, so can subordinates support their superior if they understand the superior's goals and objectives. Relatedly, knowing a superior's values, preferences, and personality can help followers better understand why superiors act the way they do and can give followers insights into how they might strengthen relationships with superiors.

Second, followers need to realize that superiors are not supermen or superwomen; superiors do not have all the answers, and they have both strengths and weaknesses. Subordinates can make a great contribution to the overall success of a team by recognizing and complementing a superior's weaknesses, and understanding his constraints and limitations. For example, a highly successful management consultant might spend over 200 days a year conducting executive development workshops, providing organizational feedback to clients, or giving speeches at various public events. This same consultant, however, might not be skilled in designing and making effective visual aids for presentations, or she might dislike having to make her own travel and accommodation arrangements. A follower could make both the consultant and the consulting firm more successful through his own good organization and planning, attention to detail, computer graphics skills, and understanding that the consultant is most effective when she has at least a one-day break between engagements. A similar process can take place in other contexts, as when subordinates help orient and educate a newly assigned superior whose expertise and prior experience may have been in a different field or activity.

In an even more general sense, subordinates can enhance superior–follower relationships by keeping superiors informed about various activities in the work group or new developments or opportunities in the field. Few superiors like surprises, and any news should come from the person with responsibility for a particular area—especially if the news is potentially bad or concerns unfavorable developments. Followers wishing to develop good superior-follower relationships should never put their superior in the embarrassing situation of having someone else know more about her terrain than she does (her own boss, for instance). As Kelley (1988) maintained, the best followers think critically and play an active role in their organizations, which means that followers should keep their superiors informed about critical information and pertinent opinions concerning organizational issues.

Adapting to the Superior's Style

Research has shown that some executives fail to get promoted (i.e., are derailed) because they are unable or unwilling to adapt to superiors with leadership styles different from their own (McCall & Lombardo, 1983). Followers need to keep in mind that it is their responsibility to adapt to their superior's style, not vice versa. For example, followers might prefer to interact with superiors face-to-face, but if their superior appreciates written memos, then written memos it should be. Similarly, a follower might be accustomed to informal interactions with superiors, but a new superior might prefer a more businesslike and formal style. Followers need to be flexible in adapting to their superiors' decision-making styles, problem-solving strategies, modes of communication, styles of interaction, and so on.

One way followers can better adapt to a superior's style is to clarify expectations about their role on the team, committee, or work group. Young workers often do not appreciate the difference between a job description and one's role in a job. A job description is a formalized statement of tasks and activities; a role describes the personal signature an incumbent gives to a job. For example, the job description of a high school athletic coach might specify such responsibilities as selecting and training a team or making decisions about lineups. Two different coaches, however, might accomplish those basic responsibilities in quite different ways. One might emphasize player development in the broadest sense, getting to know her players personally and using sports as a vehicle for their individual growth; another might see his role simply to produce the most winning team possible. Therefore, just because followers know what their job is does not mean their role is clear.

Although some superiors take the initiative to explicitly spell out the roles they expect subordinates to play, most do not. Usually it is the subordinate's task to discern his or her role. One way followers can do this is to make a list of major responsibilities and use it to guide a discussion with the superior about different ways the tasks might be accomplished and the relative priorities of the tasks. Relatedly, followers will also find it helpful to talk to others who have worked with a particular superior before.

Finally, followers interested in developing effective relationships with superiors need to be honest and dependable. Whatever other qualities or talents a subordinate might have, a lack of integrity is an absolutely fatal flaw. No one—superior, peer, or subordinate—wants to work with someone who is untrustworthy. After integrity, superiors value dependability. Superiors value workers who have reliable work habits, accomplish assigned tasks at the right time in the right order, and do what they promise (Kouzes & Posner, 1987).

Building Effective Relationships with Peers

Recognizing Common Interests and Goals
Understanding Peers' Tasks, Problems, and Rewards
Practicing a Theory Y Attitude

The phrase *influence without authority* (Cohen & Bradford, 1990) captures a key element of the work life of increasing numbers of individuals. More and more people are finding that their jobs require them to influence others despite having no formal authority over them. No man is an island, it is said, and perhaps no worker in today's organizations can survive alone. Virtually everyone needs a co-worker's assistance or resources at one time or another. Along these lines, some researchers have maintained that one of the fundamental requirements of leadership effectiveness is the ability to build strong alliances with others, and groups of peers generally wield more influence (and can get more things done) than individuals working separately (R. T. Hogan, J. Hogan, & Curphy, 1992). Similarly, investing the time and effort to develop effective relationships with peers not only has immediate dividends but also can have long-term benefits if a peer ends up in a position of power in the future. Many times, leaders are selected from among the members of a group, committee, club, or team, and having previously spent time developing a friendly rather than an antagonistic relationship with other work group members will lay the groundwork for building effective relationships with superiors and becoming a member of superiors' in-groups. Given the benefits of strong relationships with peers, the following are a few ideas about how to establish and maintain good peer relationships.

Recognizing Common Interests and Goals

Although Chapters 7 through 11 described a variety of ways people vary, one of the best ways to establish effective working relationships with peers is to acknowledge shared interests, values, goals, and expectations (Cohen & Bradford, 1990). In order to acknowledge shared aspirations and interests, however, one must know what peers' goals, values, and interests actually are. Establishing informal communication links is one of the best ways to discover common interests and values. To do so, one needs to be open and honest in communicating one's own needs, values, and goals, as well as being willing to acknowledge others' needs, aspirations, and interests. Little can destroy a relationship with peers more quickly than a person who is overly willing to share his own problems and beliefs but unwilling to listen to others' ideas about the same issues. Moreover, although some people believe that participating in social gatherings, parties, committee meetings, lunches, company sport teams, or community activities can be a waste of time, peers with considerable referent power often see such activities as opportunities to establish and improve relationships with others. Thus, an effective way to establish relationships with other members of a team, committee, or organization is to meet with them in contexts outside of normal working relationships.

Understanding Peers' Tasks, Problems, and Rewards

Few things reinforce respect between co-workers better than understanding the nature of each other's work. Building a cooperative relationship with others depends, therefore, on knowing the sorts of tasks others perform in the organization. It also depends on understanding what their problems and rewards are. With the former, one of the best ways to establish strong relationships is by lending a hand whenever peers face personal or organizational problems. With the latter, it is especially important to remember that people tend to repeat those behaviors that are rewarded and are less likely to repeat behaviors that go unrewarded. A person's counterproductive or negative behaviors may be due less to his personal characteristics (e.g., "He is just uncooperative") than to the way his rewards are structured. For example, a teacher may be less likely to share successful classroom exercises with others if teachers are awarded merit pay on the basis of classroom effectiveness. To secure cooperation from others, it helps to know which situational factors reinforce both positive and negative behaviors in others (Cohen & Bradford, 1990). By better understanding the situation facing others, people can determine whether their own positive feedback (or lack thereof) is contributing to, or hindering the establishment of, effective relationships with peers. People should not underestimate the power of their own sincere encouragement, thanks, and compliments in positively influencing the behavior of their colleagues.

Practicing a Theory Y Attitude

Another way to build effective working relationships with peers is to view them from a Theory Y perspective (see Chapter 7). When a person assumes that others are competent, trustworthy, willing to cooperate if they can, and proud of their work, peers will look on that person in the same light. Even if one practices a Theory Y attitude, however, it may still be difficult to get along with a few co-workers. In such cases, it is easy to become preoccupied with the qualities one dislikes. This should be resisted as much as possible. A vicious cycle can develop in which people become enemies, putting more and more energy into criticizing each other or making the other person look bad than into doing constructive work on the task at hand. The costs of severely strained relationships also can extend beyond the individual parties involved. Cliques, or sides, can develop among other co-workers as well, which can impair the larger group's effectiveness. The point here is not to overlook interpersonal problems, but rather to not let the problems get out of hand.

Practicing Theory Y does **not** mean looking at the world through rose-colored glasses, but it *does* mean recognizing someone else's strengths as well as weaknesses. Nevertheless, sometimes peers will be assigned to work on a task together when they don't get along with each other, and the advice "Practice a Theory Y attitude" may seem too idealistic. At such times, it is important to decide whether to focus energy first on improving the relationship (before addressing the task) or to focus it solely on the task (essentially ignoring the problem in the relationship).

Cohen and Bradford (1990) suggested several guidelines for resolving this problem. They said it is best to work on the task if there is little animosity between the parties, if success can be achieved despite existing animosities, if group norms inhibit openness, if success on the task will improve the feelings between the parties, if the other person handles directness poorly, or if you handle directness poorly. Conversely, they said it is best to work on the relationship if there is great animosity between the parties, if negative feelings make task success unlikely, if group norms favor openness, if feelings between the parties are not likely to improve even with success on the task, if the other person handles directness well, *and* if you handle directness well.

Setting Goals

Goals Should Be Specific and Observable
Goals Should Be Attainable but Challenging
Goals Require Commitment
Goals Require Feedback

The Roman philosopher Seneca wrote, "When a man does not know what harbor he is making for, no wind is the right wind." Setting goals and developing plans of action to attain them are important for individuals and for groups. For example, the purpose or goal is often the predominant norm in any group. Once group goals are agreed on, they serve to induce member compliance, act as a criterion for evaluating the leadership potential of group members, and become the criteria for evaluating group performance (Bass, 1990).

Perhaps the most important step in accomplishing a personal or group goal is stating it right in the first place. The reason many people become frustrated with the outcomes of their New Year's resolutions is not because of any character flaw on their part (e.g., "I don't have any willpower"), but because their resolutions are so vague or unrealistic that they are unlikely to ever lead to demonstrable results. It is possible to keep New Year's resolutions, but one must set them intelligently. In a more general sense, some ways of writing goal statements increase the likelihood that someone will successfully achieve the desired goals. Goals should be specific and observable, attainable and challenging, based on top-to-bottom commitment, and designed to provide feedback to personnel about their progress toward them. The following is a more detailed discussion of each of these points.

Goals Should Be Specific and Observable

As described in Chapter 14, research provides strong support for the idea that specific goals lead to higher levels of effort and performance than general goals. General goals do not work as well because they often do not provide enough information regarding which particular behaviors are to be changed or when a clear end-state has been attained. This may be easiest to see with a personal example.

Assume that a student is not satisfied with her academic performance and wants to do something about it. She might set a very general goal, such as "I will do my best next year" or "I will do better in school next year." At first, such a goal may seem fine; after all, as long as she is motivated to do well, what more would be needed? However, on further thought you can see that "do my best" or "do better" are so ambiguous as to be unhelpful in directing her behavior and ultimately assessing her success. General goals have relatively little impact on energizing and directing immediate behavior, and they make it difficult to assess, in the end, whether someone has attained them or not. A better goal statement for this student would be, for example, to attain a B average or to get no deficient grades this semester. Specific goals like these make it easier to chart one's progress. A more business-oriented example might deal with improving productivity at work. Specific goal statements in this case might include a 20 percent increase in the number of products being produced by the work unit over the next three months or a 40 percent decrease in the number of products being returned by quality control next year.

The idea of having specific goals is closely related to that of having observable goals. It should be clear to everyone when the goal has or has not been reached. It is easy to say your goal is to go on a diet, but a much better goal is "to lose 10 pounds by March." Similarly, it is easy to say the team should do better next season, but a better goal is to say the team will win more than half of next season's games. It is important to note that specific, observable goals are also time limited. Without time limits for accomplishing goals, there would be little urgency associated with them. Neither would there be a finite point at which it is clear a person or group has or has not accomplished the goals. For example, it is better to set a goal of improving the next quarter's sales figures than just improving sales.

Goals Should Be Attainable but Challenging

Some people seem to treat goals as a sort of loyalty oath they must pass, as if it would be a break with one's ideals or be a reflection of insufficient motivation if any but the loftiest, highest goals were set for oneself or one's organization. Yet to be useful, goals must be realistic. The struggling high school student who sets a goal of getting into Harvard may be unrealistic; but it may be realistic to set a goal of getting into the local state university. A civil rights activist may *wish* to eliminate prejudice completely, but a more attainable goal might be to eliminate racial discrimination in the local housing project over the next five years. A track team is not likely to win every race, but it may be realistic to aim to win the league championship.

The corollary to the preceding point is that goals should also be challenging. If goals merely needed to be attainable, then there would be nothing wrong with setting goals so easy that accomplishing them would be virtually guaranteed. As we have seen previously, setting easy goals does not result in high levels of performance; higher levels of performance come about when goals stretch and inspire people toward doing more than they thought they could. Goals need to be challenging but attainable to get the best out of oneself and others.

Goals Require Commitment

There is nothing magical about having goals; having goals per se does not guarantee success. Unless supported by real human commitment, goal statements are mere words. Organizational goals are most likely to be achieved if there is commitment to them at both the top and the bottom of the organization. Top leadership needs to make clear that it is willing to put its money where its mouth is. When top leadership sets goals, it should provide the resources workers need to achieve the goals and then should reward those who do. Subordinates often become committed to goals simply by seeing the sincere and enthusiastic commitment of top leadership to them. Another way to build subordinate acceptance and commitment to goals is to have subordinates participate in setting the goals in the first place. Research on the effects of goal setting demonstrates that worker acceptance and satisfaction tend to increase when workers are allowed to participate in setting goals (Erez, Earley, & Hulin, 1985; Locke, Latham, & Erez, 1987).

On the other hand, research is less conclusive about whether participation in goal setting actually increases performance or productivity. These mixed findings about participation and performance may be due to various qualities of the group and the leader. In terms of the group, groupthink may cause highly cohesive groups to commit to goals that are unrealistic and unachievable. Group members may not have realistically considered equipment or resource constraints, nor have the technical skills needed to successfully accomplish the goal. In addition, group members may not have any special enthusiasm for accomplishing a goal if the leader is perceived to have little expert power or is unsupportive, curt, or inept (House, 1984; Latham & Lee, 1986; Locke, Latham, & Erez, 1987). However, if leaders are perceived to be competent and supportive, then followers may have as much goal commitment as they would if they had participated in setting the goal. Thus, participation in goal setting often leads to higher levels of commitment and performance if the leader is perceived to be incompetent, but it will not necessarily lead to greater commitment and performance than is achieved when a competent leader assigns a goal. Again, these findings lend credence to the importance of technical competence in leadership effectiveness.

Goals Require Feedback

One of the most effective ways to improve any kind of performance is to provide feedback about how closely a person's behavior matches some criterion, and research shows that performance was much higher when goals were accompanied by feedback than when either goals or feedback were used alone. Goals that are specific, observable, and time limited are conducive to ongoing assessment and performance-based feedback, and leaders and followers should strive to provide and/or seek feedback on a fairly regular basis. Moreover, people should seek feedback from a variety of sources or provide feedback using a variety of criteria. Often, different sources and criteria can paint very different pictures about goal progress, and people can get a better idea of the true level of their progress by examining the information provided and integrating it across the different sources and criteria.

Punishment

Myths Surrounding the Use of Punishment
Punishment, Satisfaction, and Performance
Administering Punishment

In an ideal world, perhaps everyone would be dependable, achievement oriented, and committed to the organization's goals. The fact is, however, that leaders sometimes will need to deal with followers who are openly hostile or insubordinate, create conflicts among co-workers, do not work up to standards, or openly violate important rules or policies. In such cases leaders may need to administer punishment to change the follower's behavior.

Of all of the different aspects of leadership, few are as controversial as punishment. Some of the primary reasons for this controversy stem from myths surrounding the use of punishment, as well as the lack of knowledge regarding the effects of punishment on followers' motivation, satisfaction, and performance. This section is designed to shed light on the punishment controversy by (*a*) addressing several myths about the use of punishment, (*b*) reviewing research findings concerning the relationships between punishment and various organizational variables, and (*c*) providing leadership practitioners with advice on how to properly administer punishment.

Myths Affecting the Use of Punishment

We should begin by repeating the definition of punishment stated earlier in the book. Punishment is the administration of an aversive event or the withdrawal of a positive event or stimulus, which in turn *decreases* the likelihood a particular behavior will be repeated (Arvey & Ivancevich, 1980). Examples of punishment might include verbal reprimands, being moved to a less prestigious office, having pay docked, being fired, being made to run several laps around the athletic field, or losing eligibility for a sport entirely. We should note that according to this definition, only those aversive events administered on a contingent basis are considered to be forms of punishment; aversive events administered on a noncontingent basis may constitute harsh and abusive treatment but are not punishment. Additionally, punishment appears to be in the eye of the beholder; aversive events that effectively change the direction, intensity, or persistence of one follower's behavior may have no effect on another's (Curphy, Gibson, Asiu, McCown, & Brown, 1992). It is even possible that some followers may find the administration of a noxious event or the removal of a positive event to be reinforcing. For example, it is not uncommon for some children to misbehave if that increases the attention they receive from parents, even if the latter's behavior outwardly may seem punishing to others. (To the children, some parental attention of any kind may be preferable to no attention.) Similarly, some followers may see the verbal reprimands and notoriety they receive by being insubordinate or violating company policies as forms of attention. Because these followers enjoy being the center of attention, they may find this notoriety rewarding. From an operant perspective, they may be even more likely to be insubordinate in the future.

We will examine four myths surrounding the use of punishment. Three of these myths were reviewed by Arvey and Ivancevich (1980) and included beliefs that the use of punishment resulted in undesirable emotional side effects on the part of the recipient, was unethical and inhumane, and rarely worked anyway (i.e., seldom eliminated the undesirable behavior).

B. F. Skinner's (1938) work in behavioral psychology lent support to the idea that punishment was ineffective and caused undesirable side effects. He based his conclusions on the unnatural behaviors manifested by rats and pigeons punished in various conditioning experiments. Despite the dangers of generalizing from the behavior of rats to humans, many people accepted Skinner's contention that punishment was a futile and typically counterproductive tool for controlling human behavior. This was so despite the fact that considerable research regarding the emotional effects of punishment on humans did not support Skinner's claim (Kazdin, 1975; Johnston, 1972; Solomon, 1964). Parke (1972), for example, suggested that undesirable emotional side effects of punishment might occur only when punishment was administered indiscriminately or was particularly harsh.

With respect to the myth that punishment is unethical or inhumane, Arvey and Ivancevich (1980) maintained there is an ethical distinction between "future-oriented" and "past-oriented" punishment. Future-oriented punishment, intended to help improve behavior, may be effective in diminishing or eliminating undesirable behavior. Past-oriented punishment, or what we commonly think of as retribution, on the other hand, is simply a payback for past misdeeds. This sort of punishment may be more questionable ethically, especially when it is intended *only* as payback and not, say, as deterrent to others. Moreover, when considering the ethics of administering punishment, one must also consider the ethics of *failing* to administer punishment. The costs of *failing* to punish a potentially harmful behavior, such as unsafe workplace practices, may far outweigh those associated with the punishment itself (Arvey & Ivancevich, 1980).

A third myth concerns the efficacy of punishment. Skinner (1938, 1985), and more recently Campbell (1977) and Luthans (1989), claimed that punishment did not result in a permanent behavior change but instead only temporarily suppressed behavior. Evidence to support this claim was found by Huberman (1964), who reported that incarcerated prisoners had a recidivism rate of 85 percent. However, this high recidivism rate may be due to the fact that criminals may have received punishment primarily for retribution rather than for corrective purposes. Judicious administration of sanctions, combined with advice about how to avoid punishment in the future, may successfully eliminate undesirable behaviors on a more permanent basis (Arvey & Ivancevich, 1980). Furthermore, it may be a moot point to argue (as Skinner did) that punishment only temporarily suppresses behavior; so long as sanctions for misdeeds remain in place, their impact on behavior should continue. In that regard, it's relevant to note that the "temporary" effects of punishment on behavior are no different from the "temporary" effects of reinforcement on behavior.

Punishment, Satisfaction, and Performance

It appears that properly administered punishment does not cause undesirable emotional side effects, is not unethical, and may effectively suppress undesirable behavior. However, we also should ask what effect punishment has on followers' satisfaction and performance. Most people probably would predict that leaders who use punishment more frequently will probably have less-satisfied and lower-performing followers. Interestingly, this does not appear to be the case—at least when punishment is used appropriately. Let us look a little more closely at this issue.

Several researchers have looked at whether leaders who administer punishment on a contingent basis also administered rewards on a contingent basis. Generally, researchers have found that there is a moderate positive relationship between leaders' contingent reward behaviors and contingent punishment behaviors (Arvey, Davis, & Nelson, 1984; Podsakoff & Todor, 1985; Strasser, Dailey, & Bateman, 1981). There also are consistently strong negative correlations found between leaders' contingent reward and noncontingent punishment behaviors. Thus, leaders meting out rewards on a contingent basis were also more likely to administer punishment only when followers behaved inappropriately or were not performing up to standards.

Keller and Szilagyi (1976, 1978) maintained that punishment can serve several constructive organizational purposes. They said it can help clarify roles and expectations, as well as reduce role ambiguity. Several other authors have found contingent punishment either was unrelated to followers' satisfaction with their supervisor ratings or had a low positive relationship with it (Arvey, Davis, & Nelson, 1984; Podsakoff, Todor, Grover, & Huber, 1984). In other words, leaders who follow certain rules in administering punishment need not have dissatisfied subordinates. As a matter of fact, judicious and appropriate use of punishment by leaders may result in somewhat *higher* satisfaction of followers overall. These findings make sense when the entire work unit is considered; failing to use punishment when it seems called for in most followers' eyes may lead to perceptions of inequity, which may in turn lead to lower group cohesiveness and satisfaction (Curphy et al., 1992; Dobbins & Russell, 1986).

With respect to followers' work behaviors, Arvey and Jones (1985) reported that punishment has generally been found to reduce absenteeism and tardiness rates. Nevertheless, the evidence about punishment's impact on performance appears mixed. Some authors report a strong positive relationship between punishment and performance (Beyer & Trice, 1984; Katz, Maccoby, Gurin, & Floor, 1951; Podsakoff & Todor, 1985; Schnake, 1986), whereas others found either no relationship between punishment and performance or a negative one (Curphy et al., 1992; Curtis, Smith, & Smoll, 1979).

Despite such mixed findings, there are several points about the relationship between punishment and performance findings still worth noting. First, the level of punishment as well as the manner in which it was administered across studies could have differed dramatically, and these factors could have affected the results. Second, of the studies reporting positive results, Schnake's (1986) experiment of the vicarious effects of punishment is by far the most provocative. Schnake hired college students for a temporary job, and after several hours at work, publicly reduced the pay or threatened to reduce the pay of a confederate in the work group. As predicted, the more severe the punishment witnessed (either the threat of reduced pay or the reduction of pay), the higher the subsequent performance of other work-group members.

Although these findings demonstrated that merely witnessing rather than receiving punishment could result in increased performance, these results should be interpreted with some caution. Because most of the individuals in the experiment did not know each other and had only been working together for several hours, there was probably not enough time for group cohesiveness or norms to develop. It is not at all clear whether members of cohesive groups or groups with strong norms would react in the same way if they had observed another group member being punished (Curphy et al., 1992).

Third, of the studies reporting less favorable punishment-performance results, the Curtis, Smith, and Smoll (1979) study made an important point about the opportunities to punish. Curtis, Smith, and Smoll examined the relationships between Little League coaches' behaviors and their teams' win–loss records. They found coaches who punished more often had less-successful teams. These coaches also, however, had less-talented players and therefore had many more opportunities to use punishment. Coaches of successful teams had little if any reason to use punishment. Fourth, many behaviors that do get punished may not have a direct link to job performance. For example, being insubordinate, violating company dress codes, and arriving late to meetings are all punishable behaviors that may not be directly linked to solving work-related problems or producing goods or services.

Finally, almost all these studies implicitly assumed punishment enhanced performance (by correcting problem behaviors), but Curphy et al. (1992) were the only researchers who actually tested this assumption. Curphy et al. collected over 4,500 incidents of documented punishment and performance data from 40 identical organizations over a three-month period. (The punishment and performance data were collected monthly.) They found that low performance led to higher levels of punishment. Moreover, they found that inexperienced leaders administered almost twice as much punishment as experienced leaders. The authors hypothesized that inexperienced leaders used punishment (i.e., relied on their coercive power) more frequently because by being the newest arrivals to the organization, they lacked knowledge of the organizational norms, rules, and policies (i.e., expert power); had not yet established relationships with followers (i.e., referent power); and were severely limited in the rewards they could provide to followers (i.e., reward power).

In summary, the research evidence shows that punishment can lead to positive organizational outcomes if administered properly. When administered on a contingent basis, it may help increase job satisfaction; may decrease role ambiguity and absenteeism rates; and depending on the behaviors being punished, may have a positive effect on performance. However, administering intense levels of punishment in a noncontingent or capricious manner can have a devastating effect on the work unit. Group cohesiveness may suffer, followers are likely to become more dissatisfied and less apt to come to work, and they may perform at a lower level in the long term. Thus, learning how to properly administer punishment may be the key to maximizing the benefits associated with its use.

Administering Punishment

Usually, leaders administer punishment in order to rectify some type of behavioral or performance problem at work. However, not every behavior or performance problem is punished, and leaders probably weigh several different factors before deciding whether or not to administer punishment. Green and Mitchell (1979) maintained that leaders' decisions concerning punishment depended on whether leaders made internal or external attributions about a subordinate's substandard performance. Leaders making internal attributions were more likely to administer punishment; leaders making external attributions were more likely to blame the substandard performance on situational factors beyond the follower's control.

Attribution theory (Mitchell, Green, & Wood, 1981; Mitchell & Wood, 1980) maintains that leaders weigh three factors when making internal or external attributions about a follower's substandard performance. More specifically, leaders would be more likely to make an internal attribution about a follower's substandard performance (and administer punishment) if the follower had previously completed the task before, if other followers had successfully completed the task, and if the follower had successfully completed other tasks in the past. Moreover, Mitchell, Green, and Wood (1981) and Mitchell and Wood (1980) reported that leaders were biased toward making internal attributions about followers' poor performance (i.e., the fundamental attribution error) and thus more likely to use punishment to modify a follower's behavior.

Because leaders are biased toward making internal attributions about followers' substandard performance, leaders can administer punishment more effectively by being aware of this bias and getting as many facts as possible *before* deciding whether or not to administer punishment. Leaders also can improve the manner or skill with which they administer punishment by using tips provided by Arvey and Ivancevich (1980), who said punishment is administered most effectively when it focuses on the act, not the person. Followers probably cannot change their personalities, values, or preferences, but they can change their behaviors. By focusing on specific behaviors, leaders minimize the threat to followers' self-concepts. Also, punishment needs to be consistent across *both* behaviors and leaders; the same actions need to have the same consequences across work groups, or feelings of inequity and favoritism will pervade the organization. One way to increase the consistency in punishment is through the establishment of clearly specified organizational policies and procedures.

Administering punishment properly depends on effective two-way communication between the leader and follower. Leaders need to provide a clear rationale for punishment and indicate the consequences for unacceptable behavior in the future. Finally, leaders need to provide followers with guidance about how to improve. This guidance may entail role-modeling proper behaviors for followers, suggesting followers take additional training courses, or just giving followers accurate feedback about their behavior at work (Arvey & Ivancevich, 1980).

Overall, it may be the manner in which punishment is administered, rather than the level of punishment, that has the greatest effect on followers' satisfaction and performance. Leaders need to realize that they may be biased toward administering punishment to rectify followers' substandard performance, and the best way to get around this bias is to collect as much information as possible before deciding whether or not to punish. By collecting the facts, leaders will be better able to focus on the act, not the person; be able to administer a punishment consistent with company policy; provide the rationale for the punishment; and give guidance to followers on how to improve.

A final caution which leaders need to be aware of concerns the reinforcing or rewarding nature of punishment. As stated earlier in the discussion of the operant approach to motivation, behaviors that are rewarded are likely to be repeated. When leaders administer punishment and subsequently see improvement in a follower's behavior, the leader will be rewarded and be more apt to use punishment in the future. Over time, this may lead to an overreliance on punishment and an underemphasis of the other motivational strategies as the means for correcting performance problems. Again, by collecting as much information as possible and by carefully considering the applicability of goal setting, the operant approach, job characteristics theory, and so on, to the problem, leaders may be able to successfully avoid having only one tool in their motivational tool kit.

Conducting Meetings

Determine whether It Is Necessary

List the Objectives

Stick to the Agenda

Provide Pertinent Materials in Advance

Make It Convenient

Encourage Participation

Keep a Record

Meetings are a fact of organizational life. It is difficult to imagine a leader who could (or should) avoid them, particularly when groups, committees, or teams have high levels of task or lateral interdependence. Well-planned and well-led meetings are a valuable mechanism for accomplishing diverse goals and are an important way of exchanging information and keeping open lines of communication within and between work groups or volunteer organizations (Bass, 1990; O'Reilly, 1977). Although meetings have many advantages, they also cost time and money. The annual cost of meetings in the corporate sector alone may well be in the billions of dollars. Furthermore, unnecessary or inefficient meetings can be frustrating and are often a source of dissatisfaction for participants. Given the investment of time and energy meetings require, leaders have a responsibility to make them as productive as possible. Guth and Shaw (1980) provided seven helpful tips for running meetings, which follow.

Determine whether It Is Necessary

Perhaps the most important step in conducting a meeting is to take the time to *determine whether or not a meeting is really necessary.* If you are evaluating whether or not to have a meeting, assess what it can accomplish. Have a meeting only if the potential benefits outweigh the costs. As part of this process, get the opinions of the other participants beforehand if that is possible. Moreover, if meetings are regularly scheduled, then you should have significant business to conduct in each meeting. If not, then these meetings should probably be scheduled less frequently.

List the Objectives

Once you have decided that a meeting is necessary, you should then *list your objectives for the meeting and develop a plan for attaining them* in an orderly manner. Prioritize what you hope to accomplish at the meeting. It is often helpful to indicate approximately how much time will be spent on each agenda item. Finally, get the agenda and issues to be covered to the participants well in advance; also let them know who else will be attending.

Stick to the Agenda

Once the meeting gets started, is it important for leaders to *stick to the agenda.* It is easy for groups to get sidetracked by tangential issues or good-natured story-telling. Although you should try to keep a cooperative and comfortable climate in the meeting, it is better to err on the side of being organized and businesslike than being lax and laissez-faire. If items were important enough to put on the agenda, they are important enough to get to in the time allotted for the meeting.

Provide Pertinent Materials in Advance

Besides an agenda, a meeting is often more effective if leaders also provide the other participants with *pertinent reports or support materials well in advance.* Passing out materials and waiting for people to read them at the meeting itself wastes valuable time. Most people will come prepared, having read relevant material beforehand, if you have given it to them, and almost everyone will resent making a meeting longer than necessary doing work that could and should have been done earlier. In a similar vein, prepare well in advance for any presentations you will make. If you did not provide reports before the meeting, then it is often helpful to provide an outline of your presentation for others to take notes on. Finally, of course, be sure the information you pass out is accurate.

Make It Convenient

Another way to maximize the benefits of meetings is to *pick a time and place as convenient as possible for all participants.* Besides maximizing attendance, this will also keep key participants from being distracted with thoughts of other pressing issues. Similarly, choose a place that is convenient for the participants and suitable for the nature of the meeting. Be sure to consider whether you need such things as a table for the meeting (that has adequate seating); a blackboard, an overhead projector, or similar audiovisual aids; coffee or other refreshments; and directions on how to find the meeting place. And start on time; waiting for stragglers is unfair to those who were punctual, and it sends the wrong signal about the seriousness of the meeting. Also plan and announce a time limit on the meeting beforehand and stick to it.

Encourage Participation

Leaders have a responsibility to *encourage participation;* everyone at the meeting should have an opportunity to be heard and should feel some ownership in the meeting's outcome. In some cases, you may need to solicit participation from quieter participants at the meeting, as these members often make valuable contributions to the group when given the chance. Furthermore, ensuring that the quieter members participate will also help you to avoid interpreting someone's quietness as implied consent or agreement. By the same token, you sometimes may need to curtail the participation of more verbal and outspoken participants. You can do this respectfully by merely indicating that the group has a good idea of their position and that it would be useful also to hear from some others. You also help encourage relevant participation by providing interim summaries of the group's discussion.

Keep a Record

During a meeting, the points of discussion and various decisions or actions taken may seem clear to you. However, do not trust your memory to preserve them all. *Take minutes for the record* so you and others can reconstruct what the participants were thinking and why you did or did not take some action. Record decisions and actions to be taken, including *who* will be responsible for doing it and *when* it is supposed to be accomplished. Such records are also very useful for preparing future meeting agendas.

By following the preceding simple steps, both leaders and followers are likely to get much more out of their meetings, as well as appear well organized and effective.

ADVANCED LEADERSHIP SKILLS

Delegating

Why Delegating Is Important
Common Reasons for Avoiding Delegation
Principles of Effective Delegation

Although delegation is a relatively simple way for leaders to free themselves of time-consuming chores; provide followers with developmental opportunities; and increase the number of tasks accomplished by the work group, team, or committee, delegation is often an overlooked and underused management option (Bass, 1990; Leana, 1986). Delegation implies that one has been empowered by one's leader, boss, or coach to take responsibility for completing certain tasks or engaging in certain activities (Bass, 1990). Delegation gives the responsibility for decisions to those individuals most likely to be affected by or to implement the decision, and delegation is more concerned with autonomy, responsibility, and follower development than with participation (Leana, 1987).

Research has shown that leaders who delegate authority more frequently often have higher-performing businesses (Miller & Toulouse, 1986), but followers are not necessarily happier when their leaders frequently delegate tasks (Stogdill & Shartle, 1955). Bass (1990) maintained that the latter findings were due to subordinates who felt they were (*a*) not delegated the authority needed to accomplish delegated tasks, (*b*) monitored too closely, or (*c*) only delegated tasks leaders did not want to do. Nevertheless, Wilcox (1982) showed that leaders who delegated skillfully had more satisfied followers than leaders who did not delegate well. Because leaders who delegate skillfully often have more satisfied and higher-performing work groups, teams, or committees, the following suggestions from Taylor (1989) are provided to help leadership practitioners delegate more effectively and successfully. Taylor provided useful ideas about why delegating is important, common reasons for avoiding delegation, and principles of effective delegation.

Why Delegating Is Important

Delegation Frees Time for Other Activities.   The essence of leadership is achieving goals through others, not trying to accomplish them by oneself. Learning to think like a leader partly involves developing a frame of mind wherein one thinks in terms of the whole group's or organization's capabilities and not just one's own. This requires a new frame of reference for many individuals, especially those whose past successes resulted primarily from personal achievement in interpersonally competitive situations. Still, leaders typically have so many different responsibilities they invariably must delegate some of them to others.

It is not just the mere quantity of work that makes delegation necessary. There is a qualitative aspect, too. Because leaders determine what responsibilities will be delegated, the process is one by which leaders can ensure that their time is allocated most judiciously to meet group needs. The leader's time is a precious commodity that should be invested wisely in those activities for which the leader is uniquely suited or situated to accomplish and that will provide the greatest long-term benefits to the group. What the leader *can* delegate, the leader *should* delegate.

Delegation Develops Followers.   Developing subordinates is one of the most important responsibilities any leader has, and delegating significant tasks to them is one of the best ways to support their growth. It does so by providing opportunities for initiative, problem solving, innovation, administration, and decision making. By providing practical experience in a controlled fashion, delegation allows subordinates the best training experience of all: learning by doing.

Delegation Strengthens the Organization.   Delegation is an important way to develop individual subordinates, but doing so also strengthens the entire organization. For one thing, an organization that uses delegation skillfully will be a motivating one to work in. Delegation sends an organizational signal that subordinates are trusted and their development is important. Moreover, skillful delegation inherently tends to increase the significance and satisfaction levels of most jobs, thus making subordinates' jobs better. Delegation also can be seen as a way of developing the entire organization, not just the individuals within it. To the extent that a whole organization systematically develops its personnel using delegation, its overall experience level, capability, and vitality increase. Finally, delegation stimulates innovation and generates fresh ideas and new approaches throughout the whole organization.

Common Reasons for Avoiding Delegation

Delegation Takes Too Much Time.   Delegation saves time for the leader in the long run, but it costs time for the leader in the short run. It takes time to train a subordinate to perform any new task, so it often really does take less time for a leader to do the task herself than to put in the effort to train someone else to do it. When a task is a recurring or repetitive one, however, the long-term savings will make the additional effort in initial training worth it—both for the leader and for the subordinate.

Delegation Is Risky.   It can feel threatening to delegate a significant responsibility to another person because doing so reduces direct personal control over the work one will be judged by (Dewhirst, Metts, & Ladd, 1987). Delegation may be perceived as a career risk by staking one's own reputation on the motivation, skill, and performance of others. It is the essence of leadership, though, that the leader will be evaluated in part by the success of the entire team. Furthermore, delegation need not and should not involve a complete loss of control by the leader over work delegated to others. The leader has a responsibility to set performance expectations, ensure that the task is understood and accepted, provide training, and regularly monitor the status of all delegated tasks and responsibilities (Bass, 1990).

The Job Will Not Be Done as Well.   Often the leader can do many specific tasks or jobs better than anyone else. That is not surprising, as the leader is often the most experienced person in the group. This fact, however, can become an obstacle to delegation. The leader may rationalize not delegating a task to someone else because the follower lacks technical competence and the job would subsequently suffer (Dewhirst, Metts, & Ladd, 1987). However, this may be true only in the short term, and letting subordinates make a few mistakes is a necessary part of their development, just as it was for the leader at an earlier stage in her own development. Few things are likely to be so stifling to an organization as a leader's perfectionistic fear of mistakes. When thinking about delegating tasks to others, leaders should remember what their own skill levels used to be, not what they are now. Leaders should assess subordinates' readiness to handle new responsibilities in terms of the former, not the latter.

The Task Is a Desirable One.   A leader may resist delegating tasks that are a source of power or prestige. He may be quite willing to delegate relatively unimportant responsibilities but may balk at the prospect of delegating a significant one having high visibility (Bass, 1990; Dewhirst, Metts, & Ladd, 1987). The greater the importance and visibility of the delegated task, though, the greater will be the potential developmental gains for the subordinate. Furthermore, actions always speak louder than words, and nothing conveys trust more genuinely than a leader's willingness to delegate major responsibilities to subordinates.

Others Are Already Too Busy.   A leader may feel guilty about increasing a subordinate's already full workload. It is the leader's responsibility, though, to continually review the relative priority of all the tasks performed across the organization. Such a review might identify existing activities that could be eliminated, modified, or reassigned. A discussion with the subordinate about her workload and career goals would be a better basis for a decision than an arbitrary and unilateral determination by the leader that the subordinate could not handle more work. The new responsibility could well be something the subordinate wants and needs, and she might also have some helpful ideas about alternative ways to manage her present duties.

Principles of Effective Delegation

Decide What to Delegate. The first step leaders should take when deciding what to delegate is to identify all of their present activities. This should include those functions regularly performed and decisions regularly made. Next, leaders should estimate the actual time spent on these activities. This can be done fairly easily by developing and maintaining a temporary log. After collecting this information, leaders need to assess whether each activity justifies the time they are spending on it. In all likelihood, at least some of the most time-consuming recurring activities should be delegated to others. This process will probably also identify some activities that could be done more efficiently (either by the leader or someone else) and other activities that provide so little benefit they could be eliminated completely.

Decide Whom to Delegate To. There might be one individual whose talent and experience makes her the logical best choice for any assignment. However, leaders must be careful not to overburden someone merely because that individual always happens to be the best worker. Additionally, leaders have a responsibility to balance developmental opportunities among all their followers. Leaders should look for ways to optimize, over a series of assignments, the growth of all subordinates by matching particular opportunities to their respective individual needs, skills, and goals.

Make the Assignment Clear and Specific. As with setting goals, leaders delegating an assignment must be sure the subordinate understands just what the task involves and what is expected of him. Nevertheless, at times leaders provide too brief an explanation of the task to be delegated. A common communication error is overestimating one's own clarity, and in the case of delegation this can happen when the leader already knows the ins and outs of the particular task. Some of the essential steps or potential pitfalls in an assignment that seem self-evident to the leader may not be as obvious to someone who has never done the assignment before. Leaders should welcome questions and provide a complete explanation of the task. The time leaders invest during this initial training will pay dividends later on. When giving an assignment, leaders should ensure that they cover all of the points listed in Highlight D–1.

Assign an Objective, Not a Procedure. Indicate what is to be accomplished, not *how* the task is to be accomplished. End results are usually more important

Highlight D–1

Points to Cover When Delegating a Task

How does the task relate to organizational goals?

When does the subordinate's responsibility for the task begin?

How has the task been accomplished in the past?

What problems were encountered with the task in the past?

What sources of help are available?

What unusual situations might arise in the future?

What are the limits of the subordinate's authority?

How will the leader monitor the task (e.g., provide feedback)?

Finally, in covering the above points, always convey high confidence and expectations.

---

than the methods. It is helpful to demonstrate procedures that have worked before, but not to specify rigid methods to follow in the future. Leaders should not assume their ways always were and always will be best. Leaders need to be clear about the criteria by which success will be measured, but allowing subordinates to achieve it in their own ways will increase their satisfaction and encourage fresh ideas.

Allow Autonomy, but Monitor Performance.   Effective delegation is neither micromanagement of everything the subordinate does nor laissez-faire indifference toward the subordinate's performance. Leaders need to give subordinates a degree of autonomy (as well as time, resources, and authority) in carrying out their new responsibilities, and this includes the freedom to make certain kinds of mistakes. An organizational climate where mistakes are punished suppresses initiative and innovation. Furthermore, mistakes are important sources of development. Knowing this, one wise executive reassured a subordinate who expected to be fired for a gigantic mistake by saying, "Why should I fire you when I've just invested $100,000 in your development?" (McCall, Lombardo, & Morrison, 1988, p. 154).

Once a task has been delegated, even though the subordinate's training and development are continuing, the leader should be cautious about providing too much unsolicited advice or engaging in "rescue" activities. An exception would be when a subordinate's mistake would put significant organizational assets at risk. On the other hand, the leader needs to establish specific procedures for periodically reviewing the subordinate's performance of the delegated task. Leaders need to maintain good records of all the assignments they have delegated, including appropriate milestone and completion dates for each one.

Give Credit, Not Blame. Whenever leaders delegate, they must give subordinates *authority* along with responsibility. In the final analysis, however, leaders always remain fully responsible and accountable for any delegated task. If things should go wrong, then *leaders* should accept responsibility for failure fully and completely and never try to pass blame on to subordinates. On the other hand, if things go well, as they usually will, then leaders should give all the public credit to the subordinates. Also, when providing performance feedback privately to a subordinate, emphasize what went right rather than what went wrong. Leaders should not ignore errors in judgment or implementation, but they need not dwell on them, either. One helpful approach to performance feedback is called the sandwich technique. With this technique, negative feedback is placed in between two "pieces" of positive feedback. It affirms the subordinate's good work, puts the subordinate at least somewhat at ease, and keeps the ratio of positive and negative comments in balance. The idea of a sandwich, however, should not be taken too literally. There is nothing magical about two pieces of positive feedback for one piece of negative feedback. In fact, from the receiver's point of view the balance between positive and negative feedback may seem "about right" when the ratio is considerably higher than 2:1.

In summary, Taylor (1989) has provided useful insight about the importance of delegation as well as specific and helpful suggestions for delegating more effectively.

Managing Conflict

What Is Conflict?

Is Conflict Always Bad?

Conflict Resolution Strategies

We read or hear every day in the news about various types of negotiations. Nations often negotiate with each other over land or fishing rights, trade agreements, or diplomatic relations. Land developers often negotiate with city councils for variances on local zoning laws for their projects. Businesses often spend considerable time negotiating employee salaries and fringe benefits with labor unions. In a similar fashion, negotiations go on every day about matters ranging from high school athletic schedules to where a new office copying machine will be located. In one sense, all these negotiations, big or small, are similar. In every case, representatives from different groups meet to resolve some sort of conflict. Conflict is an inevitable fact of life and an inevitable fact of leadership. Researchers have found that first-line supervisors and middle-level managers can spend more than 25 percent of their time dealing with conflict (Thomas & Schmidt, 1976), and resolving conflicts has been found to be an important factor in leadership effectiveness (Morse & Wagner, 1978). In fact, successfully resolving conflicts is so important that it is a central theme in some of the literature about organizations (Brown, 1983; Ouchi, 1981; Peters & Waterman, 1982). Moreover, successfully resolving conflicts will become an increasingly important skill as leadership and management practice moves away from authoritarian directives and toward cooperative approaches emphasizing rational persuasion, collaboration, compromise, and solutions of mutual gain.

What Is Conflict?

> There are times in life when we confront values worth fighting for. This is one such time.
>
> George Bush (before the allied attack on Iraq)
> *Time,* January 21,1991.

> Should the Americans become embroiled, we will make them swim in their own blood.
>
> Saddam Hussein (before the allied attack on Iraq)
> *Time,* January 21, 1991.

Conflict occurs when two opposing parties have interests or goals that appear to be incompatible (Robbins, 1986). There are a variety of sources of conflict in team, committee, work-group, and organizational settings. For example, conflict can occur when group or team members (*a*) have strong differences in values, beliefs, or goals; (*b*) have high levels of task or lateral interdependence; (*c*) are competing for scarce resources or rewards; (*d*) are under high levels of stress; or (*e*) face uncertain or incompatible demands (i.e., role ambiguity and role conflict) (Yukl, 1989). Conflict can also occur when leaders act in a manner inconsistent with the vision and goals they have articulated for the organization (Kets de Vries & Miller, 1984). Of these factors contributing to the level of conflict within or between groups, teams, or committees, probably the most important source of conflict is the lack of communication between parties (Thomas & Schmidt, 1976). Because many conflicts are the result of misunderstandings and communication breakdowns, leaders can minimize the level of conflict within and between groups by improving their communication and listening skills, as well as spending time networking with others (Yukl, 1989).

Before reviewing specific negotiation tips and conflict resolution strategies, it is necessary to describe several aspects of conflict that can have an impact on the resolution process. First, the size of an issue (bigger issues are more difficult to resolve), the extent to which parties define the problem egocentrically (how much they have personally invested in the problem), and the existence of hidden agendas (unstated but important concerns or objectives) can all affect the conflict resolution process. Second, seeing a conflict situation in win/lose or either/or terms restricts the (perceived) possible outcomes to either total satisfaction or total frustration. A similar but less-extreme variant is to see a situation in zero-sum terms. A zero-sum situation is one in which intermediate degrees of satisfaction are possible (i.e., not either/or), but increases in one party's satisfaction inherently decrease the other party's satisfaction, and vice versa. Still another variant can be when parties perceive a conflict as unresolvable. In such

Highlight MC–1

Possible Effects of Conflict

Possible Positive Effects of Conflict	Possible Negative Effects of Conflict
Increased effort	Reduced productivity
Feelings get aired	Decreased communication
Better understanding of others	Negative feelings
Impetus for change	Stress
Better decision making	Poorer decision making
Key issues surfaced	Decreased cooperation
Critical thinking stimulated	Political backstabbing

cases neither party gains at the expense of the other, but each continues to perceive the other as an obstacle to satisfaction (Thomas, 1976).

Is Conflict Always Bad?

So far, we have described conflict as an inherently negative aspect of any group, team, committee, or organization. This certainly was the prevailing view of conflict among researchers during the 1930s and 40s, and it probably also represents the way many people are raised today (i.e., most people have a strong value of minimizing or avoiding conflict). Today, researchers studying group effectiveness have come to a different conclusion. Some level of conflict may be helpful in order to bolster innovation and performance (Robbins, 1986). Conflict that enhances group productivity is viewed as useful, and conflict that hinders group performance is viewed as counterproductive (Robbins, 1986). Various possible positive and negative effects of conflict are listed in Highlight MC–1.

Along these lines, researchers have found that conflict can cause a radical change in political power (Bass, 1985; Weber, 1947; Willner, 1984), as well as dramatic changes in organizational structure and design, group cohesiveness, and group or organizational effectiveness (Roberts & Bradley, 1988; Kanter, 1983). Nevertheless, it is important to realize that this current conceptualization of conflict is still somewhat limited in scope. For example, increasing the level of conflict within a group or team may enhance immediate performance but may also have a disastrous effect on organizational climate and turnover. As we noted in Chapter 5, however, leaders may be evaluated in terms of many criteria, only one of which is group performance. Thus, leaders should probably use criteria such as turnover and absenteeism rates and followers' satisfaction or organizational climate ratings in addition to measures of group performance when trying to determine whether conflict is good or bad. Leaders are cautioned against

Figure MC–1

*Five Conflict-
Handling
Orientations,
Plotted
According to
Party's Desire
to Satisfy Own
and Other's
Concerns*

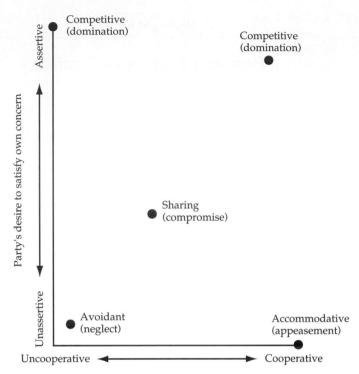

Source: K. W. Thomas, "Conflict and Conflict Management," in *Handbook of Industrial and Organizational Psychology,* ed. M. D. Dunnette (Chicago: Rand McNally, 1976. Used by permission of Marvin D. Dunnette.

using group performance alone, as these indices may not reveal the overall effects of conflict on the group or team.

Conflict Resolution Strategies

In addition to spending time understanding and clarifying positions, separating people from the problem, and focusing on interests, there are five strategies or approaches leaders can use to resolve conflicts. Perhaps the best way to differentiate between these five strategies is to think of conflict resolution in terms of two independent dimensions: cooperativeness/uncooperativeness and assertiveness/unassertiveness (see Figure MC–1). Parties in conflict do vary in their commitment to satisfy the other's concerns, but they also vary in the extent to which they assertively stand up for their own concerns (Thomas, 1976). Thus, conflict resolution can be understood in terms of how cooperative or uncooperative the parties are and how assertive or unassertive they are.

Using this two-dimension scheme, Thomas (1976) described five general approaches to managing conflict:

1. **Competition** reflects a desire to achieve one's own ends at the expense of someone else. This is domination, also known as a win–lose orientation.

2. **Accommodation** reflects a mirror image of competition, entirely giving in to someone else's concerns without making any effort to achieve one's own ends. This is a tactic of appeasement.

3. **Sharing** is an approach that represents a compromise between domination and appeasement. Both parties give up something, yet both parties get something. Both parties are moderately, but incompletely, satisfied.

4. **Collaboration** reflects an effort to fully satisfy both parties. This is a problem-solving approach that requires the integration of each party's concerns.

5. **Avoidance** involves indifference to the concerns of both parties. It reflects a withdrawal from or neglect of any party's interests.

Does one of these approaches seem clearly a better method than the other to you? Each of them does, at least, reflect certain culturally valued modes of behavior (Thomas, 1977). For example, the esteem many people hold for athletic, business, and military heroes reflects our cultural valuation of competition. Valuation of a pragmatic approach to settling problems is reflected in the compromising approach. Cultural values of unselfishness, kindness, and generosity are reflected in accommodation, and even avoidance has roots in philosophies that emphasize caution, diplomacy, and turning away from worldly concerns. These cultural roots to each of the approaches to managing conflict suggest that no single one is likely to be the right one all the time. There probably are circumstances when each of the modes of conflict resolution can be appropriate. Rather than seeking to find some single best approach to managing conflict, it may be wisest to appreciate the relative advantages and disadvantages of all approaches, and the circumstances when each may be most appropriate. A summary of experienced leaders' recommendations for when to use each strategy is presented in Highlight MC–2 (Thomas, 1977).

Negotiation

Prepare for the Negotiation
Separate the People from the Problem
Focus on Interests, Not Positions

Negotiation is an approach that may help resolve some conflicts. The following negotiating tips, from Fisher and Ury (1981), include taking the time to prepare for a negotiating session; keeping the people and problems separate; focusing on issues, not positions; and seeking win–win outcomes.

Situations in Which to Use the Five Approaches to Conflict Management

Competing

1. When quick, decisive action is vital—e.g., emergencies.
2. On important issues where unpopular actions need implementing—e.g., cost cutting, enforcing unpopular rules, discipline.
3. On issues vital to company welfare when you know you're right.
4. Against people who take advantage of noncompetitive behavior.

Collaborating

1. To find an integrative solution when both sets of concerns are too important to be compromised.
2. When your objective is to learn.
3. To merge insights from people with different perspectives.
4. To gain commitment by incorporating concerns into a consensus.
5. To work through feelings which have interfered with a relationship.

Compromising

1. When goals are important, but not worth the effort or potential disruption of more assertive modes.
2. When opponents with equal power are committed to mutually exclusive goals.
3. To achieve temporary settlements of complex issues.
4. To arrive at expedient solutions under time pressure.
5. As a backup when collaboration or competition is unsuccessful.

Avoiding

1. When an issue is trivial or more important issues are pressing.
2. When you perceive no chance of satisfying your concerns.
3. When potential disruption outweighs the benefits of resolution.
4. To let people cool down and regain perspective.
5. When gathering information supersedes immediate decision.
6. When others can resolve the conflict more effectively.
7. When issues seem tangential to or symptomatic of other issues.

> ### Accommodating
>
> 1. When you find you are wrong—to allow a better position to be heard, to learn, and to show your reasonableness.
> 2. When issues are more important to others than yourself—to satisfy others and maintain cooperation.
> 3. To build social credits for later issues.
> 4. To minimize loss when you are outmatched and losing.
> 5. When harmony and stability are especially important.
> 6. To allow subordinates to develop by learning from mistakes.
>
> Source: K. W. Thomas, "Toward Multidimensional Values in Teaching: The Example of Conflict Management," *Academy of Management Review* 2, no. 3, (1977), 484–90. Used with permission.

Prepare for the Negotiation

To successfully resolve conflicts, leaders may need to *spend considerable time preparing for a negotiating session.* Leaders should anticipate each side's key concerns and issues, attitudes, possible negotiating strategies, and goals.

Separate the People from the Problem

Fisher and Ury (1981) also advise negotiators to *separate the people from the problem.* Because all negotiations involve substantive issues and relationships between negotiators, it is easy for these parts to become entangled. When that happens, parties may inadvertently treat the people *and* the problem as though they were the same. For example, a group of teachers angry that their salary has not been raised for the fourth year in a row may direct their personal bitterness toward the school board president. However, reactions such as these are usually a mistake, as the decision may be out of the other party's hands, and personally attacking the other party often only serves to make the conflict even more difficult to resolve.

There are several things leaders can do to separate the people from the problem. First, leaders should not let their fears color their perceptions of each side's intentions. It is easy to attribute negative qualities to others when one feels threatened. Similarly, it does no good to blame the other side for one's own problems (Blake, Shepard, & Mouton, 1964). Even if it is justified, it is still usually counterproductive. Another thing leaders can do to separate the people from the problem is to communicate clearly. Earlier in this text, we suggested techniques for active listening. Those guidelines are especially helpful in negotiating and resolving conflicts.

Focus on Interests, Not Positions

Another of Fisher and Ury's (1981) main points is to *focus on interests, not positions.* Focusing on interests depends on understanding the difference between interests and positions. Here is one example. Say Raoul has had the same reserved seats to the local symphony every season for several years and he was just notified he will no longer get his usual tickets. Feeling irate, he goes to the ticket office to complain. One approach he could take would be to demand the same seats he has always had; this would be his *position*. A different approach would be to find alternative seats that are just as satisfactory as his old seats had been; this would be his *interest*. In negotiating, it is much more constructive to satisfy interests than to fight over positions. Furthermore, it is important to focus both on your counterpart's interests (not position) and on your own interests (not position).

Finally, winning a negotiation at your counterpart's expense is likely to be only a short-term gain. Leaders should attempt to work out a resolution by looking at long-term rather than short-term goals, and they should try to build a working relationship that will endure and be mutually trusting and beneficial beyond the present negotiation. Along these lines, leaders should always seek win–win outcomes, which try to satisfy both sides' needs and continuing interests. It often takes creative problem solving to find new options that provide gains for both sides. Realistically, however, not all situations may be conducive to seeking win–win outcomes (see Highlight N–1).

Problem Solving

Identifying Problems or Opportunities for Improvement
Analyzing the Causes
Developing Alternative Solutions
Selecting and Implementing the Best Solution
Assessing the Impact of the Solution

Identifying Problems or Opportunities for Improvement

The first step in problem solving is to state the problem so that everyone involved in developing a solution has an informed and common appreciation and understanding of the task. This is a critical stage in problem solving and will take time and probably group discussion. It is dangerous to assume that everyone (or anyone!) knows at the outset what the problem is. A hurried or premature definition of the problem (e.g., as a result of groupthink) may lead to considerable frustration and wasted effort. In counseling and advising, for example, a significant portion of the work with a client is devoted to clarifying the problem. A student may seek help at the school counseling center to improve his study skills because he is spending what seems to be plenty of time studying yet is still doing poorly on examinations. A little discussion, however, may reveal that he is having difficulty concentrating on schoolwork because of problems at home. If the counselor had moved immediately to developing the client's study skills, the real cause of his dif-

How to Swim with Sharks

It is dangerous to swim with sharks, but not all sharks are found in the water. Some people may behave like sharks, and a best-selling book for executives written a few years ago took its title from that theme. However, an article appeared in the journal *Perspectives in Biology and Medicine* nearly two decades ago claiming to be a translated version of an essay written in France more than a century earlier for sponge divers (Cousteau, 1973). The essay notes that while no one wants to swim with sharks, it is an occupational hazard for certain people. For those who must swim with sharks, it can be essential to follow certain rules. See if you think the following rules for interacting with the sharks of the sea serve as useful analogies for interacting with the sharks of everyday life.

Rule 1: Assume any unidentified fish is a shark. Just because a fish may be acting in a docile manner does not mean it is not a shark. The real test is how it will act when blood is in the water.

Rule 2: Don't bleed. Bleeding will prompt even more aggressive behavior and the involvement of even more sharks. Of course, it is not easy to keep from bleeding when injured. Those who cannot do so are advised not to swim with sharks at all

Rule 3: Confront aggression quickly. Sharks usually give warning before attacking a swimmer. Swimmers should watch for indications an attack is imminent and take prompt counteraction. A blow to the nose is often appropriate since it shows you understand the shark's intentions and will respond in kind. It is particularly dangerous to behave in an ingratiating manner toward sharks. People who once held this erroneous view often can be identified by a missing limb.

Rule 4: Get out of the water if anyone starts bleeding. Previously docile sharks may begin attacking if blood is in the water. Their behavior can become so irrational, even including attacking themselves, that it is safest to remove yourself entirely from the situation.

Rule 5: Create dissension among the attackers. Sharks are self-centered and rarely act in an organized fashion with other sharks. This significantly reduces the risk of swimming with sharks. Every now and then, however, sharks may launch a coordinated attack. The best strategy then is to create internal dissension among them since they already are quite prone to it; often sharks will fight among themselves over trivial or minor things. By the time their internal conflict is settled, sharks often have forgotten about their organized attack.

Rule 6: Never divert a shark attack toward another swimmer. Please observe this final item of swimming etiquette.

ficulties would have gone untreated, and the client might have become even more pessimistic about his abilities and the possibility that others can help him. Or consider the case of a police chief who is concerned about the few volunteers willing to serve on a citizen's advisory committee to her department. There are many problems she might identify here, such as citizen apathy or poor publicity concerning the need and importance of the committee. The real problem, however, might be her own reputation for rarely listening to or heeding recommendations made by similar advisory committees in the past. If the chief were to take the time to explore and clarify the problem at the outset, then she *could* discover this important fact and take steps to solve the *real* problem (her own behavior). If, on the other hand, she pressed ahead aggressively, trusting her own appraisal of the problem, then nothing likely would change.

The reason it helps to take time to define a problem carefully is that sometimes people mistake symptoms for causes. In the case of the student, his poor studying was a symptom of another cause (family difficulties), not the cause of his poor grades. In the case of the police chief, lack of citizen participation on the advisory committee was a symptom of a problem, not the problem itself. If a plan addresses a symptom rather than the causes of a problem, the desired results will not be attained. It also is important during this stage to avoid scapegoating or blaming individuals or groups for the problem, which may just engender defensiveness and reduce creative thinking. This is a stage where conflict resolution techniques and negotiating skills can be very important. Finally, the statement of a problem should not imply that any particular solution is the correct one.

As an application of these considerations, let us consider two pairs of problem statements that a teacher might present to his class as a first step in addressing what he considers to be an unsatisfactory situation. These samples of dialogue touch on many aspects of communication, listening, and feedback skills addressed earlier in this book. Here, however, our focus is on differences in defining problems. In each case, the second statement is the one more likely to lead to constructive problem solving.

A: I don't think you care enough about this course. No one is ever prepared. What do I have to do to get you to put in more time on your homework?

B: What things are interfering with your doing well in this course?

A: Your test grades are too low. I'm going to cancel the field trip unless they improve. Do you have any questions?

B: I'm concerned about your test scores. They're lower than I expected them to be, and I'm not sure what's going on. What do you think the problem is?

Another aspect of this first stage of problem solving involves identifying those factors that, when corrected, are likely to have the greatest impact on improving an unsatisfactory situation. Since there are almost always more problems or opportunities for improvement than time or energy to devote to them

FIGURE PS–1

A Cause-and-Effect Diagram

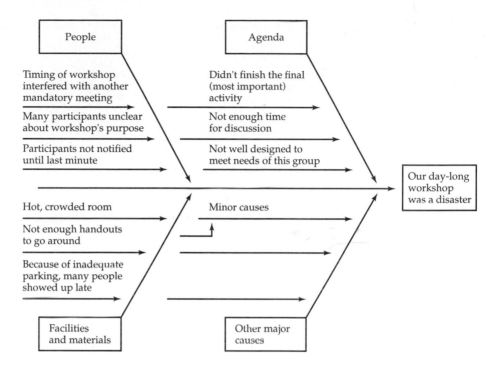

all, it is crucial to identify those whose solutions offer the greatest potential pay-off. A useful concept here is known as the Pareto principle. It states that about 80 percent of the problems in any system are the result of about 20 percent of the causes. In school, for example, most of the discipline problems are caused by a minority of the students. Of all the errors people make on income tax returns, just a few kinds of errors (e.g., forgetting to sign them) account for a disproportionately high percentage of returned forms. We would expect about 20 percent of the total mechanical problems in a city bus fleet to account for about 80 percent of the fleet's downtime. The Pareto principle can be used to focus problem-solving efforts on those causes that have the greatest overall impact.

Analyzing the Causes

Once a problem is identified, the next step is to analyze its causes. Analysis of a problem's causes should precede a search for its solutions. Two helpful tools for identifying the key elements affecting a problem situation are the cause-and-effect diagram (also called the "fishbone" diagram because of its shape, or the Ishikawa diagram after the person who developed it) and force field analysis. The cause-and-effect diagram uses a graphic approach to depict systematically the root causes of a problem, the relationships between different causes, and potentially a prioritization of which causes are most important (see Figure PS–1).

Force field analysis (see Figure PS–2) also uses a graphic approach, this time to depict the opposing forces that tend to perpetuate a present state of affairs. It

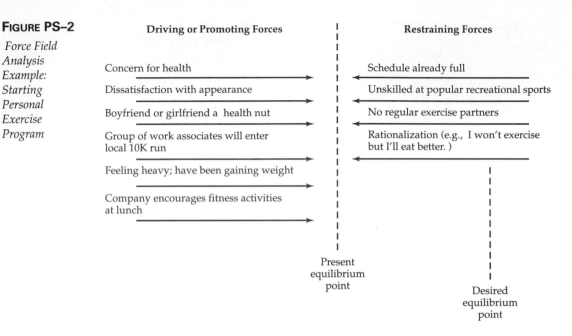

FIGURE PS–2

Force Field Analysis Example: Starting Personal Exercise Program

is a way of depicting any stable situation in terms of dynamic balance, or equilibrium, between those forces that tend to press toward movement in one direction and those other forces that tend to restrain movement in that direction. So long as the net sum of all those forces is zero, no movement occurs. When a change is desirable, force field analysis can be used to identify the best way to upset the balance between positive and negative forces so that a different equilibrium can be reached.

Developing Alternative Solutions

Several ideas we've examined previously are relevant here (e.g., brainstorming), as is the importance of solutions meeting criteria for quality and acceptance. A procedure called Nominal Group Technique (NGT) (Delbecq, Van de Ven, & Gustafson, 1975) is another way to generate a lot of ideas pertinent to a problem. This procedure is similar to brainstorming in that it is an idea-generating activity conducted in a group setting. With NGT, however, group members write down ideas on individual slips of paper, which are later transferred to a blackboard or flipchart for the entire group to work with.

Selecting and Implementing the Best Solution

The first solution one thinks of is not necessarily the best solution, even if everyone involved finds it acceptable. It is better to select a solution on the basis of established criteria. These include such questions as the following: Have the advantages and disadvantages of all possible solutions been considered? Have all the possible solutions been evaluated in terms of their respective impacts on the whole organization, not just a particular team or department? Is the information needed to make a good decision among the alternatives available?

Assessing the Impact of the Solution

One should not assume that just by going through the preceding steps the actions implemented will solve the problem. The solution's continuing impact must be assessed, preferably in terms of measurable criteria of success that all parties involved can agree on.

Improving Creativity

Seeing Things in New Ways
Using Power Constructively
Forming Diverse Problem-Solving Groups

Seeing Things in New Ways

There are several things leaders can do to increase their own and their followers' creativity. Some of these facilitating factors have already been discussed and include assuring adequate levels of technical expertise, delaying and minimizing the evaluation or judgment of solutions, focusing on the intrinsic motivation of the task, removing unnecessary constraints on followers, and giving followers more latitude in making decisions. One popular technique for stimulating creative thinking in groups is called brainstorming (see Highlight IC–1).

An additional thing leaders can do to enhance creativity is to *see things in new ways*, or to look at problems from as many perspectives as possible. This is, though, easier said than done. It can be difficult to see novel uses for things we are very familiar with, or to see such in novel ways. Psychologists call this kind of mental block functional fixedness (Duncker, 1945). Creative thinking depends on overcoming the functional fixedness associated with the rigid and stereotyped perceptions we have of the things around us.

One way to see things differently is to think in terms of analogies. Thinking in terms of analogies is a practical extension of Cronbach's (1984) definition of creativity—making fresh observations, or seeing one thing as something else. In this case, the active search for analogies is the essence of the problem-solving method. In fact, finding analogies is the foundation of a commercial creative-problem-solving approach called Synectics (W. J. J. Gordon, 1961). An actual example of use of analogies in a Synectics problem-solving group concerned designing a new roofing material that would adjust its color to the season, turning white in the summer to reflect heat and black in the winter to absorb heat. The group's first task was to find an analogy in nature, and it thought of fishes

Highlight IC–1

Steps for Enhancing Creativity through Brainstorming

Brainstorming is a technique designed to enhance the creative potential of any group trying to solve a problem. Leaders should use the following rules when conducting a brainstorming session:

1. Groups should consist of five to seven people: Fewer than five limits the number of ideas generated, but more than seven often can make the session unwieldy. It may be more important to carefully decide who should attend a session than how many people should attend.

2. Everybody should be given the chance to contribute. The first phase of brainstorming is idea generation, and members should be encouraged to spontaneously contribute ideas as soon as they get them. The objective in the first phase is quantity, not quality.

3. No criticism is allowed during the idea generation phase. This helps to clearly separate the activities of imaginative thinking and idea production from idea evaluation.

4. Freewheeling and outlandish ideas should be encouraged. With some modification, these ideas may be eventually adopted.

5. "Piggybacking" off others' ideas should be encouraged. Combining ideas or extending others' ideas often results in better solutions.

6. The greater the quantity and variety of ideas, the better. The more ideas generated, the greater the probability a good solution will be found.

7. Ideas should be recorded. Ideally, ideas should be recorded on a blackboard or butcher paper so that members can review all of the ideas generated.

8. After all of the ideas have been generated, each idea should be evaluated in terms of pros and cons, costs and benefits, feasibility, and so on. Choosing the final solution often depends on the results of these analyses.

Source: A. F. Osborn, *Applied Imagination* (New York: Scribner's, 1963).

whose colors change to match their surroundings. The mechanism for such changes in fish is the movement of tiny compartments of pigments closer to or farther away from the skin's surface, thus changing its color. After some discussion, the group designed a black roof impregnated with little white plastic balls which would expand when it is hot, making the roof lighter, and contract when it is cold, making the roof darker (W. J. J. Gordon, 1961).

Another way to see things differently is to try putting an idea or problem into a picture rather than into words. Feelings or relationships that have eluded verbal description may come out in a drawing, bringing fresh insights to an issue.

Using Power Constructively

In addition to getting followers to see problems from as many perspectives as possible, a leader can also *use her power constructively to enhance creativity.* As noted earlier, groups may suppress creative thinking by being overly critical or by passing judgment during the solution generation stage. This effect may be even more pronounced when strong authority relationships and status differences are present. Group members may be reluctant to take the risk of raising a "crazy" idea when superiors are present, especially if the leader is generally perceived as unreceptive to new ideas, or they may be reluctant to offer the idea if they believe others in the group will take potshots at it in front of the leader. Leaders who wish to create a favorable climate for fostering creativity need to use their power to encourage the open expression of ideas and to suppress uncooperative or aggressive reactions (overt or covert) between group members. Further, leaders can use their power to encourage creativity by rewarding successes and by not punishing mistakes. Leaders can also use their power to delegate authority and responsibility, relax followers' constraints, and empower followers to take risks. By taking these steps, leaders can help followers to build idiosyncratic credits, which in turn will encourage them to take risks and to be more creative. Along these same lines, the entire climate of an organization can be either more or less conducive to creative thinking, differences that may be due to the use of power within the organization. In an insightful turn of the familiar adage, "Power corrupts," Kanter (1982) noted how powerlessness also corrupts. She pointed out how managers who feel powerless in an organization may spend more energy guarding their territory than collaborating with others in productive action. The need to actively support followers' creativity may be especially important for leaders in bureaucratic organizations, as such organizations tend to be so inflexible, formalized, and centralized as to make many people in them feel relatively powerless.

Forming Diverse Problem-Solving Groups

Leaders can enhance creativity by *forming diverse problem-solving groups.* Group members with similar experiences, values, and preferences will be less likely to create a wide variety of solutions and more apt to agree on a solution prematurely than more diverse groups. Thus, selecting people for a group or committee with a variety of experiences, values, and preferences should increase the creativity of the group, although these differences may also increase the level of conflict within the group and make it more difficult for the leader to get consensus on a final solution. One technique for increasing group diversity and, in turn, creativity in problem-solving groups involves the use of the four preference dimensions of the Myers-Briggs Type Indicator (MBTI). Actual evidence to support this specific approach appears scanty (Thayer, 1988), but perhaps preferences only assume significance after certain other conditions for group creativity already have been met. For example, diversity cannot make up for an absence of technical expertise. Although the MBTI dimensions may be useful in selecting diverse groups, this instrument should only be used after ensuring that all potential members have high levels of technical expertise. Choosing members based solely on MBTI preferences ignores the crucial role that technical expertise and intrinsic motivation play in creativity. Another aspect of the relationship between creativity and leadership are described in Highlight IC–2.

Diagnosing Performance Problems in Individuals, Groups, and Organizations

Abilities
Skills
Task Understanding
Choice to Perform
Level of Effort and Persistence
Necessary Resources
Group Factors
Organizational and Environmental Factors
Concluding Comments on the Diagnostic Model

One way to integrate many of the topics covered in Parts I through IV is to discuss how they can impact individual, group, and organizational performance. The model in Figure DPP–1 provides a framework for these topics and is a modification of models developed by J. P. Campbell (1977) and J. P. Campbell, McCloy, Oppler, and Sager (in press). We hypothesize that performance is a function of abilities, skills, task understanding, choice to perform, level of effort and persistence, resources, group factors, and organizational and environmental factors. As a multiplicative rather than compensatory model, a deficit in any one component should result in a substantial decrement in performance that cannot easily be made up by increasing other components. Like the example described earlier of the high school basketball team playing the Chicago Bulls, exerting more effort will not always compensate for lacking the abilities or skills needed for performance.

The model provides general guidance about the actions leaders can take to improve follower, group, or organizational performance. The model also indicates how certain leader actions actually may disrupt performance. Primarily, though, we offer the model as a tool to show how ideas from several preceding chapters all play a part in performance.

Abilities

Abilities include such individual-difference variables as athleticism, intelligence, and creativity, and are characteristics that are relatively difficult to change with training. In other words, abilities represent raw talent. For example, it would

Highlight IC–2

Managing Creativity

T. Hogan and Morrison (1993) maintained that people who are seen as more creative tend to have several distinguishing personality characteristics. In general, creative people are open to information and experience, have high energy, can be personally assertive and even domineering, react emotionally to events, are impulsive, are more interested in music and art than in hunting and sports, and finally are very motivated to prove themselves (i.e., are concerned with personal adequacy). Thus, creative people tend to be independent, willful, impractical, unconcerned with money, idealistic, and nonconforming. Given that these tendencies may not make them ideal followers, the interesting question raised by Hogan and Morrison is: How does one lead or manage creative individuals? This question becomes even more interesting when considering the qualities of successful leaders or managers. As discussed earlier, successful leaders tend to be intelligent, dominant, conscientious, stable, calm, goal-oriented, outgoing, and somewhat conventional. Thus, one might think that the personalities of creative followers and successful leaders might be the source of considerable conflict and make them natural enemies in organizational settings. Because many organizations depend on creativity to grow and prosper, being able to successfully lead creative individuals may be a crucial aspect of success for these organizations. Given that creative people already possess technical expertise, imaginative thinking skills, and intrinsic motivation, Hogan and Morrison suggested that leaders take the following steps to successfully lead creative followers:

1. Set goals. Because creative people value freedom and independence, this step will be best accomplished if leaders use a high level of participation in the goal-setting process. Leaders should ask followers what they can accomplish in a particular time frame.

2. Provide adequate resources. Followers will be much more creative if they have the proper equipment to work with, as they can devote their time to resolving the problem rather than spending time finding the equipment to get the job done.

3. Reduce time pressures, but keep followers on track. Try to set realistic milestones when setting goals, and make organizational rewards contingent on reaching these milestones. Moreover, leaders need to be well organized to acquire necessary resources and to keep the project on track.

4. Consider nonmonetary as well as monetary rewards. Creative people often gain satisfaction from resolving the problem at hand, not from monetary rewards. Thus, feedback should be aimed at enhancing their feelings of personal adequacy. Monetary rewards perceived to be controlling may decrease rather than increase motivation toward the task.

5. Recognize that creativity is evolutionary, not revolutionary. Although followers can create truly novel products (such as the Xerox machine), often the key to creativity is continuous product improvement. Making

> next year's product faster, lighter, cheaper, or more efficient requires minor modifications that can, over time, culminate in major revolutions. Thus, it may be helpful if leaders think of creativity more in terms of small innovations than major breakthroughs.
>
> Source: R. T. Hogan and J. Morrison, "Managing Creativity," in *Create & Be Free: Essays in Honor of Frank Barron*, ed. A. Montouri (Amsterdam: J. C. Gieben, 1993).

FIGURE DPP–1

A Model of Performance

Performance = f (Abilities × Skills × Task understanding × Choice to perform × Level of effort and persistence × Necessary resources × Group factors × Organizational and environmental factors)

probably be impossible to take a person off the street and train him to be as good a hockey player as Wayne Gretzky or Mario Lemieux, just as it would be very difficult to train people to have extremely high levels of intelligence or creativity. Because abilities are relatively insensitive to training interventions, sending people who lack the required abilities to more training or motivating them to work harder will have relatively little effect on performance. Instead, performance deficits in this area can be more easily resolved by selecting those individuals with the abilities needed for performance.

Skills

As discussed in Chapter 10, skills consist of a well-defined body of knowledge, a set of related behaviors, and clear criteria of competent performance. Individuals or groups often have the abilities but lack the necessary skills to perform at a high level. Such is the case with many athletic teams or musical groups at the beginning of a season or when a work group gets a new set of equipment or responsibility for tasks they have no previous experience with. Skills are very amenable to training, and leaders with high levels of technical expertise may perform the training themselves, see that it is obtained in other ways on the job, or send their people to training programs in order to improve followers' skill levels.

Task Understanding

Performance problems often occur because individuals or groups do not understand what they are supposed to do. There are many instances where talented, skilled groups accomplished the wrong objective because of miscommunication or sat idly by waiting for instructions that never arrived. Leaders can minimize the effects of communication breakdowns on performance by improving their own communication and listening skills. Leaders must do more than communicate clearly; they must ensure that their messages are fully understood.

Choice to Perform

Sometimes people will choose not to perform a task even when they have the necessary abilities, skills, and task understanding. If this occurs, leaders should first try to learn why. For example, the task may involve risks the leader is unaware of. Another possibility, of course, is that motivation is low. If this is the case, leaders should replace nonperformers with others who are more intrinsically interested in the task or more achievement oriented. Leaders could also increase followers' choice to perform by setting goals, restructuring rewards to encourage performance, making the paths between effort-to-performance and performance-to-reward clearer, or redesigning the task to increase skill variety, autonomy, or feedback. If all these interventions fail, and the tasks to be performed are reasonable, then leaders may need to use punishment as a sanction for choosing not to perform.

Level of Effort and Persistence

Sometimes individuals or groups just seem to run out of steam. If this happens, then leaders need to communicate with followers to find out why their effort has dropped off. They may find that more periodic feedback is all that is needed to increase the level of effort or return effort to prior levels. Other interventions to enhance the level of effort and persistence include selecting followers who are intrinsically motivated by the task, setting longer-term goals, changing rewards to promote long-term rather than short-term effort, and redesigning the job to provide greater responsibility, autonomy, task significance, or task identity.

Necessary Resources

Performance also can be limited when followers lack the resources needed to get the job done. These may include equipment, computers, supplies, or even time, money, and additional manpower. Effective two-way communication is a key aspect of determining what followers need. Beyond that, leaders need good relationships with suppliers and some means of influence or exchange for securing resources.

Group Factors

Factors such as norms and cohesiveness can affect both individual and group performance. For example, leaders may run into situations where the group is not very cohesive or where the group has a low performance norm. In either case, leaders may need to create superordinate goals in order to increase group cohesiveness and performance. Superordinate goals are those that are achievable only when all group members exert effort; individual effort alone will not result in goal achievement. Moreover, group cohesiveness and performance might also be enhanced by de-emphasizing individual rewards and promoting group rewards. Group norms can also be changed by changing the group's membership or composition.

Organizational and Environmental Factors

Leaders, particularly those in senior positions, need to consider how the design, structure, or culture of the organization affects individual, group, and organizational performance. There are limits, however, to how much even the most senior or high-ranking leaders can change these factors. Particularly with regard to environmental factors, perhaps the best leaders can do is recognize how they can affect individual, group, or organizational performance. By recognizing that political, legal, and social factors sometimes may be the primary factors affecting performance, leaders can at least avoid taking actions based on a misdiagnosis of the problem, which may, in fact, turn out to be detrimental to performance in the long term.

Concluding Comments on the Diagnostic Model

In summary, this model provides an integrative framework for many of the topics affecting performance previously reviewed in this text. It reviews some of the factors that affect performance and suggests ideas for rectifying performance problems. It should be emphasized, however, that this model concerns only follower, group, or organizational performance. Leaders need to be mindful that there are other desirable outcomes, too, such as organizational climate and job satisfaction, and that actions designed to increase performance (especially just in the short term) may adversely impact these other desirable outcomes.

Team Building for Work Teams

Team-Building Interventions
What Does a Team-Building Workshop Involve?
Examples of Interventions

Few activities have become more commonplace in organizations these days than "team-building workshops." One reason for this level of activity is the powerful shift that has occurred in the workplace from a focus primarily on individual work to team-centered work. Unfortunately, however, they do not always achieve their objectives. As noted earlier in this text, it doesn't make sense to hold teams responsible for work if nothing else in the organizational environment changes. Team-building interventions, at the team level, may help team members understand why they are having so much difficulty in achieving team objectives, and even suggest coping strategies for an intolerable situation. They are not, however, very likely to remove root causes of the problem. In order to better understand the importance of looking at teams this way, let's use an example of this kind of erroneous thinking from a quite different context.

Team-Building Interventions

Suppose you have decided that the next car you drive must have outstanding ride and handling characteristics. Some cars you test, such as some huge American-made automobiles, have outstanding ride characteristics, but you are not happy with their handling. They sway and "float" in tight slalom courses. Other cars you test have just the opposite characteristics. They are as tight and as stable as you could hope for in turns and stops, but their ride is so hard that your dental work is in serious jeopardy. But you do find one car that seems to meet your requirements. In fact, a Mercedes-Benz does provide both an extremely comfortable ride *and* tremendous road handling characteristics in high-performance situations. There is, however, one small problem. The Mercedes costs a lot of money up front—more than you are willing to put into this project. So you arrive at an alternative solution. You find a used Yugo, a little car built in Yugoslavia and no longer imported into the United States, largely because of inferior quality. But it is really cheap, and after purchasing it, you know you will have lots of money left over to beef up the suspension, steering, and braking systems to provide you with the Mercedes-Benz ride you really want.

Ludicrous! Obviously, you are never going to get a Mercedes-Benz ride unless you are willing to put in considerable money and effort *up front* rather than doing little up front and putting all your money into repair work. But that is precisely what many organizations are attempting to do with teams. They do not seem willing to create the conditions necessary for teamwork to occur naturally (a point we will discuss in the section "Team Building at the Top"), but when the teams struggle in a hostile environment, as they invariably will, the leaders seem more than willing to pour tremendous amounts of money into team-building interventions to fix the problem. (And there are lots of team-building consultants out there willing to take their money.) These types of team-building problems are those we would categorize as "top-down."

An equally vexing problem occurs when organizations are committed to teamwork, are willing to change structures and systems to support it, but are not committed to the "bottom-up" work that will be required. This is best illustrated in the rationale for team training shown in Figure TW–1. In our work with organizations, we are frequently asked to help teams that are struggling. In Figure TW–1 we would place these requests at the "TEAM" level, which is the third platform up from the bottom. We believe this type of intervention will work only if the team members have achieved a stable platform from which to work. In this case, that would include the two previous platforms in Figure TW–1. If the foundation is not well established, the solely team-based intervention often leads to intrateam competition or apathy and withdrawal.

As a basis for any work at the team level, individual team members must first be comfortable with themselves. They must be able to answer the questions, "What do *I* bring to the team and what do *I* need from the team?" Not to answer these questions breeds inherent fear and mistrust. When these questions have been answered, team members are then in a position to begin dealing at the

FIGURE TW–1

*A Rationale for
Individual,
Interpersonal,
Team, and
Organizational
Training*

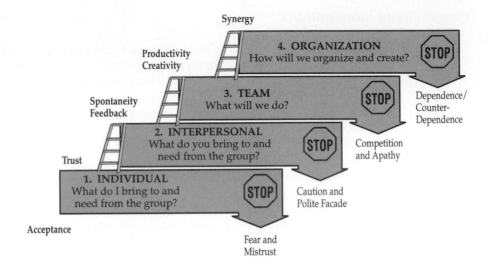

interpersonal level, where they may now comfortably ask, "What do *you* bring to the team and what do *you* need from the team?" Not to resolve these issues results in caution in dealing with other members, and interactions at the "polite-façade" level rather than at the level of truth and understanding. If the first- and second-level platforms are in place, a true team-building intervention can be useful. (Incidentally, just because team members have not stabilized themselves at levels 1 and 2 does not mean an intervention can not be conducted. Rather, it means a more extensive intervention will be required than a solely team-based effort.)

What Does a Team-Building Workshop Involve?

There are literally hundreds, if not thousands, of team-building interventions that are being conducted today. There are many good sources, such as the *Team and Organization Development Sourcebook,* which contain team-based activities such as conflict resolution, problem solving, development of norms, building trust, or goal setting, to name but a few. Rather than trying to describe all of these suggestions, however, we will give you a few recommendations that we have found to be useful and then share a few examples of interventions we have used.

At the Center for Creative Leadership, staff are frequently asked to design custom team interventions for mid- to upper-level teams. While we enter these design meetings with no agenda of activities, neither do we enter with a completely blank slate. We believe an intervention at the team level must meet three general requirements to be successful, and at least one activity must be included in the intervention pertaining to each of those three requirements.

The first requirement involves awareness raising. As we noted in our previous chapters, not all cultures are equally prepared or nurtured in the concepts of teamwork. In fact, many of the lessons we think we have learned about teams are incorrect. So we believe we need to dispel such myths and include a healthy dose of team-based research findings about how teams *really* work as a critical element of a workshop. Second, we need some diagnostic, instrument-based feedback so team members can have a reasonably valid map of where they and their teammates now are located. Finally, each intervention must include a practice field, to use Senge's (1990) term. Practice is necessary for athletic success, and it is necessary in organizations too. It would be foolish to design a whole new series of plays for a hockey team to implement, talk about them in the locker room, but never actually practice any of them before expecting the team to implement them in a game. Similarly, if you are asking people to change their behaviors in the way they interact to improve teamwork, then it is only fair to provide them with a practice field upon which they can test their new behaviors in a reasonably risk-free, protected environment. This is where experiential exercises can be extremely useful. And it is here that the quality of the team-building facilitator is most critical. Conducting a pencil-and-paper exercise in the classroom does not require the same facilitator skill set as that required to conduct, say, a team-rappelling exercise off the face of a cliff—few facilitators get those requirements wrong and we have seldom discovered problems here. Where we have seen a significant breakdown in facilitator skills is in being able to make the link between the exercise that is conducted and the real world in which the team will be asked to perform. Here facilitators must have not only a good sense of real-time team dynamics, but also a sense of the business in which the team operates. They must help the participants make the links back to team dynamics that occur on the manufacturing floor or in the board room, and this seems to be the skill that separates highly effective facilitators from the pack.

Examples of Interventions

Now let us provide a few examples of the range of interventions that can be included in team building. Ginnett (1984) conducted an intervention with three interdependent teams from a state youth psychiatric hospital. The teams included members of the administrative services, the professional staff, and the direct care providers. The members of each team were dedicated to their roles in providing high-quality service to the youths under their care, but the three groups experienced great difficulty in working with each other. Extensive diagnosis of the groups revealed two underlying problems. First, each group had a very different vision of what the hospital was or should be. Second, each of the groups defined themselves as "care givers," thus making it very difficult for them to ask others for help since, in their minds, asking for help tended to put them in the role of their patients. We conducted a series of workshops to arrive at a common vision for the hospital, but the second problem required considerably more work. Since the staff members needed to experientially understand that asking for help did not place them in an inherently inferior position, a "Wilderness Experience" was designed where the entire staff was asked to spend four days together in a primitive wilderness environment with difficult hiking, climbing, and mountaineering requirements. By the end of the experience, everyone had found an occasion to ask someone else for help. Even more importantly, everyone found that actually asking others for help—something they had previously resisted—moved the overall team much higher in its ability to perform. Considerable time was spent each evening linking the lessons of the day with the work in the hospital.

In one of the more interesting programs we've conducted, a team of senior executives spent a week together at a ranch in Colorado. Each morning, the team met for a series of awareness sessions and data feedback sessions. Afternoons were reserved by the chief operating officer for fun and relation, with the only requirement being that attendees participate in them as a team or subteams. As facilitators, we actively participated with the teams, and related their team experiences each day to the lessons of the next morning, and to challenges facing the team in its normal work. In interventions like this we have learned that team building can be fun, and that the venues for it are almost limitless. Second, we have learned that being able to observe and process team activity in a real-time mode is critical for team-building facilitators. There is no substitute for first-hand observation as a basis for discerning group dynamics and noting the variety of revealing behaviors that emerge in unstructured team activities.

Team Building at the Top

Executive Teams Are Different
Applying Individual Skills and Team Skills

In certain ways, executive teams are similar to any other teams. For example, just about any group of senior executives that has faced a dire crisis and survived will note that teamwork was essential for their survival. In a nutshell, then, *when teamwork is critical*, all the lessons of the previous section apply. More specifically, to really be able to benefit from a team-building intervention, individual members must be comfortable with their own strengths and weaknesses and the strengths and weaknesses of their peers. But this raises a question: If all this is true, why do we include a separate section on team building for top teams? Because there are two critical differences between most teams and "teams at the top" that should be addressed.

Executive Teams Are Different

As opposed to other kinds of work teams, not all the work at the executive level requires all (or even any) of the team to be present. An example might help. In our research on teams we studied the air crews who fly the B-1 bomber. These are four-person teams comprising an aircraft commander, a copilot, an offensive systems officer, and a defensive systems officer. While each has individual responsibilities, in every single bombing run we observed, it was absolutely essential that the team work together to accomplish the mission. They had all of the components of a true team (complex and common goal, differentiated skills, interdependence) and no individual acting alone could have achieved success. But this is not always the case for executive teams.

As Katzenbach (1998) has observed, many top leadership challenges do not really require teamwork at all. Furthermore, many top leadership challenges that do constitute real team opportunities do not require or warrant full involvement by everyone who is officially on the team. In fact, an official "team at the top" rarely functions as a collective whole involving all the formal members. Thus, the real trick for executive teams is to be able to apply both the technical individual skills that probably got the individuals to the team in the first place *and* the skills required for high-performance teamwork when a team situation presents itself.

Applying Individual Skills and Team Skills

There are two critical requirements if this is to work. First, one must have the diagnostic skills to discern whether the challenge presenting itself involves an individual situation or a team situation. Then, it requires that leaders "stay the course" when a team situation is present. This means, for example, when pressure for results intensifies, not slipping back into the traditional modes of assigning work to an individual (e.g., one member of that top team), but rather allowing the team to complete the work as a team. Again, Katzenbach (1998) states this clearly:

> Some leadership groups, of course, err in the opposite way, by attempting to forge a team around performance opportunities that do not call for a team approach. In fact, the increasing emphasis that team proponents place on "team-based organizations" creates real frustrations as top leadership groups try to rationalize good executive leadership instincts into time-consuming team building that has no performance purpose. Catalyzing real team performances at the top does not mean replacing executive leadership with executive teams, it means being rigorous about the distinction between opportunities that require single-leader efforts and those that require team efforts—and applying the discipline that fits.

To summarize this point, executives do not always need to perform as a team to be effective. But when they do need to perform as a team, the same lessons of team building discussed earlier can be very useful in helping them to enhance their team performance.

The second difference with executive teams is that they have an opportunity to enhance teamwork throughout their organization that few others have. It is our experience that *only the executive team can change organizational systems*. Recall from a chapter earlier in the book that we described the Team Effectiveness Leadership Model and mentioned there were four system issues critical to team performance. These systems were all located at the organizational level and consisted of reward systems, education systems, information systems, and control systems. The impact of these systems can be so pervasive across the entire organization that a small change in a system can have monumental impact in the organization. In a sense, then, the executive team has within its control the power to do widespread "team building" in a very different manner than we have discussed to this point. Just consider the impact of changing a compensation system (one element of a reward system) from an individual-based bonus plan to a team-based bonus plan!

Tripwire Lessons

Finally, our experience in working with executives has taught us that leaders at this level have some important lessons to learn about team building at the top. Richard Hackman, in preparing the huge editorial task of having many people produce one coherent book (by his own admission, not necessarily the best of team tasks), assembled the various authors at a conference center. As one of the contributors, one of this text's authors (RCG) recalls a most frustrating task of attempting to put together the simple checklist of steps to ensure a team developed properly. As this arduous process dragged on and tempers flared, it became obvious that "Teamwork for Dummies" was never going to emerge. But something else did start to emerge. It became clear *that some behaviors leaders engaged in could virtually guarantee failure for their teams.* While not our intent, this experience yielded a worthwhile set of lessons. A condensed version of those lessons, labeled "tripwires" by Hackman (1990), concludes our discussion of team building at the top.

Trip Wire 1: Call the Performing Unit a Team but Really Manage Members as Individuals.   One way to set up work is to assign specific responsibilities to specific individuals and then choreograph individuals' activities so their products coalesce into a team product. A contrasting strategy is to assign a team responsibility and accountability for an entire piece of work and let members decide among themselves how they will proceed to accomplish the work. While either of these strategies can be effective, a choice must be made between them. A mixed model, in which people are *told* they are a team but are *treated* as individual performers with their own specific jobs to do, sends mixed signals to members, is likely to confuse everyone, and in the long run is probably untenable.

To reap the benefits of teamwork, one must actually build a team. Calling a set of people a team or exhorting them to work together is insufficient. Instead, explicit action must be taken to establish the team's boundaries, to define the task as one for which members are collectively responsible and accountable, and to give members the authority to manage both their internal processes and the team's relations with external entities such as clients and co-workers. Once this is done, management behavior and organizational systems gradually can be changed as necessary to support teamwork.

Trip Wire 2: Create an Inappropriate Authority Balance.   The exercise of authority creates anxiety, especially when one must balance between assigning a team authority for some parts of the work and withholding it for other parts.

Because both managers and team members tend to be uncomfortable in such situations, they may collude to "clarify" them. Sometimes the result is the assignment of virtually all authority to the team—which can result in anarchy or a team that heads off in an inappropriate direction. At other times, managers retain virtually all authority, dictating work procedures in detail to team members and, in the process, losing many of the advantages that can accrue from teamwork. In both cases, the anxieties that accompany a mixed model are reduced, but at significant cost to team effectiveness.

To achieve a good balance of managerial and team authority is difficult. Moreover, merely deciding how much authority will be assigned to the group and how much will be retained by management are insufficient. Equally important are the domains of authority that are assigned and retained. Our findings suggest that managers should be unapologetic and insistent about exercising their authority about *direction*—the end states the team is to pursue—and about *outer-limit constraints* on team behavior—the things the team must always do or never do. At the same time, managers should assign to the team full authority for the *means* by which it accomplishes its work—and then do whatever they can to ensure that team members understand and accept their responsibility and accountability for deciding how they will execute the work.

Few managerial behaviors are more consequential for the long-term being of teams than those that address the partitioning of authority between managers and teams. It takes skill to accomplish this well, and it is a skill that has emotional and behavioral as well as cognitive components. Just knowing the rules for partitioning authority is insufficient; one also needs some practice in applying those rules in situations where anxieties, including one's own, are likely to be high. Especially challenging for managers are the early stages in the life of a team (when managers often are tempted to give away too much authority) and when the going gets rough (when the temptation is to take authority back too soon). The management of authority relations with task-performing teams is indeed much like walking a balance beam, and our evidence suggests that it takes a good measure of knowledge, skill, and perseverance to keep from falling off.

Trip Wire 3: Assemble a Large Group of People, Tell Them in General Terms What Needs to Be Accomplished, and Let Them "Work Out the Details." Traditionally, individually focused designs for work are plagued by constraining structures that have built up over the years to monitor and control employee behavior. When groups are used to perform work, such structures tend to be viewed as unnecessary bureaucratic impediments to team functioning. Thus, just as managers sometimes (and mistakenly) attempt to empower teams by relinquishing all authority to them, so do some attempt to get rid of the dysfunctional features of existing organizational structures simply by taking down all the structures they can. Apparently, the hope is that removing structures will release teams and enable members to work together creatively and effectively.

Managers who hold this view often wind up providing teams with less structure than they actually need. Tasks are defined only in vague, general terms. Group composition is unclear or fluid. The limits of the team's authority are kept deliberately fuzzy. The unstated assumption is that there is some magic in group interaction process and that, by working together, members will evolve any structures that the team actually needs.

It is a false hope; there is no such magic. Indeed, our findings suggest the opposite: groups that have appropriate structures tend to develop healthy internal processes, whereas groups with insufficient or inappropriate structures tend to have process problems. Worse, coaching and process consultation are unlikely to resolve these problems, precisely because they are rooted in the team structure. For members to learn how to interact well within a flawed or underspecified structure is to swim upstream against a very strong current.

Trip Wire 4: Specify Challenging Team Objectives, but Skimp on Organizational Supports. Even if a work team has clear, engaging direction and an enabling structure, its performance can go sour—or, at least, it can fall below the group's potential—if the team is not well supported. Teams in high-commitment organizations (Walton, 1985) fall victim to this trip wire when they given "stretch" objectives but not the wherewithal to accomplish them; high initial enthusiasm soon changes into disillusionment.

It is no small undertaking to provide these supports to teams, especially in organizations designed to support work by individuals. Corporate compensation policy, for example, may make no provision for team bonuses and, indeed, may explicitly prohibit them. Human resource departments may be primed to identify individuals' training needs and provide first-rate courses to fill those needs, but training in team skills may not be available at all. Existing performance appraisal systems, which may be state-of-the-art for measuring individual contributions, are likely to be wholly inappropriate for assessing and rewarding work done by teams. Information systems and control systems may provide managers with the data they need to monitor and control work processes, but they may be neither available nor appropriate for use by work teams. Finally, the material resources required for the work may have been prespecified by those who originally designed it, and there may be no procedure in place for a team to secure the special configuration of resources it needs to execute the particular performance strategy it has developed.

To align existing organizational systems with the needs of teams often requires managers to exercise power and influence upward and laterally in the organization.

An organization set up to provide teams with full support for their work is noticeably different from one whose systems and policies are intended to support and control individual work, and many managers may find the prospect of changing to a group-oriented organization both unsettling and perhaps even vaguely revolutionary.

It is hard to provide good organizational support for task-performing teams, but generally it is worth the trouble. The potential of a well-directed, well-structured, well-supported team is tremendous. Moreover, to stumble over the organizational support trip wire is, perhaps, the saddest of all team failures. When a group is both excited about its work and all set up to execute it superbly, it is especially shattering to fail merely because the organizational supports required cannot be obtained. It is like being all dressed up and ready to go to the prom only to have the car break down en route.

Trip Wire 5: Assume that Members Already Have All the Competence They Need to Work Well as a Team.   Once a team is launched and operating under its own steam, managers sometimes assume their work is done. As we have seen, there are indeed some good reasons for giving a team ample room to go about its business in its own way: inappropriate or poorly timed managerial interventions impaired the work of more than one group in our research. However, a strict, hands-off managerial stance also can limit a team's effectiveness, particularly when members are not already skilled and experienced in teamwork.

Development Planning

Conducting a GAPS Analysis
Identifying and Prioritizing Development Needs: Gaps of GAPS
Bridging the Gaps: Building a Development Plan
Reflecting on Learnings: Modifying Development Plans
Transfer Learnings to New Environments

> Change before you have to.
>
> Jack Welch
> General Electric CEO

Development planning is the systematic process of building knowledge and experience or changing behavior. Two people who have done a considerable amount of cutting-edge research in the development-planning process are Peterson and Hicks (1995). These two researchers believe development planning consists of five interrelated phases. The first phase of development planning is identifying development needs. Here leadership practitioners identify career goals, assess their abilities in light of career goals, seek feedback about how their behaviors are affecting others, and review the organizational standards pertaining to their career goals. Once this information has been gathered, the second phase consists of analyzing this data to identify and prioritize development needs. The prioritized development needs in turn are used to create a highly focused and achievable development plan, the third phase of this process. To help ensure permanent behavioral change takes place, the plan itself must utilize many of the best-practices techniques described in Chapter 10. Some of these best practices include having a plan that is limited to no more than two or three objectives, that capitalizes on on-the-job activities, and that incorporates multiple sources of feedback. The fourth phase in development planning is periodically reviewing the plan, reflecting on learnings, and modifying or updating the plan as appropriate. As you might expect, the AOR model, described in Chapter 4, is a key component during this phase of the development planning process. The last phase in development planning is transferring learnings to new environments. Just because a leadership practitioner can successfully delegate activities to his 3-person team may not mean he will effectively delegate tasks or utilize his staff efficiently when he is leading a group of 25 people. In that case, the leader will need to build and expand on the delegation skills he learned when leading a much smaller team. These five phases are well grounded in research—Hazucha, Hezlett, and Schneider (1993), Peterson (1993b), and Hezlett and Koonce (1995) show that approximately 75 percent of the leadership practitioners adopting these phases were successful in either changing their behaviors permanently or developing new skills. Because these five phases are so important to the development planning process, the remainder of this section will describe each phase in more detail.

Conducting a GAPS Analysis

The first phase in the development-planning process is to conduct a GAPS analysis. A GAPS analysis helps leadership practitioners to gather and categorize all pertinent development planning information. A sample GAPS analysis for an engineer working in a manufacturing company can be found in Figure DP–1. This individual wants to get promoted into a first-line supervisor position within the next year, and all of the information pertinent to this promotion can be found in her GAPS analysis. The specific steps for conducting a GAPS analysis are as follows:

- *Step 1: Goals.* The first step in a GAPS analysis is to clearly identify what you want to do or where you want to go with your career over the next year or so. This does not necessarily mean moving up or getting promoted to the next level. An alternative career objective might be to master one's current job, as you may have just gotten promoted and advancing to the next level is not as important at the moment. Other career objectives might include taking on more responsibilities in your current position, taking a lateral assignment in another part of the company, taking an overseas assignment, or even cutting back on job responsibilities to gain more work-life balance. This latter career objective may be very appropriate for leaders who are just starting a family or are taking care of loved ones who are suffering from poor health. The two most important aspects of this step in the GAPS analysis are that leadership practitioners will have a lot more energy to work on development needs that are aligned with career goals, and in many cases advancing to the next level may not be a viable or particularly energizing career goal. This latter point may be especially true with organizations that have been recently downsized. Management

FIGURE DP–1

*A Sample
GAPS Analysis*

Goals: Where do you want to go?	Abilities: What can you do now?
Step 1: Career objectives: Career strategies:	*Step 2:* What strengths do you have for your career objectives? *Step 3:* What development needs will you have to overcome?
Standards: What does your boss or the organization expect?	Perceptions: How do others see you?
Step 5: Expectations:	*Step 4:* 360 and Performance Review Results, and feedback from others: • *Boss* • *Peers* • *Direct Reports*

Sources: D. B. Peterson and M. D. Hicks, *Leader as Coach* (Minneapolis: Personnel Decisions International, 1996); and G. J. Curphy, *Career and Development Planning Workshop: Planning for Individual Development* (Minneapolis: Personnel Decisions International, 1998).

positions often bear the brunt of downsizing initiatives, resulting in fewer available positions for those wishing to advance.

· *Step 2: Abilities.* People bring a number of strengths and development needs to their career goals. Over the years, you may have developed specialized knowledge or a number of skills that have helped you to be successful in your current and previous jobs. Similarly, you may also have received feedback over the years that there are certain skills you need to develop or behaviors you need to change. Good leaders know themselves—over the years they know which strengths they need to leverage and which skills they need to develop.

- *Step 3. Perceptions.* The perceptions component of the GAPS model concerns how your abilities, skills, and behaviors impact others. What are others saying about your various attributes? What are their reactions to both your strengths and development needs? A great way of obtaining this information is by asking others for feedback or through performance reviews or 360-degree feedback instruments.
- *Step 4: Standards.* The last step in a GAPS analysis concerns the standards your boss or the organization has for your career objectives. For example, your boss may say that you may need to develop better public speaking, delegation, or coaching skills before you can get promoted. Similarly, the organization may have policies stating that people in certain overseas positions must be proficient in the country's native language, or it may have educational or experience requirements for various jobs.

When completing a GAPS analysis you may discover that you do not have all the information you need. If you do not, then you need to get it before you complete the next step of the development-planning process. Only you can decide upon your career objectives, but you can solicit advice from others on whether these objectives are realistic given your abilities, the perceptions of others, and organizational standards. You may find that your one-year objectives are unrealistic given your development needs, organizational standards, or job opportunities. In this case, you may need to either reassess your career goals or consider taking a number of smaller career steps that will ultimately help you achieve your career goal. If you are lacking information about the other quadrants, then you can ask your boss or others whose opinions you value about your abilities, perceptions, or organizational standards. Getting as much up-to-date and pertinent information for your GAPS analysis will help ensure that your development plan is focusing on high-priority objectives.

Identifying and Prioritizing Development Needs: Gaps of GAPS

As seen in Figure DP–2, the Goals and Standards quadrants are future oriented; these quadrants ask where you want to go and what your boss or your organization expects of people in these positions. The Abilities and Perceptions quadrants are focused on the present; what strengths and development needs do you currently have and how are these attributes affecting others? Given what you currently have and where you want to go, what are the gaps in your GAPS? In other words, after looking at all of the information in your GAPS analysis, what are your biggest development needs? And how should these development needs be prioritized? You need to review the information from the GAPS model, look for underlying themes and patterns, and determine what behaviors, knowledge, experiences, or skills will be the most important to change or develop if you are to accomplish your career goals.

FIGURE DP–2

A Gaps-of-the-GAPS Analysis

Where you want to go

Goals

Where you are now

Abilities

←—— Gaps? ——→

Standards

Perceptions

Developmental Objectives

Current Position: _____

_____
_____
_____
_____
_____

Next Proposed Position: _____

_____
_____
_____
_____
_____

Sources: D. B. Peterson and M. D. Hicks, *Leader as Coach* (Minneapolis: Personnel Decisions International, 1996); and G. J. Curphy, *The Leadership Development Process Manual* (Minneapolis: Personnel Decisions International, 1998).

Bridging the Gaps: Building a Development Plan

A gaps-of-the-GAPS analysis helps leadership practitioners identify high-priority development needs, but does not spell out what leaders need to do to overcome these needs. A good development plan is like a roadmap; it clearly describes the final destination, lays out the steps or interim checkpoints, builds in regular feedback to keep people on track, identifies where additional resources are needed, and builds in reflection time so that people can periodically review progress and determine whether an alternative route is needed. The specific steps for creating a high-impact development plan are as follows:

- *Step 1: Career and Development Objectives.* Your career objective comes directly from the Goals quadrant of the GAPS analysis; it is where you want to be or what you want to be doing in your career a year or so in the future. The development objective comes from your gaps of the GAPS analysis; it should be a high-priority development need pertaining to your career objective. People should be working on no more than 2–3 development needs at any one time.

- *Step 2: Criteria for Success.* What would it look like if you developed a particular skill, acquired technical expertise, or changed the behavior outlined in your development objective? This can be a difficult step in development planning, particularly with "softer" skills, such as listening, managing conflict, or building relationships with others.

- *Step 3: Action Steps.* The focus in the development plan should be on the specific, on-the-job action steps leadership practitioners will take in order to overcome their development need. However, sometimes it is difficult for leaders to think of the on-the-job action steps to overcome their development needs. Three excellent resources that provide on-the-job action steps for overcoming a variety of development needs are two books, *The Successful Manager's Handbook* (Davis, Skube, Hellervik, Gebelein, & Sheard, 1996) and *For Your Improvement* (Lombardo & Eichinger, 1996), and the development planning and coaching software *DevelopMentor* (PDI, 1995). These three resources can be likened to restaurant menus in that they provide leadership practitioners with a wide variety of action steps to overcome just about any development need.

- *Step 4: Whom to Involve and Reassess Dates.* This step in a development plan involves feedback—whom do you need to get it from and how often do you need to get it? This step in the development plan is important as it helps to keep you on track. Are your efforts being noticed? Do people see any improvement? Are there things you need to do differently? Do you need to refocus your efforts?

- *Step 5: Stretch Assignments.* When people reflect on when they have learned the most, they often talk about situations where they felt they were in over their heads. These situations stretched their knowledge and skills and often are seen as extremely beneficial to learning. If you know of a potential assignment, such as a task force, a project management team, or a rotational assignment, that would emphasize the knowledge and skills you need to develop and accelerate your learning, you should include it in your development plan.

- *Step 6: Resources.* Oftentimes people find it useful to read a book, attend a course, or watch a videotaped program to gain foundational knowledge about a particular development need. These methods generally describe the how-to steps for a particular skill or behavior.

• *Step 7: Reflect with a Partner.* In accordance with the Action-Observation-Reflection model of Chapter 4, people should periodically review their learnings and progress with a partner. The identity of the partner is not particularly important, as long as you trust his or her opinion and the partner is familiar with your work situation and development plan.

Reflecting on Learnings: Modifying Development Plans

Just as the development plan is a roadmap, this phase of development planning helps leaders to see whether the final destination is still the right one, if an alternative route might be better, and whether there is need for more resources or equipment. Reflecting on your learnings with a partner is also a form of public commitment, and people who make public commitments are much more likely to fulfill them. All things considered, in most cases it is probably better to periodically review your progress with your boss. Your boss should not be left in the dark with respect to your development, and periodically reviewing progress with your boss will help ensure there are no surprises at your performance appraisal.

Transfer Learnings to New Environments

The last phase in development planning concerns on-going development. Your development plan should be a "live" document; it should be changed, modified, or updated as you learn from your experiences, receive feedback, acquire new skills, and overcome targeted development needs. There are basically three ways to transfer learnings to new environments. The first way is to constantly update your development plan. Another way to enhance your learning is to practice your newly acquired skills to a new environment. A final way to hone and refine your skills is to coach others in the development of your newly acquired skills. Moving from the student role to that of a master is an excellent way to reinforce your learnings.

Credibility

The Two Components of Credibility
Building Expertise
Building Trust
Expertise × Trust

Leaders know that while their position may give them authority, their behavior earns them respect. Leaders go first. They set an example and build commitment through simple, daily acts that create progress and momentum.

Jim Kouzes and Barry Posner

Interviews with thousands of followers as well as the results of over half a million 360-degree feedback reports indicate that credibility may be one of the most important components of leadership success and effectiveness (Kouzes & Posner, 1987, 1996; PDI, 1992). Employees working for leaders they thought were credible were willing to work longer hours, felt more of a sense of ownership in the company, felt more personally involved in work, and were less likely to leave the company over the next two years (Kouzes & Posner, 1996). Given the difficulties companies are having finding and retaining talented leaders and workers and the role intellectual capital and bench strength play in organizational success, it would appear that credibility could have a strong bottom-line impact on many organizations. Credibility is a little like leadership in that many people have ideas of what credibility is (or is not), but there may not be a lot of consensus on one "true" definition of credibility. This section will define what we believe credibility is, present the two components of credibility, and explore what leadership practitioners can do (and avoid doing) if they want to build their credibility.

The Two Components of Credibility

Credibility can be defined as the ability to engender trust in others. Leaders with high levels of credibility are seen as trustworthy; they have a strong sense of right and wrong, stand up and speak up for what they believe in, protect confidential information, encourage ethical discussions of business or work issues, and follow through with commitments. Sometimes dishonest leaders, personalized charismatic leaders, or power wielders can initially be seen by followers to be credible, but their selfish and self-serving interests usually come to light over time. Credibility is made up of two components, which include expertise and trust. Followers will not trust leaders if they feel their leaders do not know what they are talking about. Similarly, followers will not trust leaders if they feel confidential information will be leaked, if their leaders are unwilling to take stands on moral issues, or if their leaders do not follow through with their promises. Much about these two components of credibility have already been discussed in the sections on "Building Technical Competence," "Building Effective Relationships with Superiors," and "Building Effective Relationships with Peers." What follows is a brief overview of these three skills as well as some additional considerations that can help leadership practitioners build their credibility.

Building Expertise

Expertise consists of technical competence as well as organizational and industry knowledge, so building expertise means increasing your knowledge and skills in these three areas. Building technical competence, described earlier in Part V, concerns increasing the knowledge and repertoire of behaviors one can bring to bear to successfully complete a task. To build technical competence, leadership practitioners must determine how their job contributes to the overall mission of the company or organization, become an expert in the job through formal training or teaching others, and seek opportunities to broaden their technical expertise.

Nonetheless, building expertise takes more than just technical competence. Leaders also need to understand the company and the industry they are in. Many followers are not only looking for leaders to coach them on their skills, they are also looking to their leaders to provide some context for organizational, industry, and market events. Building one's organizational or industry knowledge may be just as important as building technical competence. However, the ways in which leadership practitioners build these two knowledge bases is somewhat different from building technical competence. Building technical competence often takes more of a hands-on approach to development, but it is hard to do this when building organizational or industry knowledge. One way to build your organizational or industry knowledge is by regularly reading industry-related journals, annual reports, *The Wall Street Journal, Fortune, Inc.*, or various Web sites. Many leaders spend 5–10 hours a week building their industry and organizational knowledge bases using this approach. Getting a mentor or being coached by your boss are other ways to build these knowledge bases. Other leadership practitioners have taken stretch assignments where they work on special projects with senior executives. Often these assignments allow them to work closely with executives, and through this contact they better understand the competitive landscape, the organization's history and business strategies, and organizational politics. The bottom line is that your learning is not over once you have obtained your degree. In many ways, it will have just started.

Finally, it is important to remember that expertise is more than experience. As noted previously, some leaders get one year's worth of experience out of five years' work, whereas others get five years' worth of experience after one year's work. Leaders who get the most from their experience regularly discuss what they have been learning with a partner, and they frequently update their development plans as a result of these discussions.

Building Trust

The second component of credibility is building trust, which can be broken down into clarifying and communicating your values, and building relationships with others. In many ways leadership is a moral exercise. For example, one of the key differences between charismatic and transformational leaders is that the latter base their vision on their own and their followers' values, whereas the former base their vision on their own possibly selfish needs. Having a strong values system is an important component both in the Building Blocks Model of Skills and in leadership success. Because of the importance of values and relationships in building trust, the remainder of this section explores these two topics in more depth.

Chapter 7 defined values as generalized behaviors or states of affairs that an individual considers to be important. Provided that leaders make ethical decisions and abide by organizational rules, however, differences in values among leaders and followers may be difficult to discern. Since people do not come to work with their values tattooed to their foreheads, others typically make inferences about a leader's values based on their day-to-day behaviors (or just as importantly, their absence of certain day-to-day behaviors). Unfortunately, in many cases leaders' day-to-day behaviors are misaligned with their personal values; they are not living their life (at work, at least) in a manner consistent with their values.

An example of a leader not living life according to his values might be illustrative. An executive with an oil and gas firm was responsible for all exploration (i.e., drilling) operations in western Canada. Because he felt the discovery of new oil and gas fields was the key to the company's long-term success, he worked up to 18 hours a day, pushed his followers to work similar sorts of hours, had little patience for and would publicly disparage those oil rig operators who were behind schedule, and almost fired a manager who gave one of his followers a week off to see the birth of his son back in the United States. As these behaviors continued over time, more and more of his followers either requested transfers or quit to join other companies. Because of these problems with turnover and morale, he was asked to participate in a formal coaching program. Not surprisingly, his 360-degree feedback showed that his boss, peers, and followers found him very difficult to work with or for. These results indicated that he put a premium on getting results, getting ahead, and economic rewards, yet when he was asked to name the things he felt were most important to him as a leader, his priorities were his family, his religion, getting along with others, and developing his followers (altruism). Obviously, there was huge gap between what he truly believed in and how he behaved. He felt the company expected him to hold people's feet to the fire and get results no matter what the cost, yet neither the boss nor his peers felt that this was the case. The executive had misconstrued the situation and was exhibiting behaviors that were misaligned with his values.

Although the case above was somewhat extreme, it is not unusual to find leaders acting in ways that are misaligned with their personal values. One way to assess the degree to which leaders are living their lives according to their personal values is by asking what they truly believe in and what they spend their time and money on. For example, you could write down the five things you believe most strongly in (i.e., your top five values), and then review your calendar, daytimer, checkbook, and credit card statements to determine where you spend your time and money. If the two lists are aligned, then you are likely to be living your life according to your values. If not, then you may be living your life according to how others think you should act. And if there is some level of discrepancy between the two lists, what should you do? Of course, some level of discrepancy is likely to occur, as situational demands and constraints can often influence the way leaders behave. On the other hand, large discrepancies between the lists may indicate that you are not living life consistently with your values, and those you interact with may infer that you have a

Highlight CR–1

Sample Leadership Credos

As a leader, I . . .

. . . believe in the concept of whole persons and will seek to use the full range of talents and abilities of colleagues whenever possible.

. . . will seek to keep people fully informed.

. . . will more consistently express appreciation to others for a job well done.

. . . will take risks in challenging policies or protocol when they do not permit us to effectively serve our customers.

. . . will selectively choose battles to fight—rather than trying to fight all of the possible battles.

. . . will actively support those providing the most effective direction for our company.

. . . will seek to change the things I can in a positive direction and accept those things I have no chance or opportunity to change.

Source: *Impact Leadership* (Minneapolis: Personnel Decisions International, 1995).

---

very different set of values than those you personally believe in. A good first step in clarifying this discrepancy is to craft a personal mission statement or a leadership credo, a statement that describes what you truly believe in as a leader.

Examples of different leadership credos for managers across corporate America can be found in Highlight CR–1. There are several aspects of leadership credos worth additional comment. First, leadership credos are personal and are closely linked with a leader's values—a credo should describe what the leader believes in and will (or will not) stand for. Second, it should also describe an ideal state. A leader's behavior may never be perfectly aligned with his or her personal mission statement, but it should be a set of day-to-day behaviors that he or she will strive to achieve. Third, leadership credos should be motivating; leaders should be passionate and enthusiastic about the kind of leader they aspire to be. If the leader does not find his or her personal mission statement to be particularly inspiring, then it is hard to see how followers will be motivated by it. Much of the inspiration of a leadership credo stems from its being personal and values-based. Fourth, personal mission statements should be made public. Leaders need to communicate their values to others, and a good way to do this is to display their leadership credos prominently in their offices. This not only lets others know what you as a leader think is important, it also is a form of public commitment to your leadership credo.

Another key way to build trust is to form strong relationships with others. There is apt to be a high level of mutual trust if leaders and followers share strong relationships; if these relationships are weak, then the level of mutual trust is apt to be low. Techniques for building relationships with peers and superiors have already been described in this section of the text. Perhaps the best way to build relationships with followers is to spend time listening to what they have to say. Because many leaders tend to be action oriented and get paid to solve (rather than listen to) problems, some leaders overlook the importance of spending time with followers. Yet leaders who take the time to build relationships with followers are much more likely to understand their followers' perspectives of organizational issues, intrinsic motivators, values, level of competence for different tasks, or career aspirations. Leaders armed with this knowledge may be better able to influence and get work done through others. More on building relationships with followers can be found in the "Coaching" section of Part V.

Expertise × Trust

Leaders vary tremendously in their levels of both expertise and trust, and these differences have distinct implications for leaders wanting to improve their credibility. Take leaders who fall into the first quadrant of Figure CR–1. These individuals have a high level of trust and a high level of expertise; they would likely be seen by others as highly credible. Individuals falling into the second quadrant might include leaders who have spent little time with followers, who do not follow through with commitments, or who are new to the organization and have had little time to build relationships with co-workers. In all three cases, leaders wanting to improve their credibility should include building relationships with co-workers as key development objectives. Leaders falling into the third quadrant may be new college hires or people joining the company from an entirely different industry. It is unlikely that either type of leader would have the technical competence, organizational or industry knowledge, or time to build relationships with co-workers. These leaders may be in touch with their values and have a personal mission statement, but they will need to share their statement with others and act in a manner consistent with this statement in order to build their credibility. Other development objectives could include building expertise and strong relationships with others. Leaders falling into the fourth quadrant might include those promoted from among peers or transferring from another department within the company. Both sets of leaders may be in touch with their values, have a leadership credo, share strong relationships with co-workers, and have organizational and industry knowledge, but the former may need to develop leadership knowledge or skills and the latter technical competence if they wish to increase their credibility. Finally, it is important to note that leadership credos and development plans also have credibility implications because leaders who do not strive to live up to their ideals or fail to follow through with their developmental commitments are likely to be seen as less trustworthy than those who do.

FIGURE CR–1

The Credibility Matrix

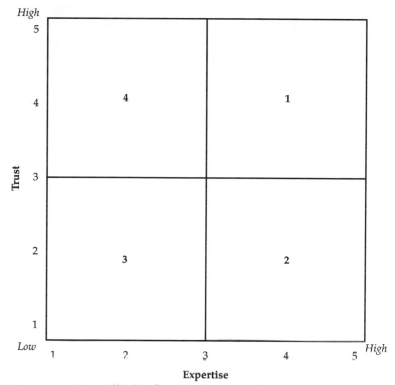

Source: G. J. Curphy, *Credibility: Building Your Reputation throughout the Organization* (Minneapolis: Personnel Decisions International, 1997).

Coaching

Forging a Partnership
Inspiring Commitment: Conducting a GAPS Analysis
Growing Skills: Creating Development and Coaching Plans
Promoting Persistence: Helping Followers Stick to Their Plans
Transferring Skills: Creating a Learning Environment
Concluding Comments

People who are coaches will be the norm. Other people won't get promoted.

Jack Welch
General Electric CEO

A key success factor in most organizations today is having leaders and followers with the right knowledge and skills. More and more, companies are looking at "bench strength" as a competitive advantage moving into the next century. There are essentially two ways to acquire bench strength; employers can either buy (i.e., hire) the talent they need, or they can build their existing talent through development and coaching programs. Given that many employers are currently facing an acute labor shortage in a number of critical positions, as well as a tight labor market, most are looking to build their own internal talent (Tichy & Cohen, 1997). Much of this talent is being developed through informal coaching. As we noted in Chapter 10, most leaders engage in some form of informal coaching. But how good of a coach are they? The authors' conversations with a multitude of leaders indicate that almost every single one was unsure what to do as a coach. Some thought it involved directing their employees on how to do tasks. Others thought it involved counseling employees on personal problems. One stated that his only example of coaching came from his high school football coach, and he wouldn't want to wish that on anyone.

Two thought leaders in this area are Peterson and Hicks (1996), who describe coaching as the "process of equipping people with the tools, knowledge, and opportunities they need to develop themselves and become more successful" (p. 14). According to Peterson and Hicks, good coaches orchestrate rather than dictate development. Good coaches help followers clarify career goals, identify and prioritize development needs, create and stick to development plans, and create environments that support learning and coaching. To some extent, many of the steps to coaching have been described under some of the other skills in Part V. Thus, coaching is really a blend of several different leadership skills. Being a good coach means having well developed skills, determining where a follower is in the coaching process, and intervening as appropriate. The five steps of coaching provide leaders with both a good road map and a diagnostic model for improving the bench strength of their followers.

Peterson and Hicks (1996) point out that this model works particularly well for high performers—individuals who tend to benefit the most from, but are often overlooked by, leaders when coaching. We noted in Chapter 14 that high performers produce 20–50 percent more than average employees (Hunter, Schmidt, & Judiesch, 1990), so coaching can have a considerable impact on the bottom line if it is targeted at high performers. Further support for the idea that top performers may benefit the most from coaching comes from athletics. If you watched any of the 1996 Summer Olympics in Atlanta or the 1998 Winter Olympics in Nagano, Japan, then you would have seen that many of the world's top athletes had at least one and sometimes two or three coaches. If these world-class athletes feel that coaching can enhance their performance, then it is likely that good coaches can also enhance the performance of any organization's top employees. Although the five-step model also works with poorly performing employees, more appropriate interventions might also include diagnosing performance problems, goal setting, providing rewards and constructive feedback, and punishing these individuals, particularly if informal coaching is not achieving desired results.

Forging a Partnership

The first step in informal coaching involves establishing a relationship built on mutual trust and respect with a follower. If a follower does not trust or respect her leader, then it will be very unlikely that she will pay much attention to his ideas for her development. There are several things leaders can do to forge a partnership with coachees. First, it will be much easier for leaders with high credibility to build strong partnerships with followers than for leaders with low credibility. Therefore, leaders need to determine where they are on the credibility matrix (Figure CR–1), and they may need to take appropriate developmental steps to improve their credibility before their coaching suggestions will have much impact. These developmental steps may include building technical and organizational knowledge as well as building strong relationships with the individuals they want to coach. Having an understanding of the context in which the employee operates can be as important as the relationship the leader shares with the employee. In the "Credibility" section, we noted that leaders will also need to spend time listening to their coachees; they need to understand coachees' career aspirations, values, intrinsic motivators, view of the organization, and current work situation. Good coaches can put themselves in their coachees' shoes, and can understand how coachees may view issues or opportunities differently from themselves. While forging a partnership, leaders can also provide coachees with realistic career advice, as sometimes coachees have unrealistic estimations of their skills and opportunities. For example, a new graduate from a top MBA program might want to be a partner at a consulting firm after two years with the company, but company policy may dictate that this decision will not be made until she has been with the firm for at least eight years. Her coach should inform her of this policy, and then work with her to map out a series of shorter-term career objectives that would help her become a partner in eight years. If coaches do not know what drives their coachees' behaviors, then another step to forging a partnership is to start asking a lot of questions. This is an excellent opportunity for leaders to practice their listening skills so as to better understand their coachees' career aspirations and intrinsic motivators.

Inspiring Commitment: Conducting a GAPS Analysis

This step in the coaching process is very similar to the GAPS analysis and the gaps-of-the-GAPS analysis, discussed in "Development Planning." The only difference is that these two analyses are now done from the coachee's perspective. Figure CH–1 might help to clarify this difference in perspective. Thus, in the Goals quadrant of the GAPS analysis the leader should write down the coachee's career objectives, and in the Perceptions quadrant the leader would write down how the coachee's behavior is impacting others. It is entirely possible that the leader may not be able to complete all of the quadrants of the GAPS for a coachee. If so, then the leader will need to gather more information before going any further. This information gathering may include discussing career goals and abilities with the coachee, reviewing the coachee's 360-degree feedback results, asking peers about how the coachee comes across or impacts others, or asking human resources about the educational or experience standards relevant to the coachee's career goals. One way to gather additional

Figure CH–1

A GAPS Analysis for an Employee

Goals: What does the employee want to do?	Abilities: What can the employee do now?
Step 1: Career objectives: —To become an Engineering Supervisor	*Step 2:* What strengths does the employee have for his or her career objectives? — Understand operational side of the business — Good planning skills — Good job function definition skills — Set clear individual and team goals *Step 3:* What development needs will he or she have to overcome? — Multidirection communication; may need to improve listening skills — May need to improve conflict resolution skills
Standards: What do you or the organization expect?	Perceptions: How do others see the employee?
Step 5: Expectations: • *Boss:* To be promoted, will need to: — Get along better with peers — Develop stronger listening skills	*Step 4:* PPRP and feedback from others: • *Boss* — Good technician — Develops good plans and holds people accountable — More interested in own rather than others' ideas • *Peers* — Can be counted on to get the job done — Can be too set in ways; too argumentative • *Direct Reports* — Has clear goals — Understands technical side of business — Doesn't value our ideas and opinions

Source: D. B. Peterson, and M. D. Hicks, *Leader as Coach* (Minneapolis: Personnel Decisions International, 1996); and G. J. Curphy, *The Leadership Development Process Manual* (Minneapolis: Personnel Decisions International, 1998).

information is to have both the leader and the coach complete a GAPS analysis independently, and then get together and discuss areas of agreement and disagreement. This can help ensure that the best information is available for the GAPS analysis and also help to build the partnership between the leader and coachee. During this discussion the leader and coachee should also do a gaps-of-the-GAPS analysis to identify and prioritize development needs. Usually leaders will get more commitment to development needs if coachees feel they had an important role in determining these needs, and a gaps-of-the-GAPS discussion is a way to build buy-in. This discussion can also help ensure that development needs are aligned with career goals.

TABLE CH–1 DEVELOPMENT PLAN CHECKLIST

Objectives:
❑ One-year career objective identified?
❑ No more than a total of two or three development goals?
❑ Areas in which the employee is motivated and committed to change and develop?

Criteria for Success:
❑ Is the new behavior clearly described?
❑ Can the behavior be measured or observed?

Action Steps:
❑ Specific, attainable, and measurable steps?
❑ Mostly on-the-job activities?
❑ Includes a variety of types of activities?
❑ Are activities divided into small, doable steps?

Seek Feedback and Support:
❑ Involvement of a variety of others?
❑ Includes requests for management support?
❑ Are reassess dates realistic?

Stretch Assignments:
❑ Do the stretch assignments relate to the employee's career objectives?

Resources:
❑ Uses a variety of books, seminars, and other resources?

Reflect with a Partner:
❑ Includes periodic reviews of learnings?

Source: G. J. Curphy, *The Leadership Development Process Manual* (Minneapolis: Personnel Decisions International, 1998).

Growing Skills: Creating Development and Coaching Plans

Once the coachee's development needs are identified and prioritized, coachees will need to build development plans to overcome targeted needs. These plans are identical to those described in the "Development Planning" section. Leaders generally do not build development plans for their coachees. Instead, they may want to go over a sample (or their own) development plan and coach their coachees on the seven steps in building a plan. They can then either jointly build a plan or have the coachee individually build a plan for the leader to review. Providing coachees with an important role in development planning should increase their level of commitment to the plan. Once a draft development plan is created, the leader and coach can then use the development planning checklist in Table CH–1 to review the plan.

In addition to the development plan, leaders will need to build a coaching plan that outlines the actions they will take to support their coachees' development. Some of these actions might include meeting with the coachees on a regular basis to provide developmental feedback, identifying developmental resources or opportunities, or helping the coachee reflect on what they have learned. As with development plans, leaders should share their coaching plans so that coachees know what kind of support they will be getting. This will also publicly commit the leaders to the coachees' development, which will make it more likely that they will follow through with the coaching plan.

Promoting Persistence: Helping Followers Stick to their Plans

Just because development and coaching plans are in place is no guarantee that development will occur. Sometimes coachees build development plans with great enthusiasm, but then never take any further action. This step in the coaching process is designed to help coachees "manage the mundane." An example of managing the mundane might be illustrative. One of the authors successfully completed a triathlon. The most difficult part of this accomplishment was not the event itself, but rather doing all of the training needed to successfully complete the event. Similarly, the inability to stick to a diet or keep a New Year's resolution is primarily due to an inability to manage the mundane; people are initially committed to these goals but have a difficult time sticking to them. The same is true with development planning. Conducting a GAPS analysis and creating a development plan are relatively easy; sticking to the plan is much more difficult. From the leader's perspective, a large part of coaching is helping followers stick to their development plan.

Several development-planning steps were specifically designed to promote persistence. For example, ensuring alignment between career and development objectives, getting feedback from multiple sources on a regular basis, and reflecting with a partner can help keep coachees focused on their development. If the leader is a coachee's developmental partner, then reflection sessions can help followers persist with their development. If leaders are not designated as partners in the development plan, then they should commit to meeting regularly with the coachees to discuss progress, what the leaders can do to support development, developmental opportunities, developmental feedback, and so forth.

Leaders can also help to promote persistence by capitalizing on coachable moments. Say a coachee was working on listening skills, and the leader and coach were in a staff meeting together. If the leader provides feedback to the coachee about her listening skills immediately after the staff meeting, then the leader has capitalized on a coachable moment. To capitalize on a coachable moment, leaders must know the followers' developmental objectives, be in situations where they can observe followers practicing their objectives, and then provide immediate feedback on their observations. Few coaches capitalize on coachable moments, but they can go a long way toward promoting persistence in coachees. It is important to note that capitalizing on coachable moments should take little time, often less than two minutes. In the example above, the leader could provide feedback to the coachee during their walk back to the office after the staff meeting.

Transferring Skills: Creating a Learning Environment

To build bench strength, leaders need to create a learning environment so that personal development becomes an on-going process rather than a one time event. As Tichy and Cohen (1997) aptly point out, the most successful organizations are those that emphasize the learning and teaching process—they focus on constantly creating leaders throughout the company. In reality, leaders have quite a bit of control over the kind of learning environments they want to create for their followers, and there are several interventions they can take to ensure that development becomes an on-going process. Perhaps the most important intervention is for leaders to role-model development. In that regard, if leaders are not getting regular feedback from followers, then they are probably not doing a good job of role-modeling development. By regularly soliciting feedback from followers, leaders are also likely to create a feedback-rich work environment. Once feedback becomes a group norm, people will be much more willing to help build team member skills, which in turn can have a catalytic effect on group performance. It is important to note that the leader will play a large role in this group norm, because if the leader is feedback averse, it will be difficult to see how this norm will be adopted by followers.

Leaders can also create learning environments by regularly reviewing their followers' development. Perhaps the easiest way to do this is by making leaders and followers development partners; then both parties can provide regular feedback and on-going support. During these discussions leaders and followers should review and update their development plans to capitalize on new development opportunities or acquire new skills. Leaders and followers can also review coaching plans to see what is and is not working and make the necessary adjustments.

Concluding Comments

Perhaps one of the greatest misperceptions of coaching, and the primary reason why leaders state they do not coach others, is that it takes a lot of time. In reality, nothing could be further from the truth. Leaders are working to build credibility, build relationships with followers, and understand followers' career aspirations and view of the world. Although these do take time, they are also activities leaders should be engaged in even if they are not coaching followers. Doing a GAPS analysis, identifying and prioritizing development needs, helping followers create development plans, and creating coaching plans often takes less than four hours. Although leaders will need to take these steps with all their followers, these four hours can be spread out over a four- to six-week period. As stated earlier, meeting with followers on a regular basis to review development (perhaps monthly) and capitalizing on coachable moments also take little time.

Finally, many of the actions outlined in "Create a Learning Environment" either take little time or are extensions of actions outlined earlier. The bottom line is that coaching really can take little additional time; it is really more a function of changing how you spend time with followers so that you can maximize their development.

Another note about the coaching model is that good coaches are equally versatile at all five steps of coaching. Some leaders are very good at forging a partnership, but then fail to carry development to the next level by conducting a GAPS analysis or helping followers build a development plan. Other leaders may help followers build a development plan but do not do anything to promote persistence or create a learning environment. Just as leaders need to develop their technical skills, so might they need to assess and in turn develop certain coaching skills. It is also important to remember that coaching is a very dynamic process—good coaches assess where followers are in the coaching process and intervene appropriately. By regularly assessing where they are with followers, they may determine that the relationship with a particular follower is not as strong as they thought, and this lack of relationship is why followers are not sticking to their development plan. In this case, a good coach would go back to forging a partnership with the follower and, once a trusting relationship had been created, go through another GAPS analysis, and so forth.

Finally, it is important to note that people can and do develop skills on their own. Nevertheless, leaders who commit to the five steps of informal coaching outlined above will both create learning organizations and help to raise development to a new level. Given the competitive advantage of companies that have a well-developed and capable workforce, in the future it will be hard to imagine leadership excellence without coaching. Good leaders are those that create successors, and coaching may be the best way to make this happen.

Empowerment

What is Empowerment?
The Psychological Components of Empowerment
Six Best Practices of Empowerment

Do what you can, where you are at, with what you have.

Teddy Roosevelt

Inside every old company is a new company waiting to be born.

Alvin Toffler

Empowerment has become a very popular concept over the past 10 years. Many companies have embarked on various types of empowerment programs to improve results, yet the success of these programs has been mixed at best (Howard, 1996). One of the reasons for the mixed results is that empowerment often means different things to different people. This section describes what empowerment is (and is not), as well as some of the psychological constructs underlying empowerment and some of the best practices of empowering others.

What Is Empowerment?

In general, people seem to fall into one of two camps with respect to empowerment. Some people believe empowerment is all about delegation and accountability, a top-down process where senior leaders articulate a vision and specific goals, and hold followers responsible for achieving them. Others believe empowerment is more of a bottom-up approach that focuses on intelligent risk taking, growth, change, trust, and ownership; followers act as entrepreneurs and owners that questioned rules and make intelligent decisions. Leaders tolerate mistakes and encourage cooperative behavior in this approach to empowerment (Quinn & Spreitzer, 1997). Needless to say, these two conceptualizations of empowerment have very different implications for leaders and followers. And it is precisely this conceptual confusion which has caused empowerment programs to fail in many organizations (Quinn & Spreitzer, 1997). Because of the conceptual confusion surrounding empowerment, companies such as Motorola will not use this term to describe programs that push decision making to lower organizational levels. These companies would rather coin their own terms to describe these programs, thus avoiding the confusion surrounding empowerment.

We define empowerment as having two key components. For leaders to truly empower employees, they must delegate leadership and decision making down to the lowest level possible. Employees are often the closest to the problem and have the most information, and as such can often make the best decisions. A classic example was the UPS employee who ordered an extra 737 to haul presents that had been forgotten in the last-minute Christmas rush. This decision was clearly beyond the employee's level of authority, but UPS praised his initiative for seeing the problem and making the right decision. The second component of empowerment, and the one most often overlooked, is equipping followers with the resources, knowledge, and skills necessary to make good decisions. All too often companies adopt an empowerment program and push decision making down to the employee level, but employees have no experience creating business plans, submitting budgets, dealing with other departments within the company, or directly dealing with customers or vendors. Not surprisingly, ill-equipped employees often make poor, uninformed decisions, and managers in turn are likely to believe that empowerment was not all it was cracked up to be. The same happens with downsizing, as employees are asked to take on additional responsibilities but are provided with little training or support. As we stated in Chapter 14, this "forced" empowerment may lead to some short-term stock gains but tends to be disastrous in the long run. Thus, empowerment has both delegation and developmental components; delegation without development is often perceived as abandonment, and development without delegation can often be perceived as micromanagement. Leaders wishing to empower followers must determine what followers are capable of doing, enhance and broaden these capabilities, and give followers commensurate increases in authority and accountability.

The Psychological Components of Empowerment

The psychological components of empowerment can be examined at both macro and micro levels. There are three macro psychological components underlying empowerment, and these are motivation, learning, and stress (Howard, 1996). As a concept, empowerment has been around since at least the 1920s, and the vast majority of companies that have implemented empowerment programs have done so to increase employee motivation and, in turn, productivity. As a motivational technique, however, empowerment has not lived up to its promise; empowered workers may not be any more productive than unempowered workers (Howard, 1996). There are several reasons why this may be the case. First, senior leaders tend to see empowerment through rose-colored glasses. They hear about the benefits an empowerment program is having in another company, but do not consider the time, effort, and changes needed to create a truly empowered workforce. Relatedly, many empowerment programs are poorly implemented—the program is announced with great fanfare, but little real guidance, training, or support is provided and managers are quick to pull the plug on the program as soon as followers start making poor decisions. Adopting an effective empowerment program takes training, trust, and time (Offermann, 1996), but companies most likely to implement an empowerment program (as a panacea for their poor financial situation) often lack these three attributes. Third, as described in Chapter 14, worker productivity and job dissatisfaction in the United States are at an all-time high. Many companies are dealing with high levels of employee burnout, and adding additional responsibilities to already overfilled plates is likely to be counterproductive. As reported by Xie and Johns (1995), some empowerment programs create positions that are just too big for a person to handle effectively, and job burnout is usually the result.

Although the motivational benefits of empowerment seem questionable, the learning and stress reduction benefits of empowerment seem more clear-cut. Given that properly designed and implemented empowerment programs include a strong developmental component, one of the key benefits to these programs is that they help employees learn more about their jobs, company, and industry. These knowledge and skill gains increase the intellectual capital of the company and can be a competitive advantage in moving ahead. In addition to the learning benefits, well designed empowerment programs can actually help to reduce burnout. People can tolerate high levels of stress when they have a high level of control. Given that many employees are putting in longer hours than ever before and work demands are at an all-time high, empowerment can help followers gain some control over their lives and better cope with stress. Although an empowered worker may have the same high work demands as an unempowered worker, the empowered worker will have more choices on how and when to accomplish these demands and as such will suffer from less stress. And because stress is a key component of dysfunctional turnover, giving workers more control over their work demands can reduce turnover and in turn positively impact the company's bottom line.

There are also four micro components of empowerment. These components can be used to determine whether employees are empowered or unempowered, and include self-determination, meaning, competence, and influence (Quinn & Spreitzer, 1997; Spreitzer, 1995). Empowered employees have a sense of self-determination; they can make choices about what they do, how they do it, and when they need to get it done. Empowered employees also have a strong sense of meaning; they believe what they do is important to them and to the company's success. Empowered employees have a high level of competence in that they know what they are doing and are confident they can get the job done. Finally, empowered employees have an impact on others and believe that they can influence their teams or work units and that co-workers and leaders will listen to their ideas. In summary, empowered employees have latitude to make decisions, are comfortable making these decisions, believe what they do is important, and are seen as influential members of their team. Unempowered employees may have little latitude to make decisions, may feel ill-equipped and may not want to make decisions, and may have little impact on their work unit, even if they have good ideas. Most employees probably fall somewhere in between the two extremes of the empowerment continuum, depicted in Figure EM–1. Leaders wanting to create more empowered followers may want to adopt some of the best practices techniques outlined below:

Six Best Practices of Empowerment

Do We Really Want or Need Empowerment?   Perhaps the first question leaders should ask before adopting an empowerment program is whether the company wants or needs empowerment. Leaders may agree that empowerment is important but may have fundamental differences as to the actions leaders need to take to create an empowered organization. Having a clear initial understanding of just what empowerment is will make the implementation of the program that much easier.

Leaders wanting to adopt an empowerment program must also consider how their own jobs and roles will be affected. They may need to fundamentally change their leadership style to better tolerate employee mistakes, play more of

FIGURE EM–1

The Empowerment Continuum

Empowered Employees ←——————→ **Unempowered Employees**

Empowered Employees	Unempowered Employees
¥ Self-determined	¥ Other-determined
¥ Sense of meaning	¥ Not sure if what they do is important
¥ High competence	¥ Low competence
¥ High influence	¥ Low influence

a coaching than directing role, and be willing to be challenged on a regular basis. Because empowered employees have access to considerably more information, they will be much more likely to question past or current decisions, and leaders will need to exert more personal power in order to get decisions adopted. Leaders feeling that this role transition is too much of a stretch will not enthusiastically embrace an empowerment program, making companywide adoption of the program difficult.

Creating a Clear Vision, Goals, and Accountabilities.   Once a decision is made to develop and implement an empowerment program, top management must ensure that the company's vision, business strategies, and operational goals are clear and are understood by everyone in the company. It is difficult to ask employees to make wise decisions if they do not know where the company is headed. Employees should know what the company and work unit are trying to accomplish and how these accomplishments will be measured, and they should be given regular feedback on progress. In addition, employees will need to understand how their own goals are related to work unit and company goals.

Developing Others.   Just because employees have a clear understanding of their work goals does not mean they have the knowledge, skills, and resources necessary to get them accomplished. Leaders will need to determine what employees can currently do, what they need to be able to do, and how they will help employees bridge the gaps between current and future capabilities. Perhaps the best way to do this is for leaders to adopt the five steps described in the "Coaching" section of the text. A key component of empowerment is trust, and leaders can build trust by taking the actions prescribed in "Forging a Partnership." Leaders can identify and prioritize development needs through a GAPS analysis, and can work to increase knowledge and skills through development plans, coaching plans, and the actions outlined under "Promote Persistence" and "Transferring Skills." The five steps of informal coaching give leaders a road map for improving the bench strength of their followers and systematically equipping them to meet the increased challenges of empowerment. Taking these development steps helps with the competence component of empowerment.

Delegating Decision Making to Followers.   Once followers are starting to develop the skills, knowledge, and experience necessary to make wise decisions, leaders must systematically increase the degree of latitude and autonomy employees are given to make decisions. Although this sounds fairly straightforward, in practice it can be fairly difficult. Some of the typical mistakes leaders make in this area are pushing followers into decision making too quickly, holding on to decision-making power too long, or taking decision-making power away from followers during a crisis. Other difficulties include the fact that many leaders associate decision making with leadership and may feel personally threatened by delegating decision-making authority to others. This may be particularly true when organizations have recently gone through a downsizing or when the level of trust between leaders and followers is low. Some followers may also feel reluctant to take on increased decision-making responsibility, as their level of skill may be exposed in ways it never had before (Offermann, 1996). Another complication is that some employees may feel that because they are taking on additional responsibilities, they should be paid more. This is particularly true when empowerment programs are introduced in union environments.

One way to determine how much latitude and authority to provide followers is to use the Situational Leadership Theory, described in Chapter 3. This theory provides a useful heuristic for developing employees and determining when they are ready to take on additional decision-making responsibilities. Another way to effectively delegate decision making to followers is to provide clear boundaries around the decisions they make. For example, employees at the Ritz-Carlton hotels have fixed limits on the amounts employees can spend to satisfy disgruntled guests. As the level of followers' knowledge and experience increases, the scope of the decisions can be increased and their boundaries loosened. Leaders delegating tasks and responsibilities should also follow the tenets of setting goals and delegating described earlier in this section of the text. Because followers will not be very skilled in making wise decisions, leaders will need to be prepared to tolerate followers' mistakes and help them learn from these experiences. The actions outlined under this best practice will help with the self-determination and influence components of empowerment.

Leading by Example. Leaders must be an example of empowerment if they want to successfully empower their employees. An illustration of how a leader could role-model empowerment will be useful. A multi-million-dollar consulting firm, run by one of the authors, was facing an acute labor shortage. Customer requests for additional services created enough work for four new positions. The office had a strong financial track record, and financial analyses provided solid support for the additional positions. Moreover, employee workload was extremely high, and the office was in desperate need of additional help. Armed with these facts, the author submitted job requisitions for the four additional positions to corporate headquarters. But after two months and numerous phone calls to corporate staff, the positions did not seem to be any closer to being approved. The author went ahead and hired the four additional staff, and informed corporate headquarters of his decision once the new personnel were onboard. Although the author took a considerable amount of heat from the COO and the vice president of human resources, the office continued to be financially successful, office morale dramatically improved, and the author sent a clear signal to his staff to seek forgiveness rather than permission.

Quinn and Spreitzer (1997) claim that it is nearly impossible for unempowered leaders to empower followers. Although there is some truth to this statement, empowerment needs to start somewhere, and it is all too easy for leaders to say that "they" are not allowing us to empower our followers. All too often "they" are very same people who are making these statements, and it is their own preconceived notions of leadership and misunderstandings of empowerment that are getting in the way. When this occurs, it is all too easy for leaders to waste time finger pointing and overlook the areas where they *can* empower followers. In the above example the author was not empowered to make these hiring decisions, yet he went ahead and did it anyway. This could have been a career-ending decision for the author, but he weighed the consequences of failing to hire additional help and thought the benefits were greater than the political costs. There is a certain amount of risk taking to leadership, and good leaders are those who themselves take, and allow their followers to take, intelligent risks. Like UPS and the employee who ordered the additional 737, good leaders reward intelligent risk taking and do not punish decisions that were well thought out but failed.

Empowerment Must Be Systemic to Be Successful.   Although individual leaders who take initiative can empower their followers, it will be much easier and more effective if senior leadership embraces empowerment as a key business strategy. When reward and performance appraisal systems, selection systems, work processes, training programs, organizational structure, and information systems are strongly aligned with the organization's definition of empowerment, then all these programs will be very successful. On the other hand, merely introducing an empowerment program but failing to make the necessary adjustments in the organizational systems, processes, and structure will likely be a recipe for failure.

REFERENCES

Adams, J.; H. T. Prince; D. Instone; and R. W. Rice. "West Point: Critical Incidents of Leadership." *Armed Forces and Society* 10 (1984), pp. 597-611.

Adams, J. L. *Conceptual Blockbusting*. New York: W. W. Norton, 1979.

Adams, J. S. "Toward an Understanding of Inequity." *Journal of Abnormal and Social Psychology* 67 (1963), pp. 422-36.

Adams, J. S. "Inequity in Social Exchange." In *Advances in Experimental Social Psychology*. ed. L. Berkowitz. Vol. 2. New York: Academic Press, 1965, pp. 267-96.

Adler, S., and H. M. Weiss. "Criterion Aggregation in Personality Research: A Demonstration Looking at Self-Esteem and Goal Setting." *Human Performance* 1, no. 2 (1988), pp. 99-109.

Aguayo, R. *Dr. Deming: The Man Who Taught the Japanese about Quality*. New York: Carol Publishing Group, 1990.

Alberti, R. E., and M. L. Emmons. *Your Perfect Right*. San Luis Obispo, CA: Impact, 1974.

Albrecht, K. *Stress and the Manager*. Englewood Cliffs, NJ: Prentice Hall, 1979.

Alderfer, C. P. "An Empirical Test of a New Theory of Human Needs." *Organizational Behavior and Human Performance* 4 (1969), pp. 142-75.

———. "Group and Intergroup Relations." In *Improving Life at Work*. ed. J. R. Hackman and J. L. Suttle, Santa Monica, CA: Goodyear, 1977.

Aldrich, H. E. *Organizations and Environments*. Englewood Cliffs, NJ: Prentice Hall, 1979.

Allen, T. H. "Situational Management Roles: A Conceptual Model." *Dissertation Abstracts International* 42, no. 2A (1981), p. 465.

Allport, G. W., and H. S. Odbert, "Trait-names: A Psycho-Lexical Study." *Psychological Monographs* 47 (1936), 171-220.

Amabile, T. M., and R. Conti. "What Downsizing Does to Creativity." *Issues & Observations* 15, no. 3 (1995), pp. 1-6.

Amabile, T. M. *The Social Psychology of Creativity*. New York: Springer-Verlag, 1983.

———. "Motivation and Creativity: Effects of Motivation Orientation on Creative Writers." *Journal of Personal and Social Psychology*, 48 (1985), pp. 393-99.

———. "The Motivation to be Creative." In *Frontiers in Creativity: Beyond the Basics*. ed. S. Isaksen. Buffalo, NY: Bearly Limited. 1987.

Amabile, T. M., and B. A. Hennessey. "The Motivation for Creativity in Children." In *Achievement and Motivation: A Social-Developmental Perspective*, ed. A. K. Boggiano and T. Pittman. New York: Cambridge University Press, 1988.

Amabile, T. M., and S. S. Gryskiewicz. "Creativity in the R&D Laboratory." Greensboro, N.C.: Center for Creative Leadership, (Tech Report No. 30), 1987.

Anastasi, A. *Psychological Testing*. 5th ed. New York: Macmillian, 1982.

Anderson, C. R., and C. E. Schneier. "Locus of Control, Leader Behavior, and Leader Performance among Management Students." *Academy of Management Journal* 21 (1978), pp. 690-98.

Andrews, P. H. "Performance, Self-Esteem and Perceptions of Leadership Emergence: A Comparative Study of Men and Women." *Western Journal of Speech Communication* 48 (1984), pp. 1-13.

Andrews, R. L., and R. Soder. "Principal Leadership and Student Achievement." *Educational Leadership* 44 (1987), pp. 9-11.

Argyris, C. *Increasing Leadership Effectiveness*. New York: Wiley, 1976.

Arvey, R. D. et al. "Mainstream Science on Intelligence." *The Wall Street Journal*, December 13, 1994.

Arvey, R. D.; T. J. Bouchard Jr.; N. L. Segal; and L. M. Abraham. "Job Satisfaction: Environmental and Genetic Components." *Journal of Applied Psychology* 74 (1989), pp. 187-92.

Arvey, R. D.; G. A. Davis; and S. M. Nelson. "Use of Discipline in an Organization: A Field Study." *Journal of Applied Psychology* 69 (1984), pp. 448-60.

Arvey, R. D., and J. M. Ivancevich. "Punishment in Organizations: A Review, Propositions, and Research Suggestions." *Academy of Management Review* 5 (1980), pp. 123-32.

Arvey, R. D., and A. P. Jones. "The Use of Discipline in Organizational Settings; A Framework for Future Research." In *Research in Organizational Behavior*. ed. L. L. Cummings and B. M. Staw, vol. 7. Greenwich, CT: JAI, 1985, pp. 367-408.

Astin, H. S., and C. Leland. *Women of Influence, Women of Vision*. San Francisco: Jossey-Bass, 1991.

Atkinson, J. W. "Motivational Determinants of Risk Taking Behavior." *Psychological Review* 64 (1957), pp. 359-72.

Atwater, L.; P. Roush; and A. Fischthal. "The Influence of Upward Feedback on Self- and Follower Ratings of Leadership." *Personnel Psychology* 48, no. 1 (1995), pp. 35-60.

Atwater, L. E.; J. F. Camobreco; S. D. Dionne; B. J. Avolio; and A. N. Lau. "Effects of Rewards and Punishments on Leader Charisma, Leader Effectiveness, and Follower Reactions." *Leadership Quarterly* 8 no. 2 (1997), pp. 133-52.

Austin, J. S.; E. J. Conlon; and R. L. Daft. "Organizing for Effectiveness: A Guide to Using Structural Design for Mission Accomplishment." (LMDC-TR-84-3-0). Maxwell AFB, AL: Leadership and Management Development Center, Air University, 1986.

Avolio, B. J., and B. M. Bass. "Charisma and Beyond." In *Emerging Leadership Vistas*. ed. J. G. Hunt, B. R. Baliga, H. P. Dachler, and C. A. Schriesheim. Lexington, MA: D. C. Heath, 1987.

―――. "Transformational Leadership, Charisma, and Beyond." In *Emerging Leadership Vista*. ed. J. G. Hunt, B. R. Baliga, and C. A. Schriesheim. Lexington. MA: D. C. Heath, 1988.

Avolio, B. J., and T. C. Gibbons. "Developing Transformational Leaders: A Life Span Approach." In *Charismatic Leadership: The Elusive Factor in Organizational Effectiveness.* ed. J. A. Conger and R. N. Kanungo. San Francisco: Jossey-Bass, 1988.

Ayman R., and M. M. Chemers. "The Effect of Leadership Match on Subordinate Satisfaction in Mexican Organizations: Some Moderating Influences of Self-Monitoring." *Applied Psychology: An International Review* 40 no. 3 (1991), pp. 229-314.

Azar, B. "Corporations Seek Help Fitting Goals Together." *APA Monitor*, July 1997, pp. 14-15.

Azar, B. "Corporations Seek Help Fitting Goals Together." *APA Monitor*, July 1997, pp. 14-15.

Azar, B. "Searching for Intelligence Beyond G." *APA Monitor* 26, no. 1 (1995), p. 1.

Azar, B. "Which Traits Predict Job Performance?" *APA Monitor*, July 1995, pp. 30-31.

Back, K., and K. Back. *Assertiveness at Work.* London: McGraw-Hill. 1982.

Badin, I. J. "Some Moderator Influences on Relationships between Consideration, Initiating Structure, and Organizational Criteria." *Journal of Applied Psychology* 59 (1974), pp. 380-82.

Bales, R. F. "Task Roles and Social Roles in Problem-Solving Groups." In *Readings in Social Psychology.* ed. E. E. Maccoby, T. M. Newcomb, and E. L. Hartley. New York: Holt, 1958.

Baltzell, E. D. *Puritan Boston and Quaker Philadelphia.* New York: The Free Press, 1980.

Bandura, A. "Self-Efficacy: Toward a Unifying Theory of Behavioral Change." *Psychological Review* 84 (1977), pp. 191-215.

Barling, J.; T. Weber; and E. K. Kelloway. "Effects of Transformational Leadership Training on Attitudinal and Financial Outcomes: A Field Experiment." *Journal of Applied Psychology* 81, no. 6, (1996), pp. 827-32.

Barnes, F. "Mistakes New Presidents Make" *Reader's Digest* (January 1989), p. 43.

Barnum, D. F. "Effective Membership in the Global Business Community." In *New Traditions in Business.* ed. J. Renesch. San Francisco: Berrett-Koehler, 1992.

Barrick, M. R. and M. K. Mount. "The Big Five Personality Dimensions and Job Performance: A Meta-analysis." *Personal Psychology* 44 (1991), pp. 1-26.

Barrick, M. R., and M. K. Mount, "Effects of Impression Management and Self-Deception on the Predictive Validity of Personality Constructs." *Journal of Applied Psychology* 81, no. 3 (1996), pp. 261-72.

Barron, F., and D. M. Harrington. "Creativity, Intelligence, and Personality." *Annual Review of Psychology* 32 (1981), pp. 439-76.

Bass, B. M., and B. J. Avolio (Eds.). *Increasing Organizational Effectiveness through Transformational Leadership.* Thousand Oaks, CA: Sage, 1994.

Bass, B. M. *Leadership, Psychology, and Organizational Behavior.* New York: Harper, 1960.

———. *Leadership and Performance Beyond Expectations.* New York: The Free Press, 1985.

———. "Evolving Perspectives of Charismatic Leadership." In *Charismatic Leadership: The Elusive Factor in Organizational Effectiveness.* ed. J. A. Conger and R. N. Kanungo. San Francisco: Jossey-Bass, 1988.

———. *Bass and Stogdill's Handbook of Leadership.* 3rd ed. New York: Free Press, 1990.

Bass, B. M. "Does the Transactional-Transformational Leadership Paradigm Transcend Organizational and National Boundaries?" *American Psychologist* 52, no. 3 (1997), pp. 130-39.

Bass, B. M., and B. J. Avolio. *The Multifactor Leadership Questionnaire Report.* Palo Alto, CA: Mind Garden, Inc., 1996.

Bass, B. M.; B. J. Avolio; and L. E. Atwater. "The Transformational and Transactional Leadership of Men and Women." *Applied Psychology: An International Review* 45 (1996), pp. 5-34.

Bass, B. M., and F. J. Yammarino. *Long-term Forecasting of Transformational Leadership and Its Effects among Naval Officers: Some Preliminary Findings.* (Technical Report No. ONR-TR-2). Arlington, VA: Office of Naval Research, 1988.

Bedeian, A. G., and A. A. Armenakis. "The Cesspool Syndrome: How Dreck Floats to the Top of Declining Organizations." *Academy of Management Executive* 12, no. 1 (1998), pp. 58-63.

Benne, K. D., and P. Sheats. "Functional Roles of Group Members." *Journal of Social Issues* 4 (1948), pp. 41-49.

Benner, P. E. *Stress and Satisfaction on the Job.* New York: Praeger, 1984.

Bennis, W. G. *On Becoming a Leader.* Reading, MA: Addison-Wesley, 1989.

Bennis, W. G. "Leadership Theory and Administrative Behavior: The Problem of Authority." *Administrative Science Quarterly* 4 (1959).

Berkman, L., and S. L. Syme. "Social Networks, Host Resistance, and Mortality: A Nine-Year Follow-up Study of Alameda County Residents." *American Journal of Epidemiology* 109 (1979), pp. 186-204.

Berlew, D. E. " Leadership and Organizational Excitement." In *Organizational Psychology: A Book of Readings.* ed. D. A. Kolb, I. M. Rubin, and J.M. McIntyre. 2nd ed. Englewood Cliffs, NJ: Prentice-Hall, 1974.

———. "Leadership and Empowerment." Workshop presented at the Seventh Annual Society for Industrial and Organizational Psychologists Convention, Montreal, May 1992.

Bernardin, H. J., and R. W. Beatty. *Performance Appraisal: Assessing Human Behavior at Work*. Boston: Kent, 1984.

Berry, J. K. "Linking Management Development to Business Strategies." *Training and Development Journal*, August 1990, pp. 20-22.

Betz, E. L. "Two Tests of Maslow's Theory of Need Fulfillment." *Journal of Vocational Behavior*, 24 (1984), pp. 204-20.

Beyer, J. M., and H. M. Trice. "A Field Study in the Use and Perceived Effects of Discipline in Controlling Work Performance." *Academy of Management Journal* 27 (1984), pp. 743-64.

Bickman, L. "The Social Power of a Uniform." *Journal of Applied Social Psychology* (1974), pp. 47-61.

Blake, P. "Walt Disney World: No Mere Amusement Park." *The Architectural Forum* 136, no. 5 (1972), pp. 24-40.

———. "The Lessons of the Parks." In *The Art of Walt Disney: From Mickey Mouse to the Magic Kingdom*. ed. C. Finch. New York: Harry N. Abrams, 1973, pp. 423-49.

Blake, R. J. "Relations between Worker Satisfactories and Personality." In R. T. Hogan (Chair), *Personality and Organizational Behavior*. Symposium presented at the 104th Annual Meeting of the American Psychological Association, Toronto, Canada, 1996.

Blake, R. J., and E. H. Potter III. "Novice Leaders, Novice Behaviors, and Strong Culture: Promoting Leadership Change Beyond the Classroom." In *Impact of Leadership*. ed. K. E. Clark, M. B. Clark, and D. P. Campbell. Greensboro, NC: The Center for Creative Leadership, 1992.

Blake, R. R., and A. A. McCanse. *Leadership Dilemmas—Grid Solutions*. Houston, TX: Gulf, 1991.

Blake, R. R., and J. S. Mouton. *The Managerial Grid*. Houston, TX: Gulf, 1964.

———. *The Managerial Grid III*. Houston, TX: Gulf, 1985.

Blake, R. R.; H. A. Shepard; and J. S. Mouton, *Managing Intergroup Conflict in Industry*. Houston, TX: Gulf, 1964.

Blanchard, K.; P. Zigami; and P. Zigami. *Leadership: The One Minute Manager*. New York: Morrow, 1985.

Blank, T. O. "What High School Leaders Think of Leadership." *High School Journal* 63 (1986), pp. 207-13.

Blankenship, L. V., and R. E. Miles. "Organizational Structure and Managerial Decision Behavior." *Administrative Science Quarterly* 13 (1968), pp. 106-20.

Blau, P. M. "Critical Remarks on Weber's Theory of Authority." *American Political Science Review* 57, no. 2 (1963), pp. 305-15.

Blau, P. M. "The Hierarchy of Authority in Organizations." *American Journal of Sociology* 73 (1968), pp. 453-67.

Block, P. *Stewardship*. San Francisco: Berrett-Koehler, 1993.

Blum, R. E.; J. A. Butler; and N. L. Olson. "Leadership for Excellence: Research-based Training for Principals." *Educational Leadership,* 45, no. 1 (1987), pp. 25-29.

Boal, K. M., and J. M. Bryson. "Charismatic Leadership: A Phenomenal and Structural Approach." In Emerging Leadership Vista. ed. J. G. Hunt, B. R. Baliga, H. P. Dachler, and C. A. Schriesheim. Lexington, MA: Heath Company.

Borman, W. C.; M. A. Hanson; S. H. Oppler; and E. D. Pulakos. "The Role of Early Supervisory Experience in Supervisor Performance." *Journal of Applied Psychology* (in press).

Borman, W. C.; L. A. White; E. D. Pulakos; and S. A. Oppler. "Models Evaluating the Effects of Rated Ability, Knowledge, Proficiency, Temperament, Awards, and Problem Behavior on Supervisor Ratings." *Journal of Applied Psychology* 76 (1991), pp. 863-72.

Bottger, P. C. "Expertise and Air Time as Bases of Actual and Perceived Influence in Problem-Solving Groups." *Journal of Applied Psychology* 69 (1984), pp. 214-21.

Bowers, D. G., and S. E. Seashore. "Predicting Organizational Effectiveness with a Four Factor Theory of Leadership." *Administrative Science Quarterly* 11 (1966), pp. 238-63.

Boyatzis, R. E., and F. R. Skelly. "The Impact of Changing Values on Organizational Life." In *Organizational Behavior Readings.* ed. D. A. Kolb, I. M. Rubin, and J. Osland, 5th ed. Englewood Cliffs, NJ: Prentice Hall, 1991, pp. 1-16.

Bracken, D. W. "Straight Talk about Multi-rater Feedback." *Training & Development,* September 1994.

Bradley, R. T. *Charisma and Social Power: A Study of Love and Power, Wholeness and Transformation.* New York: Paragon, 1987.

Brandt, R. "On Leadership and Student Achievement: A Conversation with Richard Andrews." *Educational Leadership* 45, no. 1 (1987), pp. 9-16.

Bray, D. W., and A. Howard. "The AT&T Longitudinal Study of Managers. In *Longitudinal Studies of Adult Psychological Development.* Ed. K. W. Schaiel. New York: Guilford, 1983.

Bray, D. W.; R. J. Campbell; and D. L. Grant. *Formative Years in Business: A Long-term AT&T Study of Managerial Lives.* New York: Wiley-Interscience, 1974.

Brenner, O. C.; J. Tomkiewicz; and V. E. Schein. "The Relationship between Sex Role Stereotypes and Requisite Management Characteristics Revisited." *Academy of Management Journal,* 32 (1989), pp. 662-669.

Brief, A. P.; R. S. Schuler; and M. Van Sell. *Managing Job Stress.* Boston: Little, Brown, 1981.

Brinkmeyer, K. R., and R. T. Hogan. "An Exploration of the Structure of Individual Differences." In R. T. Hogan (Chair), *Personality Applications in the Workplace: Thinking outside the Dots.* Symposium presented at the 12th Annual Conference of the Society of Industrial and Organizational Psychology, St. Louis, 1997.

Brockner, J., and L. Adsit. "The Moderating Impact of Sex on the Equity-Satisfaction Relationship." *Journal of Applied Psychology* 71 (1986), pp. 585-90.

Brody, N. "Intelligence, Schooling, and Society." *American Psychologist* 52, no. 10, (1997), pp. 1046-50.

Brody, N. *Intelligence.* San Diego: Academic Press, 1992.

Brown, A. D. "Narcissism, Identity, and Legitimacy." *Academy of Management Review* 22, no. 3 (1997), pp. 643-86.

Brown, L. D. *Managing Conflict at Organizational Interfaces.* Reading, MA: Addison-Wesley, 1983.

Brumback, G. "Institutionalizing Ethics in Government." *Public Personnel Management* 20, 3 (1991), pp. 353-364.

Brungardt, C. "The Making of Leaders: A Review of the Research in Leadership Development and Education." *Journal of Leadership Studies* 3, no. 3. (1996), pp. 81-95.

————. "Benchmarking Employee Attitudes." *Training and Development*, June 1992, 49-53.

Bugental, D. E. "A Study of Attempted and Successful Social Influence in Small Groups as a Function of Goal-Relevant Skills," *Dissertation Abstracts* 25 (1964), p. 660.

Bunker, K. A., & Webb, A. *Learning How to Learn from Experience: Impact of Stress and Coping.* Report No. 154. Greensboro, NC: Center for Creative Leadership, 1992.

Burke, M. J., and R. R. Day. " A Cumulative Study of the Effectiveness of Managerial Training." *Journal of Applied Psychology* 71 (1986), pp. 242-45.

Burke, P. J. "The Development of Task and Socio-Emotional Role Differentiation." *Sociometry* 30 (1967), pp. 379-92.

Burns, J. M. *Leadership.* New York: Harper & Row, 1978.

Burns, T., and G. M. Stalker. *The Management of Innovation.* London: Tavistock, 1961.

Bycio, P.; R. D. Hackett; and J. S. Allen. "Further Assessments of Bass's (1985) Conceptualization of Transformational and Transactional Leadership." *Journal of Applied Psychology* 80 (1995), pp. 468-78.

Calder, B. J. and B. M. Staw. "Self-Perception of Intrinsic and Extrinsic Motivation." *Journal of Personality and Social Psychology* 31 (1975), pp. 599-605.

Campbell, D. P. *Handbook for the Strong Vocational Interest Blank.* Stanford, CA: Stanford University Press, 1971.

————. "The Psychological Test Profiles of Brigadier Generals: Warmongers or Decisive Warriors?" Invited address presented to Division 14 of the American Psychological Association, New York, 1987.

————. *Campbell Leadership Index Manual.* Minneapolis: National Computer Systems, 1991.

Campbell, D. P., and S. Hyne. *Manual for the Revised Campbell Organizational Survey*. Minneapolis, MN: National Computer Systems, 1995.

Campbell, D. P., Curphy, G. J., & Tuggle, T. *360 Degree Feedback Instruments: Beyond Theory*. Workshop presented at the Tenth Annual Conference of the Society for Industrial and Organizational Psychology. Orlando, FL. May, 1995.

Campbell, D. P.; S. Hyne; and D. L. Nilsen. *Campbell Interests and Skill Survey Manual*. Minneapolis, MN: National Computer Systems, 1992.

Campbell, J. P. The Cutting Edge of Leadership: An Overview. In *Leadership: The Cutting Edge*, ed. J. G. Hunt and L. L. Larson. Carbondale, IL: Southern Illinois University Press, 1977.

————. "Training design for performance improvement." In *Productivity in Organizations: New Perspectives from Industrial and Organizational Psychology*. ed. J. P. Campbell, R. J. Campbell, and Associates. San Francisco: Jossey-Bass, 1988, pp. 177-216.

Campbell, J. P.; M. D. Dunnette; E. E. Lawler; and K. E. Weick. *Managerial Behavior, Performance, and Effectiveness*. New York: McGraw-Hill, 1970.

Campbell, J. P.; R. A. McCloy; S. H. Oppler; and C. E. Sager. "A Theory of Performance." In *Frontiers in Industrial/Organizational Psychology and Personnel Selection*. ed. N. Schmitt and W. C. Borman. San Francisco: Jossey-Bass, 1993, pp. 35-70.

Campbell, J. P., and R. D. Pritchard. "Motivation Theory in Industrial and Organizational Psychology." In *Handbook for Industrial and Organizational Psychology*. ed. M. D. Dunnette. Chicago: Rand McNally, 1976, pp. 60-130.

Cascio, W. F. *A Guide to Responsible Restructuring*. Washington, DC: U.S. Government Printing Office, 1995.

Case, T.; L. Dosier; G. Murkison; and B. Keys. "How Managers Influence Superiors: A Study of Upward Influence Tactics." *Leadership and Organization Development Journal* 9(4), (1988), pp. 4, 25-31.

Ceci, S. J., and W. M. Williams. "Schooling, Intelligence, and Income." *American Psychologist* 52, no. 10 (1997), pp. 1051-58.

Cellar, D. F.; M. L. Miller; D. D. Doverspike; and J. D. Klawsky. "Comparison of Factor Structures and Criterion-Related Validity Coefficients for Two Measures of Personality Based on the Five-Factor Model." *Journal of Applied Psychology* 81, no. 6 (1996), pp. 694-704.

Chaleff, I. *The Courageous Follower*. San Francisco: Berrett-Koehler, 1995.

Chandler, A. D. *Scale and Scope: The Dynamics of Industrial Capitalism*. Cambridge, MA: Harvard University Press, 1990.

Charters, W. W., and N. J. Pitner. "The Application of the Management Behavior Survey to the Measurement of Principle Leadership Behaviors." *Education and Psychological Measurement*, 46 (1986), pp. 811-25.

Chemers, M. M. "The Social, Organizational, and Cultural Contest of Effective Leadership." In *Leadership: Multidisciplinary Perspectives*. ed. B. Kellerman. Englewood Cliffs, NJ: Prentice-Hall, 1984.

Chinoy, E. *Society* New York: Random House, 1961.

Chitayat, G., and I. Venezia. "Determinates of Management Styles in Business and Nonbusiness Organizations." *Journal of Applied Psychology* 69 (1984), pp. 437-47.

Church, A. H. "From Both Sides Now: The Utility of Individual Personality Theory in I/O Psychology." *The Industrial-Organizational Psychologist* 32. no. 3 (1995), pp. 55-63.

———. "From Both Sides Now: The Utility of Individual Personality Theory in I/O Psychology." *The Industrial-Organizational Psychologist* 31, no. 3 (1994), pg. 108-116.

Church, A. H. "Managerial Self-Awareness in High-Performing Individuals in Organizations." *Journal of Applied Psychology* 82 no. 2 (1997) pp. 281-92.

Cialdini, R. B. *Influence.* New York: William Morrow, 1984.

Clark, B. R. "The Organizational Saga in Higher Education." *Administrative Science Quarterly* 17 (1972), pp. 178-84.

Cleland, D. I. *Strategic Management of Teams.* New York: John Wiley & Sons, 1996.

Cleveland, H. *The Knowledge Executive: Leadership in an Information Society.* New York: Dutton, 1985.

Clover, W. H. "Transformational Leaders: Team Performance Leadership Ratings and Firsthand Impressions." In *Measures of Leadership.* ed. K. E. Clark and M. B. Clark. West Orange, NJ: Leadership Library of America, 1990.

———. "At TRW, Executive Training Contributes to Quality." *The Human Resources Professional* (Winter 1991), pp. 16-20.

Clutterbuck, D. "How Much Does Success Depend upon a Helping Hand from Above?" *International Management* 37 (1982), pp. 17-19.

Cohen, A. R., and D. L. Bradford. *Influence without Authority.* New York: Wiley, 1990.

Conference Board. "Global Management Teams: A Perspective." *HR Executive Review* 4 (1996).

Conger, J. A. *The Charismatic Leader.* San Francisco: Jossey-Bass, 1989.

Conger, J. A., and R. N. Kanungo. *Charismatic Leadership: The Elusive Factor in Organizational Effectiveness.* San Francisco: Jossey-Bass, 1988.

Conway, F., and J. Siegalman. *Snapping.* New York: Delta, 1979.

Cornwell, J. M. "A Meta-Analysis of Selected Trait Research in the Leadership Literature." Paper presented at the Southeastern Psychological Association, Atlanta, Ga., 1983.

Cosell, H. *I Never Played the Game.* New York: William Morrow, 1985.

Costa, P. T., Jr., and R. R. McCrae. *The NEO Personality Inventory.* Odessa, FL: Psychological Assessment Resources, 1985.

Costa, R. R., and P. T. McCrae. "The Stability of Personality: Observations and Evaluations." *Current Directions in Psychological Science* 3, no. 6 (1994), pp. 173-175.

Couch, A., and P. W. Yetton. "Manager Behavior, Leadership Style, and Subordinate Performance: An Empirical Extension of the Broom-Yetton Conflict Rule." *Organizational Behavior and Human Decision Processes* 39 (1987), pp. 384-96.

Cousteau, V. "How to Swim with Sharks: A Primer." *Perspectives in Biology and Medicine* (summer 1973), pp. 525-28.

Coye, R. W. "Subordinate Responses to Ineffective Leadership." *Dissertation Abstracts International* 43, 6A (1982), p. 2070.

Cronbach, L. J. *Essentials of Psychological Testing.* 4th ed. San Francisco: Harper & Row, 1984.

Cronshaw, S. F., and R. J. Ellis. "A Process Investigation of Self-Monitoring and Leader Emergence." Paper presented at the Academy of Management Annual Meeting, San Francisco, 1990.

Csikszentmihalyi, M. *Flow: The Psychology of Optimal Experience.* New York: Harper & Row, 1990.

Cudney, M. R., and R. E. Hardy. *Self-Defeating Behaviors.* San Francisco, CA: Harper Collins, 1993.

Cummings, R. C. "Job Stress and the Buffering Effect of Supervisory Support." *Group and Organizational Studies* 15, no. 1, pp. 92-104.

Cummings, W. H. "Age Group Differences and Estimated Frequencies of the MBTI Types: Proposed Changes." *Proceedings of the Psychology in the Department of Defense Thirteenth Symposium*, U. S. Air Force Academy, Colorado Springs, CO, April 1992.

Curphy, G. J. "A Commentary on Moral Character Screening." In W. Sellman (Chair), *Moral Character Screening: Sorting Good and Bad Apples.* Symposium presented at the 105th Annual Meeting of the American Psychological Association, Chicago, 1997d.

———. "An empirical investigation of Bass' (1985) theory of transformational and transactional leadership." Ph.D. dissertation University of Minnesota, 1991a.

Curphy, G. J. "Career and Development Planning." Television presentation given at National Technical University, Ft. Collins, CO, 1997b.

Curphy, G. J. "Executive Coaching: How to Achieve Long-Term Leadership Behavioral Change." Panel presentation at the 15th Annual Applied Behavioral Sciences Symposium, United States Air Force Academy, CO, 1996.

Curphy, G. J. "In-Depth Assessments, 360-Degree Feedback, and Development: Key Research Results and Recommended Next Steps." Presentation given at the Annual Conference for HR Managers at U S WEST Communications, Inc., Denver, CO, January 1998a.

Curphy, G. J. "New Directions in Personality." In R. T. Hogan (Chair), *Personality and Organizational Behavior.* Symposium presented at the 104th Annual Meeting of the American Psychological Association, Toronto, Canada, 1996b.

Curphy, G. J. "Personality and Work: Some Food for Thought." In R. T. Hogan (Chair), *Personality Applications in the Workplace: Thinking outside the Dots.* Symposium presented at the 12th Annual Conference of the Society of Industrial and Organizational Psychology, St. Louis, 1997c.

Curphy G. J. "Personality, Intelligence, and Leadership." Presentation given to the Pioneer Leadership Program at Denver University, Denver, CO, 1997a.

————. "Some closing remarks about the use of self- and other-ratings of personality and behaviors." In *Multirater assessment systems: What we've learned*, chair M. D. Dunnette. Symposium conducted at the 99th American Psychological Association Convention, San Francisco, August 1991b.

————. "The Effects of Transformational and Transactional Leadership on Organizational Climate, Attrition, and Performance." In *Impact of Leadership*, ed. K. E. Clark, M. B. Clark, and D. P. Campbell. Greensboro, NC: Center for Creative Leadership, 1992a.

Curphy, G. J. "Transformational, Charismatic, and Transactional Leadership: A Literature Review." Unpublished manuscript, University of Minnesota, Department of Psychology, Minneapolis, 1990.

Curphy, G. J. *Users Guide and Interpretive Report for the Leadership Personality Survey*. Minneapolis: Personnel Decisions International, 1998b.

————. "Using Low Fidelity Simulations to Predict Future Leadership Success." In *Selections in Leadership: Some New Research Directions*, chair R. T. Hogan. Symposium conducted at the 13th Biennial Psychology in the DoD Conference, United States Air Force Academy, 1992b.

Curphy, G. J.; F. W. Gibson; B. W. Asiu; C. P. McCown; and C. Brown. "A Field Study of the Causal Relationships between Organizational Performance, Punishment, and Justice." Submitted for publication, 1992.

Curphy, G. J., F. W. Gibson; B. Asiu; J. Horn; and G. Macomber. The Attaché Selection Project. Technical Report no. 94-2. Colorado Springs, CO: U.S. Air Force Academy, 1994.

Curphy, G. J., and K. D. Osten. *Technical Manual for the Leadership Development Survey*. Technical Report no. 93-14. Colorado Springs, CO: U.S. Air Force Academy, 1993.

Curtis, B.; R. E. Smith; and F. L. Smoll. "Scrutinizing the Skipper: A Study of Behaviors in the Dugout." *Journal of Applied Psychology* 64 (1979), pp. 391-400.

Dansereau, F., Jr.; G. Graen; and J. W. Haga. "A Vertical Dyad Linkage Approach to Leadership within Formal Organizations: A Longitudinal Investigation of the Role Making Process." *Organizational Behavior and Human Performance*, 13 (1975), pp. 46-78.

Davis, B. L.; C. J. Skube; L. W. Hellervik; S. H. Gelelein; and J. L. Sheard. *The Successful Manager's Handbook*. Minneapolis, MN: Personnel Decisions Incorporated, 1992.

Davis, B. L.; L. W. Hellervik; and J. L. Sheard. *Successful Manager's Handbook*. 3rd ed. Minneapolis, MN: Personnel Decisions, 1989.

Davis, R. C. *The Fundamentals of Top Management*. New York: Harper, 1942.

Deary, J. J. "A (Latent) Big-Five Personality Model in 1915? A Reanalysis of Webb's Data." *Journal of Applied Psychology* 71, no. 5, (1996), pp. 992-1005.

DeBolt, J. W.; A. E. Liska; and B. R. Weng, "Replications of Associations between Internal Locus of Control and Leadership in Small Groups." *Psychological Reports* 38 (1976), p. 470.

Deci, E. L. "Effects of Contingent and Noncontingent Rewards and Controls on Intrinsic Motivation." *Organizational Behavior and Human Performance* 22 (1972), pp. 113-20.

————. *Intrinsic Motivation*. New York: Plenum, 1975.

————. *The Psychology of Self-Determination*. Lexington, MA: Lexington Books, 1980.

Deci, E. L., and R. M. Ryan. "The Support of Autonomy and the Control of Behavior." *Journal of Personality and Social Psychology* 53 (1987), pp. 1024-37.

Decker, P. J. "Social Learning Theory and Leadership." *Journal of Management* 5 (1986), pp. 46-58.

Deep, S., and L. Sussman. *Smart Moves*. Reading MA: Addison-Wesley, 1990.

Delbecq, A. L.; A. H. Van de Ven; and D. H. Gustafson. *Group Techniques for Program Planning: A Guide to Nominal and Delphi Processes*. Glenview, IL: Scott, Foresman, 1975.

Deluga, R. J. "Relationship among America Presidential Charismatic Leadership, Narcissism, and Rated Performance." *Leadership Quarterly* 8, no. 1, (1997), pp. 51-68.

Den Hartog, D. N., and R. M. Verburg. Charisma and Rhetoric: Communicative Techniques of International Business Leaders." *Leadership Quarterly* 8, no. 4 (1997), pp. 355-92.

Deveraux, G. "Charismatic Leadership and Crisis." In *Psychoanalysis and the Social Sciences*. Ed. W. Muensterberger and S. Axelrod. New York: International University Press, 1955.

Dewhirst, H. D.; V. Metts; and R. T. Ladd. "Exploring the Delegation Decision: Managerial Responses to Multiple Contingencies." Paper presented at the Academy of Management Convention, New Orleans, LA, 1987.

Dienesch, R. M., and R. C. Liden. "Leader-Member Exchange Model of Leadership: A Critique and Further Development." *Academy of Management Review* 11 (1986), pp. 618-34.

Dobbins, G. H., and J. M. Russell. "The Biasing Effects of Subordinate Likeableness on Leaders' Responses to Poor Performance." *Personnel Psychology* 39 (1986), pp. 759-77.

Donley, R. E., and D. G. Winter. "Measuring the Motives of Public Officials at a Distance: An Exploratory Study of American Presidents." *Behavioral Science* 15 (1970), pp. 227-36.

Donno, D. "Introduction." In *The Prince and Selected Discourses: Machiavelli*, ed. and trans. D. Dunno. New York: Bantam, 1966.

Dosier, L.; T. Case; B. Keys. "How Managers Influence Subordinates: An Empirical Study of Downward Influence Tactics." *Leadership and Organization Development Journal* 9, no. 5 (1988), pp. 22-31.

Dow, T. E. "The Theory of Charisma." *Sociological Quarterly* 10 (1969), pp. 306-18.

Downton, J. V. *Rebel Leadership: Commitment and Charisma in the Revolutionary Process*. New York: Free Press, 1973.

Druskat, V. U. "Gender and Leadership Style: Transformational and Transactional Leadership in the Roman Catholic Church." *Leadership Quarterly* 5(1), (1994), 99-120.

Dubois, P. H. "A Test Dominated Society: China 1115 BC–1905. In *Testing Problems in Perspective*. Ed. A. Anastasi. American Council on Education, 1964.

Duchon, D.; S. G. Green; and T. D. Taber. "Vertical Dyad Linkage: A Longitudinal Assessment of Antecedents, Measures, and Consequences." *Journal of Applied Psychology* 71 (1986), pp. 56-60.

Dukerich, J. M.; M. L. Nichols; D. R. Elm; and D. A. Vollrath. "Moral Reasoning in Groups: Leaders Make a Difference," *Human Relations* 43 (1990), pp. 473-93.

Dumaine, B. "Creating a New Company Culture." *Fortune*. 121, no. 2 (1990), pp. 127-131.

Duncker, K. "On Problem Solving." *Psychological Monographs* 58, no. 5, Whole No. 270.

Durand, D. E., and W. R. Nord. "Perceived Leader Behavior as a Function of Personality Characteristics of Supervisors and Subordinates." *Academy of Management Journal* 19 (1976), pp. 427-38.

Eagly, A. H. *Sex Differences in Social Behavior: A Social Role Interpretation*. Hillsdale, NJ: Erlbaum. 1987.

Eagly, A. H.; S. J. Karau; and M. G. Makhijani. "Gender and the Effectiveness of Leaders: A Meta-Analysis." *Psychological Bulletin* 117 (1995), pp. 125-45.

Eagly, A. H.; M. G. Makhijani; and B. G. Klonsky. "Gender and the Effectiveness of Leaders: A Meta-Analysis." *Psychological Bulletin* 111 (1992), pp. 3-22.

Eden, D., and A. B. Shani. "Pygmalion Goes to Boot Camp: Expectancy, Leadership, and Trainee Performance." *Journal of Applied Psychology* 67 (1982), pp. 194-99.

Edwards, B. *Drawing on the Right Side of the Brain*. Los Angeles, CA: J. P. Tarcher, 1979.

———. *Drawing on the Artist Within*. New York: Simon & Schuster, 1986.

Ehrlichman, J. *Witness to Power*. New York: Simon & Schuster, 1982.

Einstein, A. *On Education, Ideas and Opinions*. New York: Bonanza Books, 1954.

Eisenberger, R., and J. Cameron. "Detrimental Effects of Reward: Reality or Myth?" *American Psychologist* 51, no. 11 (1996), pp. 1153-66.

Ellis, A., and R. Harper. *A New Guide to Rational Living*. Englewood Cliffs, NJ: Prentice Hall, 1975.

Ellis, R. J.; R. S. Adamson; G. Deszca; and T. F. Cawsey. "Self-Monitoring and Leadership Emergence." *Small Group Behavior* 19 (1988), pp. 312-24.

Emery, F. E. and E. L. Trist. "The Causal Texture of Organizational Environments." *Human Relations* 18 (1965), pp. 21-32.

———. *Towards a Social Ecology*. London: Plenum, 1973.

England, G. W., and R. Lee. "The Relationship between Managerial Values and Managerial Success in the United States, Japan, India, and Australia." *Journal of Applied Psychology* 59 (1974), 411-19.

Erez, M.; P. C. Earley; and C. L. Hulin. "The Impact of Participation on Goal Acceptance and Performance: A Two-Step Model." *Academy of Management Journal* (1985), pp. 359-72.

Etzioni, A. *A Comparative Analysis of Complex Organizations*. New York: Free Press, 1961.

Evans, M. G. "The Effects of Supervisory Behavior on the Path-Goal Relationship." *Organizational Behavior and Human Performance* 5 (1970), pp. 277-98.

Fadiman, C. *The Little, Brown Book of Anecdotes*. Boston: Little, Brown, 1985.

Fairholm, G. W. *Values Leadership*. Praeger: New York, 1991.

Farris, G. F. "Colleagues' Roles and Innovation in Scientific Teams." (Working paper No. 552-71). Cambridge, MA: Alfred P. Sloan School of Management, M.I.T., 1971.

Feldman, D. C. "The Development and Enforcement of Group Norms," *Academy of Management Review*, January 1984, pp. 47-53.

Ferlise, W. G. "Violence in the Workplace." *Labor and Employment Newsletter*, Winter, 1995. Washington, D.C.: Semmes, Bowen, & Semmes.

Ferris, G. R. "Role of Leadership in the Employee Withdrawal Process: A Constructive Replication." *Journal of Applied Psychology* 70 (1985), pp. 777-81.

Fiechtner, B., and J. J. Krayer, "Variations in Dogmatism and Leader-Supplied Information: Determinants of Perceived Behavior in Task-Oriented Groups." *Group and Organizational Studies* 11 (1986), 403-18.

Fiedler, F. E. *A Theory of Leadership Effectiveness*. New York: McGraw-Hill, 1967.

———. "The Contingency Model and the Dynamics of the Leadership Process." In *Advances in Experimental Social Psychology*, ed. L. Berkowitz. New York: Academic Press, 1978.

———. "The Effect and Meaning of Leadership Experience: A Review of Research and a Preliminary Model." In *Impact of Leadership*. ed. K. E. Clark, M. B. Clark, and D. P. Campbell. Greensboro, NC: Center for Creative Leadership, 1992.

Fiedler, F. E., and M. M. Chemers. *Improving Leadership Effectiveness: The Leader Match Concept*. 2nd Ed. New York: Wiley, 1982.

Fiedler, F. E. "Cognitive Resources and Leadership Performance." *Applied Psychology: An International Review* 44, no. 1 (1995), pp. 5-28.

Fiedler, F. E., and J. E. Garcia. *New Approaches to Leadership: Cognitive Resources and Organizational Performance.* New York: Wiley, 1987.

Fiedler, F. E. "Reflections by an Accidental Theorist." *Leadership Quarterly* 6, no. 4 (1995), pp. 453-61.

Field, R. H. G. "A Test of the Vroom-Yetton Normative Model of Leadership." *Journal of Applied Psychology* 67 (1982), pp. 523-32.

Filley, A. C., and L. A. Pace. "Making Judgments Descriptive." In *The 1976 Annual Handbook for Group Facilitators.* ed. J. E. Jones and J. W. Pfeiffer. La Jolla, CA: University Associates Press, 1976.

Fishbein, M., and I. Azjen. *Belief, Attitude, Intention, and Behavior: An Introduction to Theory and Research.* Reading, MA: Addison-Wesley, 1975.

Fisher, C. D. "The Effects of Personal Control, Competence, and Extrinsic Reward Systems on Intrinsic Motivation." *Organizational Behavior and Human Performance* 21 (1978), pp. 273-288.

Fisher, C. D., and R. Gitleson. "A Meta-Analysis of the Correlates of Role Conflict and Ambiguity." *Journal of Applied Psychology* 68 (1983), pp. 320-33.

Fisher, R., and W. Ury. *Getting to Yes.* Boston: Houghton Mifflin, 1981.

Flanagan, J. C. "Defining the Requirements of the Executive's Job." *Personnel* 28, no. 1 (1951), pp. 28-35.

Fleishman, E. A. *Examiner's manual for the Supervisory Behavior Description Questionnaire.* Washington, D.C.: Management Research Institute, 1972.

———. "Twenty Years of Consideration and Structure." In *Current Developments in the Study of Leadership.* ed. E. A. Fleishman and J. G. Hunt. Carbondale, IL: Southern Illinois University Press, 1973.

———. *Examiner's Manual for the Leadership Opinion Questionnaire.* rev. ed. Chicago: Science Research Associates, 1989.

Fodor, E. "Motive Pattern as an Influence on Leadership in Small Groups." Paper presented at the meeting of the American Psychological Association, New York, August, 1987.

"Focus on Personality Tests." *Individual Employment Rights.* Washington, DC: Bureau of National Affairs (April 23, 1996), p. 4.

Fleenor, J. W.; C. D. McCauley; and S. Brutus. "Self-Other Rating Agreement and Leader Effectiveness." *Leadership Quarterly* 7, no. 4 (1996), pp. 487-506.

Folkman, S., and R. S. Lazarus. "An Analysis of Coping in a Middle-Aged Community Sample." *Journal of Health and Social Behavior* 21 (1980), pp. 219-39.

Ford, J. D. "Department Context and Formal Structure as Constraints on Leader Behavior." *Academy of Management Journal* 24 (1981), pp. 274-88.

Foushee, H. C. "Dyads and Triads at 35,000 Feet: Factors Affecting Group Process and Aircrew Performance." *American Psychologist* 39 (1984), pp. 885-93.

French, J., and B. H. Raven. "The Bases of Social Power." In *Studies of Social Power*. ed. D. Cartwright. Ann Arbor, MI: Institute for Social Research, 1959.

Freud, S. *Group Psychology and the Analysis of the Ego*, trans. J. Strachey. 2nd ed. The standard edition of the complete psychological works of Sigmund Freud, Vol. 2. London: Hogarth Institute for Psychoanalysis.

Friedland, W. H. "For a Sociological Concept of Charisma." *Social Forces* no. 1 (1964), pp. 18-26.

Friedman, M., and D. Ulmer. *Treating Type A Behavior—and Your Heart*. New York: Knopf, 1984.

Fry, L.; W. Kerr; and C. Lee. "Effects of Different Leader Behaviors under Different Levels of Task Interdependence." *Human Relations* 39 (1986), pp. 1067-82.

Funder, D. C. "Errors and Mistakes: Evaluating the Accuracy of Social Judgement." *Psychological Bulletin* 101 (1987), pp. 75-90.

Gabarro, J. J., and J. P. Kotter. "Managing Your Boss." *Harvard Business Review* 58, no. 1 (1980), pp. 92-100.

Gabor, A. *The Man Who Discovered Quality*. New York: Penguin, 1990.

Gabrenya, W. K., and R. M. Arkin. "Self-Monitoring Scale: Factor Structure and Correlates." *Personality and Social Psychology Bulletin* 6 (1980), pp. 12-22.

Gal, R. *A Portrait of the Israeli Soldier*. New York: Greenwood Press, 1986.

Galbraith, J. *Designing Complex Organizations*. Menlo Park, CA: Addison-Wesley, 1973.

Gardner, H. Frames of Mind: The Theory of Multiple Intelligences. New York: Basic Books, 1983.

Gardner, J. W. "The Antileadership Vaccine." Essay in the Carnegie Corporation of New York annual report, 1965.

———. The Tasks of Leadership. (Leadership paper No. 2). Washington, D.C.: Independent Sector, 1986.

———. *On Leadership*. New York: Free Press, 1990.

Garforth, F. I. De la P. "War Office Selection Boards." *Occupational Psychology* 19 (1945), pp. 97-108.

Gaugler, B. B.; D. B. Rosenthal; G. C. Thornton III; and C. Bentson. "Meta-Analysis of Assessment Center Validity." *Journal of Applied Psychology* 72 (1987), pp. 493-511.

Gebelein, S. H. *Multi-rater Performance Appraisal: The Promise, the Pitfalls, and the Steps*. Paper presented at the American Society of Training and Development Convention. Anaheim, CA, May, 1994.

Gebelein, S. H. "360-Degree Feedback Goes Strategic." *PDI Portfolio,* Summer 1996, pp. 1-3.

General Accounting Office. "Managerial Practices—U.S. Companies Improve Performance through Quality Efforts," (1990).

Gerth, H. H., and C. W. Mills. *Max Weber: Essays in Sociology*. New York: Oxford University Press, 1946.

Ghiselli, E. E. "Intelligence and Managerial Success." *Psychological Reports* 12 (1963), pp. 89.

Gibson, F. W., and G. J. Curphy. "The MBTI: Skewering A Sacred Cow." Presentation given to the Colorado Organizational Development Network, Denver, CO, 1996.

Ginnett, R. C. "To the Wilderness and Beyond: The Application of a Model for Transformal Change." *Proceedings of the 9th Psychology in the Department of Defense Symposium*. Colorado Springs, CO. 1984.

———. "Interaction of Traits and Motivational Factors in the Determination of the Success of Managers." *Journal of Applied Psychology* 52 (1968), pp. 480-83.

Gibb, C. A. "Leadership." In *The Handbook of Social Psychology*. ed. G. Lindzey and E. Aronson. 2nd ed., vol. 4. Reading, MA: Addison-Wesley, 1968, pp. 205-82.

Gibb, J. R. "Defensive Communication." *Journal of Communication*, XIII no. 3 (1961), pp. 141-48.

Gibbard, G. S.; J. J. Hartman; and R. D. Mann. *Analysis of Groups: Contribution to the Theory, Research, and Practice*. San Francisco: Jossey-Bass, 1974.

Gibble, J. L., and J. D. Lawrence. "Peer Coaching for Principals." *Educational Leadership* 45 (1987), pp. 72-73.

Gibson, F. W. "A Taxonomy of Leader Abilities and Their Influence on Group Performance as a Function of Interpersonal Stress." In *Impact of Leadership*. ed. K. E. Clark, M. B. Clark, and D. P. Campbell. Greensboro, NC: Center for Creative Leadership, 1992.

Gilligan, C. *In a Different Voice*. Cambridge, MA: Harvard University Press, 1982.

Ginnett, R. C. "The Formation Process of Airline Flight Crews." *Proceedings of the Fourth International Symposium on Aviation Psychology*. Columbus, OH, 1987.

———. "Cockpit Crew Effectiveness from the Inside Out: A Micro-Analysis Leading to Macro Considerations." *Proceedings of the Eleventh Psychology in the Department of Defense Symposium*. Colorado Springs, CO, 1988.

———. "Behavioral Characteristics of Effective Crew Leaders." *Human Error Avoidance Techniques: Proceedings of the Second Conference*. Herndon, VA: Society of Automotive Engineers, 1989.

———. "Airline Cockpit Crew." In *Groups that Work (and Those that Don't)*, ed. J. Richard Hackman. San Francisco: Jossey-Bass, 1990.

———. "Crews as Groups: Their Formation and Their Leadership." In *Cockpit Resource Management*, ed. E. Wiener; B. Banki; and R. Helmreich. Orlando, FL: Academic Press, 1993.

———. "Effectiveness Begins Early: The Leadership Role in the Formation of Intra-Organizational Task Groups." (unpublished manuscript, 1992).

Ginnett, R. C. "Team Effectiveness Leadership Model: Identifying Leverage Points for Change." *Proceedings of the 1996 National Leadership Institute Conference*. College Park, MD: National Leadership Institute, 1996.

Glasser, W. *The Quality School*. New York: Harper & Row, 1990.

Goldstein, I. L. *Training in Organizations: Needs Assessments, Development, and Evaluation*. End ed. Monterey, CA: Brooks/Cole, 1986.

Goodstadt, B. E., and L. A. Hjelle. "Power to the Powerless: Locus of Control and the Use of Power." *Journal of Personality and Social Psychology* 27 (1973), pp. 190-96.

Goodstadt, B. E., and D. Kipnis. "Situational Influences on the Use of Power." *Journal of Applied Psychology* 54 (1970), pp. 201-07.

Gordon, L. V. *Measurement of Interpersonal Values*. Chicago: Science Research Associates, 1975.

Gordon, W. J. J. *Synectics*. New York: Harper & Row, 1961.

Gough, H. G. "A Leadership Index on the California Psychological Inventory." *Journal of Counseling Psychology* 16 (1969), pp. 283-89.

———. "A Managerial Potential Scale for the California Psychological Inventory." In *Measures of Leadership*. ed. K. E. Clark and M. B. Clark. West Orange, NJ: Leadership Library of America, 1989.

Gough, H. G., and A. B. Heilbrun, Jr. *The Adjective Check List Manual*. Palo Alto, CA: Consulting Psychologist Press, 1983.

Gould, S. J. *The Mismeasure of Man*. New York: W. W. Horton, 1981.

Graeff, C. L. "The Situational Judgement Theory: A Critical Review." *Academy of Management Journal* 8 (1983), pp. 285-96.

Graen, G. B., and J. F. Cashman. "A Role-Making Model of Leadership in Formal Organizations: A Developmental Approach." In *Leadership Frontiers*. Ed. J. G. Hunt and L. L. Larson. Kent, OH: Kent State University Press, 1975.

Graen, G. B. and T. A. Scandura. "Toward a Psychology of Dyadic Organizing." In *Research in Organizational Behavior*, vol. 9 L. L. Cummings and B. M. Staw. Greenwich, CT: JAI Press, 1987.

Graen, G. B.; R. C. Linden; and W. Hoel. "Role of Leadership in the Employee Withdrawal Process." *Journal of Applied Psychology* 67 (1982), pp. 868-72.

Green, S. G.; G. T. Fairhurst; and B. K. Snavely. "Chains of Poor Performance and Supervisory Control." *Organizational Behavior and Human Decision Processes* 38 (1986), pp. 7-27.

Green, S. G., and T. R. Mitchell. "Attributional Processes of Leaders in Leader-Member Interactions." *Organizational Behavior and Human Performances* 23 (1979), pp. 429-58.

Greller, M. M. "Evaluation of Feedback Sources as a Function of Role and Organizational Development." *Journal of Applied Psychology* 65 (1980), pp. 24-27.

Grey, R. J. and G. G. Gordon. "Risk-Taking Managers: Who Gets the top Jobs?" *Management Review* 67 (1978), pp. 8-13.

Griffin, R. W.; A. Welsh; and G. Moorehead. "Perceived Task Characteristics and Employee Performance: A Literature Review." *Academy of Management Review* 6 (1981), pp. 655-64.

Guilford, J. P. *The Nature of Human Intelligence*. New York: McGraw-Hill, 1967.

Guion, R. M. "Personnel Assessment, Selection, and Placement." In *Handbook of Industrial and Organizational Psychology*. ed. M. D. Dunnette and L. M. Hough, Vol. 2, Palo Alto, CA: Consulting Psychologists Press, Inc., 1991, pp. 327-98.

Guion, R. M., and R. F. Gotter. "Validity of Personality Measures in Personnel Selection." *Personnel Psychology* 18 (1965), pp. 135-64.

Guth, C. K., and S. S. Shaw. *How to Put on Dynamic Meetings*. Reston, VA: Reston, 1980.

Guzzo, R. A.; P. R. Yost; R. J. Campbell; and G. P. Shea. "Potency in teams: Articulating a construct." *British Journal of Social Psychology* 32 (1993), pp. 87-106.

Hackman, J. R. "Group Influences on Individuals." In *Handbook of Industrial and Organizational Psychology*. ed. M. D. Dunnette. Chicago: Rand McNally, 1976.

————. "Group Level Issues in the Design and Training of cockpit Crews." In *Proceedings of the NASA/MAC Workshop on Cockpit Resource Management*, ed. H. H. Orlady and H. C. Foushee. Moffett Field, CA: NASA Ames Research Center, 1986.

Hackman, J. R. *Groups that Work (and Those that Don't)*. San Francisco: Jossey-Bass, 1990.

Hackman, J. R., and G. R. Oldham. "Motivation through the Design of Work: Test of a Theory." *Organizational Behavior and Human Performance* 16 (1976), pp. 250-79.

————. *Work Redesign*. Reading, MA: Addison Wesley, 1980.

Hall, J., S. M. Donnell. "Managerial Achievement: The Personal Side of Behavioral Theory." *Human Relations* 32 (1979), pp. 77-101.

Hallam, G. L., and D. P. Campbell. "Selecting Team Members? Start with a Theory of Team Effectiveness." Paper presented at the seventh annual meeting of the Society of Industrial/Organizational Psychologists, Montreal, Canada, May 1992.

Halpin, A. W., and B. J. Winer. "A Factorial Study of the Leader Behavior Descriptions." In *Leader Behavior: It's Descriptions and Measurement*. Ed. R. M. Stogdill and A. E. Coons. Columbus, OH: Ohio State University, Bureau of Business Research, 1957.

Hambrick, D. C. "Environment, Strategy and Power Within Top Management Teams." *Administrative Science Quarterly* 26 (1981), pp. 253-275.

Hambuger, K. E. "Leadership in Combat." Unpublished report. Department of History, U.S. Military Academy, 1984.

Hammer, M., and J. Champy. *Reengineering the Corporation*. New York: Harper Business, 1993.

Hammer, T. H., and J. Turk. "Organizational Determinants of Leader Behavior and Authority." *Journal of Applied Psychology* 71 (1987), pp. 674-82.

Haney, C.; C. Banks; and P. G. Zimbardo. "Interpersonal Dynamics in a Simulated Prison." *International Journal of Criminology and Penology*, 1 (1973), pp. 69-97.

Hansen, J. C. and D. P. Campbell. *Manual for the Strong Interest Inventory*, 4th ed. Stanford, CA: Stanford University Press, 1985.

Harris, T. A. *I'm OK—You're OK: A Practical Guide to Transactional Analysis.* New York: Harper & Row, 1967.

Harrison, E. L. "Training Supervisors to Discipline Effectively." *Training and Development Journal* 36, no. 11 (1982), pp. 111-13.

Hart, M. H. *The 100: A Ranking of the Most Influential Persons in History.* New York: Hart, 1978.

Harvey, J. B. "The Abilene Paradox: The Management of Agreement." *Organizational Dynamics* 3 (1974), pp. 63-80.

Hazucha, J. F. *PDI Indicator: Competence, Potential, and Jeopardy. What Gets Managers Ahead May Not Keep Them Out of Trouble.* Minneapolis, MN: Personnel Decisions, Inc., September, 1992.

Hazucha, J. F.; S. A. Hezlett; and R. J. Schneider. "The Impact of 360-Degree Feedback on Management Skills Development." *Human Resource Management* 32 (1993), pp. 325-351.

Health, Education, and Welfare Task Force. *Work in America.* Cambridge, MA: MIT Press, 1973.

Heckman, R. J., and B. W. Roberts. "Personality Profiles of Effective Managers across Functions: A Person-Centered Approach." In R. T. Hogan (Chair), *Personality Applications in the Workplace: Thinking outside the Dots.* Symposium presented at the 12th Annual Conference of the Society of Industrial and Organizational Psychology, St. Louis, 1997.

Hegarty, W. H., and H. P. Sims. "Some Determinants of Unethical Decision Behavior: An Experiment." *Journal of Applied Psychology* 63 (1978), pp. 451-57.

———. "Organizational Philosophy, Policies, and Objectives Related to Unethical Decision Behavior: A Laboratory Experiment." *Journal of Applied Psychology* 64 (1979), pp. 331-38.

Heller, T., and J. Van Til. "Leadership and Followership: Some Summary Propositions." *Journal of Applied Behavioral Science* 18, 405-14.

Helson, R. "Women Mathematicians and Creative Personality" *Journal of Consulting and Clinical Psychology* 36 (1971), pp. 210-20.

Hemphill, J. K. "The Leader and His Group" *Journal of Educational Research* 28 (1949), pp. 225-29, 245-46.

Hemphill, J. K. and A. E. Coons. "Development of the Leader Behavior Description Questionnaire." In *Leader Behavior: Its Description and Measurement.* ed. R. M. Stogdill and A. E. Coons. Columbus, OH: Ohio State University, Bureau of Business Research, 1957.

Herrnstein, R. J., and C. Murray. *The Bell Curve: Intelligence and Class Structure in American Life.* New York: The Free Press, 1994.

Hersey, P. and K. H. Blanchard. "Life Cycle Theory of Leadership." *Training and Development Journal* 23 (1969), pp. 26-34.

———. *Management of Organizational Behavior: Utilizing Human Resources*. 3rd ed. Englewood Cliffs, NJ: Prentice Hall, 1977.

———. *Management of Organizational Behavior: Utilizing Human Resources*. 4th ed. Englewood Cliffs, NJ: Prentice Hall, 1977.

Herzberg, F. "The Motivation-Hygiene Concept and Problems of Manpower." *Personnel Administrator* 27 (1964), pp. 3-7.

Herzberg, F. *Work and the Nature of Man*. Cleveland, OH: World Publishing, 1966.

Hezlett, S. A., and B. A. Koonce. *"Now that I've Been Assessed, What do I do? Facilitating Development after Individual Assessments."* Paper presented at the IPMA Assessment Council Conference on Public Personnel Assessment, New Orleans, LA, June, 1995.

Hill, C. W. "Leadership and Symbolic Authority in Psychoanalysis." In *Multidisciplinary Perspectives*, ed. B. Kellerman. Englewood Cliffs, NJ: Prentice Hall, 1984.

Hill, N. "Self Esteem: The Key to Effective Leadership." *Administrative Management* 40, no. 9, (1985), pp. 71-76.

Hinkin, T. R., and C. A. Schriesheim. "Development and Application of New Scales to Measure the French and Raven (1959) Bases of Social Power." *Journal of Applied Psychology* 74 (1989), pp. 561-67.

Hirsh, S. K., and J. M. Kummerow. *Introduction to Type in Organizations*. Palo Alto, CA: Consulting Psychologists Press, 1990.

Hogan, J. "The Mask of Integrity." Paper presented at the 13th Biennial Psychology in the Department of Defense Symposium, United States Air Force Academy, Colorado Springs, CO, 1992a.

———. "The View from Below." In *The Future of Leadership Selection*, chair, R. T. Hogan. Symposium conducted at the 13th Biennial Psychology in the DoD Conference, United States Air Force Academy, Colorado Springs, CO, 1992b.

Hogan, R. T. *Hogan Personality Inventory Manual*. Minneapolis, MN: National Computer Systems, 1986.

———. "Personality and Personality Measurement." In *Handbook of Industrial and Organizational Psychology*. ed. M. D. Dunnette and L. M. Hough. Vol. 2, Palo Alto, CA: Consulting Psychologists Press, Inc. 1991, pp. 873-919.

Hogan, R. T., and A. M. Morrison. "The Psychology of Managerial Incompetence." Paper presented at a joint American Psychological Association-National Institute of Occupational Safety and Health conference. Washington, D. C., October, 1991.

Hogan, R. J.; G. J. Curphy; and J. Hogan. "What Do We Know about Personality: Leadership and Effectiveness?" *American Psychologist* 49 (1994), pp. 493-504.

Hogan, R. T.; J. Hogan; and B. W. Roberts. "Personality Measurement and Employment Decisions: Questions and Answers." *American Psychologist* 51, no. 5 (1996), pp. 469-77.

Hogan, R. T., and J. Morrison. "Managing Creativity," In *Create to Be Free: Essays in Honor of Frank Barron*, ed. A. Montouri. Amsterdam: J. C. Gieben, 1993.

Hogan, R. T., and J. Hogan. *Manual for the Hogan Personality Inventory*. Tulsa, OK: Hogan Assessment Systems, 1992.

Hogan, R. T., and J. Morrison; and G. J. Curphy. *The Necessary and Sufficient Traits for Leadership Effectiveness*. Manuscript submitted for publication.

Hogan, R. T.; R. Raskin; and D. Fazzini. "The Dark Side of Charisma." In *Measures of Leadership*. ed. K. E. Clark and M. B. Clark. West Orange, NJ: Leadership Library of America, 1989.

Holladay, S. J., and W. T. Coombs. "Speaking of Visions and Visions Being Spoken: An Exploration of the Effects of Content and Delivery on Perceptions of Leader Charisma." *Management Communication Quarterly* 7 (1994), pp. 165-89.

Hollander, E. P. *Leadership Dynamics: A Practical Guide to Effective Relationships*. New York: Free Press, 1978.

———. "Relationships between Subordinate Perceptions of Supervisory Influence Tactics and Attributed Bases of Supervisory Power." *Human Relations* 43 (1990), pp. 221-37.

———. "Leadership and Power." In *Handbook of Social Psychology*. ed. G. Lindzey and E. Aronson. 3rd ed., vol. 2. New York: Random House, 1985.

Hollander, E. P., and J. W. Julian." Contemporary Trends in the Analysis of Leadership Processes." *Psychological Bulletin* 71 (1969), pp. 387-91.

Hollander, E. P., and L. R. Offermann. "Power and Leadership in Organizations." *American Psychologist* 45 (1990), pp. 179-89.

Holloman, C. R. "Leadership and Headship: There is a Difference." *Personal Administration* 31, no. 4 (1968), pp. 38-44.

Hoppock, R. *Job Satisfaction*. New York: Harper, 1935.

Hough, L. "Personality Measurement, Response Distortion, and Issues of Implementation." In J. Hogan (Chair), *Personality Measurement and Employment Decisions: Questions and Answers*. Symposium presented at the 12th Annual Conference of the Society of Industrial and Organizational Psychology, St. Louis, 1997.

Hough, L. M. "The Big Five Personality Variables—Construct Confusion: Description Versus Prediction." *Human Performance* 5 (1992), pp. 139-155.

House, R. J. "A 1976 Theory of Charismatic Leadership." In *Leadership: The Cutting Edge*. Ed. J. G. Hunt and L. L. Larson. Carbondale, IL: Southern Illinois University Press, 1977.

———. "Power in Organizations: A Social Psychological Perspective." Unpublished manuscript, University of Toronto, 1984.

House, R. J., and G. Dressler. "The Path-Goal Theory of Leadership: Some Posthoc and A Priori Tests." In *Contingency Approaches to Leadership*. ed. J. G. Hunt and L. L. Larson. Carbondale, IL: Southern Illinois University Press, 1974.

House, R. J.; R. S. Schuler; and E. Levanoni. "Role Conflict and Ambiguity Scales: Reality or Artifact?" *Journal of Applied Psychology* 68 (1983), pp. 334-37.

House, R. J.; W. D. Spangler; and J. Woycke. "Personality and Charisma in the U.S. Presidency: A Psychological Theory of Leadership Effectiveness." *Administrative Science Quarterly* 36 (1991), pp. 364-96.

House, R. J.; J. Woycke; and E. M. Fodor. "Charismatic and Noncharismatic Leaders: Differences in Behavior and Effectiveness." In *Charismatic Leadership: The Elusive Factor in Organizational Effectiveness*. ed. J. A. Conger and R. N. Kanungo. San Francisco: Jossey-Bass, 1988, pp. 98-121.

House, R. J., and T. R. Mitchell. "Path-Goal Theory of Leadership." *Contemporary Business* 3 (Fall 1974), pp. 81-98.

Howard, A. "College Experiences and Managerial Performance." *Journal of Applied Psychology* 71 (1986), pp. 530-52.

Howard, A., and D. W. Bray. "Predictors of Managerial Success Over Long Periods of Time." In *Measures of Leadership*. ed. M. B. Clark and K. E. Clark. West Orange, NJ: Leadership Library of America, 1989.

Howard, P. J., and J. M. Howard. "Buddy, Can You Paradigm?" *Training & Development*, September 1995, pp. 28-34.

Howard, A; T.A. Judge; E. A. Locke; C. C. Durham; and A. N. Kluger. "Dispositional Effects on Job and Life Satisfaction: The Role of Core Evaluations." *Journal of Applied Psychology* 83, no. 1 (1998), pp. 17-34.

Howell, J. M. "Two Faces of Charisma: Socialized and Personalized Leadership in Organizations." In *Charismatic Leadership: The Elusive Factor in Organizational Effectiveness*. ed. J. A. Conger and R. N. Kanungo. San Francisco: Jossey-Bass, 1988.

Howell, J. M., and B. J. Avolio. "Transformational Leadership, Transactional Leadership, Focus of Control, and Support for Innovation: Key Predictors of Consolidated Business Unit Performance." *Journal of Applied Psychology* 78 (1993), pp. 891-902.

Howell, J. M., and P. Frost. "A Laboratory Study of Charismatic Leadership." *Organizational Behavior and Human Decision Processes* 43 (1988), pp. 243-69.

Howell, J. P., and P. W. Dorfman. "Substitute for Leadership: Test of a Construct." *Academy of Management Journal* 24 (1981), pp. 714-28.

———. "Leadership and Substitutes for Leadership among Professional and Nonprofessional Workers." *Journal of Applied Behavioral Science* 22, (1986), pp. 29-46.

Huberman, J. "Discipline without Punishment." *Harvard Business Review* July-August 1964, p. 62.

Hughes, R. L., and R. LaScala. *Helper Effectiveness Learning Program*. Chicago: Instructional Dynamics, Inc., 1977.

Humphreys, L. G. "General Intelligence." In *Perspectives on Bias in Mental Testing*, ed. C. R. Reynolds and R. T. Brown. New York: Plenum, 1984, pp. 221-47.

———. "Intelligence: Three Kinds of Instability and Their Consequences for Policy." In *Intelligence: Measurement, Theory, and Public Policy*. ed. R. L. Linn. Chicago: University of Illinois Press, 1989, pp. 193-216.

Hunt, J. G., and R. N. Osborn. "Toward a Macro-oriented Model of Leadership: An Odyssey." In *Leadership: Beyond Establishment Views*. ed. J. G. Hunt, U. Sekaran, and C. A. Schriesheim. Carbondale, IL: Southern Illinois University Press, 1982, pp. 196-221.

Hunter, J. E., and R. F. Hunter. "Validity and Utility of Alternative Predictors of Job Performance." *Psychological Bulletin* 96 (1984), pp. 72-98.

Hunter, J. E.; F. L. Schmidt; and M. K. Judiesch. "Individual Differences in Output Variability as a Function of Job Complexity." *Journal of Applied Psychology* 74 (1990), pp. 28-42.

Hymowitz, C. "Five Main Reasons Why Managers Fail." *The Wall Street Journal*. May 2, 1988.

Iacocca, L., with W. Novack. *Iacocca: An Autobiography*. New York: Bantam, 1984.

Iaffaldano, M. T., and P. M. Muchinsky. "Job Satisfaction and Job Performance: A Meta-Analysis." *Psychological Bulletin* 97 (1985), pp. 251-273.

Imai, M. *Kaizen: The Key to Japan's Competitive Success*. New York: Random House, 1986.

Indik, B. P. "Organizational Size and Member Participation: Some Empirical Tests of Alternative Explanations." *Human Relations* 18 (1965), pp. 339-50.

Instone, D.; B. R. Major; and B. B. Bunker. "Gender, Self-Confidence, and Social Influence Strategies: An Organizational Simulation." *Journal of Personality and Social Psychology* 44 (1983), pp. 322-33.

Ivancevich, J. M.; D. M. Schweiger; and J. W. Ragan. "Employee Stress, Health, and Attitudes: A comparison of American, Indian, and Japanese Managers." Paper presented at the Academy of Management convention, Chicago, 1986.

Jago, A. G. "Leadership: Perspectives in Theory and Research." *Management Science* 28 (1982), pp. 315-36.

Jago, A. G., and J. W. Ragan. "The Trouble with LEADER MATCH Is that It Doesn't Match Fiedler's Contingency Model." *Journal of Applied Psychology* 71 (1986a), pp. 555-59.

———. "Some Assumptions Are More Troubling than Others: Rejoinder to Chemers and Fiedler." *Journal of Applied Psychology* 71 (1986b), pp. 564-65.

Jamal, M. "Job Stress and Job Performance Controversy: An Empirical Assessment." *Organizational Behavior and Human Performance* 33 (1984), pp. 1-21.

Janda, K. F. "Towards the Explication of the Concept of Leadership in Terms of the Concept of Power." *Human Relations* 13 (1960), pp. 345-63.

Janis, I. L. *Groupthink*. 2nd ed. Boston: Houghton Mifflin, 1982.

———. *Stress and Frustration*. New York: Harcourt Brace Jovanovich, 1971.

Jaques, E. "Assessing Creative Leaders." In *Proceedings of the Creativity and innovation Symposium*. National Defense University. ed. V. E. Hendrix, D. B. Chapla, and W. Mizzle. Washington, D.C., 1985, pp. 145-56.

Jayaratne, S.; D. Himle; and W. A. Chess. "Dealing with Work Stress and Strain: Is the Perception of Support More Important than Its use?" *Journal of Applied Behavioral Science* 24, no. 2 (1988), pp. 34-45.

Jennings, G. *The Mobile Manager*. New York: McGraw-Hill, 1971.

Johnson, A. L.; F. Luthans; and H. W. Hennessey. "The Role of Locus of Control in Leader Influence Behavior." *Personal Psychology* 37 (1984), pp. 61-75.

Johnson, C. "Japanese-Style Management in America." *California Management Review* 30 (1988), pp. 34-45.

Johnson, J. "Towards a Taxonomy of Managerial Profiles." *Human Performance*, in press.

Johnston, J. M. "Punishment of Human Behavior." *American Psychologist* 27 (1972), pp. 1033-54.

Johnson, J. C., and M. D. Dunnette. "Validity and Test-Retest Stability of the Nash Managerial Effectiveness Scale on the Revised Form of the Strong Vocational Interest Blank." *Personnel Psychology* (1968), pp. 283-93.

Jones, E. E. "Interpreting Interpersonal Behavior: The Effects of Expectancies." *Science* 234 (1986), pp. 41-46.

Jones, E. E., and R. E. Nisbett. "The Actor and the Observer: Divergent Perceptions of the Causes of Behavior." In *Attribution: Perceiving the causes of behavior*. ed. E. E. Jones, D. E. Kanouse, H. H. Kelley, R. E. Nisbett, S. Valins, and B. Weiner. Morristown, NJ: General Learning Press, 1972.

Jones, J. E. "Criteria of Effective Goal-Setting: The Spiro Model." In *The 1972 Annual Handbook for Group Facilitators*. ed. J. E. Jones and J. W. Pfeiffer. LaJolla, CA: University of Associates Press, 1972, pp. 133-34.

Judge, T. A., and C. L. Hulin. "Job Satisfaction as a Reflection of Disposition: A Multiple Source Causal Analysis." *Organizational Behavior and Human Decision Processes* 56 (1993), pp. 388-421.

Judge, T. A., and E. A. Locke. "Effect of Dysfunctional Thought Processes on Subjective Well-Being and Job Satisfaction." *Journal of Applied Psychology* 78 (1993), pp. 475-490.

Judge, T. A., and S. Watanabe. "Another Look at the Job Satisfaction-Life Satisfaction Relationship." *Journal of Applied Psychology* 78 (1993), pp. 939-948.

Judge, T. A.; J. W. Boudreau; R. D. Bretz. "Job and Life Attitudes of Male Executives." *Journal of Applied Psychology* 79 (1994), pp. 767-782.

Jung, C. G. *Psychological Types*, trans. R. F. C. Hall. Princeton, NJ: Princeton University Press, 1971.

Jung, D. I., Bass, B. M., & Sosik, J. Collectivism and Transformational Leadership. *Journal of Management Inquiry* 2 (1995), pp. 3-18.

Juran, J. M. "The QC Circle Phenomenon." *Industrial Quality Control*, January 1967, pp. 329-36.

————. *Juran on Leadership for Quality*. New York: Free Press, 1989.

Justice, A. "Review of the Effects of Stress on Cancer in Laboratory Animals: Importance of Time of Stress Application and Type of Tumor." *Psychological Bulletin* 98 (1985), pp. 108-38.

Kanfer, R. "Motivation Theory in Industrial and Organizational Psychology." In *Handbook of Industrial and Organizational Psychology*. ed. M. D. Dunnette and L.

M. Hough. Vol. 1. Palo Alto, CA: Consulting Psychologists Press, 1990, pp. 75-170.

Kanter, R. M. *Commitment and Community.* Cambridge, MA: Harvard University Press, 1972.

Kaplan, R. S., and D. P. Norton. *The Balanced Scorecard: Translating Strategy into Action.* Boston: Harvard Business School Press, 1996.

Karplan, R. E. "The Warp and Woof of the General Manager's Jobs." In *Facilitating Work Effectiveness.* ed. B. Schneider and D. Schoorman. Lexington, MA: Lexington Books, 1986.

Karp, D. A., and W. C. Yoels. *Symbols, Selves, and Society.* New York: Lippincott, 1979.

Katz, D.; N. Maccoby; G. Gurin; and L. G. Floor. *Productivity, Supervision, and Morale Among Railroad Workers.* Ann Arbor, MI: University of Michigan, Survey Research Center, Institute of Social Research, 1951.

Katzell, R. A., and R. A. Guzzo. "Psychological Approaches to Productivity Improvement." *American Psychologist* 38 (1983), pp. 468-72.

Katzenbach, J. R. *Teams at the Top.* Boston: Harvard Business School Press, 1998.

———. "Dilemmas of Managing Participation." *Organizational Dynamics* 11, no. 1 (1982), pp. 5-27.

———. *The Change Masters.* New York: Simon & Schuster, 1983.

Katzenbach, J. R., and B. K. Smith. *The Wisdom of Teams.* Boston: Harper Business, 1994.

Kazdin, A. E. *Behavior Modification in Applied Settings.* Homewood, IL: Dorsey, 1975.

Keller, G. "Increasing Quality on Campus." *Change* 24, no. 3 (1992), pp. 48-51.

Keller, R. T. *Toward a Contingency Theory of Leader Behavior and Creative versus Incremental Innovative Outcomes in Research and Development Project Groups: Report on the First Wave of Data.* Bethelehem, PA: Lehigh University, Center for Innovative Management, 1989.

Keller, R. T., and A. D. Szilagyi. "Employee Reactions for Leader Reward Behavior." *Academy of Management Journal* 19 (1976), pp. 619-27.

———. "A Longitudinal Study of Leader Reward Behavior, Subordinate Expectancies, and Satisfaction." *Personnel Psychology* 11 (1978), pp. 119-29.

Kelley, R. *The Power of Followership.* New York: Doubleday Currency, 1992.

Kelley, R. E. "In Praise of Followers." *Harvard Business Review* 66, no. 6 (1988), pp. 142-48.

Kelly, G. *The Psychology of Personal Constructs.* New York: W. W. Norton, 1955.

Kennedy, J. K. "Middle LPC Leaders and the Contingency Model of Leader Effectiveness." *Organizational Behavior and Human Performance* 30 (1982), pp. 1-14.

Kerr, S., and J. M. Jermier. "Substitutes for Leadership: Their Meaning and Measurement." *Organizational Behavior and Human Performance* 22 (1978), pp. 375-403.

Kets de Vries, M. F. R. "Crises Leadership and the Paranoid Potential: An Organizational Perspective." *Bulletin of the Menninger Clinic* 41 (1977), pp. 349-65.

Kets de Vries, M. F. R., and D. Miller. "Managers Can Drive Their Subordinates Mad." In *The Irrational Executive: Psychoanalytic Explorations in Management*, ed. M. F. R. Kets de Vries. New York: International Universities Press, 1984.

Keys, B.; T. Case; T. Miller; K. E. Curran; and C. Jones. "Lateral Influence Tactics in Organizations." *International Journal of Management* 4 (1987), pp. 425-37.

Kilmann, R. H., and M. J. Saxton. *Organizational Cultures: Their Assessment and Change*. San Francisco: Jossey-Bass, 1983.

Kincheloe, J. L. *Measured Lies: The Bell Curve Examined*. New York: St. Martins, 1996.

Kinni, T. B. "The Empowered Workforce." *Industry Week,* September 19, 1994 pp. 37-41.

Kipnis, D. "Technology, Power, and Control." *Research in the Sociology of Organizations* 3 (1984a), pp. 125-56.

———. "The View from the Top." *Psychology Today* 18, no. 12 (1984b), pp. 30-36.

Kipnis, D. and S. M. Schmidt. *Profiles of Organizational Strategies* (Form M). San Diego, Calif.: University Associates, 1982.

———. "The Language of Persuasion." *Psychology Today* 19, no. 4 (1985), pp. 40-46.

Kipnis, D.; S. M. Schmidt; and I. Wilkinson. "Intraorganizational Influence Tactics: Explorations in Getting One's Way." *Journal of Applied Psychology* 65 (1980), pp. 440-52.

Kirkpatrick, D. L. "Evaluation of Training." In *Training and Development Handbook*, ed. R. L. Craig and L. R. Bittel. New York: McGraw-Hill, 1967.

Kirkpatrick, S. A., and E. A. Locke. "Direct and Indirect Effects of Three Core Charismatic Leadership Components on Performance and Attitudes." *Journal of Applied Psychology* 81, no. 1, pp. 36-51.

Kirton, M. J. *Test Manual for the Kirton Adaptation-Innovation Inventory*. Hatfield, United Kingdom: Occupational Research Centre, 1987.

Kleiman, C. "Majority of Management Rates Salary as Very Good." *Denver Post*, January 4, 1998b, L-1.

Kleiman, C. "Survey: Job Satisfaction Can Be Costly to Employers." *Denver Post*, June 22, 1997, p. J-4.

Klein, S. B. *Learning*. 2nd ed. New York: McGraw-Hill, 1991.

Klimoski, R. J., and N. J. Hayes. "Leader Behavior and Subordinate Motivation." *Personnel Psychology* 33 (1980), pp. 543-55.

Koestler, A. *The Act of Creation*. New York: Macmillan, 1964.

Kohl, L. R. *Survival Kit for Overseas Living*. 2nd ed. Yarmouth, ME: Intercultural Press.

Kohlberg, L. *The Philosophy of Moral Development: Essays on Moral Development.* Vol. I. San Francisco: Harper & Row, 1981.

———. "The Psychology of Moral Development: Essays on Moral Development" Vol. II San Francisco: Harper & Row, 1984.

Kohn, A. "It's Hard to Get Left Out of a Pair." *Psychology Today,* October 1987, pp. 53-57.

Kojimoto, C. "The Kids-Eye View of Effective Principals." *Educational Leadership,* September 1987, pp. 69-74.

Kolb, D. *Experiential Learning: Experience as the Source of Learning and Development.* Englewood Cliffs, NJ: Prentice-Hall, 1983.

Komacki, J. L. "Why We Don't Reinforce: The Issues." *Journal of Organizational Behavior Management* 4, no. 3-4 (1982), pp. 97-100.

———. "Toward Effective Supervision: An Operant Analysis and Comparison of Managers at Work." *Journal of Applied Psychology* 71 (1986), pp. 270-79.

Komacki, J. L.; S. Zlotnick; and M. Jensen. "Development of an Operant-based Taxonomy and Observational Index on Supervisory Behavior." *Journal of Applied Psychology* 71 (1986), pp. 260-69.

Kossler, M., and S. Prestridge. "Geographically Dispersed Teams." *Issues and Observations* 16 (1996), pp. 2, 3.

Kotter, J. *Matsushista Leadership.* New York: Free Press, New York. 1997.

Kotter, J. P. "What Leaders Really Do." *Harvard Business Review.* May-June 1990, 103-111.

———. "Power and Influence: Beyond Formal Authority. *Macmillan Executive Summary Program,* September 1985, pp. 1-8.

Kouzes, J. M., and B. Z. Posner. *The Credibility Factor.* San Francisco: Jossey-Bass, 1996.

Kouzes, J. M., and B. Z. Posner. *The Leadership Challenge: How to Get Extraordinary Things Done in Organizations.* San Francisco: Jossey-Bass, 1987.

Kozlowski, S. W. J., and M. L. Doherty. "Integration of Climate and Leadership: Examination of a Neglected Issue." *Journal of Applied Psychology* 74 (1989), pp. 546-53.

Kraiger, K.; J. K. Ford; and E. Salas. *Integration of Cognitive, Behavioral, and Affective Theories of Learning into New Methods of Training Evaluation.* Manuscript submitted for publication.

Kroeger, O., and J. M. Thuesen. *Type Talk.* New York: Delacourt, 1988.

Kubler-Ross, E. *Living with Death and Dying.* New York: Macmillan, 1981.

Kuhn, R. *The Structure of Scientific Revolutions.* Chicago: The University of Chicago Press, 1962.

Kuncel, N. *"Personality and Cognitive Differences among Management Levels."* Unpublished manuscript. Minneapolis: Personnel Decisions International, 1996.

Kurke, L. B., and H. E. Aldrich. "Mintzberg Was Right! A Replication and Extension of 'The Nature of Managerial Work.'" *Management Science* 29 (1983), pp. 975-84.

Labak, A. S. "The Study of Charismatic College Teachers." *Dissertation Abstracts International* 34 (1973), pp. 1258B.

Landy, F. J. *Psychology of Work Behavior*. 3rd ed. Homewood, IL: Dorsey, 1985.

Larson, J. R., Jr. "Supervisors' Performance Feedback to Subordinates: The Impact of Subordinate Performance Valence and Outcome Dependence." *Organizational Behavior and Human Decision Processes* 37 (1986), pp. 391-408.

Latack, J. C. "Coping with Job Stress: Measures and Future Decisions for Scale Development." *Journal of Applied Psychology* 71 (1986), pp. 377-85.

Latane, B.; K. Williams; and S. Harkins. "Social Loafing." *Psychology Today* 13, no. 4 (1979), p. 104.

Latham, G. P., and T. W. Lee. "Goal Setting." In *Generalizing from Laboratory to Field Settings*. ed. E. A. Locke. Lexington, MA: Lexington Books, 1986.

Lawler, E. E. III. *Motivation in Work Organizations*. Pacific Grove, CA: Brooks/Cole, 1973.

Lawrence, P. R., and J. W. Lorsch. "Differentiation and Integration in Complex Organizations." *Administrative Science Quarterly* 12 (1967a), pp. 1-47.

———. *Organization and Environment*. Boston: Harvard University, 1967b.

———. *Organization and Environment: Managing Differentiation and Integration*. Homewood, IL: Irwin, 1969.

Lazarsfeld, P. F. "The American Soldier: An Expository Review." *Public Opinion Quarterly* 13 (1949), pp. 377-404.

Leana, C. R. "Predictors and Consequences of Delegation." *Academy of Management Journal* 29 (1986), pp. 754-74.

———. "Power Relinquishment vs. Power Sharing: Theoretical Clarification and Empirical Comparison of Delegation and Participation." *Journal of Applied Psychology* 72 (1987), pp. 228-33.

Lee, David B. "War Gaming: Thinking for the Future." *Airpower Journal* 3 (1990), pp. 40-51.

Lepper, M. R.; D. Greene; and R. E. Nisbett. "Undermining Children's Intrinsic Interests with Extrinsic Rewards: A Test of the 'Overjustification' Hypothesis." *Journal of Personality and Social Psychology* 28 (1973), pp. 128-37.

Lepsinger, R., and A. D. Lucia. *The Art and Science of 360° Feedback*. San Francisco: Pfeiffer, 1997.

Levering, R., M. Moskowitz, and M. Katz. *The 100 Best Companies to Work for in America*. Reading, MA: Addison-Wesley, 1984.

Levy, J. "Right Brain, Left Brain: Fact and Fiction." *Psychology Today*, May 1985, pp. 38-44.

Levy-Leboyer, C. "Leadership Performance: Towards a More Complex Model." *Applied Psychology: An International Review* 44, no. 1 (1995), pp. 43-44.

Liden, R. C, and G. B. Graen. "Generalizability of the Vertical Dyad Linkage Model of Leadership." *Academy of Management Journal* 23 (1980), pp. 451-65.

Liden, R. C.; R. W. Sparrowe, R. T. and S. J. Wayne. Leader-Member Exchange Theory: The Past and Potential for the Future." In *Research in Personnel and Human Resource Management*, vol. . 15, ed. G. R. Ferris. Greenwich, CT: JAI Press, 1997.

Likert, R. *New Patterns of Management*. New York: McGraw-Hill, 1961.

Lindsley, D. H.; D. J. Brass.; and J. B. Thomas. "Efficacy-Performance Spirals: A Multilevel Perspective." *Academy of Management Review* 20 (1995), pp. 645-78.

Linn, R. L., ed. *Intelligence: Measurement, Theory, and Public Policy*. Chicago: University of Illinois Press, 1989.

Linville, P. W. "Self-Complexity as a Cognitive Buffer Against Stress-Related Illness and Depression." *Journal of Personality and Social Psychology* 52, no. 4 (1987), pp. 663-76.

Lipnack, J., and J. Stamps. *Virtual Teams: Reaching across Space, Time and Organizations with Technology*. New York: John Wiley & Sons, 1997.

Lippitt, R. "The Changing Leader-Follower Relationships of the 1980s." *Journal of Applied Behavioral Science* 18 (1982), pp. 395-403.

Litzinger, W., and T. Schaefer. "Leadership through Followership." *Business Horizons*, 25, no. 5 (1982), pp. 78-81.

Locke, E. A., and G. P. Latham. *Goal Setting: A Motivational Technique that Works*. Englewood Cliffs, NJ: Prentice Hall, 1984.

————. "Work Motivation and Satisfaction: Light at the End of the Tunnel." *Psychological Science* 1 (1990), pp. 240-46.

Locke, E. A.; G. P. Latham; and M. Erez. "3-way Interactive Presentation and Discussion; A Unique Approach to Resolving Scientific Disputes; Designing Crucial Experiments." Papers presented at the Society of Industrial and Organizational Psychology Convention, Atlanta, GA, 1987.

Locke, E. A.; S. J. Motowidlo; and P. Bobko. "Using Self-Efficacy Theory to Resolve the Conflict between Goal-Setting Theory and Expectancy Theory in Organizational Behavior and Industrial/Organizational Psychology." *Journal of Social and Clinical Psychology* 4 (1985), pp. 280-89.

Lombardo, M. M., and R. W. Eichinger. *Eighty-eight Assignments for Development in Place: Enhancing the Developmental Challenge of Existing Jobs*. Greensboro, NC: Center for Creative Leadership, 1990.

Lombardo, M. M., and R. W. Eichinger. *For Your Improvement: A Development and Coaching Guide*. Minneapolis: Lominger Limited, 1996.

Lombardo, M. M., M. N. Ruderman; and C. D. McCauley. "Explorations of Success and Derailment in Upper-Level Management Positions." Paper presented at meeting of the Academy of Management, New York, 1987.

London, M., and J. W. Smither. "Can Multi-source Feedback Change Perceptions of Goal Accomplishment, Self-Evaluations, and Performance-Related Outcomes? Theory-Based Applications and Directions for Research." *Personnel Psychology* 48, no. 4 (1995), pp. 803-39.

Lord, R. G.; C. L. DeVader; G. M. Allinger. "A Meta-Analysis of the Relationship between Personality Traits and Leadership Perceptions: An Application of Validity Generalization Procedures." *Journal of Applied Psychology* 71 (1986), pp. 402-10.

Lowe, K. B.; K. G. Kroeck; and N. Sivasubramaniam. "Effectiveness Correlates of Transformational and Transactional Leadership: A Meta-Analytic Review of the MLQ Literature." *Leadership Quarterly* 7, no. 3 (1996), pp. 385-425.

Lowin, A., and J. R. Craig. "The Influence of Level of Performance on Managerial Style: An Experimental Object-Lesson in the Ambiguity of Correlational Data." *Organizational Behavior and Human Performance* 3 (1968), pp. 68-106.

Lundin, S. C., and L. C. Lancaster. "Beyond Leadership . . . The Importance of Followership." *The Futurist*, May-June 1990, pp. 18-22.

Luthans, F. 1989. *Organizational Behavior*. 5th ed. San Francisco: McGraw-Hill, 1992.

Luthans, F., and R. Kreitner. *Organizational Behavior Modification and Beyond: An Operant and Social Learning Approach*. Glenview, IL: Scott, Foresman, 1985.

Luthans, F., and J. K. Larsen. "How Managers Really Communicate." *Human Relations* 39 (1986), pp. 161-78.

Luthans, F.; S. A. Rosenkrantz; and H. W. Hennessey. "What Do Successful Managers Really Do? An Observational Study of Managerial Activities." *Journal of Applied Behavioral Science* 21 (1985), pp. 255-70.

Lytle, C. F., ed. *Leaves of Gold*. Williamsport, PA: Coslett, 1948.

Maccoby, M. "Management: Leadership and the Work Ethic." *Modern Office Procedures* 28, no. 5 (1983), pp. 14, 16, 18.

MacKenzie, R. A. "The Management Process in 3-D." *Harvard Business Review* 47, no. 6 (1969s), pp. 80-87.

Macrorie, K. *20 Teachers*. Oxford: Oxford University Press, 1984.

Madsen, D., and P. G. Snow. "The Dispersion of Charisma." *Comparative Political Studies* 16, no. 3 (1983), pp. 337-62.

Mahoney, T. A.; T. H. Jerdee; and S. J. Carroll. "The Job(s) of Management." *Industrial Relations* 4 (1965), pp. 97-110.

Main, J. "Is the Baldridge Overblown?" *Fortune*, July 1, 1991, pp. 62-65.

Malinkowski, C. I., and C. P. Smith. "Moral Reasoning and Moral Conduct: An Investigation Prompted by Kohlberg's Theory." *Journal of Personality and Social Psychology* 49 (1985), pp. 1016-27.

Mann, F. C. "Toward an Understanding of the Leadership Role in a Formal Organization." In *Leadership and Productivity*, ed. R. Dubin. San Francisco: Chandler, 1965.

Mann, R. D. "A Review of the Relationships between Personality and Performance in Small Groups." *Psychological Bulletin* 56 (1959), pp. 241-70.

Manz, C. C. "Self-Leadership: Toward an Expanded Theory of Self-Influence Process in Organizations." *Academy of Management Review* 11 (1986), pp. 585-600.

Marcus, J. T. "Transcendence and Charisma." *The Western Political Quarterly* 16 (1961), pp. 236-41.

Margerison, C. J. "Action Learning and Excellence in Management Development." *Journal of Management Development* 7 no. 2 (1983), pp. 52-64.

Martinko, M. J., and W. L. Gardner. " Beyond Structured Observation: Methodological Issues and New Directions." *Academy of Management Review* 10 (1985), pp. 676-95.

Maslow, A. H. *Motivation and Personality*. New York: Harper & Row, 1954.

Massey, M. *The People Puzzle: Understanding Yourself and Others*. Reston: VA: Reston, 1979.

Mayer, R. E. *Thinking, Problem Solving, Cognition*. New York: W. H. Freeman, 1983.

Maynard, H. B., and S. E. Mehrtens. *The Fourth Wave: Business in the 21ˢᵗ Century*. San Francisco: Berrett-Koehler, 1993.

Mayo, E. *The Human Problems of an Industrial Civilization*. New York: Macmillan, 1933.

McCall, M. W., Jr., and M. M. Lombardo. "Using Simulation for Leadership and Management Research: Through the Looking Glass." *Management Science* 28 (1982), pp. 533-49.

———. "Off the Track: Why and How Successful Executives Get Derailed." (Tech. Rep. No. 21). Greensboro, NC: Center for Creative Leadership, 1983.

McCall, M. W.; M. M. Lombardo; and A. M. Morrison. *The Lessons of Experience: How Successful Executives Develop on the Job*. Lexington, MA: Lexington Books, 1988.

McCarley, N., and T. G. Carskadon. "Test-Retest Reliabilities of Scales and Subscales of the Myers-Briggs Type Indicator and of Criteria for Clinical Interpretive Hypothesis Involving Them." *Research in Psychological Type* 6 (1983), pp. 24-36.

McCauley, C. D. "Stress and the Eye of the Beholder." *Issues & Observations* 7, no. 3 (1987), pp. 1-16.

McCaulley, M. H. "The Myers-Briggs Type Indicator and Leadership." In *Measures of Leadership*, ed. K. E. Clark and M. B. Clark. Greensboro, NC: Center for Creative Leadership, 1988.

McClelland, D. C. "Intelligence Is Not the Best Predictor of Job Performance." *Current Directions in Psychological Science* 2, no. 1 (1993), pp. 5-6.

———. *Power: The Inner Experience*. New York: Irvington (distributed by Halstead Press), 1975.

———. *Human Motivation*. Glenview, IL: Scott Foresman, 1985.

McClelland, D. C., and R. E. Boyatzis. "Leadership Motive Pattern and Long-Term Success in Management." *Journal of Applied Psychology* 67 (1982), pp. 737-43.

McClelland, D. C., and D. H. Burnham. "Power Is the Great Motivator." *Harvard Business Review*, 54, no. 2 (1976), pp. 100-110.

McCormick, J., and B. Powell. "Management for the 1990s" *Newsweek*, April 1988, pp. 47-48.

McCrae, R. R., and Costa, P. T. "The Stability of Personality: Observations and Evaluations." *Current Directions in Psychological Science* 3, no. 6, (1994), pp. 173-75.

McFarlin, D. B., and P. D. Sweeney. "Distributive and Procedural Justice as Predictors of Satisfaction with Personal and Organizational Outcomes." *Academy of Management Journal* 35 (1992), pp. 626-637.

McGrath, J. E. *Leadership Behavior: Some Requirements for Leadership Training.* Washington, D.C.: Office of Career Development, U. S. Civil Service Commission, 1964.

McGregor, D. *Leadership and Motivation.* Cambridge, MA: MIT Press, 1966.

McGue, M., and T. J. Bouchard, Jr. "Genetic and Environmental Determinants of Information Processing and Special Mental Abilities: A Twin Analysis." In *Advances in the Psychology of Human Intelligence.* ed. R. J. Sternberg. Hillsdale, NJ: Erlbaum, 1989, pp. 7-45.

McKay, H. "Author Encourages Creativity, Risk Taking on Road to Success." *Denver Post*, December 21, 1997, p. J-8.

McKay, M.; M. Davis; and P. Fanning. *Thoughts & Feelings: The Art of Cognitive Stress Intervention.* Richmond, CA: New Harbinger, 1981.

Meindl, J. R., and S. B. Ehrlich. "The Romance of Leadership and the Evaluation of Organizational Performance." *Academy of Management Journal* 30 (1987), pp. 90-109.

Meindl, J. R.; S. B. Ehrlich; and J. M. Dukerich. "The Romance of Leadership." *Administrative Science Quarterly* 30 (1985), pp. 78-102.

Merton, R. K. *Social Theory and Social Structure.* New York: Free Press, 1957.

———. "The Social Nature of Leadership." *American Journal of Nursing*, 69 (1969), pp. 2614-18.

Michel. R., and R. T. Hogan. "Personality and Organizational Behavior." In R. T. Hogan (Chair), *Personality and Organizational Behavior.* Symposium presented at the 104th Annual Meeting of the American Psychological Association, Toronto, Canada, 1996.

Michener, H. A., and M. R. Burt. "Use of Social Influence under Varying Conditions of Legitimacy." *Journal of Personality and Social Psychology* 32 (1975), pp. 398-407.

Milgram, S. "Behavioral Study of Obedience." *Journal of Personality and Social Psychology* 67 (1963), pp. 371-78.

Miller, D. D. *The Story of Walt Disney.* New York: Henry Holt, 1956.

Miller, D., and J. M. Toulouse. "Strategy, Structure, CEO Personality and Performance in Small Firms." *American Journal of Small Business*. Winter 1986, pp. 47-62.

Miller, W. R., and S. Rollnick. *Motivational Interviewing: Preparing People to Change Addictive Behavior*. New York: Guilford Press, 1991.

Miller, D. T., and M. Ross. "Self-Serving Biases in the Attribution of Causality: Fact or Fiction?" *Psychological Bulletin* 82 (1975), pp. 213-25.

Mindell, M., and W. Gorden. *Employee Values in a Changing Society: An AMA Management Briefing*. New York: American Management Associations, 1981.

Miner, J. B. "Student Attitudes toward Bureaucratic Role Prescriptions and the Prospects for Managerial Shortages." *Personnel Psychology* 27 (1974), pp. 605-13.

———. "The Uncertain Future of the Leadership Concept: An Overview." In *Leadership Frontiers*. ed. J. G. Hunt and L. L. Larson. Kent, OH: Kent State University, 1975.

———. "Twenty Years of Research on Role Motivation Theory of Managerial Effectiveness." *Personnel Psychology* 31 (1978), pp. 739-60.

———. "If You're Not Serving Bill or Barbara, Then You're Not Serving Leadership." In *Leadership: Beyond Establishment Views*. ed. J. G. Hunt, U. Sekaran, and C. A. Schriesheim. Carbondale IL: Southern Illinois University Press, 1982.

Mitchell, T. R. "Review of *In Search of Excellence* versus *The 100 Best Companies to Work for in America*: A Question of Perspective and Values." *Academy of Management Review* 10 (1985), pp. 350-55.

Mitchell, T. R.; S. G. Green; and R. E. Wood. "An Attributional Model of Leadership and the Poor Performing Subordinate: Development and Validation." In *Research in Organizational Behavior*. ed. B. M. Staw and L. L. Cummings. Greenwich, CN: JAI, 1981, pp. 197-234.

Mitchell, R. R.; C. M. Smyser; and S. E. Weed. "Locus of Control: Supervision and Work Satisfaction." *Academy of Management Journal*. 18 (1975), pp. 623-30.

Mitchell, T. R., and R. E. Wood. "Supervisors' Responses to Subordinate Poor Performance: A Test of an Attributional Model." *Organizational Behavior and Human Performance* 25 (1980), pp. 123-38.

Moore, L. I. "The FMI: Dimensions of Follower Maturity." *Group and Organizational Studies* 1 (1976), pp. 203-22.

Moorman, R. H. "Relationships between Organizational Justice and Organizational Citizenship Behaviors: Do Fairness Perceptions Influence Employee Citizenship?" *Journal of Applied Psychology* 76 (1991), pp. 845-55.

Morabito, M. A., B. L. Dilla. "Leadership Development of USAF Aircraft Maintenance Officers." Presented at the 27th Annual Meeting of the Military Testing Association, San Diego, CA, October 1985.

Moreno, J. L. *Sociodrama: A Method of Analysis for Social Conflicts*. Beacon, NY: Beacon House, 1955.

Morrison, A. M.; R. P. White; and E. Van Velsor. *Breaking the Glass Ceiling.* Reading, MA: Addison-Wesley, 1987.

Morse, J. J., and F. R. Wagner. "Measuring the Process of Managerial Effectiveness." *Academy of Management Journal* 21 (1978), pp. 23-35.

Motowidlo, S. J.; M. D. Dunnette; and G. W. Carter. "An Alternative Selection Procedure: The Low-Fidelity Simulation." *Journal of Applied Psychology* 75 (1990), pp. 640-47.

Mount, M. K.; M. R. Sytsma; J. F. Hazucha; and K. E. Holt. "Rater-Ratee Effects in Development Performance Ratings of Managers." *Personnel Psychology* 50, no. 1, pp. 51-70.

Mount, M. K.; M. R. Barrick; J. K. Strauss. "Validity of Observers Ratings of the Big Five Personality Factors." *Journal of Applied Psychology* 79 (1994), pp. 272-80.

Mowday, R. T. "Leader Characteristics, Self-Confidence, and Methods of Upward Influence in Organizational Decision Situations." *Academy of Management Journal* 22, no. 4 (1979), pp. 709-25.

Mulder, M. and A. Stemerding. "Threat, Attraction to Group, and Need for Strong Leadership." *Human Relations* 16 (1963), pp. 317-34.

Mulder, M., R. D. de Jong; L. Koppelar; and J. Verhage. "Power, Situation, and Leaders' Effectiveness: An Organizational Study." *Journal of Applied Psychology* 71 (1986), pp. 566-70.

Munson, C. E. "Style and Structure in Supervision." *Journal of Education for Social Work* 17 (1981), pp. 65-72.

Murphy, A. J. "A Study of the Leadership Process." *American Sociological Review* 6 (1941), pp. 674-87.

Murray, H. A., and D. W. MacKinnon. "Assessment of OSS Personnel." *Journal of Consulting Psychology* 10 (1946), pp. 76-80.

Murray, M., and M. A. Owen. *Beyond the Myths and Magic of Mentoring.* San Francisco. Jossey-Bass, 1991.

Mussen, P. H., and L. W. Porter, "Personal Motivations and Self-Conceptions Associated with Effectiveness and Ineffectiveness in Emergent Groups." *Journal of Abnormal and Social Psychology* 59 (1959), pp. 23-27.

Myers, D. G. *Psychology.* 2nd ed. New York: Worth, 1989.

Myers, I. *Gifts Differing.* Palo Alto, CA: Consulting Psychologists Press, 1980.

Myers, I. B. *Introduction to Type.* Palo Alto, CA: Consulting Psychologists Press, 1976.

Myers, I. B. *The Myers-Briggs Type Indicator: Supplementary Manual.* Palo Alto, CA: Consulting Psychologists Press, 1977.

Myers, I. B., and B. H. McCaulley. *Manual: A Guide to the Development and Use of the Myers-Briggs Type Indicator.* Palo Alto, Calif.: Consulting Psychologists Press, 1985.

Myers, I. B., and K. C. Briggs. *The Myers-Briggs Type Indicator.* Palo Alto, CA: Consulting Psychologists Press, 1943/1962.

Naisbitt, J., and P. Aburdene. *Re-inventing the Corporation*. New York: Warner Books, 1985.

———. *Megatrends 2000*. New York: William Morrow, 1990.

Nash, A. N. "Vocational Interests of Effective Managers: A Review of the Literature." *Personnel Psychology* 18 (1965), pp. 21-37.

Neilson, E. H., and J. Gypen. "The Subordinate's Predicament." *Harvard Business Review* 57, no. 5 (1979), pp. 133-43.

Nierenberg, G. I. *The Art of Creative Thinking*. New York: Simon & Schuster, 1982.

Neisser, U.; G. Boodoo; T. J. Bouchard; A. W. Boykin; N. Brody; S. J. Ceci, D. F. Halpern; J. C. Loehlin; R. Perloff; R. J. Sternberg; and S. Urbina. "Intelligence: Knowns and Unknowns." *American Psychologist* 51, no. 2 (1996), pp. 77-101.

———. "Development of a SVIB Key for Selecting Managers." *Journal of Applied Psychology* 50 (1966), pp. 250-54.

Newman, R. G. "Thoughts on Superstars of Charisma: Pipers in Our Midst." *American Journal of Orthopsychiatry* 53 (1983), pp. 201-08.

Nilsen, D. L. *Using Self and Observers' Rating of Personality to Predict Leadership Performance*. Unpublished doctoral dissertation, The University of Minnesota, 1995.

———. "Using Observer Judgments for Selection." In *The Future of Leadership Section*, chair, R. L. Hughes. Symposium conducted at the 13th Biennial Psychology in the DoD Conference, U.S. Air Force Academy, April 1992.

Nixon, R. M. *Leaders*. New York: Warner Books, 1982.

Nystrom, P. C. "Comparing Beliefs of Line and Technostructure Managers." *Academy of Management Journal* 29 (1986), pp. 812-19.

O'Brien, B. "Designing an Organization's Governing Ideas." In *The Fifth Discipline Fieldbook*. ed. P. Senge, A. Kleiner, C. Roberts, R. Ross, and B. Smith. New York: Doubleday, 1994.

O'Connor, J.; M. D. Mumford; T. C. Clifton; T. L. Gessner; and M. S. Connelly. "Charismatic Leaders and Destructiveness: An Historiometric Study." *Leadership Quarterly* 6, no. 4 (1995), pp. 529-40.

Offermann, L. R. "Leading and Empowering Diverse Followers." In *The Balance of Leadership and Followership*, Kellogg Leadership Studies Project, ed. E. P. Hollander, and L. R. Offerman. College Park, MD: University of Maryland, 1997, pp. 31-46.

Oldham, G. R., and A. Cummings. "Employee Creativity: Personal and Contextual Factors at Work." *Academy of Management Journal* 39 (1996), pp. 607-34.

O'Leary-Kelly, A. M.; J. J. Martocchio; and D. D. Frink. "A Review of the Influence of Group Goals on Group Performance." *Academy of Management Journal* 37 (1994), pp. 1285-1301.

Ones, D. S.; C. Viswesvaran; and A. D. Reiss. "Role of Social Desirability in Personality Testing for Personnel Selection: The Red Herring. "*Journal of Applied Psychology* 81, no. 6 (1996), pp. 660-79.

Ones, D. S.; M. K. Mount; M. R. Barrick; and J. E. Hunter. "Personality and Job Performance: A Critique of Tett, Jackson, and Rothstein (1991) Meta-Analysis." *Personnel Psychology* 47 (1994), pp. 147-156.

O'Reilly, B. "360-Degree Feedback Can Change Your Life." *Fortune*. October 17, 1994.

O'Reilly, C. A. "Supervisors and Peers as Informative Sources, Group Supportiveness, and Individual Decision-Making Performance." *Journal of Applied Psychology* 62 (1977), pp. 632-35.

Organ, D. W., and K. Ryan. "A Meta-Analytic Review of Attitudinal and Dispositional Predictors of Organizational Citizenship Behavior." *Personnel Psychology* 48 (1995), pp. 775-802.

Osborn, A. F. *Applied Imagination*. New York: Scribner's, 1963.

Ouchi, W. G. *Theory Z*. Reading, MA: Addison-Wesley, 1981.

———. *How American Business Can Meet the Japanese Challenge*. Reading, MA: Addison-Wesley, 1981.

Paajanen, G. E.; T. L. Hansen; and R. A. McLellan. *PDI Employment Inventory and PDI Customer Service Inventory Manual*. Minneapolis, MN Personnel Decisions, Inc., 1993.

Page, R. C., and W. W. Tornow. "Managerial Job Analysis: Are We Any Further Along?" *Paper presented at a meeting of the Society of Industrial Organizational Psychology*, Atlanta, GA, 1987.

Parke, R. D. "Some Effects of Punishment on Children's Behavior." In *The Young Child: Reviews of Research*. ed. W. W. Hartup. Vol. 2. Washington, D.C.: National Association for the Education of Young Children, 1972.

Parks, M. R. "Interpersonal Communication and the Quest for Personal Competence." In *Handbook of Interpersonal Communication*. ed. M. L. Knapp and G. R. Miller. Beverly Hills, CA: Sage, 1985.

Parsons, C. K.; D. M. Herold; and M. L. Leatherwood. "Turnover during Initial Employment: A Longitudinal Study of the Role of Causal Attributions." *Journal of Applied Psychology* 70 (1985), pp. 337-41.

Paunonen, S. V. "Sense, Nonsense, and the Big Five Factors of Personality." *The Score* vol. XVI, no. 1 (1993), pp. 8-9.

Pawar, B. S., & K. K. Eastman. "The Nature and Implications of Contextual Influences on Transformational Leadership: A Conceptual Examination." *Academy of Management Review* 22, no. 1 (1997), pp. 80-109.

Pearson, C. S. *The Hero Within*. San Francisco: Harper-Collins, 1986.

Penner, D. D.; D. M. Malone; T. M. Coughlin; and J. A. Herz. *Satisfaction with U.S. Army Leadership*. U.S. Army War College, Leadership Monograph Series, no. 2, 1973.

Perkins, D. N. "Thinking Frames." *Educational Leadership* 43 (1986), pp. 4-10.

Perkins, D. N., and T. A. Grotzer. "Teaching Intelligence." *American Psychologist* 52, no. 10 (1997), pp. 1125-1134.

Person, H. S. "Leadership as a Response to Environment." *Educational Record Supplement* no. 6 (1928), pp. 9, 10-21.

Personnel Decisions Inc. *Managerial Job Satisfaction*. Minneapolis, MN: Author, 1991.

———. *PROFILER® Certification Workshop Manual*. Minneapolis, MN: Author, 1992.

———. *Successful Managers Handbook: Development Suggestions for Today's Managers*. Minneapolis, MN: Author, 1983.

———. *The Management Skills Profile*. Minneapolis, MN: Author, 1983.

Personnel Decisions International. *Develop Mentor: Assessment, Development, and Coaching Software*. Minneapolis, MN: Personnel Decisions International, 1995.

Peter, L., and R. Hull. *The Peter Principle*. New York: Morrow, 1969.

Peters, L. H.; D. D. Hartke; and J. T. Pohlmann. "Fielder's Contingency Theory of Leadership: An Application of the Meta-Analytic Procedures of Schmidt and Hunter." *Psychological Bulletin* 97 (1985), pp. 274-85.

Peters, T. *The Circle of Innovation: You Can't Shrink Your Way to Greatness*. New York: Random House. 1997.

Peters, T. J., and R. H. Waterman. *In Search of Excellence*. New York: Harper & Row, 1982.

Peterson, D. B. "Executive Coaching at Work: The Art of One-on-One Change." *Consulting Psychology Journal* 48 no. 2 (1996), pp. 78-86.

Peterson, D. B. *Positive Coaching Manual*. Unpublished manuscript. Minneapolis, MN: Personnel Decisions, Inc., 1994.

———. *A Psychometric Approach to Evaluating Individual Training Outcomes*. Paper presented at the Eighth Annual Conference of the Society of Industrial and Organizational Psychology. San Francisco, CA, April, 1993a.

———. "Skill Learning and Behavioral Change in an Individually Tailored Management Coaching and Training Program." Unpublished doctoral dissertation. University of Minnesota, 1993b.

Peterson, D. B., and M. D. Hicks. *Development FIRST: Strategies for Self-Development*. Minneapolis: Personnel Decisions International, 1995.

Peterson, D. B., and M. D. Hicks. *Leader as Coach: Strategies for Coaching and Developing Others*. Minneapolis: Personnel Decisions International, 1996.

Peterson, D. B., and M. D. Hicks. "Coaching across Borders: It's Probably a Long Distance Call." *Development Matters* no. 9, (1997), pp. 1-4.

Petrick, J. A., and G. E. Manning. "Developing an Ethical Climate for Excellence." *Journal of Quality and Participation*. March 1990, pp. 13-18.

Petty, R. E., and J. T. Cacioppo. *Attitudes and Persuasion: Classic and Contemporary Approaches*. Dubuque, IA: Wm. C. Brown, 1981.

Pfeffer, J. "The Ambiguity of Leadership." In *Leadership: Where Else Can We Go?*, ed. M. W. McCall, Jr., and M. M. Lombardo. Durham, NC: Duke University Press, 1977.

Pfeffer, J., and G. R. Salancik. "Determinants of Supervisory Behavior: A Role Set Analysis." *Human Relations* 28 (1975), pp. 139-54.

Pitt, L. F. "Managerial Attitudes Towards Corruption: A Pilot Study." *South African Journal of Business Management* 16 (1985), pp. 27-30.

Pittman, T. S.; W. E. Rosenbach; and E. H. Potter. "Followers as Partners: Taking the Initiative for Action." In *Contemporary Issues in Leadership*, 4th ed., W. E. Rosenback and R. L. Taylor. Boulder, CO: Westview Press, 1998.

Ployhart, R. E., and A. M. Ryan. "Applicants' Reactions to the Fairness of Selection Procedures: The Effects of Positive Rule Violations and Time of Measurement." *Journal of Applied Psychology* 83, no. 1 (1998), pp. 3-16.

Podsakoff, P. M. "Determinants of a Supervisor's Use of Rewards and Punishments: A Literature Review and Suggestions for Future Research." *Organizational Behavior and Human Performance* 29 (1982), pp. 58-83.

Podsakoff, P. M., and L. J. Williams. "The relationship between Job Performance and Job Satisfaction." In *Generalizing from Laboratory to Field Setting*. ed. E. A. Locke. Lexington, MA: Lexington, 1986.

Podsakoff, P. M., and C. A. Schriesheim. "Field Studies of French and Raven's Bases of Power: Critique, Reanalysis, and Suggestions for Future Research." *Psychological Bulletin* 97 (1985), pp. 387-411.

Podsakoff, P. M., and W. D. Todor. "Relationships between Leader Reward and Punishment Behavior and Group Process and Productivity." *Journal of Management.* 11 (1985), pp. 55-73.

Podsakoff, P. M.; W. D. Todor; R. A. Grover; and V. L. Huber. "Situational Moderators of Leader Reward and Punishment Behaviors: Fact or Fiction?" *Organizational Behavior and Human Performance* 34 (1984), pp. 21-63.

Podsakoff, P. M.; W. D. Todor; and R. S. Schuler. "Leadership Expertise as a Moderator of the Effects of Instrumental and Supportive Leader Behaviors." *Journal of Management* 9 (1983), pp. 173-85.

Podsakoff, P. M.; W. D. Todor; and R. Skov. "Effects of Leader Contingent and Noncontigent Reward and Punishment Behaviors on Subordinate Performance and Satisfaction." *Academy of Management Journal.* 25 (1982), pp. 810-25.

Polanyi, M. *Personal Knowledge*. Chicago: University of Chicago Press, 1962.

Pomerleau, O. F., and J. Rodin. "Behavioral Medicine and Health Psychology." In *Handbook of Psychotherapy and Behavior Change*. ed. S. L. Garfield and A. E. Bergin. 3rd ed. New York: Wiley, 1986.

Popper, M.; O. Landau; and U. M. Gluskinos. "The Israeli Defense Forces: An Example of Transformational Leadership." *Leadership and Organizational Development Journal,* 13, no. 1 (1992), pp. 3-8.

Porter, D. A. "Student Course Critiques: A Case Study in Total Quality in the Classroom." Proceedings of the 13th Biennial Psychology in DoD Conference, U.S. Air Force Academy, Colorado Springs, CO, 1992, pp. 26-30.

Porter, L. W., and E. E. Lawler, III. *Managerial Attitudes and Performance.* Homewood, IL: Dorsey, 1968.

Porter, D. B.; M. Bird; and A. Wunder. "Competition, Cooperation, Satisfaction, and the Performance of Complex Tasks among Air Force Cadets." *Current Psychology Research and Reviews* 9, no. 4 (1991), pp. 347-54.

Posner, B. Z., and J. M. Kouzes. "Leadership Practices: An Alternative to the Psychological Perspective." In *Measures of Leadership.* ed. K. E. Clark and M. B. Clark. West Orange, NJ: Leadership Library of America, 1990, pp. 205-15.

Powell, C., with Joe Pirsico. *My American Journey.* New York: Random House, 1995.

Potter, E. H.; W. E. Rosenbach; and T. S. Pittman. "Leading the New Professional." In *Military Leadership,* 3rd ed., ed. R. L. Taylor and W. E. Rosenbach. Boulder, CO: Westview Press, 1996.

Posner, B. Z., and W. H. Schmidt. "Values and the American Manager: An Update." *California Management Review* 3 (1984), pp. 206-16.

Prince, G. M. "Creative Meetings through Power Sharing." *Harvard Business Review* 50, no. 4 (1972), pp. 47-54.

Pritchard, R. D.; J. Hollenback; P. J. DeLeo. "The Effects of Continuous and Partial Schedules of Reinforcement of Effort, Performance, and Satisfaction." *Organizational Behavior and Human Performance* 16 (1976), pp. 205-30.

Pritchard, R. D.; S. D. Jones; P. L. Roth; K. K. Stuebing; and S. E. Ekeberg. "Effects of Group Feedback, Goal Setting, and Incentives on Organizational Productivity." *Journal of Applied Psychology* 73, no. 2 (1988), pp. 337-58.

Pryer, M. W., and M. K. DiStefano. "Perceptions of Leadership Behavior, Job Satisfaction, and Internal-External Control across Three Nursing Levels." *Nursing Review* 20 (1971), pp. 534-37.

Pulakos, E. D., and K. N. Wexley. "The Relationship among Perceptual Similarity, Sex, and Performance Ratings in Manager-Subordinate Dyads." *Academy of Management Journal* 26 (1983), pp. 129-39.

Quaglieri, P. L., and J. P. Carnazza. "Critical Inferences and the Multidimensionality of Feedback." *Canadian Journal of Behavioral Science* 17 (1985), pp. 284-93.

Quast, L. N., and T. L. Hansen. *The Relationship between MBTI Expanded Analysis Report (EAR) Scores and Leaders' Management Behaviors.* Minneapolis: Personnel Decisions International, 1996.

Quayle, D. "American Productivity: The Devastating Effect of Alcoholism and Drug Use." *American Psychologist* 38 (1983), pp. 454-58.

Quinn, R. E., and G. M. Spreitzer. "The Road to Empowerment: Seven Questions Every Leader Should Consider." *Organizational Dynamics,* Autumn 1997, pp. 37-49.

Ragins, B. R.; B. Townsend; and M. Mattis. "Gender Gap in the Executive Suite: CEOs and Female Executives Report on Breaking the Glass Ceiling." *Academy of Management Executive* 12, no. 1 (1998), pp. 28-42.

Rath, G. J., and K. S. Stoyanoff. "Understanding and Improving Communication Effectiveness." In *The 1982 Annual for Facilitators, Trainers, and Consultants*. ed. J. W. Pfeiffer and L. D. Goodstein. San Diego, CA: University Associates, 1982.

Read, P. P. *Alive*. New York: J. B. Lippincott, 1974.

Reason, J., and K. Mycielska. *Absent-Minded? The Psychology of Mental Lapses and Everyday Errors*. Englewood Cliffs, NJ: Prentice Hall, 1982, p. 183.

Ree, M. J., and J. A. Earles. "G Is to Psychology What Carbon Is to Chemistry: A Reply to Sternberg and Wagner, McClelland, and Calfee." *Current Directions in Psychological Science* vol. 2, no. 1 (1993), pp. 11-12.

———. "Intelligence Is the Best Predictor of Job Performance." *Current Directions in Psychological Science* 1, no. 3 (1992), pp. 86-89.

Remland, M. S. "Developing Leadership Skills in Nonverbal Communication: A Situation Perspective." *Journal of Business Communication* 18, no. 3 (1981), pp. 17-29.

Rest, J. "Research on Moral Judgment in College Students." In *Approaches to Moral Development, New Research and Emerging Themes*. ed. A. Garrod. New York: Teachers College Press, Columbia University, 1993, pp. 201-213.

Reykowski, J. "Social Motivation." *Annual Review of Psychology* 33 (1982), pp. 123-54.

Rice, R. W. "Construct Validity of the Least Preferred Co-Worker Score." *Psychological Bulletin* 85 (1978), pp. 1199-1237.

Richardson, R. J., and S. K. Thayer. *The Charisma Factor: How to Develop Your Natural Leadership Ability*. Englewood Cliffs, NJ: Prentice Hall.

Rizzo, J. R.; R. J. House; and S. I. Lirtzman. "Role Conflict and Ambiguity in Complex Organizations." *Administrative Science Quarterly* 15 (1970), pp. 150-63.

Roach, C. F., and O. Behling. "Functionalism: Basis for an alternate Approach to the Study of Leadership." In *Leaders and Managers: International Perspectives on Managerial Behavior and Leadership*. ed. J. G. Hunt, D. M. Hosking, C. A. Schriesheim, and R. Stewar. Elmsford, NY: Pergamon, 1984.

Robbins, S. P. *Organizational Behavior: Concepts, Controversies, and Applications*. Englewood Cliffs, NJ: Prentice Hall, 1986.

———. *Training in Interpersonal Skills*. Englewood Cliffs, NJ: Prentice Hall, 1989.

Roberts, N. C., and R. T. Bradley. "Limits of Charisma." In *Charismatic Leadership: The Elusive Factor in Organizational Effectiveness*. ed. J. A. Conger and R. N. Kanungo. San Francisco: Jossey-Bass, 1988, pp. 253-75.

Roberts, B. W. "An Alternative Perspective on the Relation between Work and Psychological Functioning: The Reciprocal Model of Person–Environment Interaction." In R. T. Hogan (Chair), *Personality and Organizational Behavior*. Symposium presented at the 104th Annual Meeting of the American Psychological Association, Toronto, Canada, 1996.

Roethlisberger, F. J.; and W. J. Dickson. *Management and the Worker: An Account of a Research Program Conducted by the Western Electric Company, Hawthorne Works, Chicago*. Cambridge, MA: Harvard University Press, 1939.

Rogers, C., and R. E. Farson. "Active Listening." In *Organizational Psychology.* ed. D. A. Kolb, I. M. Rubin, and J. M. McIntyre. Englewood Cliffs, NJ: Prentice Hall, 1984, pp. 255-66.

Rokeach, M. *The Nature of Human Values.* New York: Free Press, 1973.

Rorabaugh, W. J. *Berkeley at War.* New York: Oxford University Press, 1989.

Rosen, B., and T. H. Jerdee. "Influence of Subordinate Characteristics on Trust and Use of Participative Decision Strategies in a Management Simulation. " *Journal of Applied Psychology* 59 (1977), pp. 9-14.

Rosenbach, W. E.; T. S. Pittman; and E. H. Potter. "The Performance and Relationship Questionnaire." Gettysburg, PA, 1997.

Rosenback, W. E. "Mentoring: A Gateway to Leader Development." In *Contemporary Issues in Leadership.* ed. W. E. Rosenbach and R. L. Taylor. 2nd ed. Boulder, CO: Westview, 1989, pp. 139-48.

Rosener, J. B. "Ways Women Lead." *Harvard Business Review* 68 (1990), pp. 119-125.

Ross, L. "The Intuitive Psychologist and His Shortcomings." *Advances in Experimental Social Psychology.* vol. 10. ed. L. Berkowitz. New York: Academic Press, 1977.

Ross, S. M., and L. R. Offermann. "Transformational Leaders: Measurement of Personality Attributes and Work Group Performance." Paper presented at the Sixth Annual Society of Industrial and Organizational Psychologists Convention, St. Louis, MO, April 1991.

Rost, J. C. *Leadership in the 21st Century.* New York; Praeger, 1991.

Rotter, J. B. "Generalized Expectancies for Internal versus External Control of Reinforcement." *Psychological Monographs* 80, Whole No. 609, 1966.

Roush, P. E. "The Myers-Briggs Type Indicator and Perceptions of Leadership Effectiveness." Paper presented at the Center for Creative Leadership's Impact of Leadership Conference, Colorado Springs, CO, July 1991.

Rushton, J. P. "Race, IQ, and the APA Report on the Bell Curve." *American Psychologist* 52, no. 1 (1997), pp. 69-70.

Rusmore, J. T. *Executive Performance and Intellectual Ability in Organizational Levels.* San Jose, Calif.: San Jose University, Advanced Human Systems Institution, 1984.

Rusmore, J. T. and H. Baker. "Executive Performance in Four Organizational Levels and Two Kinds of Intellectual Ability." Paper presented at Society of Industrial and Organizational Psychology Convention, Atlanta, GA, 1987.

Rutan, J. S., and C. A. Rice. "The Charismatic Leader: Asset or Liability?" *Psychotherapy: Theory, Research, and Practice* 18 (1981), pp. 487-92.

Ryan, E. M.; V. Mims; and R. Koestner. "Relation of Reward Contingency and Interpersonal Context to Intrinsic Motivation: A Review and Test Using Cognitive Evaluation Theory." *Journal of Personality and Social Psychology* 45 (1983), pp. 736-50.

Rybicki, S. L., and D. D. Klippel. "Exploring the Impact of Personality Syndromes on Job Performance." In R. T. Hogan (Chair), *Personality Applications in the Workplace: Thinking outside the Dots.* Dymposium presented at the 12th Annual Conference of the Society of Industrial and Organizational Psychology, St. Louis, 1997.

Saal, F. E., and P. A. Knight. *Industrial Organizational Psychology: Science and Practice.* Belmont, CA: Brooks/Cole, 1988.

Sadler, P. J., and G. H. Hofstede. "Leadership Styles: Preferences and Perceptions of Employees of an International Company in Different Countries." *Mens en Onderneming* 26 (1972), pp. 43-63.

Safire, W., and L. Safir, eds. *Leadership.* New York: Simon & Schuster, 1990.

Sagie, A. "The Effects of Leader's Communications Style and Participative Goal Setting on Performance and Attitudes." Manuscript submitted to *Human Performance*, 1994.

Sales, C. A.; E. Levanoni; and D. H. Saleh. "Satisfaction and Stress as a Function of Job Orientation, Style of Supervision, and the Nature of the Task." *Engineering Management International* 2 (1984), pp. 145-53.

Salgado, J. F. "The Five-Factor Model of Personality and Job Performance in the European Community." *Journal of Applied Psychology* 82, no. 1 (1997), pp. 30-43.

Sanford, A., and S. Garrod. *Understanding Written Language.* New York: Wiley, 1981.

Sarason, I. "Stress, Anxiety, and Cognitive Interference: Reactions to Stress." *Journal of Personality and Social Psychology* 46 (1986), pp. 929-39.

Sashkin, M. *A Manager's Guide to Performance Management.* New York: American Management Association Publications Division, 1986.

———. "A New Vision of Leadership." *Journal of Management Development* 6, no. 4 (1987), pp. 19-28.

———. "The Visionary Leader." In *Charismatic Leadership: The Elusive Factor in Organizational Effectiveness,* ed. J. A. Conger and R. N. Kanungo. San Francisco: Jossey-Bass, 1988.

Sashkin, M., and G. Huddle. "Recruit Top Principals." *School Administrator* 45, no. 2 (1988), pp. 8-15.

Sayles, L. *Leadership: What Effective Managers Really Do . . . and How They Do It.* New York: McGraw-Hill, 1979.

Scandura, T. A.; G. B. Braen; and M. A. Novak. "When Managers Decide Not to Decide Autocratically: An Investigation of Leader-Member Exchange and Decision Influence." *Journal of Applied Psychology* 71 (1986), pp. 579-84.

Scandura, T. A; G. B. Graen; and M. A. Novak. "When Managers Decide Not to Decide Autocratically: An Investigation of Leader-Member Exchange and Decision Influence." *Journal of Applied Psychology* 52 (1986), pp. 135-47.

Scarr, S. "Protecting General Intelligence: Constructs and Consequences for Interventions." In *Intelligence: Measurement, Theory, and Public Policy.* ed. R. L. Linn. Chicago: University of Illinois Press, 1989.

Schein, E. *Career Dynamics: Matching Individual and Organizational Needs.* Reading, MA: Addison-Wesley, 1978.

Schein, E. H. *Organizational Culture and Leadership: A Dynamic View.* San Francisco: Jossey-Bass, 1985.

Schein, V. E. "The Relationship Between Sex-Role Stereotypes and Requisite Management Characteristics: A Cross-Cultural Look." Paper presented at the *22nd International Congress of Applied Psychology*, Kyoto, Japan, July 1990.

Schellenbarger, S. "Investors Seem Attracted to Firms with Happy Employees." *Wall Street Journal*, March 19, 1997, p. I2.

Schmidt, F. L.; I. Gast-Rosenberg; and J. E. Hunter. "Validity Generalization Results for Computer Programmers." *Journal of Applied Psychology* 65 (1980), pp. 643-61.

Schmidt, F. L., and J. E. Hunter. "Tacit Knowledge, Practical Intelligence, General Mental Ability and Job Knowledge." *Current Directions in Psychological Science.* vol. 2, no. 1 (1993), pp. 8-9.

————. "Development of a Causal Model of Job Performance." *Current Directions in Psychological Science* 1, no. 3 (1992), pp. 89-92.

Schmidt, W. H., and B. Z. Posner. "Values and Expectations of Federal Service Executives." *Public Administrative Review* 46 (1986), pp. 447-54.

Schnake, M. E. "Vicarious Punishment in a Work Setting." *Journal of Applied Psychology* 71 (1986), pp. 343-45.

Schneider, B. "Interactional Psychology and Organizational Behavior," In *Research in Organizational Behavior.* ed. L. L. Cummings and B. M. Staw. New York: Praeger, 1983, pp. 106-28.

Schneider, J. "The Cultural Situation as a Condition for the Condition of Fame." *American Sociology Review* 2 (1937), pp. 480-91.

Schonpflug, W. "The Noncharismatic Leader-Vulnerable." *Applied Psychology: An International Review* 44, no. 1 (1995), pp. 39-42.

Schriesheim, C. A., and A. S. DeNisi. "Task Dimensions as Moderators of the Effects of Instrumental Leadership: A Two Sample Replicated Test of Path-Goal Leadership Theory." *Journal of Applied Psychology* 66 (19981), pp. 589-97.

Schriesheim, C. A., and T. R. Hinkin. "Influence Tactics Used by Subordinates: A Theoretical and Empirical Analysis and Refinement of the Kipnis, Schmidt, and Wilkinson Subscales." *Journal of Applied Psychology* 75 (1990), pp. 246-57.

Schriesheim, C. A., and S. Kerr. "Theories and Measures of Leadership: A Critical Appraisal of Current and Future Directions." In *Leadership: The Cutting Edge.* ed. J. G. Hunt and L. L. Larson. Carbondale, IL : Southern Illinois University Press, 1977.

Schriesheim, C. A.; R. T. Mowday; and R. M. Stogdill. "Crucial Dimensions in Leader-Group Interactions." In *Cross-Currents in Leadership*, ed. J. G. Hunt and L. L. Larsen. Carbondale, IL: Southern Illinois University Press, 1979.

Scully, J. A.; H. P. Sims, Jr.; J. D. Olian; E. R. Schneell; and K. A. Smith. "Tough Times Make Tough Bosses: A Meso-Analysis of CEO Leader Behavior." *Leadership Quarterly* 5 (1994), pp. 59-83.

Segal, D. "Management, Leadership, and the Future Battlefield." In *Leadership on the Future Battlefield*. ed. J. Hunt and J. Blair. Washington, D.C.: Permagon-Brassey, 1985, pp. 201-213.

Seldes, G. ed. *The Great Quotations*. Seacanus, NJ: Citadel, 1983.

Senge, P. M. *The Fifth Discipline*. New York: Doubleday, 1990.

Shamir, B.; M. B. Arthur; and R. J. House. "The Rhetoric of Charismatic Leadership: A Theoretical Extension, a Case Study, and Implications for Research." *Leadership Quarterly* 5 (1994), pp. 25-42.

Shamir, B.; R. J. House; and M. B. Arthur. "The Motivational Effects of Charismatic Leadership: A Self-Concept Based Theory." *Organizational Science.* (in press).

Shaver, K. G. *Principles of Social Psychology*. 2nd ed. Hillsdale, NJ: Erlbaum, 1985.

Shaw, M. *Group Dynamics: The Psychology of Small Group Dynamics*. 3rd ed. New York: McGraw-Hill, 1981.

Shephard, J. E. "Thomas Becket, Ollie North, and You." *Military Review* 71, no. 5 (991), pp. 20-33.

Sheppard, B. H.; R. J. Lewicki; and J. W. Minton. *Organizational Justice: The Search for Fairness in the Workplace*. New York: Lexington Books, 1972.

Shils, E. "Charisma, Order, and Status." *American Sociological Review* 30 (1965), pp. 199-213.

Shipper, F., and C. L. Wilson. "The Impact of Managerial Behaviors on Group Performance, Stress, and Commitment." In *Impact of Leadership*. ed. K. E. Clark, M. B. Clark, D. P. Campbell. Greensboro, NC: Center for Creative Leadership, 1992.

Shostrom, E. L. *Man, the Manipulator*. New York: Bantam, 1967.

Siegall, M., and L. L. Cummings. "Task Role Ambiguity, Satisfaction, and the Moderating Effect of Task Instruction Source." *Human Relations* 39 (1986), pp. 1017-32.

Silberman, M. *Team and Organization Development Sourcebook*. New York: McGraw-Hill, 1996, 1997, 1998.

Simon, H. A. "Making Management Decisions: The Role of Intuition and Emotion." *Academy of Management Executive* 1 (1987), pp. 57-64.

Simoneit, M. *Grundris de Charakterologischen Diagnostik*. Leipzig: Teubner, 1944.

Simonton, D. "Creativity and Leadership: Convergence and Divergence." In *National Defense University, Proceedings of the Creativity and Innovation Symposium*. ed. V. E. Hendrix, D. B. Chapla, and W. Mizzelle. Washington, D.C., 1985, pp. 157-70.

———. "Presidential Style: Personality, Biography, and Performance." *Journal of Personality and Social Psychology* 55 (1988), pp. 928-36.

Simpson, W. G., and T. C. Ireland. "Managerial Excellence and Shareholder Returns." *American Association of Individual Investors Journal* 9 (1987), pp. 4-8.

Sims, H. P., and A. D. Szilagyi. "Leader Reward Behavior and Subordinate Satisfaction and Performance." *Organizational Behavior and Human Performance* 14 (1975), pp. 426-38.

Skinner, B. F. *The Behavior of Organisms*. New York: Appleton-Century-Crofts, 1938.

————. *Walden Two*. New York: MacMillan, 1948.

Sloane, E. B.; S. A. Hezlett; N. R. Kuncel; and M. R. Systma. "Performance, Potential, and Peril: What it Takes to Succeed at the Top." Paper presented at the 11th Annual Conference of the Society for Industrial/Organizational Psychology, San Diego, CA, April 1996.

Slovic, P., and B. Fischoff. "On the Psychology of Experimental Surprises." *Journal of Experimental Social Psychology* 22 (1977), pp. 544-51.

Smith, F. J.; K. D. Scott; and C. L. Hulin. "Trends in Job-Related Attitudes in Managerial and Professional Employees." *Academy of Management Journal* 20 (1977), pp. 454-60.

Smith, J. E.; K. P. Carson; and R. A. Alexander. "Leadership: It Can Make a Difference." *Academy of Management Journal* 27 (1984), pp. 765-76.

Smith, K. W.; E. Salas; and M. T. Brannick. Leadership Style as a Predictor of Teamwork Behavior: Setting the Stage by Managing Team Climate. Paper presented at the Ninth Annual Conference of the Society for Industrial and Organizational Psychology, Nashville, TN, 1994.

Smith, L. "The Executive's New Coach." *Fortune*. December 27, 1993.

Smith, M. J. *When I Say No I Feel Guilty*. New York: Dial, 1975.

Smith, P. C. "Behaviors, Results, and Organizational Effectiveness: The Problem of Criteria." In *Handbook of Industrial and Organizational Psychology*. ed. M. D. Dunnette Chicago: Rand, 1976.

Smither, J. W.; M. London; N. L. Vasilopoulis; R. R. Reilly; R. E. Millsap; and N. Salvemini. An Examination of the Effects of an Upward Feedback Program over Time." *Personnel Psychology* 48, no. 1 (1995), pp. 1-34.

Snyder, N. H.; J. J. Dowd and D. M. Houghton. *Vision, Values, and Courage*. New York: Free Press, 1994.

Snyder, M. "Self-Monitoring of Expressive Behavior." *Journal of Personality and Social Psychology* 30 (1974), pp. 526-37.

Snyder, R. A., and J. H. Morris. "Organizational Communication and Performance." *Journal of Applied Psychology* 69 (1984), pp. 461-65.

Solomon, R. L. "Punishment." *American Psychologist* 19 (1964), pp. 239-53.

Sparrowe, R. T., and R. C. Liden. "Process and Structure in Leader-Member Exchange." *Academy of Management Review* 22 (1997).

Spearman, C. S. "General Intelligence, Objectively Determined and Measured." *American Journal of Psychology* 15 (1994), pp. 201-09.

Spector, B., and M. Beer. "Beyond TQM Programmes." *Journal of Organizational Change Management* 7 (1994), pp. 63-70.

Sperry, R. W. "Some Effects of Disconnecting the Cerebral Hemispheres." *Science* 217 (1968), pp. 1223-26.

Spiller, G. "The Dynamics of Greatness." *Sociological Review* 21 (1929), pp. 218-32.

Spitzberg, I. J. "Paths of Inquiry into Leadership." *Liberal Education* 73, no. 2 (1987), pp. 24-28.

Spreitzer, G. M. "Psychological Empowerment in the Workplace: Dimensions, Measurement, and Validation." *Academy of Management Journal* 38, no. 5 (1995), pp. 1442-65.

Springer, S.; and G. Deutsch. *Left Brain, Right Brain.* San Francisco: W. H. Freeman, 1981.

Stahl, M. J. "Achievement, Power, and Managerial Motivation: Selecting Managerial Talent with the Job Choice Exercise." *Personnel Psychology* 36 (1983), pp. 775-89.

Staines, G. L., and R. P. Quinn. "American Workers Evaluate the Quality of Their Jobs." *Monthly Labor Review* 102, no. 1 (1979), pp. 3-12.

Stamps, D. "Are We Smart for Our Jobs?" *Training*, April 1996, pp. 44-50.

Staw, B. M. "Organizational Behavior: A Review and Reformulation of the Field's Outcome Variables." *Annual Review of Psychology* 35 (1984), pp. 627-66.

Stech, E. L. *Leadership Communication.* Chicago: Nelson-Hall, 1983.

Steele, R. S. "Power Motivation, Activation, and Inspirational Speeches." *Journal of Personality* 45 (1977), pp. 53-64.

Steiner, I. D. *Group Process and Productivity.* New York: Academic Press, 1972.

Steinmetz, J.; J. Blankenship; L. Brown; D. Hall; and G. Miller. *Managing Stress before It Manages You.* Palo Alto, CA: Bull, 1980.

Sternberg, R. J. *Beyond IQ: A Triarchic Theory of Human Intelligence.* New York: Cambridge University Press, 1985.

Sternberg, R. J. "The Concept of Intelligence: Its Role in Lifelong Learning and Success." *American Psychologist* 52, no. 10 (1997), pp. 1030-37.

Sternberg, R. J., and E. L. Grigorenko. "Are Cognitive Styles Still in Style?" *American Psychologist* 51, no. 7 (1996), pp. 677-88.

Sternberg, R. J., and T. I. Lubart. "Investing in Creativity." *American Psychologist* 52, no. 10 (1997), pp. 1046-50.

Sternberg, R. J.; R. K. Wagner; W. M. Williams; and J. A. Horvath. "Testing Common Sense." *American Psychologist* 50, no. 11 (1995), pp. 912-927.

Stewart, R. *Managers and Their Jobs.* London: MacMillan, 1967.

———. *Contrasts in Management.* Maidenhead, Berkshire, England: McGraw-Hill UK, 1976.

———. *Choices for the Manager: A guide to Understanding Managerial Work.* Englewood Cliffs, NJ: Prentice Hall, 1982.

Stock, G. *The Book of Questions: Business, Politics, and Ethics*. New York: Workman Publishing Co., 1991.

Stogdill, R. M. "Personal Factors Associated with Leadership: A Review of the Literature." *Journal of Psychology* 25 (1948), pp. 35-71.

———. *Individual Behavior and Group Achievement*. New York: Oxford University Press, 1959.

———. "Group Productivity, Drive, and Cohesiveness." *Organizational Behavior and Human Performance* 8 (1972), pp. 26-43.

———. *Handbook of Leadership*. 1st ed. New York: Free Press, 1974.

Stogdill, R. M.; O. S. Goode; and D. R. Day. "The Leader Behavior of Presidents of Labor Unions." *Personnel Psychology* 17 (1964), pp. 49-57.

Stogdill, R. M., and C. L. Shartle. *Methods in the Study of Administrative Performance*. Columbus, OH: Ohio State University, Bureau of Business Research, 1955.

Stone, D. L.; H. G. Gueutal; and B. MacIntosh. "The Effects of Feedback Sequence and Expertise of Rater of Perceived Feedback Accuracy." *Personal Psychology* 37 (1984), pp. 487-506.

Strasser, S; R. C. Dailey; and T. S. Bateman. "Attitudinal Moderators and Effects of Leaders' Punitive Behavior." *Psychological Reports* 49 (1981), pp. 695-98.

Strickland, B. R. "Internal-External Expectancies and Health-Related Behaviors." *Journal of Consulting and Clinical Psychology* 46 (1978), pp. 1192-1211.

Strube, M. J., and J. E. Garcia. "A Meta-Analytic Investigation of Fielder's Contingency Model of Leadership Effectiveness." *Psychological Bulletin* 90 (1981), pp. 307-21.

Sutton, C. D., and R. W. Woodman. "Pygmalion Goes to Work: The Effects of Supervisor Expectations in the Retail Setting." *Journal of Applied Psychology* 74 (1989), pp. 943-50.

Swets, J. A.; and R. A. Bjork. "Enhancing Human Performance: An Evaluation of "New Age" Techniques Considered by the U.S. Army." *Psychological Science* 1, no. 2 (1990), pp. 85-96.

Taylor, H. L. *Delegate: The Key to Successful Management*. New York: Warner Books, 1989.

Tellegen, A.; D. T. Lykken; T. J. Bouchard, J.; K. J. Wilcox; N. L. Segal; and S. Rich. "Personality Similarity in Twins Reared Apart and Together." *Journal of Personality and Social Psychology* 54 (1988), pp. 1031-39.

Terborg, J. R.; C. H. Castore; and J. A. DeNinno. "A Longitudinal Field Investigation of the Impact of Group Composition on Group Performance and Cohesion." Paper presented at the meeting of the Midwestern Psychological Association, Chicago, 1975.

Tett, R. R.; D. N. Jackson; M. Rothstein; J. R. Reddon. "Meta-Analysis of Personality-Job Performance Relations: A Reply on Ones, Mount, Barrick, and Hunter, 1994" *Personnel Psychology* 47 (1994), pp. 157-79.

Tett, R. P., and J. P. Meyer. "Job Satisfaction, Organizational Commitment, Turnover Intention, and Turnover: Path Analyses Based on Meta-Analytic Findings." *Personnel Psychology* 44 (1991), pp. 703-42.

Thayer, P. W. "The Myers-Briggs Type Indicator and Enhancing Human Performance." Report prepared for the Committee on Techniques for the Enhancement of Human Performance of the National Academy of Sciences, 1988.

Thomas, B. *Walt Disney*. New York: Simon and Schuster., 1976.

Thomas, K. W. "Conflict and Conflict Management." In *Handbook of Industrial and Organizational Psychology*. ed. M. D. Dunnette. Chicago: Rand McNally, 1976.

———. "Toward Multidimensional Values in Teaching: The Example of Conflict Management." *Academy of Management Review* 2, no. 3 (1977), pp. 484-90.

Thomas, K. W.; and W. H. Schmidt. "A Survey of Managerial Interests with Respect to Conflict." *Academy of Management Journal* 19 (1976), pp. 315-18.

Thurstone, L. L. "The Factors of the Mind." *Psychological Review* 41 (1934), pp. 1-32.

Tichy, N. M., and M. A. Devanna. *The Transformational Leader*. New York: Wiley, 1986.

Tichy, N. M., and E. Cohen. *The Leadership Engine: How Winning Companies Build Leaders at Every Level*. New York: HarperCollins, 1997.

Tjosvold, D. "Stress Dosage for Problem Solvers." *Working Smart*, August 1995, p. 5.

Toffler, A. *Future Shock*. New York: Random House, 1970.

Tolman, E. C. *Purposeful Behavior in Animals and Men*. New York: Appleton-Century-Crofts, 1932.

Trevino, L. K. "The Social Effects of Punishment in Organizations: A Justice Perspective." *Academy of Management Review* 17 (1992), pp. 647-76.

Trevino, L. K., and S. A. Youngblood. "Bad Apples in Bad Barrels: A Causal Analysis of Ethical Decision-Making Behavior." *Journal of Applied Psychology* 75 (1990), pp. 378-85.

Trice, H. M. and J. M. Beyer. "Charisma and Its Routinization in Two Social Movement Organizations." In *Research in Organizational Behavior*. ed. B. M. Staw and L. L. Cummings. Vol. 8 Greenwich, CN: JAI, 1986.

Trist, E. L., and K. W. Bamforth. "Some Social and Psychological Consequences of the Longwall Method of Goal Setting." *Human Relations* 4 (1951), pp. 1-38.

Tsui, A. "A Role Set Analysis of Managerial Reputation." *Organizational Behavior and Human Performance* 34 (1984), pp. 64-96.

Tucker, R. C. "The Theory of Charismatic Leadership." *Daedalus* 97 (1968), pp. 731-56.

Tuckman, B. W. "Developmental Sequence in Small Groups." *Psychological Bulletin* 63 (1965), pp. 384-99.

Udell, J. G. "An Empirical Test of Hypotheses Relating to Span of Control." *Administrative Science Quarterly* 12 (1967), pp. 420-39.

Uecker, M. E., and B. L. Dilla. "Mentoring as a Leadership Development Tool in the United States Air Force." *Proceedings of the 26th Annual Meeting of the Military Testing Association*, Munich, Germany, 1985, pp. 423-28.

Ungson, G. R.; C. James; and B. H. Spicer. "The Effects of Regulatory Agencies on Organizations in Wood Products and High Technology/Electronics Organizations." *Academy of Management Journal* 28 (1985), pp. 426-45.

Urwick, L. F. *Notes on the Theory of Organization.* New York: American Management Association, 1952.

Van Velsor, E., and J. B. Leslie. "Why Executives Derail: Perspectives across Time and Cultures." *Academy of Management Executive* 9, no. 4 (1995), pp. 62-71.

Vecchio, R. P. "Predicting Worker Performance in Inequitable Settings." *Academy of Management Review* 7 (1982), pp. 103-10.

————. "Assessing the Validity of Fiedler's Contingency Model of Leadership Effectiveness: A Closer Look at Strube and Garcia." *Psychological Bulletin* 93 (1983), pp. 404-08.

————. "Situational Leadership Theory: An Examination of a Prescriptive Theory." *Journal of Applied Psychology* 72 (1987), pp. 444-51.

Vroom, V. H. *Work and Motivation.* New York: Wiley, 1964.

Vroom, V. H., and A. G. Jago. "Leadership and Decision Making: A Revised Normative Model. Paper presented at the Academy of Management Convention, Boston, MA, 1974.

————. *The New Theory of Leadership: Managing Participation in Organizations.* Englewood Cliffs, NJ: Prentice Hall, 1988.

Vroom, V. H., and P. W. Yetton. *Leadership and Decision Making.* Pittsburgh: University of Pittsburgh Press, 1973.

Wagner, J. A. "Participation's Effect on Performance and Satisfaction: A Reconsideration of Research Evidence." *Academy of Management Review* 19 (1994), pp. 312-30.

Wainer, H. A., and I. M. Rubin. "Motivation of Research and Development Entrepreneurs: Determinants of Company Success." *Journal of Applied Psychology* 53 (1969), pp. 178-84.

Wakabayashi, M., and G. B. Graen. "The Japanese Career Progress Study: A Seven-Year Follow-up." *Journal of Applied Psychology* 69 (1984), pp. 603-14.

Wakin, M. M. "Ethics of Leadership." In *Military Leadership.* ed. J. H. Buck and L. J. Korb. Beverly Hills, CA: Sage, 1981.

Walker, T. G. "Leader Selection and Behavior in Small Political Groups." *Small Group Behavior* 7 (1976), pp. 363-68.

Wall, T. D.; N. J. Kemp; P. R. Jackson; and C. W. Clegg. "Outcomes of Autonomous Work Groups: A Long-Term Field Experiment." *Academy of Management Journal* 29 (1986), pp. 280-304.

Wallach, M. A., and N. Kogan. *Modes of Thinking in Young Children.* New York: Holt, Rinehart & Winston, 1965.

Wallas, G. *The Art of Thought*. New York: Harcourt Brace Jovanovich., 1926.

Wanous, J. P.; T. L. Keon; and J. C. Latack. "Expectancy Theory and Occupational/Organizational Choices: A Review and Test." *Organizational Behavior and Human Performance* 32 (1983), pp. 66-86.

Wayne, S. J.; L. M. Shore; and R. C. Liden. "Perceived Organizational Support and Leader-Member Exchange: A Social Exchange Perspective." "*Academy of Management Journal*" 40 (1997) pg. 82-111.

Weber, J. "Managers' Moral Meaning: An Exploratory Look at Managers' Responses to the Moral Dilemmas." *Proceedings of the Academy of Management Convention*, Washington, D.C., 1989, pp. 333-337.

Weber, M. *The Theory of Social and Economic Organization*. Ed. and trans. A. M. Henderson and T. Parsons. (Original work published in 1923). New York: The Free Press.

Weber, M. *The Theory of Social and Economic Organization*, ed. Talcott Parsons; trans. A. M. Henderson and T. Parsons. New York: Free Press, 1964.

Weiss, H. M. "Subordinate Imitation of Supervisor Behavior: The Role of Modeling in Organizational Socialization." *Organizational Behavior and Human Performance* 19 (1977), pp. 89-105.

Weschler, D. *Weschler Adult Intelligence Scale: Manual*. New York: Psychological Corporation, 1955.

West Point Associates, the Department of Behavior Sciences and Leadership, United States Military Academy. *Leadership in Organizations*. Garden City Park, NY: Avery, 1988.

West, M. A. and N. R. Anderson. "Innovation in Top Management Teams." *Journal of Applied Psychology* 81, no. 6, pp. 680-93.

Westley, F. R., and H. Mintzberg. "Profiles of Strategic Vision: Levesque and Iacocca." In *Charismatic Leadership: The Elusive Factor in Organizational Effectiveness*. ed. J. A. Conger and R. N. Kanungo. San Francisco: Jossey-Bass, 1988.

Wexley, K. N., and G. P. Latham. *Developing and Training Human Resources in Organizations*. Glenview, IL: Scott Foresman, 1981.

Wheelan, S. A. *Group Processes*. Needham Heights, MA: Allyn & Bacon, 1994.

Whitely, W.; T. W. Dougherty; and G. F. Dreher. "The Relationship of Mentoring and Socioeconomic Origin to Managers' and Professionals' Early Career Progress." *Proceedings, Academy of Management*. Anaheim, CA: 1988, pp. 58-62.

Whiteside, D. E. *Command Excellence: What It Takes to Be the Best!* Department of the Navy, Washington, D.C.: Leadership Division, Naval Military Personnel Command, 1985.

Wilcox, W. H. "Assistant Superintendents' Perceptions of the Effectiveness of the Superintendent, Job Satisfaction, and Satisfaction with the Superintendent's Supervisory Skills." Ph.D. dissertation, University of Missouri, Columbia, MO, 1982.

Wiley, J., and T. Comacho. "Life-Style and Future Health: Evidence from the Alameda County Study." *Preventive Medicine* 9 (1980), pp. 1-21.

Willerman, L. *The Psychology of Individual and Group Differences.* San Francisco: W. H. Freeman, 1979.

Willner, A. R. *The Spellbinders: Charismatic Political Leadership.* New Haven, CN: Yale University Press, 1984.

Wilson, J. A., and N. S. Elman. "Organizational Benefits of Mentoring." *Academy of Management Executive* 4 (1990), pp. 88-93.

Wilson, P. R. "The Perceptual Distortion of Height as a Function of Ascribed Academic Status." *Journal of Social Psychology* 74 (1968), pp. 97-102.

Winter, D. G. "Leader Appeal, Leader Performance, and the Motive Profiles of Leaders and Followers: A Study of American Presidents and Elections." *Journal of Personality and Social Psychology* 52 (1987), pp. 196-202.

Wofford, J. C., and V. L. Goodwin. "A Cognitive Interpretation of Transformational and Transactional Leadership Theories." *Leadership Quarterly* 5 (1994), pp. 161-86.

Wolpe, H. "A Critical Analysis of Some Aspects of Charisma." *The Sociological Review* 16 (1968), pp. 305-18.

Wood, G. "The Knew-It-All-Along Effect." *Journal of Experimental Psychology: Human Perception and Performance* 4 (1979), pp. 345-53.

Woodward, J. *Industrial Organization.* London: Oxford University Press, 1965.

Xie, J. L., and G. Johns. "Job Scope and Stress: Can Job Scope Be Too High?" *Academy of Management Journal* 38, no. 5 (1995), pp. 1288-1309.

Yammarino, F. J., and A. J. Dubinsky. "Transformational Leadership Theory: Using Levels of Analysis to Determine Boundary Conditions." *Personnel Psychology* 47 (1994), pp. 787-812.

Yammarino, F. J.; A. J. Dubinsky; L. B. Comer; M. A. Jolson. "Women and Transformational and Contingent Reward Leadership: A Multiple-Levels-of-Analysis Perspective." *Academy of Management Journal* 40, no. 1 (1997), pp. 205-22.

Yammarino, F. J.; W. D. Spangler; and B. M. Bass. "Transformational Leadership and Performance: A Longitudinal Investigation." *Leadership Quarterly* 4 (1993), pp. 81-102.

Yoshida, K. "Deming Management Philosophy: Does It Work in the U.S. as Well as in Japan?" *Columbia Journal of World Business* (1989), pp. 10-16.

Yukl, G. A. *Leadership in Organizations.* 2nd ed. Englewood Cliffs, NJ: Prentice Hall, 1989.

Yukl, G. A., and C. M. Falbe. "Importance of Different Power Sources in Downward and Lateral Relations." *Journal of Applied Psychology* 76 (1991), pp. 416-23.

Yukl, G. A., and D. D. Van Fleet. "Cross-Situational Multi-Method Research on Military Leader Effectiveness." *Organizational Behavior and Human Performance* 30 (1982), pp. 87-108.

————. "Theory and Research on Leadership in Organizations." In *Handbook of Industrial & Organizational Psychology*. ed. M. D. Dunnette and L. M. Hough. Vol. 3. Palo Alto, CA: Consulting Psychologists Press, 1992, pp. 1-51.

Yukl, G. A.; R. Lepsinger; and T. Lucia. "Preliminary Report on the Development and Validation of the Influence Behavior Questionnaire." In *Impact of Leadership*. ed. K. E. Clark, M. B. Clark, and D. P. Campbell. Greensboro, NC: Center for Creative Leadership, 1992.

Yukl, G. A.; S. Wall; and R. Lepsinger. "Preliminary Report on Validation of the Managerial Practices Survey." In *Measures of Leadership*. ed. K. E. Clark and M. B. Clark. Greensboro, NC: Center for Creative Leadership, 1989.

Zaccaro, S. J. "Leader Resources and the Nature of Organizational Problems." *Applied Psychology: An International Review* 44, no. 1 (1995), pp. 32-36.

Zaccaro, S. J.; R. J. Foti; and D. A. Kenny. "Self-Monitoring and Trait-Based Variance in Leadership: An Investigation of Leader Flexibility across Multiple Group Situations." *Journal of Applied Psychology* 76 (1991), pp. 308-15.

Zajonc, R. "Social Facilitation," *Science* 149 (1965), pp. 269-74.

Zaleznik, A. "Charismatic and Consensus Leaders: A Psychological Comparison." *Bulletin of the Menninger Clinic* 38 (1974), pp. 22-38.

————. "The Leadership Gap." *The Washington Quarterly* 6, no. 1 (1983), pp. 32-39.

Zey, M. G. *The Mentor Connection*. Homewood, IL: Dow Jones-Irwin, 1984.

Zimbardo, P.; C. Haney; W. Banks; and D. Jafe. "The Mind Is a Formidable Jailer: A Pirandellian Prison." *The New York Times Magazine*, April 8, 1973, pp. 38-60.

Zonana, V. E. "Teaming Up—When It Comes to Foreign Alliances, Japan Proves a More Willing Partner." *Los Angeles Times*, February 22.